Communications
in Computer and Information Science   819

Commenced Publication in 2007
Founding and Former Series Editors:
Alfredo Cuzzocrea, Xiaoyong Du, Orhun Kara, Ting Liu, Dominik Ślęzak,
and Xiaokang Yang

More information about this series at http://www.springer.com/series/7899

Benoit Huet · Liqiang Nie
Richang Hong (Eds.)

Internet Multimedia Computing and Service

9th International Conference, ICIMCS 2017
Qingdao, China, August 23–25, 2017
Revised Selected Papers

 Springer

Editors
Benoit Huet
Multimedia Communications Department
EURECOM
Sophia Antipolis
France

Richang Hong
Hefei University of Technology
Hefei
China

Liqiang Nie
Shandong University
Qingdao
China

ISSN 1865-0929   ISSN 1865-0937 (electronic)
Communications in Computer and Information Science
ISBN 978-981-10-8529-1   ISBN 978-981-10-8530-7 (eBook)
https://doi.org/10.1007/978-981-10-8530-7

Library of Congress Control Number: 2018934345

This Springer imprint is published by the registered company Springer Nature Singapore Pte Ltd.
part of Springer Nature
The registered company address is: 152 Beach Road, #21-01/04 Gateway East, Singapore 189721, Singapore

Preface

The 9th International Conference on Internet Multimedia Computing and Service (ICIMCS 2017) was held during August 23–25, 2017, at Tsingtao, China. ICIMCS focuses on pushing the frontier of multimedia computing technology in a variety of application domains. During the past 8 years, ICIMCS has successfully facilitated the communications of state-of-the-art progress made by multimedia researchers and participants worldwide. With the venue mainly based in China, ICIMCS presents highly-quality research papers and technical presentations organized by influential scholars in the multimedia community. Therefore, ICIMCS offers a great opportunity for the international community to know and get involved in the fast development of Chinese research in multimedia such as computer vision, natural language processing, and data knowledge understanding.

ICIMCS 2017 was organized at Shandong University of Science and Technology, Qingdao, Shandong. We gratefully thank Shandong University of Science and Technology for its generous support of ICIMCS 2017. Perched on the southern tip of the Shandong Peninsula, Qingdao is well-known to the West by its postal map spelling of Tsingtao. It is known as "Pearl on the Yellow River" and "China's Switzerland." The most famous beer of China—Tsingtao Beer—is produced here. We hope that our venue made ICIMCS 2017 a memorable experience for all participants.

We received 103 paper submissions, covering topics of multimedia information fusion, image processing and object recognition, machine learning and representation learning, as well as multimedia retrieval. The submitted papers were reviewed by the Technical Program Committee, consisting of 68 reviewers. Each paper was reviewed by at least two reviewers. The program chairs carefully considered the input and feedback from the reviewers and accepted 48 papers (46.6%) to the main conference. Among the accepted papers, 20 were oral papers and 28 were poster papers. This volume of the conference proceedings contains all the oral and poster papers.

The technical program is an important aspect but only achieves its full impact if complemented by challenging keynotes. We are extremely pleased and grateful to have had three exceptional keynote speakers, Bin Hu, Jingdong Wang, and Xiansheng Hua, accept our invitation and present interesting ideas and insights at ICIMCS 2017.

We are heavily indebted to many individuals for their significant contributions. First, we are very grateful to all the authors who contributed their high-quality research and shared their knowledge with our scientific community. Second, we wish to thank all Organizing and Program Committee members, reviewers, session chairs, student volunteers, and supporters. Their contributions are much appreciated. We hope you all enjoy the proceedings of ICIMCS 2017.

September 2017

Benoit Huet
Liqiang Nie
Richang Hong

Organization

General Chairs

Alex Hauptmann   Carnegie Mellon University, USA
Baoquan Chen   Shandong University, China
Donghua Zhou   Shandong University of Science and Technology, China

Technical Program Chairs

Benoit Huet   EURECOM, France
Liqiang Nie   Shandong University, China
Richang Hong   Hefei University of Technology, China

Sponsorship Chair

Xinshun Xu   Shandong University, China

Publication Chairs

Tian Gan   Shandong University, China
Hanwang Zhang   Columbia University, USA

Special Session Chairs

Liang Li   Chinese Academy of Sciences, China
Xuemeng Song   Shandong University, China

Registration Chair

Weifeng Liu   China University of Petroleum (East China), China

Finance Chair

Weijian Ni   Shandong University of Science and Technology, China

Local Chair

Qingtian Zeng   Shandong University of Science and Technology, China

Publicity Chair

Yongquan Liang   Shandong University of Science and Technology, China

Program Committee

Lamberto Ballan	University of Florence, Italy
Kseniya Buraya	National University of Singapore, Singapore
Da Cao	Xiamen University, China
Jingjing Chen	City University of Hong Kong, Hong Kong, SAR China
Jingyuan Chen	National University of Singapore, Singapore
Zhumin Chen	Shandong University, China
Wen-Huang Cheng	Academia Sinica, Taiwan
Zhiyong Cheng	National University of Singapore, Singapore
Wei-Ta Chu	National Chung Cheng University, Taiwan
Noel Codella	IBM Research, USA
Chaoran Cui	Shandong University of Finance and Economics, China
Yuming Fang	Nanyang Technological University, Singapore
Aleksandr Farseev	National University of Singapore, Singapore
Fuli Feng	National University of Singapore, Singapore
Tian Gan	Shandong University, China
Ke Gao	Institute of Computing Technology, Chinese, China
Lianli Gao	The University of Electronic Science and Technology of China, China
Zan Gao	Tianjing University of Technology, China
Francesco Gelli	National University of Singapore, Singapore
Xue Geng	National University of Singapore, Singapore
Kailing Guo	University of Technology Sydney, Australia
Jungong Han	Civolution Technology, The Netherlands
Shijie Hao	HeFei University of Technology, China
Steven Hoi	Singapore Management University, Singapore
Wolfgang Huerst	Utrecht University, The Netherlands
Muwei Jian	Ocean University of China, China
Tae Hoon Joseph Kim	National University of Singapore, Singapore
Duy-Dinh Le	National Institute of Informatics, Japan
Liang Li	University of Chinese Academy of Sciences, China
Xirong Li	Renmin University of China, China
Zechao Li	Nanjing University of Science and Technology, China
Zhen Li	University of Illinois Urbana-Champaign, USA
Anan Liu	Tianjing University, China
Bo Liu	Rutgers University, USA
Meng Liu	Shandong University, China
Weifeng Liu	China University of Petroleum (East China), China
Xueliang Liu	Hefei University of Technology, China
Zhu Liu	AT&T Labs Research, USA
He Ma	Northeastern University, China
Qirong Mao	Jiangsu University, China
Yadong Mu	Columbia University, USA
Chong-Wah Ngo	City University of Hong Kong, Hong Kong, SAR China

Weijian Ni	Shandong University of Science and Technology, China
Weizhi Nie	Tianjing University, China
Xiushan Nie	Shandong University of Finance and Economics, China
Tongwei Ren	Nanjing University, China
Jitao Sang	Chinese Academy of Sciences, China
Xiangjun Shen	Jiangsu University, China
Xiangbo Shu	Nanjing University of Science and Technology, China
Jiande Sun	Shandong University, China
Sheng Tang	University of Chinese Academy of Sciences, China
Qi Tian	University of Texas at San Antonio, USA
Xiang Wang	National University of Singapore, Singapore
Xiangyu Wang	Facebook, USA
Xiaochi Wei	Beijing Institute of Technology, China
Lynn Wilcox	FXPAL, USA
Yang Wu	Kyoto University, Japan
Hongtao Xie	University of Chinese Academy of Sciences, China
Xinshun Xu	Shandong University, China
Feng Xue	HeFei University of Technology, China
Yi Yang	University of Technology Sydney, Australia
Chunyun Zhang	Shandong University of Finance and Economics, China
Jianglong Zhang	Communication University of China, China
Wanlei Zhao	Inria, France
Lei Zhu	The University of Queensland, Australia

Contents

Machine Learning and Representation Learning

Multimedia Retrieval

Regular Poster Papers

Best Paper

Joint Deep Learning and Gaussian Representation for Person Re-identification

Nan Song[1(✉)], Xianglei Zhu[2], and Yahong Han[1]

[1] School of Computer Science and Technology, Tianjin University, Tianjin, China
{songnan,yahong}@tju.edu.cn
[2] China Automotive Technology and Research Center, Tianjin, China
zhuxianglei@catarc.ac.cn

Abstract. Person re-identification (re-id) has attracted extensive attention worldwide in the computer vision. Unlike other images retrieval tasks, the color and texture information of pedestrian clothing is an important clue of person re-id. However, these special features of re-id are not focused in the process of extracting features by deep learning. We find that some traditional methods of extracting features are better than deep learning in color and texture. Therefore, in this paper, we propose a model of jointing Deep learning and Gaussian representation (JDAG), which is the fusion of CNN network and Gaussian descriptor to enrich the person re-id features. We also adjust the parameters of our model to achieve an optimal performance and obtain more discriminative features. The experimental results generated on two representative and public datasets (a large-scale dataset Market1501 and a small dataset VIPeR) are evaluated using three different distance metric learning strategies. The comparisons show that our method is superior than other existing methods.

Keywords: Deep learning · Fusion strategy · Person re-identification

1 Introduction

Recent years, person re-identification (re-id) is a new technology in computer vision and intelligent surveillance systems, which is mainly applied on person recognition and pedestrian similarity matching in a complex and changeful environment. The key of problems is described as a task of matching same person ID between gallery images and index query images from different camera views. However, intra-personal variations such as blur, illumination, occlusion, person pose, resolution, and the images intercepted from different camera views, bring great challenges. Therefore, researchers are concerned with improving the accuracy and efficiency in recognition and retrieval. Some effective methods are proposed [1–10].

© Springer Nature Singapore Pte Ltd. 2018
B. Huet et al. (Eds.): ICIMCS 2017, CCIS 819, pp. 3–12, 2018.
https://doi.org/10.1007/978-981-10-8530-7_1

Feature extraction, similarity computation and evaluation are three main steps to solve the person re-id problems generally. Firstly, the convolutional neural network (CNN) has been widely applied on image feature extraction and achieved state-of-the-art results [11–13]. However, there are two difficulties: (1) Training set of re-id is relatively small so that it is prone to over-fitting. (2) Re-id problem is mainly based on the color and texture information of person. While these characteristics are not mainly focused by CNN, instead, semantic features are extracted. Although semantic features may be more accurate and rich, small datasets have a better performance for special features using traditional machine learning, which motivates us to combine them to improve features discrimination. As known, the features from traditional machine learning are also studied as a hot spot at present, included Local Maximal Occurrence (LOMO) features [1], Covariance-of-Covariance feature [14], Gaussian Of Gaussian (GOG) features recently proposed in [4] which can combine mean and covariance information in region hierarchies and achieve the state-of-the-art performances, so we regard it as traditional branches in our work.

Similarity computation and evaluation can be treat as a whole by distance metrics learning (DML) for a pair of images. At present, there are many DML methods which have been proved to be effective for person re-id. Davis et al. [15] presented an information-theoretic approach (ITML) to handle a variety constraints problem and Guillaumin et al. [16] raised a logistic discriminant method to learn the labeled image pairs (LDM). In addition of that, it also includes: person re-id methods (eSDC) [3], KISSME [17], XQDA [1] and using Euclidean distance to compute the score of similarity directly. In our paper, we used the last three methods to evaluate results and the contrast results also were listed in experiment section.

As mentioned above, a small dataset trained by deep learning model such as ResNet [18] gets a bad result due to over-fitting. Therefore, traditional methods had been employed in the high-dimensional feature vectors to express the person features of small datasets. However, these features need to be extracted based on special attributes (color, texture), so that it is more deficient to extract discriminative features than deep learning. In order to solve the problems, we consider the color and texture of pedestrian clothing as a focus jointing the CNN features and training in ImageNet model. The fusion can not only solve the problem of over-fitting, but also solve the attention problem of color and texture information.

In this paper, the important contributions of our work are: (1) we discover the issue that small datasets (VIPeR [19]) tend to over-fitting in CNN model. However, the special features of color and texture enhanced by traditional machine learning have applicability to solve this problem of person re-id. (2) We propose a fusion model of jointing Deep learning and Gaussian representation (JDAG). The traditional features and CNN features are trained in the network by fusion strategy. (3) Our method is tested on two benchmarks (a large dataset Market1501 [20] and a small dataset VIPeR) and achieved a good performance. Besides, we use the three kinds of relatively common DML strategies (XQDA, KISSME, Euclidean distance) to find out a most suitable one for our JDAG model.

The organization of this paper is as follows: Firstly, we describe the two branches of JDAG model about the two features in fusion respectively and how to concatenate the features in a 2stream siamese network [21] in Sect. 2. In Sect. 3, we present our experimental details and show the comparison results on representative datasets. At last, we conclude our method in Sect. 4.

2 Methodology

In this section, we introduce our network architecture. At first, we extract the GOG features of four different color channels (HSV, Lab, RnG, RGB) for a pair of images as the traditional features inputs, then the mean and L2 normalization can be used next. Secondly, the features which are fusions of GOG and CNN for a pair of images are fed into the identification network and verification network to train together simultaneously. Finally, we test and evaluate our method in public datasets using state-of-the-art metric learning strategies.

2.1 Branch of CNN Features

In the previous works of person re-id, verification models and identification models are trained separately. Verification models are mainly used to calculate the similarity of images, which allow a pair of images as inputs and then similarity scores are obtained by cosine distance between the features of outputs in order to predict whether the IDs are same or not. Identification models are developed for classification and the number of categories varies with the number of person IDs in datasets, so it can be treated as a large-scale multi-classification problem where an image as input can be predicted for the corresponding person ID.

It is difficult to improve the accuracy of similarity scores, because of only considering optimizing verification models and that person ID can be only treated as a ground truth label of loss function in the previous works. Recently, a method of combining the two models was proposed [21] to take advantages of both networks and form a unified framework, so we select this network to train datasets. However, the difference is that ours method adds GOG features as input data to predict person ID and calculate similarity in stead of only using the outputs from the pool5 layer in ResNet50. It is necessary to remove mean and L2 normalization before GOG features are fed into the network.

The architecture of JDAG model is shown in Fig. 1: we introduce the 2stream siamese of Resnet50 to extract the features of *pool5* layer for the inputs of pairs. Meanwhile, the traditional features represented by GOG descriptor f_g and f_{g_2} can be fed into the respective FC layers and the outputs are indicated by f_1 and f_2 respectively. Next, we combine the *pool5* features and GOG features into fusion features indicated by f_1^* and f_2^*. On the one hand, the fusion features are applied on identifying person ID for the pairs of images by FC layers of multi classification. On the other hand, we use the Euclidean distance layer to compare the fusion features and predict similarity scores by the next FC layer of binary classification. The Euclidean distance layer is denoted as

$$f = (f_1^* - f_2^*)^2 \tag{1}$$

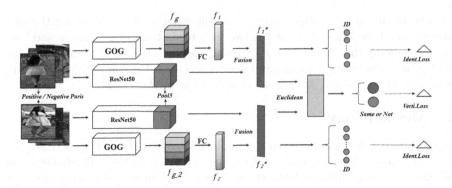

Fig. 1. JDAG model structure. Positive or Negative pairs of images of size 256 × 256 input ResNet50 network and GOG model and the features of *pool5* and f_g are outputs respectively. The fusion features which achieved by FC layers and Concat layers can be fed into Identification model and Verification model. Finally, the three loss can be obtained.

Finally, two identification losses and a verification loss computed by softmax layers are used back propagation. Identification loss and verification loss can be computed by cross-entropy loss which is

$$H(p,q) = -\sum_{i=1}^{n} p(x) log q(x) \tag{2}$$

x is the features vector. $p(x)$ and $q(x)$ are the probability of predicting and target by softmax layer respectively and H is the cross-entropy loss.

2.2   Branch of GOG Features

We select GOG feature as traditional features to combine with CNN features, because GOG feature is more concerned about the color and texture attributes of pedestrian images, which is more suitable for person features extraction. We briefly review the GOG features extraction method as follow: firstly, an image is divided into n regions. M patches of size k × k are selected in a region. Then, a 8 dimensional feature vector f_i is extracted for each pixel i in a patch.

$$f_i = [y, M_{0°}, M_{90°}, M_{180°}, M_{270°}, R, G, B]^T$$

y denotes the features of the vertical direction. Due to that people walk upright normally on the road, the person images tend to be consistent in the vertical direction but great changeful in the horizontal when pose or view is changed. M denotes gradient magnitude for different angles which can describe the texture information of person clothing effectively. R, G, B denote the color information of clothing, so they are the most important cue for person re-id. Therefore, four different color channels are selected to extend the color space, which include

HSV, Lab, RnG and RGB. After extracting the features of the pixels, each pixel information is summarized in a patch feature vector by Gaussian distribution. Next, a region feature can be represented by summarizing all the patches features with Gaussian expression. At last, n regions features are concatenated to describe the whole image. So, the feature is called Gaussian of Gaussian (GOG) feature.

It is not difficult to find that GOG feature is mainly based on color and texture attributes, and this is a state-of-the-art method for person feature extraction. After extracting the GOG feature, removing mean value and L2 normalization are utilized at next stage in order to make it easier to combine with CNN features. For more algorithmic details, please refer to [4].

2.3   Strategies of Fusion

Processing Data with PCA. An image processed by the GOG method can transform into a 1×7567 dimensional feature vector and in the CNN branch, can transform into a $1 \times 1 \times 2048$ dimensional features in the pool5 layer of resnet50 network. In order to balance the GOG features and CNN features and reduce impacts for redundancy results, PCA method for reducing dimension is applied on our work. Before the GOG features are fed into the ResNet50, the dimension can be handled by PCA, so that the dimension is $1 \times 1 \times D_{PCA}$.

The advantages of processing GOG features by PCA are reduction of features dimension and effective balance between GOG and CNN. What's more, PCA can reduce parameters for the network and improve the speed for training. However, the disadvantage is that magnifying the dimensions of noise which causes a small standard deviation so that the deviation of whole is increased.

Processing Data with Full Connection. As above section, although PCA method is helpful for reducing dimension of features, the deviations can be magnified. So, we propose to replace the PCA with a fully connected layer to reduce the dimension. In fact, the fully connection layer can be regarded as a special convolution layer. After the GOG features are processed by reshape layer, $1 \times 1 \times 7567 \times D_{FC}$ filter of FC layer can be set and the concatenation of outputs and pool5 features is fed into identification layer and verification layer as their inputs. In our experiment, the D_{FC} filter size is changed to balance the fusion feature.

The advantages of FC layer are that all the information of the GOG features is retained, and the weights are learned well by training the network. But the speed of training is slow because of the parameters increased.

3   Experimental Results

In order to verify the effectiveness of our proposed method, we make experiments on a large scale dataset market1501 and a small dataset VIPeR. We report the results which are compared with the current state-of-the-art results on two datasets and show that our method performs best.

Table 1. Impact of different dropout parameters on Market1501 dataset in three DML.

D	Our + Euclidean		Our + XQDA		Our + KISSME	
	MAP	Rank-1	MAP	Rank-1	MAP	Rank-1
0.4	64.7	83.4	64.2	82.1	65.6	84.8
0.5	**65.7**	**84.4**	**65.0**	**83.2**	**66.0**	**84.8**
0.6	65.7	83.8	64.8	81.7	65.9	83.9
0.7	**66.1**	**83.9**	**65.2**	**82.2**	**66.0**	**84.2**
0.8	65.4	83.8	64.8	81.7	65.9	84.0
0.9	61.9	81.3	62.7	81.2	63.8	82.9

Market1501 dataset contains 32,668 detected bounding boxes of 1,501 person IDs and the images corresponded each ID are captured by DPM method from the videos of 6 cameras. The dataset is divided into three parts: the training set consists of 12,936 cropped images and 751 person IDs, the test set consists of 19,732 cropped images and 750 person IDs, and a single query set includes 3,368 person images. The task is to select the ground truth images of the corresponding query set from all candidate images of the test set. The settings of the training and testing process are same as [22] in single query and multiple query evaluated.

We train the 2stream siamese JDAG model which is consisted of two ResNet50 and fine-tune it on ImageNet. FC layer filter size is set to $1 \times 1 \times 7567 \times 256$. The dropout parameters are adjusted as shown in Table 1 to reduce the the occurrence of over-fitting phenomenon. We report the mean average precision (MAP) and Rank-1 on Market1501 in three different DML when the dropout parameter is changed from 0.4 to 0.9. It is not difficult to find that when dropout is set to 0.7, our results perform best by the Euclidean distance and KISSME.

We also compare our method with other state-of-the-art method which are published within a year in terms of MAP and Rank-1 on Market1501 dataset in single query and multi query as Table 2. The dropout fixed is set to 0.7. (a) group denotes the latest results obtained by the existing method in a year. (b) and (c) groups denote the results evaluating the pool5 layer features and fusion layer features, respectively. We note that compared to the result obtained without using the person special features, our result has a 6% advantage on hard level. (d) group denotes the results adding re-ranking method [23], we were surprised to find that MAP of our results have improved about 13% and the rank-1 has a 3% advantage than the results only using CNN features and re-ranking in the Euclidean distance and the XQDA evaluation strategies. According the comparison of Table 2, our method performs better than the state-of-the-art results no matter which evaluation strategies.

VIPeR is a challenging dataset which includes 1,264 person images and 632 person IDs from two cameras. Because the scale of training set is small, the

Table 2. Comparison with state-of-the-art results of person re-identification on Market1501 dataset. (a) Previous works and results. (b) Our results by evaluating the features of pool5 layer (c) Our results by evaluating the features of fusion. The MAP and Rank-1 are listed for single query and multi query, respectively.

Method		Year of Publication	Single Query		Multi Query	
			MAP	Rank-1	MAP	Rank-1
(a)	Gate Reid	ECCV 2016 [24]	39.6	65.9	48.5	76.0
	CRAFT − MFA + LOMO	TPAMI 2017 [25]	45.5	71.8	54.3	79.7
	SOMAnet	Arxiv 2017 [26]	47.9	73.9	57.0	81.3
	IDE + Re-ranking	CVPR 2017 [23]	63.6	77.1	-	-
	PIE descriptor + KISSME	Arxiv 2017 [27]	56.0	79.3	-	-
	Re-id based CNN Embedding	Arxiv 2016 [21]	59.9	79.5	70.3	85.8
	SVDNet	Arxiv 2017 [28]	62.1	82.3	-	-
	Deep transfer learning	Arxiv 2016 [29]	65.5	83.7	73.8	89.6
(b)	JDAG(pool5) + Euclidean	Ours	66.5	84.4	72.3	86.1
	JDAG (pool5) + XQDA	Ours	65.0	82.1	70.2	85.1
	JDAG (pool5) + KISSME	Ours	65.9	83.4	71.0	85.4
(c)	JDAG (fusion) + Euclidean	Ours	66.1	83.4	71.5	85.9
	JDAG (fusion) + XQDA	Ours	65.2	82.2	71.0	84.9
	JDAG (fusion) + KISSME	Ours	66.0	84.2	71.6	85.7
(d)	JDAG (fusion) + Euclidean + Re-ranking	Ours	**79.3**	**86.3**	**81.2**	**88.5**
	JDAG (fusion) + XQDA + Re-ranking	Ours	**76.7**	**84.0**	**79.4**	**87.0**

Table 3. Comparison of state-of-the-art results on VIPeR dataset.

Method	Rank-1	Rank-5	Rank-10	Rank-20
MLFL [11]	29.1	-	65.9	70.9
SCNCD [30]	37.8	68.5	81.2	90.4
Semantic [12]	31.1	68.6	82.8	94.9
LOMO + XQDA [1]	40.0	-	80.5	91.1
MetricEnsemble [13]	45.9	77.5	88.9	95.8
GOG + XQDA [4]	49.7	79.7	88.7	94.5
Ours + XQDA	**57.2**	**84.5**	**91.5**	**96.2**

features are extracted by Market1501 training model. Then, we randomly select 316 images for testing and evaluation by XQDA and the procedure is conducted for 10 splits. The comparison with other method is reported in Table 3. We can observe that our result is superior to existing results. The precision is improved by 8% in Rank-1 than only using GOG features.

In order to explain this result intuitively, we choose an example in VIPeR dataset to compare the accuracy of the matching between GOG + XQDA and JDAG + XQDA, as Fig. 2. A ground truth image from a query is ranked the fourth position in GOG + XQDA, however it is ranked the first in JDAG + XQDA, which fully shows that our performance is more outstanding.

Fig. 2. Person re-id samples on VIPeR dataset. The images in left column is query images. The tested images are ranked according to the similarity scores. The retrieval images in top row are from GOG method and the bottom is from our method. The red boxes denote error detection and the green boxes denote exactness. (Color figure online)

The result above on two datasets indicate that discriminative features extracted by JDAG model are more suitable for application to the large scale datasets and small datasets.

4   Conclusions

In this work, we introduce a novel model called JDAG which is a fusion network of 2stream ResNet50 and GOG. When the JDAG model is trained, the traditional GOG features is fed into the model to play an important role in emphasizing special features. The features trained and extracted by JDAG model are more discriminative than the single features extracted. We utilize the JDAG features to improve the robustness of matching score. We verify the results on two public datasets and achieve a state-of-the-art performance. In the future work, we will continue to explore the robust feature extraction method based on JDAG model. We also consider applying our method on more areas, such as person search, re-id in video and some related retrieval tasks.

Acknowledgment. This work was supported by the NSFC (under Grant U1509 206, 61472276).

References

1. Liao, S., Hu, Y., Zhu, X., Li, S.Z.: Person re-identification by local maximal occurrence representation and metric learning. In: Proceedings of the IEEE Conference on Computer Vision and Pattern Recognition, pp. 2197–2206 (2015)
2. Zhao, R., Ouyang, W., Wang, X.: Person re-identification by salience matching. In: Proceedings of the IEEE International Conference on Computer Vision, pp. 2528–2535 (2013)
3. Zhao, R., Ouyang, W., Wang, X.: Unsupervised salience learning for person re-identification. In: Proceedings of the IEEE Conference on Computer Vision and Pattern Recognition, pp. 3586–3593 (2013)

4. Matsukawa, T., Okabe, T., Suzuki, E., Sato, Y.: Hierarchical Gaussian descriptor for person re-identification. In: Proceedings of the IEEE Conference on Computer Vision and Pattern Recognition, pp. 1363–1372 (2016)
5. Hong, R., Zhang, L., Zhang, C., Zimmermann, R.: Flickr circles: aesthetic tendency discovery by multi-view regularized topic modeling. IEEE Trans. Multimedia **18**(8), 1555–1567 (2016)
6. Hong, R., Hu, Z., Wang, R., Wang, M., Tao, D.: Multi-view object retrieval via multi-scale topic models. IEEE Trans. Image Process. **25**(12), 5814–5827 (2016)
7. Hong, R., Yang, Y., Wang, M., Hua, X.S.: Learning visual semantic relationships for efficient visual retrieval. IEEE Trans. Big Data **1**(4), 152–161 (2015)
8. Nie, L., Yan, S., Wang, M., Hong, R., Chua, T.S.: Harvesting visual concepts for image search with complex queries. In: Proceedings of the 20th ACM international conference on Multimedia, pp. 59–68 (2012)
9. Nie, L., Wang, M., Zha, Z., Li, G., Chua, T.S.: Multimedia answering: enriching text QA with media information. In: Proceedings of the 34th International ACM SIGIR Conference on Research and Development in Information Retrieval, pp. 695–704 (2011)
10. Nie, L., Wang, M., Zha, Z.J., Chua, T.S.: Oracle in image search: a content-based approach to performance prediction. ACM Trans. Inf. Syst. (TOIS) **30**(2), 13 (2012)
11. Zhao, R., Ouyang, W., Wang, X.: Learning mid-level filters for person re-identification. In: Proceedings of the IEEE Conference on Computer Vision and Pattern Recognition, pp. 144–151 (2014)
12. Shi, Z., Hospedales, T.M., Xiang, T.: Transferring a semantic representation for person re-identification and search. In: Proceedings of the IEEE Conference on Computer Vision and Pattern Recognition, pp. 4184–4193 (2015)
13. Paisitkriangkrai, S., Shen, C., van den Hengel, A.: Learning to rank in person re-identification with metric ensembles. In: Proceedings of the IEEE Conference on Computer Vision and Pattern Recognition, pp. 1846–1855 (2015)
14. Serra, G., Grana, C., Manfredi, M., Cucchiara, R.: Covariance of covariance features for image classification. In: Proceedings of International Conference on Multimedia Retrieval, p. 411 (2014)
15. Davis, J.V., Kulis, B., Jain, P., Sra, S., Dhillon, I.S.: Information-theoretic metric learning. In: Proceedings of the 24th International Conference on Machine Learning, pp. 209–216 (2007)
16. Guillaumin, M., Verbeek, J., Schmid, C.: Is that you? metric learning approaches for face identification. In: 2009 IEEE 12th International Conference on Computer Vision, pp. 498–505 (2009)
17. Koestinger, M., Hirzer, M., Wohlhart, P., Roth, P.M., Bischof, H.: Large scale metric learning from equivalence constraints. In: 2012 IEEE Conference on Computer Vision and Pattern Recognition (CVPR), pp. 2288–2295 (2012)
18. He, K., Zhang, X., Ren, S., Sun, J.: Deep residual learning for image recognition. In: Proceedings of the IEEE Conference on Computer Vision and Pattern Recognition, pp. 770–778 (2016)
19. Gray, D., Tao, H.: Viewpoint invariant pedestrian recognition with an ensemble of localized features. In: Forsyth, D., Torr, P., Zisserman, A. (eds.) ECCV 2008. LNCS, vol. 5302, pp. 262–275. Springer, Heidelberg (2008). https://doi.org/10.1007/978-3-540-88682-2_21
20. Zheng, L., Shen, L., Tian, L., Wang, S., Wang, J., Tian, Q.: Scalable person re-identification: a benchmark. In: Proceedings of the IEEE International Conference on Computer Vision, pp. 1116–1124 (2015)

21. Zheng, Z., Zheng, L., Yang, Y.: A discriminatively learned CNN embedding for person re-identification. arXiv preprint arXiv:1611.05666 (2016)
22. Zagoruyko, S., Komodakis, N.: Learning to compare image patches via convolutional neural networks. In: Proceedings of the IEEE Conference on Computer Vision and Pattern Recognition, pp. 4353–4361 (2015)
23. Zhong, Z., Zheng, L., Cao, D., Li, S.: Re-ranking Person Re-identification with k-reciprocal Encoding. arXiv preprint arXiv:1701.08398 (2017)
24. Varior, R.R., Haloi, M., Wang, G.: Gated siamese convolutional neural network architecture for human re-identification. In: Leibe, B., Matas, J., Sebe, N., Welling, M. (eds.) ECCV 2016. LNCS, vol. 9912, pp. 791–808. Springer, Cham (2016). https://doi.org/10.1007/978-3-319-46484-8_48
25. Chen, Y.C., Zhu, X., Zheng, W.S., Lai, J.H.: Person re-identification by camera correlation aware feature augmentation. IEEE Trans. Pattern Anal. Mach. Intell. (2017)
26. Barbosa, I.B., Cristani, M., Caputo, B., Rognhaugen, A., Theoharis, T.: Looking beyond appearances: synthetic training data for deep CNNs in re-identification. arXiv preprint arXiv:1701.03153 (2017)
27. Zheng, L., Huang, Y., Lu, H., Yang, Y.: Pose invariant embedding for deep person re-identification. arXiv preprint arXiv:1701.07732 (2017)
28. Sun, Y., Zheng, L., Deng, W., Wang, S.: SVDNet for Pedestrian Retrieval. arXiv preprint arXiv:1703.05693 (2017)
29. Geng, M., Wang, Y., Xiang, T., Tian, Y.: Deep transfer learning for person re-identification. arXiv preprint arXiv:1611.05244 (2016)
30. Yang, Y., Yang, J., Yan, J., Liao, S., Yi, D., Li, S.Z.: Salient color names for person re-identification. In: Fleet, D., Pajdla, T., Schiele, B., Tuytelaars, T. (eds.) ECCV 2014. LNCS, vol. 8689, pp. 536–551. Springer, Cham (2014). https://doi.org/10.1007/978-3-319-10590-1_35

Blind Image Deblurring Using Adaptive Priors

Bingwang Zhang[1,2], Risheng Liu[1,2], Haojie Li[1,2($\boxtimes$)], Qi Yuan[1,2], Xin Fan[1,2], and Zhongxuan Luo[1,2]

[1] DUT-RU International School of Information and Software Engineering, Dalian University of Technology, Dalian, China
bwzhang@mail.dlut.edu.cn , hjli@dlut.edu.cn
[2] Key Laboratory for Ubiquitous Network and Service Software of Liaoning Province, Dalian, China

Abstract. For blind image deblurring, a good prior knowledge can guide the maximum a posterior (MAP) based algorithms to be away from the trivial solution. Therefore, many existing methods focus on designing effective priors to constrain the solution space. However, blind deconvolution with fixed priors is not robust. And many priors are extremely costly to design and compute. In this paper, we proposed a blind deconvolution method with adaptive priors under the MAP framework. Specifically, we carry out our algorithm under the multi-scale, and at each scale we add specific sparse regularization to standard deblurring formulation. By tunning both the priors and the weights we can give more flexible sparse regularization constraint. After iteration, our algorithm output both latent image and estimated blur kernel, simultaneously. We prove the convergence of the proposed algorithm. Extensive experiments show the effectiveness of our proposed approach.

Keywords: Blind deblurring · Sparsely constraint · Adaptive priors
MAP

1 Introduction

Blind image deblurring aims to recover a latent sharp image and a blur kernel from a blurred image. And it has recently attracted increasing attention in computer vision. Generally, the deblurring problem can be represented as

$$y = k \otimes x + n$$

where y represents the blur image, x is the latent image, k is the blur kernel, n is Gaussian noise, $\otimes$ denotes convolution operator. The problem is how to recover both x and k from single input y, which is highly ill-posed and non-convex.

Most previous works used regularization term method for solving above problem. The formulation of regularization term method for image deblurring as

$$J(x, k) = \phi(k \otimes x, y) + \lambda \varphi(x, k)$$

© Springer Nature Singapore Pte Ltd. 2018
B. Huet et al. (Eds.): ICIMCS 2017, CCIS 819, pp. 13–22, 2018.
https://doi.org/10.1007/978-981-10-8530-7_2

where $\phi(k \otimes x, y)$ is data term, $\varphi(x, k)$ denotes regularization constraint term, and λ are weights.

When n denotes Gaussian noise, the data term

$$\phi(k \otimes x, y) = \|k \otimes x - y\|_2^2$$

So, many previous methods obtained satisfactory results by carefully designed $\varphi(x, k)$ and empirically tuned λ. Priors on the statistics of both image and kernel determine the selection of regularization term. Specifically, many methods focus on designing effective priors for x, while k is usually restricted to be smooth. So, priors on the statistics of image are crucial.

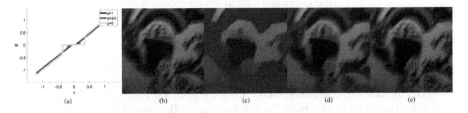

Fig. 1. Example of different p value in L_p-norm. The curves in (a) show the solution space of shrinkage function $\min_g (g-v)^2 + \lambda|g|^p, p = 0$ (yellow), $p = 2/3$ (red), $p = 1$ (black). $(c) - (e)$ represents the solution of the image denoising equation $\min_x \|x - y\|_2^2 + \lambda\|\nabla x\|_p^p$. (b) Blurry image, (c) $p = 0, (d)$ $p = 2/3$, (e) $p = 1$. The regularizer with smaller p value smooth many small-scale textures, larger p value retain more details. (Color figure online)

In this paper, we propose a blind image deblurring method with adaptive priors. We introduce a family of priors (L_p-regularized gradient priors) as sparse regularization. We select different priors along iterations. Different priors corresponds to different energy functions. And we minimize them via our modified ADMM[1] algorithm. We will prove the convergence of our algorithm for any L_p-norm. In other words, we can select any L_p-norm along with iterations. Specifically, at the initial stage, we select L_0-norm, which can be used to smooth small-scale textures and select salient edges, so that we can estimate coarse shape of blur kernel rapidly. Then we refine the estimated blur kernel by gradually increasing the p value of L_p-norm along with iteration. Finally, we model the heavy-tailed distribution of gradients in natural scenes via L_p-norm ($p = 0.8$). Figure 1 shows one example. The regularizer with smaller p value can smooth many small-scale textures, and with the increase of p value, the intermediate images include more gradient details.

The contributions of this work are as follows: (1) we proposed a method for blind image deblurring with adaptive priors. Specifically it is adaptive L_p-regularized gradient priors; (2) we proved the convergence of the proposed algorithm; (3) our approach achieved competitive results on widely-used natural image deblurring benchmarks [7,9,13] and some challenging images.

---

[1] Alternating direction method of multiplier.

2   Related Work

Most image deblurring methods are based on Bayesian theory, which can be divided into two classes: variational Bayes (VB)-based and maximum a posterior (MAP)-based. VB-based is more robust, but computationally inefficient.

In recent years, many MAP-based approaches are developed and achieved promising performance. The priors for MAP-based is critical. In [2] Chan and Wong used total variation (TV) regularizer for blind image deblurring. Xu *et al.* [16] used the L_0-regularizer on the image gradient. Krishnan *et al.* [8] introduced L_1/L_2 in image gradient prior. However, these approaches failed to address specific images such as face and low-illumination images.

Different from the method of iteration wise priors [18], which learned iteration wise parameters of the hyper Laplacian prior for kernel estimation. Our method design adaptive priors for both kernel and latent image estimation, and we are not only limited to use hyper Laplace ($0 < p < 1$) priors but also select L_p-norm where $p \in \{[0, 1] \cup 2\}$. Furthermore, our method can be directly applied to any blurry images while do not need to train. [11,17] are some other related works.

3   Blind Image Deblurring with Adaptive Priors

In this section, we describe our algorithm and analyze its convergence. Firstly we prove the convergence of modified ADMM algorithm with two assumptions. Then we apply the modified ADMM algorithm to image deblurring problems. And we prove that for any L_p-norm ($p \in \{[0, 1] \cup 2\}$) satisfies the assumptions.

3.1   Our Algorithm Framework

Model Statement. We describe our algorithm by solving a widely-concerned problem. We consider optimization problem:

$$\hat{x} = \arg\min_{x} \ f(x) + \lambda g(x) \qquad (1)$$

where $f(x)$ has second order continuous derivative on R. General, $g(x)$ is non-convex. It is difficult to solve the problem directly. We introduce an auxiliary variable v, and convert Eq. (1) into a constrained problem:

$$(\hat{x}, \hat{v}) = \arg\min_{x,v} \ f(x) + \lambda g(v), \ subject\,to\ x = v \qquad (2)$$

General, we obtain the solution for Eq. (2) by alternatively solving

$$\begin{aligned} &\min_{x} \ f(x) + \tfrac{\rho_t}{2}\big\|x - \tilde{x}^{(t)}\big\|^2, \\ &\min_{v} \ \lambda g(v) + \tfrac{\rho_t}{2}\big\|v - \tilde{v}^{(t)}\big\|^2 \end{aligned} \qquad (3)$$

where $\tilde{x}^{(t)} = \tilde{v}^{(t)} - u^{(t)}, \tilde{v}^{(t)} = x^{(t+1)} + u^{(t)}$ is known as ADMM. And $u^{(t+1)} = u^{(t)} + \big(x^{(t+1)} - v^{(t+1)}\big), \rho_{t+1} = \gamma\rho_t \ (\gamma > 1)$ are updated.

Convergence. To ensure global convergence, one sufficient condition is that $g(v)$ is convex. But in many cases, $g(v)$ is a complex nonsmooth and even nonconvex function. We assume a mild condition for $g(v)$ and expect a weaker form of convergence. Before providing the convergence of our algorithm, we first give some essential assumptions:

1. $f : [0,1]^n \to R$ has bounded gradients, i.e., $\|\nabla f(x)\| \leq C_0$, for some universal constant C_0.
2. $\left\|v^{(t+1)} - \tilde{v}^{(t)}\right\|^2 = \left\|G_{\sigma_t}\left(\tilde{v}^{(t)}\right) - \tilde{v}^{(t)}\right\|^2 \leq \frac{\lambda M}{\rho_t}$, for some universal, nonnegative constant M. Where $G_{\sigma_t}\left(\tilde{v}^{(t)}\right) = \min_v g(v) + \frac{\rho_t}{2}\left\|v - \tilde{v}^{(t)}\right\|^2$ for updating v in Eq. (3) and $\sigma_t = \sqrt{\lambda/\rho_t}$. Under two assumptions, the iterates of our algorithm in Eq. (3) is convergent.

Proof. Comes from the assumptions, the iterative sequence generated by our algorithm have the following estimations:

$$\left\|x^{(t+1)} - x^{(t)}\right\| \leq \frac{1}{\sqrt{\rho_{t-2}}}\left(5\sqrt{C_1} + \frac{C_0}{\sqrt{\rho_0}}\right) \tag{4}$$

$$\left\|v^{(t+1)} - v^{(t)}\right\| \leq \frac{1}{\sqrt{\rho_{t-2}}}\left(\sqrt{C_1} + \frac{C_0}{\sqrt{\rho_0}}\right) \tag{5}$$

$$\left\|u^{(t+1)} - u^{(t)}\right\| \leq \frac{2\sqrt{C_1}}{\sqrt{\rho_{t-2}}} \tag{6}$$

So, for any t we have

$$\left\|x^{(t+1)} - x^{(t)}\right\| + \left\|v^{(t+1)} - v^{(t)}\right\| + \left\|u^{(t+1)} - u^{(t)}\right\|$$
$$\leq \frac{1}{\sqrt{\rho_0}}\left(8\sqrt{C_1} + \frac{C_0}{\sqrt{\rho_0}}\right)\left(\sqrt{\frac{1}{\gamma}}\right)^{t-2} \tag{7}$$
$$= C'\delta^{t-2}$$

where the notation $C' = \frac{1}{\sqrt{\rho_0}}\left(8\sqrt{C_1} + \frac{C_0}{\sqrt{\rho_0}}\right)$ and $\delta = \left(\sqrt{\frac{1}{\gamma}}\right)$ $(0 < \delta < 1)$. From any $n < t \leq N$, we have that

$$\sum_{t=n+1}^{N} \left\|x^{(t+1)} - x^{(t)}\right\| + \left\|v^{(t+1)} - v^{(t)}\right\| + \left\|u^{(t+1)} - u^{(t)}\right\|$$
$$\leq C'\left(\delta^{n-1} + \delta^n + \cdots + \delta^{N-2}\right) \tag{8}$$
$$= C'\delta^{n-1}\frac{1-\delta^{N-n}}{1-\delta}$$

When $n \to \infty$, the sequence tends to 0. Hence the sequence generated by our algorithm is a Cauchy sequence.

3.2 Image Deblurring Algorithm

Different priors corresponds to different energy functions. So we will minimize a series of energy functions along iterations. For each energy function, we obtain the solution by estimating sharp latent image and blur kernel, alternately. For estimating sharp latent image, we use our modified ADMM algorithm.

Models. Our adaptive image deblurring algorithm is carried out using multi-scale $(S, S-1, \ldots, s, \ldots, 1)$. At each scale, we add specific prior $P_s(x)$ to a standard formulation for image deblurring as

$$\min_{x,k} \|k \otimes x - y\|_2^2 + \omega \|k\|_2^2 + \lambda P_s(x) \tag{9}$$

where x and y denote the latent and blurred images, respectively; k is a blur kernel with the convolution operator $\otimes$ and L_2 regularized term $\|k\|_2^2$; γ and ω are weights. Specific priors $P_s(x)$ are L_p-regularized gradient priors

$$P_s(x) = \|\nabla x\|_{p_s}^{p_s} \tag{10}$$

Inner Iterations for Estimating Image. We update intermediate images via our algorithm. We define $f(x) = \|k \otimes x - y\|_2^2$ as data term, and $g(v) = P_s(v)$ as prior term. And the iteration form

$$x^{(t+1)} = \arg\min_x \frac{1}{2} \|k \otimes x - y\|_2^2 + \frac{\rho_t}{2} \left\| x - \tilde{x}^{(t)} \right\|_2^2 \tag{11}$$

$$v^{(t+1)} = G_{\sigma_t}\left(\tilde{v}^{(t)} \right) \tag{12}$$

$$u^{(t+1)} = u^{(t)} + \left(x^{(t+1)} - v^{(t+1)} \right) \tag{13}$$

where $\tilde{x}^{(t)} = v^{(t)} - u^{(t)}, \tilde{v}^{(t)} = x^{(t+1)} + u^{(t)}$ and $\sigma_t = \sqrt{\lambda/\rho_t}$. $\rho_{t+1} = \gamma \rho_t$ as a continuation scheme.

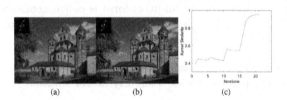

(a)   (b)   (c)

Fig. 2. Convergence of our algorithm. (a) is input image and kernel, (b) is the result of our algorithm, and (c) is kernel similarity plot. With the increase of iterations, the kernel estimation is better.

Equation (11) can be regarded as an inversion step as it involves the forward imaging model $f(x)$, and it can be efficiently computed by Fast Fourier transforms (FFTs).

Note, $f(x)$ is required to satisfy the first assumption. We prove that $f(x) = \|k \otimes x - y\|_2^2$ has bounded gradients.

Proof. For $K \in R^{n \times n}$ with eigenvalues bounded between 0 and 1. The gradient of f is $\nabla f(x) = 2K^T (Kx - y)$ and

$$\|\nabla f(x)\| \leq 2\lambda_{\max}(K)^2 (\|x\| + \|y\|)$$

Table 1. Quantitative comparisons on image sets (Levin *et al.*'s image set/Sun *et al.*'s image sets).

Methods	PSNR	SSIM
Cho and Lee [3]	27.63/26.19	0.85/0.81
Krishnan *et al.* [8]	24.87/22.92	0.74/0.75
Levin *et al.* [10]	29.03/24.90	0.89/0.80
Sun *et al.* [13]	29.71/29.48	0.90/**0.85**
Xu *et al.* [16]	26.71/28.27	0.83/0.85
Ours	**30.73/29.85**	**0.91**/0.84

Equation (12) can be regarded as a denoising step as it involves the prior $g(v)$. So, G_{σ_t} can be regarded as a denoiser. Different priors $g(v)$ corresponds to different denoisers. G_{σ_t} is required to satisfy the second assumption. We prove that G_{σ_t} with L_p-regularized gradient priors ($p \in \{[0,1] \cup 2\}$) satisfy the second assumption.

Proof. When $p = 2, g(v)$ is convex, so our algorithm have global convergence. When $p \neq 2$, we update v by

$$v^{(t+1)} = \arg\min_v \frac{\lambda}{2} \|\nabla v\|_{p_s}^{p_s} + \frac{\rho_t}{2} \left\|v - \tilde{v}^{(t)}\right\|_2^2 \tag{14}$$

We solve above problem via half-quadratic optimization algorithm. [14] proved that half-quadratic approaches of additive form is convergence. So, We can get the inequality $\left\|v^{(t+1)} - \tilde{v}^t\right\| < \infty$. So, there exist a positive integer M make $\left\|v^{(t+1)} - \tilde{v}^t\right\| < (\lambda M)/\rho_t$.

In practice, we return v as intermediate latent image for estimating blur kernel k, because v tends to provide a slightly better solution.

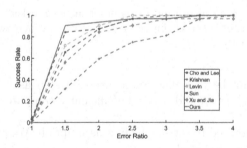

Fig. 3. Results on Levin *et al.*'s image sets.

Convergence of the Whole Algorithm. Our algorithm is carried out using multi-scale. At each scale, we ensure each that sub-problem either is convergent or has a closed-form solution. So, the whole algorithm has the fast convergence property. Figure 2 shows kernel similarity [6] with respect to iterations.

4   Experiments

4.1   Experimental Setup

We present experimental results of the proposed method against the several state-of-the-art deblurring approaches in this section. All the experiments are carried out on a desktop computer with an Intel Core i5-4460 processor and 8 GB RAM. And all the results of compared methods are provided by the authors or generated using their codes with default parameter setting. At each scale, we set $\lambda = 4e^{-3}, \omega = 2$. And, we set $\rho_0 = 0.1, \gamma = 1.12$. At the coarsest level, we set $p = 0$, and gradually add p value. At the last level, we set $p = 0.8$. As for the quantitative comparison, we follow recent works to report the average peak signal to noise ratio (PSNR), structural similarity (SSIM), error ratio (ER) and kernel similarity (KS) on image sets.

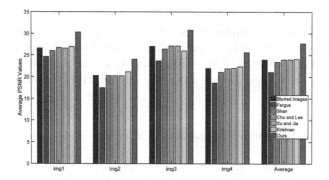

Fig. 4. Results on dataset [7]. Our method has the highest average PSNR among all the methods evaluated.

4.2   Results and Analysis on Benchmark Datasets

We first evaluate our method on two benchmark datasets. And we compare our proposed method with 5 state-of-the-art approaches [3, 8, 10, 13, 16] on these two datasets.

Results on Levin *et al.*'s Image Sets. The results on Levin *et al.*'s image sets are shown in the left part of "/" of Table 1. Our method achieved the highest average PSNR and SSIM among all these compared methods. Time comparisons are shown in Table 2, we can see that although our proposed system isn't the

Table 2. Time comparisons on Levin *et al.*'s image sets (time in seconds).

Methods	[3]	[8]	[10]	[13]	[16]	Ours
Time(s)	1.16	17.74	107.98	494.70	2.44	9.45

fastest, it is still faster than [13]. Table 3 shows the results of PSNR and runtime on Levin *et al.*'s image set using different denoisers. We use these four state-of-the-art denoisers for updating v. Compared to four fixed priors denoisers (BM3D [5], RF (Recursive Filter), TV [2], NLM [1]), our method achieved the highest average PSNR. Time comparisons show that our method with adaptive L_p-regularized gradient priors is efficient. The results further validate the correctness of our methodology. Figure 3 shows the curves of the accumulated error ratios.

Table 3. Comparison between our method and four fixed priors approaches on Levin *et al.*'s image set (time in seconds).

	BM3D	RF	NLM	TV	Ours
PSNR	27.94	27.28	29.02	27.27	30.73
Time(s)	211.98	18.37	50.31	131.88	9.45

Results on Sun *et al.*'s Image Sets. The right part of "/" of Table 1 shows the results on Sun *et al.*'s image sets. Our method achieved better results than almost all the competing methods. The results show that our method also performs well on large scale images. Table 4 shows the quantitative comparisons of kernel similarity.

Table 4. Quantitative comparisons (KS) on Sun *et al.*'s image sets.

Methods	[3]	[8]	[10]	[13]	[16]	Ours
KS(s)	0.783	0.722	0.711	0.819	0.835	0.857

Results on Köhler *et al.*'s Image Sets. We evaluate our method using the image dataset by Köhler *et al.* [7]. We compare with five methods [3,4,8,12,15]. As shown in Fig. 4, our method achieved the highest average PSNR among all the methods evaluated.

4.3   Evaluation on Nature Blurred Images

To demonstrate the flexibility of the proposed method, we test our method on nature blurred images, and compare with four methods [3,8,13,16]. Figure 5 shows the deconvolution results of three different types of real blurred photographes. (*a*) is face image. Blurred face images are challenging for methods designed for natural images, because they contain fewer edges for kernel estimation. (*b*) is wall image with heavy blur. (*c*) is a car image. Our method has a better presentation.

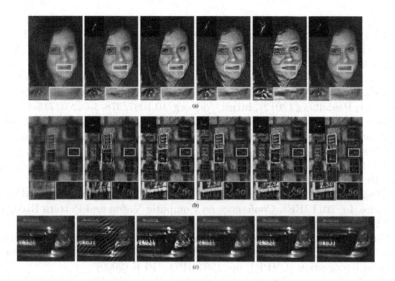

Fig. 5. Comparisons on different nature blurred images. In each row, from left to right, there are input, results of [3], results of [8], results of [13], results of [16], Ours, respectively.

5 Conclusions

In this paper, we proposed a novel method for blind image deblurring with adaptive priors. Our algorithm is carried out under the multi-scale. At each scale, we design different prior in objective function, and minimize it via our optimize algorithm. Extensive experiments demonstrate that our method is effective and efficient. Our approach achieved competitive results on three benchmarks and some challenging images. In the future, we are interested to extend our method for text image deblurring.

Acknowledgement. This work was partially supported by National Natural Science Funds of China (61472059, 61632019 and 61672125).

References

1. Buades, A., Coll, B., Morel, J.M.: Non-local means denoising. Image Process. Line **1**, 208–212 (2011)
2. Chan, T.F., Wong, C.K.: Total variation blind deconvolution. IEEE Trans. Image Process. **7**(3), 370–375 (1998)

3. Cho, S., Lee, S.: Fast motion deblurring. ACM Trans. Graph. (TOG) **28**, 145 (2009)
4. Fergus, R., Singh, B., Hertzmann, A., Roweis, S.T., Freeman, W.T.: Removing camera shake from a single photograph. ACM Trans. Graph. (TOG) **25**, 787–794 (2006)
5. Foi, A.: Image and video denoising by sparse 3D transform-domain collaborative filtering. Transforms and Spectral Methods Group, Department of Signal Processing, Tampere University (2014). http://www.cs.tut.fi/foi/GCF-BM3D/. Accessed 3 Aug 2014
6. Hu, Z., Yang, M.-H.: Good regions to deblur. In: Fitzgibbon, A., Lazebnik, S., Perona, P., Sato, Y., Schmid, C. (eds.) ECCV 2012. LNCS, vol. 7576, pp. 59–72. Springer, Heidelberg (2012). https://doi.org/10.1007/978-3-642-33715-4_5
7. Köhler, R., Hirsch, M., Mohler, B., Schölkopf, B., Harmeling, S.: Recording and playback of camera shake: benchmarking blind deconvolution with a real-world database. In: Fitzgibbon, A., Lazebnik, S., Perona, P., Sato, Y., Schmid, C. (eds.) ECCV 2012. LNCS, vol. 7578, pp. 27–40. Springer, Heidelberg (2012). https://doi.org/10.1007/978-3-642-33786-4_3
8. Krishnan, D., Tay, T., Fergus, R.: Blind deconvolution using a normalized sparsity measure. In: 2011 IEEE Conference on Computer Vision and Pattern Recognition (CVPR), pp. 233–240. IEEE (2011)
9. Levin, A., Weiss, Y., Durand, F., Freeman, W.T.: Understanding and evaluating blind deconvolution algorithms. In: IEEE Conference on Computer Vision and Pattern Recognition (CVPR), pp. 1964–1971. IEEE (2009)
10. Levin, A., Weiss, Y., Durand, F., Freeman, W.T.: Efficient marginal likelihood optimization in blind deconvolution. In: 2011 IEEE Conference on Computer Vision and Pattern Recognition (CVPR), pp. 2657–2664. IEEE (2011)
11. Nie, L., Yan, S., Wang, M., Hong, R., Chua, T.S.: Harvesting visual concepts for image search with complex queries. In: Proceedings of the 20th ACM International Conference on Multimedia, pp. 59–68. ACM (2012)
12. Shan, Q., Jia, J., Agarwala, A.: High-quality motion deblurring from a single image. ACM Trans. Graph. (TOG) **27**, 73 (2008)
13. Sun, L., Cho, S., Wang, J., Hays, J.: Edge-based blur kernel estimation using patch priors. In: Proceedings of the IEEE International Conference on Computational Photography (2013)
14. Wang, Y., Yin, W.: Compressed sensing via iterative support detection. Rice University CAAM Technical report TR09-30 (2009)
15. Xu, L., Jia, J.: Two-phase kernel estimation for robust motion deblurring. In: Daniilidis, K., Maragos, P., Paragios, N. (eds.) ECCV 2010. LNCS, vol. 6311, pp. 157–170. Springer, Heidelberg (2010). https://doi.org/10.1007/978-3-642-15549-9_12
16. Xu, L., Zheng, S., Jia, J.: Unnatural L0 sparse representation for natural image deblurring. In: Proceedings of the IEEE Conference on Computer Vision and Pattern Recognition, pp. 1107–1114 (2013)
17. Zhang, H., Zha, Z.J., Yang, Y., Yan, S., Gao, Y., Chua, T.S.: Attribute-augmented semantic hierarchy: towards bridging semantic gap and intention gap in image retrieval. In: Proceedings of the 21st ACM International Conference on Multimedia, pp. 33–42. ACM (2013)
18. Zuo, W., Ren, D., Gu, S., Lin, L., Zhang, L.: Discriminative learning of iteration-wise priors for blind deconvolution. In: Proceedings of the IEEE Conference on Computer Vision and Pattern Recognition, pp. 3232–3240 (2015)

Joint Latent Space and Multi-view Feature Learning

Kailing Guo, Xiangmin Xu$^{(\boxtimes)}$, Bolun Cai, and Tong Zhang

South China University of Techonology, 381 Wushan Road, Guangzhou, China
eecollinguo@gmail.com, caibolun@gmail.com,
{xmxu,tony}@scut.edu.cn

Abstract. GoDec+ shows its robustness in low-rank matrix decomposition but only deals with single-view data. This paper extends GoDec+ to multi-view data by jointly learning latent space and multi-view fusion feature. The proposed method factorizes the low-rank matrix in GoDec+ into the product of a basis matrix of the latent space and a shared representation given by a transformation matrix. By constraining the basis matrix to be group sparse, the proposed method treats the effects of different views differently. Extensive experiments show that the proposed method learns a good fusion feature and outperforms the compared methods in image classification and annotation.

Keywords: Low-rank · Multi-view · Correntropy

1 Introduction

In real applications, multi-view data are common since data are usually collected from different domains or obtained from various feature extrators. For examples, images of one human face taken in different directions, and shape, texture, and color properties of one image. Multi-view learning aims to make good use of the information from different views and is a classic problem in machine learning [1–3].

Canonical correlation analysis (CCA) is commonly used for multi-view data analysis [4]. For two observation vectors x_1 and x_2, CCA finds transformation matrix B_1 and B_2 such that the transformed data $B_1^T x_1$ and $B_2^T x_2$ are maximally correlated. Its probablistic interpretation is that there exists a latent variable z satisfying $x_1 = B_1 z + \epsilon_1$ and $x_2 = B_2 z + \epsilon_2$, where ϵ_1 and ϵ_1 are Gaussian noise [5]. It means that CCA intrinsically finds a common latent representation. Some recent multi-view learning methods also adopt a common latent intrinsic representation and show great success [6,7].

Low-rank is a good property for capturing the intrinsic representation. GoDec+ [8] is a robust and fast low-rank approximation method that maximizing the sum of correntropy of the difference between the original data X and the low-rank approximation $\tilde{X}$. Discriminative GoDec+ (D-GoDec+) [9]

B. Huet et al. (Eds.): ICIMCS 2017, CCIS 819, pp. 23–31, 2018.
https://doi.org/10.1007/978-981-10-8530-7_3

extends GoDec+ for classification by replacing $\widetilde{X}$ with a matrix factorization form $BW^T X$. Since it is easy to add more information for learning by enforcing constraints on the factor matrices B and W, D-GoDec+ successfully incorporates label information for classification. Motivated by this, we replace $\widetilde{X}$ in GoDec+ by $BW^T X$ and add constraints on B and W for multi-view learning in this paper. Here B is treated as the view generation matrix (i.e., the basis of the latent space) and W is treated as the transformation matrix that extracts the latent intrinsic representation.

Comprehensive experiments on face recognition, digit classification and image annotation demonstrate the effectiveness of the proposed multi-view learning method.

2 Problem Formulation

2.1 Brief Review of GoDec+

Given a data matrix $X \in \mathbb{R}^{m \times n}$, GoDec+ represents the data by a low-rank matrix $\widetilde{X}$ and the error E modeled by a nonlinear similarity measurement correntropy [10]. The definition of correntropy is given as $C(E) = \sum_i^m \sum_j^n g_\sigma(E_{i,j})$, where g_σ is Gaussian kernel $g_\sigma(x) = \exp(-x^2/\sigma^2)$. Maximizing correntropy is equivalent to minimizing the sum of the Welsch M-estimator, which is defined as

$$w(E) = \sum_i^m \sum_j^n [1 - g_\sigma(E_{i,j})]. \tag{1}$$

The model of GoDec+ is given as

$$\min_{\widetilde{X}} w(X - \widetilde{X}), \quad s.t. \quad \text{rank}(\widetilde{X}) \leq r, \tag{2}$$

where $\widetilde{X}$ is the low-rank matrix and r is the given rank.

2.2 The Proposed Model

Following [6], group sparsity is enforced on the view generation matrix B to achieve view specific generation sub-matrices. The proposed model is given as follows.

$$\min_{B,W} w(X - BW^T X) + \alpha \sum_{v=1}^{V} \|B_v\|_{2,1} + \frac{\beta}{2} \|W\|_F^2, \tag{3}$$

$$\min_{B,W} w(x_i^v - B_v W^T x_i^v) + \frac{\alpha}{2} \|B\|_F^2 + \frac{\beta}{2} \|W\|_F^2, \tag{4}$$

$$\min_{B,W} w(x_i^v - B_v(W_s^T x_i + W_v^T x_i^v)) + \frac{\alpha}{2} \|B\|_F^2 + \frac{\beta}{2} \|W_s\|_F^2 + \frac{\gamma}{2} \sum_{v=1}^{V} \|W_v\|_F^2, \tag{5}$$

where $B = [B_1; B_2; \cdots ; B_V]$ with B_i's are the view-specific generation sub-matrices, α and β are positive trade-off parameters, $\| \cdot \|_{2,1}$ denotes $\ell_{2,1}$ norm, and $\| \cdot \|_F$ is Frobenius norm. The $\ell_{2,1}$ norm is defined as

$$\|A\|_{2,1} = \sum_j \sqrt{\sum_i A_{i,j}^2} = \sum_j \|a_{:,j}\|_2. \tag{6}$$

The $\ell_{2,1}$ norm encourages group sparsity and the columns of the matrix tend to be zeroed-out. Thus, each view depends on only a subset of the latent dimensions. By the competitions of the views for data reconstruction, we can learn view-specific generation sub-matrices. The last term in the objective function is regularization term for stable solution.

2.3 Optimization

Since half-quadratic (HQ) optimization is a commonly used optimization method for dealing with correntropy, we give a short review of the main ideas of HQ. Let $\phi(v)$ be a objective function of v that satisfies the preliminary facts [11] of HQ. Then, we have

$$\phi(v) = \min_p \frac{1}{2}(v\sqrt{c} - \frac{p}{\sqrt{c}})^2 + \varphi(p). \tag{7}$$

where c is a constant satisfying that $c > 0$ and $cv^2 - \phi(v)$ is convex, p is an auxiliary variable determined, and $\varphi(.)$ is the dual potential function of $\phi(.)$. It follows that

$$\min_v \phi(v) = \min_{v,p} \frac{1}{2}(v\sqrt{c} - \frac{p}{\sqrt{c}})^2 + \varphi(p). \tag{8}$$

Although the exact formulation of $\varphi(p)$ is often unknown, the minimizer of Eq. (7) can be determined by a specific function $\delta(.)$ only related to $\phi(.)$ with the form

$$p = \delta(v) = cv - \phi'(v). \tag{9}$$

With this solution, minimizing $\phi(v)$ can be solved by iteratively optimizing v and p. When p is given, the sub-problem of minimizing v is a quadratic problem. This is why this method is called half-quadratic optimization. We refer interested readers to [11] for more details.

For our specific problem, $w(v)$ is $\phi(v)$ in (7). According to (9), the function $\delta(\cdot)$ for the Welsch M-estimator is

$$\delta(v) = cv - \frac{2}{\sigma^2}v\exp(-\frac{v^2}{\sigma^2}). \tag{10}$$

In this case, $c = \frac{2}{\sigma^2}$. Define $\alpha_1 = \alpha/c$, $\beta_1 = \beta/c$ and $\hat{X} = X - \frac{T}{c}$, problem (5) changes into

$$\min_{B,W,T} \frac{1}{2}\|\hat{X} - BW^T X\|_F^2 + \frac{\varphi_s(T)}{c} + \alpha_1 \sum_{i=1}^{V} \|B_i\|_{2,1} + \frac{\beta_1}{2}\|W\|_F^2, \tag{11}$$

where T_i is the auxiliary variable introduced by HQ and $\varphi_s(T)$ is defined as $\varphi_s(T) = \sum_{i,j} \varphi(T_{i,j})$. When the other variables are given, it is easy to obtain T by

$$T = cE - \frac{2}{\sigma^2} E \circ g_\sigma(E), \tag{12}$$

where $\circ$ denotes the Hadamard product and $E = X - BW^T X$. Thus, problem (5) can be solved by alternately optimizing the variables.

In order to deal with the term $BW^T X$, the inexact augmented Lagrange multiplier (ALM) method [12] is adopted. Auxiliary variables D and K are introduced and the problem (11) changes into

$$\min_{\substack{B,W,T \\ D,K}} \frac{1}{2} \|\hat{X} - BK\|_F^2 + \frac{\varphi_s(T)}{c} + \alpha_1 \sum_{i=1}^{V} \|D_i\|_{2,1} + \frac{\beta_1}{2} \|W\|_F^2,$$

$$s.t. \quad B = D, \quad W^T X = K.$$

The augmented Lagrange function of this new optimization problem is

$$L(B, W, T, D, K, Y_1, Y_2, \mu)$$

$$= \frac{c}{2} \|X - BK - \frac{T}{1}\|_F^2 + \frac{\varphi_s(T)}{c} + \alpha_1 \sum_{i=1}^{V} \|D_i\|_{2,1} + \frac{\beta_1}{2} \|W\|_F^2$$

$$+ \langle Y_1, B - D \rangle + \frac{\mu}{2} \|B - D\|_F^2 + \langle Y_2, W^T X - K \rangle$$

$$+ \frac{\mu}{2} \|W^T X - K\|_F^2,$$

where Y_1 and Y_2 are the Lagrange multipliers and μ is a positive scalar. When the other variables are fixed, the solutions of B, W, K are given as

$$B = (\hat{X}K^T + \mu(D - \frac{1}{\mu}Y_2))(KK^T + \mu I)^{-1}, \tag{13}$$

$$W = (\mu XX^T + \beta_1 I)^{-1}(\mu X(K - \frac{1}{\mu}Y)^T), \tag{14}$$

and

$$K = (B^T B + \mu I)^{-1}(B^T \hat{X} + \mu W^T X + Y_1). \tag{15}$$

When the other variables are fixed, the minimization of L with respect to D_i is to solve the following problem

$$\alpha_2 \|D_i\|_{2,1} + \frac{1}{2} \|B_i - D_i + \frac{1}{\mu} Y_{1,i}\|_F^2, \tag{16}$$

where $\alpha_2 = \alpha_1/\mu$. Define $Q_i = B_i + \frac{1}{\mu} Y_{1,i}\|_F^2$. Following [13], the jth column of the optimal solution is given by

$$[D_i]_{:,j} = \begin{cases} \frac{\|[Q_i]_{:,j}\|_2 - \alpha_2}{\|[Q_i]_{:,j}\|_2}[Q_i]_{:,j}, & \text{if } \|[Q_i]_{:,j}\|_2 > \alpha_2; \\ 0, & \text{otherwise.} \end{cases} \tag{17}$$

Y_1, Y_2 and μ are updated following [12]. Algorithm 1 summarizes the solution to problem (5).

Algorithm 1. The proposed multi-view learning method

Input: $X \in \mathbb{R}^{m \times n}, r, \sigma, \alpha, \beta, \rho, \mu_0, \mu_{max}$
Output: B, W
1: Initialize $Y_1 = 0, Y_2 = 0, E = 0, k = 0$.
2: Generate standard Gaussian matrix $B, W \in \mathbb{R}^{m \times n}$.
3: Compute $D = B$ and $K = W^T X$.
4: **while** not converged **do**
5:      Update W as (14);
6:      **for** $i = 1$ to v **do**
7:          Update D_i as (17);
8:      **end for**
9:      Update K, B and E as (15), (13), and (12).
10:     Update the Lagrange multipliers as follows:
        $Y_{1,k+1} = Y_{1,k} + \mu_k(B - D)$
        $Y_{2,k+1} = Y_{2,k} + \mu_k(W^T X - K)$
11:     Update μ as follows: $\mu_{k+1} = \min(\mu_{\max}, \rho\mu_k)$.
12:     Update k : $k \leftarrow k + 1$.
13: **end while**

---

3 Experiments

Here we conduct experiments on several popular datasets to verify the effectiveness of the proposed method. It is compared with multi-view intact space learning (MISL) [7], multi-view embedding (MSE) [14], and GoDec+ [8]. For GoDec+, the fusion feature is obtained by projecting the concatenated multi-view data onto the column space of the low-rank matrix learned by GoDec+. The data of each view are rescaled to range in [0,1]. The parameters are tuned for optimal performance and all the experiments are repeated for ten times.

3.1 Face Recognition

The CMU PIE face images dataset [15] contains 68 individuals under 13 different poses, 42 illumination and four expressions. We select two near frontal poses (C9 and C29) as two views to construct the multi-view setting. Each image is reshaped to 32×32. K-nearest neighbor (KNN) method based on the Euclidean distance is used for face recognition. We randomly select 50 percent of one individual for training and the rest for test. To study the effectiveness of multi-view learning, experiments results with various combinations are summarized in Table 1. Here C9 and C29 mean using single view, and C9 + C29 means multi-view learning. All methods achieve improvement when combining the two views and the proposed method is the best. The recognition rate is illustrated in Fig. 2 with varying dimension. Even the worst case of the proposed method is better than the best cases of the other methods. The convergence of the variables and the objective value of the proposed method is shown in Fig. 1, which shows that Algorithm 1 converges quite well.

Table 1. Face recognition rate (%) on CMU PIE

Views	C9	C29	C9 + C29
MISL	72.62	72.95	75.75
MSE	79.57	78.49	80.16
GoDec+	70.38	72.50	74.42
Model1	**86.03**	**84.36**	**88.65**

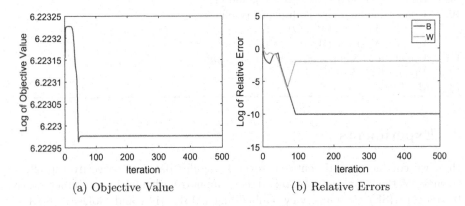

(a) Objective Value   (b) Relative Errors

Fig. 1. Convergence plot of the proposed method on CMU PIE

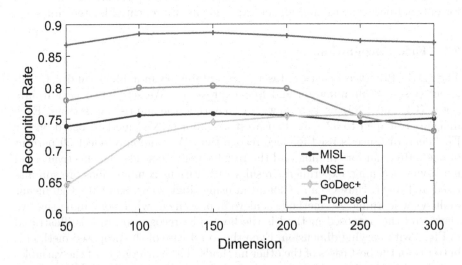

Fig. 2. Recognition rate on CMU PIE with varying dimension

3.2   Digit Classification

The multiple features (MFeat) dataset [16] is a handwritten numeral dataset with 10 categories (i.e., "0–9") and 200 samples per category. The samples are represented by six kinds of features and the total dimensions of all the features are 649. For each category, 20% of the data are selected for training and the rest for testing. The classification accuracy is reported in Table 2. The proposed method outperforms the other compared method. The confusion matrix of the proposed method is given in Fig. 3. It shows that most categories are classified with high accuracy.

Table 2. Digit classification accuracy (%)

Methods	Accuracy	Methods	Accuracy
MISL	92.67	GoDec+	93.78
MSE	85.01	Model1	**93.83**

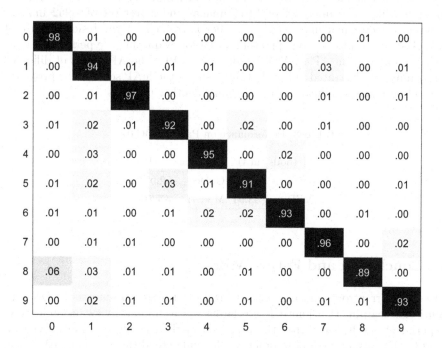

Fig. 3. Confusion matrix

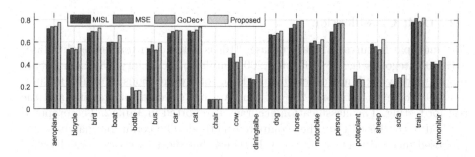

Fig. 4. AP scores of different algorithms for Pascal VOC'07

3.3 Image Annotation

The Pascal VOC'07 dataset [17] contains 9963 images of 20 classes. To simulate a multi-view setting, we choose four types of features including 1000-dimensional "DenseSift", 512-dimensional "Gist", 100-dimensional "DenseHue" and 804-dimensional "Tag" from [18]. Following common setting [17], the images are spited into a training set of 5,011 images and a test set of 4,952 images. A support vector machine (SVM) classifier is trained for the fusion feature of each class. We utilize average precision (AP) for evaluating the performance for each class and mean AP (mAP) for all classes [19]. The AP scores of different algorithms are illustrated in Fig. 4. Table 3 shows the mAP scores. The proposed method performs significantly better than the other methods.

Table 3. Performance on Pascal VOC'07

Methods	mAP	Methods	mAP
MISL	51.19	GoDec+	52.97
MSE	53.94	Model1	**55.76**

4 Conclusion and Future Work

Based on correntropy and matrix factorization, this paper extends GoDec+ to multi-view learning that jointly learns latent space and multi-view fusion feature. Experiment results show that the proposed method is efficient and provides a good feature fusion method in practice. We will extend this method with kernel function in the future.

Acknowledgments. This work is supported in part by the National Natural Science Founding of China (61170192, U1636218), Science and Technology Planning Project of Guangzhou (201704020043), the Fundamental Research Funds for the Central Universities (2017MS045), and Guangzhou Key Lab of Body Data Science (201605030011).

References

1. Zhao, J., Xie, X., Xu, X., Sun, S.: Multi-view learning overview: recent progress and new challenges. Inf. Fusion **38**, 43–54 (2017)
2. Hong, R., Zhang, L., Zhang, C., Zimmermann, R.: Flickr circles: aesthetic tendency discovery by multi-view regularized topic modeling. IEEE Trans. Multimedia **18**(8), 1555–1567 (2016)
3. Hong, R., Hu, Z., Wang, R., Wang, M., Tao, D.: Multi-view object retrieval via multi-scale topic models. IEEE Trans. Image Process. **25**(12), 5814–5827 (2016)
4. Podosinnikova, A., Bach, F., Lacoste-Julien, S.: Beyond CCA: moment matching for multi-view models. In: Proceedings of 33rd International Conference on Machine Learning (2016)
5. Bach, F.R., Jordan, M.I.: A probabilistic interpretation of canonical correlation analysis (2005)
6. Guan, N., Tao, D., Luo, Z., Shawe-Taylor, J.: MahNMF: Manhattan non-negative matrix factorization. arXiv preprint arXiv:1207.3438 (2012)
7. Xu, C., Tao, D., Xu, C.: Multi-view intact space learning. IEEE Trans. Pattern Anal. Mach. Intell. **37**(12), 2531–2544 (2015)
8. Guo, K., Liu, L., Xu, X., Xu, D., Tao, D.: Godec+: fast and robust low-rank matrix decomposition based on maximum correntropy. IEEE Trans. Neural Netw. Learn. Syst. (2017)
9. Guo, K., Xu, X., Tao, D.: Discriminative Godec+ for classification. IEEE Trans. Sig. Process. (2017)
10. Liu, W., Pokharel, P.P., Príncipe, J.C.: Correntropy: properties and applications in non-Gaussian signal processing. IEEE Trans. Sig. Process. **55**(11), 5286–5298 (2007)
11. Nikolova, M., Ng, M.K.: Analysis of half-quadratic minimization methods for signal and image recovery. SIAM J. Sci. Comput. **27**(3), 937–966 (2005)
12. Lin, Z., Chen, M., Ma, Y.: The augmented Lagrange multiplier method for exact recovery of corrupted low-rank matrices. arXiv preprint arXiv:1009.5055 (2010)
13. Liu, G., Lin, Z., Yan, S., Sun, J., Yu, Y., Ma, Y.: Robust recovery of subspace structures by low-rank representation. IEEE Trans. Pattern Anal. Mach. Intell. **35**(1), 171–184 (2013)
14. Xia, T., Tao, D., Mei, T., Zhang, Y.: Multiview spectral embedding. IEEE Trans. Syst. Man Cybern. Part B (Cybern.) **40**(6), 1438–1446 (2010)
15. Sim, T., Baker, S., Bsat, M.: The CMU pose, illumination, and expression (PIE) database. In: Proceedings of IEEE International Conference on Automatic Face and Gesture Recognition, pp. 46–51 (2002)
16. Lichman, M.: UCI machine learning repository (2013)
17. Everingham, M., Van Gool, L., Williams, C.K., Winn, J., Zisserman, A.: The Pascal visual object classes (VOC) challenge. Int. J. Comput. Vis. **88**(2), 303–338 (2010)
18. Guillaumin, M., Verbeek, J., Schmid, C.: Multimodal semi-supervised learning for image classification. In: 2010 IEEE Conference on Computer Vision and Pattern Recognition (CVPR), pp. 902–909. IEEE (2010)
19. Hong, R., Yang, Y., Wang, M., Hua, X.S.: Learning visual semantic relationships for efficient visual retrieval. IEEE Trans. Big Data **1**(4), 152–161 (2015)

Sketch-Based Image Retrieval
with Multiple Binary HoG Descriptor

Tianqi Wang[1], Liyan Zhang[2]([✉]), and Jinhui Tang[1]

[1] Nanjing University of Science and Technology, Nanjing, China
tianqi537@163.com, jinhuitang@njust.edu.cn
[2] Nanjing University of Aeronautics and Astronautics, Nanjing, China
zhangliyan@nuaa.edu.cn

Abstract. The proliferation of touch screen devices has enabled Sketch-Based Image Retrieval (SBIR) to become an effective method for image retrieval. Although prior research efforts have ex-tensively explored the methods for SBIR, the appropriate descriptor which can accurately and efficiently describe sketch and natural images is still unavailable. To further improve the accuracy and efficiency of SBIR, in this paper, we pro-pose a novel sketch-based image retrieval method leveraging Multiple Binary HoG (MBHoG) descriptor. In this method, two novel binary descriptors named Primary Binary HoG (PBHoG) and Discrete Binary HoG (DBHoG), are proposed and combined, together with the color feature as an extra condition to enhance the accuracy of results. We use Ham-ming distance with two binary masks as constraint to re-trieve images. The method ensures time and space efficiency. The experimental results performed on the public dataset demonstrate that the proposed method has the superiority of accuracy.

Keywords: Sketch retrieval · Multiple binary HoG
Hamming distance

1 Introduction

Sketch-based image retrieval (SBIR), which leverages sketch content as query input to retrieve images from database, has become an effective image retrieval method, especially with the proliferation of touch screen devices. Compared with the traditional text-based image retrieval which requires massive tedious labeling work and accurate words to describe query images, SBIR can better understand user's intention by allowing users to draw simple sketch as input. Sketch-based image retrieval systems can be extensively applied to a wide range of applications including digital library, sensing remote systems, medical diagnosis, crime prevention, photo sharing sites, etc.

In the prior literature, research efforts have extensively explored the techniques for SBIR since 1990s [1]. Most research work concentrates on searching

© Springer Nature Singapore Pte Ltd. 2018
B. Huet et al. (Eds.): ICIMCS 2017, CCIS 819, pp. 32–42, 2018.
https://doi.org/10.1007/978-981-10-8530-7_4

appropriate descriptor to eliminate the difference between sketch images and natural images. Hu et al. [2,3] proposed a Gradient Field HoG (GF-HoG) descriptor to capture local structure, and created an efficient codebook based retrieval method by clustering algorithm. Tu and Collomosse [4] improved GF-HoG with color feature to get more detailed retrieval results. The disadvantage of GF-HoG lies in it's difficulties of finding an excellent clustering center for good codebook. Eitz et al. [5] proposed edge histogram descriptor (EHD) and Tensor descriptor, then clustered best matching images based on color histograms. This method can be applied to a large database with images over one million, but it's accuracy needs improvement. In order to improve retrieval results with complex natural images, Tseng et al. [6] focus on the main object in natural images through salient boundaries extraction method, while Zhou et al. [7] extract the most salient contour region of images. Take storage cost and time cost into consideration, Fu et al. [8] proposed a method named BHoG. In this method, binary descriptor is used for feature storage, and Hamming distance is used for retrieval. Eitz et al. [9] proposed Bag-of-Features descriptors for 2D and 3D images search. Cao et al. [10] proposed a method named edgel (edge pixels) index, using Chamfer Matching [11] for feature extraction and inverted index for retrieval structure. MindFinder [12] is a SBIR system based on this method. Some other applications of SBIR are also realized, such as Sketch2Photo [13], PhotoSketch [14].

Although plenty of research efforts have been dedicated to exploring appropriate feature extraction method, the effective and efficient descriptor is still unavailable. Therefore, in this paper, we propose an effective descriptor named Multiple Binary HoG (MBHoG) considering both storage cost and time cost. As illustrated in Fig. 1, we first leverage Structured Forests [15] method to acquire edge images. Then we propose two novel binary descriptors named Primary Binary HoG (PBHoG) and Discrete Binary HoG (DBHoG), used for outer distance descriptor and inner distance descriptor respectively. Second, we retrieve images through Hamming distance with our special binary mask. In addition, color feature is used for more detailed result. To evaluate the proposed method, we perform a series of experiments on public dataset. Experimental results demonstrate the superiority of our approach in both effectiveness and efficiency.

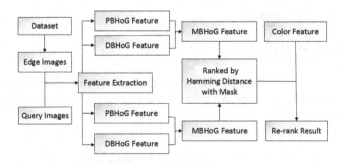

Fig. 1. The fundamental steps of our proposed sketch-based image retrieval algorithm.

The rest of this paper is organized as follows. We propose two novel feature extraction methods in Sect. 2. In Sect. 3, we describe image retrieval methods using Hamming distance. The proposed approach is empirically evaluated in Sect. 4. Finally, we conclude in Sect. 5 by highlighting key points of our work.

2   Feature Extraction

In this section, we will introduce two binary feature descriptors. We choose Structured Forests [15] as edge detection method instead of traditional edge detection descriptor, the result generated by this method is smoother and more detailed. We extract two kinds of texture features, Primary Binary HoG (PBHoG) and Discrete Binary HoG (DBHoG), by two transformative histogram of oriented gradient descriptors. In addition, we extract color feature from RGB color space as extra retrieval parameter.

2.1   PBHoG Descriptor

Our PBHoG is the improvement of BHoG [8]. Firstly, we introduce BHoG to you, including the main idea and steps.

Among all gradient orientations, there always exists an orientation whose amplitude is obviously higher than others when the patch is not empty. Based on this fact, there is no need to save all the gradient orientations. BHoG method only selects the main orientation of gradient from cells. As shown in Fig. 2, the whole sketch image is taken as an BHoG detection window. The region surrounded by thick red lines is the first block composed by four cells in which we will extract our partial BHoG feature. The blue lines indicate the horizontal sliding of the block and the green ones indicate vertical sliding. W_h and W_w are the height and width of the whole image. B_h and B_w are the height and width of the block. S_h and S_w are the vertical and horizon sliding incremental of the block. D is the dimension of the BHoG feature, the gradient is quantified as Bin directions.

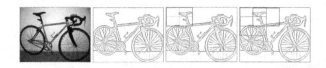

Fig. 2. The steps of BHoG feature descriptor. The images form left to right: a natural image, an edge image, an image with first block, an image with slide of block. (Color figure online)

According to [8], the feature extraction includes following steps, which are introduced briefly. Firstly, we calculate the gradient orientation and amplitude. Then, we build the histogram of oriented gradient for each cell. The edge image is divided into 36 cell units with the following equations, $C_w = W_w/6$ and $C_h = W_h/6$. The range of the gradient orientation is $[0,180]$ degree, the method quantify the orientation as 8 bins. Finally, we choose one main orientation from 8 bins for each cell and combine 2×2 cell units into a block, one cell for overlapped step length. The dimension of the BHoG feature is:

$$D = \frac{B_w B_h}{C_w C_h} \times \left(\frac{W_w - B_w}{S_w} + 1\right) \times \left(\frac{W_h - B_h}{S_h} + 1\right) \tag{1}$$

In proposed BHoG in [8], the dimension is 100. The dimension of the feature reduces to $1/Bin$ compared to traditional HoG.

The BHoG method selects the orientation which has the largest amplitude as the HoG principal component of the cell unit. The key question is how to store these orientation features. Consider of retrieval speed and storage, Fu et al. [8] proposed a binary code to describe the main orientation of cells. As shown in Table 1, the Hamming distance between the orientations belong to 0, 2, 4, 6, 8. The distance between adjacent orientations is 2. The empty cell unit has an all-0 encoding and it's Hamming distance to any orientation is 4.

Table 1. Cyclic binary code of BHoG

Index	Encoding	Index	Encoding
1	11110000	6	10000111
2	01111000	7	11000011
3	00111100	8	11100001
4	00011110	0	00000000
5	00001111		

According to experiments, we find that use one main orientation to describe the feature is lacking. In view of the advantage of binary code in storage cost and retrieval time cost, we make improvement in BHoG. We find the best amount of orientation is 2, which means we save two primary orientations of the cell units. The distance of orientation with largest amplitude between two cells is called $d1$, the distance of orientation with secondary amplitude is called $d2$, and the whole Hamming distance $d = d1 + d2$. Finally, the dimension of PBHoG is double of BHoG. In our experiment, each image is represented as a set of 1600-bit binary codes, which occupies 0.2 KB memory.

PBHoG describes distance between primary orientation, which ignoring the specific amplitude value, so we call it outer distance. Next, we introduce DBHoG descriptor which calculates distance about amplitude in the same orientation called inner distance.

2.2 DBHoG Descriptor

We propose Discrete Binary HoG (DBHoG) descriptor, which is the transformation of traditional HoG descriptor and decreases storage cost and retrieval time cost.

Now, we consider traditional HoG descriptor firstly. We divide the edge image into $n \times n$ cells. The range of the gradient orientation is $[0,180]$ degree, and the gradient orientation is quantified as Bin directions. We calculate the HoG descriptor of each cell. After normalization, we combine all the HoG to form the descriptor of the edge image. In our method, we set $n = 8$ and $Bin = 8$, the dimension of the HoG feature is $D = n \times n \times Bin = 512$.

As we know, we can't get a perfect edge image from natural image, there are always errors with edge images, so there is no need to store precise amplitude values. For the improvement of the retrieval accuracy and speed, we propose a binary code for amplitude values. As shown in Table 2, for each cell, we normalize the amplitude values into the range of $[0,1]$, narrowing the range to $[0, 0.8]$ through multiply by 0.8, then each range is encoded using 8-bit binary. We naturally take 0.1 as a fragment, we attribute the amplitude below 0.05 to all 0 and above 0.75 to all 1. The distance between the adjacent range is 1, the empty cell units have an all-0 encoding. By this way, we get discrete descriptors of images. The dimension of DBHoG is 512, and we use 1 byte for each binary memory, so the memory of an edge image is 0.5 KB. Hamming distance is used for distance criterion.

Table 2. Binary code of DBHoG

Range	Encoding	Range	Encoding
[0.00, 0.05)	00000000	[0.45, 0.55)	00011111
[0.05, 0.15)	00000001	[0.55, 0.65)	00111111
[0.15, 0.25)	00000011	[0.65, 0.75)	01111111
[0.25, 0.35)	00000111	[0.75, 0.80)	11111111
[0.35, 0.45)	00001111		

2.3 Color Feature

For better retrieval performance, the previous retrieval results are re-ranked through color feature using RGB color space. In our method, the image is split into three channels R, G and B respectively, the value of each channel is divided into 16 segments. We calculate three histograms of color and map to a 4096 dimensional vector. RGB values are used for query parameters, obviously, single color parameter for query is lacking. For example, we set [100, 200, 50] for RGB parameters, but we can't form an effective 4096 dimensional vector because each value only belongs to one segment. In this situation, we create a gradient color image around the RGB value as query image. Our method is to extend the value in each channel around original value, and different segment with new value has different weight according to the distance between new segment and the original segment. The shorter the distance, the bigger the weight [16]. Finally, we create a gradient color image and an effective 4096 dimensional vector, we use Bhattacharyya Distance as color distance criterion.

3   Retrieval Method

After extracting features, an appropriate retrieval method is necessary. We use two special binary masks for retrieval constraint condition, and we use Hamming distance for distance criterion.

3.1   Two Types of Masks

Firstly, we introduce masks to you. In our proposed method, masks are used for query images. As shown in Fig. 3, in the middle image, the sketch is divided into 6×6 cells for PBHoG, we combine 2×2 cell units into a block such as the blue region. In the right image, the sketch is divided into 8×8 for DBHoG. We create 6×6 and 8×8 masks respectively. There are edge pixels in the gray cells, we set mask value to 1 for these cells, and we set mask value to 0 for other empty cells. The computation of mask is:

$$mask(i, j) = \begin{cases} 1, & \text{if } cell(i, j) \text{ is not empty} \\ 0, & \text{if } cell(i, j) \text{ is empty} \end{cases} \tag{2}$$

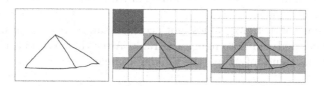

Fig. 3. Two kinds of masks, the images from left to right: an original sketch, a mask of PBHoG, a mask of DBHoG. (Color figure online)

3.2   Distance Calculation Criterion

When we calculate Hamming distance, we use masks as constraint condition for sketches. For PBHoG, we have already set 2×2 cells for a block, one cell for overlapped step length. We only compute with these blocks whose mask values in 4 cells are not all 0. We set $mask\_b(i, j) = 0$, if the mask values of cells in a block are all 0, otherwise, $mask\_b(i, j) = 1$. Variable b_d1 is the distance of orientation with largest amplitude between two blocks in sketch and edge image, b_d2 is the distance of orientation with secondary amplitude between two blocks.

We set $A1$ for the distance between two blocks in sketch and edge image, $D1$ for the PBHoG distance between sketch and edge image.

$$A1(i,j) = \begin{cases} b\_d1(i,j) + b\_d2(i,j), & \text{if } mask\_b(i,j) = 1 \\ 0, & \text{if } mask\_b(i,j) = 0 \end{cases} \tag{3}$$

$$D1 = \sum_{i=1}^{5} \sum_{j=1}^{5} A1(i,j) \tag{4}$$

Analogously, for DBHoG, d is the distance between two cells without masks, $A2$ is the distance between two cells with masks. $D2$ is the DBHoG distance between two images.

$$A2(i,j) = \begin{cases} d(i,j), & \text{if } mask(i,j) = 1 \\ 0, & \text{if } mask(i,j) = 0 \end{cases} \tag{5}$$

$$D2 = \sum_{i=1}^{8} \sum_{j=1}^{8} A2(i,j) \tag{6}$$

By this way, we can focus on the most significant part of the sketch and images, while ignoring the influence of uncorrelated edge pixels, and we can improve the accuracy of retrieval results.

Finally, for N images in the dataset, we get a N dimensional matrix $M1$ that stores N distance values depending PBHoG, and N dimensional matrix $M2$ for DBHoG. Now, the two distance results should be combined with each other through suitable method for more accurate results. In consideration of that different feature descriptors have different significance and different distance matrixes have different value range, adding them together directly is unreasonable. To solve this problem, $M1$ and $M2$ should be normalized firstly. What we need is the rank of distance values, not accurate values, so we can use normalization method and will not change the rank. After that, we add $M1$ and $M2$ to make M, the values of M are the ranking of images.

4   Experiments

We demonstrate our method on a public dataset and use an effective benchmark [9].

4.1   Benchmark

Rank correlation is the benchmark in the experiments [9]. This benchmark compares the rank of images with human subjective feelings. There are 31 sketch images for query, with exactly 40 images associated with each sketch. For each sketch, the corresponding 40 images have different degree from 1 to 7 by experimenters. The lower the degree is, the higher the similarity is. There are 28 participants for the rank of images. Finally a standard human feeling ordered dataset is formed. The evaluation method compares the difference between query results and human feelings. Let x_i and y_i denote the rank of image i in two image sets x and y, x_j and y_j denote the rank of image j in x and y as well. We use the pairs of ranks (x_i, y_i) and (x_j, y_j) for computing. A pair is concordant if $(x_i - x_j)(y_i - y_j) > 0$ and discordant if $(x_i - x_j)(y_i - y_j) < 0$. Given n pairs of ranks in x and y, let n_c denotes the number of concordant pairs and n_d denotes the number of discordant pairs, then the rank correlation coefficient of x and y is defined as:

$$\tau = \frac{n_c - n_d}{n(n-1)/2} \qquad (7)$$

According to the definition, the value of τ belongs to $[-1, 1]$, the larger τ is, the better the system performs.

4.2   Experimental Results

In our experiments, we test retrieval results with different parameters. There are many parameters that have important consequences for the results, we test the number of cell, the number of orientation, and whether the overlapping block is necessary and so on. As shown in Table 3, there are some test results for the division of cells.

All images and sketches must be scaled to the same size, so we set the largest length of size to 400. Firstly, we test the performance of our PBHoG. The rank correlation coefficient of BHoG is 0.298 in [8] when using one primary orientation, but we get terrible result 0.237 when we use the same method. We find that the BHoG feature descriptor may be too sparse to describe the image. Therefore, we decide to use two primary orientations in our experiment. The method ensures enough feature and reduces the influence of uncorrelated edge pixels and the rank correlation coefficient is 0.270 in our experiment. We find two primary orientations are best for our PBHoG through experiment. Secondly, we test the performance of our DBHoG. We attempt different divided method and consider if overlapped block is necessary. We choose 8×8 cells for our DBHoG, and the rank correlation coefficient is 0.273.

Consider that the two descriptors represent different distance measure criterion, so they can supplement each other for better results. The finally rank correlation coefficient of MBHoG is 0.326. Figure 4 shows some results of different methods. We compare MBHoG with EHD [17], HoG [18], SHoG [9] and

Table 3. Some test results for the division of cells

PBHoG		DBHoG	
Cells	Result	Cells	Result
5×5	0.234	6×6	0.266
6×6	0.270	8×8	0.273
7×7	0.246	10×10	0.261

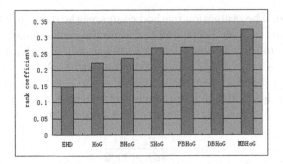

Fig. 4. The rank correlation coefficient of seven methods in our experiment.

Fig. 5. Some examples in our experiments using MBHoG.

BHoG [8]. Obviously, our method has best performance among these methods. It is worth mentioning that the performance on DBHoG is about 8% higher than traditional HoG, and DBHoG has less storage cost and faster retrieval speed. The performance of MBHoG is 18% higher than EHD, 11% higher than HoG, 9% higher than BHoG and 6% higher than SHoG. Figure 5 shows some examples of MBHoG retrieval results. For MBHoG feature, the memory of an image is 0.7 KB, which is suitable for large dataset retrieval.

4.3   Result Analysis

Actually, we can also get good retrieval result without masks on the dataset, but when we test our method without masks on other dataset, the performance may be worse than our expectation. As shown in Fig. 6, we demonstrate our viewpoint on public irregular mirflickr100k dataset. When the query images have only simple outlines such as circle, the retrieval results may contain many uncorrelated images which have nearly no edge pixels. When the query images have complicated outlines, the images in retrieval result may influence by irrelevant pixels. So we use masks for both higher retrieval accuracy and wider applicability.

In addition, we can use color feature for more accurate results. Firstly, we acquire retrieval results through MBHoG without color feature. Then for top N results, we use gradient color feature to get re-rank retrieval result. Figure 7 shows some examples in our experiments.

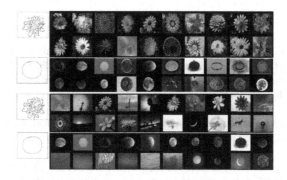

Fig. 6. The upper two examples are results with masks, the under two examples are results without masks.

Fig. 7. Examples of MBHoG with color feature. (Color figure online)

5 Conclusion

In this paper, we propose PBHoG and DBHoG feature descriptor, then a MBHoG descriptor is formed for sketch-based image retrieval. We use masks as constraint condition for more precise retrieval results and wider applicability. In the method, binary code is used for feature storage, and we calculate distance between sketch and natural images by Hamming distance. The experiment demonstrates that our method can get more accurate retrieval result than other methods. Our method has faster calculation speed and occupy less storage space, which is suitable for real-time retrieval on large dataset. Moreover, we propose a RGB color space method for color feature retrieval, and it makes our result more accurately.

For the future work, we focus on improving retrieval result. We will explore better edge detection algorithm and the invariance for image scale and location. We also attempt to employ better file structure for feature storage to improve retrieval speed.

Acknowledgement. This work was partially supported by the National Natural Science Foundation of China (Grant No. 61522203 and 61572252), the Natural Science Foundation of Jiangsu Province (Grant No. BK20140058 and BK20150755).

References

1. Tang, J., Li, Z., Wang, M., Zhao, R.: Neighborhood discriminant hashing for large-scale image retrieval. IEEE Trans. Image Process. **24**(9), 2827–2840 (2015)
2. Hu, R., Barnard, M., Collomosse, J.: Gradient field descriptor for sketch based retrieval and localization. In: IEEE International Conference on Image Processing, pp. 1025–1028 (2010)
3. Hu, R., Collomosse, J.: A performance evaluation of gradient field hog descriptor for sketch based image retrieval. Comput. Vis. Image Underst. **117**(7), 790–806 (2013)
4. Tu, B., Collomosse, J.: Scalable sketch-based image retrieval using color gradient features. In: IEEE International Conference on Computer Vision Workshop, pp. 1012–1019 (2016)
5. Eitz, M., Hildebrand, K., Boubekeur, T., Alexa, M.: A descriptor for large scale image retrieval based on sketched feature lines. In: Eurographics Symposium on Sketch-Based Interfaces and Modeling, pp. 29–36 (2009)
6. Lin, Y.L., Hsu, W.H.: Sketch-based image retrieval on mobile devices using compact hash bits. In: ACM International Conference on Multimedia, pp. 913–916 (2012)
7. Zhou, R., Chen, L., Zhang, L.: Sketch-based image retrieval on a large scale database. In: ACM International Conference on Multimedia, pp. 973–976 (2012)
8. Fu, H., Zhao, H., Kong, X., Zhang, X.: BHoG: binary descriptor for sketch-based image retrieval. Multimed. Syst. **22**(1), 127–136 (2016)
9. Eitz, M., Hildebrand, K., Boubekeur, T., Alexa, M.: Sketch-based image retrieval: benchmark and bag-of-features descriptors. IEEE Trans. Visual Comput. Graph. **17**(11), 1624–1636 (2011)
10. Cao, Y., Wang, C., Zhang, L., Zhang, L.: Edgel index for large-scale sketch-based image search. In: IEEE Conference on Computer Vision and Pattern Recognition, pp. 761–768 (2011)
11. Aarthi, R., Amudha, J.: Saliency based modified chamfers matching method for sketch based image retrieval. In: International Conference on Innovations in Information, Embedded and Communication Systems, pp. 1–4 (2015)
12. Cao, Y., Wang, H., Wang, C., Li, Z., Zhang, L., Zhang, L.: MindFinder: interactive sketch-based image search on millions of images. In: International Conference on Multimedia 2010, Firenze, Italy, pp. 1605–1608, October 2010
13. Chen, T., Cheng, M.M., Tan, P., Shamir, A., Hu, S.M.: Sketch2Photo: internet image montage. ACM Trans. Graph. **28**(5), 1–10 (2009)
14. Eitz, M., Hildebrand, K., Boubekeur, T., Alexa, M.: PhotoSketch: a sketch based image query and compositing system. In: SIGGRAPH 2009: Talks, p. 60 (2009)
15. Dollar, P., Zitnick, C.L.: Fast edge detection using structured forests. IEEE Trans. Pattern Anal. Mach. Intell. **37**(8), 1558–1570 (2015)
16. Li, Z., Liu, J., Yang, Y., Zhou, X., Lu, H.: Clustering-guided sparse structural learning for unsupervised feature selection. IEEE Trans. Knowl. Data Eng. **26**(9), 2138–2150 (2014)
17. Won, C.S., Park, D.K., Park, S.J.: Efficient use of MPEG7 edge histogram descriptor. ETRI J. **24**(1), 23–30 (2002)
18. Dalal, N., Triggs, B.: Histograms of oriented gradients for human detection. In: IEEE Computer Society Conference on Computer Vision and Pattern Recognition, CVPR 2005, pp. 886–893 (2005)

Multimedia Information Fusion

Joint Visual Context for Pedestrian Captioning

Quan Liu[1,2,4](✉), Yingying Chen[3,4], Jinqiao Wang[3,4], and Sijiong Zhang[1,2,4]

[1] National Astronomical Observatories/Nanjing Institute of Astronomical Optics
and Technology, Chinese Academy of Sciences, Nanjing 210042, China
{quanliu,sjzhang}@niaot.ac.cn
[2] Key Laboratory of Astronomical Optics and Technology,
Nanjing Institute of Astronomical Optics and Technology,
Chinese Academy of Sciences, Nanjing 210042, China
[3] National Lab of Pattern Recognition, Institute of Automation,
Chinese Academy of Sciences, Beijing, China
{yingying.chen,jqwang}@nlpr.ia.ac.cn
[4] University of Chinese Academy of Sciences, Beijing 100190, China

Abstract. Image captioning is a fundamental task connecting computer
vision and natural language processing. Recent researches usually concentrate on generic image captioning or video captioning among thousands of classes. However, they can not effectively deal with a specific
class of objects, such as pedestrian. Pedestrian captioning is critical for
analysis, identification and retrieval in massive collections of data. Therefore, in this paper, we propose a novel approach for pedestrian captioning
with joint visual context. Firstly, a deep convolutional neural network
(CNN) is employed to obtain the global attributes of a pedestrian (e.g.,
gender, age, and actions), and a Faster R-CNN is utilized to detect the
local parts of interest for identification of the local attributes of a pedestrian (e.g., cloth type, color type, and the belongings). Then, we splice
the global and local attributes into a fixed length vector and input it
into a Long-Short Term Memory network (LSTM) to generate descriptions. Finally, a dataset of 5000 pedestrian images is collected to evaluate
the performance of pedestrian captioning. Experimental results show the
superiority of the proposed approach.

Keywords: Image captioning · Pedestrian description

1 Introduction

Effectively describing the content of an image relies on rich semantic knowledge
of a visual scene including the location, objects, attributes and actions etc. This
is a particular challenging task in computer vision, but simultaneously it could
help people understand the content of an image more directly compared to the
fixed-categories image classification or object detection tasks. The majority of
recent researches [1–3] have attempted to describe generic images with fixed

© Springer Nature Singapore Pte Ltd. 2018
B. Huet et al. (Eds.): ICIMCS 2017, CCIS 819, pp. 45–53, 2018.
https://doi.org/10.1007/978-981-10-8530-7_5

vocabularies of visual concepts. Some object detection and region description methods [4,5] have been added to expand the label space.

However, due to the limitation of the collected visual concepts and sentence templates of existing models, it has difficulties in generating detailed description for a specific target, such as pedestrian. In this paper, we strive to take a step for generating dense captions for a pedestrian image. Pedestrian captioning is to help a machine "understanding" a pedestrian image by several sentences. The rich description includes global attributes (e.g., gender, age, and action) and local attributes (e.g., cloth type, color type, and the belongings). Pedestrian captioning is critical for many applications. Taking video surveillance as an example, detailed description of the pedestrian is conducive to quickly retrieve the target of interest. Moreover, it's a basic part of our task to describe the dressing of a person, as a result, this technology can also provide intelligent recommendation for online shopping such as buying clothes, bags etc. For image captioning, many previous methods have attempted to go from an image to caption by combining a deep Convolutional Neural Network (CNN) with a Recurrent Neural Network (RNN). Mao et al. [1] proposed a multi-modal Recurrent Neural Network model (m-RNN) for generating novel sentence descriptions of images, which was the first work incorporating the RNN in a deep multimodal architecture. Karpathy and Fei-Fei [4] also put forward an m-RNN model. However, their RNN inputs the image information only at the first time step in comparison to [1]. Since Long Short-Term Memory network (LSTM), as a special variation of RNN, has achieved remarkable results on nature language processing tasks such as speech recognition [6] and machine translation [7,8], recent approaches introduced LSTM to image caption and achieved a significant improvement, such as NIC model [2] and LRCN model [3]. Wu et al. [9] incorporated high-level attribute vector instead of high-level image features into a CNN-RNN framework and made further progress in image caption task.

In this paper, to generate a rich description for a pedestrian image, we pay attention to the description of a specific object class, then generate individual and particular description for a pedestrian image, including global and local attribute information as well as the pedestrian activities. Figure 1 gives an example of pedestrian caption, where we can see that the two sentences give a more detail description including the global and local characteristic for this girl. To obtain these personalized attributes, we first train a global attribute classifier based on CNN to predict the global characteristics of pedestrians, and use a part detector based on Faster R-CNN [10] with a deep CNN to locate each part of the pedestrian for the local attributes. Then, we splice the global and local predictive probability distributions into a fixed length attribute vector and input it into a LSTM-based language model to generate a structured and detailed description of the pedestrian. To evaluate the proposed approach, a dataset of 5000 pedestrian images is collected and published online and this is the first dataset for pedestrian captioning[1].

---

[1] Dataset can be downloaded at: www.nlpr.ia.ac.cn/iva/homepage/jqwang/pedestr ian_caption_dataset.zip.

Global attribute:
Woman
Walking
Under an umbrella

Local attribute:
Top: coat black
Down: skirt black
Shoes: boots black
Bag: handbag black

A woman wearing a black coat, a black skirt and black boots, a woman carrying a black handbag under an umbrella is walking

Fig. 1. An example of pedestrian captioning.

2 Methodology

The architecture of our approach is illustrated in Fig. 2. The model consists of two parts: attribute analysis and sentence generation. The attribute analysis is decomposed into global and local attribute classification, which eventually generates the prediction probability for each attribute. To generate sentences, a recurrent neural network (RNN) is trained to predict each word of the sentence we adopt the LSTM architecture for the RNN. Recent researches [1–3] usually input the high level image features into the LSTM model, however this approach cannot work well in describing local features. Inspired by [9], we input a high-level attribute vector that contains the prediction probabilities for particular attributes generated by the image analysis part into the LSTM model to generate the sentence. $S_{0:N}$ is the words that the LSTM model generated at every time step, more details about the prediction procedure will be illustrated in Sect. 2.2.

2.1 Global and Local Attributes

The salient context extracted from an entire image is often treated as the global attribute. The global attribute recognition can be seen as a traditional classification problem, so we design a deep CNN to predict the probability of a particular attribute, which is a part of the attribute vector. We use a powerful VGGNet [11] pretrained on ImageNet [12] to extract the global attribute. This model is finetuned on the pedestrian dataset that we created and labeled and will be illustrated in Sect. 3.

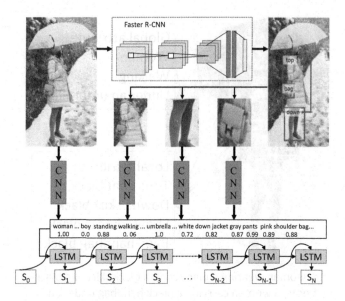

Fig. 2. Overview of pedestrian captioning. The model includes attribute analysis and sentence generation.

Table 1. Global and local attributes samples for pedestrian

	Attribute	Words
Global	Gender	Girl, boy, man, woman, old man/woman etc.
	Actions	Walking, running, holding a baby/umbrella etc.
Local	Top	T-shirt, shirt, coat, down jacket, suit etc.
	Down	Pants, shorts, skirt, dress etc.
	Bag	Handbag, shoulder bag, backpack, suitcase etc.
	Color	Black, white, red, blue, yellow, gray, green etc.

To obtain local attribute, we detect the important parts of a pedestrian and then recognize the categories and color attributes. In this paper, we detect the local attributes with a Faster Region Convolutional Neural Network (Faster R-CNN). Following the common training method of object detection, our detection model is finetuned on the pedestrian dataset with annotated groundings to regions of different parts of the pedestrian. Then, we design a deep CNN to analyze the category and color of each part in a pedestrian image. Thereby, we achieve local information like what kind of clothes the man is wearing and what color it is. Both global and local attributes are shown in Table 1. At last, we splice the global and local predictive probability distributions into a fixed length attribute vector whose length is the size of the attribute set. Then, we will be able to take the vector as an input and apply a LSTM-based language model to generate pedestrian captions.

2.2 Sentence Generator

Recent advances in machine translation have shown that a powerful sequence model is the guarantee to achieve state-of-the-art results. Thus, we use a Long-Short Term Memory (LSTM) network for sequence generation. LSTM is a particular variant of RNN and has achieved great success in translation [7,8] and sequence generation [13] tasks. The choice of LSTM is up to its ability to deal with gradient vanishing and exploding, the most common challenge in designing and training RNNs. Similar to [9], given the image and annotation sentence, we train the LSTM model by maximizing the probability of the correct captions. However, unlike typical approaches, we utilize the attribute vector described in the previous section rather than high level image features as the input. The formulation can be written as follows:

$$\log p(S|V_{attr}) = \sum_{t=1}^{N} \log p(S_t|S_{0:t-1}, V_{attr}) \tag{1}$$

where $S_0, \ldots, S_L$ is a sequence of words, each word S_t is represented in one-hot vector whose dimension is equal to the size of words dictionary. Note that S_0 and S_N respectively represent the special start and end token which donates the start and end of the sentence. $p(S_t|S_{0:t-1}, V_{attr})$ is the probability of the next word S_t given the previous words $S_{0:t-1}$ and the attribute vector V_{attr}.

We train the LSTM language generation model to predict each word of the final caption sentence in an unrolled form. Given the attribute vector V_{attr} and previous sentence $S_{1:t-1}$, the probability distribution of the next word is predicted in a sequence by iterating the following recurrence relation:

$$b_v = W_{hv}V_{attr} \tag{2}$$

$$h_t = LSTM(W_{hx}x_t, W_{hh}h_{t-1}, b_v(t=1), b_h) \tag{3}$$

$$p_t = softmax(W_{ho}h_t + b_o) \tag{4}$$

where $W_{hv}, W_{hx}, W_{hh}, W_{ho}$ and b_h, b_o are the learnable parameters and we provide the embedded atrributes vector b_v to the RNN only at the first iteration, because we found it works better than at each time step. At each time step the hidden state (h_t) of the LSTM layer is used to predict a distribution (p_t) over the words in the vocabulary. Particularly, if the stop word is predicted, a complete sentence has been generated.

All the parameters in LSTM are leant by minimizing the following loss function which is the sum of negative log likelihood of the correct word at each step:

$$L(S, V_{attr}) = -\sum_{t=1}^{N} log p_t(S_t) \tag{5}$$

Stochastic Gradient Descent (SGD) is used to solve Eq. 5 with mini-batches of 10 image-sentence pairs. The embedding size of attributes is set to 65, while the sizes of the embedding word and hidden state are set to 1000 in all the experiments. At time step $t = -1$, we set $x_{-1} = 0$ and $h_{-1} = 0$. The LSTM memory state is initialized to the range $(-0.1, 0.1)$ with a uniform distribution. In inference process, the first sentence uses beam search (beam size = 3) and the second is sampled from the output distribution and choose the most probable caption which is different to the first sentence.

3   Experiments

Since we are stepping towards generating a well-structured description of a specific pedestrian, there is no public dataset available for pedestrian captioning. Therefore, we establish a new dataset of pedestrian caption to evaluate our approach. For fair comparison, we implement some representative methods trained on our dataset for comparison. The generated captions are evaluated on multiple widely used evaluation metrics.

3.1   Dataset

Most previous works in image captioning [1–4] are evaluated on Flickr8k [14], Flickr30k [15] and Microsoft COCO [16] dataset. However, these datasets describe the diversity of the multiple objectives, and there is no detailed descriptions for each pedestrian, thus it is not suitable for evaluating our proposed generation method. Therefore, we initially select 5,000 pedestrian images under different scenes, manually adding descriptions as the ground truth. Of which, 4500 images are randomly selected to train our LSTM-based language model and 500 images for testing. These pictures cover a variety of seasons, time, and back-ground locations. Each image has two descriptions, the format can be described with reference to Fig. 1.

3.2   Main Results

To evaluate the quality of sentences generated by the language model for the given images and their reference sentences, we adopt the following four widely used evaluation metrics in image caption: BLEU [17], METEOR [18], ROUGE [19], and CIDEr [20]. All the scores are calculated using the coco-evaluation code, so the format of our ground truth file is similar to MS COCO dataset's test file format. To demonstrate the effectiveness of our approach, we first evaluate our approach by using different attributes as the input to the LSTM model, "global attributes", "local attributes" and "global+local attribute" respectively denote model with global attributes input, local attributes input and all the attributes input. Results are shown in Table 2. Obviously, local attributes plays a crucial role in the caption task. With all the attributes inputted into the LSTM model, we achieve a better performance. We also implement some baseline models that are representative approaches in the field of image captioning on our dataset. We show the results of baseline models and our approach on our own datasets in Table 3. As shown in the table, our method has achieved remarkable results in the

Table 2. Results of our approach with only global attributes, local attributes input and global+local attributes input on BLEU-1, 2, 3, 4, METEOR, ROUGE and CIDEr metrics.

Model	BLEU-1	BLEU-2	BLEU-3	BLEU-4	METEOR	ROUGE	CIDEr
Global attributes	0.743	0.616	0.525	0.439	0.325	0.677	1.001
Local attributes	0.802	0.711	0.646	0.586	0.455	0.817	2.620
Global+local attributes	0.866	0.806	0.755	0.702	0.516	0.871	3.084

Table 3. BLEU-1, 2, 3, 4, METEOR, ROUGE and CIDEr metrics compared with the typical methods and our approach on our own dataset. High is good in all columns.

Model	BLEU-1	BLEU-2	BLEU-3	BLEU-4	METEOR	ROUGE	CIDEr
LRCN [3]	0.774	0.677	0.600	0.531	0.405	0.773	2.207
Google-NIC [2]	0.803	0.735	0.679	0.633	0.436	0.804	2.880
Ours-all attributes	**0.866**	**0.806**	**0.755**	**0.702**	**0.516**	**0.871**	**3.084**

Fig. 3. Examples of pedestrian captioning with our approach.

mainstream of several evaluation metrics and the scores are much higher than the LRCN [3] and NIC [2] model. We also show some example pedestrian captions generated by our approach in Fig. 3. We can see that our method can generate descriptions with high quality for both global or local information, which mainly benefits from utilizing the Faster R-CNN model to detect local attributes as well as inputting the attributes vector to the LSTM language model directly.

4   Conclusions

In this paper, we propose a novel caption approach to generate descriptions for pedestrian on joint visual context. We pay more attention to personalized descriptions for pedestrians, thus we use a Faster R-CNN model along with deep CNNs to classify the different parts of the pedestrian body to get the local attributes. Along with the global attributes, we create an attribute vector which contains the probabilities of various attributes and input it into a LSTM-based language model to generate sentences. Experiments and comparison with multiple popular evaluation metrics on our own dataset show the promise of the proposed approach.

References

1. Mao, J., Xu, W., Yang, Y., Wang, J., Huang, Z., Yuille, A.: Deep captioning with multimodal recurrent neural networks (m-RNN). arXiv preprint arXiv:1412.6632 (2014)
2. Vinyals, O., Toshev, A., Bengio, S., Erhan, D.: Show and tell: a neural image caption generator. In: Proceedings of the IEEE Conference on Computer Vision and Pattern Recognition, pp. 3156–3164 (2015)
3. Donahue, J., Anne Hendricks, L., Guadarrama, S., Rohrbach, M., Venugopalan, S., Saenko, K., Darrell, T.: Long-term recurrent convolutional networks for visual recognition and description. In: Proceedings of the IEEE Conference on Computer Vision and Pattern Recognition, pp. 2625–2634 (2015)
4. Karpathy, A., Fei-Fei, L.: Deep visual-semantic alignments for generating image descriptions. In: Proceedings of the IEEE Conference on Computer Vision and Pattern Recognition, pp. 3128–3137 (2015)
5. Fang, H., Gupta, S., Iandola, F., Srivastava, R.K., Deng, L., Dollár, P., Gao, J., He, X., Mitchell, M., Platt, J.C., et al.: From captions to visual concepts and back. In: Proceedings of the IEEE Conference on Computer Vision and Pattern Recognition, pp. 1473–1482 (2015)
6. Graves, A., Jaitly, N.: Towards end-to-end speech recognition with recurrent neural networks. In: ICML 2014, pp. 1764–1772 (2014)
7. Sutskever, I., Vinyals, O., Le, Q.V.: Sequence to sequence learning with neural networks. In: Advances in Neural Information Processing Systems, pp. 3104–3112 (2014)
8. Cho, K., Van Merriënboer, B., Bahdanau, D., Bengio, Y.: On the properties of neural machine translation: encoder-decoder approaches. arXiv preprint arXiv:1409.1259 (2014)
9. Wu, Q., Shen, C., Liu, L., Dick, A., van den Hengel, A.: What value do explicit high level concepts have in vision to language problems? In: Proceedings of the IEEE Conference on Computer Vision and Pattern Recognition, pp. 203–212 (2016)
10. Ren, S., He, K., Girshick, R., Sun, J.: Faster R-CNN: towards real-time object detection with region proposal networks. In: Advances in Neural Information Processing Systems, pp. 91–99 (2015)
11. Simonyan, K., Zisserman, A.: Very deep convolutional networks for large-scale image recognition. arXiv preprint arXiv:1409.1556 (2014)
12. Deng, J., Dong, W., Socher, R., Li, L.-J., Li, K., Fei-Fei, L.: Imagenet: a large-scale hierarchical image database. In: Proceedings of the IEEE Conference on Computer Vision and Pattern Recognition, pp. 248–255 (2009)
13. Graves, A.: Generating sequences with recurrent neural networks. arXiv preprint arXiv:1308.0850 (2013)
14. Hodosh, M., Young, P., Hockenmaier, J.: Framing image description as a ranking task: data, models and evaluation metrics. J. Artif. Intell. Res. **47**, 853–899 (2013)

15. Young, P., Lai, A., Hodosh, M., Hockenmaier, J.: From image descriptions to visual denotations: new similarity metrics for semantic inference over event descriptions. Trans. Assoc. Comput. Linguist. **2**, 67–78 (2014)
16. Lin, T.-Y., Maire, M., Belongie, S., Hays, J., Perona, P., Ramanan, D., Dollár, P., Zitnick, C.L.: Microsoft COCO: common objects in context. In: Fleet, D., Pajdla, T., Schiele, B., Tuytelaars, T. (eds.) ECCV 2014. LNCS, vol. 8693, pp. 740–755. Springer, Cham (2014). https://doi.org/10.1007/978-3-319-10602-1_48
17. Papineni, K., Roukos, S., Ward, T., Zhu, W.-J.: BLEU: a method for automatic evaluation of machine translation. In: Proceedings of the 40th Annual Meeting on Association for Computational Linguistics, pp. 311–318 (2002)
18. Denkowski, M., Lavie, A.: Meteor universal: language specific translation evaluation for any target language. In: ACL 2014, p. 376 (2014)
19. Lin, C.-Y.: Rouge: a package for automatic evaluation of summaries. In: Text Summarization Branches Out: Proceedings of the ACL 2004 Workshop, p. 8 (2004)
20. Vedantam, R., Lawrence Zitnick, C., Parikh, D.: Cider: consensus-based image description evaluation. In: Proceedings of the IEEE Conference on Computer Vision and Pattern Recognition, pp. 4566–4575 (2015)

Choose the Largest Contributor:
A Fusion Coefficient Learning Network
for Semantic Segmentation

Jianzhuang Yu[1], Shuai Zhao[2], and Yahong Han[1(✉)]

[1] School of Computer Science and Technology, Tianjin University,
Tianjin 300350, China
{jzyu,yahong}@tju.edu.cn
[2] China Automotive Technology and Research Center, Tianjin, China
zhaoshuai@catarc.ac.cn

Abstract. Among many semantic segmentation works using deep learning methods, fusing multiple layer features usually could boost performance. Multi-layer feature fusion could obtain more comprehensive context information. However, fusing different layers leads to different experiment results. There is no unified method to select effective layers to fuse in previous works, which mostly relied on intuition or experience. In this paper, we propose a fusion coefficient learning method that can guide us to select effective layers. What's more, our approaches can be added to other works that require multi-scale fusion to further boost their performance. We proposed three principles for preliminary screening of layers and presented the fusion coefficient learning algorithm. Then, We could select the most effective layer through three steps. Our approaches are verified by massive experiments and proved to be effective on the PASCAL VOC2012, PASCAL Context data set.

Keywords: Semantic segmentation · Fusion layer
Learnable coefficients

1 Introduction

In the past a few years, Deep Convolutional Neural Network (DCNN) has achieved great successes in vision recognition tasks, including image classification [13,16,18], object detection [6,8,9], pose estimation [24], and semantic image segmentation [1,5,14]. Because of its ability on feature extraction and context information abstraction, DCNN has greatly enhanced the performance of semantic segmentation, compared to feature engineering by hand.

Currently, the main method of semantic segmentation is DCNN-based, and partly combined with the graphic model. A number of existing DCNN-based methods are region proposal based methods [6,10,17], which first generate region proposals and then assign category labels to each region. More recently, Fully Convolutional Networks [14] have become a popular choice for semantic segmentation, which are capable for pixelwise prediction and end-to-end training.

© Springer Nature Singapore Pte Ltd. 2018
B. Huet et al. (Eds.): ICIMCS 2017, CCIS 819, pp. 54–64, 2018.
https://doi.org/10.1007/978-981-10-8530-7_6

DeepLab-CRF in [1] trains FCNNs and applies the dense CRFs [12] method as a post-processing step.

For the purpose of higher performance, many DCNN-based works obtained richer context information through the way of fusion multiple layer features. Long et al. [14] performance improved by 3.3% mIOU on Pascal VOC2012 validation set through fusion two more layer features, and obtained more fine-grained segment results. Xie and Tu [25] improved about 10% percentage performance in the edge detection tasks through fusion all layers outputs. Chen et al. [1] mIOU performance from 70.3% (DeepLab-CRF-LargeFOV) improved to 72.6% (DeepLab-V2-VGG16) through fusion four different scale features. Noh et al. [19] fused all the pooling layer outputs and then through deconvolution to obtain high resolution feature maps. Shuai et al. [22] got a excellent performance through stitching a context net after pool5 layers and fusing all the context layer outputs.

Fusion features has become a basic way to improve semantic image segmentation performance. That is because fusing skip layer features could pick up more context information than a single layer. Typically, all of these features are treated equally to fuse as same proportion in most previous works, and the fusion coefficient is 1. Each layer has a different Receptive Of Field, and contains different context information. The contribution to the final semantic segmentation must be different. Choosing which layer to fuse does not have a uniform approach so far. Some works relied on experiment results after fusing this layer, some relied on intuition or experience to select layers. That experiment result as the basis of selecting layer, has great blindness and is time-consuming. While relying on intuition or experience, exists the serious arbitrariness and has not much use for reference.

As discussion above, to select the effective layer on fusing features more efficiently, we provide some basics for selecting layers. We proposed three principles for preliminary screening of layers, presented the fusion coefficient learning algorithm, and showed complete layer selection procedures.

This paper is organized as follows. In Sect. 2, We will describe our approaches in detail. Section 3 presents the experimental results. The paper is concluded in Sect. 4.

2   Method

In this section, we will describe our layer selection approach in detail. We use the Deeplab-V2-VGG16 net [1] as the base network in our method.

2.1   Multi-scale Large Filed of View

Deeplab exploits multi-scale features by employing multiple parallel filters with different atrous convolution rates. Atrous convolution skip several elements to convolution. Detailed atrous convolution definition which can be refered to [1]. Atrous convolution has a very big advantage. It could increase the size field of view (FOV) to arbitrary size, and the convolution kernel scale is enlarged at the same time, without increasing the number of convolution parameters. Kernel scale computing method, as follows:

$$k_s = k_e + (k_e - 1)(r - 1) \tag{1}$$

where k_s is the kernel scale, k_e is the kernel size, and r is atrous convolution rate.

Large field of view is very helpful to improve the segment performance. Deeplab chose and fused four different scale features through four different rates to boost segmentation results. Figure 2 shows multi-scale atrous convolution (Deeplab called Atrous Spatial Pyramid Pooling, ASPP). But why and how choose these four rates, we didn't find a very good basis in [1]. We will discuss some principles on making choice of rates in the next section.

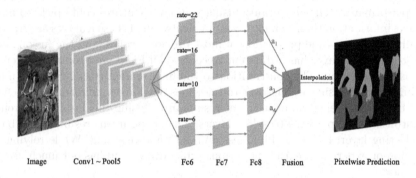

Fig. 1. The whole network structure of Learnable CoeffNet has 4 branches of different scale after pool5 layer. Kernel size in fc6 is 3. Fc8 layer output features multiplied by the corresponding coefficient, then sum fusion together. a_i is the learnable coefficients.

2.2 Making Choice of Layer

In our framework, there are three steps to choose the certain layer.

Scale Range. Table 1 shows the single scale performance comparison. It can be seen that the performance of large FOV (rate = 12) is much higher than the small FOV (rate = 1). Large field of view could bring performance improve. But field of view is not the bigger the better. With the increase of FOV, the performance shows a downward trend. We know that the actual upper limit size of Receptive Of View is the input image size. So we suggest that the size of field of view shouldn't bigger than the previous layer's feature maps size too much (Principle one).

Layer Group. We divide all the layers found in the first step into different groups. Within the layer group, features of different layer should have similar distribution (Principle two). While selecting layer, we rely on the size of the learned coefficients. In order to make the bigger coefficient reflect the greater

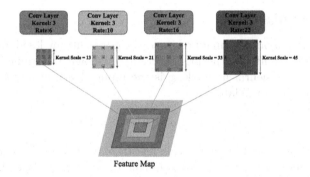

Fig. 2. Multi-scale atrous convolution with kernel size 3, rate = {6, 10, 16, 22}.

contribution of this layer to the segmentation results, these features should have similar distribution. That is because, while fusing features will be multiplied by the coefficient. So if their distribution is very different, the size of the coefficient could not approximately reflect the importance of the contribution. Only when the features are approximately distributed, the value of the coefficients could reflect the contribution of the features. So, what kind of layer's outputs have similar distribution? Layers nearby or kernel scales close will have similar distribution. Between layer groups, kernel scale should have a certain span (Principle three). Neighbor layers or scales have similar features distribution. That is to say that they have similar context information. After fusion, there will be many redundant information which are no useful for performance improving. There is a certain span between the layers or scales, which could take the advantages of complementary information.

Coefficients Learning. We will learn a fusion coefficient for each layer through coefficient learning algorithm. The layer with maximum coefficients in each group is which we want exactly. Figure 1 shows the whole coefficients learning network structure, which has four different scale branches after pool5 layer. The low-dimension fusion feature maps are directly upsampled to the original feature map size via bilinear interpolation. The coefficients learning algorithm will be introduced in the next section.

Table 1. Single scale mIOU results. Kernel size is 3 with different rate in fc6 layer.

Rate	1	6	12	18
mIOU	54.65%	61.39%	65.71%	64.73%
Rate	24	30	40	-
mIOU	62.10%	59.30%	55.06%	-

2.3   Learning Algorithm

The loss function in our learning process is the cross entropy loss function, same as [1]. Let $L(*)$ stands for the loss function, as shown in formula 2, where w is the parameter of neural network, x is the input of neural network, y is the prediction score, Y is the label.

$$Loss Function : L(w, x, y, Y) \tag{2}$$

The fusion formula of different scale features is shown in Eq. 3. $f_k(*)$ is the k-th layer process function. w_k is the weight parameters of layer k, x_k is the input of layer k. a_k is the k-th layer fusion coefficient. There are N layers to fusion totally.

$$Fusion_l = \sum_{k}^{N} a_k f_k(w_k, x_k) \tag{3}$$

Table 2. Step training single layer fc6 kernel size 3, rate 1.

Init mode	Train mode	Iteration	mIOU
VGG-16	Non-step	20,000	53.7
Gaussian	Non-step	20,000	50.2
Gaussian	Non-step	30,000	51.5
Gaussian	Step	10,000/20,000	53.36

Our goal is to make a_k learnable while training. We use the stochastic gradient descent algorithm to update coefficients. Therefore, we need to calculate the gradient of a_k. In Eq. 4, G is the transition matrix for the a_k gradient. By combining Eq. 3, we get the Eq. 5. We achieve the gradient of a_k by summing all the elements g_{ij} of the gradient matrix G, as shown in Eq. 6.

$$G = \frac{\partial L}{\partial Fusion_l} \cdot \frac{\partial Fusion_l}{\partial a_k} \tag{4}$$

$$G = \frac{\partial L}{\partial Fusion_l} \cdot \left[f_k(w, x) \right]^T \tag{5}$$

$$\Delta a_k = \sum_{ij} g_{ij} \tag{6}$$

During the experiments, we found that the coefficients are not sensitive to the segmentation results. After training, the coefficients can only get the approximate of optimal value, it is difficult to acquire the optimal value. However, the segment results are very sensitive to the coefficients. The impact of coefficients fluctuation on the segmentation results is relatively large. In order to make the distribution of features do not have too much fluctuation, we add a constrain item on coefficients, shown in formula 7.

$$\sum_{k}^{N} a_k = N \tag{7}$$

The coefficients update rules are as follows. Where i is the iteration index, v_i is the momentum variable, α is the learning rate. η is the momentum parameter, μ is the weight decay parameter.

$$v_{i+1} := \eta * v_i - \mu * \alpha * (a_k)_i - \alpha * (\Delta a_k)_i \tag{8}$$

$$(a_k)_{i+1} := (a_k)_i + v_{i+1} \tag{9}$$

$$(a_k)_{i+1} := (a_k)_{i+1} * \frac{N}{\sum_{k}^{N} (a_k)_{i+1}} \tag{10}$$

3 Experiments and Results

In this section, we will describe the details of our experiment. We use Caffe [11] as our experimental platform to implement our learning algorithm.

3.1 PASCAL VOC 2012

Dataset

The Pascal VOC 2012 [4] dataset consists of 1,464 training images, 1,449 validation images, and 1,456 test images, involves 20 foreground object classes and one background class. For training, we used the augmented PASCAL VOC training data including 10,582 images provided by Hariharan et al. [7] in the same way as the other works [1,14,20]. The performance is measured in the standard metric of mean pixel intersection over union (mIOU), with the mean taken over all classes, including background.

Rate Selection and Setting

Rate Range. Deeplab-v2-VGG16 as our basic network, has four branches at fc6 layer with rate {6, 12, 18, 24}, which is modified from VGG-16 [23] to fully convolutional network [14]. The input image width and height in the training network are both 321, and the output size of the pool5 layer is 41. Thus, the actual maximum kernel scale of fc6 layer is 41 with kernel size 3. According to the Eq. 1, the corresponding rate is 20. On the basis of Principle one in Sect. 2.2, we suggest that rate should not exceed 20 too much. Besides, due to the increase of pad size, excessive rate will bring additional the consumption of computation resources. At last, our rate range is set at [1, 30]. For different network, the method setting up the rate range is the same. The range values of rate is determined by the input size of current layer.

Table 3. Coefficients learned results in 4 rates combination groups.

Rate combination/mIOU	Learned coefficients
4, 5, 6, 7, 8/60.57	0.916, 0.947, 1.068, 1.006, 1.061
10, 11, 12, 13, 14/64.13	1.079, 1.041, 0.920, 0.934, 1.023
16, 17, 18, 19, 20/62.78	1.101, 0.957, 0.958, 0.960, 1.022
22, 23, 24, 25, 26/60.55	1.056, 0.982, 0.955, 0.968, 1.037

Scale Combination. Deeplab Multi-Scale net uses four different scale {6, 12, 18, 24}. In order to verify our learning algorithm under the same conditions, we also select 4 scales to fusing features. We can see that among the four scales of Deeplab-V2-VGG16 net, there has been a certain span. It has already met the third principle of select scales. In order to satisfy the second principle, we choose the size of the nearest neighbor range at the four scales to set scale combination. At last, we choose four different combinations of scale {4, 5, 6, 7, 8}, {11, 12, 13, 14, 15}, {16, 17, 18, 19, 20}, {22, 23, 24, 25, 26}.

Table 4. Results on fusion rates without CRF. Results on DeepLab was reimplement.

Rate combination	mIOU	Note
6, 12, 18, 24 (DeepLab)	64.58	VGG-16 (conv1–conv5)
6, 10, 16, 22 (Ours)	**64.87**	VGG-16 (conv1–conv5)
6, 12, 18, 24 (DeepLab)	69.48	VGG-16, COCO
6, 10, 16, 22 (Ours)	**69.77**	VGG-16, COCO

Coefficients Learning

In the previous section, We got 4 groups of scale combination. Next, we will learn the fusion coefficient in each group.

Initialization Mode. We use Imagenet-pretrained VGG-16 [23] as our initial weights. The fc6 layer weights of VGG-16 are equal to atrous convolution with kernel size 7, rate 4. In order to avoid the scale effects among different rates, we only use VGG-16 pre-trained model to initialize the conv1 layer to conv5 layer weights of our network. Layers after fc6, we use Gaussian random initialization with std 0.01. However, Gaussian random initialization bring us a drop in performance. To alleviate such impact as much as possible, we use two step training same as [21].

Step Training. First step, we fixed conv1-conv5 weights, only fine-tune layers after pool5 with 10,000 iterations. Second step, we release the fixed weights. All weights get fine-tuned for 20,000 iterations. Table 2 shows step training and non-step training segmentation results. We employed a single scale network with kernel size 3, rate 1 in fc6 layer. As can be see, performance has dropped 3.5%

by using Gauss initialization. Increasing training times, there is still a large performance gap. While using step training, the performance gap is much smaller. In the following experiments, when encountered Gaussian random initialization, we use the step training method.

Experimental Setup. We first fix fusion coefficients to 1 using step training to train, with batch size 10, learning rate 0.001, learning policy "poly", momentum 0.9 and weight decay 0.0005 follows [1]. Then, we fix the network weights, and loose fusion coefficients with lr_mult 100 in fc6 layer, batch 120, training 2500 iterations. The results of 4 rate combination groups and related segmentation results shown in Table 3.

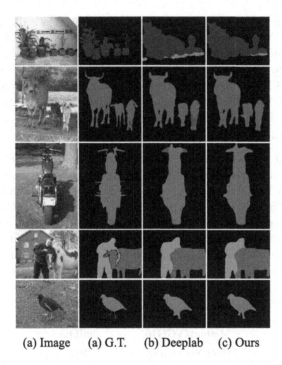

(a) Image   (a) G.T.   (b) Deeplab   (c) Ours

Fig. 3. Results on PASCAL VOC 2012 val set. Input image, Deeplab-V2-VGG16 net and our Learnable CoeffNet best model results.

Rates Fusion

From the above experiments, we obtained the fusion coefficient of each rate combination. We chose one rate which has the maximum coefficient in each group and got the final rate combination {6, 10, 16, 22}. Table 4 shows the performance of the final 4 selected rate combination. Here we put two groups of experiments. The first experiment network initialize its conv1 layer to conv5 layer with pre-trained VGG-16, and the layers after fc6 are used Gaussian random initialization. It shows that our algorithm has a 0.29% improvement. The second

Table 5. Results on PASCAL VOC2012 testing set.

Method/VGG16	mIOU
CoeffNet (ours)	72.8
CoeffNet-MSC (ours)	**73.2**
FCN-8s [14]	62.2
CRF-RNN [26]	72.0
DeconvNet [19]	72.5
Deeplab-v2-VGG16 [1]	72.6

is initialized with VGG-16 pre-trained model to all layers' weights, and then fine-tuned with COCO datasets follows [1], which also has a 0.29% improvement. Both experiment results show that our method is effective. We also explored multi-scale fusion [2] and CRF post-processing [12]. Table 5 shows our method on PASCAL VOC2012 testing set results. We provide qualitative visual comparisons of our Learnable CoeffNet and Deeplab-V2-VGG16 net results in Fig. 3.

3.2   PASCAL-Context

We also verified our approaches on the PASCAL-Context dataset [15]. The PASCAL-Context dataset are re-labeled as pixel-wise to the whole scene, which images are from Pascal VOC 2010. This dataset totally contain 4,998 training images and 5,105 validation images, including 459 semantic classes. Following [15], our proposed models are trained with the most frequent 59 classes along with the background category. Experiment results are shown in Table 6. Compared to Deeplab-V2-VGG16, our approaches has only a slightly improvement. After fusion additional scales feature [2], we have a 1.1% improvement.

Table 6. Results on PASCAL-context val set.

Method/VGG16	mIOU
CoeffNet (ours)	39.6
CoeffNet-MSC (ours)	**40.7**
FCN-8s [14]	37.8
CRF-RNN [26]	39.3
Deeplab-v2-VGG16 [1]	39.5
BoxSup [3]	40.5

4   Conclusions

In this paper, we propose a method to guide us selecting layers, so that we have a basis in fusion features. At the same time, the experiments also verified that the contribution of different scale to the segmentation results is different, and it is not the best choice to carry out feature fusion with same coefficients. Through the coefficient learning, and determination of optimal scales combination, we have further improved the performance of semantic segmentation results.

Acknowledgement. This work was supported by the NSFC (under Grant U1509206, 61472276).

References

1. Chen, L.C., Papandreou, G., Kokkinos, I., Murphy, K., Yuille, A.L.: DeepLab: semantic image segmentation with deep convolutional nets, atrous convolution, and fully connected CRFs. arXiv preprint arXiv:1606.00915 (2016)
2. Chen, L.C., Yang, Y., Wang, J., Xu, W., Yuille, A.L.: Attention to scale: scale-aware semantic image segmentation. In: Proceedings of the IEEE Conference on Computer Vision and Pattern Recognition, pp. 3640–3649 (2016)
3. Dai, J., He, K., Sun, J.: BoxSup: exploiting bounding boxes to supervise convolutional networks for semantic segmentation. In: Proceedings of the IEEE International Conference on Computer Vision, pp. 1635–1643 (2015)
4. Everingham, M., Eslami, S.A., Van Gool, L., Williams, C.K., Winn, J., Zisserman, A.: The pascal visual object classes challenge: a retrospective. Int. J. Comput. Vision **111**(1), 98–136 (2015)
5. Farabet, C., Couprie, C., Najman, L., LeCun, Y.: Learning hierarchical features for scene labeling. IEEE Trans. Pattern Anal. Mach. Intell. **35**(8), 1915–1929 (2013)
6. Girshick, R., Donahue, J., Darrell, T., Malik, J.: Rich feature hierarchies for accurate object detection and semantic segmentation. In: Proceedings of the IEEE Conference on Computer Vision and Pattern Recognition, pp. 580–587 (2014)
7. Hariharan, B., Arbeláez, P., Bourdev, L., Maji, S., Malik, J.: Semantic contours from inverse detectors. In: 2011 IEEE International Conference on Computer Vision (ICCV), pp. 991–998. IEEE (2011)
8. Hong, R., Hu, Z., Wang, R., Wang, M., Tao, D.: Multi-view object retrieval via multi-scale topic models. IEEE Trans. Image Process. **25**(12), 5814–5827 (2016)
9. Hong, R., Yang, Y., Wang, M., Hua, X.S.: Learning visual semantic relationships for efficient visual retrieval. IEEE Trans. Big Data **1**(4), 152–161 (2015)
10. Hong, R., Zhang, L., Zhang, C., Zimmermann, R.: Flickr circles: aesthetic tendency discovery by multi-view regularized topic modeling. IEEE Trans. Multimed. **18**(8), 1555–1567 (2016)
11. Jia, Y., Shelhamer, E., Donahue, J., Karayev, S., Long, J., Girshick, R., Guadarrama, S., Darrell, T.: Caffe: convolutional architecture for fast feature embedding. In: Proceedings of the 22nd ACM International Conference on Multimedia, pp. 675–678. ACM (2014)
12. Koltun, V.: Efficient inference in fully connected CRFs with Gaussian edge potentials. Adv. Neural Inf. Process. Syst. **2**(3), 4 (2011)
13. Krizhevsky, A., Sutskever, I., Hinton, G.E.: Imagenet classification with deep convolutional neural networks. In: Advances in Neural Information Processing Systems, pp. 1097–1105 (2012)
14. Long, J., Shelhamer, E., Darrell, T.: Fully convolutional networks for semantic segmentation. In: Proceedings of the IEEE Conference on Computer Vision and Pattern Recognition, pp. 3431–3440 (2015)

15. Mottaghi, R., Chen, X., Liu, X., Cho, N.G., Lee, S.W., Fidler, S., Urtasun, R., Yuille, A.: The role of context for object detection and semantic segmentation in the wild. In: Proceedings of the IEEE Conference on Computer Vision and Pattern Recognition, pp. 891–898 (2014)

16. Nie, L., Wang, M., Zha, Z.J., Chua, T.S.: Oracle in image search: a content-based approach to performance prediction. ACM Trans. Inf. Syst. (TOIS) **30**(2), 13 (2012)

17. Nie, L., Wang, M., Zha, Z., Li, G., Chua, T.S.: Multimedia answering: enriching text QA with media information. In: Proceedings of the 34th International ACM SIGIR Conference on Research and Development in Information Retrieval, pp. 695–704. ACM (2011)

18. Nie, L., Yan, S., Wang, M., Hong, R., Chua, T.S.: Harvesting visual concepts for image search with complex queries. In: Proceedings of the 20th ACM International Conference on Multimedia, pp. 59–68. ACM (2012)

19. Noh, H., Hong, S., Han, B.: Learning deconvolution network for semantic segmentation. In: Proceedings of the IEEE International Conference on Computer Vision, pp. 1520–1528 (2015)

20. Oquab, M., Bottou, L., Laptev, I., Sivic, J.: Is object localization for free? -weakly-supervised learning with convolutional neural networks. In: Proceedings of the IEEE Conference on Computer Vision and Pattern Recognition, pp. 685–694 (2015)

21. Shimoda, W., Yanai, K.: Distinct class-specific saliency maps for weakly supervised semantic segmentation. In: Leibe, B., Matas, J., Sebe, N., Welling, M. (eds.) ECCV 2016. LNCS, vol. 9908, pp. 218–234. Springer, Cham (2016). https://doi.org/10.1007/978-3-319-46493-0_14

22. Shuai, B., Liu, T., Wang, G.: Improving fully convolution network for semantic segmentation. arXiv preprint arXiv:1611.08986 (2016)

23. Simonyan, K., Zisserman, A.: Very deep convolutional networks for large-scale image recognition. arXiv preprint arXiv:1409.1556 (2014)

24. Tompson, J.J., Jain, A., LeCun, Y., Bregler, C.: Joint training of a convolutional network and a graphical model for human pose estimation. In: Advances in Neural Information Processing Systems, pp. 1799–1807 (2014)

25. Xie, S., Tu, Z.: Holistically-nested edge detection. In: Proceedings of the IEEE International Conference on Computer Vision, pp. 1395–1403 (2015)

26. Zheng, S., Jayasumana, S., Romera-Paredes, B., Vineet, V., Su, Z., Du, D., Huang, C., Torr, P.H.: Conditional random fields as recurrent neural networks. In: Proceedings of the IEEE International Conference on Computer Vision, pp. 1529–1537 (2015)

Clothing Matching Based on Multi-modal Data

Zekun Li, Xuemeng Song[✉], Tian Gan, Zhumin Chen, and Xiaoyu Zhu

Shandong University, Jinan, China
lizekunlee@gmail.com, sxmustc@gmail.com, xiaoyu.lorraine@gmail.com,
{gantian,chenzhumin}@sdu.edu.cn

Abstract. Clothing, as a kind of beauty-enhancing product, plays an important role in people's daily life. People want to look good by dressing properly. Nevertheless, not everyone is good at clothing matching and thus is able to make aesthetic outfits. Fortunately, certain fashion-oriented online community (e.g., Polyvore) allows fashion experts to share their outfit compositions to the public. Each outfit composition there usually consists of several complementary items (e.g., tops, bottoms and shoes), where both the visual image and textual title are available for each item. In this work, we aim to take fully advantage of such rich fashion data to decode the secret of clothing matching. Essentially, we propose a method (CMVT) to comprehensively measure the compatibility among fashion items by integrating the multi-modal data of items. Extensive experiments have been conducted on a real-world dataset to evaluate the effectiveness of the proposed model.

Keywords: Clothing matching · Multi-modal

1 Introduction

In modern society, people pay more and more attention to their clothing, as proper outfits would enhance their beauty greatly. However, not everyone is good at clothing matching and making aesthetic outfits. It thus draws our attention to develop a clothing matching model to help people match clothes well. In fact, with the proliferation of fashion-oriented online communities (e.g., Polyvore[1] and Chictopia[2]), many fashion experts are enabled to share their outfit compositions to the public. As shown in Fig. 1, the outfit composition on Polyvore usually involves several complementary items (e.g., tops, bottoms and shoes). Each item is associated with not only a visual image, but also textual description (i.e., title). Currently, there are over 3 million outfits created per month on Polyvore. These rich data provide us a good opportunity to decode the secret of clothing matching. Without loss of generality, in this work, we focus on matching bottoms for tops, both of which are the most basic components of an outfit.

---

[1] http://www.polyvore.com/.

[2] http://www.chictopia.net/.

© Springer Nature Singapore Pte Ltd. 2018
B. Huet et al. (Eds.): ICIMCS 2017, CCIS 819, pp. 65–74, 2018.
https://doi.org/10.1007/978-981-10-8530-7_7

Fig. 1. Example outfit composition on Polyvore. Each item has an visual image and a textual title.

In a sense, clothing matching heavily depends on the compatibility between clothes. As a matter of fact, a handful existing efforts [13,17,22] have been dedicated to this area. However, they mainly focused on the visual signals of clothing, but overlooked the other modalities. In fact, the visual information maybe effective in capturing certain intuitive features of clothes such as the color and shape, but not for features like material and functionality. Therefore, visual signals maybe insufficient to model the compatibility between fashion items. In that case, the textual modality which usually concisely summarize the key features of items can be a good supplement for visual signals. For example, for a top titled `Black Leather Look Biker Jacket`, we can easily find that the bottom titled `Black Stretch Leather Pants` would match the top better than the bottom titled `High Waisted Shorts` based on their textual descriptions. Therefore, in this work, we focus on the comprehensive compatibility modeling between fashion items by exploring both visual and textual modality.

However, the compatibility modeling with the multi-modal data is non-trivial due to the following challenges. First, factors affecting the compatibility between fashion items usually ranging from the color, material, to the shape and pattern. Therefore, how to accurately model such factors and hence measure the compatibility between items poses us a tough challenge. Second, due to that different modalities come from heterogenous spaces, how to seamlessly integrate the heterogenous visual and textual information of fashion items is another crucial challenge.

To address these challenges, in this work, we propose a model for clothing matching (matching tops with bottoms) based on visual and textual information (CMVT) as shown in Fig. 2. We first extract the input visual and textual features of tops and bottoms with the help of a pre-trained CNN [12] and the bag-of-words scheme [10], respectively. We then seamlessly integrate the heterogeneous visual and textual modalities by mapping them into the same latent style space, where the simple Euclidean distance can be used to model the compatibility between fashion items.

The remainder of this paper is structured as follows. Section 2 presents the proposed model. Section 3 details the dataset and feature extraction. Section 4 shows the experiment results and analysis, followed by the conclusion remarks in Sect. 5.

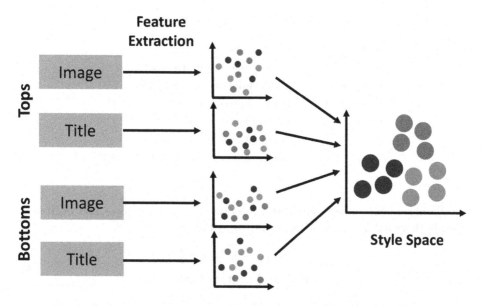

Fig. 2. Framework of the proposed CMVT model.

2   The Model

We first declare certain notations. In particular, we employ bold capital letters (e.g., $\mathbf{X}$) and bold lowercase letters (e.g., $\mathbf{x}$) to denote matrices and vectors, respectively. We utilize non-bold letters (e.g., x) to represent scalars and Greek letters (e.g., β) to denote parameters. If not clarified, all vectors are in the column form. Let $\|\mathbf{x}\|_2$ refers to the Euclidean norm of vector $\mathbf{x}$.

Table 1 summarizes of the key notations. Let $\mathbf{v}_i^1 \in \mathcal{R}^{D_v^1}$ and $\mathbf{t}_i^1 \in \mathcal{R}^{D_t^1}$ denote the visual and textual features of top i, while $\mathbf{v}_j^2 \in \mathcal{R}^{D_v^2}$ and $\mathbf{t}_j^2 \in \mathcal{R}^{D_t^2}$ stand for that of bottom j, where D_v^1, D_t^1, D_v^2 and D_t^2 are the corresponding feature dimensions. Inspired by [13], we assume that there exists a latent style space that can better model the compatibility between tops and bottoms, as compared to the raw feature space. One apparent advantage is that the latent style space can relate the compatible tops and bottoms who are not visually or textually similar. We simply employ the linear transformations to map each fashion item into a latent style space, which has been proven to be effective to representation learning [2,20]. In particular, we aim to learn four transformation matrices $\mathbf{Y}_v^1 \in \mathbb{R}^{D_v^1 \times D_0}$, $\mathbf{Y}_t^1 \in \mathbb{R}^{D_t^1 \times D_0}$, $\mathbf{Y}_v^2 \in \mathbb{R}^{D_v^2 \times D_0}$ and $\mathbf{Y}_t^2 \in \mathbb{R}^{D_t^2 \times D_0}$ which can map the visual and textual modalities of tops and bottoms to a latent style space. D_0 is the dimension for the latent style space.

Given top i and bottom j, we can obtain their latent representations $\tilde{\mathbf{v}}_i^1$, $\tilde{\mathbf{t}}_i^1$, $\tilde{\mathbf{v}}_j^2$ and $\tilde{\mathbf{t}}_j^2$ as follows,

$$\begin{cases} \tilde{\mathbf{v}}_i^1 = \mathbf{v}_i^1 \mathbf{Y}_v^1, & \tilde{\mathbf{t}}_i^1 = \mathbf{t}_i^1 \mathbf{Y}_t^1, \\ \tilde{\mathbf{v}}_j^2 = \mathbf{v}_j^2 \mathbf{Y}_v^2, & \tilde{\mathbf{t}}_j^2 = \mathbf{t}_j^2 \mathbf{Y}_t^2. \end{cases} \tag{1}$$

Table 1. Notations

Notation	Explanation
$\mathcal{P}, \mathcal{N}$	Positive and negative datasets
$\mathbf{v}_i^1, \mathbf{t}_i^1, \mathbf{v}_j^2, \mathbf{t}_j^2$	Input visual and textual features
$\tilde{\mathbf{v}}_i^1, \tilde{\mathbf{t}}_i^1, \tilde{\mathbf{v}}_j^2, \tilde{\mathbf{t}}_j^2$	Latent representations
$\mathbf{Y}_v^1, \mathbf{Y}_t^1, \mathbf{Y}_v^2, \mathbf{Y}_t^2$	Linear transformations
β	Trade-off weight coefficient
$c(i,j)$	Compatibility between items i and j

We hence can measure the distance between any given top i and bottom j from both visual and textual perspectives as follows,

$$\begin{cases} d_v(i,j) = ||\tilde{\mathbf{v}}_i^1 - \tilde{\mathbf{v}}_j^2||_2^2, \\ d_t(i,j) = ||\tilde{\mathbf{t}}_i^1 - \tilde{\mathbf{t}}_j^2||_2^2. \end{cases} \tag{2}$$

Due to the fact that the visual and textual signals may both affect the compatibility between fashion items i and j, we thus linearly fuse [19,20] the distances generated with multi-modal data to comprehensively measure the compatibility as follows,

$$d(i,j) = (1 - \beta)d_v(i,j) + \beta d_t(i,j), \tag{3}$$

where $\beta \in [0,1]$ is a trade-off weight coefficient and plays an important role in modulating the effect of these two modalities. Specifically, when β approaches zero, the compatibility would be evaluated solely by the visual cues. On the contrary, when $\beta = 1$, the textual cues would determine the compatibility measurement.

Furthermore, in order to relate the distance to the compatibility between fashion items, we employ the sigmoid function which monotonically grows with the $d(i,j)$ as follows,

$$c(i,j) = \sigma(-d(i,j)) = \frac{1}{1 + e^{d(i,j)}}, \tag{4}$$

where $c(i,j)$ refers to the compatibility between top i and bottom j. It is apparent that the lower the distance, the higher the compatibility.

So far we have defined the compatibility between fashion items, and we can proceed to the training by maximizing the likelihood of the observed matching set of fashion items. In particular, suppose we have a set of outfit compositions created by fashion experts on Polyvore, each of which consists of a top i and a bottom j. Based on these compositions, we thus can develop a positive set $\mathcal{P} = \{(i,j)|$ top i and bottom j have once been paired$\}$ regarding the matching between tops and bottoms. Meanwhile, we can also construct a neutral set $\mathcal{N}$, where we randomly mix up a top i and a bottom k and make sure that $(i,k) \notin \mathcal{P}$.

In other words, top i and bottom k have never been paired in our dataset. In order to maximize the likelihood of the observed two sets $\mathcal{P}$ and $\mathcal{N}$, we have the following loss function,

$$\mathcal{L} = - \sum_{(i,j)\in\mathcal{P}} c(i,j) + \sum_{(i,k)\in\mathcal{N}} c(i,k). \tag{5}$$

In a sense, we aim to maximize the compatibility between fashion items in $\mathcal{P}$ while minimize that in $\mathcal{N}$. In terms of the optimization, we employed the stochastic gradient descent (SGD) [1,23] with the momentum factor as 0.9.

3 Dataset and Features

3.1 Dataset

In this work, we collected the dataset from the popular fashion-oriented online community—Polyvore. We first collected 14,094 outfit compositions, each of which consists of several complementary fashion items such as tops, bottoms and shoes. In case of the accident inaesthetic outfit compositions created on Polyvore, we filtered out the compositions that had been liked by less than 50 times to ensure the quality of the dataset. In the end, based on these outfits, we obtained 10, 000 positive top-bottom pairs for $\mathcal{P}$. For each top and bottom, we collected their images and titles.

3.2 Feature Extraction

We extract both visual and textual features for tops and bottoms, respectively.

Visual Feature. We utilize the advanced deep convolutional neural networks, which have been proven to be effective for image representation learning [24], rather than the traditional handcrafted features, such as SIFT descriptors [14,16], visual word [8], topic model based representation [7] and histogram of gradient [9]. In particular, we choose the pre-trained ImageNet deep neural network provided by the Caffe software package [11]. We feed the image of each fashion item to the CNNs, and adopt the fc7 layer output as the visual feature. Ultimately, for each item, the visual modality is represented by a 4096-D vector.

Textual Feature. Analogous to [15], we take advantage of the bag-of-words scheme [10], which has been proven to be effective to encode contextual metadata [4]. As such user-generated data can be inevitably noisy [19], we thus filter out the words in titles that appeared in less than 5 items as well as those whose length is shorter than 3 characters. We ultimately obtain a vocabulary of $1,511$ words, and thus compile the textual modality of each fashion item with a $1,511$-D boolean vector.

4   Experiment

4.1   Experiment Setting

In this work, we apply the proposed method to the application of clothing matching, where we cast the problem of clothing matching as the complementary fashion item retrieval. Given a top, we aim to generate a ranking list of the bottoms. In particular, we first split the positive top-bottom pairs in $\mathcal{P}$ into three parts: 80% for training, 10% for validation, and 10% for testing, which are denoted as $\mathcal{P}_{train}$, $\mathcal{P}_{valid}$ and $\mathcal{P}_{test}$, respectively. For each pair $(i,j) \in \mathcal{P}_{train}$, we randomly sample a bottom k that has never been paired with top i and make a pair (i,k) for the neutral set $\mathcal{N}_{train}$. We then train our model with $\mathcal{P}_{train}$ and $\mathcal{N}_{train}$ and learn the matrices $\mathbf{Y}_v^1$, $\mathbf{Y}_t^1$, $\mathbf{Y}_v^2$ and $\mathbf{Y}_t^2$. Afterwards, given any two testing fashion items, we can measure their compatibility according to Eq. (4). We can thus generate a ranking list of bottoms for a given top based on their compatibility. For efficient evaluation, we here adopt the common strategy [5] that feeds each testing top as a query, and randomly samples K bottom candidates, where only one of them is the positive bottom. We thus adopt the widely used metric MRR (Mean Reciprocal Rank) [18,21], which is defined as,

$$MRR = \frac{1}{K} \sum_{i=1}^{K} \frac{1}{rank_i}, \tag{6}$$

where $rank_i$ refers to the ranking of the positive bottom for the i-th top query. Specifically, we set $K = 10$.

In terms of training, we adopt the grid search strategy to obtain the optimal parameters β and D_0. In particular, we search β in the range of $[0, 1.0]$ with the step of 0.2, and D_0 in the range of $[10, 100]$ with a step of 10. All the results reported in this work are based on the optimal parameters. In addition, as the input features of tops and bottoms are extracted in the same way and hence come from the same feature spaces, we impose that $\mathbf{Y}_v^1 = \mathbf{Y}_v^2$, and $\mathbf{Y}_t^1 = \mathbf{Y}_t^2$.

4.2   Experiment Results

We first experimentally verify that the convergence of the proposed model. The change of the training loss and MRR of our model is shown in Fig. 3. As we can see, the loss and MRR both change rapidly within a few iterations and then tend to be steady, which well demonstrates the convergence of our model and reflects the efficiency of our model to certain extent.

To evaluate the effectiveness of the proposed model, we select the following state-of-the-art baselines.

RAW: We calculate the compatibility of top i and bottom j based on their raw features as follows,

$$c(i,j) = (1 - \gamma)\mathbf{v}_i^1(\mathbf{v}_j^2)^T + \gamma \mathbf{t}_i^1(\mathbf{t}_j^2)^T, \tag{7}$$

where γ is the nonnegative trade-off weight coefficient.

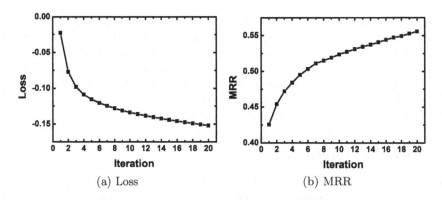

(a) Loss   (b) MRR

Fig. 3. The training loss and MRR of each iteration.

SVR: SVR is a version of the support vector machines (SVMs) for regression problems. For each pair $(i, j) \in \mathcal{P}$, we concatenate their feature vectors, and assign class 1. Similarly, we generate the negative samples labeled as 0 based on $\mathcal{N}$. Then the compatibility thus can be measured as the regression score. We ultimately fuse the compatibility measured by different modalities.

IBR: IBR refers to the image-based clothing recommendation model [13], which models the relationships between items via a latent linear style space solely based on the visual data.

Table 2 shows the performance of different models in terms of MRR. As can be seen, our model shows superiority over **RAW** and **SVR**, which suggests that it is necessary to seek a latent space to bridge the gap between heterogenous

Table 2. Performance of different models.

Model	RAW	SVR	IBR	CMVT
MRR	0.3006	0.3268	0.3639	**0.4509**

Top	1	2	3	4	5	6	7	8	9	10

Fig. 4. Illustration of the ranking results. The bottoms highlighted in the red boxes are the positive ones.

fashion items. In addition, we observed that our model outperforms **IBR**, and this enables us to draw the conclusion that integration of the multi-modal data can boost the performance significantly. Several intuitive retrieval results are listed in Fig. 4. As can be seen, although in certain cases that our model failed to rank the positive one at the first place, the neutral bottoms ranked before the positive one are also much compatible with the query top. This demonstrates the usefulness of the proposed model in real applications.

4.3   Sensitivity Analysis

As all the above analysis reported is based on the optimal results achieved by parameter tuning, we here take a closer look at the key parameters (i.e., β and D_0) and explore their effects on the performance. Figure 5 shows the sensitivity curves of performance with different fusion coefficient β and the dimension of the latent space D_0. We observed that the performance reaches the best at $\beta = 0.9$. According to Eq. (3), this implies that the textual modality of fashion items on Polyvore is more powerful in terms of compatibility measurement than the visual modality. In addition, we observed that with D_0 increasing, the performance first increases sharply at $D_0 = 20$, followed by a drop afterwards. This suggests that the factors that affect the latent space are not too many.

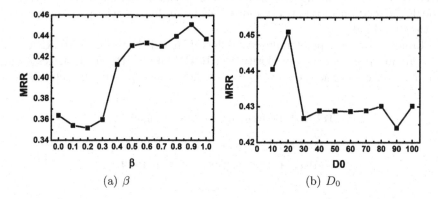

(a) β (b) D_0

Fig. 5. Parameter tuning of the fusion parameter β and the dimension of the latent space D_0.

5   Conclusion and Future Work

In this work, we propose a model (CMVT) for clothing matching based on both the visual and textual information of fashion items. CMVT seamlessly integrates the complementary visual and textual information of fashion items and then comprehensively measures the compatibility of any given two items. In particular, we apply CMVT to solve the practical problem of matching bottoms for a given top. Experimental results demonstrate the superiority of our model over other state-of-the-art baselines. Currently, we only consider the general clothing matching but overlook the personalization. In the future, we will further explore the sensor data [3] to take users' figure into consideration. In addition, the implicit feedback [6] regarding outfit compositions can be exploited.

Acknowledgments. The work is supported by the National Natural Science Foundation of China under Grant No.: 61702300.

References

1. Bottou, L.: Stochastic gradient learning in neural networks. Proc. Neuro-Nımes **91**(8) (1991)
2. Chen, J., Song, X., Nie, L., Wang, X., Zhang, H., Chua, T.-S.: Micro tells macro: predicting the popularity of micro-videos via a transductive model. In: Proceedings of the ACM International Conference on Multimedia, pp. 898–907. ACM (2016)
3. Gan, T., Wong, Y., Zhang, D., Kankanhalli, M.S.: Temporal encoded f-formation system for social interaction detection. In: Proceedings of the ACM International Conference on Multimedia, pp. 937–946. ACM (2013)
4. Gao, Y., Wang, M., Zha, Z.-J., Shen, J., Li, X., Xindong, W.: Visual-textual joint relevance learning for tag-based social image search. IEEE Trans. Image Process. **22**(1), 363–376 (2013)
5. He, X., Liao, L., Zhang, H., Nie, L., Hu, X., Chua, T.-S.: Neural collaborative filtering. In: Proceedings of the ACM International Conference on World Wide Web, pp. 173–182. ACM (2017)
6. He, X., Zhang, H., Kan, M.-Y., Chua, T.-S.: Fast matrix factorization for online recommendation with implicit feedback. In: Proceedings of the International ACM SIGIR Conference on Research and Development in Information Retrieval, pp. 549–558. ACM (2016)
7. Hong, R., Zhenzhen, H., Wang, R., Wang, M., Tao, D.: Multi-view object retrieval via multi-scale topic models. IEEE Trans. Image Process. **25**(12), 5814–5827 (2016)
8. Hong, R., Yang, Y., Wang, M., Hua, X.-S.: Learning visual semantic relationships for efficient visual retrieval. IEEE Trans. Big Data **1**(4), 152–161 (2015)
9. Hong, R., Zhang, L., Zhang, C., Zimmermann, R.: Flickr circles: aesthetic tendency discovery by multi-view regularized topic modeling. IEEE Trans. Multimed. **18**(8), 1555–1567 (2016)
10. Ji, R., Xie, X., Yao, H., Ma, W.-Y.: Mining city landmarks from blogs by graph modeling. In: Proceedings of the ACM International Conference on Multimedia, pp. 105–114. ACM (2009)
11. Jia, Y., Shelhamer, E., Donahue, J., Karayev, S., Long, J., Girshick, R., Guadarrama, S., Darrell, T.: Caffe: convolutional architecture for fast feature embedding. In: Proceedings of the ACM International Conference on Multimedia, pp. 675–678. ACM (2014)
12. Krizhevsky, A., Sutskever, I., Hinton, G.E.: Imagenet classification with deep convolutional neural networks. In: Proceedings of the Advances in Neural Information Processing Systems, pp. 1097–1105 (2012)
13. McAuley, J., Targett, C., Shi, Q., Van Den Hengel, A.: Image-based recommendations on styles and substitutes. In: Proceedings of the International ACM SIGIR Conference on Research and Development in Information Retrieval, pp. 43–52. ACM (2015)

14. Nie, L., Wang, M., Zha, Z.-J., Chua, T.-S.: Oracle in image search: a content-based approach to performance prediction. ACM Trans. Inf. Syst. **30**, 13:1–13:23 (2012)
15. Nie, L., Wang, M., Zha, Z., Li, G., Chua, T.-S.: Multimedia answering: enriching text QA with media information. In: Proceedings of the International ACM SIGIR Conference on Research and Development in Information Retrieval, pp. 695–704. ACM (2011)
16. Nie, L., Yan, S., Wang, M., Hong, R., Chua, T.-S.: Harvesting visual concepts for image search with complex queries. In: Proceedings of the ACM International Conference on Multimedia, pp. 59–68. ACM (2012)
17. Jagadeesh, V., Piramuthu, R., Bhardwaj, A., Di, W., Sundaresan, N.: Large scale visual recommendations from street fashion images. In: Proceedings of the ACM SIGKDD International Conference on Knowledge Discovery and Data Mining, pp. 1925–1934. ACM (2014)
18. Song, X., Feng, F., Liu, J., Li, Z., Nie, L., Ma, J.: Neurostylist: neural compatibility modeling for clothing matching. In: Proceedings of the ACM International Conference on Multimedia. ACM (2017)
19. Song, X., Ming, Z.-Y., Nie, L., Zhao, Y.-L., Chua, T.-S.: Volunteerism tendency prediction via harvesting multiple social networks. ACM Trans. Inf. Syst. **34**(2), 10 (2016)
20. Song, X., Nie, L., Zhang, L., Akbari, M., Chua, T.-S.: Multiple social network learning and its application in volunteerism tendency prediction. In: Proceedings of the International ACM SIGIR Conference on Research and Development in Information Retrieval, pp. 213–222. ACM (2015)
21. Voorhees, E.M., et al.: The TREC-8 question answering track report. In: TREC, vol. 99, pp. 77–82 (1999)
22. Iwata, T., Wanatabe, S., Sawada, H.: Fashion coordinates recommender system using photographs from fashion magazines. In: Proceedings of the International Joint Conference on Artificial Intelligence, vol. 22 (2011)
23. Wang, X., He, X., Nie, L., Chua, T.-S.: Item silk road: recommending items from information domains to social users. In: Proceedings of the International ACM SIGIR Conference on Research and Development in Information Retrieval. ACM (2017)
24. Zhang, H., Shang, X., Yang, W., Xu, H., Luan, H., Chua, T.-S.: Online collaborative learning for open-vocabulary visual classifiers. In: Proceedings of the IEEE Conference on Computer Vision and Pattern Recognition, pp. 2809–2817. IEEE (2016)

Bidirectional Multimodal Recurrent Neural Networks with Refined Visual Features for Image Captioning

Yanwu Shu[1], Liyan Zhang[2(✉)], Zechao Li[1], and Jinhui Tang[1]

[1] Nanjing University of Science and Technology, Nanjing, China
sywcumt@163.com, {zechao.li,jinhuitang}@njust.edu.cn
[2] Nanjing University of Aeronautics and Astronautics, Nanjing, China
zhangliyan@nuaa.edu.cn

Abstract. Image captioning which aims to automatically describe the content of an image using sentences, has become an attractive task in computer vision and natural language processing domain. Recently, neural network approaches have been proposed and proved to be the most efficient methods for image captioning. However, most of the prior work only considers past semantic context information to generate words in the sentence, lacking the consideration of future textual context. Therefore, in this paper, we propose a bidirectional multimodal Recurrent Neural Network (m-RNN) model which considers both history and future semantic context through a bidirectional recurrent layer. We first employ a pre-trained Convolution Neural Network (CNN) to extract image features and then leverage the bidirectional m-RNN to generate the sentences to describe each input image. Besides, we refine visual features by combining word embedding features and raw image features together to further improve the performance. Experimental results performed on the MS-COCO dataset have demonstrated the superiority of our proposed model compared with the original m-RNN model.

Keywords: Image captioning · Bidirectional · Refined visual features

1 Introduction

The rapid advances in computer vision and knowledge learning [1,2] have enabled the possibility of image captioning, which aims to automatically describe the content of an image using sentences. Compared with the traditional tasks, such as image classification, object recognition and image annotation, the goal of image captioning tends to be more challenging and complex. It aims to not only recognize the object in an image, but also express the attributes of these objects and corresponding relationships. Besides, the sentence description for an image can contain richer information than the traditional tag description.

In this work, we propose a bidirectional multimodal Recurrent Neural Network model which considers both history and future semantic context through a

© Springer Nature Singapore Pte Ltd. 2018
B. Huet et al. (Eds.): ICIMCS 2017, CCIS 819, pp. 75–84, 2018.
https://doi.org/10.1007/978-981-10-8530-7_8

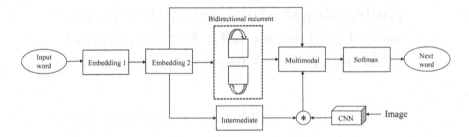

Fig. 1. The process of our bidirectional multimodal Recurrent Neural Network with refined visual features at one time step.

bidirectional recurrent layer. Figure 1 illustrates the general architecture of the proposed model. It contains several layers including the two word embedding layers, a bidirectional recurrent layer, a multimodal layer, an intermediate layer and a softmax layer. The inputs of the model involve image features extracted from a pre-trained CNN model and words corresponding to each image, and the output is the probability distribution of next word. And then the generated words at each time step are combined into a sentence. Here, the bidirectional recurrent layer consists of two recurrent layers, one for learning history textual context and the other for learning future textual context. After obtaining two sentences from both directions, we select the final caption from them according to the probability summation of every word in the sentence.

In addition, to further improve the results, we refine visual features by combining word embedding features and raw image features together. In the original m-RNN model, visual features extracted from the pre-trained CNN model are sent into the multimodal layer directly, along with the word embedding features and bidirectional recurrent layer activation. However, it is unreasonable to keep the image features unchanged, while the generated words are different at each time step. When generating a new word, existing textual context features are closely linked with visual features and can be regarded as a supplementary for visual features. Therefore, instead of sending image features into the multimodal layer directly, we refine image features on the basis of textual context in advance and then leverage the new visual features to generate sentences for images.

The main contribution of this paper can be summarized as follows. First, we propose a bidirectional m-RNN model which considers both history textual context and future textual context to generate sentences. Second, image features extracted from the CNN model can be refined on the basis of textual features to further improve the performance. To evaluate performance of the proposed methods, we perform a series of experiments on the public MS-COCO dataset. The experimental results have demonstrated the superiority of our proposed model compared with the original m-RNN model.

2   Related Work

There are a lot of research about image captioning and all these work can be divided into three categories. The first category is template-based methods [3,4], which predefine some sentence templates and fill in the blanks in the template. What this kind of methods considers about is detecting objects, attributes and actions appearing in pictures and putting these words into a proper template. Although template-based methods can generate sentences with correct grammar, they can't generate sentences with rich semantics due to limited number of templates. These sentences are also robotic and unable to achieve human's fluency.

The second category is retrieval-based methods [5,6], which is related to image retrieval. Retrieval-based methods aim to choose the best sentence of visually similar images in the database to describe target pictures. These methods can generate fluent and human-like sentences, but these sentences may be unable to describe the content accurately. It is easy to see that all these generated sentences already exist in the database. If there are some novel objects which don't appear in the database, retrieval-based methods can't describe them well.

Different from template-based methods and retrieval-based methods, neural network approaches are most popular among these methods because it can produce novel sentences for images and these sentences are fluent and natural [7]. There have been much work using neural network models in recent years. In the work of Mao et al. [8], they propose a multimodal Recurrent Neural Network model. Similar architectures are proposed in the work of Vinyals et al. [9], they use LSTM, a variant of RNN, to learn textual context information. Karpathy and Fei-Fei [10] use region-CNN to generate descriptions of image regions, while Xu et al. [11] integrate visual attention through the hidden state of the LSTM model in order to focus on different image regions when generating corresponds words. Our work draws on some ideas from the work of Wang et al. [12] who present a deep bidirectional LSTM model by stacking multiple LSTM layers. Most recently, existing models with visual attributes and attention mechanism make the results better.

3   Methods

In this section, we introduce our extended model of m-RNN which is a bidirectional m-RNN model with refined visual features. There are two parts in this section, one is how to make original m-RNN model learn textual context from two directions, and the other is how to generate refined visual features.

3.1   Bidirectional m-RNN Model

The idea of learning semantic context information from two directions is from the work of Wang et al. [12]. However, instead of boosting the performance by

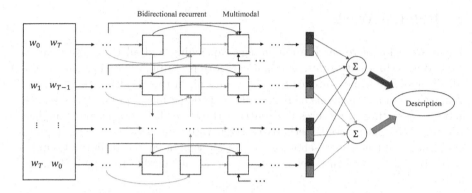

Fig. 2. The unfolded model of our bidirectional multimodal Recurrent Neural Network at different time steps. (Color figure online)

increasing the depth of LSTM network and using data augmentation, our model is much simpler which contains no stacked LSTM layers. Therefore, we don't need to augment the training set in the dataset.

The architecture of our model is similar to the m-RNN model. It contains a language model part, a vision model part and a multimodal layer part. The language model part can produce a dense representation of each word that appears in a sentence and store semantic context information in a bidirectional recurrent layer. The vision model part can extract feature vectors of every picture in the dataset. And the multimodal layer part is used for combining these factors into a softmax layer to generate the current word.

The input words in the model are encoded in one-hot code and are embedded into dense word representations which require less memory space. After the two embedding layers, there is a bidirectional recurrent layer which combines its own hidden state at time $t-1$ with the word embedding vectors at time t. As shown in Fig. 2, the model learns semantic context information from two directions, where the blue arrows represent the forward direction and the red arrows represent the backward direction. The bidirectional RNN layer here is made up of two separated RNN layers for learning sequence of word embedding from both forwards and backwards as shown below:

$$\overrightarrow{r}(t) = R(\overrightarrow{w}(t), \overrightarrow{r}(t-1)) \tag{1}$$

$$\overleftarrow{r}(t) = R(\overleftarrow{w}(t), \overleftarrow{r}(t-1)) \tag{2}$$

where $R()$ represents the bidirectional recurrent layer, $w(t)$ are the word embedding features at time t, $r(t)$ and $r(t-1)$ are the hidden state of the bidirectional recurrent layer. Then similar to the m-RNN model, we also send the word embedding representation, bidirectional recurrent layer activation and visual features extracted from a CNN model into a multimodal layer:

$$m(t) = f(\overrightarrow{w}(t), \overrightarrow{r}(t), \overleftarrow{w}(T-t), \overleftarrow{r}(T-t), I) \tag{3}$$

where $f()$ is a Rectified Linear Unit (ReLU) activation function and I represent image features. Particularly, w and r in the formula contains word embedding features and hidden state of the recurrent layer from two directions. At last, there is a softmax layer to generate the probability distribution of next word at each time step and we choose the word with highest probability till the end.

The goal of the image captioning task is to maximize the probability of the correct sentence for an image. Similar to previous work [9], our model also needs to set optimal parameters to minimize the cost function as the following formula:

$$\theta^* = \arg\min_{\theta} \sum_{(S,I)} -\log P(S|I,\theta) \tag{4}$$

where θ are parameters of each layer in the model, S is a sentence corresponding to an image I.

Existing models only generate one word at each time step, so the whole sentence S with length T can be divided into several words represented as $w_0, w_1, \cdots, w_T$. Therefore, the cost function can be replaced by the sum of log probability for every word. When generating a word, it is not only related to previous words before time t, but also related to those words that follow word w_t. In other words, the probability $P(S|I)$ can be replaced in another form as follows:

$$P(S|I) = \max\left(\sum_{t=0}^{T} P(w_t|I, w_{0:t-1}), \sum_{t=0}^{T} P(w_t|I, w_{t+1:T})\right) \tag{5}$$

where $w_{0:t-1}$ are the words from the beginning to time $t-1$, $w_{t+1:T}$ are the words from time $t+1$ to the end. Both of them are related to the word w_t at time t.

We choose the sentence with the higher sum of probability between two directions as the final description for the input image. Figure 3 shows an example for

Forward direction:
A group of people standing on top of a sandy beach.

Backward direction:
A group of people with surfboards on a beach.

Fig. 3. Results of two generated captions from forward direction and backward direction.

two sentences from forward direction and backward direction. In our experiments for the example, we choose the description of forward direction because it has higher probability.

3.2 Refined Visual Features

In the m-RNN model, image features are involved in the multimodal layer at each time step. In the later research [9,13], it is recognized that feeding image features only at first time step can get superior results. They attribute this phenomenon to that extra input of image features can make noise for the network. However, feeding image features only at first time step may cause another problem which is the lack of image representation information at last few time steps.

In our model, we also feed image features at each time step. As we can see, it is unreasonable that the input word and the output word are different at each time step in the model while the image features are always same. Therefore, instead of directly feeding image features to the multimodal layer, we refine image features by combining the raw image features and its corresponding word embedding features at each time step. In this way, image features and word embedding features are related to each other and the model can learn the relationship between them. In order to combine the two kind of features conveniently, we first make the word embedding features have the same dimension with image features through an intermediate layer and then integrate them into the new features followed by a ReLU activation as shown below:

$$I'(t) = f(inter(w(t)) * I) \tag{6}$$

where $f()$ is a ReLU activation function, $inter()$ is an intermediate layer used to change the dimension of word embedding features at time t, and $*$ represents the element-wise multiplication. Thus, the refined visual features are changing at different time steps. And as the result of using time-dependent image features, the activation of the multimodal layer is also transformed into another form:

$$m(t) = f\left(\overrightarrow{w}(t), \overrightarrow{r}(t), \overleftarrow{w}(T-t), \overleftarrow{r}(T-t), \overrightarrow{I'}(t), \overleftarrow{I'}(T-t)\right) \tag{7}$$

where $m(t)$ is related to the time-dependent image features $I'(t)$ in the forward direction and $I'(T-t)$ in the backward direction, which contains richer information at different time step.

4 Experiments

We conduct the experiments using the method as mentioned above on the MS-COCO dataset [14]. The following sections are some experimental details and final results.

4.1   Dataset

The MS-COCO dataset is the most popular dataset which is widely used for the image captioning task. It contains 82783 images for training and 40504 images for validation. There are five sentences annotated manually for every image. Since the unreasonable provided split of dataset, we use 82783 images for training and randomly choose 5000 images for validation and testing from original validation set which is the same as previous work.

4.2   Implementation Details

Following previous work, we divide every sentence in the dataset into words and these words are used to build a vocabulary. In order to decrease the quantity of the vocabulary size, we just keep the words occurring more than 3 times. In addition, we add three words which are $\langle begin \rangle$, $\langle end \rangle$ and $\langle unknown \rangle$ into the vocabulary. Here, $\langle begin \rangle$ and $\langle end \rangle$ represent the start and end sign of a sentence, and $\langle unknown \rangle$ represents those deleted words which don't exist in the vocabulary. Thus, we get a final vocabulary with 13694 words. The generated sentence of a new image is made up of the words in the vocabulary.

For the vision part, we extract image features by a pre-trained inception_v3 network [15] on ImageNet dataset which is an advanced CNN model for image classification. We use the 2048 dimensional vectors produced by the last fully-connected layer of a pre-trained inception_v3 model.

There are two ways for generating a sentence in the evaluation step of the model. One is to select the word with maximum probability at each time step until the end sign appears or the sentence reaches the maximum length. The other is called beam search which is to iteratively consider k best sentences up to time t as candidates to generate the next word and produce the new k best sentences. Finally, the sentence with highest sum of probability is selected as final description. We use beam search which is proved to be more efficient and set $k = 3$ in our experiments.

4.3   Results

As shown in Fig. 4, there are some examples of image descriptions using three methods: the original m-RNN model, our bidirectional m-RNN model and our model with refined visual features. Our methods can recognize the object in an image more accurately than the original m-RNN model such as the "girl" in the first image, the "umbrella" in the third image and the "sandwich" in the fourth image, while the original m-RNN model makes mistakes. And our methods can also generate richer and more specific information. For example, our model can generate the words "a red jacket" for the fifth image and "a frisbee" for the last image, which don't exist in the description created by the original m-RNN model.

Although the most effective evaluation method for image captioning is human evaluation, it is common to use automatic evaluation metrics which are BLEU

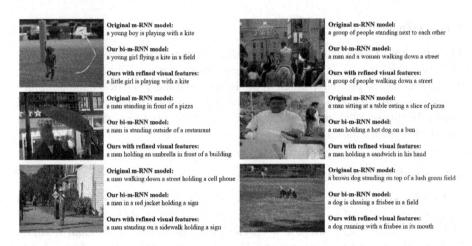

Fig. 4. Results of descriptions for some pictures generated by different models. (Color figure online)

score [16], METEOR [17], ROUGE_L [18] and CIDEr [19]. As shown in Table 1, B-N, M, R, and C represent BLEU-N, METEOR, ROUGE_L, and CIDEr scores respectively. "-" represents that the scores are not released. It is easy to see that the results of our bidirectional m-RNN model are better than other models.

Inspired by retrieval-based methods using nearest neighbor approaches to find the best caption in the training set for an image, there is a supplementary in the work of Mao et al. [8] where the sentences generated by the m-RNN model using beam search can be reordered to find the most precise sentence. We also apply this tip to our model and use the same number of nearest neighbor images and captions as their work. Table 2 shows that our model with consensus reranking is better than the original m-RNN too.

Table 1. Results of our proposed models and other methods on MS-COCO dataset.

Model	B-1	B-2	B-3	B-4	M	R	C
m-RNN [8]	0.67	0.49	0.35	0.25	-	-	-
Google NIC [9]	0.666	0.461	0.329	0.246	-	-	-
NeuralTalk [10]	0.625	0.450	0.321	0.230	0.195	-	0.660
Bi-LSTM [12]	0.672	0.492	0.352	0.244	-	-	-
Soft-Attention [11]	0.707	0.492	0.344	0.243	0.239	-	-
Hard-Attention [11]	0.718	0.504	0.357	0.250	0.230	-	-
Bi-m-RNN	0.698	0.524	0.386	0.287	0.244	0.517	0.922
Bi-m-RNN with refined features	0.708	0.538	0.403	0.304	0.249	0.527	0.955

Table 2. Results of the models after using nearest neighbor captions in the training set as references for consensus reranking.

	B-1	B-2	B-3	B-4	M	R	C
m-RNN-shared-NNref-BLEU [8]	0.718	0.550	0.409	0.305	0.235	0.519	0.909
m-RNN-shared-NNref-CIDEr [8]	0.714	0.543	0.406	0.304	0.239	0.519	0.938
Ours-NNref-BLEU	0.733	0.570	0.431	0.326	0.254	0.540	1.001
Ours-NNref-CIDEr	0.722	0.556	0.420	0.319	0.254	0.535	1.020

5   Conclusion

In this paper, we propose a bidirectional m-RNN model for image captioning. The model is made up of a language model part, a vision model part and a multimodal layer. In the language model part, we use a bidirectional recurrent layer to take both history and future textual context information into consideration. In the vision mode part, we refine the image features extracted from a pre-trained CNN model on the basis of the corresponding word embedding features. The language model part and the vision model part are connected by a multimodal layer to generate words at each time step. Results of the experiments show that our model is not only more effective than the original m-RNN model, but also achieves better performances with consensus reranking. In the future work, we will try to add the methods existing in state-of-the-art work into our model to make the results get further improved.

Acknowledgement. This work was partially supported by the National Natural Science Foundation of China (Grant No. 61522203, 61572252 and 61672285), the Natural Science Foundation of Jiangsu Province (Grant No. BK20140058 and BK20150755).

References

1. Tang, J., Shu, X., Qi, Q.J., Li, Z., Wang, M., Yan, S., Jain, R.: Tri-clustered tensor completion for social-aware image tag refinement. IEEE Trans. Pattern Anal. Mach. Intell. **39**(8), 1662–1674 (2017)
2. Tang, J., Shu, X., Li, Z., Qi, Q.J., Wang, J.: Generalized deep transfer networks for knowledge propagation in heterogeneous domains. ACM Trans. Multimed. Comput. Commun. Appl. **12**(4) (2016)
3. Kulkarni, G., Premraj, V., Ordonez, V., Dhar, S., Li, S., Choi, Y., Berg, A.C., Berg, T.L.: Babytalk: understanding and generating simple image descriptions. IEEE Trans. Pattern Anal. Mach. Intell. **35**(12), 2891–2903 (2013)
4. Yang, Y., Teo, C.L., Daumé III, H., Aloimonos, Y.: Corpus-guided sentence generation of natural images. In: Proceedings of the Conference on Empirical Methods in Natural Language Processing, pp. 444–454. Association for Computational Linguistics (2011)
5. Farhadi, A., Hejrati, M., Sadeghi, M.A., Young, P., Rashtchian, C., Hockenmaier, J., Forsyth, D.: Every picture tells a story: generating sentences from images. In: Daniilidis, K., Maragos, P., Paragios, N. (eds.) ECCV 2010. LNCS, vol. 6314, pp. 15–29. Springer, Heidelberg (2010). https://doi.org/10.1007/978-3-642-15561-1_2

6. Kuznetsova, P., Ordonez, V., Berg, A.C., Berg, T.L., Choi, Y.: Collective generation of natural image descriptions. In: Proceedings of the 50th Annual Meeting of the Association for Computational Linguistics: Long Papers, vol. 1, pp. 359–368. Association for Computational Linguistics (2012)

7. Li, Z., Tang, J.: Weakly supervised deep matrix factorization for social image understanding. IEEE Trans. Image Process. **26**(1), 276–288 (2017)

8. Mao, J., Xu, W., Yang, Y., Wang, J., Huang, Z., Yuille, A.: Deep captioning with multimodal recurrent neural networks (m-RNN). In: ICLR (2015)

9. Vinyals, O., Toshev, A., Bengio, S., Erhan, D.: Show and tell: a neural image caption generator. In: Proceedings of the IEEE Conference on Computer Vision and Pattern Recognition, pp. 3156–3164 (2015)

10. Karpathy, A., Fei-Fei, L.: Deep visual-semantic alignments for generating image descriptions. In: Proceedings of the IEEE Conference on Computer Vision and Pattern Recognition, pp. 3128–3137 (2015)

11. Xu, K., Ba, J., Kiros, R., Cho, K., Courville, A., Salakhudinov, R., Zemel, R., Bengio, Y.: Show, attend and tell: neural image caption generation with visual attention. In: International Conference on Machine Learning, pp. 2048–2057 (2015)

12. Wang, C., Yang, H., Bartz, C., Meinel, C.: Image captioning with deep bidirectional LSTMs. In: Proceedings of the 2016 ACM on Multimedia Conference, pp. 988–997. ACM (2016)

13. Li, Z., Liu, J., Tang, J., Lu, H.: Robust structured subspace learning for data representation. IEEE Trans. Pattern Anal. Mach. Intell. **37**(10), 2085–2098 (2015)

14. Chen, X., Fang, H., Lin, T.Y., Vedantam, R., Gupta, S., Dollár, P., Zitnick, C.L.: Microsoft COCO captions: data collection and evaluation server (2015). arXiv preprint: arXiv:1504.00325

15. Szegedy, C., Vanhoucke, V., Ioffe, S., Shlens, J., Wojna, Z.: Rethinking the inception architecture for computer vision. In: Proceedings of the IEEE Conference on Computer Vision and Pattern Recognition, pp. 2818–2826 (2016)

16. Papineni, K., Roukos, S., Ward, T., Zhu, W.J.: BLEU: a method for automatic evaluation of machine translation. In: Proceedings of the 40th Annual Meeting on Association for Computational Linguistics, pp. 311–318. Association for Computational Linguistics (2002)

17. Banerjee, S., Lavie, A.: METEOR: an automatic metric for MT evaluation with improved correlation with human judgments, pp. 228–231 (2005)

18. Lin, C.Y.: ROUGE: a package for automatic evaluation of summaries. In: Text Summarization Branches Out: Proceedings of the ACL-2004 Workshop, vol. 8, Barcelona, Spain (2004)

19. Vedantam, R., Lawrence Zitnick, C., Parikh, D.: CIDEr: consensus-based image description evaluation. In: Proceedings of the IEEE Conference on Computer Vision and Pattern Recognition, pp. 4566–4575 (2015)

Image Processing and Object Recognition

Automatic Watermeter Digit Recognition on Mobile Devices

Yunze Gao[1,2]([⊠]), Chaoyang Zhao[1,2], Jinqiao Wang[1,2], and Hanqing Lu[1,2]

[1] National Lab of Pattern Recognition, Institute of Automation,
Chinese Academy of Sciences, Beijing, China
{yunze.gao,chaoyang.zhao,jqwang,luhq}@nlpr.ia.ac.cn
[2] University of Chinese Academy of Sciences, Beijing 100190, China

Abstract. Automatic watermeter digit recognition in the wild is a challenging task, which is an application of scene text recognition in the field of computer vision. In this paper, we propose an automatic watermeter digit recognition approach on mobile devices which consists of digit detection and recognition. Specifically, we adopt Adaboost with aggregated channel features (ACF) to detect watermeter digital regions, where the computation is accelerated by the fast feature pyramid technology. Then a small attention bidirectional long short-term memory (BLSTM) is designed for end-to-end digit sequence recognition. Convolutional Neural network (CNN) is exploited to extract discriminative feature and BLSTM is able to capture the rich context in both directions within sequence data. Moreover, an attention mechanism is added to weight the most important part of incoming image features. We validate the performace of our approach on the collected complex dataset. It contains various watermeter images in real scenario which has illumination changes, messy environment, half-digit and blurring. It is observed that the proposed algorithm outperforms existing methods. Our approach runs 10 fps with 96.1% accuracy on HUAWEI Mate 8.

Keywords: Watermeter digit recognition · BLSTM · Attention model

1 Introduction

It is very time consuming and labor intensive to record the digital number of watermeter manually from house to house. Therefore, if we can take a photo and recognize its digital value automatically, recoding the value of watermeter becomes much convenient and less mistakes caused by meter reader. Traditional approaches for watermeter recognition are mainly based on template matching [1] or BP neural networks [2]. These approaches usually involve several steps including detection, segmentation, binarization and recognition. Each step has several experienced parameters and rigid rules. Therefore, they cannot deal with complex scenes such as various watermeter types, different views and messy environment.

© Springer Nature Singapore Pte Ltd. 2018
B. Huet et al. (Eds.): ICIMCS 2017, CCIS 819, pp. 87–95, 2018.
https://doi.org/10.1007/978-981-10-8530-7_9

Watermeter digit recognition is an application of scene text recognition. Nowadays, text recognition in the wild has received intensive concerns from numerous researchers [3,4], which has a variety of applications, such as automatic car license plate recognition, sign reading in the driveless vehicle, and image retrieval. Traditional approaches [5,6] focused on the conventional Optical Character Recognition (OCR) method by first segmenting individual characters and then recognizing these characters separately. The diversity of text patterns and blurring, backlight increase the difficulty of character segmentation. So the performance is confined to the inaccuracy of character-level segmentation. Furthermore, recognizing each character individually ignores the relationship between the characters. Recent studies regard scene text recognition as a sequence recognition problem without segmentation. Shi *et al.* [7] proposed a Convolutional Recurrent Neural Network (CRNN) to integrate CNN and RNN for text recognition. Lee *et al.* [8] designed an attention-based RNN approach model for OCR in the wild by weighted sequence modeling.

Different from the scene text, each digit of watermeter is surrounded by a rectangular box, and there exist some partial occlusions since the digits roll in the watermeter. Furthermore, the environment of watermeter is complicated and messy, which also increases the challenge of watermeter digit recognition. Liu *et al.* [1] captured watermeter images through a camera at a fixed angle to obtain the digit region directly, and used template matching to recognize each digit. Rui *et al.* [2] used feature pattern matching method to segment watermeter digits and trained two BP neural networks to classify full digits and half digits, respectively. Conventional watermeter digit recognition methods are inaccurate and inflexible, because the segmentation errors do harm to the recognition accuracy. Besides, the fixed viewpoint and the same feature pattern cannot be generalized to other situations, such as mobile devices and different kinds of watermeters.

In this paper, we propose an automatic watermeter digit recognition approach on mobile devices, which consists of digital region detection and recognition. To extract the feature efficiently in the detection, we adopt the ACF features which are single pixel values in the aggregated channels [9]. Then Adaboost is used to combine decision trees over these features to distinguish digits and background [10]. At the same time, the feature pyramid estimation is applied to accelerate the computation. For the digital recognition, we employ a sequential attention-based model that is specifically designed for sequential recognition. To begin with, a sequence of feature vectors is extracted by the BLSTM [11,12] which is on top of CNN. According to the feature representation, the watermeter digits are predicted recurrently by an attention decoder [13]. The attention mechanism [14] can perform feature selection and recurrent network can learn the sequential dynamics of digits. Our system performs well in the task of automatic watermeter reading on mobile devices and can achieve higher accuracy than traditional methods.

2   The Proposed Approach

As shown in Fig. 1, the watermeter image is captured by a mobile phone. The digital region of watermeter is detected by boosting ACF features. Then the features of cropped digital region are extracted by CNN and BLSTM, and input into the attention decoder to obtain the meter reading.

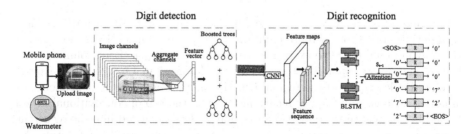

Fig. 1. Overview of mobile watermeter digit recognition.

2.1   Digit Detection

We adopt adaboost with ACF features to detect the digital region from a captured watermeter image. Since a cell phone often provides limited computational power in CPU, our detection part has to be realized with small computational complexity. Methods such as DPM or CNN based approaches are far beyond our option. In this paper, we choose ACF features and boosting framework for both fast-to-compute and high accuracy properties. To begin with, given an input image, several channels including normalized gradient magnitude, histogram of oriented gradients and LUV color channels are computed. These channels are divided into 4 × 4 blocks. Afterwards, the pixels in each block are summed, resulting in aggregate channel features. All pixel values are vectorized to form a pixel lookup table as the feature description of the image. To increase the accuracy, we use adaboost to train and combine multiple decision trees over these features to distinguish digits from background. Based on sliding windows over multiscale feature pyramid, the digital region of watermeter can be detected accurately.

When constructing the feature pyramid, we utilize a pyramid scale estimation [9] to accelerate the computation. Only the features for a sparse set of scales are computed by resampling the image and recomputing the channel features $C_s = \Omega(R(I, s))$, where C_s are the channel features at scale s, I is the original image, R is the sampling function and Ω is the channel computation function. For intermediate scales, C_s is computed by $C_s \approx R(C_{s'}, s/s')(s/s')^{-\lambda_\Omega}$, where s' is the nearest scale and λ_Ω is a channel specific power-law factor. With this method, the cost of feature computation is greatly reduced. The fast feature pyramid construction and scale estimation not only provide good performance but also guarantee the speed.

2.2   Digit Recognition

After digital detection, we adopt an end-to-end sequence recognition network to obtain the digit sequence. First, a feature sequence is generated by a network that combines convolutional layers and recurrent layers. Next, an attention decoder predicts one digit at each step recurrently according to the feature representation.

Sequence Feature. CNN has demonstrated strong ability to learn rich semantic description and robust representation from an input image [15], so we employ the convolutional layers to extract features of digital region. Each column of the feature map is corresponding to a receptive field of original image, which can be seen as the descriptor of the region. But this method ignores the dependence of adjacent regions, so we apply recurrent layer on the top of convolutional layers to obtain the long term context information. Before being fed into the recurrent layer, the feature maps are converted to a feature sequence, by extracting the same column of all feature maps and concatenating these columns into a vector as one element of feature sequence.

Considering the context information in the left and right are both helpful to recognize digits, we use the BLSTM to model the dependencies within the sequence in both directions. Then the BLSTM outputs the feature sequence that contains the latent relationship of these digits. The output sequence is denoted by $f = (f_1, f_2, \cdots, f_n)$, where n is the width of feature maps. The combination of convolutional layer and recurrent layer can effectively generate the discriminative feature for sequence recognition.

Attention Decoder. According to the feature sequence, the digits can be predicted recurrently by an attention-based decoder, which is also a recurrent network with attention mechanism like [14]. At each step t, the LSTM cell is applied to decode the weighted feature and predict the digit. First, conditioning on feature sequence and previous recurrent cell state, attention weights are computed by scoring each element in f separately and normalizing the scores:

$$e_{tj} = w^T tanh(W^T s_{t-1} + V^T f_j + b) \tag{1}$$

$$\alpha_{tj} = \frac{exp(e_{tj})}{\sum_{j=1}^{n} exp(e_{tj})} \tag{2}$$

where $\alpha_t \in R^n$ is a vector of attention weights; s_{t-1} is the recurrent cell state of previous frame; f_j is a vector of feature sequence; and W, V are weight matrices; w, b are weight vectors. The attention weight α_{tj} can be regarded as the relative importance of feature vector f_j. Then the input g_t of recurrent cell is computed by weighted sum of feature vectors based on the attention weights:

$$g_t = \sum_{j=1}^{n} \alpha_{tj} f_j \tag{3}$$

Following that, the internal state s_t of the recurrent cell is updated by taking input g_t, previous state s_{t-1} and output y_{t-1} into account. Next, the probability estimation over the label is computed by:

$$y_t = softmax(U^T s_t) \qquad (4)$$

The class with the highest probability is output as the predicted digit. Besides of ten digits, the labels also include "start of sequence" (SOS) which starts the prediction and "end of sequence" (EOS) which ends the prediction procedure. In this approach, at each step, we can focus on the most relevant content to make more accurate prediction. In addition, the recognition network also allows that the input and output sequence have arbitrary length, thus we can recognize various watermeters with different number of digits.

3 Experiment

3.1 Experiment Setting

There is no public watermeter images dataset to evaluate the performance. Therefore, we collect watermeter images by mobile phones in the wild and establish a complex dataset including 8781 watermeter images with five digits. These images are captured in the horizon or vertical angle including various illumination, messy situations, complicated environment, half digit and blurring. We randomly divide 8781 images into two parts: 7781 images are as train set and 1000 images are as test set.

Table 1. Network architecture of the digit recognition network.

attention-decoder 2 layers, 256 units per layer
BLSTM 1 layer, 512 units
Cov7 512, 2×2, stride 1×1, bn
Maxpooling 2×1, stride 2×1
Cov6 512, 3×3, stride 1×1
Cov5 512, 3×3, stride 1×1, bn
Maxpooling 2×1, stride 2×1
Cov4 256, 3×3, stride 1×1
Cov3 256, 3×3, stride 1×1, bn
Maxpooling 2×2, stride 2×2
Cov2 128, 3×3, stride 1×1
Maxpooling 2×2, stride 2×2
Cov1 64, 3×3, stride 1×1

In the experiment, we set 2048 decision trees with depth-two in the detection module. And we show the proposed digit recognition network in Table 1. Convolutions are performed with zero padding and ReLU activation function. During the phrase of training and testing, all the images are resized to 32-pixel height and meanwhile maintains original aspect ratio.

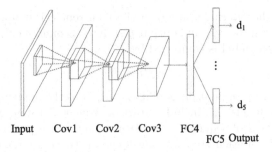

Input   Cov1   Cov2   Cov3   FC4

FC5 Output

Fig. 2. The structure of Multi-softmax network.

3.2   Experiment Results

To verify the efficiency of the digital detection part, here we compare the ACF detector with boosting methods that combined with several other features, including HOG [16] and LBP [17]. The detection performance is shown in Fig. 3. Here we use log-average miss rate for evaluation (lower the better). As shown in Fig. 3, the ACF feature shows most promising result. Although boosting with HOG shows comparable result, its computation of 31 gradient orientations suffers more computational complexity compared to ACF. LBP shows the worst result on the digit detection task.

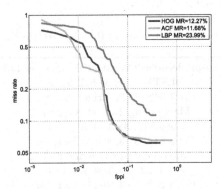

Fig. 3. Comparison of watermeter digits detection by different features.

We also conduct two baseline approaches even segmentation and Multi-softmax for recognition on the same test dataset. Even segmentation is to divide the character region into five parts evenly and each part is classified by an ordinary convolutional neural network. Multi-softmax is a method to recognize digits directly without segmentation, but no recurrent unit and attention mechanism. As shown in Table 2, our approach outperforms even segmentation. For even segmentation, the poor performance indicates that segmentation mistakes could influence the final recognition result greatly.

Table 2. Comparison results with traditional methods.

Method	Accuracy (%)
Even segmentation	51.2
Multi-softmax	91.6
Ours	96.1

For Multi-softmax approach, the network is illustrated in Fig. 2. We use the cifar network, which consists of three convolutional layers and two fully connected layers. To predict multiple labels for an input image, the last fully connected layer and softmax are copied according to the number of watermeter digits. As shown in Table 2, our approach outperforms the Multi-softmax approach by 4.5%. This can be explained that more relevant context information is obtained by recurrent network and the attention mechanism.

Fig. 4. Examples of watermeter digits detection and recognition results.

Some examples of watermeter detection and recognition results are shown in Fig. 4. By analyzing the mistake results, we find most of recognition errors appear in the case of half digits. As mentioned before, half-digit recognition is a difficult issue because of the various patterns.

Table 3. The time of each section.

	Detection	Recognition	Total
Time (ms)	50	70	120

Furthermore, the computation time of the watermeter digit recognition on HUAWEI Mate 8 is shown in Table 3. The digit detection spends 50 ms and the digit recognition spends 70 ms. We can get the recognition result of an image within 120 ms.

4   Conclusions

In this paper, we propose an automatic watermeter digit recognition method on mobile devices which is composed of digit detection and recognition. For the detection part, the ACF detector with boosting method can extract the digital region accurately and efficiently. During digit recognition, BLSTM is utilized for the context information and attention mechanism is also employed for weighting image features. With this method, the digits can be recognized without segmentation, which improves recognition accuracy greatly. Some comparative experimental results show that our approach performs well on validity and practicability. Next, we will add Spatial Transform Network to recognize tilted and rotated watermeter images.

References

1. Liu, Y., Han, Y.-B., Zhang, Y.-L.: Image type water meter character recognition based on Embedded DSP. arXiv preprint arXiv:1508.06725 (2015)
2. Xiao-ping, R., Xian-feng, S.: A character recognition algorithm adapt to a specific kind of water meter. In: 2009 WRI World Congress on Computer Science and Information Engineering, vol. 5, pp. 632–636 (2009)
3. Neumann, L., Matas, J.: Real-time scene text localization and recognition. In: 2012 IEEE Conference on Computer Vision and Pattern Recognition (CVPR), pp. 3538–3545. IEEE (2012)
4. Jaderberg, M., Simonyan, K., Vedaldi, A., Zisserman, A.: Synthetic data and artificial neural networks for natural scene text recognition. arXiv preprint arXiv:1406.2227 (2014)
5. Wang, T., Wu, D.J., Coates, A., Ng, A.Y.: End-to-end text recognition with convolutional neural networks. In: 2012 21st International Conference on, Pattern Recognition (ICPR), pp. 3304–3308 (2012)
6. Bissacco, A., Cummins, M., Netzer, Y., Neven, H.: Photoocr: reading text in uncontrolled conditions. In: Proceedings of the IEEE International Conference on Computer Vision, pp. 785–792 (2013)
7. Shi, B., Bai, X., Yao, C.: An end-to-end trainable neural network for image-based sequence recognition and its application to scene text recognition. IEEE Trans. Pattern Anal. Mach. Intell. **39**, 2298–2304 (2016)
8. Lee, C.-Y., Osindero, S.: Recursive recurrent nets with attention modeling for OCR in the wild. In: Proceedings of the IEEE Conference on Computer Vision and Pattern Recognition, pp. 2231–2239 (2016)
9. Dollár, P., Appel, R., Belongie, S., Perona, P.: Fast feature pyramids for object detection. IEEE Trans. Pattern Anal. Mach. Intell. **36**(8), 1532–1545 (2014)
10. Friedman, J., Hastie, T., Tibshirani, R.: Additive logistic regression: a statistical view of boosting. Ann. Stat. **28**(2), 337–407 (2000)
11. Graves, A., Mohamed, A.-R., Hinton, G.: Speech recognition with deep recurrent neural networks. In: 2013 IEEE International Conference on Acoustics, Speech and Signal Processing (ICASSP), pp. 6645–6649 (2013)
12. Hochreiter, S., Schmidhuber, J.: Long short-term memory. Neural Comput. **9**(8), 1735–1780 (1997)
13. Shi, B., Wang, X., Lyu, P., Yao, C., Bai, X.: Robust scene text recognition with automatic rectification. In: Proceedings of the IEEE Conference on Computer Vision and Pattern Recognition, pp. 4168–4176 (2016)
14. Chorowski, J.K., Bahdanau, D., Serdyuk, D., Cho, K., Bengio, Y.: Attention-based models for speech recognition. In: Advances in Neural Information Processing Systems, pp. 577–585 (2015)

15. Krizhevsky, A., Sutskever, I., Hinton, G.E.: Imagenet classification with deep convolutional neural networks. In: Advances in Neural Information Processing Systems, pp. 1097–1105 (2012)
16. Dalal, N., Triggs, B.: Histograms of oriented gradients for human detection. In: 2005 IEEE Computer Society Conference on Computer Vision and Pattern Recognition, CVPR 2005, vol. 1, pp. 886–893 (2005)
17. Ahonen, T., Hadid, A., Pietikäinen, M.: Face recognition with local binary patterns. In: European Conference on Computer Vision, pp. 469–481 (2004)

3D Human Body Reshaping
with Anthropometric Modeling

Yanhong Zeng[1], Jianlong Fu[2(✉)], and Hongyang Chao[1]

[1] School of Data and Computer Science, Sun Yat-sen University,
Guangzhou 510006, People's Republic of China
[2] Microsoft Research, Beijing 100080, People's Republic of China
jianf@microsoft.com

Abstract. Reshaping accurate and realistic 3D human bodies from anthropometric parameters (e.g., height, chest size, etc.) poses a fundamental challenge for person identification, online shopping and virtual reality. Existing approaches for creating such 3D shapes often suffer from complex measurement by range cameras or high-end scanners, which either involve heavy expense cost or result in low quality. However, these high-quality equipments limit existing approaches in real applications, because the equipments are not easily accessible for common users. In this paper, we have designed a 3D human body reshaping system by proposing a novel feature-selection-based local mapping technique, which enables automatic anthropometric parameter modeling for each body facet. It is worth nothing that the proposed approach can take as input limited anthropometric parameters (i.e., 3–5 measurements), which avoids complex measurement, and thus better user-friendly experience can be achieved in real scenarios. Specifically, the proposed reshaping model consists of three steps. First, we calculate full-body anthropometric parameters from limited user inputs by imputation technique, and thus essential anthropometric parameters for 3D body reshaping can be obtained. Second, we select the most relevant anthropometric parameters for each facet by adopting relevance masks, which are learned offline by the proposed local mapping technique. Third, we generate the 3D body meshes by mapping matrices, which are learned by linear regression from the selected parameters to mesh based body representation. We conduct experiments by anthropomorphic evaluation and a user study from 68 volunteers. Experiments show the superior results of the proposed system in terms of mean reconstruction error against the state-of-the-art approaches.

Keywords: 3D human body shape · Local mapping · Deformation

Y. Zeng—This work is partially supported by NSF of China under Grant 61672548, U1611461, and the Guangzhou Science and Technology Program, China, under Grant 201510010165. This work was performed when Yanhong Zeng was visiting Microsoft Research as a research intern.

B. Huet et al. (Eds.): ICIMCS 2017, CCIS 819, pp. 96–107, 2018.
https://doi.org/10.1007/978-981-10-8530-7_10

1   Introduction

Reshaping accurate and realistic 3D human bodies from anthropometric parameters plays a key role for real users, and can benefit a broad range of applications for person identification, health monitoring, online shopping and virtual reality. For example, reshaping an appropriate 3D human body can help people choose suitable clothes by fitting clothes into the 3D model, and thus the high refund rate for online shops and the waste of time for users can be largely reduced. However, building such a system is challenging, because the body shape of each person is unique, which is hard to be expressed by traditional anthropometric parameters (e.g., height, weight, chest size, etc.) even for the users themselves.

Significant progress has been made by introducing datasets on 3D human body reshaping (e.g., CAESAR dataset [1]), which provides opportunities for representing human bodies by 3D models and motivates great number of research works on learning statistical models for 3D human bodies. These works mainly focus on learning linear regression models from anthropometric parameters and PCA coefficients from vertex information in 3D body shapes [2–4]. Furthermore, Sumner et al. proposed to reformulate the deformation transfer problem in terms of the triangles' vertex positions in their work [5]. Such an approach introduced more complex models for 3D body reshaping by a deformation transfer method for the first time. Later, Yang et al. proposed the SPRING model, which outperforms deformation-based global mapping methods with a significant margin [6]. However, the SPRING model requires segmenting the body shape into fixed rigid parts beforehand (e.g., 16 parts) and binding anthropometric parameters to each part manually for calculating mapping relationship, which brings several limitations. First, defining the relationships among these parts and more than 20 parameters manually often involves heavy human efforts. Second, the definition can vary a lot among different people, which may bring inconsistent results using the same algorithm. Third, binding parameters to facets by hand totally loses the statistic information among the parameters, which may cause some error-prone results. Moreover, creating such 3D shapes from range cameras [7,8] or high-end scanners [9–11] often requires complex measurement devices that are not widely available. A high precision 3D scanner usually costs thousands of dollars, which limits the applications for common users in real scenarios.

To address the above problems, we have designed a 3D human body reshaping system by proposing a novel feature-selection-based local mapping technique with limited user inputs. First, we propose to adopt Multivariate Imputation by Chained Equations (MICE) technique to fill in the missing parameters from the limited user's input [12], which improves the precision of model and enables better user experience in real scenarios. Second, the proposed feature-selection-based local mapping method takes advantage of recursive feature elimination techniques to remove irrelevant anthropometric parameters recursively based on the linear regression weights from a parameter set to mesh based body representation for each facet [13]. As a result, an optimal relevant subset of features will be selected automatically, which eliminates the heavy human involvement from manually binding parameters into body parts. Third, we conduct anthropomorphic evaluation and a user study from 68 volunteers for the proposed system. From these experiments, we find that the proposed system outperforms the state-of-the-art approaches with a clear margin. Figure 1 shows an exemplar screenshot of our system. The contributions are summarized as follows:

(a) Our system provides users with an accurate body shape by using limited parameters as inputs, which ensures better user experience in real scenarios.
(b) We propose a feature-selection-based local mapping method for anthropometric modeling, which can jointly bind relevant parameters to each facet.
(c) We design comprehensive experiments from objective and subjective aspects to show the superiority of our system.

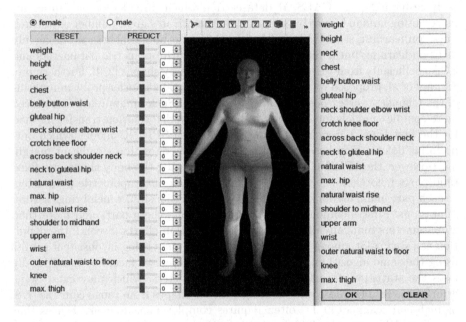

Fig. 1. A screenshot of the proposed system. User can (1) enter a few anthropometric parameters in the right panel; (2) view the generated body shape inside the center window; (3) refine the current body shape slightly by using the slide controls on the left panel as they expected.

The rest of the paper is organized as follows. Section 2 introduces the proposed system. Section 3 describes the evaluation and analysis, followed by the conclusion in Sect. 4.

2   System

To develop an accurate and user-friendly 3D human body reshaping system, we propose to leverage MICE and propose the feature-selection-based local mapping method for anthropometric modeling in our system. Specifically, our system consists of three modules in offline stage and online stage, i.e., the Imputer, the Selector and the Mapper. The overview of our system can be found in Fig. 2. Several relevant data are marked as (a–g) in Fig. 2.

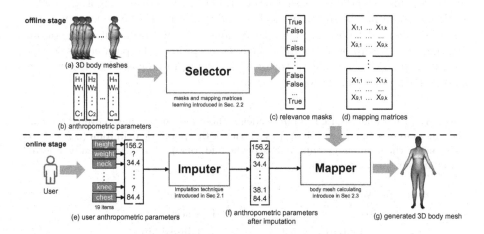

Fig. 2. The overview of the proposed 3D human body reshaping system. The system consists of three parts, i.e., the Imputer, the Selector and the Mapper in both online stage and offline stage. In offline stage, the Selector takes the dataset of 3D body meshes (a) and corresponding anthropometric parameters (b) as inputs to learn the relevance masks (c) by the proposed feature-selection-based local mapping technique. The mapping matrices (d) are further learned by linear regression from the parameters selected by (c) to mesh based body representation. The details of the Selector are introduced in Sect. 2.2. In online stage, MICE is leveraged in the Imputer for the imputation of the parameters from user input (e), which is introduced in Sect. 2.1. '?' in (e) indicates the missing parameters from user inputs, yet could be complemented in (f) by the proposed approach. After imputation, the vector of parameters (f) will be passed to the Mapper. By adopting (c) and (d), 3D body mesh (g) will be generated from (f) in the Mapper, which is introduced in Sect. 2.3.

The Imputer module is responsible for imputation of user's input (Fig. 2(e)), which may contain missing data. After imputation, the vector of parameters (f) will be passed to the Mapper module. The Mapper module selects the most relevance parameters from (f) by adopting relevance masks (c) for each facet, and then generates a final body mesh (g) by mapping matrices (d). (c) and (d) are learned offline by the proposed feature-selection-based local mapping technique in the Selector module. The Selector module takes as inputs the dataset of body mesh (a) and corresponding anthropometric parameters (b) to learn (c) and (d) offline. The details of these modules will be introduced in Sects. 2.1, 2.2 and 2.3.

2.1 Imputer

Since more anthropometric parameters contained in the reshaping model, more constrains will be used when generating the 3D body mesh, which results in a more approximate body mesh. Our system allows users to enter as up to 19 items of anthropometric parameters as listed in Table 1 (e.g., height, weight, chest etc.) so that more approximate body meshes can be obtained. In case most users do not remember all values of these 19 parameters and the input may contain missing data, the Imputer module needs to preprocess the parameters so that a completed 19 dimensional vector of parameters can be passed to the Mapper module for further calculation.

Table 1. 19 parameters used in our models. These parameters have covered primary body measurements, and each item has a strict anthropometric definition (e.g. natural waist means the minimum circumference of the mid torso). More details can be referred in the measurement guide [14].

1	Weight	2	Height
3	Neck	4	Chest
5	Belly button waist	6	Gluteal hip
7	Neck shoulder elbow wrist	8	Crotch knee floor
9	Across back shoulder neck	10	Neck to gluteal hip
11	Natural waist	12	Maximum hip
13	Natural waist rise	14	Shoulder to midhand
15	Upper arm	16	Wrist
17	Outer natural waist to floor	18	Knee
19	Maximum thigh		

Imputation is a task to predict and interpolate the missing item in dataset with statistical analysis of dataset. The most common imputation techniques are mean substitution method, similarity coefficients simple average method, K nearest method, MICE etc. [15]. Specifically, MICE is considered to be one of the best ways to impute missing data. To simulate the uncertainty of missing data, Rubin et al. established this method by generating a series of possible values instead of each missing value [16], and the results of each missing data will be predicted after a standard statistical analysis on the generated datasets.

In order to choose the optimal imputation technique for the Imputer module, we have designed experiments to evaluate the above four imputation techniques. We have 19 parameters in our system, which means that there are 2^{19} possible input cases. To try out all these possible situations is meaningless. So we designed five sets of experiments, which involve most common situations and most important parameters used in [17]. Under the same time consumption, we found that MICE performs best in our experiments, so we choose MICE as the core technique of the Imputer. In our system, the Imputer takes the parameters from user input together with our datasets to run MICE process for imputation.

2.2   Selector

The Selector module takes as inputs the datasets of 3D body meshes and corresponding anthropometric parameters to learn the relevance masks and mapping matrices for each facet by the feature-selection-based local mapping method.

The analysis of 3D human body shape can be divided into two paradigms as point based and mesh based [18]. Our system adopts the latter one, which analyzes the deformations of each triangle facet. Mesh based analysis can factor out other variations (e.g. pose etc.) in some complex models and enables us to use local mapping method in simple body reshaping models. The deformations of each triangle facets can be computed using the similar method in [5].

After obtaining the deformations across of all bodies in the dataset, we denote the deformation of each facet in each body mesh as a 3×3 transformation matrix:

$$Q = \begin{bmatrix} q_{1,1} & q_{1,2} & q_{1,3} \\ q_{2,1} & q_{2,2} & q_{2,3} \\ q_{3,1} & q_{3,2} & q_{3,3} \end{bmatrix}, \tag{1}$$

then the deformations of body mesh $i \in 1, \cdots, n$ can be expressed as $S_i = [Q_{i,1}, Q_{i,2}, \ldots, Q_{i,m}]^T$, where m is the number of facets in a body mesh, n is the size of datasets. For each body mesh in our datasets, there is a 19 dimensional vector of anthropometric parameters value P, which are extracted from the body mesh by point-to-point distance with sets of control points.

SPRING proposed to segment the body mesh into 16 rigid parts, then bind a vector of the most relevant parameters P' from P to the parts. It learns the linear regression model between deformation matrix Q and the relevant parameters P' for each facets, which utilizes the topology information of the human body shape and outperforms global mapping method with a large margin [6]. Such an approach has limits in binding parameters to the parts manually, which results in inconsistent results by different binding set and involves heavy human efforts.

To address the problems above, we propose the feature-selection-based local mapping method, which can bind parameters to the parts automatically. There is no need for our method to segment the body mesh and specify the relevant parameters for each facet. Our method propose to analyze the statistic information between parameters and deformations to select the most relevant parameters for each facets automatically. The details are introduced as follows.

Consider only one facet. Here we denote the matrix of anthropometric parameters for n body meshes as

$$X = \begin{bmatrix} p_{1,1} & \cdots & p_{1,19} \\ \vdots & \cdots & \vdots \\ p_{n,1} & \cdots & p_{n,19} \end{bmatrix}, \tag{2}$$

where $p_{i,j}$ means the jth ($j \in 1, \cdots, 19$) parameter of body $i \in 1, \cdots, n$. Since Q is a linear transformation matrix, the absolute value of the determinant of Q, $det(Q)$, can reflect how much the transformation expands the "volume" of the facet, so we can calculate the determinant of each transformation matrices as a feature of each deformation. The determinants of transformation matrices of a facet for n body meshes is given by:

$$Y = \begin{bmatrix} det(Q_1) \\ det(Q_2) \\ \vdots \\ det(Q_n) \end{bmatrix} = \begin{bmatrix} d_1 \\ d_2 \\ \vdots \\ d_n \end{bmatrix}. \tag{3}$$

For a facet, our method learns linear regression between X and Y to select the most important parameters from 19 items by recursive feature elimination algorithm [13]. The recursive feature elimination algorithm learns linear regression on the whole set of features at first. Then, features with smallest absolute weights will be pruned and a new linear regression model is then retrained until the desired number of features to select is eventually reached. Our method binds the optimal relevant subsets of parameters in this way, at the same time a vector of corresponding relevance mask will be generated. If the parameter is selected for this facet, then the label in the vector of this facet will be true, otherwise it will be false. After selection, we reshape the top k relevant parameters as a k dimensional vector P'. Then a linear regression model can be learned from P' to a transformation matrix Q. The mapping matrix M for a facet is a $9 \times k$ dimensional. From experiments, we found that, the results of feature selection are consistent with the topology knowledge of human body shape.

2.3 Mapper

The Mapper module synthesizes a final 3D human body mesh for users in our system. It maps the 19 dimensional vector of anthropometric parameters after imputation to a mesh based body representation, which consists of a list of deformations for each facets. The vertex positions of the mesh based representation can be computed from the deformations using the method in [5]. The details of this module are introduced as follows.

Specifically, the Mapper module consists of two steps. First, the Mapper module selects a subset of parameters for each facet from the 19 dimensional vector of anthropometric parameters by adopting the relevance masks, which are learned in the Selector (details in Sect. 2.2). It reshapes the selected k parameters ($k < 19$) as a k dimensional vector P'. Second, we obtain the deformation by multiplying P' with specific mapping matrix M for each facet separately. M is mentioned in Sect. 2.2 as a $9 \times k$ dimensional matrix. The mapping for a facet can be represented as:

$$Q' = MP' = \begin{bmatrix} m_{1,1} & m_{1,2} & \cdots & m_{1,k} \\ m_{2,1} & m_{2,2} & \cdots & m_{2,k} \\ \vdots & \vdots & \vdots & \vdots \\ m_{9,1} & m_{9,2} & \cdots & m_{9,k} \end{bmatrix} \begin{bmatrix} p_1 \\ p_2 \\ \vdots \\ p_k \end{bmatrix} = \begin{bmatrix} q_1 \\ q_2 \\ \vdots \\ q_9 \end{bmatrix}. \tag{4}$$

Here the transformation matrix can be obtained by reshaping Q' to a 3×3 dimensional matrix.

Finally, vertex positions can be solved from the list of deformations by a more efficient method proposed by Sumner and Popović [5], which reformulates the deformation transfer optimization problem in terms of vertex positions.

3   Evaluation

Here we conduct extensive objective and subjective evaluations by anthropomorphic evaluation and a user study for our system. We also trained state-of-art global mapping method and the SPRING model for comparison. The global mapping method learns the linear regression on anthropometric parameters and PCA coefficients of deformation matrices [2]. As for the SPRING model, we conduct a survey on the relationship between each rigid part and anthropometric parameters, then we bind the relevant parameters to each part according to the analysis of the results of the survey.

These models are trained on the pose-independent dataset published by Yang et al. [6]. The dataset contains 1531 female meshes and 1517 male meshes. The resolution of each mesh is 12500 vertices and 25000 facets.

3.1   Anthropomorphic Evaluation

Since anthropometric measurements are important in applications such as clothing sizing and our system generates 3D body meshes from anthropometric parameters, the error evaluation in such anthropometric parameters is necessary. We conduct an anthropomorphic error evaluation by calculating the mean absolute errors (MAE) in anthropometric measurements of reconstructed body mesh using a similar method used by Streuber et al. [19].

Taking the original anthropometric parameters of the bodies in the dataset as input, our experiments reconstruct the bodies with the global mapping method, the SPRING model and our system. To evaluate the accuracy of these three methods, we extract the anthropometric measurements from the generated meshes by calculating the point-to-point distance with sets of control points. Then for each model we calculate the mean absolute error between the measurements of generated meshes and those from the dataset. Table 2 shows the mean absolute errors of reconstructing meshes using 19 parameters with three models. Evaluation results shows that our proposed model outperforms the state-of-the-art approaches in terms of mean reconstruction error.

3.2   User Study

Anthropomorphic evaluation does not always reflect the performance of shaping models. Here we adjust the value of a certain parameter from mean shape to see whether the change in the mesh is similar as we expected, and we also conduct a user study on these three models from 68 volunteers. The age distribution, gender distribution and body type [20] distribution are shown in Fig. 3.

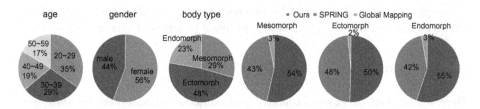

Fig. 3. The distribution of volunteers.   **Fig. 4.** The result of satisfaction survey.

We increase the number of gluteal hip circumstance by 12 cm. We analyze the results generated by different models in Fig. 5, and we find that the upper part of the result generated by the global mapping method changes a lot including chest size, belly button waist size etc. Our model produces a similar result with the one generated by SPRING model. Specifically, when the value of gluteal hip circumstance is increased, our model can keep the irrelevant parts (e.g., chest part, thigh part, shoulder part etc.) unchanged.

When the value of chest circumstance is increased by 10 cm, we observe from Fig. 6 that the global mapping method is unable to reshape the 3D body mesh as expected. The result generated by the global mapping method seems unchanged compared with the mean body shape. The results generated by our system and the SPRING model both change significantly in the chest part of body, which outperforms the global mapping method dramatically.

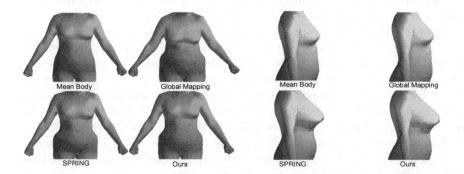

Fig. 5. Increasing gluteal hip by 12 cm.   **Fig. 6.** Increasing chest size by 10 cm.

We also conduct a user study on three models. 68 volunteers are invited to experience these models. Volunteers are asked which model can generates the most resembling body mesh after experiencing all three models. The results shown in Fig. 4 according to three body types proves the advantages of our system.

Table 2. Reconstruction errors of anthropomorphic evaluation. Mean absolute errors (MAE) for anthropometric parameters used in models: length error in mm, weight error in kg, and the numbers are listed as female/male. (The smaller, the better)

Parameter	Global [2]	SPRING [6]	Ours
Weight	1.4/1.4	1.2/1.4	**0.9/0.9**
Height	15.1/16.6	12.2/13.4	**4.5/4.7**
Neck	8.5/11	2.9/3.5	3.2/4.0
Chest	28.1/25.6	11/11.8	**10.3/11.4**
Belly button waist	23.8/25.0	10.3/13.3	10.7/14.1
Gluteal hip	20.6/22.3	9.01/9.9	9.5/10.4
Neck shoulder elbow wrist	11.4/11.7	7.9/7.5	**7.3/6.8**
Crotch knee floor	15.4/15.4	10.4/9.2	**10.4/9.1**
Across back shoulder neck	11.5/11.8	3.3/3.6	4.7/4.7
Neck to gluteal hip	15.1/18.7	10.5/12.6	**9.7/12**
Natural waist	23/23.2	10.5/11.9	10.6/12.3
Max. hip	21.7/21	10.1/9.3	10.3/9.7
Natural waist rise	28.6/33.67	16.4/21.7	16.7/22.4
Shoulder to midhand	8.3/9.0	3.8/4.1	3.8/4.3
Upper arm	10.5/11.3	5.4/6.8	**4.8/5.9**
Wrist	4.5/4.9	2.4/2.1	**2.4/2.1**
Outer natural waist to floor	14.4/12.9	9.9/10	**9.1/8.4**
Knee	9.9/8.4	4.5/3.5	4.7/3.6
Max. thigh	18.5/18.2	16.1/14	**14.7/12.7**
Length average error	16.1/16.7	8.7/9.3	**8.3/8.8**

4   Conclusion

In this paper, we have design a user-friendly and accurate system for 3D human body reshaping with limited anthropometric parameters by leveraging MICE technique for imputation and proposing a feature-selection-based local mapping method for shape modeling. The feature-selection-based local mapping method we proposed here can select the most relevant parameters for each facet automatically for linear regression learning, which eliminates heavy human efforts for utilizing topology information of body shape, and thus a more approximate body mesh can be obtained. We also conduct anthropomorphic evaluation and a user study for our system. The results compared with other methods shows the advantages of our system. In future work, we plan to combine local methods with global methods for a faster and more accurate system.

References

1. Robinette, K.M., Blackwell, S., Daanen, H., Boehmer, M., Fleming, S.: Civilian American and European Surface Anthropometry Resource (CAESAR), Final Report. Technical report, June 2002
2. Allen, B., Curless, B., Popović, Z.: The space of human body shapes: reconstruction and parameterization from range scans. In: ACM SIGGRAPH 2003 Papers, SIGGRAPH 2003, pp. 587–594. ACM (2003)
3. Seo, H., Magnenat-Thalmann, N.: An automatic modeling of human bodies from sizing parameters. In: Proceedings of the 2003 Symposium on Interactive 3D Graphics, pp. 19–26. ACM (2003)
4. Allen, B., Curless, B., Popović, Z.: Exploring the space of human body shapes: data-driven synthesis under anthropometric control. SAE Trans. **113**(1), 245–248 (2004)
5. Sumner, R.W., Popović, J.: Deformation transfer for triangle meshes. In: ACM SIGGRAPH 2004 Papers, SIGGRAPH 2004, pp. 399–405. ACM (2004)
6. Yang, Y., Yu, Y., Zhou, Y., Du, S., Davis, J., Yang, R.: Semantic parametric reshaping of human body models. In: 2014 2nd International Conference on 3D Vision, vol. 2, pp. 41–48, December 2014
7. Bogo, F., Black, M.J., Loper, M., Romero, J.: Detailed full-body reconstructions of moving people from monocular RGB-D sequences, pp. 2300–2308 (2015)
8. Li, H., Vouga, E., Gudym, A., Luo, L., Barron, J.T., Gusev, G.: 3D self-portraits. ACM Trans. Graph. **32**(6), 187:1–187:9 (2013)
9. Allen, B., Curless, B., Popović, Z., Hertzmann, A.: Learning a correlated model of identity and pose-dependent body shape variation for real-time synthesis. In: Proceedings of the 2006 ACM SIGGRAPH/Eurographics Symposium on Computer Animation, SCA 2006, pp. 147–156. Eurographics Association (2006)
10. Anguelov, D., Srinivasan, P., Koller, D., Thrun, S., Rodgers, J., Davis, J.: SCAPE: shape completion and animation of people. In: ACM SIGGRAPH 2005 Papers, SIGGRAPH 2005, pp. 408–416. ACM (2005)
11. Loper, M., Mahmood, N., Romero, J., Pons-Moll, G., Black, M.J.: SMPL: a skinned multi-person linear model. ACM Trans. Graph. **34**(6), 248:1–248:16 (2015)
12. Azur, M.J., Stuart, E.A., Frangakis, C., Leaf, P.J.: Multiple imputation by chained equations: what is it and how does it work? Int. J. Methods Psychiatr. Res. **20**(1), 40–49 (2011)
13. Guyon, I., Weston, J., Barnhill, S., Vapnik, V.: Gene selection for cancer classification using support vector machines. Mach. Learn. **46**(1), 389–422 (2002)
14. BodyLabs-Developer, June 2017
15. Su, X., Khoshgoftaar, T.M.: A survey of collaborative filtering techniques. Adv. Artif. Intell. **2009**, 4:2 (2009)
16. Royston, P.: Multiple imputation of missing values. Stata J. **4**(3), 227–241 (2004)
17. Seo, H., Magnenat-Thalmann, N.: An example-based approach to human body manipulation. Graph. Models **66**(1), 1–23 (2004)

18. Tsoli, A.: Modeling the human body in 3D: data registration and human shape representation. Ph.D. thesis, Brown University, Department of Computer Science Providence, RI, USA (2014)
19. Streuber, S., Quiros-Ramirez, M.A., Hill, M.Q., Hahn, C.A., Zuffi, S., O'Toole, A., Black, M.J.: Body talk: crowdshaping realistic 3D avatars with words. ACM Trans. Graph. **35**(4), 54:1–54:14 (2016)
20. Sheldon, W.H., Stevens, S.S., Tucker, W.B.: The varieties of human physique: an introduction to constitutional psychology, vol. 1. Harper (1940)

Learning Multi-Scale Shrinkage Fields for Blind Image Deblurring

Bingwang Zhang[1,2], Risheng Liu[1,2], Haojie Li[1,2(✉)], Qi Yuan[1,2], Xin Fan[1,2], and Zhongxuan Luo[1,2]

[1] DUT-RU International School of Information & Software Engineering, Dalian University of Technology, Dalian, China
`bwzhang@mail.dlut.edu.cn` , `hjli@dlut.edu.cn`
[2] Key Laboratory for Ubiquitous Network and Service Software of Liaoning Province, Dalian, China

Abstract. For blind image deblurring problem, regularization term met-hod is effective and efficient. Many existing approaches usually rely on carefully designed regularization terms and handcrafted parameter tuning to obtain satisfactory solution. It is complex and difficult. In this paper, we proposed a novel learning-based blind deconvolution method. We learn a Multi-Scale Shrinkage Fields model (MSSF). At each scale, we obtain the nonlinear functions and parameters through the data-driven way. Our method achieved strong robustness against others. It was evaluated on several widely-used natural image deblurring benchmarks, and achieved competitive results.

Keywords: Blind deconvolution · Shrinkage field · Regularization

1 Introduction

Blind image deblurring is an important branch of image processing. It aims to restore both latent image and blur kernel from single input. We can model the blur process with convolution $\otimes$

$$y = k \otimes x + n$$

where y represents the blur image, x is the latent image, k is the blur kernel, n is Gaussian noise. This problem is highly ill-posed and non-convex.

Currently, there are mainly two groups of methods for blind image deblurring, variational Bayes (VB)-based and maximum a posterior (MAP)-based methods. The VB-based methods are more robust [7], but they are computionally ineffi-cient. MAP-based methods are easy to get close to trivial delta kernel solution. Many previous works show that good priors knowledge of both image and ker-nel is crucial. The prior is also called regularization, which is used to constrain solution space.

© Springer Nature Singapore Pte Ltd. 2018
B. Huet et al. (Eds.): ICIMCS 2017, CCIS 819, pp. 108–115, 2018.
https://doi.org/10.1007/978-981-10-8530-7_11

Regularization term is a nonlinear function (known as shrinkage function), is used to model the filter responses. The existing methods manually design regularization term and tune parameters to obtain satisfactory solution. It is heavily engineered and empirically. We consider using nonlinear function and parameters which are obtained by training.

In this paper, we proposed a discriminative learning method to learn nonlinear functions and parameters from the training dataset. In the training phase, we learn a Multi-Scale Shrinkage Fields model (MSSF). At each scale, we obtain the nonlinear functions and parameters through the data-driven way. Figure 1 shows an example, on one scale, we learned nonlinear functions and parameters. During the testing phase, our MSSF can be directly applied to other datasets.

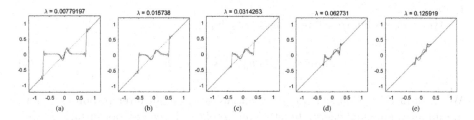

Fig. 1. Learned nonlinear functions and parameters. The curves are nonlinear functions, and λ denotes parameters. From (a) to (e) are the middle process of training.

2   Related Work

2.1   MAP-Based

In recent years, many MAP-based approaches has been developed and achieved promising performance. The priors for MAP-based is critical. In [1] Chan et al. used total variation (TV) regularizer for image blind deblurring. Xu et al. [18] applied a heuristic edge selection step, this is often necessary to achieve state-of-the-art results in the MAP framework. Xu et al. [19] used the L_0-regularizer on the image gradient. Wipf et al. [16] used L_p-regularized where $p \ll 1$. Krishnan et al. [6] introduced L_1/L_2 in image gradient prior. Pan et al. [10] proposed dark channel prior, which has obtained good results. [9, 15, 20, 21] are some other related works.

2.2   Learning-Based

Schelten et al. [11] trained cascaded interleaved regression tree field (RTF) for natural images deblurring. Zuo [22] learned iteration-wise parameters of the hyper-Laplacian prior for kernel estimation. Shrinkage Fields [12] achieve both high quality and high efficiency for non-blind image restoration. And Xiao et al. [17] extended the idea to more challenging blind text images deconvolution problem. In this paper we learn a Multi-Scale Shrinkage Fields model for blind image deblurring.

3   Multi-Scale Shrinkage Fields

3.1   Model Statement

Our algorithm is carried out under multi-scale which like an image pyramid [3]. At each scale, we solve

$$\min_{x,k} \|x \otimes k - y\|_2^2 + \gamma \|k\|_2^2 + \lambda \sum_{i=1}^{N} \rho_i (F_i x) \qquad (1)$$

where x and y denote the latent and blurred images, respectively; k is a blur kernel with the convolution operator $\otimes$ and L$_2$-regularized term $\|k\|_2^2$; ρ_i denote potential function that model the responses $F_i x$ of filters F_i; and γ and λ are the weights.

We estimate intermediate images by solving

$$\min_{x} \|x \otimes k - y\|_2^2 + \lambda \sum_{i=1}^{N} \rho_i (F_i x) \qquad (2)$$

We introduce independent auxiliary variables u_i for all filter responses $F_i x$ to obtain an augmented energy function and replace the energy optimization problem Eq. (2) with a quadratic relaxation:

$$\arg\min_{x,u} \|x \otimes k - y\|_2^2 + \sum_{i=1}^{N} \left(\frac{\beta}{2}(F_i x - u_i)^2 + \rho_i (u_i) \right) \qquad (3)$$

Intuitively, when $\beta \to \infty$, the auxiliary $u_i \to F_i x$ approach their corresponding filter responses, and Eq. (3) converges to the original problem in Eq. (2). The minimizer of the second term w.r.t. u_i can be replaced by a flexible shrinkage function f_{π_i} modeled as a linear combination of Gaussian RBF kernels:

$$f_{\pi_i} (F_i x) = \sum_{j=1}^{M} \pi_{ij} \exp \left(-\frac{\gamma}{2}(F_i x - \mu_j)^2 \right) \qquad (4)$$

with shared precision γ and M Gaussian kernels placed at equidistant positions μ_j. Directly modeling the shrinkage function can reduce the optimization procedure to a single quadratic minimization in each iteration, which can be solved efficiently as:

$$x^t = Ft^{-1} \left[\frac{Ft \left(K^T y + \frac{\beta^t}{2} \sum_{i=1}^{N} F_i^T f_{\pi_i}^t \left(F_i x^{t-1} \right) \right)}{Ft \left(K^T \right) Ft \left(K \right) + \frac{\beta^t}{2} \sum_{i=1}^{N} Ft \left(F_i^T \right) Ft \left(F_i \right)} \right] \qquad (5)$$

where t is iteration index, K is the blur kernel matrix, Ft and Ft^{-1} indicate Fourier transform and its inverse, and f_{π_i} the shrinkage function. We set $\eta^t = \beta^t/2$. The model parameters $\Theta^t = \{\eta^t, \pi_i^t, f_i^t\}_{i=1}^{N}$ are trained by loss function.

We estimate blur kernel via FFTs in the gradient space.

3.2 Learning

We use fixed filters i.e. $[1, -1], [1, -1]^T$. The model parameters $\Theta^t = \{\eta^t, \pi^t{}_i\}_{i=1}^2$ in our multi-scale shrinkage fields model are learned through loss minimization.

On one scale, in addition to the blurry input image, each model also receives the previous image and estimated blur kernel as input. This is different from the non-blind deconvolution setting of [12], where the blur kernel is known. To greedily learn the model, we minimize the L_2 error between the current estimated image and the ground truth image x_{gt}, i.e.

$$\ell\left(x^t, x_{gt}\right) = \left\| x^t - x_{gt} \right\|_2^2 \tag{6}$$

where x^t is obtained via Eq. (5). We minimize the overall cost with the gradient-based L-BFGS method.

We derive the generic gradients for the given loss function. For brevity, we define

$$A_t = K^T K + \eta^t \sum_{i=1}^2 F_i^T F_i$$

and

$$B_t = K^T y + \eta^t \sum_{i=1}^2 F_i^T f_{\pi_i}^t \left(F_i x^{t-1}\right)$$

$$\frac{\partial \ell}{\partial \Theta^t} = \frac{\partial \ell}{\partial x^t} A_t^{-1} \left(\frac{\partial B_t}{\partial \Theta^t} - \frac{\partial A_t}{\partial \Theta^t} x^t \right) \tag{7}$$

We derive the specific gradients w.r.t. the model parameters $\Theta^t = \{\eta^t, \pi^t{}_i\}_{i=1}^2$. We define $\hat{c}_t^T = \frac{\partial \ell}{\partial x^t} A_t^{-1}$.

Parameter η. We define $\eta^t = \exp\left(\tilde{\eta}^t\right)$ to ensure positive values of η^t. And we define $u^t = f_\pi^t \left(F x^{t-1}\right)$.

$$\frac{\partial \ell}{\partial \tilde{\eta}^t} = \eta^t \sum_{i=1}^2 (F_i \hat{c}_t)^T \left(u_i^t - F_i x^t\right) \tag{8}$$

Shrinkage function. For each filter

$$\frac{\partial \ell}{\partial \pi_t} = \eta^t (F \hat{c}_t)^T \frac{\partial f_\pi^t}{\partial \pi_t} \tag{9}$$

where $\frac{\partial f_\pi^t}{\partial \pi_t} \in R^{N \times M}$ is a matrix, N denotes the number of pixels of x, M denotes the number of Gaussian RBF kernels.

4   Experiments

4.1   Experimental Setup

We used 400 training images from Chen *et al.* [2], they cropped a 180×180 region from each image from [12]. The kernels we obtain from Levin *et al.*'s image set [7]. We set $\lambda = 4e^{-3}$, $\omega = 2$. We set maximal kernel size to 27. Accordingly, the numbers of scales are five, and the kernel widths that are used at different scales are 7, 11, 15, 21, 27 pixels, respectively. For Shrinkage Fields, we set 97 radial basis functions (RBFs) of each filters, horizontal and vertical directions. We used the L-BFGS in MATLAB for training and all the experiments are carried out on a desktop computer with an AMD Athlon processor. The training of 400 images took about 15.7 h. Note, we trained our models in five scales. So, we address all blur images in five scales although they may blured with larger kernel.

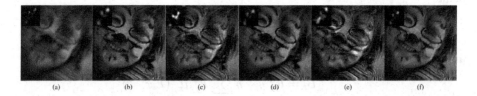

(a)   (b)   (c)   (d)   (e)   (f)

Fig. 2. One example of deblurring results on Levin *et al.*'s image sets. (*a*) is input image and kernel, (*b*) is the results of Cho and Lee [3] (PSNR 26.64 / SSIM 0.83), (*c*) is the results of Krishnan *et al.* [6] (PSNR 21.37 / SSIM 0.59). (*d*) is the results of Sun [14] (PSNR 28.23 / SSIM 0.88). (*e*) is the results of Xu and Jia [19] (PSNR 18.58 / SSIM 0.55) and our results are shown in (*f*) (PSNR 28.42 / SSIM 0.89).

All the results of compared methods are provided by the authors or generated using their codes with default parameter setting. We follow recent work to report the average peak signal to noise ratio (PSNR), structural similarity (SSIM), error ratio (ER) and kernel similarity (KS) on image sets.

4.2   Evaluation

We evaluate our method on three benchmark data sets.

Table 1. Quantitative comparisons on Levin *et al.*'s image set.

Methods	[3]	[6]	[8]	[14]	[19]	Our MSSF
PSNR	27.63	24.87	29.03	29.71	26.71	**30.00**
SSIM	0.85	0.74	0.89	0.90	0.83	**0.91**

Table 2. Quantitative comparisons on Sun *et al.*'s image set.

Methods	[3]	[6]	[8]	[14]	[19]	Our MSSF
PSNR	26.19	22.92	24.90	29.48	28.27	**29.55**
SSIM	0.81	0.75	0.80	**0.85**	0.85	0.83
KS	0.783	0.722	0.711	0.819	0.835	**0.836**

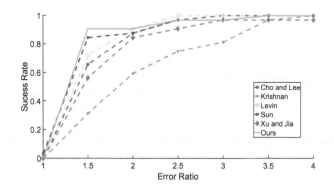

Fig. 3. Results on Levin *et al.*'s image sets.

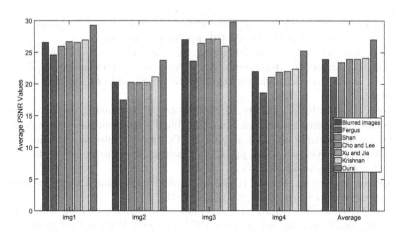

Fig. 4. Results on Köhler *et al.*'s dataset [5]. Our method has the highest average PSNR among all the methods evaluated.

Results on Levin *et al.*'s Image Set. The results on Levin *et al.*'s image set are shown in Table 1 and Fig. 3. One example is shown in Fig. 2. Our method achieved the highest average PSNR and SSIM among all these compared methods.

Results on Sun *et al.*'s Image Set. Table 2 shows the results on Sun *et al.*'s image set. Our method achieved better results than almost all the competing methods. The results show that our method also performs well on large scale images.

Results on Köhler *et al.*'s Image Set. We evaluate our method using the image dataset by Köhler *et al.* [5]. We compare with five methods [3,4,6,13,18]. As shown in Fig. 4, our method achieved the highest average PSNR among all the methods evaluated.

5   Conclusions

In this paper, we learn a Multi-Scale Shrinkage Fields model for blind image deblurring. We obtain the nonlinear functions and parameters through the data-driven way. And we evaluate our MSSF model on three benchmark data sets. Experimental results show the effectiveness of our method.

Acknowledgement. This work was partially supported by National Natural Science Funds of China (61472059, 61632019 and 61672125).

References

1. Chan, T.F., Wong, C.K.: Total variation blind deconvolution. TIP **7**(3), 370–375 (1998)
2. Chen, Y., Yu, W., Pock, T.: On learning optimized reaction diffusion processes for effective image restoration. In: CVPR, pp. 5261–5269 (2015)
3. Cho, S., Lee, S.: Fast motion deblurring. In: TOG, vol. 28, p. 145. ACM (2009)
4. Fergus, R., Singh, B., Hertzmann, A., Roweis, S.T., Freeman, W.T.: Removing camera shake from a single photograph. In: TOG, vol. 25, pp. 787–794. ACM (2006)
5. Köhler, R., Hirsch, M., Mohler, B., Schölkopf, B., Harmeling, S.: Recording and playback of camera shake: benchmarking blind deconvolution with a real-world database. In: Fitzgibbon, A., Lazebnik, S., Perona, P., Sato, Y., Schmid, C. (eds.) ECCV 2012. LNCS, vol. 7578, pp. 27–40. Springer, Heidelberg (2012). https://doi.org/10.1007/978-3-642-33786-4_3
6. Krishnan, D., Tay, T., Fergus, R.: Blind deconvolution using a normalized sparsity measure. In: CVPR, pp. 233–240. IEEE (2011)
7. Levin, A., Weiss, Y., Durand, F., Freeman, W.T.: Understanding and evaluating blind deconvolution algorithms. In: CVPR, pp. 1964–1971. IEEE (2009)
8. Levin, A., Weiss, Y., Durand, F., Freeman, W.T.: Efficient marginal likelihood optimization in blind deconvolution. In: CVPR, pp. 2657–2664. IEEE (2011)
9. Nie, L., Yan, S., Wang, M., Hong, R., Chua, T.S.: Harvesting visual concepts for image search with complex queries. In: Proceedings of the 20th ACM international conference on Multimedia, pp. 59–68. ACM (2012)
10. Pan, J., Sun, D., Pfister, H., Yang, M.H.: Blind image deblurring using dark channel prior. In: CVPR, pp. 1628–1636 (2016)
11. Schelten, K., Nowozin, S., Jancsary, J., Rother, C., Roth, S.: Interleaved regression tree field cascades for blind image deconvolution. In: 2015 IEEE Winter Conference on Applications of Computer Vision (WACV), pp. 494–501. IEEE (2015)

12. Schmidt, U., Roth, S.: Shrinkage fields for effective image restoration. In: CVPR, pp. 2774–2781 (2014)
13. Shan, Q., Jia, J., Agarwala, A.: High-quality motion deblurring from a single image. In: TOG, vol. 27, p. 73. ACM (2008)
14. Sun, L., Cho, S., Wang, J., Hays, J.: Edge-based blur kernel estimation using patch priors. In: Proceedings of the IEEE International Conference on Computational Photography (2013)
15. Tang, J., Shu, X., Qi, G.J., Li, Z., Wang, M., Yan, S., Jain, R.: Tri-clustered tensor completion for social-aware image tag refinement. TPAMI **39**(8), 1662–1674 (2017)
16. Wipf, D., Zhang, H.: Analysis of Bayesian blind deconvolution. In: Heyden, A., Kahl, F., Olsson, C., Oskarsson, M., Tai, X.-C. (eds.) EMMCVPR 2013. LNCS, vol. 8081, pp. 40–53. Springer, Heidelberg (2013). https://doi.org/10.1007/978-3-642-40395-8_4
17. Xiao, L., Wang, J., Heidrich, W., Hirsch, M.: Learning high-order filters for efficient blind deconvolution of document photographs. In: Leibe, B., Matas, J., Sebe, N., Welling, M. (eds.) ECCV 2016. LNCS, vol. 9907, pp. 734–749. Springer, Cham (2016). https://doi.org/10.1007/978-3-319-46487-9_45
18. Xu, L., Jia, J.: Two-phase kernel estimation for robust motion deblurring. In: Daniilidis, K., Maragos, P., Paragios, N. (eds.) ECCV 2010. LNCS, vol. 6311, pp. 157–170. Springer, Heidelberg (2010). https://doi.org/10.1007/978-3-642-15549-9_12
19. Xu, L., Zheng, S., Jia, J.: Unnatural l0 sparse representation for natural image deblurring. In: CVPR, pp. 1107–1114 (2013)
20. Zhang, H., Shen, F., Liu, W., He, X., Luan, H., Chua, T.S.: Discrete collaborative filtering. In: Proceedings of SIGIR, vol. 16 (2016)
21. Zhang, H., Zha, Z.J., Yang, Y., Yan, S., Gao, Y., Chua, T.S.: Attribute-augmented semantic hierarchy: towards bridging semantic gap and intention gap in image retrieval. In: Proceedings of the 21st ACM international conference on Multimedia, pp. 33–42. ACM (2013)
22. Zuo, W., Ren, D., Gu, S., Lin, L., Zhang, L.: Discriminative learning of iteration-wise priors for blind deconvolution. In: CVPR, pp. 3232–3240 (2015)

Indoor RGB-D Object Detection
with the Guidance of Hand-Held Objects

Leixian Qiao[1,2(✉)], Yaohui Zhu[1,2], Runze Li[1,2], Weiqing Min[1],
and Shuqiang Jiang[1,2]

[1] Key Laboratory of Intelligent Information Processing,
Institute of Computing Technology, Chinese Academy of Sciences,
Beijing 100190, China
{leixian.qiao,yaohui.zhu,runze.li}@vipl.ict.ac.cn,
{minweiqing,sqjiang}@ict.ac.cn
[2] University of Chinese Academy of Sciences, Beijing 100049, China

Abstract. In this paper, towards intelligent learning like human for
robots, we propose a novel framework to detect indoor objects with the
guidance of hand-held objects. In this framework, firstly, we leverage
the segmentation algorithm to obtain hand-held objects proposals, and
propose another segmentation algorithm based on depth information to
obtain object proposals in the indoor scene. Second, to solve the problem of the diversity of data distribution between hand-held objects and
indoor objects, we employ the unsupervised adaptive deep neural networks to learn adaptive features on the RGB and depth modality. To
evaluate the proposed framework, we conduct experiments on the HOD-
16 dataset and indoor scene dataset. The experimental results demonstrate that the proposed framework improves the performance of the
indoor object detection in RGB, depth and fused modality respectively.

Keywords: RGB-D object detection · Hand-held object learning
Unsupervised domain adaption

1   Introduction

With the development of intelligent indoor robots, the perception of robots is
becoming more and more important. In the process of human-machine interaction, the intelligent robot often needs to detect objects to enhance the understanding of scenes, which assists robot Simultaneous Localization and Mapping
(SLAM), navigation, path planning, motion control, and other functions. Therefore, the study of the object detection of intelligent robots is of great research
and practical value.

In a real scenario, an intelligent robot employs a 2D or 3D camera to perceive
and understand the indoor scene. Traditional methods are to apply a trained
object detection system to the target indoor object detection. But these methods

© Springer Nature Singapore Pte Ltd. 2018
B. Huet et al. (Eds.): ICIMCS 2017, CCIS 819, pp. 116–127, 2018.
https://doi.org/10.1007/978-981-10-8530-7_12

are not friendly for an intelligent robot. Because the intelligent robot does not actively learn from the original concept to the final actual testing application, especially for a lack of transferable perceptual knowledge. A friendly approach is to learn the concept of knowledge actively under human's guidance, just like the process of human learning. Therefore, a complete process from the learning to the application needs to be done in an interactive environment. With the development of the field of natural language processing and understanding, the robot has the ability to parse natural language in speech interaction with people, so as to obtain concepts, properties and other relevant information. In addition, with the aid of a vision system, a robot real-timely track to obtain the data of human skeleton, especially for the data of two hands, and obtain the image segmentation of hand-held objects for the concept learning. After the intelligent robot learned these concepts of hand-held objects, we hope that the robot robustly applies these concepts in a wide range of indoor scene. To achieve this goal, the main problem is inconsistent data distributions in the two domains. Firstly, hand-held objects contain the hand information in vision, but indoor objects do not contain this information. Secondly, postures of objects always appear vertically in the hand-held status, while appear horizontally in the indoor. Thirdly, there are some occlusions in the indoor object, but hand-held objects are hardly obscured.

Our contributions are as follows: (1) We propose a novel framework to detect indoor objects with the guidance of hand-held objects in the RGB-D scene; (2) To gain indoor object proposals, we propose an object segmentation algorithm based on depth information of images; (3) We employ deep adversarial unsupervised domain adaption neural network, to deal with the problem of inconsistent data distribution; (4) We conduct experiments in real scenarios, and experimental results demonstrate that our framework is effective.

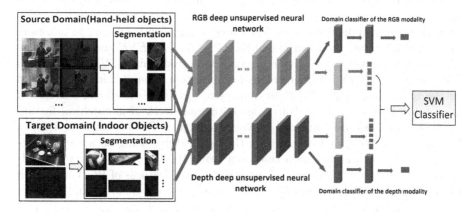

Fig. 1. The framework of indoor object recognition in RGB-D scene with the hand-held object learning

2   Related Work

Object detection. The object detection method based on deep learning has gradually become popular in research and application fields, such as RCNN [6], Fast-RCNN [5] and Faster-RCNN [17]. To speed up efficiencies of the detection, some new methods have been proposed in recent works, such as YOLO [16], SSD [9]. YOLO [16] obtain the bounding box and the classification of each region simultaneously, but does not use the region proposal network [17]. Based on YOLO, SSD [9] leverage the anchor to generate some fixed-size bounding boxes.

Robot-oriented object detection. In order to perceive scenes, robot-oriented object detection is often carried out in the 3D environment. For example, Biegelbauer and Vincze [1] proposed an approach of rapid automatic localization which is adapted to the indoor scene from one view with a laser radar to obtain objects of different shapes, and daily objects of the indoor scene are modeled in an approximate super-quadratic algorithm. This process of object detection is based on the hierarchical RANSAC to quickly obtain the test results. In addition, Sun *et al.* [18] proposed the Depth-Encoded Hough Voting (DEHV) algorithm based on the coding of depth information, which combines the depth information into the process of characterizing the feature distribution of image patches, and implement locating objects, inferring object categories, estimating spatial poses, encoding to obtain depth maps. Gupta *et al.* [7] encoded the original depth map into HHA channels: horizontal disparity, height above ground, and the angle of local surface normal making with the direction of gravity, to gain better object proposals. This method is also applied to the object detection in RGB-D indoor scene and improves the capability of RGB-D object detection.

Hand-held object learning. Lv *et al.* [12] proposed a learning framework of hand-held objects recognition. This framework leverages a fine-tuned AlexNet network to extract features from RGB images and depth images. In addition, to extract 3D point cloud features of the $C^3 - HALC$, ESF and $GRSD$, they fuse the three features as object representations, and train a SVM classifier. In addition, Lv *et al.* [13] introduced a real-time system of hand-held objects based on the above work [12]. To obtain more stronger representational features of hand-held objects, Lv *et al.* [14] proposed a framework of hierarchical feature learning, which use two different networks to extract RGB features and depth features respectively, and concatenate the two features using an advanced network. In order to interact with the robot using the hand-held object concept, Qiao *et al.* [15] used a deep neural network to learn features of RGB and depth model, and recognize objects with fused features of the two models in the scene.

Unsupervised domain adaption. In the field of unsupervised domain adaption, the most common method is mapping features to specific transformation spaces, especially for the popular reproducing kernel hilbert space [2,8]. With the development of deep learning, some works [10,19] employ a deep feed-forward neural network to map features to reproducing Kernel Hilbert Space by minimizing the average distance of data distributions between different domains. To reduce the deviation of feature distribution in source and target domains, Long et al. [10] proposed a method which appends the MMD layer to obtain self-adaptive features. In addition, Long et al. [11] used the key idea of the ResNet to train a adaptive classifier in both source domain and target domain, which alleviates the problem of inconsistent data distributions in the source and target domain.

3   Indoor Object Detection with Hand-Held Objects

In this work, we exploit the data of hand-held objects for indoor object detection. As this object detection does not use the target domain data for training, we can not use an end-to-end framework for object detection, such as faster-rcnn [17], SSD [9]. Therefore, we adopt a strategy of two steps for object detection. The first step is to obtain object proposals by using segmentations of objects, and the second step is using the SVM classifier to obtain object labels. In this process, the most important is achieving high-quality object proposals and learning domain invariant features. The overall architecture of object detection is shown in Fig. 1. First, we obtain hand-held objects proposals and indoor objects proposals. Second, we use two neural networks to obtain RGB features and depth features of images, and concatenate the features of two modalities for final classification. Finally, we use a SVM classifier to obtain labels. In the section, we will introduce the segmentation algorithm of indoor objects and how to obtain the domain invariant feature.

3.1   Object Proposals

In the process of indoor man-machine interaction, RGB-D camera is a useful device. It can not only obtain RGB images and depth images real-timely, but also capture the data of human skeleton. In this work, we exploit these real-time information and the knowledge of hand-held objects to detect indoor objects. In the hand-held object learning, the most important step is to obtain proposals of hand-held objects. Due to great differences of depth information between hand-held objects and background, the data of depth images and the coordinates of two hands tracked by the Kinect play a positive role for obtaining object proposals. For this reason, to obtain proposals of hand-held objects, we employ the hand-held object segmentation algorithm [13] based on regions of depth information and the data of human skeleton.

To detect indoor objects, we firstly need to obtain object proposals. In this paper, we exploit the object segmentation algorithm based on point clouds to capture proposals of objects, and this algorithm is built on that robot's angle is above or near the ground. The target of this algorithm is to obtain the distribution of objects, and the process of segmentations mainly contains the following four steps: (1) The first step contains synthesizing indoor scene point clouds and down-sampling these point clouds; (2) We use the RANSAC algorithm [3] detecting the ground, and along the normal vector of the ground to obtain a set of points for clustering; (3) Kd-tree is constructed to search similar points of proximity, and reasonable distance between clusters need to be set. Subsequently, point clusters are obtained by clustering; (4) The mask region of RGB and depth images are obtained by using the camera. Through the above processes, objects are automatically segmented in the indoor scene.

3.2   Domain Invariant Features

Hand-held objects are different from objects in the indoor scene. Firstly, hand-held objects contain the hand information in vision. Second, the postures of some of objects are apparently different in the two domains. Therefore, we need to solve the problem, which is gaps of data distributions in the two domains.

According to ideas of unsupervised domain adaption in deep architectures proposed in [4], we solve the above problem of different data distributions in different domains by combining the framework of the adversarial network and the technology of deep learning. Unsupervised domain adaption deep neural network [4] bring a domain classifier, which is an adversarial framework to a feature extractor. The domain classifier also is a classifier, whose target is to learn domain invariant features. To learn the domain invariant representation, the domain classifier is required that domain can't be classified correctly. Therefore, the optimization goal of the domain classifier is to maximize the loss of cross entropy; On the other hand, the goal of the label classifier is to learn features with categorical discriminant information as soon as possible, and it's optimization goal is to minimize the softmax classification loss. The overall loss function is:

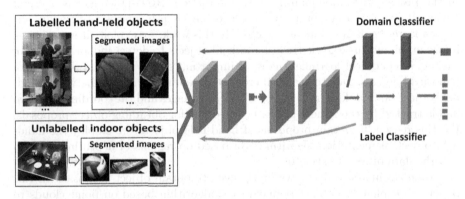

Fig. 2. RGB deep adversarial unsupervised domain adaption neural network (Color figure online)

$$E(\theta_f, \theta_d, \theta_y) = \sum_{i=1...N, d=0} L_y(G_y(G_f(x_i; \theta_f); \theta_y), y_i)$$

$$- \lambda \sum_{i=1...N} L_d(G_d(G_f(x_i; \theta_f); \theta_d), d_i)$$

$$= \sum_{i=1...N, d_i=0} L_y^i(\theta_f, \theta_y) - \lambda \sum_{i=1...N} L_d^i(\theta_f, \theta_d)$$

where θ_f is the parameters of feature extractor, θ_y is the parameters of label classifier, θ_d is the parameters of domain classifier, L_y is the loss of label classifier, L_d is the loss of domain classifier, N is the number of Instances, G_* is a neural network, d_i is tag of domain, $d_i = 0$ represent source domain, $d_i = 1$ represent target domain, λ is a hyper-parameter. The details can be referred to [4].

Table 1. The total number of instance for each object and the total number of RGB-D frame for each object in five scenes

Object	Instances	RGB-D frames
Apple	2	274
Book	3	196
Ball	3	83
Box	3	131
Bottle	2	114
Calculator	2	89
Can	2	143
Cup	2	150
Disk	2	54
Fan	2	85
Glove	2	60
Handbag	2	65
Hat	2	65
Keyboard	2	95
Trashcan	3	82

3.3 Proposed System

We leverage the adversarial unsupervised domain adaption deep neural network to detect indoor objects with the guidance of the hand-held object. The data of source domain is proposals of hand-held objects, and the target domain data is indoor object proposals. The process of training RGB model is demonstrated in Fig. 2. In the process of training model, to learn a common feature space, the source domain data and target domain data enter the same neural network with two classification layers. For target domain data, only domain classification layer (blue) work; For source domain data, the label classification layer (yellow) also work to ensure the classification accuracy of source domain data. In the test phase, we get the label of target domain data from the label classification layer. In a word, the object detection in the indoor scene contains three steps. (1) Proposals of source objects and target objects are obtained. (2) Training deep neural network extracts features. (3) A SVM classification needs to be trained for the final decision. In particular, firstly, we employ the above algorithm to get object proposals of both domains; Secondly, using these proposals, we train RGB and depth adversarial unsupervised domain adaption deep neural network respectively, which are pre-trained on the ImageNet dataset; Finally, we exploit the RGB and depth model to extract RGB features and depth features concatenated as object representations, and train a SVM classifier with the source domain data.

4   Experiments

4.1   Experimental Datasets

HOD-16 datasets. The HOD-16 dataset is a RGB-D object dataset [13], which is collected by using Microsoft Kinect v1 in the human-machine interaction. These objects proposals, containing RGB modality and depth modality, is obtained by the algorithm of object segmentation proposed in [13]. The hand-held object dataset contains 12800 video frames and 16 common object classes, and each object class has 4 instances, 64 instances totally. Each instance is captured by two persons in two different scenes, and each instance is collected up to 50 RGB-D frames in every scene.

Fig. 3. The five instances in different indoor scenes

Table 2. The accuracy of object recognition of three methods in different modalities

	M1	M2	M3 (our)
RGB	50.1%	92.8%	54.5%
Depth	40.2%	90.8%	41.9%
RGB-D	52.2%	93.5%	56.7%

Indoor scene datasets. To conduct experiment for indoor RGB-D object detection, we use Microsoft Kinect v1 to collect a dataset of five indoor scenes, which contains meeting table, ping pang table, ground, wash-basin and tea table. The object distributions of five indoor scenes are shown in Fig. 3. In the process of collection, for the configuration of Microsoft Kinect v1, frame rate is set up to 30Fp to save two frames RGB-D image per second. The object classes in the HOD-16 dataset and the indoor scene dataset are the same, but the instances of each object class in the two datasets are different. As shown in Fig. 3, there are apparently different postures of some objects in the two datasets, especially for these objects such as book, handbag, dish, keyboard and so on. Due to this reason, proposals of the same class in the two datasets exist differences. In this paper, we leverage the above segmentation algorithm to obtain proposals of RGB images and depth images of objects in the five indoor scenes. Finally, we obtain 16 object classes totally, which contains 1835 frames of RGB-D images and the detail information of each object class is listed in Table 1.

4.2 Experimental Setup

In this work, we train convolutional neural network in Caffe environment, and use the AlexNet network as the basic architecture for both RGB and depth adversarial unsupervised domain adaption deep neural network. For the configuration of the input of the two networks, we resize each image into 256 * 256 and change channel sequence of RGB images into B-G-R sequence. In addition, we subtract the mean value of images to improve performance of classification.

In the configuration of adversarial unsupervised domain adaption deep neural network. The domain classifier and the label classifier share weights of the first five convolutional layers. For the domain classifier, the number of neurons of the last three connectional layers are 1024, 1024 and 2, and the loss function is the cross entropy function. For the label classifier, the number of neurons of the last three connectional layers are 4096, 4096 and 16, and the loss function is the softmax loss function. In addition, the initial weights of our network come from the AlexNet network trained in the ImageNet ILSVRC 2012 dataset. We also use the policy of batch optimization, and set up a batch images, where the half come from source domain data and the other come from target domain data. In order to suppress noisy signal from the domain classifier at the early stages of the training procedure, we use $\lambda_p = \frac{2}{1+exp(-\gamma \cdot p)} - 1$ instead of fixing the adaptation factor λ, where $\gamma = 10$, $p > 0$. For the SVM classifier, we use RBF kernel in LIBSVM, where the value of C is fixed into 1000, and σ is 0.0001.

Table 3. The accuracy of object recognition of our method of each class

Object	Apple	Book	Ball	Box
Acc.	72.1%	58.8%	70.7%	62.2%
Object	Bottle	Calculator	Can	Cup
Acc.	60.6%	60.6%	57.4%	68.3%
Object	Dish	Disk	Fan	Glove
Acc.	50.6%	63.3%	69.5%	54.7%
Object	Handbag	Keyboard	Trashcan	Hat
Acc.	47.4%	52.5%	58.7%	56.5%

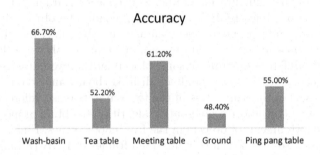

Fig. 4. The accuracy of object recognition of our method of each scene

4.3 Experimental Result

To evaluate the proposed method for the task of object detection in the indoor RGB-D scene, we conduct experiments using the following three methods:

1. M1 is training RGB and depth AlexNet respectively only using the data of hand-held objects without the domain classification layer. Subsequently, we exploit the two networks to extract RGB features and depth features concatenated as object representations, and train a SVM classifier with the features of hand-held objects. For indoor object recognition, we also obtain the feature representation with the two networks, and use the trained SVM for decision.
2. M2 is training RGB and depth AlexNet respectively using the data of hand-held objects and the data of indoor objects without the domain classification layer. Similarly with the above method, we extract RGB features and depth features concatenated as object representations, but we train the SVM classifier using two domain datasets and use the trained SVM for indoor object recognition.

3. M3 is proposed by this paper, which is training RGB and depth adversarial unsupervised domain adaption deep neural network respectively using the labeled data of hand-held objects and the unlabeled data of indoor objects. Similarly with the above methods, we extract RGB features and depth features concatenated as object representations, and train a SVM classifier with the data of hand-held objects, and use the trained SVM for indoor object recognition.

From the above experimental results, we obtain the following conclusions:

1. From the view of M1 and M2 in Table 2, we improve the accuracy of object recognition with the adversarial unsupervised domain adaption deep neural network. This experimental result illuminates that adversarial unsupervised domain adaption deep neural network can reduce differences of data distributions in different domains and obtain more robust feature representations.
2. From the column of Table 2, the accuracy of the fused feature have improved for the any single one. This illuminates that the fusion of RGB features and depth features improves representational ability of objects.
3. In Table 3, some objects, such as handbag, keyboard, book, plate, obtain a low accuracy. The main reason is that postures of these objects are large different in the two domains. For example, these objects mostly appear vertically in the hand-held object dataset, but appear horizontally in the indoor object dataset.
4. In Fig. 4, the accuracy of wash-basin, meeting table and ping pang table are better than the rest two scenes. The main reason is that there are occlusions between objects and complicated background in the ground and tea table, which leads to a low quality of object proposals.

5   Conclusion

In this paper, we have proposed a framework for indoor object detection with the guidance of hand-held objects. Using the adversarial unsupervised domain adaption deep neural network, we obtain domain invariant features from labeled hand-held objects and unlabeled indoor objects. In addition, we demonstrate the feasibility of our framework detecting objects in five indoor scenes. The segmentation of indoor objects is important for object detection, we will enhance the robustness of the segmentation algorithm in the further work.

Acknowledgment. This work was supported in part by the National Natural Science Foundation of China (61532018, 61322212, 61602437 and 61672497), in part by the Beijing Municipal Commission of Science and Technology (D161100001816001), in part by Beijing Natural Science Foundation (4174106), in part by the Lenovo Outstanding Young Scientists Program, in part by National Program for Special Support of Eminent Professionals and National Program for Support of Top-notch Young Professionals, and in part by China Postdoctoral Science Foundation (2016M590135, 2017T100110).

References

1. Biegelbauer, G., Vincze, M.: Efficient 3D object detection by fitting superquadrics to range image data for robot's object manipulation. In: 2007 IEEE International Conference on Robotics and Automation, pp. 1086–1091. IEEE (2007)
2. Borgwardt, K.M., Gretton, A., Rasch, M.J., Kriegel, H.P., Schölkopf, B., Smola, A.J.: Integrating structured biological data by kernel maximum mean discrepancy. Bioinformatics **22**(14), e49–e57 (2006)
3. Fischler, M.A., Bolles, R.C.: A paradigm for model fitting with applications to image analysis and automated cartography. Commun. ACM **24**(6), 381–395 (1981). (Reprinted in Readings in Computer Vision, Ed. by M.A. Fischler)
4. Ganin, Y., Lempitsky, V.: Unsupervised domain adaptation by backpropagation. In: International Conference on Machine Learning, pp. 1180–1189 (2015)
5. Girshick, R.: Fast R-CNN. In: Proceedings of the IEEE International Conference on Computer Vision, pp. 1440–1448 (2015)
6. Girshick, R., Donahue, J., Darrell, T., Malik, J.: Rich feature hierarchies for accurate object detection and semantic segmentation. In: Proceedings of the IEEE Conference on Computer Vision and Pattern Recognition, pp. 580–587 (2014)
7. Gupta, S., Girshick, R., Arbeláez, P., Malik, J.: Learning rich features from RGB-D images for object detection and segmentation. In: Fleet, D., Pajdla, T., Schiele, B., Tuytelaars, T. (eds.) ECCV 2014, Part VII. LNCS, vol. 8695, pp. 345–360. Springer, Cham (2014). https://doi.org/10.1007/978-3-319-10584-0_23
8. Huang, J., Gretton, A., Borgwardt, K.M., Schölkopf, B., Smola, A.J.: Correcting sample selection bias by unlabeled data. In: Advances in Neural Information Processing Systems, pp. 601–608 (2007)
9. Liu, W., Anguelov, D., Erhan, D., Szegedy, C., Reed, S., Fu, C.-Y., Berg, A.C.: SSD: single shot multibox detector. In: Leibe, B., Matas, J., Sebe, N., Welling, M. (eds.) ECCV 2016, Part I. LNCS, vol. 9905, pp. 21–37. Springer, Cham (2016). https://doi.org/10.1007/978-3-319-46448-0_2
10. Long, M., Cao, Y., Wang, J., Jordan, M.: Learning transferable features with deep adaptation networks. In: International Conference on Machine Learning, pp. 97–105 (2015)
11. Long, M., Zhu, H., Wang, J., Jordan, M.I.: Unsupervised domain adaptation with residual transfer networks. In: Advances in Neural Information Processing Systems, pp. 136–144 (2016)
12. Lv, X., Jiang, S.Q., Herranz, L., Wang, S.: RGB-D hand-held object recognition based on heterogeneous feature fusion. J. Comput. Sci. Technol. **30**(2), 340 (2015)
13. Lv, X., Jiang, S., Herranz, L., Wang, S.: Hand-object sense: a hand-held object recognition system based on RGB-D information. In: Proceedings of the 23rd ACM International Conference on Multimedia, pp. 765–766. ACM (2015)
14. Lv, X., Liu, X., Li, X., Li, X., Jiang, S., He, Z.: Modality-specific and hierarchical feature learning for RGB-D hand-held object recognition. Multimed. Tools Appl. **76**(3), 4273–4290 (2017)
15. Qiao, L., Li, X., Jiang, S.: RGB-D object recognition from hand-held object teaching. In: Proceedings of the International Conference on Internet Multimedia Computing and Service, pp. 31–34. ACM (2016)
16. Redmon, J., Divvala, S., Girshick, R., Farhadi, A.: You only look once: unified, real-time object detection. In: Proceedings of the IEEE Conference on Computer Vision and Pattern Recognition, pp. 779–788 (2016)

17. Ren, S., He, K., Girshick, R., Sun, J.: Faster R-CNN: towards real-time object detection with region proposal networks. In: Advances in Neural Information Processing Systems, pp. 91–99 (2015)
18. Sun, M., Bradski, G., Xu, B.-X., Savarese, S.: Depth-encoded hough voting for joint object detection and shape recovery. In: Daniilidis, K., Maragos, P., Paragios, N. (eds.) ECCV 2010, Part V. LNCS, vol. 6315, pp. 658–671. Springer, Heidelberg (2010). https://doi.org/10.1007/978-3-642-15555-0_48
19. Tzeng, E., Hoffman, J., Zhang, N., Saenko, K., Darrell, T.: Deep domain confusion: maximizing for domain invariance. arXiv preprint arXiv:1412.3474 (2014)

Machine Learning and Representation Learning

Building Weighted Classifier Ensembles Through Classifiers Pruning

ChenWei Cai, Dickson Keddy Wornyo, Liangjun Wang, and XiangJun Shen[(✉)]

School of Computer Science and Communication Engineering,
Jiangsu University, Zhenjiang, China
xjshen@ujs.edu.cn

Abstract. Many theoretical or experimental studies has shown that ensemble learning is an effective technique to achieve better classification accuracy and stability than individual classifiers. In this paper, we propose a novel weighted classifier ensemble method through classifiers pruning with two stages. In the first stage, we use canonical correlation analysis (CCA) to model maximum correlation relationships between training data points and base classifiers. Based on such globally multilinear projections, a sparse regression method is proposed to prune base classifiers so that each test data point will dynamically select a subset of classifiers to form a unique classifier ensemble, to decrease effects of noisy input data and incorrect classifiers in such a global view. In the second stage, the pruned classifiers are weighted locally by a fusion method, which utilizes the generalization ability of pruned classifiers among nearest neighbors of testing data points. By this way, each test data point can build a unique locally weighted classifier ensemble. Analysis of experimental results on several UCI data sets shows that the classification results of our method are better than other ensemble methods such as Random Forests, Majority Voting, AdaBoost and DREP.

Keywords: Ensemble learning · Classification · Classifier pruning
Classifier weighting

1 Introduction

Ensemble learning [1] is a machine learning method that combines the results of a set of classifiers to achieve better results. Ensemble learning has been proven to achieve better classification accuracy than individual classifier, supported by theoretical or experimental results [2–4]. Due to its good generalization performance, ensemble learning methods are amongst the state-of-the-art machine learning approaches and a variety of ensemble based approaches have being investigated and proposed, such as Bagging [5], Boosting [6] and Random Forests [7].

It is well-accepted that no significant performance can be obtained by combining multiple identical learning models. On the other hand, an ensemble whose members make errors on different samples reaches higher prediction performance.

© Springer Nature Singapore Pte Ltd. 2018
B. Huet et al. (Eds.): ICIMCS 2017, CCIS 819, pp. 131–139, 2018.
https://doi.org/10.1007/978-981-10-8530-7_13

This is important, for we can select one or a subset of base classifiers to build an ensemble. This selective ensemble is also named classifiers pruning. The principle of pruning base classifiers is that it must be both accurate and diverse, so as to achieve better performance. Many ensemble pruning methods [8] are proposed to select representative classifiers. For instance, Munoz et al. [9] introduced some methods on ordered aggregation for selecting a subset of base classifiers. Another static ensemble pruning technique is the diversity regularized ensemble pruning (DREP) proposed in [10]. Zhang and Zhou proposed a framework of sparse ensembles [11] that deals with new linear weighted combination methods for sparse ensembles.

In addition to pruning classifiers, another important direction in ensemble learning is how to weight base classifiers. Recent research shows that there are three different ways of weighting classifiers: majority vote, weight vote and soft vote. This can help to combine the output of these base classifiers. Many combination rules have been proposed. And weight voting is the most frequent used rule [11, 12] in these combination rules. For example majority voting is a popular rule used in [11], which combines all base classifiers outputs with same weight. Other methods proposed for weighted voting combination rule classifiers that have different contributions for improving the performance, and hence assign base classifiers with different weights. Mao et al. Proposed a weighted classifier ensemble method based on quadratic forms (QFWEC) [13].

The above observations motivated our research on classifiers pruning and weighting. We propose a sparse fusion method by combining classifiers pruning and weighting together to improve accuracy of classification. The motivation for our proposed method is to prune base classifiers in a global sparse regression model and weight pruned classifiers in a local fusion model. In the first stage, we model maximum correlation relationship between training data points and base classifiers by canonical correlation analysis (CCA) [14]. Therefore canonical output classifiers and input data points are modeled in multi-linear projections globally so that it can decrease effects of noisy input data and incorrect classifiers. Then, based on that projection's direction, we propose a sparse regression method to prune base classifiers. Therefore each test data points will dynamically select a subset of classifiers to form a unique classifier ensemble, by decreasing effects of noisy input data and incorrect classifiers in such a global view. However, these pruned classifiers don't have weights because we just find global correlation between training data points and base classifiers in this stage. In the second stage, we assign the pruned classifiers with different weights. As we all know, different classifiers have impact on the final output. If we evaluate a test data point, its nearest training data points have great impact on the final decision. This gives us the motivation on building a local ensemble by a classifier fusion method. Our proposed method applies a fusion method to learn weights of pruned base classifiers. When nearest neighbors of training points are considered, we can utilize the generalization ability of pruned base classifiers to obtain different weights in such a local view. Based on those local classifier results, locally discriminative classifiers are assigned heavy weights to form a locally classifier ensemble.

To demonstrate the validity and the effectiveness of our proposed method, we performed extensive statistical comparisons with several ensemble techniques based on several UCI datasets. The results indicate that our proposed method achieves best classification performance among several ensemble methods (such as Random Forest, Adaboost, QFWEC and DREP).

The rest of the paper is organized as follows: Sect. 2 introduces our proposed method in detail. The experimental results of several UCI datasets are shown to illustrate that our proposed method improves the classification performance in Sect. 3 and the last section concludes our work and proposes some future works.

2   Proposed Method

In this section, to present our proposed method in detail, we introduce the method from two stages in Subsects. 2.1 and 2.2.

2.1   Classifiers Pruning by Sparse Regression Globally

Assuming that $\mathbf{X} = \{\mathbf{x}_1, \mathbf{x}_2, \ldots, \mathbf{x}_N\}$ is the training datasets, where $\mathbf{x}_N \in R^q$ is one sample of training dataset, N is the number of training datasets with the dimension of R^q and $\mathbf{M} = \{\mu_1, \mu_2, \ldots, \mu_s\}$ is the set of class labels, where μ_s is one label of all labels and s is number of labels. We also have l base classifiers $\mathbf{C} = (\mathbf{C}_1, \mathbf{C}_2, \ldots, \mathbf{C}_l)^T$, $\mathbf{C}$ is a column vector. The classification result of l base classifiers on dataset $\mathbf{X}$ is $\mathbf{C}(\mathbf{X})$, which is named $\mathbf{K} \in R^{n \times l}$. The base classifiers $\mathbf{H} = \{h_1, h_2, \ldots h_s\}$ denote the set of s classifiers, which are selected from $\mathbf{C}$. Each basic classifier h_j gives a weight w_j, we define the vector of classifier weights as $\mathbf{W} = \{w_1, w_2, \ldots, w_s\}$, where $\sum_{j=1}^{s} w_j = 1, w_j \geq 0$. And our proposed model is used as follows:

$$\underset{\mathbf{y}_t \in \{0,1\}^p}{\arg\min} \sum_{k=1}^{d} \|\mathbf{v}_k^T \mathbf{y}_t - \mathbf{v}_k^T h(\mathbf{x}_t)\|^2 + \alpha|\mathbf{y}_t|_1 - \beta \mathbf{y}_t^T \mathbf{D} \mathbf{y}_t$$

$$h(\mathbf{x}_t) = \sum_{KX} \sum_{XX}^{-1} \mathbf{x}_t = \mathbf{K}^T \mathbf{X} (\mathbf{X}^T \mathbf{X})^{-1} \mathbf{x}_t \qquad (1)$$

$$\mathbf{D} = \frac{1}{2N}(n\mathbf{1}_{p \times p} - \mathbf{O}^T \mathbf{O})$$

Where $h(\mathbf{x}_t)$ is regression function of $\mathbf{K}$ given $\mathbf{X}$. And $\mathbf{x}_t$ is a test data point. $\{\mathbf{v}_k\}_{k=1}^{d}$ is d projection vectors of matrix $\mathbf{K}$. Therefore $\sum_{k=1}^{d} \|\mathbf{v}_k^T \mathbf{y} - \mathbf{v}_k^T h(\mathbf{x})\|^2 + \alpha|\mathbf{y}|_1$ is to find a sparse least squares regression solution between projection vectors of $\{\mathbf{v}_k\}_{k=1}^{d}$ and test data points $\mathbf{x}_t$. To enforce classifier selection, the values of $\mathbf{y}_t \in \{0, 1\}^d$ is 0 or 1. And 1 means the corresponding classifier is selected and 0 means the classifier is not selected. $\mathbf{D}$ is a diversity matrix of base classifiers, and each element in the matrix represents the difference between two base classifiers. So diagonal element of matrix $\mathbf{D}$ is zero.

In our proposed method, we apply CCA technique to find maximized projection directions between input data points and output classifiers in order to model relationship between input data points $\mathbf{X}$ and output classifiers $\mathbf{K}$. And d pairs of projection vectors: $\{(\mathbf{u}_k, \mathbf{v}_k)\}_{k=1}^d$ is obtained. Through applying CCA technique, the impact of noisy input data and incorrect classifiers are decreased to a minimum degree in such a global view. From the formula 1, we use a sparse regression method to prune base classifiers so as to select representative classifiers among training data variables. The regulation term $\mathbf{y}^T \mathbf{D} \mathbf{y}$ is added to make classifier ensemble robust as well, where $\mathbf{D}$ is classifier diversity measurement. This regulation term (α, β are regulation parameters) will result in choosing diversified base classifiers.

From above model, we can see that sparse classifiers are dynamically pruned based on the regression model between training data points and base classifiers. Also, this classifier pruning is evaluated with maximizing classifiers diversity. Based on this method, each test data variable will dynamically select a subset of classifiers in such a global view.

2.2   Weighting Pruned Classifiers Locally in a Fusion Model

To build a unique locally weighted classifier ensemble, we propose a fusion method. For each test data point, we choose its ϕ nearest neighbors from the training datasets. These ϕ nearest neighbors are chosen by calculating the Euclidean distance between the test data point $\mathbf{x}_t$ and each training data point. The ϕ nearest neighbors of $\mathbf{x}_t$ compose a set $\phi_D = \{\mathbf{x}_i | \mathbf{x}_i \in \mathbf{X}\}$, where $\mathbf{x}_i$ is a data point of training datasets. Then, we classify the ϕ nearest neighbors with the selected base classifiers. The classification errors are collected, and the weight w_j for base classifiers was assigned.

Each base classifier h_j in our local ensemble outputs confidence levels of class labels with which a data point is classified. For convenience, we assume that the level is the interval $[0, 1]$. The class confidence level of a training data point $\mathbf{x}_i$ which is classified by base classifiers h_j to classes μ_k denoted by $\rho_{j,k}(\mathbf{x}_i)$. Obviously, the greater the value of $\rho_{j,k}(\mathbf{x}_i)$, the more likely a data point will belong to the class μ_k. Base classifiers output a confidence level matrix $B(\mathbf{x}_i)$ for each nearest neighbor $\mathbf{x}_i$ in the set of ϕ_D. Each row of $B(\mathbf{x}_i)$ represents a row vector of confidence level of class labels that $\mathbf{x}_i$ is classified in n^{th} base classifier in the above matrix. For example, $\mathbf{B}_n(\mathbf{x}_i) = (\rho_{n,1}(\mathbf{x}_i), ..., \rho_{n,j}(\mathbf{x}_i))$ denotes the confidence level of class labels that $\mathbf{x}_i$ is classified to n^{th} base classifier.

For a test data point t, its class confidence level matrix $\mathbf{B}(t)$ is calculated, and the similarity distance $\|\mathbf{BT}_\phi^n - \mathbf{B}_n(t)\|$, between $\mathbf{BT}_\phi^n$ and $\mathbf{B}_n(t)$ is calculated. The $\|.\|$ is the Euclidean distance which reflects the local errors that are collected in the nth classifier. The smaller the distance, The better the nth base classifier. This shows that the nth base classifier could achieve a similar performance just like that of data points in ϕ_D. Based on the training data points in ϕ_D, the similarity distance that the nth classifier classifies the test sample t to the class label μ_ϕ is defined as follows:

$$\psi_{\phi,n}(t) = \frac{(1 + ||\mathbf{BT}_\phi^n - \mathbf{B}_n(t)||)^{-1}}{\sum_{\phi=1}^s (1 + ||\mathbf{BT}_\phi^n - \mathbf{B}_n(t)||)^{-1}} \tag{2}$$

Where $\mathbf{B}_n(t)$ is the row vector of confidence level of the test data point t which is classified by the nth base classifier. $\mathbf{BT}_\phi^n$ is the vector of confidence level of class labels that data points in ϕ_D are trained in n^{th} base classifier. The numerator shows the similarity between test data point and training datasets in ϕ_D, and the denominator is a normalized factor that ranges the formulation from 0 to 1. Obviously, the smaller the distance, more possible the testing data point t classified to class label μ_ϕ, through the nth base classifier.

Then, based on the distance definition in formula 2, each base classifier is weighted as follows:

$$w_\phi^n(t) = \frac{\psi_{\phi,n}(t) \prod_{m \neq \phi}(1 - \psi_{m,n}(t))}{\sum_{n=1}^s \psi_{\phi,n}(t) \prod_{m \neq \phi}(1 - \psi_{m,n}(t))} \tag{3}$$

Where $w_\phi^n(t)$ is the weight of the nth base classifier which classifies the test data point t to class label μ_ϕ. The numerator is the base classifier's confidence level for classifying the test data point t to class label μ_ϕ, based on formula 2. And the denominator is a normalized factor to make the confidence level in the interval $[0,1]$. Apparently, the larger the weight, the better contribution of the base classifier.

When this weight method is applied to base classifiers, a unique locally classifier ensemble is obtained by combining these weighted base classifiers. For each test data point t, the weighted result is calculated from the local classifier ensemble for each class μ_ϕ, and then the maximum class label is outputted. Our local weighted classifier ensemble for classifying test data point t is as follows:

$$\arg\max_\iota : \sum_{n=1}^s w_\phi^n(t)\mathbf{B}_n^\phi(t) \tag{4}$$

Where $w_\phi^n(t)$ is the weight defined in formula 3 and $\mathbf{B}_n^\phi(t)$ is the ϕth component of row vector. The formula above gives the maximum output as the class label for the test data point t.

3   Experimental Results

In order to validate the classification performance of the proposed method, experiments are performed on several UCI datasets [15]. The detailed descriptions of experimental datasets are shown in the following parts. In this section, all algorithms are implemented by MATLAB R2014a and all numerical experiments are performed on a personal computer with a 2.8 GHz Intel Core2 Duo and 4G bytes of memory with Windows7 64 bit operation system.

Table 1. Descriptions of UCI datasets used in experiments

Datasets	Instances	Feature	Class
Australian	690	2	14
Pima	768	2	8
cmc	1473	3	9
Heart	270	2	13
Scene	2407	2	294
Waveform	5000	3	21
Magic04	19020	2	10
wdbc	569	2	30
Balance	625	3	4
Eyes	238	3	2

3.1   Datasets

We performed our experiment on 10 UCI datasets. Basic descriptive information about UCI datasets used in experimental analysis appears in Table 1. Each dataset is presented in one row in Table 1 including the number of instances, features and classes.

3.2   Experimental Results and Discussion

Our proposed method emphasizes on how to prune and combine base classifiers to achieve better classification performance. The basic classifier models of ensemble is the Decision tree C4.5 [16]. For each dataset, the optimal parameters of basic classifier algorithms are obtained by 10-fold cross validation in experiments. Furthermore, we compare the classification performance of our proposed method with five other ensemble methods, such as DREP [10], QFWEC [13], random forest (RF), simple vote (SV) and Adaboost. In these compared 5 methods, simple vote, Adaboost and random forest are the widely used ensemble methods. And QFWEC is an ensemble method that tries to achieve a balance between diversity and accuracy among base classifiers. Furthermore DREP is the recently proposed method that uses pruning technique and diversity measure, which is very similar to our proposed method.

In our experiments, the values of parameters L which is the number of base classifiers are decided based on each dataset. Each base classifier should have different contribution to a classifier ensemble. By standard, the generalization ability of an ensemble will be good if there are enough base classifiers. However, excessive base classifiers may lead to low performance because many poor base classifiers are working. Therefore the classification performances of different $L \in \{10, 20, 50, 100, 200\}$ are considered to our experiments. Figure 1 shows that average accuracy of our experiments on different L.

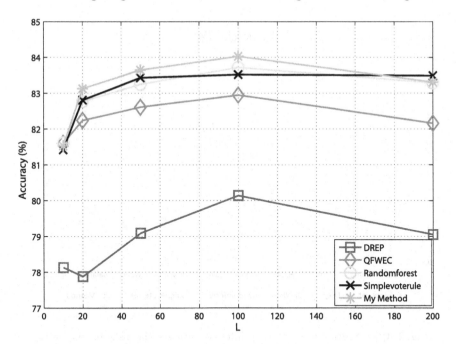

Fig. 1. Classification accuracy changes with the value of different L

Table 2. Classification accuracies on test sets of 10 UCI datasets by 100 classifiers ensemble

Datasets	RF	VR	Adaboost	QFWEC	Drep	Our method
Australia	86.54 ± 0.60	86.53 ± 0.61	84.78 ± 1.55	86.05 ± 0.70	85.79 ± 0.65	$\mathbf{88.23 \pm 0.54}$
Pima	81.10 ± 0.61	81.00 ± 1.18	72.89 ± 1.52	79.05 ± 1.46	80.38 ± 1.32	$\mathbf{82.07 \pm 0.69}$
cmc	54.62 ± 0.44	54.75 ± 1.59	54.80 ± 3.57	54.22 ± 1.43	54.34 ± 1.13	$\mathbf{55.03 \pm 0.53}$
Heart	83.75 ± 0.70	83.75 ± 0.70	72.36 ± 4.25	83.17 ± 0.70	80.42 ± 1.08	$\mathbf{83.81 \pm 0.61}$
Scene	83.00 ± 0.26	83.08 ± 0.32	77.36 ± 1.62	83.05 ± 0.22	81.29 ± 0.51	$\mathbf{83.23 \pm 0.21}$
Waveform	83.72 ± 0.22	83.52 ± 0.37	71.07 ± 1.79	82.95 ± 0.82	80.14 ± 0.85	$\mathbf{84.03 \pm 0.17}$
Magic04	87.62 ± 0.25	87.39 ± 0.22	79.95 ± 2.23	87.48 ± 0.34	87.44 ± 0.18	$\mathbf{87.82 \pm 0.19}$
wdbc	95.77 ± 0.37	95.03 ± 1.10	95.24 ± 0.71	94.18 ± 1.98	93.23 ± 2.29	$\mathbf{96.08 \pm 0.71}$
Balance	86.50 ± 0.86	86.99 ± 0.86	72.44 ± 2.36	77.99 ± 1.44	84.50 ± 3.26	$\mathbf{87.23 \pm 1.09}$
Vehicle	75.96 ± 1.31	76.03 ± 1.39	67.33 ± 3.65	74.04 ± 1.59	70.50 ± 2.42	$\mathbf{77.09 \pm 0.64}$

It could be seen from the Fig. 1 that, a better clarification accuracy is achieved when L is 100 hence the number of base classifiers were fixed at 100 and served as the appropriate value for experiments on other UCI datasets.

On each dataset, each experiment is executed for twenty times. At each time, the accuracy rates on test dataset are recorded, and finally the averaged results with standard deviation over multiple runs are reported. The experimental results of ensemble 100 classifiers by the proposed method and comparative 5 ensemble methods are described in Fig. 2 and detailed data are shown in Table 2.

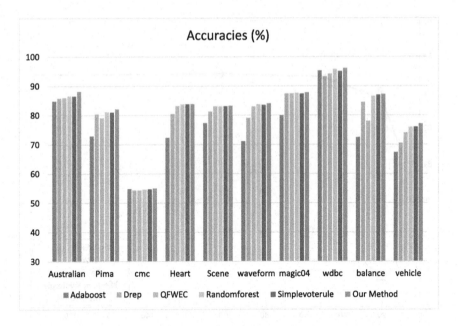

Fig. 2. Classification accuracies of different datasets via ensemble methods

In Table 2, the result is shown by $(A \pm B)$. A and B express the mean of classification accuracy (%) and the standard deviation of classification accuracy (%) on the test set of each dataset, respectively. From the result of Fig. 2 and Table 2, we can see that our proposed method achieves the best classification performance and higher stability among other five ensemble methods.

4   Conclusions

In this paper, we investigate the problem of how to prune and combine different base classifiers. In order to avoid the problem generated by constructing an ensemble algorithm, we propose a method that builds weighted classifier ensembles through classifiers pruning and this comprises of two stages. In the first stage, we model maximum correlation relationship between training data points and base classifiers by canonical correlation analysis (CCA). Then we use a sparse regression method to prune base classifiers so that each test data point will dynamically select a subset of classifiers to form a unique classifier ensemble, by decreasing effects of noisy input data and incorrect classifiers in such a global view. In the second stage, we assign the pruned classifiers with different weights. A fusion method is applied to learn weights locally of pruned base classifiers, which utilizes the generalization ability of pruned classifiers among nearest neighbors of testing data points. The experimental results on a variety of UCI datasets demonstrate that our proposed method outperforms other ensemble methods such as random forests, majority voting, Adaboost and DREP.

Acknowledgments. This work was funded in part by the National Natural Science Foundation of China (No. 61572240, 61601202), Natural Science Foundation of Jiangsu Province (Grant No. BK20140571), the Open Project Program of the National Laboratory of Pattern Recognition (NLPR) (No. 201600005), and the Research Innovation Program for College Graduates of Jiangsu Province (Grant No. SJLX16_0440).

References

1. Zhou, Z.H.: Ensemble Methods: Foundations and Algorithms. Taylor & Francis, Abingdon (2012)
2. Liu, J., Shang, S., Zheng, K., Wen, J.R.: Multi-view ensemble learning for dementia diagnosis from neuroimaging: an artificial neural network approach. Neurocomputing **195**, 112–116 (2016)
3. Ghorai, S., Mukherjee, A., Sengupta, S., Dutta, P.K.: Cancer classification from gene expression data by NPPC ensemble. IEEE/ACM Trans. Comput. Biol. Bioinform. **8**(3), 659–671 (2010)
4. Liu, L., Shao, L., Rockett, P.: Boosted key-frame selection and correlated pyramidal motion-feature representation for human action recognition. Pattern Recogn. **46**(7), 1810–1818 (2013)
5. Breiman, L.: Bagging predictors. Mach. Learn. **24**(2), 123–140 (1996)
6. Schapire, R.E.: The Boosting Approach to Machine Learning: An Overview. Springer, New York (2002). https://doi.org/10.1007/978-0-387-21579-2_9
7. Liaw, A., Wiener, M.: Classification and regression by randomforest. R News **2**(3), 18–22 (2002)
8. Tsoumakas, G., Partalas, I., Vlahavas, I.: An ensemble pruning primer. Stud. Comput. Intell. **245**, 1–13 (2009)
9. Martinezmuoz, G., Hernandezlobato, D., Suarez, A.: An analysis of ensemble pruning techniques based on ordered aggregation. IEEE Trans. Pattern Anal. Mach. Intell. **31**(2), 245–259 (2009)
10. Li, N., Yu, Y., Zhou, Z.-H.: Diversity regularized ensemble pruning. In: Flach, P.A., De Bie, T., Cristianini, N. (eds.) ECML PKDD 2012. LNCS (LNAI), vol. 7523, pp. 330–345. Springer, Heidelberg (2012). https://doi.org/10.1007/978-3-642-33460-3_27
11. Zhang, L., Zhou, W.D.: Sparse ensembles using weighted combination methods based on linear programming. Pattern Recogn. **44**(1), 97–106 (2011)
12. Liu, T., Tao, D.: Classification with noisy labels by importance reweighting. IEEE Trans. Pattern Anal. Mach. Intell. **38**(3), 447–461 (2016)
13. Mao, S., Jiao, L., Xiong, L., Gou, S., Chen, B., Yeung, S.K.: Weighted classifier ensemble based on quadratic form. Pattern Recogn. **48**(5), 1688–1706 (2014)
14. Hardoon, D.R., Szedmak, S., Shawetaylor, J.: Canonical correlation analysis: an overview with application to learning methods. Neural Comput. **16**(12), 2639–2664 (2004)
15. Blake, C.: UCI repository of machine learning databases (1998). http://www.ics.uci.edu/~mlearn/MLRepository.html
16. Quinlan, J.R.: C4.5: Programs for Machine Learning, vol. 1. Morgan Kaufmann Publishers, Burlington (1992)

Elastic Net Regularized Dictionary Learning for Face Recognition

Li Wang$^{(\boxtimes)}$, Yan-Jiang Wang, and Bao-Di Liu

College of Information and Control Engineering,
China University of Petroleum (East China),
No. 66 Changjiang West Road, Qingdao, China
b15050141@s.upc.edu.cn, yjwang@upc.edu.cn

Abstract. The sparse representation based classification (SRC) method and collaborative representation based classification (CRC) method attract more and more attention in recent years, due to their promising result and robustness for face recognition. However, both SRC and CRC algorithms directly use the training samples as the dictionary, which leads to large fitting error. Additionally, the subsequent research shows that the performance of face recognition is not only determined by the sparsity constraint (ℓ_1 regularizer), but also driven by the collaborative constraint (ℓ_2 regularizer). To overcome the issue mentioned above, in this paper, we propose an elastic net regularized dictionary learning based classification method. The proposed method is capable of improving the performance for face recognition according to class specific dictionary learning and elastic net regularizer. Moreover, to enhance the ability for handling nonlinear problems, we also extend the proposed method to arbitrary kernel space. Extensive experimental results on several face recognition benchmark datasets demonstrate the superior performance of our proposed algorithm.

Keywords: Elastic net regularizer · Sparse representation
Dictionary learning · Kernel method

1 Introduction

The past few years have witnessed the impressive performance of dictionary learning for sparse representation in visual computation areas, such as image processing [1], image segmentation [2], face recognition [3], object detection [4], transfer learning [5], and image denoising [6], due to its impressive effect. Different from the traditional decomposition methods, such as PCA, support vector machines (SVM) [7], non-negative matrix factorization [8,9], the sparse representation method extracts image features over complete dictionary bases, and forms a simple expression of the signal.

Meanwhile, face recognition based on sparse representation is one of the most important and active research topics among pattern recognition and artificial

© Springer Nature Singapore Pte Ltd. 2018
B. Huet et al. (Eds.): ICIMCS 2017, CCIS 819, pp. 140–150, 2018.
https://doi.org/10.1007/978-981-10-8530-7_14

intelligence. Normally, face recognition involves two stages: feature extraction stage and classification stage. In the feature extraction stage, PCA [10] algorithm was proposed to get the best explain of the data. LDA [11,12] algorithm was suggested to minimum within-class and maximum Between-Class Scatter. LPP [13] algorithm was proposed to find an embedding subspace that preserves local structure information, Chong et al. [14] proposed two-directional and Modular Fuzzy 2DPCA algorithm to extract two-dimensional local characteristic of face features. Tao et al. [15] develop a general tensor discriminant analysis (GTDA) as a preprocessing step for LDA. Wu et al. [16] proposed multi-feature kernel discriminant dictionary learning algorithm which fuses multi-feature in multiple kernel framework. In the procedure of classification, the subspace methods [17] proposed recently classify images through comparing the reconstruction error of each category. A sparse representation based classification (SRC) method was proposed within the framework of the nearest subspace and attracting more and more researchers'attention in computer vision due to its state-of-the-art performance in classification. The SRC [18] method firstly obtained the sparse representation of the test sample, and then measured the residual error from training samples of each class. Zhang et al. [19] proposed Collaborative representation based Classification (CRC) algorithm.

Due to their promise, both SRC and CRC algorithms directly use the training samples as the dictionary, which will lead to large fitting error. Therefore, many dictionary learning algorithms have emerged. Existing discriminative dictionary learning approaches are mainly categorized into three types: shared dictionary learning, class specific dictionary learning, and hybrid dictionary learning.

In class specific dictionary learning, Wang et al. [20] introduced a modified sparse model and a supervised class-specific dictionary learning method for classification. Liu et al. [3] proposed a class specific dictionary learning algorithm which can find the intrinsic relationship between the base vectors and the original image features. Wang et al. [21] proposed a classification-oriented dictionary learning model and applied it for face recognition. Shu et al. [22] proposed a novel Fine-grained Dictionary Learning (FDL) method to learn a high-quality discriminative dictionary. Liu [23] proposed a class specific centralized dictionary learning (CSCDL) algorithm to simultaneously consider the desired characteristics for both dictionary and sparse codes. In spite of the hybrid dictionary learning algorithm shown to be an effective method in visual recognition tasks, it is still a challenge to balance between the shared dictionary learning algorithms and the class specific dictionary learning algorithms.

Motivated by the high performance of SRC, CRC and class specific dictionary learning (CSDL), we proposed an elastic net regularized dictionary learning algorithm with kernels (KENRDL). The main contribution is listed in four aspects. (1) We propose an elastic net regularized sparse representation algorithm. It combines the advantages of SRC's discriminant ability and CRC's similarity attribute of different faces. (2) We propose an elastic net regularized dictionary learning algorithm to construct superior subspace and reduce the residual error. (3) We extend the elastic net regularized dictionary learning algorithm to arbitrary kernel space to find nonlinear structure of face images. (4) Experimental results on several benchmark datasets demonstrate the superior performance performance of our proposed algorithm.

The rest of the paper are organized as follows. Section 2 overviews the two classical face recognition algorithms. Section 3 proposes our elastic net regularized dictionary learning algorithm with kernels. The solution to the minimization of the objective function is elaborated in Sect. 4. Then, experimental results and analysis are shown in Sect. 5. Finally, discussions and conclusions are drawn in Sect. 6.

2   Overview of SRC and CRC

In this section, we will briefly overview two classical face recognition algorithms, SRC and CRC.

Wright *et al.* [18] proposed the sparse representation based classification(SRC) algorithm and achieved superior performance in face recognition task due that SRC is capable of finding the discriminant representation for a testing sample.

Assuming that X stands for the training samples, $X \in R^{D \times N}$. Here, D represents the dimension of the samples and N stands for the number of the samples. SRC algorithm uses the training samples to form the basis matrix. Assuming that y stands for a testing sample, and s represents the sparse coding of y under the basis matrix X, the objective function of SRC algorithm is presented as follows:

$$\hat{s} = \arg\min_{s}\{||y - Xs||_2^2 + 2\alpha||s||_1\} \tag{1}$$

In the formula above, α stands for the regularization parameter to control the sparsity and accuracy of the representation.

Zhang *et al.* [19] proposed the collaborative representation based classification (CRC) algorithm, which changed the ℓ_1 regularizer term to ℓ_2 regularizer term. ℓ_2 regularizer allows more training samples to participate in the description of the testing sample since different kinds of face has many similar attributes. The objective of CRC algorithm can be rewritten as follows:

$$\hat{s} = \arg\min_{s}\{||y - Xs||_2^2 + \beta||s||_2^2\} \tag{2}$$

In the formula above, β is the regularization parameter to control the fitting error of the object function.

Both SRC and CRC algorithms directly utilize the training samples X as the dictionary and the testing sample y can be encoded as:

$$y \approx Xs, \tag{3}$$

Here, X is the dictionary matrix composed by the training samples, and s is the sparse coding of the testing sample.

3 Our Proposed Approach

From the description in above section, on the one hand, both the SRC and CRC algorithms have achieved superior performance for face recognition, i.e. both ℓ_1 regularizer and ℓ_2 have the ability to improve the face recognition performance. ℓ_1 regularizer is capable of finding the sparse approximation (discriminant representation) of a testing sample with the training sample, while ℓ_2 allows more training samples to participate in the description of the testing sample to guarantee the similarity description of different kinds of faces. The combination of ℓ_1 regularizer and ℓ_2 regularizer, i.e. elastic regularizer, will provide both the spare representation (discriminant representation) ability and collaborative representation attribute when describing the testing sample. The objective function of elastic net regularized sparse representation is as follows:

$$\hat{s} = \arg\min_{s}\{||y - Xs||_2^2 + 2\alpha||s||_1\} + \beta||s||_2^2\} \tag{4}$$

On the other hand, both SRC and CRC algorithms directly utilize the training samples as the dictionary. This will lead to poor fitting, especially for isolated training samples. If there exist a weight matrix W to represent the contribution of each sample in the dictionary construction, the Eq. (3) can be rewritten as:

$$y \approx XWs. \tag{5}$$

Here, W is the weight coefficient matrix. In SRC and CRC algorithms, W represents an identity matrix. However, the test samples may be poor described by the dictionary composition of the training samples considering that the training samples of the same class should have different weights when constructing bases in the corresponding dictionary. Hence, the weight coefficient matrix could be generalized from an identity matrix to a block-diagonal matrix. The weight coefficient matrix can be obtained by class specific dictionary learning. The objective function of the elastic net regularized dictionary learning is as follows:

$$f(W^c, S^c) = ||X^c - X^c W^c S^c||_F^2 + 2\alpha \sum_{n=1}^{N_c} ||S_{\bullet n}^c||_1 + \beta ||S^c||_F^2 \tag{6}$$

$$s.t. ||X^c W_{\bullet k}^c||_2^2 \leq 1, \forall k = 1, 2, \cdots K, \forall c = 1, 2, \cdots C.$$

Here, $||\bullet||_F^2$ represents the frobenius norm. $W_{\bullet i}$ and $W_{j\bullet}$ denote the i_{th} column and j_{th} row vectors of matrix W. W^c can be obtained in the procedure of dictionary learning by the method of iteration. W^c stands for the dictionary weight matrix of class c, and S^c is the sparse representation of X^c.

From Eq. (6), the weight coefficient matrix can be learnt from the training samples. After obtaining the weight coefficient matrix, the residual error of fitting the testing sample will be greatly reduced.

Additionally, superior performance of face recognition is often achieved in Reproducing Kernel Hilbert Space due that the nonlinear structure often exist in face features. Our proposed elastic net regularized dictionary learning (ENRDL) algorithm is easily extended to arbitrary kernel space. Suppose there exists a kernel function $\phi : R^D \to R^K (D < K)$, function ϕ map the image dataset to the high dimensional feature space: $\phi(X) = [\phi(X^1), \phi(X^2), \cdots, \phi(X^C)] \in \mathrm{R}^{K \times N}$. The objective function of our proposed elastic net regularized dictionary learning algorithm with kernels is as follows:

$$f(W^c, S^c) = \|\phi(X^c) - \phi(X^c) W^c S^c\|_F^2 + 2\alpha \sum_{n=1}^{N_c} \|S_{\bullet n}^c\|_1 + \beta \|S^c\|_F^2 \tag{7}$$

$$\|\phi(X^c) W_{\bullet k}^c\|_2^2 \le 1, \forall k = 1, 2, \cdots, K$$

4   Optimization of the Objective Function

In this section, we focus on solving the optimization problem for the proposed kernel based elastic net regularized self-explanatory sparse representation algorithm. Specifically, similar to the optimization strategy adopted in [24], it is decomposed into two subproblems via alternating minimization for learning dictionary of each class. One is an elastic net regularized least-squares minimization subproblem with fixed W^c. The other one is an ℓ_2 norm constrained least-squares minimization subproblem with fixed S^c.

4.1   Elastic Net Regularized Minimization Subproblem

With W^c fixed, the objective function of the elastic net regularized least-squares minimization subproblem is cast as:

$$f(S^c) = \|\phi(X^c) - \phi(X^c) W^c S^c\|_F^2 + 2\alpha \sum_{n=1}^{N_c} \|S_{\bullet n}^c\|_1 + \beta \|S^c\|_F^2 \tag{8}$$

Ignoring the constant term, Eq. (8) can be simplified as

$$f(S^c) = trace\{\kappa(X^c, X^c)\} - 2 \sum_{n=1}^{N_c} [\kappa(X^c, X^c) W^c]_{n \bullet} S_{\bullet n}^c$$

$$+ \sum_{n=1}^{N} S_{\bullet n}^{c}{}^T [W^{cT} \kappa(X^c, X^c) W^c] S_{\bullet n}^c \tag{9}$$

$$+ 2\alpha \sum_{k=1}^{K} \sum_{n=1}^{N_c} |S_{kn}^c| + \beta \sum_{k=1}^{K} \sum_{n=1}^{N_c} (S_{kn}^c)^2$$

The formula (9) can be decomposed into a series of sub problem, in order to solve every element in formula (9), formula (9) can simplified to:

$$f(S_{kn}^c) = -2[\kappa(X^c, X^c) W^c]_{nk} S_{kn}^c$$

$$+ (S_{kn}^c)^2 [W^{cT} \kappa(X^c, X^c) W^c]_{kk}$$

$$+ 2 \sum_{l=1, l \ne k}^{K} [W^{cT} \kappa(X^c, X^c) W^c]_{lk} S_{kn}^c \tag{10}$$

$$+ 2\alpha |S_{kn}^c| + \beta(S_{kn}^c)^2$$

According to the solving method in [24], it is easy to infer that $f(S_{kn}^c)$ reaches the minimum at the unique point

$$
S_{k\bullet}^c = \frac{\min\left\{ \left[W^{cT}\kappa\left(X^c, X^c\right) \right]_{k\bullet} - \left[E\overline{S^c}^k \right]_{k\bullet}, -\alpha \right\}}{\left[W^{cT}\kappa\left(X^c, X^c\right)W^c \right]_{kk} + \beta}
$$
$$
+ \frac{\max\left\{ \left[W^{cT}\kappa\left(X^c, X^c\right) \right]_{k\bullet} - \left[E\overline{S^c}^k \right]_{k\bullet}, \alpha \right\}}{\left[W^{cT}\kappa\left(X^c, X^c\right)W^c \right]_{kk} + \beta}
\tag{11}
$$

Here, $\overline{S^c}^k = \begin{cases} S_{p\bullet}^c, & p \neq k \\ 0, & p = k \end{cases}$, $E = W^{cT}\kappa\left(X^c, X^c\right)W^c + \beta I$, I represents an identity matrix.

4.2 ℓ_2 Norm Constrained Minimization Subproblem

With S^c fixed, the objective function of the minimization subproblem becomes

$$
f(W^c) = \|\phi\left(X^c\right) - \phi\left(X^c\right)W^c S^c\|_F^2
$$
$$
s.t. \ \|\phi\left(X^c\right)W_{\bullet k}^c\|_2^2 \leq 1, \forall k = 1, 2, \cdots, K.
\tag{12}
$$

Here, the lagrange multipliers are used to solve the ℓ_2 norm constrained least-squares minimization subproblem. W^c can be obtained by optimizing each column alternately. Specifically, ignoring the constant term $trace\{\kappa(X^c, X^c)\}$, the lagrangian term is as follows:

$$
L(W^c, \lambda_k, \mu_k) = -2\sum_{k=1}^{K} [S^c\kappa(X^c, X^c)]_{k\bullet} W_{\bullet k}^c
$$
$$
+ \sum_{k=1}^{K} W_{\bullet k}^c [\kappa(X^c, X^c)W^c S^c S^{cT}]_{\bullet k}
$$
$$
+ \lambda_k(1 - [W^{cT}\kappa(X^c, X^c)W^c]_{kk}),
\tag{13}
$$

where λ_k is a variable.

According to the Karush-Kuhn-Tucker (KKT) conditions, the optimal solution $W_{\bullet k}^c$ should satisfy the following criteria:

$$
(a): \frac{\partial L(W^c, \lambda_k)}{\partial W_{\bullet k}^c} = 0
$$
$$
(b): (1 - [W^{cT}\kappa(X^c, X^c)W^c]_{kk}) = 0
\tag{14}
$$
$$
(c): \lambda_k > 0
$$

Hence, the solution to $W_{\bullet k}^c$ becomes

$$
W_{\bullet k}^c = \frac{S_{\bullet k}^c - \left[\overline{W^c}^k F\right]_{\bullet k}}{\sqrt{\left(S_{k\bullet}^{c\ T} - \left[\overline{W^c}^k F\right]_{\bullet k}\right)^T \kappa\left(X^c, X^c\right)\left(S_{k\bullet}^{c\ T} - \left[\overline{W^c}^k F\right]_{\bullet k}\right)}}
\tag{15}
$$

where $F = S^c S^{cT}$ and $\overline{W^c}^k = \begin{cases} W_{\bullet p}^c, & p \neq k \\ 0, & p = k \end{cases}$.

5   Experimental Results

In this section, we present experimental results on three benchmark datasets to illustrate the effectiveness of our method. The following subsections focus on experimental settings, parameter tuning, experimental results and some discussions.

5.1   Experimental Settings

Our proposed KENRDL algorithm is verified on three benchmark datasets, such as CMU-PIE dataset, Extended Yale B dataset and AR dataset. We resize the maximum side (width/length) of each image to 32×32 and pulled it into a column vector, we use L2-norm to normalize the feature length to 1.

For fair comparison, 5 images in each category are randomly selected as the training data and 10 images in each category are randomly selection as the testing data. The mean value and standard deviation of the face recognition rate are recorded.

The proposed KENRDL algorithm is compared with five other classical face recognition algorithms, nearest neighbor classification (NN), collaborative representation based classification (CRC) [19], sparse representation based classification (SRC) [18], kernel based class specific dictionary learning algorithm [3], and SVM [25]. For SVM, one-against-all multi-class classification strategy is adopted by LIBSVM [25].

The weight of sparsity term α is an important factor in KENRDL. α is used to adjust the trade-off between the reconstruction error and the sparsity. We increase α from 2^{-12} to 2^{-1} in each experiment and find the best α in our experiments.

β is another important factor in KENRDL. KENRDL algorithm use β to control the trade-off between the reconstruction error and the collaborative information. We increase β from 2^{-12} to 2^{-1} and find the best β in all of our experiments.

We also evaluate the effect of different kernels for KENRDL on Extended YaleB dataset, CMU-PIE dataset and AR dataset. Three different kernel functions is adopted, such as linear kernel ($\kappa(x,y) = x^T y$), Hellinger kernel ($\kappa(x,y) = \sum_{d=1}^{D} \sqrt{x_d y_d}$), and polynomial kernel ($\kappa(x,y) = (p + x^T y)^q$). Here, in our experiments, p and q are set to be 4 and 2, respectively.

5.2   CMU-PIE Dataset

The CMU-PIE dataset is often used to validate an algorithm's effectiveness because it contains many kinds of image variations. It consists of $41,368$ images of 68 individuals captured under various laboratory-controlled lighting conditions. We selected two types of images to carry out our experiment: five near frontal poses and all different illuminations. We choose $11,554$ images in total for our evaluation. Each person contains about 170 images.

Table 1 lists the performance values of all algorithms on the CMU-PIE data set with NN, SVM, CRC, SRC, KCSDL, and KENRDL. In our experiments, we set the weight of sparsity term α is 2^{-9}, 2^{-7}, and 2^{-7}, for linear kernel, Hellinger kernel and polynomial kernel, respectively. The optimal β is 2^{-4} for all three types of kernel. From Table 1, we can see that KENRDL algorithm always achieves the highest recognition rates under different kernel space. KENRDL algorithm outperforms KCSDL method, which achieves the second highest recognition rate, by more than 3% improvement of recognition rate in Hellinger kernel space.

Table 1. Recognition rate on the CMU-PIE dataset (%).

Methods Kernels	Linear	Hellinger	Poly
NN	30.09 ± 1.67	NA	NA
SVM	66.79 ± 2.63	65.71 ± 2.54	65.46 ± 2.76
CRC	72.89 ± 2.21	75.19 ± 2.09	73.19 ± 2.20
SRC	72.16 ± 2.09	70.26 ± 2.23	69.19 ± 2.17
KCSDL	74.46 ± 2.01	74.78 ± 2.05	73.49 ± 2.22
KENRDL	$\mathbf{75.74 \pm 1.98}$	$\mathbf{77.99 \pm 1.77}$	$\mathbf{77.06 \pm 1.64}$

5.3   Extended YaleB Dataset

Extended YaleB contains 38 categories, and 2414 frontal-face images. The cropped image size is 32×32. All the images are captured under varying illumination conditions. In our experiments, we set the weight of sparsity term α is 2^{-9}, 2^{-7}, and 2^{-7}, for linear kernel, Hellinger kernel and polynomial kernel, respectively. The optimal β is 2^{-5}, 2^{-5}, and 2^{-8} for linear kernel, Hellinger kernel and polynomial kernel, respectively. From Table 2, we can clearly know that KENRDL achieves the best recognition rates of 79.82%, 91.14% and 80.90% in linear kernel, Hellinger kernel and polynomial kernel space, respectively, while KCSDL, the second best method, arrives at 78.55%, 88.98% and 79.68%.

Table 2. Recognition rate on the extended YaleB dataset (%).

Methods Kernels	Linear	Hellinger	Poly
NN	33.17 ± 1.45	NA	NA
SVM	65.52 ± 2.77	79.97 ± 2.57	64.89 ± 2.43
CRC	78.07 ± 2.16	87.23 ± 1.44	76.33 ± 2.17
SRC	77.59 ± 1.59	88.58 ± 1.56	74.82 ± 2.35
KCSDL	78.55 ± 2.25	88.98 ± 1.62	79.68 ± 2.41
KENRDL	$\mathbf{79.82 \pm 1.87}$	$\mathbf{91.14 \pm 1.51}$	$\mathbf{80.90 \pm 2.04}$

Table 3. Recognition rate on the AR dataset (%).

Methods Kernels	Linear	Hellinger	Poly
NN	32.99 ± 1.97	NA	NA
SVM	80.67 ± 1.32	80.59 ± 1.26	80.84 ± 1.57
CRC	91.98 ± 0.86	92.18 ± 0.78	92.43 ± 0.75
SRC	89.17 ± 1.14	85.32 ± 1.12	85.25 ± 1.41
KCSDL	91.12 ± 1.57	89.77 ± 1.27	89.02 ± 1.31
KENRDL	$\mathbf{92.11 \pm 1.16}$	$\mathbf{91.02 \pm 0.84}$	$\mathbf{92.9 \pm 0.96}$

5.4   AR Dataset

AR dataset contains over 4000 frontal face images corresponding to 126 persons. A subset of 50 males and 50 females is selected from the AR dataset. The AR dataset has 26 faces per class and has wide variations such as facial variations, illumination change, various expressions and so on. Similar to the parameter tuning on CMU-PIE dataset, the optimal α is 2^{-10}, 2^{-7}, and 2^{-7} for linear kernel, Hellinger kernel and polynomial kernel, respectively. The optimal β is 2^{-4} for all three types of kernel. From Table 3, we can easily see that KENRDL algorithm achieves the best recognition rate of 92.90% in polynomial kernel space. In other words, KENRDL algorithm outperforms the best competitor KCSDL algorithm by more than 3% improvement of recognition rate in polynomial kernel space, 1.25% improvement of recognition rate in Hellinger kernel space, and 0.99% improvement of recognition rate in linear kernel space.

6   Conclusions

We present a novel elastic net regularized dictionary learning algorithm with kernels. The proposed KENRDL algorithm improves the classical SRC or CRC algorithm in threefold. First, it concisely combines the discriminant ability (sparse representation) and similarity attribute (collaborative representation) to enhance the interpretability of face recognition. Second, it greatly reduces the residual error according to elastic regularized dictionary learning. Third, it easily finds the nonlinear structure hidden in face images by extending the algorithm to arbitrary kernel space. Experimental results on several publicly available datasets have demonstrated that KENRDL can provide superior performance to the traditional face recognition approaches.

Acknowledgments. This paper is supported partly by the National Natural Science Foundation of China (Grant No. 61402535, No. 61271407), the Natural Science Foundation for Youths of Shandong Province, China (Grant No. ZR2014FQ001), Qingdao Science and Technology Project (No. 14-2-4-111-jch), and the Fundamental Research Funds for the Central Universities, China University of Petroleum (East China) (Grant No. 16CX02060A), International S And T Cooperation Program of China (Grant No. 2015DFG12050).

References

1. Russ, J.C.: The Image Processing Handbook. CRC Press, Boca Raton (2016)
2. Pont-Tuset, J., Arbelaez, P., Barron, J.T., Marques, F., Malik, J.: Multiscale combinatorial grouping for image segmentation and object proposal generation. IEEE Trans. Pattern Anal. Mach. Intell. **39**(1), 128–140 (2017)
3. Liu, B.-D., Shen, B., Wang, Y.-X.: Class specific dictionary learning for face recognition. In: 2014 International Conference on Security, Pattern Analysis, and Cybernetics (SPAC), pp. 229–234. IEEE (2014)
4. Redmon, J., Divvala, S., Girshick, R., Farhadi, A.: You only look once: unified, real-time object detection. In: Proceedings of the IEEE Conference on Computer Vision and Pattern Recognition, pp. 779–788 (2016)
5. Chang, H., Han, J., Zhong, C., Snijders, A., Mao, J.-H.: Unsupervised transfer learning via multi-scale convolutional sparse coding for biomedical applications. IEEE Trans. Pattern Anal. Mach. Intell. (2017)
6. Rajwade, A., Rangarajan, A., Banerjee, A.: Image denoising using the higher order singular value decomposition. IEEE Trans. Pattern Anal. Mach. Intell. **35**(4), 849–862 (2013)
7. Tao, D., Tang, X., Li, X., Wu, X.: Asymmetric bagging and random subspace for support vector machines-based relevance feedback in image retrieval. IEEE Trans. Pattern Anal. Mach. Intell. **28**(7), 1088–1099 (2006)
8. Liu, T., Gong, M., Tao, D.: Large-cone nonnegative matrix factorization. IEEE Trans. Neural Netw. Learn. Syst. **28**, 2129–2142 (2016)
9. Liu, T., Tao, D.: On the performance of manhattan nonnegative matrix factorization. IEEE Trans. Neural Netw. Learn. Syst. **27**(9), 1851–1863 (2016)
10. Shlens, J.: A tutorial on principal component analysis. arXiv preprint arXiv:1404.1100 (2014)
11. Yan, Y., Ricci, E., Subramanian, R., Liu, G., Sebe, N.: Multitask linear discriminant analysis for view invariant action recognition. IEEE Trans. Image Process. **23**(12), 5599–5611 (2014)
12. Tao, D., Li, X., Wu, X., Maybank, S.J.: Geometric mean for subspace selection. IEEE Trans. Pattern Anal. Mach. Intell. **31**(2), 260–274 (2009)
13. Zhong, F., Zhang, J., Li, D.: Discriminant locality preserving projections based on l1-norm maximization. IEEE Trans. Neural Netw. Learn. Syst. **25**(11), 2065–2074 (2014)
14. Chong, Y., He, X., Luo, Q., Peng, Y., Han, Y.: Face recognition method based on two-directional and modular fuzzy 2DPCA. In: Chinese Automation Congress (CAC), pp. 2027–2032. IEEE (2015)
15. Tao, D., Li, X., Wu, X., Maybank, S.J.: General tensor discriminant analysis and gabor features for gait recognition. IEEE Trans. Pattern Anal. Mach. Intell. 29(10) (2007)
16. Wu, X., Li, Q., Xu, L., Chen, K., Yao, L.: Multi-feature kernel discriminant dictionary learning for face recognition. Pattern Recogn. **66**, 404–411 (2017)
17. Wei, C.-P., Chao, Y.-W., Yeh, Y.-R., Wang, Y.-C.F.: Locality-sensitive dictionary learning for sparse representation based classification. Pattern Recogn. **46**(5), 1277–1287 (2013)
18. Wright, J., Yang, A.Y., Ganesh, A., Sastry, S.S., Ma, Y.: Robust face recognition via sparse representation. IEEE Trans. Pattern Anal. Mach. Intell. **31**(2), 210–227 (2009)

19. Zhang, L., Yang, M., Feng, X.: Sparse representation or collaborative representation: which helps face recognition? In: 2011 IEEE International Conference on Computer Vision (ICCV), pp. 471–478. IEEE (2011)
20. Wang, H., Yuan, C., Hu, W., Sun, C.: Supervised class-specific dictionary learning for sparse modeling in action recognition. Pattern Recogn. **45**(11), 3902–3911 (2012)
21. Wang, D., Kong, S.: A classification-oriented dictionary learning model: explicitly learning the particularity and commonality across categories. Pattern Recogn. **47**(2), 885–898 (2014)
22. Shu, X., Tang, J., Qi, G.-J., Li, Z., Jiang, Y.-G., Yan, S.: Image classification with tailored fine-grained dictionaries. IEEE Trans. Circ. Syst. Video Technol. (2016)
23. Liu, B.-D., Gui, L., Wang, Y., Wang, Y.-X., Shen, B., Li, X., Wang, Y.-J.: Class specific centralized dictionary learning for face recognition. Multimedia Tools Appl. **76**(3), 4159–4177 (2017)
24. Liu, B.-D., Wang, Y.-X., Shen, B., Zhang, Y.-J., Hebert, M.: Self-explanatory sparse representation for image classification. In: Fleet, D., Pajdla, T., Schiele, B., Tuytelaars, T. (eds.) ECCV 2014. LNCS, vol. 8690, pp. 600–616. Springer, Cham (2014). https://doi.org/10.1007/978-3-319-10605-2_39
25. Chang, C.-C., Lin, C.-J.: LIBSVM: a library for support vector machines. ACM Trans. Intell. Syst. Technol. (TIST) **2**(3), 27 (2011)

Extracting Deep Video Feature for Mobile Video Classification with ELU-3DCNN

Jihong Liu[1(✉)], Jing Zhang[1], Hui Zhang[1], Xi Liang[1], and Li Zhuo[1,2]

[1] Signal and Information Processing Laboratory,
Beijing University of Technology, Beijing, China
{kev, liangxi627}@emails.bjut.edu.cn,
{zhj, huizhang, zhuoli}@bjut.edu.cn
[2] Collaborative Innovation Center of Electric Vehicles in Beijing,
Beijing 100124, People's Republic of China

Abstract. Extracting robust video feature has always been a challenge in the field of video classification. Although existing researches on video feature extraction have been active and extensive, the classification results based on traditional video feature are always neither flexible nor satisfactory enough. Recently, deep learning has shown an excellent performance in video feature extraction. In this paper, we improve a deep learning architecture called ELU-3DCNN to extract deep video feature for video classification. Firstly, ELU-3DCNN is trained with exponential linear units (ELUs). Then a video is split into 16-frame clips with 8-frame overlaps between consecutive clips. These clips are passed to ELU-3DCNN to extract fc7 activations, which are further averaged and normalized to form a 4096-dim video feature. Experimental results on UCF-101 dataset show that ELU-3DCNN can improve the performance of video classification compared with the state-of-the-art video feature extraction methods.

Keywords: Deep learning · ELU-3DCNN · Deep video feature
Feature extraction · Video classification · Mobile video

1 Introduction

With the development of Mobile Internet, the amount of available mobile video content is growing exponentially. Mobile video is delivered and shared in mobile internet, which usually has the characteristics of being short in time and small in volume. Moreover, video sharing has become immensely popular, enabling every individual to access a vast amount of video content. Therefore, it is inevitable that such amount of videos demands an accurate video classification for tackling various applications like video recommendation [1], retrieval system [2], action recognition [3], and abnormal detection [4], etc. In general, a superior video representation depends on the video feature extraction. Thus, analyzing video content with robust video feature has become a crucial research task.

The computer vision community has studied feature representation especially for video for decades [5]. Up to now, many traditional hand-crafted video features have

© Springer Nature Singapore Pte Ltd. 2018
B. Huet et al. (Eds.): ICIMCS 2017, CCIS 819, pp. 151–159, 2018.
https://doi.org/10.1007/978-981-10-8530-7_15

been proposed. For example, Wang *et al.* proposed improved Dense Trajectories (iDT) [6] that improves its performances by considering camera motion. Currently, iDT is the state-of-the-art hand-crafted feature for action recognition. However, the disadvantage of being computationally complicated makes the iDT becomes inflexible on large-scale datasets. Inspired by the deep learning breakthroughs in feature extraction [7], some researchers have tried to apply deep learning technology to extract deep video feature. References [8, 9] extended Convolutional Neural Networks (CNNs) to video content analysis by performing convolutions in both time and space. Karen *et al.* proposed a two-stream ConvNet architecture [10] that incorporates spatial and temporal networks trained on multi-frame dense optical flow. However, deep video features above always cannot achieve satisfying results when applied to mobile video classification. Unsupervised learning schemes for extracting deep video feature have also been developed. Nitish *et al.* used multilayer Long Short Term Memory (LSTM) networks [11, 12] to extract feature from mobile video in an unsupervised way, in which LSTM is used as an encoder to map frame sequences into a fixed representation. Although these deep video features perform well in video classification, its performance can be further improved by designing a delicate neural network. Considering the structure of videos, Du *et al.* proposed a simple, yet effective approach for spati-temporal feature learning using deep 3-Dimensional Convolutional Neural Networks called ReLU-3DCNN [13] trained on a large-scale supervised video dataset. ReLU-3DCNN architecture uses the Rectified Linear Units (ReLUs) [14] as the activation function. However, ReLUs have a mean activation greater than zero because of the characteristic of being non-negative. Because units with a non-zero mean activation act as bias for the next layer, the bias will further make the speed of training be reduced. Therefore, ReLU-3DCNN have a poor efficiency and low accuracy for video classification [15].

Considering that ELUs have negative values and no bias shift, our ELU-3DCNN architecture takes a step forward by substituting Exponential Linear units (ELUs) [15] for rectified linear units (ReLUs) to produce a better result. Moreover, in order to improve the generalization of ELU-3DCNN, we utilize some regularization methods such as dropout, data augmentation and weight decay to reduce overfitting.

2   Overview of Proposed ELU-3DCNN Architecture

Commonly, deep learning architectures consist of three basic operations including activation functions, convolutions and pooling operations. Based on these basic operations in this paper, an ELU-3DCNN architecture is devised to extract deep video feature for mobile video classification. Moreover, in order to improve the generalization of ELU-3DCNN, we implement dropout [16] and weight decay to reduce overfitting.

2.1   Using Exponential Linear Units (ELUs) as Activation Function

Currently, the most popular activation function for neural networks is the rectified linear units (ReLUs). The main advantage of ReLUs is that they can alleviate the vanishing gradient problem. However, ReLUs have a mean activation greater than zero due to the characteristic of being non-negative. Units with a non-zero mean activation act as bias for the next layer. From Ref. [15], we can see that more bias shift will bring the standard gradient far more to the natural gradient and further reduce the training speed. Similar to ReLUs, ELUs [15] can also alleviate the vanishing gradient problem via identity and positive values. Moreover, because ELUs have negative values, the mean activation for every unit can be pushed to zero. Owing to the characteristic of being no bias shift, the neural networks based on ELUs are more efficient and effective. ELU is defined as:

$$f_{ELU}(x) = \begin{cases} x & if \quad x > 0 \\ \alpha(\exp(x) - 1) & if \quad x \leq 0 \end{cases} \tag{1}$$

where α is the ELU hyper parameter, it controls the convergence value when x tends to be negative infinite.

Considering the effectiveness of ELU, we use ELU as the activation function in our architecture. The comparison between ELU-3DCNN and ReLU-3DCNN are shown in Fig. 1, in which Fig. 1(a) is ReLU-3DCNN and Fig. 1(b) is ELU-3DCNN. In ELU-3DCNN, 16-frames of size 112×112 centered on the current frame will be fed into the ELU-3DCNN. ELU-3DCNN has 8 convolution layers, 5 max-pooling, 6 ELU activation functions and 2 fully connected layers followed by a softmax output layer. All 3D convolution kernels are $3 \times 3 \times 3$ with stride 1 in both spatial and temporal dimensions. The number of filters are denoted in each box in Fig. 1(b). The 3D pooling layers are denoted from Pool 1 to Pool 5. All pooling kernels are $2 \times 2 \times 2$, except for Pool 1 is $1 \times 2 \times 2$. Each fully connected layers has 4096 output units.

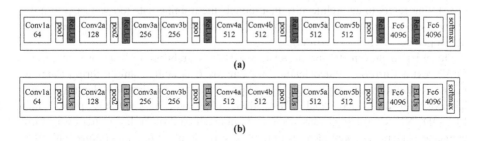

Fig. 1. Comparison of ELU-3DCNN and ReLU-3DCNN. (a) ReLU-3DCNN, (b) ELU-3DCNN.

2.2 3D-Convolution and Pooling

Compared with 2DCNNs, 3DCNNs has the ability to model temporal information better, owing to 3D convolutions and 3D pooling operations. The 3D convolution is achieved by convolving a 3D kernel to the cube formed by stacking multiple contiguous frames together. Similar to 3D convolution, the 3D pooling is achieved by performing a pooling operation to the cube after being convolved. Figure 2 illustrates the comparison between 2D convolutions and 3D convolutions. Different from 2D convolution (Fig. 2(a)), in 3D convolution (Fig. 2(b)), we convolve a 3D kernel to the cube formed by stacking multiple contiguous frames. In 3D convolutional layer, the value at position (x, y, z) on the jth feature map in the ith layer, denoted as v_{ij}^{xyz}, is given by:

$$v_{ij}^{xyz} = b_{ij} + \sum_m \sum_{p=0}^{P_i-1} \sum_q^{Q_i-1} \sum_{r=0}^{R_i-1} w_{ijm}^{pqr} v_{(i-1)m}^{(x+p)(y+q)(z+r)} \tag{2}$$

where b_{ij} is the bias for this feature map, w_{ijm}^{pqr} is the value at position (p, q, r) of the kernel connected to the mth feature map in the previous layer. P_i, Q_i and R_i are the height, width and the size of the 3D kernel along the temporal dimension, respectively.

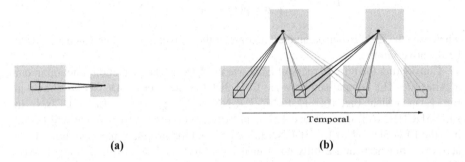

(a)   **(b)**

Fig. 2. Comparison of 2D convolutions and 3D convolutions. (a) 2D convolution, (b) 3D convolution.

2.3   Reduce Overfitting

Overfitting refers to an architecture that models the training data too well. Up to now, many methods including data augmentation, dropout, and weight decay have been developed for reducing overfitting.

In order to prevent the proposed ELU-3DCNN architecture from overfitting and further extract a robust video feature, we employ data augmentation during training. For each training video, three individual clips are extracted without overlap frames and labeled with the video label. Then, these clips will be randomly passed into ELU-3DCNN for training. Meanwhile, we implement a dropout layer after every fully connected layers. The key idea of dropout is to randomly drop units (along with their connections) from the neural networks during training. Moreover, we add weight decay as an extra term called regularization term to the cost function. The regularized cross-entropy loss function J(w) of the proposed architecture is defined as below:

$$J(w) = -\frac{1}{m} \sum_{i=1}^{m} \text{cost}\left(h_w\left(x^{(i)}\right), y^{(i)}\right) + \lambda \sum_{l=1}^{L} w_l^T w_l \tag{3}$$

where m is the number of samples, w represent the weight of the entire proposed architecture, w_l represent the weight between the layer $l - 1$ and the layer l, *cost* is the loss function between input $x^{(i)}$ which is labeled with $y^{(i)}$, and prediction $h_w\left(x^{(i)}\right)$, $\lambda > 0$ is known as the regularization parameter.

3 Application

3.1 Extracting Deep Feature from Mobile Video

After training on a large-scale supervised video dataset, we use ELU-3DCNN to extract deep video feature. The flowchart of deep video feature extraction is shown in Fig. 3. Firstly, a video is split into 16-frame long clips with 8-frame overlap between two consecutive clips. These clips are passed to the ELU-3DCNN to extract fc7 activations. Then, these clip activations are averaged to form a 4096-dim deep mobile video feature. After that, L2-normalization will be used to normalize the deep video feature. L2-normalization is defined as follows:

$$y = x / \sqrt[2]{\max\left(\sum_i^N x_i, \in\right)} \tag{4}$$

where x and y are the input and output of L2-normalization, respectively, N is the dimension of input and $\in$ is a very small number for avoiding zero denominator.

Fig. 3. The flowchart of deep video feature extraction.

3.2 Mobile Video Classification

After extracting deep feature from mobile videos, we classify mobile videos with a softmax classifier, which is denoted as:

$$y = \frac{1}{\sum_{j=1}^{k} e^{\theta_j^T x}} \left(e^{\theta_1^T x}, e^{\theta_2^T x}, \ldots, e^{\theta_k^T x}\right)^{\mathrm{T}} \tag{5}$$

where x and y are the input and output of the classifier, respectively. θ_k represents the parameters connected to the kth output unit. Figure 4 illustrates several video classification results of our proposed architecture.

Different from traditional deep architectures (i.e. the feature extraction and video classification are assembled into a single procedure), we perform the two steps separately. By adopting this strategy, we can further optimize the extracted feature by L2-normalization. Meanwhile, we can take advantage of convolutional neural networks (CNNs) to achieve video feature extraction and classification simultaneously.

Fig. 4. Several video classification results of the proposed architecture. The height of bin is the degree of probability.

4 Experiments

Mobile video usually has the characteristics of being short in time and small in volume. The statistical average duration of UCF-101 dataset is less than 8 s and the statistical average volume of UCF-101 dataset is less than 10 MB. Considering the characteristics of mobile video and the specialties of UCF-101 dataset, we utilized UCF-101 dataset to test the performance of the deep video feature. Firstly, we compared ELU-3DCNN with ReLU-3DCNN. Then, we performed experiments on the same dataset to make a comparison with other methods. The experimental platform is a PC with 3.3 GHz CPU, GeForce GTX 1080 GPU, 16 GB memory, Ubuntu 14.04 operating system and TensorFlow 1.0.

4.1 Comparison of ELU-3DCNN and ReLU-3DCNN

In order to evaluate the performance of the proposed architecture, ELU-3DCNN was compared with the original ReLU-3DCNN. Moreover, four evaluation criteria were used in our experiments, including training accuracy, validation accuracy, training loss and test accuracy. The results of ELU-3DCNN and ReLU-3DCNN are shown in Fig. 5. As can be seen that ELU-3DCNN indeed process a superior learning ability compared with ReLU-3DNN. Besides, ELU-3DCNN not only outperforms ReLU-3DCNN on the training accuracy and training loss, but also reaches a higher training efficiency. Meanwhile, the validation accuracy of ELU-3DCNN is also better than ReLU-3DCNN. Moreover, the final test accuracy of ELU-3DCNN is 84.5%, which outperforms the test accuracy of ReLU-3DCNN by 2.2%.

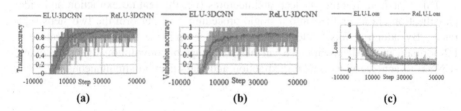

Fig. 5. The ELU-3DCNN's result compared with ReLU-3DCNN's. (a) Training accuracy. (b) Validation accuracy. (c) Training loss. The number of iterations 50000 approximately is 20 epochs.

4.2   Comparison of Other Video Feature Extraction Architectures

Next, we took a step forward to evaluate the performance of the proposed ELU-3DCNN architecture by comparing with the state-of-the-art video classification architectures. All architectures in our experiments only used RGB data (single or multiple frames). The video classification results are shown in Table 1.

Table 1. Performance comparison of video classification.

Method	Accuracy (%)
Deep networks [8]	65.4
LRCN [12]	71.1
Spatial stream network [10]	72.6
LSTM composite model [11]	75.8
iDT w/BoW + linear SVM [6]	76.2
ReLU + 3DCNN [13]	82.3
ELU + 3DCNN	**84.5**

ELU-3DCNN achieves 84.5% that is 8.3% higher than the state-of-the-art hand-crafted feature iDT [6]. In addition, compared with the deep networks [8] and spatial stream network [10], our architecture improves the accuracy by 19.1% and 11.9% respectively. Both deep networks and spatial stream network are sort of AlexNet architecture in which 2D convolution is used to extract feature. Compared with Recurrent Neural Networks (RNNs) based methods including LRCNs [12] and LSTM composite architecture [11], ELU-3DCNN outperforms Long-term Recurrent Convolutional Networks (LRCNs) and LSTM composite architecture by 13.4% and 8.7%, respectively. Moreover, compared with ReLU-3DCNN [13] the state-of-the-art method, ELU-3DCNN still make an improvement of 2.2%.

We can clearly see that, by modelling temporal and spatial information simultaneously through 3D convolution and 3D pooling operation, using 3DCNN to extract video feature is a better solution. Meanwhile, ELU-3DCNN outperforms ReLU-3DCNN by adopting exponential linear units (ELUs) as the activation function.

5   Conclusions

In this paper, in order to extract a more robust video feature for mobile video classification, we propose a 3D convolutional neural network named ELU-3DCNN trained on a large-scale video dataset UCF-101 to extract deep video feature from mobile videos. We replace rectified linear units (ReLUs) with exponential linear units (ELUs) in 3DCNN to produce a better performance. The experimental results show that our architecture can achieve a better mobile video classification performance.

In the future, considering the increasing amount of mobile video, a deeper 3D neural network will be studied to extract more abstract features. Moreover, since most videos are without labels, unsupervised deep learning for video feature extraction will become far more important in the long term. The visual semantic relationships [17] among deep video features will also be a worthy research field.

Acknowledgments. The work in this paper is supported by the National Natural Science Foundation of China (No. 61531006, No. 61602018), the Science and Technology Development Program of Beijing Education Committee (No. KM201510005004), the Importation and Development of High-Caliber Talents Project of Beijing Municipal Institutions (No. CIT&TCD20150311). Funding Project for Academic Human Resources Development in Institutions of Higher Learning Under the Jurisdiction of Beijing Municipality.

References

1. Deldjoo, Y., Elahi, M., Cremonesi, P., et al.: Content-based video recommendation system based on stylistic visual features. J. Data Semant. **5**(2), 99–113 (2016)
2. Hong, R., Hu, Z., Wang, R., Wang, M., Tao, D.: Multi-view object retrieval via multi-scale topic models. IEEE Trans. Image Process. **25**(12), 5814–5827 (2016)
3. Fernando, B., Gavves, E., Oramas, J., et al.: Rank pooling for action recognition. IEEE Trans. Pattern Anal. Mach. Intell. **39**(4), 773–787 (2017)
4. Coar, S., Donatiello, G., Bogorny, V., et al.: Toward abnormal trajectory and event detection in video surveillance. IEEE Trans. Circ. Syst. Video Technol. **27**(3), 683–695 (2017)
5. Hong, R., Zhang, L., Zhang, C., Zimmermann, R.: Flickr circles: aesthetic tendency discovery by multi-view regularized topic modeling. IEEE Trans. Multimed. **18**(8), 1555–1567 (2016)
6. Wang, H., Schmid, C.: Action recognition with improved trajectories. In: Proceedings of the IEEE International Conference on Computer Vision, pp. 3551–3558 (2013)
7. Krizhevsky, A., Sutskever, I., Hinton, G.E.: Imagenet classification with deep convolutional neural networks. In: Advances in Neural Information Processing Systems, pp. 1097–1105 (2012)
8. Karpathy, A., Toderici, G., Shetty, S., et al.: Large-scale video classification with convolutional neural networks. In: Proceedings of the IEEE Conference on Computer Vision and Pattern Recognition, pp. 1725–1732 (2014)
9. Ji, S., Xu, W., Yang, M., et al.: 3D convolutional neural networks for human action recognition. IEEE Trans. Pattern Anal. Mach. Intell. **35**(1), 221–231 (2013)
10. Simonyan, K., Zisserman, A.: Two-stream convolutional networks for action recognition in videos. In: Advances in Neural Information Processing Systems, pp. 568–576 (2014)
11. Srivastava, N., Mansimov, E., Salakhutdinov, R.: Unsupervised learning of video representations using LSTMs. In: Proceedings of the International Conference on Machine Learning, pp. 843–852 (2015)
12. Donahue, J., Anne Hendricks, L., Guadarrama, S., et al.: Long-term recurrent convolutional networks for visual recognition and description. In: Proceedings of the IEEE Conference on Computer Vision and Pattern Recognition, pp. 2625–2634 (2015)
13. Tran, D., Bourdev, L., Fergus, R., et al.: Learning spatiotemporal features with 3D convolutional networks. In: Proceedings of the IEEE International Conference on Computer Vision, pp. 4489–4497 (2015)
14. Nair, V., Hinton, G.E.: Rectified linear units improve restricted Boltzmann machines. In: Proceedings of the International Conference on Machine Learning, pp. 807–814 (2010)

15. Clevert, D.-A., Unterthiner, T., Hochreiter, S.: Fast and accurate deep network learning by exponential linear units. In: International Conferences on Learning Representations, pp. 3327–3341 (2016)
16. Srivastava, N., Hinton, G.E., Krizhevsky, A., et al.: Dropout: a simple way to prevent neural networks from overfitting. J. Mach. Learn. Res. **15**(1), 1929–1958 (2014)
17. Hong, R., Yang, Y., Wang, M., Hua, X.-S.: Learning visual semantic relationships for efficient visual retrieval. IEEE Trans. Big Data **1**(4), 152–161 (2015)

A Robust End-to-End Neural Network for Scene Text Detection

Qi Yuan[1,2], Haojie Li[1,2(✉)], Zhihui Wang[1,2], Xin Fan[1,2], and Zhongxuan Luo[1,2]

[1] DUT-RU International School of Information & Software Engineering,
Dalian University of Technology, Dalian, China
yqdlut@foxmail.com, hjli@dlut.edu.cn
[2] Key Laboratory for Ubiquitous Network and Service Software of Liaoning Province,
Dalian, China

Abstract. Scene text detection is an important task in computer vision. Many previous work require multi-step processing and are not robust against challenges, such as small-scales and blurring. In this paper, we propose a Multi-level Feature extraction Network (MLFN), which can capture more detailed information and is easy to train. We embed MLFN into the middle of an end-to-end network and achieve a better accuracy and robustness. The experiment results on ICDAR 2011 and ICDAR 2013 further demonstrate the effectiveness of our method.

Keywords: Scene text detection · Convolutional network · End-to-end

1 Introduction

Scene text detection has recently gained increasing attention from the computer vision community due to its numerous potential applications. However, this task still faces many challenges, which mainly come from significant diversity of text patterns and highly complicated background. For example, text can be in a very small size, or low quality, and even regular texts can be distorted considerably by uncontrollable environmental factors such as high light, occlusion, or blurring. Due to these challenges, text in natural scene has to be robustly detected before coming into service.

Most previous text detection methods are mainly based on sliding window and connected components. The sliding-window based [2,9] scan the image at different scales by using a sub-window, which is computationally expensive. Many connected component based methods have achieved promising results. Among them, Stroke Width Transform (SWT) [3,7] and Maximally Stable Extremal Regions [14,24] are the two most representative methods, which have high capability for detecting most character components in an image. However, these two traditional methods rely heavily on the performance of low-level text detector and well-designed parameters, and that is why they are not robust and highly sensitive to noise. Besides, they generate a large amount of false candidates and that is a great challenge to filter them out.

© Springer Nature Singapore Pte Ltd. 2018
B. Huet et al. (Eds.): ICIMCS 2017, CCIS 819, pp. 160–168, 2018.
https://doi.org/10.1007/978-981-10-8530-7_16

Recently, owning to the strong representation-capability of the deep Convolutional Neural Networks (CNN), more and more deep learning based methods [25,26] develop rapidly. Huang *et al.* [8] applied CNN model to learn high-level features from the MSERs components. He *et al.* [6] designed a text-attentional CNN model and substantially improved the previous performance. However, these methods just employ CNN models for classifying and still can not avoid multi-step processing such as filter and group, which are also not robust enough against noise and easily lead to serious error accumulation.

Inspired by the high performance method SSD [12] for object detection, we propose an end-to-end trainable neural network to detect text robustly. There are already some studies conducted based on this. For example, Liao *et al.* [11] proposed a fast and accurate text detector called TextBoxes, which is based on fully-convolutional network. Compared to TextBoxes, our proposed method has better robustness against challenging conditions such as small-scales, low resolution.

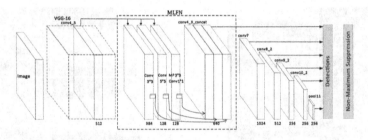

Fig. 1. Pipeline architecture of our model. Our method takes a natural image as input, directly predict text presence and bounding boxes. Our designed MLFN is shown in the red box. (Color figure online)

In this paper, we detect text by directly predicting text bounding boxes with a single neural network. Specially, we apply separate convolutional kernels to multiple feature maps from the later stages of our network, and then we jointly predict text presence and box offsets to its corresponding default boxes. With this method, we can perform text detection at multiple scales and do not need multi-step processing, which has greatly improve the detection accuracy. To handle challenging images, we designed Multi-level Feature extraction Network(MLFN) to capture more detailed information and handle text with small-scale and low resolution. It has been shown that the proposed MLFN improves the robustness of detection model, and more details are described in Sect. 4.

2   Related Work

Most current deep learning based methods for scene text detection are bottom-up. Although these methods have achieved promising results, there are still many problems, such as being sensitive to noise, requiring multi-step processing. In this research, to track the above problems caused by bottom-up strategy, inspired by SSD [12], we employ an end-to-end trainable model to directly predict text bounding boxes.

SSD is a feed-forward convolutional network for general object detection and it has outperformed other state of the art detection models such as Faster R-CNN [17], YOLO [16]. SSD procedures a fixed-size collection of bounding boxes and scores of object class instances in those boxes. However, it fails on objects that can be small or have extreme aspect ratios such as words. In this paper, we extend SSD to the more challenging scene text detection problem.

To handle more challenging texts such as small-scales, low-resolution and blurring, we propose MLFN, and embed it into the middle of aboved extended SSD framework. MLFN is inspired by GoogLeNet [21], which increases the depth and width of neural network to improve the performance. The experiments show that MLFN is essential to improve the robustness of detection model.

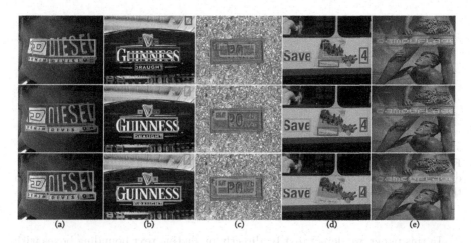

Fig. 2. Comparisons of our method (Bottom) with TextBoxes (Middle) and SSD (Top). The green bounding box are corresponding detections, and the red bounding box are missed detections. Obviously, the results suggest that our method is strongly robust against cluttered background, blurring, small-scales, and large character spacing. (Color figure online)

3   Robust Text Detection Network

3.1   Model

The architecture of our model is depicted in Fig. 1. It inherits SSD [12] architecture, which add many layers based on VGG-16 [20], namely conv6 to pool11. Based on this architecture, we insert proposed multi-level feature maps after the conv4_3 layer.

Multi-level Feature Extraction Network. In this paper, multiple feature layers are used for text classification and bounding box regression, where the layers decrease in size progressively and allow our model to predict at multiple scales. In the lower layers (the ones close to input), the feature maps correspond to the prediction of relatively small text. However, through analyzing data sets, we observed that small text often occurs with low resolution or slight blurring, which is difficult to locate accurately with a single convolutional feature layer.

To tackle this problem, we design multi-level feature layers for making full use of features of the lower layer and capturing more text information. [21] suggested that pooling operations have been an essential part of current state-of-art convolutional networks, and adding an alternative parallel pooling path before forming the input of next stage should have additional beneficial effect. Inspired by this idea, we use both pooling feature and convolutional feature to predict text location. Additionally, we use a layer of 1×1 convolution after the pooling layers to reduce dimension and keep the computational budget constant. Experiments show that our model has a better invariance against micro displacement by introducing additional pooling feature.

In the realization aspect, we apply multiple convolution and pooling kernels on a particular feature map to achieve local feature extraction. Specially, we employ 3×3 convolution, 5×5 convolution and 3×3 max pooling to extract text feature on the top of conv4_3 layer and combine these multi-level features. This method can capture more detailed text information, and it is more robust against small-scales and blurring.

Multiple Output Layers. To handle different text scales, we use multiple feature maps from different levels to simultaneously make detection predictions, following SSD [12]. For each of them, we associate a set of default boxes with every map location in a convolution manner. In other words, we predict both classification scores and shape offsets at every map location. For example, for a given location with k default boxes, we compute $2k$ scores and $4k$ offsets to its corresponding default boxes.

Considering the apparent characteristic of words, we impose 6 large aspect ratios for each default box and adopt irregular 1×5 convolutional kernels to replace the original 3×3 ones, following TextBoxes [11]. This design can better fit words and avoid noise.

3.2 Training

In the training phase, we adopt the same matching strategy and loss function as [12]. We match each ground truth to the default boxes with best or relatively large jaccard overlap, which simplify the learning process. Specially, when the i-th default box is matched to the j-th ground truth box, $x_{ij} = 1$ and $x_{ij} = 0$ otherwise. The objective loss function is as follows:

$$L\left(x, c, l, g\right) = \frac{1}{N}\left(L_{conf}\left(x, c\right) + \alpha L_{loc}\left(x, l, g\right)\right),$$

where N is the number of matched default boxes, c is the confidence, l is the predicted box, g is the ground truth box, and L_{conf} is a 2-class softmax loss. The localization loss L_{loc} applies smooth-L1 defined in [4], and α is set to 1. At the end of the network, we apply a non-maximum suppression to remove the redundant bounding boxes.

4   Experiments

4.1   Datasets and Experimental Setting

We evaluate our model on two benchmarks for text detection in natural scene: ICDAR 2011 [18], and ICDAR 2013 [10]. The ICDAR 2011 includes 229 and 255 images for training and testing, respectively. There are 229 training images and 233 test images in the ICDAR 2013. We follow the standard protocol proposed by [10,23] for evaluation.

We used the pre-trained VGG-16 [20] as initialization of our network, and trained our model on SynthText [5] for $50k$ iterations, which includes 800k synthesized text images. Then we finetune it on ICDAR 2013 using SGD with learning rate 10^{-4}, 0.9 momentum, and 5×10^{-4} weight decay for $5k$ iterations. We rescale the input image to two scales for testing our model, including 300×300 and 700×700.

4.2   Experimental Results on Full Text Detection

We compare our performance against recently published results on ICDAR 2011 and ICADR 2013 datasets, including traditional methods and CNN-based methods. The results are reported in Tables 1 and 2, where P, R and F indicate Precision, Recall and F-measure, respectively. Our method achieved the best performance among all these compared methods. Further, the high performance confirms the robustness and effectiveness of our proposed method.

Some detection examples are shown in Fig. 3, which contain many challenging conditions such as high light, shadow, small-scales and blurring. The qualitative detection results under these conditions demonstrate that our model is extremely robust against background noise, unconstrained illumination, and low resolution in natural scenes. Further, our model is also capable of detecting text with diverse patterns.

4.3   Evaluation of MLFN

To reveal the benifit of the MLFN, a comparison between our model and two most relevant detection models (namely TextBoxes [11] and SSD [12]) is conducted. Here, SSD is trained using the same procedures as ours and TextBoxes

Table 1. Experimental results on the ICDAR 2011 datasets

Methods	Year	P	R	F
Shi et al. [19]	2013	0.83	0.63	0.72
SFT-TCD [7]	2013	0.82	0.75	0.73
Yin et al. [24]	2014	0.86	0.68	0.75
MSERs-CNN [8]	2014	**0.88**	0.71	0.78
Zhang et al. [27]	2015	0.84	**0.76**	0.80
Fast TextBoxes [11]	2016	0.86	0.74	0.80
MLFN (ours)	-	0.86	0.74	**0.80**

model is offered by its author. The effect is shown in Fig. 2, from which, we can see that MLFN considerably outperforms the others.

Compared to TextBoxes and SSD, MLFN can capture more text information, which is greatly helpful to improve robustness against the challenge conditions. As shown in Fig. 2(a), our method is able to detect text with large character spacing, while TextBoxes and SSD failed. For text with low quality or blurring (see Fig. 2(c) and (d)), MLFN can locate accurately, in contrast, TextBoxes can only locate the distinct text regions and SSD generates many false positives. Moreover, even for very small-scale ones, MLFN also performs well. For example, the text in lower left of Fig. 2(b) can be detected accurately, but they are missed by TextBoxes and SSD. For dotted text in Fig. 2(e), although all the results are not good, the result by our method provides a roughly accurate detection, while there is no valuable detections for TextBoxes and SSD.

Table 2. Experimental results on the ICDAR 2013 datasets

Methods	Year	P	R	F
Text Spotter [14]	2012	0.88	0.65	0.72
Yin et al. [24]	2014	0.88	0.66	0.73
FASText [1]	2015	0.84	0.69	0.75
Neumann and Matas [15]	2015	0.82	0.72	0.78
Lu et al. [13]	2015	**0.89**	0.70	0.80
TextFlow [22]	2015	0.85	0.76	0.80
SSD [12]	2016	0.80	0.60	0.80
Fast TextBoxes [11]	2016	0.86	0.74	0.80
MLFN (ours)	-	0.87	**0.75**	**0.80**

Fig. 3. MLFN detection results on several challenging images. The green bounding box are correct detections. (Color figure online)

5   Conclusions

In this paper, we have presented an end-to-end trainable neural network for text detection in natural scenes. Our proposed Multi-level Feature Extraction Network can capture more detailed text information, and make our models more robust against some challenging conditions. Experimental results show that our approach achieved competitive performance on ICDAR 2011 and ICADR 2013 datasets. In future, we are interested to apply recurrent neural network to our framework for taking advantage of context information.

Acknowledgement. This work was partially supported by National Natural Science Funds of China (61472059, 61632019).

References

1. Busta, M., Neumann, L., Matas, J.: FASText: efficient unconstrained scene text detector. In: Proceedings of the IEEE International Conference on Computer Vision, pp. 1206–1214 (2015)
2. Chen, X., Yuille, A.L.: Detecting and reading text in natural scenes. In: Proceedings of the 2004 IEEE Computer Society Conference on Computer Vision and Pattern Recognition, CVPR 2004, vol. 2, p. II. IEEE (2004)
3. Epshtein, B., Ofek, E., Wexler, Y.: Detecting text in natural scenes with stroke width transform. In: 2010 IEEE Conference on Computer Vision and Pattern Recognition (CVPR), pp. 2963–2970. IEEE (2010)

4. Girshick, R.: Fast R-CNN. In: Proceedings of the IEEE International Conference on Computer Vision, pp. 1440–1448 (2015)
5. Gupta, A., Vedaldi, A., Zisserman, A.: Synthetic data for text localisation in natural images. In: Proceedings of the IEEE Conference on Computer Vision and Pattern Recognition, pp. 2315–2324 (2016)
6. He, T., Huang, W., Qiao, Y., Yao, J.: Text-attentional convolutional neural network for scene text detection. IEEE Trans. Image Process. **25**(6), 2529–2541 (2016)
7. Huang, W., Lin, Z., Yang, J., Wang, J.: Text localization in natural images using stroke feature transform and text covariance descriptors. In: Proceedings of the IEEE International Conference on Computer Vision, pp. 1241–1248 (2013)
8. Huang, W., Qiao, Y., Tang, X.: Robust scene text detection with convolution neural network induced MSER trees. In: Fleet, D., Pajdla, T., Schiele, B., Tuytelaars, T. (eds.) ECCV 2014. LNCS, vol. 8692, pp. 497–511. Springer, Cham (2014). https://doi.org/10.1007/978-3-319-10593-2_33
9. Jaderberg, M., Vedaldi, A., Zisserman, A.: Deep features for text spotting. In: Fleet, D., Pajdla, T., Schiele, B., Tuytelaars, T. (eds.) ECCV 2014. LNCS, vol. 8692, pp. 512–528. Springer, Cham (2014). https://doi.org/10.1007/978-3-319-10593-2_34
10. Karatzas, D., Shafait, F., Uchida, S., Iwamura, M., i Bigorda, L.G., Mestre, S.R., Mas, J., Mota, D.F., Almazan, J.A., de las Heras, L.P.: ICDAR 2013 robust reading competition. In: 2013 12th International Conference on Document Analysis and Recognition (ICDAR), pp. 1484–1493. IEEE (2013)
11. Liao, M., Shi, B., Bai, X., Wang, X., Liu, W.: TextBoxes: a fast text detector with a single deep neural network. arXiv arXiv:1611.06779 (2016)
12. Liu, W., Anguelov, D., Erhan, D., Szegedy, C., Reed, S., Fu, C.-Y., Berg, A.C.: SSD: single shot multibox detector. In: Leibe, B., Matas, J., Sebe, N., Welling, M. (eds.) ECCV 2016. LNCS, vol. 9905, pp. 21–37. Springer, Cham (2016). https://doi.org/10.1007/978-3-319-46448-0_2
13. Lu, S., Chen, T., Tian, S., Lim, J.H., Tan, C.L.: Scene text extraction based on edges and support vector regression. Int. J. Doc. Anal. Recognit. (IJDAR) **18**(2), 125–135 (2015)
14. Neumann, L., Matas, J.: Real-time scene text localization and recognition. In: 2012 IEEE Conference on Computer Vision and Pattern Recognition (CVPR), pp. 3538–3545. IEEE (2012)
15. Neumann, L., Matas, J.: Efficient scene text localization and recognition with local character refinement. In: 2015 13th International Conference on Document Analysis and Recognition (ICDAR), pp. 746–750. IEEE (2015)
16. Redmon, J., Divvala, S., Girshick, R., Farhadi, A.: You only look once: unified, real-time object detection. In: Proceedings of the IEEE Conference on Computer Vision and Pattern Recognition, pp. 779–788 (2016)
17. Ren, S., He, K., Girshick, R., Sun, J.: Faster R-CNN: towards real-time object detection with region proposal networks. In: Advances in Neural Information Processing Systems, pp. 91–99 (2015)
18. Shahab, A., Shafait, F., Dengel, A.: ICDAR 2011 robust reading competition challenge 2: reading text in scene images. In: 2011 International Conference on Document Analysis and Recognition (ICDAR), pp. 1491–1496. IEEE (2011)
19. Shi, C., Wang, C., Xiao, B., Zhang, Y., Gao, S.: Scene text detection using graph model built upon maximally stable extremal regions. Pattern Recognit. Lett. **34**(2), 107–116 (2013)
20. Simonyan, K., Zisserman, A.: Very deep convolutional networks for large-scale image recognition. arXiv preprint arXiv:1409.1556 (2014)

21. Szegedy, C., Liu, W., Jia, Y., Sermanet, P., Reed, S., Anguelov, D., Erhan, D., Vanhoucke, V., Rabinovich, A.: Going deeper with convolutions. In: Proceedings of the IEEE Conference on Computer Vision and Pattern Recognition, pp. 1–9 (2015)
22. Tian, S., Pan, Y., Huang, C., Lu, S., Yu, K., Tan, L.C.: Text flow: a unified text detection system in natural scene images. In: Proceedings of the IEEE International Conference on Computer Vision, pp. 4651–4659 (2015)
23. Wolf, C., Jolion, J.M.: Object count/area graphs for the evaluation of object detection and segmentation algorithms. IJDAR **8**(4), 280–296 (2006)
24. Yin, X.C., Yin, X., Huang, K., Hao, H.W.: Robust text detection in natural scene images. IEEE Trans. Pattern Anal. Mach. Intell. **36**(5), 970–983 (2014)
25. Zhang, H., Kyaw, Z., Chang, S.F., Chua, T.S.: Visual translation embedding network for visual relation detection. In: CVPR (2017)
26. Zhang, H., Shang, X., Luan, H., Wang, M., Chua, T.S.: Learning from collective intelligence: feature learning using social images and tags. ACM Trans. Multimed. Comput. Commun. Appl. (TOMM) **13**, 1 (2016)
27. Zhang, Z., Shen, W., Yao, C., Bai, X.: Symmetry-based text line detection in natural scenes. In: Proceedings of the IEEE Conference on Computer Vision and Pattern Recognition, pp. 2558–2567 (2015)

Multimedia Retrieval

Exploiting Concept Correlation with Attributes for Semantic Binary Representation Learning

Haiping Wu, Yang Yang, Xing Xu$^{(\boxtimes)}$ ⓘ, Fumin Shen, Ning Xie, and Yanli Ji

Center for Future Media and School of Computer Science and Engineering,
University of Electronic Science and Technology of China, Chengdu, China
xing.xu@uestc.edu.cn

Abstract. Recent years have witnessed the unprecedented efforts of visual representation for enabling various efficient and effective multimedia applications. In this paper, we propose a novel visual representation framework, which generates efficient semantic hash codes for visual samples by substantially exploring concepts, semantic attributes as well as their inter-correlations. Specifically, we construct a conceptual space, where the semantic knowledge of concepts and attributes is embedded. Then, we develop an effective on-line feature coding scheme for visual objects by leveraging the inter-concept relationships through the intermediate representative power of attributes. The code process is formulated as an overlapping group lasso problem, which can be efficiently solved. Finally, we binarize the visual representation to generate efficient hash codes. Extensive experiments have illustrated the superiority of our proposed framework on visual retrieval task as compared to state-of-the-art methods.

Keywords: Visual computing · Hashing · Semantics

1 Introduction

Recently visual representation has become a vital part of computer vision applications (*e.g.* image recognition [1–3] and image retrieval [4–7]). Methods vary from raw feature extraction, to high-level feature statistics such Bag-of-Words, and today more complex feature extraction framework like deep neural network. However, the above artificial frameworks are obvious inferior [8] compared to our humans. Further, it has been widely recognized that a good visual representation should integrate both low-level visual features addressing the more detailed perceptual aspects and high-level semantic features underlying the more general conceptual aspects of visual data [9,10]. Many efforts have been devoted to reduce this semantic gap between low-level visual features and high-level semantic features [11,12], in this work, we aim to reduce this semantic gap through finding the correlation between low-level features and high-level concepts to obtain better visual representation.

© Springer Nature Singapore Pte Ltd. 2018
B. Huet et al. (Eds.): ICIMCS 2017, CCIS 819, pp. 171–179, 2018.
https://doi.org/10.1007/978-981-10-8530-7_17

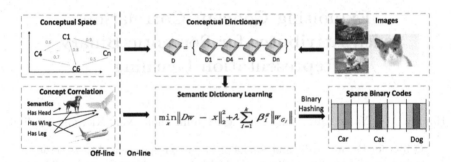

Fig. 1. The proposed visual representation framework. In the off-line stage, dictionaries in the conceptual space are learned. Then inter-concept correlation are exploited by leveraging semantic attributes. In the on-line stage, overlapping groups are formed using the correlation information and then group sparsity are imposed to generate features using dictionaries obtained in the off-line stage. At last, hashing methods are used to generate compact binary representation.

In order to capture high-level semantics and cross category properties, attributes [13] has been proposed, which offers an important intermediate representation. As human recognize objects by finding their main attributes in high-level concepts, attributes description is more explainable and could be used to describe unknown category objects. Thus, by leveraging high-level attribute information with low-level features, we could obtain more compact and discriminative features across categories and further reduce the semantic gap. Specifically, the more semantic attributes two concepts share, the similar the two concepts are, such as "cat" and "dog" share many attributes together like "fur", "has head", and they are conceptually similar. Then we could use dictionary learning scheme in the coding process to efficiently solve this correlation embedding and feature selection problem.

In this paper, we propose a novel binary visual representation learning framework which exploits the semantic attributes to reduce semantic gap and generate binary codes for visual representation. As illustrated in Fig. 1, the proposed framework exploits concept correlation relationships in the off-line stage and further encodes concept-rich sparse visual representation in the on-line stage. We summarize our contribution as follows:

Semantic Binary Learning Framework. The proposed framework adapts hashing schemes to generate binary codes for visual representation. Extensive experiments for visual retrieval tasks have been conducted compared to several state-of-art hashing methods and salient performance boost could be observed.

Dictionary Learning in Conceptual Space. The proposed framework learns dictionaries in conceptual space, which holds objects that if are conceptually similar, then they are close in the conceptual space.

Exploit Concept Correlation. The proposed framework utilizes the semantic attribute information to exploit the inter-concept correlation, which combines low-level features and high-level semantics in efficient way and thus reduce the semantic gap.

2   The Proposed Framework

In this section, we elaborate our proposed framework in terms of the off-line and on-line stages.

2.1   OFF-LINE: Dictionary Learning in the Conceptual Space

In off-line stage, we obtain the dictionary bases in the conceptual space and exploit the concepts correlation by utilizing attribute correlation information.

Conceptual Space Dictionary. In our work, we aim to construct a semantic-enriched dictionary by mapping the original images to the conceptual space. Close objects in conceptual space should be conceptual similar. Suppose we have n samples $\mathbf{X} = [\mathbf{x_1}, \mathbf{x_2}, \cdots, \mathbf{x_n}] \in \mathbb{R}^{m \times n}$. We map the samples from original space to conceptual space by the projection:

$$\|\mathbf{X} - \mathbf{D_c}\mathbf{S}\|, \tag{1}$$

where $\mathbf{D_c} \in \mathbb{R}^{m \times k}$ is the bases of the conceptual space, and $\mathbf{S} \in \mathbb{R}^{k \times n}$ is the new representation in the conceptual space.

Learning Bases of Concepts. Category is a nature choice for conceptual space, where each concept is implicitly corresponding to one category. In order to effectively exploit the images and category label information to construct conceptual space, we choose to obtain the bases' representations of each category using the classification hyperplanes learned from logistic regression, which split categories from each other:

$$\min_{\mathbf{d},c} \frac{1}{2}\mathbf{d}^\mathbf{T}\mathbf{d} + C \sum_{i=1}^{n} \log(exp(-\mathbf{y^i}(\mathbf{X_i^T}\mathbf{d} + c)) + 1), \tag{2}$$

where y^i is the category label for each sample $\mathbf{X_i}$, C is the reverse of regularization strength, and smaller C specify stronger regularization, $\mathbf{d}$ is the classification hyperplane we need ($\mathbf{D_c} = [\mathbf{d_1}, \mathbf{d_2}, \cdots, \mathbf{d_k}]$). For each category, we learn the hyperplane that could tell samples from whether belong to the category. Then, bases of conceptual space are made up of the hyperplanes. In this way, our dictionary has the natural power of generating discriminative features that could be easily used in the classification task.

Modeling Concepts Correlation with Semantic Attributes. Co-occurrence statistics contain meaningful information about correlation relationship. The more semantic attributes two concepts share, the similar the two concepts are. Thus we propose to group the conceptual dictionary bases by leveraging attribute information. In our experiment, a group is formed by selecting which bases share the same attribute, that is, if there are m attributes, there should be m groups where each group all share the same attribute. The formed groups are defined as:

$$\mathbf{G_i} = [j \text{ for } concept_j \text{ has } attribute_i]. \tag{3}$$

If two conceptual dictionary bases are divided into one group, it indicates that they are somehow conceptually connected through attributes. Groups could be overlapping due to classes often share more than one attributes, which means one concept is similar to another concept in multiple attribute aspects.

2.2   ON-LINE: Binary Visual Representation Generation

As the dictionary bases of conceptual space and the relationships of concepts have been obtained in the off-line stage, in this stage, we adapt dictionary learning and hashing methods to produce our semantic binary representation.

Semantic Visual Coding. New representation in the conceptual space could be obtained by using the projection illustrated by the Eq. (1). **S** is the reconstruction in the conceptual space. However, the conceptual space bases contain the whole classes in the dataset, out of which many bases would not be used to reconstruct the feature for one specific image. Thus, variable selection methods could be used to impose sparsity on the reconstruction weight of bases which generates more explainable features. We use group-based lasso [14] to solve the variable selection problem. The forming groups could be non-overlapping or overlapping, we obtain our new feature representation by separately handle these two situation. The lasso [15] estimate is defined by

$$\hat{\beta}^{lasso} = \arg\min_{\beta} \{\frac{1}{2}\sum_{i=1}^{N}(\mathbf{y_i} - \beta_0 - \sum_{j=1}^{p}\mathbf{x_{ij}}\beta j)^2 + \lambda\sum_{j=1}^{p}|\beta_j|\}. \tag{4}$$

Here, λ is a tuning parameter that controls the amount of shrinkage: the larger the value of λ, the greater the amount of shrinkage. The l_1-norm penalty induces sparsity in the solution. In our work, each conceptual dictionary base may be divided into one or more than one groups, thus we select our variables in two cases, non-overlapping and overlapping by imposing group sparsity and overlapping group sparsity penalty.

Visual Coding with Concept Correlation. In the case of overlapping concept correlation where formed groups are overlapped, we impose (overlapping) group sparsity penalty when learning the visual representation. The variables selection and visual representation learning process could be formalized as the follow:

$$\min_{\mathbf{v}} \|\mathbf{D_c v} - \mathbf{x}\|_2^2 + \lambda_1\|\mathbf{v}\|_1 + \lambda_2\sum_{i=1}^{k}\beta_i^g\|\mathbf{v_{G_i}}\|, \tag{5}$$

where $\mathbf{D_c} \in \mathbb{R}^{m \times k}$ is the bases of the conceptual space. $\mathbf{x} \in \mathbb{R}^{m \times 1}$ is the original feature, $\mathbf{v} \in \mathbb{R}^{k \times 1}$ is the new feature. The groups $\mathbf{G_i}$ may overlap, and β_i^g

is the weight for the i-th group. The obtained new visual representation $\mathbf{v}$ is not only sparse, but also contains salient conceptual and attribute information. Equation 5 is a standard sparse dictionary learning problem, and in practice it can be efficiently solved by the the SLEP software [16].

Binary Representation Generation. In order to generate compact binary codes, we utilize existing hashing methods to generate binary hashing codes. Unsupervised and supervised learning methods are adapted to evaluate our generated features. Take ITQ [17] for example, we first do PCA projection converting $\mathbf{V} = [\mathbf{v_1}, \mathbf{v_2}, \cdots, \mathbf{v_n}]$ obtained from Eq. (5) to $\mathbf{V}' \in \mathbb{R}^{l \times n}$, l is the code length. Then the objective function is described as:

$$\|\mathbf{B} - \mathbf{V}'^{\mathbf{T}}\mathbf{R}\|_F^2, \tag{6}$$

where $\mathbf{B} \in \{-1, 1\}^{l \times n}$ is the final binary codes, $\mathbf{R} \in \mathbb{R}^{l \times l}$ is the rotation matrix, and $\|\cdot\|_F$ denotes the Frobenuis norm.

3   Experiments

3.1   Datasets and Configuration

Animals with Attributes (AWA). The AWA dataset consists of 30475 images, 50 classes, 85 numeric attribute values. Features are 4096-dimension vectors of fc-7 layer of VGG-19, pretained on ILSVRC2014. We randomly select two-thirds of each concept (class) as the off-line stage training dataset, and the left one-third as the on-line stage testing dataset, which gives us 15226 images for the off-line stage and 10172 images for the on-line stage.

aPascal and aYahoo dataset. aYahoo dataset contains 2644 visual objects, 12 categories. In our experiment, we use the whole aPascal dataset in the off-line stage to obtain concept dictionaries and exploit concept correlation. And we use the whole aYahoo dataset in the on-line stage to evaluate our framework. This also helps evaluate the generalization abilities of our framework.

For evaluation metrics, we chose commonly used Average Precision (AP) and mean Average Precision (mAP). For AWA dataset, we randomly choose 1000 samples in the testing phase, and for aPascal dataset, we randomly choose 100 samples in the testing phase.

3.2   Results and Discussions

We evaluate our proposed framework by comparing with deep neural network representation [18] on AWA dataset, and method designed by [13] on aPascal dataset. As illustrated, Table 1 shows the results of mAP on AWA dataset using unsupervised and supervised hashing methods. We can observe from the results that our proposed framework can achieve obvious improvements in terms of retrieval performance over other methods on AWA dataset. Our proposed framework boosts the performance of unsupervised and supervised hashing methods.

Table 1. mAP Comparison on AWA dataset

Method		8 bits	16 bits	32 bits	48 bits
ITQ	Fc-7	0.6067	0.6871	0.7529	0.7926
	Ours	0.5839	0.6867	**0.7660**	**0.8064**
LSH	Fc-7	0.1934	0.2557	0.3319	0.4143
	Ours	**0.3060**	**0.4528**	**0.5609**	**0.6538**
SKLSH	Fc-7	0.1705	0.1794	0.1928	0.2677
	Ours	**0.1851**	**0.2341**	**0.2805**	**0.3123**
COSDISH	Fc-7	0.4226	0.7590	0.8317	0.8622
	Ours	**0.6970**	**0.8924**	**0.9152**	**0.8907**
KSH	Fc-7	0.4566	0.6254	0.7018	0.7385
	Ours	**0.5317**	**0.6418**	**0.7407**	**0.7619**
FastHash	Fc-7	0.7093	0.8314	0.8644	0.8835
	Ours	**0.8374**	**0.8912**	**0.9016**	**0.9084**

Take 48 bits codes for example, our proposed framework outperforms CNN representation by around 1.74%, 57.80%, 20.39% for ITQ [17], LSH [19] and SKLSH [20] hashing methods, and around 3.31%, 3.17%, 2.82% for COSDISH [21], KSH [22], and FashHash [23] hashing methods. The underlying reasons are two folds. First of all, our framework works in the conceptual space where similar concepts could be close in this space. Second, our framework efficiently exploit the concepts correlation by using semantic attribute information, thus reducing semantic gap.

Table 2. mAP on aYahoo dataset

Method		4 bits	8 bits	12 bits	16 bits	20 bits
ITQ	[13]	0.7117	0.7621	0.7872	0.8003	0.8124
	Ours	**0.8532**	**0.8721**	**0.9064**	**0.9207**	**0.9282**
LSH	[13]	0.5261	0.5242	0.5384	0.5448	0.5704
	Ours	**0.7213**	**0.7201**	**0.8090**	**0.8181**	**0.7990**
COSDISH	[13]	0.1541	0.2219	0.3082	0.3720	0.3191
	Ours	**0.3893**	**0.4701**	**0.5146**	**0.5665**	**0.5539**

Table 2 reports the mAP performance for our proposed framework and the method designed by [13] on aYahoo dataset. Figure 2 shows the detailed performance (AP) of individual concepts on aYahoo dataset. We can see from the results that our proposed framework achieve better performance of all individual concepts for all the hashing methods we use. This consistently validates the advantages of our framework. Notice that, the dictionary bases and concepts

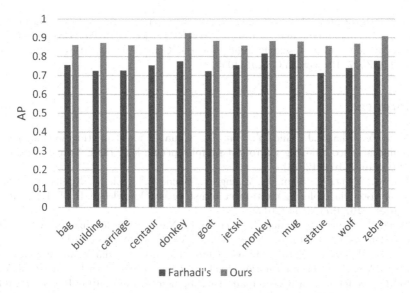

Fig. 2. Average precision of individual concepts for visual retrieval on aYahoo dataset.

correlation relationships for aYahoo dataset are not derived from the dataset itself but from aPascal dataset. This further shows the salient performance and generalization abilities of our framework.

Moreover, we can observe from Tables 1 and 2 that the improvement of our proposed framework highly depends on the hashing methods we adapt. For example, we obtain 1.74% improvement using ITQ, compared to 57.80% using LSH for 48 bits on AWA dataset. We infer that this is because some hashing methods utilize the data better than others, thus our framework boosts less using these methods compared to others. We could also observe that the improvement varies with code length. We assume the reason that there is a best code length suitable for the hashing methods to interpret the dataset, thus influencing the performance boost of our framework.

4   Conclusion

In this paper, we introduced a novel binary visual representation learning framework to effectively exploit inter-concept correlation. Through the designed framework, we generated a concept-enriched dictionary and exploit concepts correlation by utilizing semantic attribute information. We proposed to impose overlapping group sparsity on the conceptual dictionaries, which achieves a better variable selection process. Also, we show the generalization ability of our framework by using different datasets in the off-line and on-line stages. In the future, we will further investigate an automatic way for group the dictionaries as well as exploit the inter-concept correlation.

Acknowledgments. This work was supported in part by the National Natural Science Foundation of China under Project 61572108, Project 61632007, Project 61602089 and the Fundamental Research Funds for the Central Universities under Project ZYGX2014Z007, Project ZYGX2015J055.

References

1. Yang, Y., Zha, Z.J., Gao, Y., Zhu, X., Chua, T.S.: Exploiting web images for semantic video indexing via robust sample-specific loss. IEEE Trans. Multimedia **16**(6), 1677–1689 (2014)
2. Hu, M., Yang, Y., Shen, F., Zhang, L., Shen, H.T., Li, X.: Robust web image annotation via exploring multi-facet and structural knowledge. IEEE Trans. Image Process. **26**, 4871–4884 (2017)
3. Yang, Y., Yang, Y., Huang, Z., Shen, H.T., Nie, F.: Tag localization with spatial correlations and joint group sparsity. In: CVPR, pp. 881–888 (2011)
4. Nie, L., Wang, M., Zha, Z., Li, G., Chua, T.S.: Multimedia answering: enriching text QA with media information. In: Proceedings of the 34th International ACM SIGIR Conference on Research and Development in Information Retrieval, SIGIR 2011, pp. 695–704 (2011)
5. Nie, L., Wang, M., Zha, Z.J., Chua, T.S.: Oracle in image search: a content-based approach to performance prediction. ACM Trans. Inf. Syst. **30**(2), 13:1–13:23 (2012)
6. Xu, X., Shen, F., Yang, Y., Shen, H.T., Li, X.: Learning discriminative binary codes for large-scale cross-modal retrieval. IEEE Trans. Image Processing **26**(5), 2494–2507 (2017)
7. Xu, X., He, L., Shimada, A., Taniguchi, R., Lu, H.: Learning unified binary codes for cross-modal retrieval via latent semantic hashing. Neurocomputing **213**, 191–203 (2016)
8. Yang, Y., Zhang, H., Zhang, M., Shen, F., Li, X.: Visual coding in a semantic hierarchy. In: MM, pp. 59–68 (2015)
9. Shih, T.K.: Distributed Multimedia Databases: Techniques and Applications. IGI Global, Hershey (2002)
10. Yang, Y., Luo, Y., Chen, W., Shen, F., Shao, J., Shen, H.T.: Zero-shot hashing via transferring supervised knowledge. In: Proceedings of the 2016 ACM on Multimedia Conference, pp. 1286–1295 (2016)
11. Yang, Y., Zhang, H., Zhang, M., Shen, F., Li, X.: Visual coding in a semantic hierarchy. In: Proceedings of the 23rd ACM International Conference on Multimedia, MM 2015, pp. 59–68 (2015)
12. Nie, L., Yan, S., Wang, M., Hong, R., Chua, T.S.: Harvesting visual concepts for image search with complex queries. In: Proceedings of the 20th ACM International Conference on Multimedia, pp. 59–68 (2012)
13. Farhadi, A., Endres, I., Hoiem, D., Forsyth, D.: Describing objects by their attributes. In: CVPR, pp. 1778–1785 (2009)
14. Jacob, L., Obozinski, G., Vert, J.P.: Group lasso with overlap and graph lasso. In: ICML, pp. 433–440 (2009)
15. Tibshirani, R.: Regression shrinkage and selection via the lasso. J. R. Stat. Soc. Ser. B (Methodol.) 267–288 (1996)
16. Liu, J., Ji, S., Ye, J.: SLEP: Sparse Learning with Efficient Projections. Arizona State University (2009)

17. Gong, Y., Lazebnik, S.: Iterative quantization: a procrustean approach to learning binary codes. In: CVPR, pp. 817–824 (2011)
18. Simonyan, K., Zisserman, A.: Very deep convolutional networks for large-scale image recognition. arXiv preprint arXiv:1409.1556 (2014)
19. Datar, M., Immorlica, N., Indyk, P., Mirrokni, V.S.: Locality-sensitive hashing scheme based on p-stable distributions. In: SCG, pp. 253–262. ACM (2004)
20. Raginsky, M., Lazebnik, S.: Locality-sensitive binary codes from shift-invariant kernels. In: NIPS, pp. 1509–1517 (2009)
21. Kang, W.C., Li, W.J., Zhou, Z.H.: Column sampling based discrete supervised hashing. In: AAAI, pp. 1230–1236 (2016)
22. Liu, W., Wang, J., Ji, R., Jiang, Y.G., Chang, S.F.: Supervised hashing with kernels. In: CVPR, pp. 2074–2081 (2012)
23. Lin, G., Shen, C., Shi, Q., van den Hengel, A., Suter, D.: Fast supervised hashing with decision trees for high-dimensional data. In: CVPR, pp. 1963–1970 (2014)

Image Retrieval Based on Optimized Visual Dictionary and Adaptive Soft Assignment

Hui Liu[(✉)], Zechao Li, and Xiangbo Shu

Nanjing University of Science and Technology, Nanjing, China
hui_liu04@163.com, {zechao.li,shuxb}@njust.edu.cn

Abstract. In this work, we propose a new image retrieval scheme by identifying better visual representations and fusing multiple similarities based on multiple features. For visual representation, we propose a new coarse-to-fine visual dictionary construction method based on the bag-of-features model. An adaptive soft assignment technique is developed to assign one local descriptor to several nearest visual words. To leverage the advantages of different features, a fusion strategy based on similarities is introduced to fuse multiple features. Experimental results demonstrate the effectiveness of the proposed method for image retrieval.

Keywords: Bag-of-features · Visual dictionary
Adaptive soft assignment · Image retrieval · Image representation

1 Introduction

With the development of the digital technology and intelligent mobile devices, the number of images grows exponentially. It is difficult for people to find their desired images accurately and quickly. Content based image retrieval is proposed to solve the problem by analyzing the visual contents of images. Due to the well-known semantic gap [1], it is challenging to find very similar images for one query. Consequently, it is necessary to develop more effective CBIR approaches.

A number of methods have been proposed to describe the global low-level features of images, such as color, texture and shape [2,3]. However, the global features cannot well describe the visual information, which results to the limited performance. As we know, images contain several objects corresponding to different labels, while users are always interested in only one object. Local features can be used to describe the images in separate regions, and capture the important properties of some specific objects [4–6]. Thus, local features, such as Scale-invariant Feature Transform (SIFT) [7], Speed up Robust Feature (SURF) [8] and Histogram of Oriented Gradients (HOG) [9], have attracted more attention in CIBR system. Nevertheless, the superiority of global features that are able to capture the abstract semantic similarity should not be ignored. Accordingly, a graph-based query specific fusion approach is proposed to integrate the superiority of local and holistic features for different query images [10].

© Springer Nature Singapore Pte Ltd. 2018
B. Huet et al. (Eds.): ICIMCS 2017, CCIS 819, pp. 180–190, 2018.
https://doi.org/10.1007/978-981-10-8530-7_18

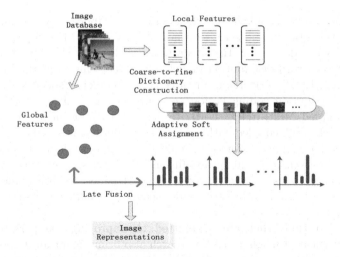

Fig. 1. The proposed framework for constructing image representations with multiple features.

To handle the massive images, some methods are proposed to improve retrieval performance based on the Bag of Features model (BoF) [11]. The BoF model first defines a visual dictionary or codebook containing numbers of visual words [11,12]. These visual words are generated by unsupervised learning such as K-means [13]. For a single image, the conventional BoF model is eventually expressed as the frequency histogram of the visual words using the hard assignment method, which is also the representation of the visual dictionary. However, both the process of generating visual dictionary and frequency histogram bring in quantization distortions, which degrades the performance.

Towards this end, we propose a new coarse-to-fine visual dictionary construction method based on the bag-of-features model for image retrieval, as shown in Fig. 1. To reduce the quantization distortions, we first introduce the optimized product quantization technique [14] into the Bag-of-Features model and propose to find a discriminative coarse-to-fine visual dictionary. Different from the previous hard assignment scheme, an adaptive soft assignment between feature points and visual words is utilized to construct image representation. In addition, to fully explore the advantages of different features, a fusion strategy is introduced to integrate the local and global features by an improved weighting strategy. Experiments are conducted and the results demonstrate the effectiveness of the proposed method for image retrieval.

2   Related Work

To improve the performance of content based image retrieval [15], a number of methods and algorithms are proposed in recent years. Yu et al. [16] proposed the features integration frameworks of image based and patch based SIFT-LBP, HOG-LBP. The weighted average k-means clustering balances the importance between the two kinds of features when training codebooks. Tian et al. [17] proposed a novel rotation and scale invariant Edge Oriented Difference Histogram (EODH) feature descriptor. He integrates it with color SIFT by constructing a weighted codeword distribution model. The feature fusion method is extracting SIFT and EODH features from three color channels respectively. Then the weighted distribution coding is done for each channel. Zheng et al. [18] proposed a coupled Multi-Index (c-MI) framework to perform feature fusion at indexing level. SFIT coupled with color features significantly reduce the impact of false positive matches. Moreover, multiple assignment, hamming embedding [19], burstiness weighting [20], graph fusion [10, 21, 22] are combined to improve the precision and recall of the retrieval results. Besides, recently some methods based on deep learning framework have achieved remarkable results in image retrieval [23, 24].

Some algorithms that are committed to improving the performance of approximate nearest neighbor (ANN) search also bring significant improvements to retrieval quality and efficiency in CIBR system. Approximate nearest neighbor (ANN) search has been applied to computer vision field such as image retrieval [25], image classification [26] and object recognition [27]. Vector quantization [28] can also construct compact codes for a large number of local features. Iterative quantization [29] proposed by Gong and Lazebnik is an efficient alternating minimization scheme for finding a rotation of zero centered data so as to minimize the quantization error of mapping this data to the vertices of a zero-centered binary hypercube. Product quantization [30] is used to map a feature vector to its nearest visual word in the predefined codebook which is composed by the Cartesian product of a finite number of sub-codebooks. Ge et al. proposed an Optimized Product Quantization [14] method that minimizes the quantization distortions by searching for optimal codebooks and space decomposition. It treats product quantization as an optimization problem and achieves little quantization distortions for approximate nearest neighbor search.

3   Proposed Method

3.1   The Coarse-to-Fine Dictionary Construction

When the vector dimension or the size of visual dictionary is large, K-means based quantization method achieves low computation efficiency and accuracy in conventional BoF model. Product quantization [30] is a semi-structured quantizer which achieves a large effective size of visual dictionary or codebook with the Cartesian product of a set of small sub codebooks. It decomposes high-dimensional feature vectors to low-dimensional subspaces and quantizes each subspace respectively. Cartesian product enables to calculate distances between codewords of each subspace which are to be stored in tables in advance. Moreover, it prevents similar feature vectors from quantizing to different clusters which leads to low quantization distortions and more precise distance computation using a set of small lookup tables. We preliminarily cluster features extracted from images and take the pre-clustering centroids

Table 1. Average retrieval precision by the proposed methods and other image retrieval system on Corel1K.

Class	[2]	[12]	[31]	[16]	[16]	Our SURF + GIST	Our SURF + denseSIFT
Africa	0.48	0.55	0.61	0.57	0.55	0.59	**0.60**
Beaches	0.34	0.47	0.49	**0.58**	0.47	0.53	0.53
Building	0.36	0.44	0.46	0.43	0.56	0.52	**0.56**
Bus	0.61	0.93	0.93	0.93	0.91	0.90	**0.93**
Dinosaur	0.95	0.98	0.99	0.98	0.94	**0.99**	0.99
Elephant	0.48	0.52	0.58	0.58	0.49	**0.77**	0.74
Flower	0.61	0.77	0.83	0.83	0.85	**0.90**	0.84
Horses	0.74	0.65	0.65	0.68	0.52	**0.89**	0.88
Mountain	0.42	0.34	0.36	0.46	0.37	**0.52**	0.46
Food	0.50	0.52	0.51	0.53	0.55	0.56	**0.59**
ARP	0.549	0.617	0.641	0.657	0.621	**0.717**	0.712

as the coarse visual dictionary. To express the principle formally [14,30], we denote the pre-clustering centroids as: $X = [x_1; x_2; ...; x_i; ...; x_N]$, where N is the number of center points and $x_i \in R^D$, $X \in R^{N \times D}$. x_i is represented as the cascade of M sub-vectors: $x_i = [x_i^1 \ x_i^2 \ ... \ x_i^m ... \ x_i^M]$, with each $x_i^m \in R^{D/M}$, the dimension of sub-vector x_i^m is D/M (D = cM, c is an integer). When all data are divided into M parts, the centroids predefined can be denoted as follows. The m-th component of all data vectors: $X^m = [X_1^m; X_2^m; ...; X_i^m; ...; X_N^m]$. At last, the aggregation of M components: $X = [X^1 \ X^2 \ ... \ X^m \ ... \ X^M]$. Take each component of all vectors as a data set and perform clustering on it. The sub-visual-dictionary V^m has k visual words: $[v_1^m; v_2^m; ...; v_j^m; ...; v_k^m]$, with each $v_j^m \in V^m$. The final visual dictionary V is the Cartesian product of each sub-visual-dictionary: $V = V^1 \times V^2 \times ... \times V^m \times ... \times V^M$. The final visual words v consists of M sub-visual-words: $v = [v^1 \ v^2 \ ... \ v^m ... \ v^M]$, with each $v^m \in V^m$. We denote a sub-quantizer: $x^m \rightarrow v^m(x^m)$. Then, the complete data vector: $x = [v^1(x^1) \ v^2(x^2)...v^m(x^m)...v^M(x^M)] \rightarrow v(x)$. The quantization distortion function can be expressed by a squared distance formula: $\sum_{i=1}^{N} ||x_i - v(x_i)||^2$. Therefore, the optimization objective function is:

$$\underset{V^1 V^2 ..., V^M}{Min} \sum_{i=1}^{N} ||x_i - v(x_i)||^2. \tag{1}$$

The optimal product quantization proposed by Ge et al. [14] is to minimize quantization distortion by searching for optimal vector space decomposition and the visual dictionary. A non-parametric algorithm which does not assume any priori information about the data distribution is used to solve the optimization problem. An orthonormal matrix R firstly transforms the feature vector of D dimensions to rotate the vector space. Then, the vectors are divided into D/M partitions. Assigning a D dimensional vector x to the nearest visual words v is equal to assigning Rx to nearest Rv. The author alternately fixes R matrix and the visual dictionary to optimize the other. Finally, we can obtain the optimal coarse-to-fine visual dictionary V.

3.2 Adaptive Soft Assignment

In the bag-of-features model, each feature vector is assigned to a nearest visual word. Counting the appearance of visual words leads to a K dimensional frequency histogram, a description of the image. K represents not only the number of clustering centers, but also the size of the visual dictionary. For a feature vector, it brings in large coding distortion that merely considering one nearest visual word and ignoring the potential relationship between the feature vector and other visual words.

To solve the problem, Philbin et al. [32] proposed a soft assignment method for constructing the statistical histogram of visual words. Each local feature is mapped to a plurality of visual words when performing soft assignment. However, most soft assignment methods use a fixed number of assignments which result in that some unambiguous local features have to be mapped to multiple visual words. This depresses the distinctiveness of unambiguous features. Moreover, the number of assignments also needs to be set in advance, which may cause artificial error.

In this paper, an adaptive soft assignment method is proposed to select the number of assignments adaptively so as to avoid introducing redundant information. We take N as the variable of assignments. An image I can be represented as $I = [y_1; y_2; ...; y_T]$, where I is composed of a set of local features y_i. T is the total number of features. We compute distances between y_i and all visual words to obtain $d = (d_1, d_2, ..., d_K)$ that is in an ascending order by distance. We define the weight of each assignment as (2), which is similar to [33] but (3) shows better performance through comparative tests.

$$\omega_n = \frac{s_n}{\sum_{n=1}^{N} s_n} \tag{2}$$

$$s_n = e^{\frac{1-n}{2}}, n = 1, 2, ..., N \tag{3}$$

The value of adaptive assignment N of each sample y_i is determined by (4), in which γ is a variable factor.

$$N = \arg \min_i \{d_i \leq \gamma \cdot d_1\}, i = 1, 2, ..., K \tag{4}$$

In the query stage, we adopt asymmetric distance calculation method [30] for calculating the distances between one local feature and all visual words with formula (5). Here, y_i is a feature vector of a query image and x are the features extracted from images in the database. For each component of y_i like y_i^m, asymmetric distance is calculated between y^m and $v^m(x^m)$. Note that the query vectors do not need to be quantized to the sub-visual-words of corresponding sub-spaces.

$$d(x, y) \approx \sum_{m=1}^{M} dist(v^m(x^m), y^m) \qquad (5)$$

3.3 The Late Fusion of Features

With the diverse ways of image acquisition and the richness of image content, single kind of descriptor sometimes ignores the intrinsic link within the images. The solution is integrating multiple features to obtain a comprehensive description of the image. Conventional weighting methods include feature vector based weighting and similarity based weighting. There are external and internal normalization problems. Here, we merely take the external normalization into consideration by similarity based weighting.

Before fusion retrieval, the similarity distances of single feature must be normalized. The process of getting the similarity distances calculated between images is stochastic. Therefore, distances distribution can be regarded as a Gaussian distribution. If the similarity distance between the query image and the image of the database is represented as D_i, the normalized Gaussian distance can be expressed as follows:

$$D_i' = \frac{D_i - \mu_D}{\delta_D} \qquad (6)$$

Where μ_D and δ_D are the mean and variance of all the distances between the query image and images from the database respectively. We implement the above normalization strategy to deal with all feature spaces. Assuming that there are J kinds of visual features. For each of them, we assign a parameter $w_j (j = 1, 2, ..., J)$ for weighting. After the Gaussian normalization, we obtain the top α nearest neighbor distances of each query image. Then, the variance of the former α distances is calculated. The variance value has negative correlation with the importance among multiple feature spaces. We take a greater w_j when the variance of corresponding feature space is smaller. Eventually, the similarity distance is represented by:

$$D = w_1 D_{i1}' + w_2 D_{i2}' + ... + w_j D_{ij}' + ... + w_J D_{iJ}' \qquad (7)$$

$$s.t. \ w_1 + w_2 + ... + w_J = 1 \qquad (8)$$

4   Experiments

To illustrate the superiority of the proposed method, we conduct experiments on the Corel1K and Caltech101 image databases. The Corel1K is composed of 10 categories like "Africa" "Beaches" "Building" etc. There are 100 similar pictures in each categories and 1K images in total. The Caltech101 has 101 categories and 9145 pictures in total. For the Corel1K database, we quantitatively analyze the performances on the integration of SURF and GIST and on the integration of SURF and Dense-SIFT respectively. Then we compare our proposed method with some other image retrieval methods by the same evaluation criteria. Moreover, we exhibit the search performance on Caltech101. In this paper, we use the average retrieval precision (ARP) [2] as the evaluation criterion of the image retrieval performance.

4.1   The Performance of Image Retrieval

We evaluate the performances for the integration of SURF [8] and GIST [34] as well as the integration of SURF and Dense-SIFT. The 64 dimension SURF descriptors of all images are divided into M = 4 subspaces. The 128 dimension Dense-SIFT descriptors are divided into M = 8 subspaces. Therefore, the dimension of each sub-vector is 16. For each quantization subspace, we adopt 8 bits to represent the centroids. Therefore, there are $k = 2^8$ clustering centers for each subspace. The Cartesian product generates k^M centers which are called sub-visual-words. The final visual words are composed of the Cartesian product of the M sub-visual-words. At the stage of forming image representation, we take adaptive soft assignment by an improved weighting strategy to enhance the discriminative power of image representation. The determinants γ of assigned number N is determined

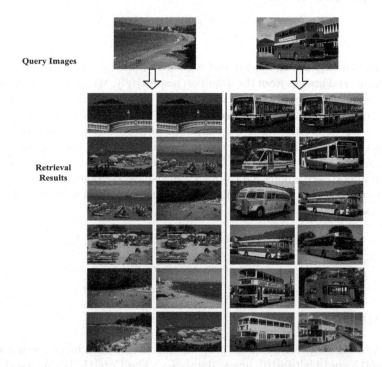

Fig. 2. Retrieval results of our two methods on Corel1K. The first column below each query image is retrieved by SUFR and GIST. The second column below each query image is retrieved by SUFR and Dense-SIFT. Note that both SURF and Dense-SIFT adopt optimized visual dictionary and adaptive soft assignment measures.

through numerous attempts. We set γ to 2.4 when the feature is SURF and set γ to 1.9 when the feature is Dense-SIFT. As shown in the Fig. 2, it is clearly to see that the SURF + GIST and SURF+ Dense-SIFT methods yield meaningful retrieval results on Corel1K. We compare the retrieval precision of our proposed method with other methods on Corel1K database. As can be observed from the Table 1, a framework for combining all the three i.e. color, texture and shape information which is a robust feature set for image retrieval, is employed in comparison [2]. A bag-of-features based SIFT method which presents a simple but effective algorithm for building codebooks is also compared in experiments [12]. The spatial pyramid matching [31] is a particular extension of the BoF model. It involves repeatedly subdividing the image and computing histograms of local features at increasingly fine resolutions. The SPM based SIFT method is also referred in the comparison. Features integration frameworks of image based SIFT-LBP and patch based HOG-LBP [16] are compared as well. Obviously, our proposed method outperforms the methods mentioned above especially in the class "Elephant", "Mountain" and "Horses". Figure 3 shows the precision-recall curve of three methods on Corel1K database: the circular ring histogram (CRH) [35], our SUFR (with proposed method) + GIST and SURF + GIST (without any optimizing measures). It is obvious that our method (the blue and red one) achieves higher accuracy when their recalls are identical. Our integration framework (the blue one) outperforms the CRH generally. Moreover, it shows greater superiority when adopting the proposed measures. The Fig. 4 exhibits the comparative results of adopting or without adopting optimized visual dictionary and adaptive soft assignment measures on Caltech101 database. For each query image, the first row is searched by SUFR (with proposed method) + GIST and the second row is searched by SURF + GIST (without any optimizing measures). Images in red frames are negative results. As can be seen, our proposed framework obtain less negative results.

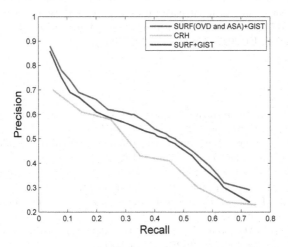

Fig. 3. Comparison of precision-recall values in CRH, SUFR (with proposed method) + GIST and SURF + GIST (without any optimizing measures). (Color figure online)

Queries Results

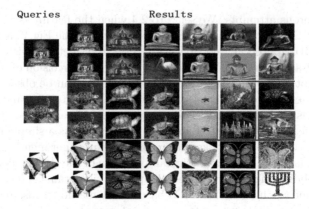

Fig. 4. The comparative retrieval results on Caltech101. For each query image, the first row is searched by SUFR (with proposed method) + GIST and the second row is searched by SURF + GIST (without any optimizing measures). Images in red frames are negative results. (Color figure online)

5 Conlusion

In this paper, we exhibit an image representation framework based on optimized visual dictionary and adaptive soft assignment. The optimized product quantization is used to reduce the quantization distortion in the generation of visual dictionary. Weighted histogram based on adaptive soft assignment is applied to obtain the optimized image representation in BoF model. As shown in the experiments, our image retrieval scheme achieves effective performance.

Acknowledgements. This work was partially supported by the 973 Program (Project No. 2014CB347600), the National Natural Science Foundation of China (Grant No. 61402228, and 61702265) and the Natural Science Foundation of Jiangsu Province (Grant BK20140058, BK20170856 and BK20170033).

References

1. Alzubi, A., Amira, A., Ramzan, N.: Semantic content-based image retrieval. J. Vis. Commun. Image Represent. **32**(C), 20–54 (2015)
2. Hiremath, P.S., Pujari, J.: Content based image retrieval using color, texture and shape features. In: ADCOM, pp. 780–784 (2007)
3. Tousch, A.M., Herbin, S., Audibert, J.Y.: Semantic hierarchies for image annotation: a survey. Pattern Recogn. **45**(1), 333–345 (2012)
4. Kusumam, K., Duckett, T.: Image features and seasons revisited. In: European Conference on Mobile Robots (2015)
5. Jian, M., Lam, K.M., Dong, J.: Facial-feature detection and localization based on hierarchical scheme. Inf. Sci. **262**(3), 1–14 (2014)
6. Jian, M., Lam, K.M.: Face-image retrieval based on singular values and potential-field representation. Signal Process. **100**(7), 9–15 (2014)

7. Lowe, D.G.: Distinctive image features from scale-invariant keypoints. In: ICCV (2004)
8. Bay, H., Ess, A., Tuytelaars, T., Gool, L.V.: Speeded-up robust features (SURF). Comput. Vis. Image Underst. **110**(3), 346–359 (2008)
9. Dalal, N., Triggs, B.: Histograms of oriented gradients for human detection. In: CVPR (2005)
10. Zhang, S., Yang, M., Cour, T.: Query specific rank fusion for image retrieval. IEEE Trans. Pattern Anal. Mach. Intell. **37**(4), 803–815 (2015)
11. Liu, J.: Image retrieval based on bag-of-words model. Computer Science (2013)
12. Jurie, F., Triggs, B.: Creating efficient codebooks for visual recognition. In: ICCV (2005)
13. Wan, T., Qin, Z.: A new technique for summarizing video sequences through histogram evolution. In: International Conference on Signal Processing and Communications, pp. 1–5 (2010)
14. Ge, T., He, K., Ke, Q.: Optimized product quantization for approximate nearest neighbor search. In: CVPR (2013)
15. Hong, R., Yang, Y., Wang, M., Hua, X.S.: Learning visual semantic relationships for efficient visual retrieval. IEEE Trans. Big Data **1**(4), 152–161 (2017)
16. Yu, J., Qin, Z., Wan, T., Zhang, X.: Feature integration analysis of bag-of-features model for image retrieval. Neurocomputing **120**(10), 355–364 (2013)
17. Tian, X., Jiao, L., Liu, X., Zhang, X.: Feature integration of eodh and color-sift: application to image retrieval based on codebook. Signal Process. Image Commun. **29**(4), 530–545 (2014)
18. Zheng, L., Wang, S., Liu, Z., Tian, Q.: Packing and padding: coupled multi-index for accurate image retrieval. In: CVPR, pp. 1947–1954 (2014)
19. Jegou, H., Douze, M., Schmid, C.: Hamming embedding and weak geometric consistency for large scale image search. In: Forsyth, D., Torr, P., Zisserman, A. (eds.) ECCV 2008. LNCS, vol. 5302, pp. 304–317. Springer, Heidelberg (2008). https://doi.org/10.1007/978-3-540-88682-2_24
20. Jégou, H., Douze, M., Schmid, C.: On the burstiness of visual elements. In: CVPR, pp. 1169–1176 (2009)
21. Liqiang, N., Yan, S., Meng, W., Richang, H., Tat-Seng, C.: Harvesting visual concepts for image search with complex queries. In: Proceedings of the 20th ACM International Conference on Multimedia, pp. 59–68. ACM (2012)
22. Nie, L., Wang, M., Zha, Z.J., Chua, T.S.: Oracle in image search: a content-based approach to performance prediction. ACM Trans. Inf. Syst. **30**(2), 1–23 (2012)
23. Li, Z., Tang, J.: Weakly supervised deep metric learning for community-contributed image retrieval. IEEE Trans. Multimedia **17**(11), 1989–1999 (2015)
24. Li, Z., Tang, J.: Weakly supervised deep matrix factorization for social image understanding. IEEE Trans. Image Process. **26**(1), 276–288 (2016)
25. Sivic, J., Zisserman, A.: Video google: a text retrieval approach to object matching in videos. In: ICCV (2003)
26. Boiman, O., Shechtman, E., Irani, M.: In defense of nearest-neighbor based image classification. In: CVPR (2008)
27. Torralba, A., Fergus, R., Weiss, Y.: Small codes and large image databases for recognition. In: CVPR (2008)
28. Sayood, K.: Vector quantization. In: Introduction to Data Compression, pp. 295–344 (2012)
29. Gong, Y., Lazebnik, S.: Iterative quantization: a procrustean approach to learning binary codes. IEEE Trans. Pattern Anal. Mach. Intell. **35**(12), 2916–2929 (2011)

30. Jégou, H., Douze, M., Schmid, C.: Product quantization for nearest neighbor search. IEEE Trans. Pattern Anal. Mach. Intell. **33**(1), 117–128 (2011)
31. Lazebnik, S., Schmid, C., Ponce, J.: Beyond bags of features: spatial pyramid matching for recognizing natural scene categories. In: CVPR (2006)
32. Philbin, J., Chum, O., Isard, M.: Lost in quantization: improving particular object retrieval in large scale image databases. In: CVPR, pp. 1–8 (2008)
33. Wang, T., Zhao, Y., Li, B.: Image classification based on adaptive soft assignment. Terahertz Sci. Electron. Inf. Technol. **13**(1), 154–159 (2015)
34. Oliva, A., Torralba, A.: Modeling the shape of the scene: a holistic representation of the spatial envelope. Int'l J. Comput. Vis. **42**(3), 145–175 (2001)
35. Wang, X.: A novel circular ring histogram for content-based image retrieval. In: International Workshop on Education Technology and Computer Science, pp. 785–788 (2009)

Query Modeling for Click Data Based Image Recognition Using Graph Based Propagation and Sparse Coding

Weichen Wu⦿, Min Tan[✉], Guangjian Zheng, and Jun Yu

Key Laboratory of Complex Systems Modeling and Simulation,
School of Computer Science and Technology,
Hangzhou Dianzi University, Hangzhou 310018, China
tanmin@hdu.edu.cn

Abstract. We address the fine-grained image recognition problem using user click data, wherein each image is represented as a semantical query-click feature vector. Usually, the query set obtained from search engines is large-scale and redundant. We propose a novel query modeling approach to merge semantically similar queries and construct a compact click feature. We represent each query as a click feature, and design a graph based propagation approach to predict the zero-clicks, ensuring similar images have similar clicks. Afterwards, using this feature, we formulate the problem as a sparse coding based recognition task, wherein the dictionary is discriminatively trained. We evaluate our method for fine-grained image recognition on the public Clickture-Dog dataset. It is shown that, the propagated click feature performs much better than the original one. Also, sparse coding performs better than K-means in query merging.

Keywords: Image recognition · Click feature · Query modeling
Graph based model · Sparse coding

1   Introduction

Fine-grained image recognition aims to distinguish images of different categories with subtle differences [1,18]. Traditional visual feature based recognition always fails in this task, and it also results in a big semantic gap [4].

To bridge this gap, many efforts have been made to design semantical features to represent images. Recently, researchers proposed to utilize user click data to represent semantics in images [20,21,24,26]. With click data, each image is represented as a click count vector based on its clicked queries, namely *query-click* feature [17]. As the query set is large-scale and noisy, the click feature based on the original query space (set) is highly sparse and redundant. Therefore, a query modeling method is desired to construct a compact and interpretable query space to represent images [25].

© Springer Nature Singapore Pte Ltd. 2018
B. Huet et al. (Eds.): ICIMCS 2017, CCIS 819, pp. 191–199, 2018.
https://doi.org/10.1007/978-981-10-8530-7_19

There are at least three kinds of query modeling schemes. One way is to ignore queries with fewer click count [4]. But it is too heuristic, and queries with fewer clicks could be rare ones rather than noisy ones. Another one is learning a feature selection model by sparse optimization [11,14,16]. The third way is to merge the semantically similar queries, and construct a compact click feature by the merged queries. Traditionally, queries are merged by their text-based similarities [2,3], but semantic gap will occur since the semantically similar queries may differ a lot in text. To this end, we propose a novel click data based query merging approach via graph based click propagation and sparse coding.

2   Our Method

As aforementioned, we utilize user click data to construct a semantical image representation for fine-grained recognition, and each image is represented as a click feature vector based on its clicked queries. To deal with the noisy and large-scale query set, we propose a novel query modeling approach to merge semantically similar queries and construct a compact query space for image representation. The click data based image recognition framework is illustrated in Fig. 1.

2.1   Formulation

Given n images $\mathbf{x}$ with category labels $\mathbf{y}$, m queries $\mathbf{q}$, and the associated user click matrix $\mathbf{C} \in \mathbb{R}^{n \times m}$, we represent the i-th image by a extremely high-dimensional click feature $\mathbf{u}_i = (c_{i,1}, c_{i,2}, \ldots, c_{i,m})$. Our task is to merge semantically similar queries and construct a compact click feature with the merged queries to represent images. This compact click feature is used to do the following recognition task.

In the follows, we describe our click data based query merging approach in detail. With click data, $\mathbf{q}_j$ can be represented as the click count vector $\mathbf{v}_j$ by its clicked images:

$$\mathbf{v}_j = (c_{1,j}, \ldots, c_{n,j}). \tag{1}$$

As the click count of similar images may vary a lot for each query due to the high sparsity in click data, we propose a graph based click propagation approach to obtain a relatively dense click feature. Afterwards, we merge queries by their propagated click features. We do image clustering by their CNN features and conduct click propagation just within each image cluster.

Image Clustering. As the visual differences of images among categories is relatively huge, we conduct image clustering within each category. For category j, we conduct K-means algorithm on the CNN features of the containing images, i.e., $\mathcal{F} = \{\phi_i | i \in \chi_j\}$, and then obtain the cluster index $\{\mathcal{A}_{j,1}, \ldots, \mathcal{A}_{j,N_I}\}$ for the N_I clusters.

With the cluster index $\mathcal{A}$, we obtain the re-ranked click feature $\widetilde{\mathbf{v}}_k$ for query k as below:

$$\widetilde{\mathbf{v}}_k = (\widetilde{\mathbf{v}}_k^{1,1}, \ldots, \widetilde{\mathbf{v}}_k^{1,N_I}, \ldots, \widetilde{\mathbf{v}}_k^{N_c,1}, \ldots, \widetilde{\mathbf{v}}_k^{N_c,N_I}), \tag{2}$$

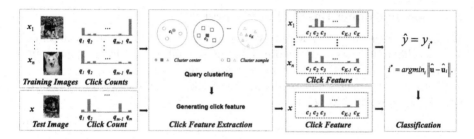

Fig. 1. Pipeline of our click data based image recognition via 1-NN. When queries with similar semantics have been merged, we convent the original sparse click feature $\mathbf{u}$ to a dense one $\widehat{\mathbf{u}}$ by the K query clusters instead of the m queries ($m \gg K$).

where $\widetilde{\mathbf{v}}_k^{j,i}$ is the click count vector related to images belong to the i-th cluster in category j, which is defined as:

$$\widetilde{\mathbf{v}}_k^{j,i} = (c_{s_1,k}, \ldots, c_{s_{N'},k}), \mathbf{s} = \mathcal{A}_{j,i}, N' = |\mathcal{A}_{j,i}|. \tag{3}$$

Note that $|\mathcal{A}_{j,i}|$ denotes the cardinal number for set $\mathcal{A}_{j,i}$, which equals to the total number of elements in $\mathcal{A}_{j,i}$.

Propagation Function. Based on image clusters, we convert the sparse click feature $\widetilde{\mathbf{v}}_k$ to a dense one $\widehat{\mathbf{v}}_k$ by a propagation function $\mathcal{P}$ as below:

$$\widehat{\mathbf{v}}_k = (\widehat{\mathbf{v}}_k^{1,1}, \ldots, \widehat{\mathbf{v}}_k^{1,N_I}, \ldots, \widehat{\mathbf{v}}_k^{N_c,1}, \ldots, \widehat{\mathbf{v}}_k^{N_c,N_I}), \widehat{\mathbf{v}}_k^{j,i} = \mathcal{P}(\widetilde{\mathbf{v}}_k^{j,i}). \tag{4}$$

We perform a weighted propagation such that the click count of an image will be allocated to its similar images based on their distances. To this end, we construct a similarity matrix within each image cluster. For images in the i-th cluster in category j, the similarity matrix $\mathbf{G}^{j,i}$ is defined as below:

$$\mathbf{G}^{j,i} = \{g_{u,v}\}, g_{u,v} = \exp(-\|\boldsymbol{\phi}_{s_u} - \boldsymbol{\phi}_{s_v}\|)), \mathbf{s} = \mathcal{A}_{j,i}, \tag{5}$$

where $\boldsymbol{\phi}_i$ is the CNN feature vector for image i.

We perform weighted click propagation as follows:

$$\begin{aligned}
\mathcal{P}(\widetilde{\mathbf{v}}_k^{j,i}) &= \sum_{u=1}^{N'} (\widetilde{\mathbf{v}}_k^{j,i}(u)(\alpha\widetilde{g}_{u,1}, \ldots, (1-\alpha), \ldots, \alpha\widetilde{g}_{u,N'}) \\
&= \widetilde{\mathbf{v}}_k^{j,i}(\alpha\widetilde{\mathbf{G}}^{j,i} + (1-\alpha)\mathbf{E} - \alpha\mathbf{M}^{j,i}),
\end{aligned} \tag{6}$$

where α is the propagation rate, $\mathbf{E}$ is the identity matrix, $\widetilde{\mathbf{G}}^{j,i}$ is the normalized graph defined as:

$$\widetilde{\mathbf{G}}^{j,i} = \{\widetilde{g}_{u,v}\}, \widetilde{g}_{u,v} = \frac{g_{u,v}}{\sum_{k \neq u} g_{u,k}}. \tag{7}$$

$\mathbf{M}^{j,i}$ is defined as:

$$\mathbf{M}^{j,i} = diag(\widetilde{g}_{1,1}, \widetilde{g}_{2,2}, \ldots, \widetilde{g}_{N',N'}). \tag{8}$$

Particularly, the evenly propagation will be conducted if $\mathbf{G}^{j,i} = \{g_{u,v} = 1 | \forall u, v\}$.

2.2   Sparse Coding Based Query Merging

We use the propagated click feature $\widehat{\mathbf{v}}$ to merge queries that are similar in semantics. As different categories denote different semantics, we divide queries into different categories, and perform per-category query merging.

With labeled images and the associated click data, the category label of $\mathbf{q}_j$, namely $\mathcal{Y}_j$, is defined as below:

$$\mathcal{Y}_j = \{y_i | c_{i,j} > 0\}. \tag{9}$$

Using $\mathcal{Y}$, we separate queries into K set $\{\pi_k | 1 \leq k \leq K\}$ with each one sharing the same category label set, i.e., $\pi_k = \{q_j | y_i = k\}$.

Directly using the classical K-means algorithm may be improper for this propagated click feature, as user click data is usually too noisy and unbalanced. In this paper, we propose a sparse coding based recognition approach for query merging and learn a category-dependent query dictionary.

Dictionary Learning. For category k, we learn the dictionary $\mathbf{D}_k$ by K-SVD. To better model intra-class variance, we divide the $\mathbf{D}_k$ into different clusters via K-means, and assign each containing query $\mathbf{q} \in \pi_k$ to the cluster with the maximum coefficient sum (refer to (11)). More specifically, we divide $\mathbf{D}_k$ into n_k subsets ensuring that $p_k^i = \min\{P, |\pi_k^i|\}$ items exist in each sub-class, i.e.,

$$\mathbf{D}_k = [\mathbf{D}_k^1, \ldots, \mathbf{D}_k^{n_k}]. \tag{10}$$

Specially, when $P = 1$ and $P > 1$, we call $\mathbf{D}_k$ is multi-template dictionary and single-template one respectively.

Sparse Coding. With fixed dictionary $\mathbf{D}_k$, each query $\mathbf{q}$ will be assigned to a cluster by solving the following sparse coding problem using its propagated click feature $\widehat{\mathbf{v}}$:

$$\mathbf{x}^* = argmin_{\mathbf{x}}(\|\widehat{\mathbf{v}} - \mathbf{x}\mathbf{D}_k\|_2^2),$$
$$s.t. \|\mathbf{x}\|_0 \leq T \sum_i p_k^i, \tag{11}$$

where T controls the non-zero coefficient in the code. The predicted cluster label of $\mathbf{q}$, i.e. $\widehat{l}$, is obtained as below:

$$\widehat{l} = argmax_j \sum_{l_k = j} x_k^*. \tag{12}$$

2.3   Click Feature Based Image Recognition

When queries are grouped into K clusters, we construct a compact click feature for each image based on the cluster index $\mathcal{G} = \{\{i | \widehat{l}_i = 1\}, \{i | \widehat{l}_i = 2\}, \ldots, \{i | \widehat{l}_i = K\}\}$ as below:

$$\widehat{\mathbf{u}}_i = (\sum_{j \in \mathcal{G}_1} c_{i,j}, \sum_{j \in \mathcal{G}_2} c_{i,j}, \ldots, \sum_{j \in \mathcal{G}_K} c_{i,j}). \tag{13}$$

The compact image representation is used for the following recognition task. The predicted label $\widehat{y}$ for an image $\mathbf{x}$ is obtained by 1-nearest-neighborhood (1-NN) classifier by $\widehat{\mathbf{u}}$:

$$\widehat{y} = y_{i^*}, i^* = argmin_i \|\widehat{\mathbf{u}} - \widehat{\mathbf{u}}_i\|. \tag{14}$$

3   Experiments

We evaluate the proposed query modeling approach by testing the image recognition accuracy using the compact click feature with merged queries. Different merging schemes are compared, and the basic 1-NN recognizer is employed.

As most publicly available dog-breed classification dataset does not involve user click data, including the Stanford Dogs Dataset [5], we only used the public Clickture-Dog dataset [4] to evaluate the proposed method. The advantages of the two main components of our approach, i.e. similarity matrix based click propagation and sparse coding based merging, are evaluated.

3.1   Experimental Settings

The Clickture-Dog dataset consists of dog images of 344 categories. As the Clickture-Dog has been rarely studied and no training/testing split of the dataset is publicly available, we randomly split the dataset into three parts: 50% for training, 30% for validation, and 20% for testing respectively. To ensure a valid split, we ignore categories containing less than 5 images. Different from [6], we conduct no pre-processing on this dataset, e.g. data cleaning, ROI extraction.

For image representation, we only utilize the click feature rather than visual feature. The clicked query set and their corresponding counts are collected from Clickture-Full [4]. Using click data, we collect a dog dataset containing (1) a set with $95,041$ images of 283 dog categories; (2) $481,998$ queries with each one having non-zero clicks for dog images.

3.2   Click Feature by Propagation

We compare the propagated click feature with original one. Both weighted propagation by the similarity matrix (Prop-W) and evenly propagation (Prop-E) are tested. For a fair comparison, we set the cluster number in each category (n_k in (10)) be 10 in the following experiments. We test different propagation rate α and select the optimize one from $\{[0.1, 0.3, \ldots, 0.9]\}$. Using the optimal α^1, we compare different click feature and list the result in Table 1.

As most existing fine-grained recognition methods are based on visual features, we just adopt one state-of-the-art vision based approach (CNN with fine-tuning) as the comparison to our click-feature-based recognition[2]. Note that the recognition accuracies by method in [6] seem much better than using the proposed one. The reason lies in that their experiments were performed on a reduced "clean" dataset which is of much higher quality than the original Clickture-Dog dataset. However, the "clean" dataset is not publicly available, and all the experiments in this paper are conducted on the original noisy Clickture-Dog dataset.

---

[1] The optimal α is 0.9 and 0.5 for Prop-E and Prop-W respectively.

[2] We use VGG-net [12] with 16-layers to learn a CNN model, including 13 convolutional layers and 3 fully connected layers. It is pre-trained on ImageNet Large-Scale Visual Recognition Challenge (ILSVRC)-2012 dataset.

For "Sum" in Table 1, the click feature is generated by directly adding the clicks within each image cluster. We see that: (1) semantical feature outperforms visual feature; (2) click propagation largely improves the click feature, besides, Prop-W outperforms Prop-E. It implies that click propagation can help to predict the zero-clicks in the sparse click data. Also, visual consistency based graph constrains can boost the prediction.

Table 1. Comparison of recognition accuracy (%) for different click features. "Org" denotes the original click feature.

Feature	CNN	Org	Sum	Prop-E	Prop-W
Acc	42.85	47.12	51.77	57.04	**58.24**

3.3 Sparse Coding Based Recognition

Using the similarity matrix based propagated click feature, we evaluate sparse coding based query clustering. We employ the Orthogonal Matching Pursuit (OMP) algorithm to solve the sparse coding problem.

Impact of Parameters. As it is known, sparse coding requires a well-built over-completed dictionary, which is hard to learn from few samples. Therefore, for categories with query number less than θ, we employ the K-means algorithms for query clustering.

With $\theta = 600$, we first we test the recognition accuracies under different combinations of T and P, and the result is shown in Fig. 2. In the following experiments, we set $P = 10, T = 0.2$ to obtain the optimal solution.

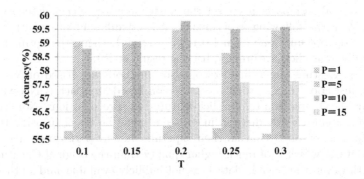

Fig. 2. Recognition accuracies (%) with varying T under different P.

Overall Performance. We compare the proposed query merging method to conventional K-means algorithm. Both multi-template dictionary $(P > 1)$ and single-template dictionary $(P = 1)$ are compared. The result is shown in Table 2. It can be found that: (1) sparse coding outperforms K-means in the click feature based query merging, due to the heavy unbalance and noise in click-feature; (2) compared with single-template dictionary (KSVD*), learning multi-template dictionary (KSVD) can improve the performance, owing to its advantage in dealing with the intra-class variance.

Table 2. Comparison of recognition accuracy (%) for different merging approaches. "A*"/"A" denotes learning a single/multiple dictionaries with "A".

Method	K-means	KSVD*	KSVD
Acc	58.24	59.40	**60.84**

4   Conclusion

We present a click data based image recognition framework, which can bridge the semantical gap. To deal with the large-scale and noisy query set, we propose a novel click data based query modeling approach to merge semantically similar queries and construct a compact click feature for images. We test our approach on the public Clickture-Dog dataset. Experimental results show the advantage of click propagated and sparse coding based query merging.

Future work will concentrate on several open problems: (1) we extend the weakly supervised training [13,15,23] method to deal with the noisy/mislabeled click data [7,19]; (2) we consider constructing a deep neural network to learn a deep click feature; (3) we will utilize the proposed feature in other tasks, such as image retrieval [8–10,22], object detection, Multimedia [8,10], etc.

Acknowledgments. This work was partly supported by National Natural Science Foundation of China (No. 61602136, No. 61622205, and No. 61472110), and Zhejiang Provincial Natural Science Foundation of China under Grant LR15F020002.

References

1. Berg, T., Liu, J., Lee, S.W., Alexander, M.L., Jacobs, D.W., Belhumeur, P.N.: Birdsnap: large-scale fine-grained visual categorization of birds. In: IEEE CVPR, pp. 2019–2026 (2014)
2. Cilibrasi, R.L., Vitanyi, P.: The Google similarity distance. IEEE Trans. Knowl. Data Eng. **19**(3), 370–383 (2007)
3. Feng, L., Bhanu, B.: Semantic concept co-occurrence patterns for image annotation and retrieval. IEEE Trans. Pattern Anal. Mach. Intell. **38**(4), 1 (2016)
4. Hua, X.-S., Yang, L., Wang, J., Wang, J., Ye, M., Wang, K., Rui, Y., Li, J.: Clickage: towards bridging semantic and intent gaps via mining click logs of search engines. In: ACM International Conference on Multimedia, pp. 243–252. ACM (2013)

5. Khosla, A., Jayadevaprakash, N., Yao, B., Fei-Fei, L.: Novel dataset for fine-grained image categorization. In: First Workshop on Fine-Grained Visual Categorization, IEEE CVPR, Colorado Springs, CO, June 2011
6. Li, C., Song, Q., Wang, Y., Song, H., Kang, Q., Cheng, J., Lu, H.: Learning to recognition from bing clickture data. In: IEEE ICME Workshops, pp. 1–4 (2016)
7. Liu, T., Tao, D.: Classification with noisy labels by importance reweighting. IEEE Trans. Pattern Anal. Mach. Intell. **38**(3), 447–461 (2016)
8. Nie, L., Wang, M., Zha, Z., Li, G., Chua, T.-S.: Multimedia answering: enriching text QA with media information. In: Proceedings of the 34th International ACM SIGIR Conference on Research and Development in Information Retrieval, SIGIR 2011, pp. 695–704. ACM (2011)
9. Nie, L., Wang, M., Zha, Z.-J., Chua, T.-S.: Oracle in image search: a content-based approach to performance prediction. ACM Trans. Inf. Syst. **30**(2), 13:1–13:23 (2012)
10. Nie, L., Yan, S., Wang, M., Hong, R., Chua, T.-S.: Harvesting visual concepts for image search with complex queries. In: Proceedings of the 20th ACM International Conference on Multimedia, MM 2012, pp. 59–68. ACM (2012)
11. Shao, H., Chen, S., Zhao, J., Cui, W., Yu, T.: Face recognition based on subset selection via metric learning on manifold. Front. Inf. Technol. Electron. Eng. **16**(12), 1046–1058 (2015)
12. Simonyan, K., Zisserman, A.: Very deep convolutional networks for large-scale image recognition. Computer Science (2014)
13. Tan, M., Hu, Z., Wang, B., Zhao, J., Wang, Y.: Robust object recognition via weakly supervised metric and template learning. Neurocomputing **101**, 96–107 (2016)
14. Tan, M., Pan, G., Wang, Y., Zhang, Y., Wu, Z.: L1-norm latent svm for compact features in object detection. Neurocomputing **139**(139), 56–64 (2014)
15. Tan, M., Wang, B., Wu, Z., Wang, J., Pan, G.: Weakly supervised metric learning for traffic sign recognition in a lidar-equipped vehicle. IEEE Trans. Intell. Transp. Syst. **17**(5), 1415–1427 (2016)
16. Tan, M., Wang, Y., Pan, G.: Feature reduction for efficient object detection via L1-norm latent SVM. In: Yang, J., Fang, F., Sun, C. (eds.) IScIDE 2012. LNCS, vol. 7751, pp. 322–329. Springer, Heidelberg (2013). https://doi.org/10.1007/978-3-642-36669-7_40
17. Tan, M., Yu, J., Zheng, G., Wu, W., Sun, K.: Deep neural network boosted large scale image recognition using user click data. In: International Conference on Internet Multimedia Computing and Service, pp. 118–121 (2016)
18. Tsung-Yu Lin, A.R., Maji, S.: Bilinear CNN models for fine-grained visual recognition. In: IEEE International Conference on Computer Vision (2015)
19. Wang, R., Liu, T., Tao, D.: Multiclass learning with partially corrupted labels. IEEE Trans. Neural Netw. Learn. Syst. **PP**(99), 1–13 (2017)
20. Yu, J., Rui, Y., Chen, B.: Exploiting click constraints and multi-view features for image re-ranking. IEEE Trans. Multimedia **16**(1), 159–168 (2014)
21. Yu, J., Rui, Y., Tao, D.: Click prediction for web image reranking using multimodal sparse coding. IEEE Trans. Image Process. **23**(5), 2019–2032 (2014)
22. Yu, J., Tao, D., Meng, W., Yong, R.: Learning to rank using user clicks and visual features for image retrieval. IEEE Trans. Cybern. **45**(4), 767–779 (2015)
23. Yu, J., Wang, M., Tao, D.: Semi supervised multiview distance metric learning for cartoon synthesis. IEEE Trans. Image Process. Publ. IEEE Sig. Process. Soc. **21**(11), 4636 (2012)

24. Yu, J., Yang, X., Gao, F., Tao, D.: Deep multimodal distance metric learning using click constraints for image ranking. IEEE Trans. Cybern. **47**, 4014–4024 (2016)
25. Zhang, J., Nie, L., Wang, X., He, X., Huang, X., Chua, T.S.: Shorter-is-better: venue category estimation from micro-video. In: ACM on Multimedia Conference, pp. 1415–1424 (2016)
26. Zheng, G., Tan, M., Yu, J., Wu, Q., Fan, J.: Fine-grained image recongnition via weakly supervised click data guided bilinear CNN model. In: IEEE ICME (Accpet). IEEE (2017)

Zero-Shot Cross-Media Retrieval with External Knowledge

Jingze Chi, Xin Huang, and Yuxin Peng$^{(\boxtimes)}$

Institute of Computer Science and Technology, Peking University,
Beijing 100871, China
pengyuxin@pku.edu.cn

Abstract. Cross-media retrieval has drawn much attention recently, by which users can retrieve results across different media types like image and text. The existing methods mainly focus on the condition where the training data covers all the categories in the testing data. However, the number of categories is infinite in real world and it is impossible to include all categories in the training data. Due to the limitation of scalability, the performance of existing methods will be not effective when retrieving with unseen categories. For addressing the issues of both "heterogeneity gap" and the gap of seen and unseen categories, this paper proposes a new approach to model both multimedia and external knowledge information. The common semantic representations are generated jointly by media features and category weight vectors which are learned by utilizing online encyclopedias. Experiment on two widely-used datasets shows the effectiveness of our approach for zero-shot cross-media retrieval.

1 Introduction

Nowadays, image, video, text, audio and other multimedia data influence everyone's daily life, and multimedia retrieval has become an active research topic for decades [1], which can obtain large number of relevant data with a single query. Past efforts mainly focus on single-media retrieval, where user's queries and retrieval results are of the same media type. However, with the development of multimedia and Internet technology, multimedia data can be easily generated and seen everywhere. Retrieval results of the same type with query, such as image retrieval and text retrieval, can not meet the needs of multimedia retrieval. In that case, the limitation of single-media retrieval is becoming increasingly obvious, and cross-media retrieval has become a highlighted research topic in multimedia community.

Cross-media retrieval is proposed to retrieve data of similar semantic but different media types with user's queries. For example, if someone is visiting the Palace Museum, he can submit one query of image, and then get relevant multimedia information, including image samples, video introductions, text descriptions, audio clips and so on. Different from single-media retrieval, the key problem of cross-media retrieval is that the distribution and representation of

© Springer Nature Singapore Pte Ltd. 2018
B. Huet et al. (Eds.): ICIMCS 2017, CCIS 819, pp. 200–211, 2018.
https://doi.org/10.1007/978-981-10-8530-7_20

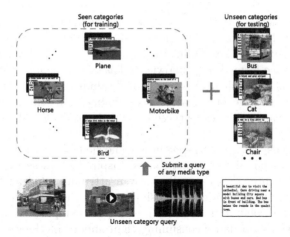

Fig. 1. The illustration of zero-shot cross-media retrieval. (Color figure online)

different media types are inconsistent, so there exists a "heterogeneity gap" which makes it hard to measure the cross-media similarity. For addressing this problem, the mainstream methods of cross-media retrieval are common representation learning. The main idea is to represent data of different media types with the same type of representation, so that cross-media similarity can be directly computed by distance measurement. Based on different models, these methods can be further divided into traditional methods [2–4] and DNN-based methods [5–7]. They all project cross-media data into a common space by learning from their correlations.

The progress of the above methods is supported by the experiment setting where categories of testing data are completely the same with training data categories. While retrieving with the data not included in training categories, the performance of existing methods will be not effective. Although cross-media datasets are growing bigger, data collecting and labeling are still heavily labor-consuming and time-consuming. More importantly, in real world, the number of categories is infinite, and it is impossible to label all categories in the training data. So it is important to support no training category data retrieval based on limited training categories in real world applications.

Zero-shot learning is proposed earlier by [8,9] to improve the scalability for no training category data. Specifically for zero-shot cross-media retrieval, it aims to address the problem where the query and retrieval data are of different media types, and the categories of testing data (unseen categories) are not overlapped with the categories of training data (seen categories). A brief illustration of zero-shot cross-media retrieval is shown in Fig. 1. It is a very challenging problem due to the issues of both "heterogeneity gap" and the gap of seen and unseen categories.

For humans, an important reason of generalization ability for recognizing lots of concepts is based on existing knowledge. So one feasible way to address zero-shot cross-media retrieval is to make use of existing external knowledge. External knowledge in this paper refers to the information source that contains human wisdom and can be obtained easily. After years of development, online encyclopedias have formed huge knowledge bases. For example, Wikipedia now contains 5,421,321 English articles that provide abundant descriptions and explanations for a lot of concepts. Besides, the number of articles is increasing over time. Everyone can easily access these resources and exploit the rich sources of information.

Some previous works [10,11] transfer knowledge for seen categories and unseen categories based on the attributes. Inspired by these thoughts, we can assume that the categories naturally contain attribute information and design methods to learn the semantic relationship between the attributes and multimedia data. However, definition of attributes is quite complicated and annotating attributes is even more labor-consuming than annotating labels, especially for multiple different media types. While the existing knowledge base like Wikipedia can provide a possible approach to get attributes of categories. In this way, unseen categories can be constructed by combining different sets of attributes which are not manually annotated. The similar setup has been previously considered in [12,13], where the attributes are extracted from text descriptions for image classification. However, to the best of our knowledge, these methods are designed for single-media scenario, and cannot support cross-media retrieval.

To address the above problems, this paper proposes to employ online encyclopedias as the external knowledge where descriptions of categories can be considered as existing attributes of them. We use textual descriptions of both seen and unseen categories, which involve rich implicit external knowledge, to learn a set of category weight vectors. Category weight vectors contain different characteristics among different categories. And the output features in a common semantic space are generated jointly by category weight vectors and features of medias, which model both multimedia and external knowledge information. Comprehensive experimental results on two widely-used cross-media retrieval datasets: Wikipedia and Pascal Sentence show the effectiveness of our proposed approach for zero-shot cross-media retrieval.

The main contributions of this paper can be concluded as follows:

- We propose a new approach to combine cross-media retrieval and zero-shot learning together.
- We utilize online encyclopedias as external knowledge to model unseen categories cross-media data.
- The experiments for zero-shot cross-media retrieval on Wikipedia and Pascal Sentence datasets show that our approach outperforms the existing methods.

2   Related Works

2.1   Cross-Media Retrieval

Cross-media retrieval aims to measure similarities among different media types, which are inconsistent and of different feature spaces. Most existing methods mainly focus on common representation learning, so that different media types can be represented in the same common space, leading to cross-media common representation. These methods can be divided into two categories: traditional methods and DNN-based methods. Traditional methods mainly learn linear projections for different media types. Canonical correlation analysis (CCA) [2] is proposed to learn cross-media common representation by maximizing the pairwise correlation, which is a classical baseline method for cross-media measurement [3]. An alternative method named cross-modal factor analysis (CFA) [4] is proposed by Li et al., which aims to find the projection functions for different media types, and minimizes the Frobenius norm between the pairwise data in the common space. Beyond pairwise correlation, joint representation learning (JRL) [14] is proposed to make use of semi-supervised regularization and semantic information, which can jointly learn common representation projections for up to five media types. Recent years, DNN-based cross-media retrieval has become an active research topic [15]. Instead of linear projection, DNN-based methods take deep neural network as the basic model for generating common representation. For example, CMDN [5] is proposed to simultaneously consider inter-modality and intra-modality information in a hierarchical multi-network architecture, which improves the retrieval accuracy. Wei et al. [6] propose to use CNN model pre-trained on ImageNet as the feature extractor for images, and show the effectiveness of CNN feature in cross-media retrieval. He et al. [16] propose a deep and bidirectional representation learning model, which trains the matched and unmatched image/text pairs simultaneously using two convolution-based networks. However, existing methods use the training set that contains all the same labeled categories as the testing set, which are not practical in real world applications and they cannot apply to the zero-shot cross-retrieval problem well.

2.2 Zero-Shot Learning

Zero-shot learning aims to address the increasing difficulty caused by insufficient training data. Most existing methods mainly take advantage of external knowledge to improve the scalability for no training category data. There are several knowledge sources can be used. Kankuekul et al. [17] utilize knowledge from interaction with users. Encyclopedias are used in [12] to learn visual classifiers for images. Wu et al. [18] make use of information from search engine to address zero-shot event detection. And many existing methods connect seen and unseen categories through attributes. Farhadi et al. [19] describe objects with manually annotated attributes to classify unseen objects. In [13], the attributes are extracted from textual descriptions for image classification. Parikh and Grauman [20] propose to learn relative visual attributes, which are more powerful than binary attributes. However, to the best of our knowledge, these methods are mostly designed for single-media scenario, and cannot support cross-media retrieval.

3 Our Approach

In this paper, we take image and text as examples to describe our approach, while it can be applied for other media types. The overview illustration of our approach is shown as Fig. 2, which can be viewed as four parts, namely (a) category weight vector prediction, (b) image representation learning, (c) text representation learning, and (d) knowledge transfer learning.

For training stage, textual descriptions for each training categories are as input with training images and texts. Dot product is done by image/text feature and category weight vectors to generate common semantic representation, which is trained through cross entropy loss function. For testing stage, image or text can serve as input independently with the textual descriptions of both seen and unseen categories, and our approach can generate common semantic representations for them to perform cross-media retrieval with distance measurement.

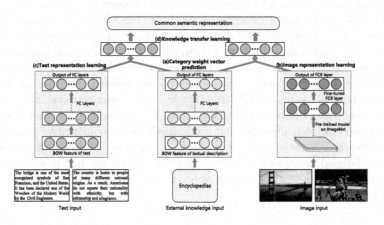

Fig. 2. The overview illustration of our approach.

3.1 Problem Definition

We take two media types X and Y as examples to give the formulation of zero-shot cross-media retrieval. x_i and y_i denote instances of X and Y, and $x_i \in R^{d_x}, y_i \in R^{d_y}$. R^{d_x} and R^{d_y} are the dimensional space of media X and Y. There are N_{sc} seen categories for training, the training labels $l^{tr} \in \{1, \ldots, N_{sc}\}$ and training set $D_{tr} = \{x_n, y_n, l_n^{tr}\}_n^{N_{tr}}$. N_{tr} is the number of training data. During testing stage, we are given additional N_{uc} unseen categories for testing, the testing labels $l^{te} \in \{N_{sc} + 1, \ldots, N_{sc} + N_{uc}\}$ and testing set $D_{te} = \{x_n, y_n, l_n^{te}\}_n^{N_{te}}$. N_{te} is the number of testing data. Our goal is to compute cross-media similarities $sim(x_a, y_b)$, and retrieve relevant instances of different media types in testing data by one query of any media type. Remarkably, there is no overlap between the seen categories and unseen categories, so it is very challenging to address "heterogeneity gap" and the gap between seen and unseen categories at the same time.

3.2 Category Weight Vector Prediction

This part aims to generate a set of category weight vectors to represent different characteristics of different categories. As discussed in Sect. 1, for seen and unseen categories of cross-media data, a direct and feasible way is to build the transfer through attributes. Formally, transform $f : S \rightarrow U$ to $f : S \rightarrow A \rightarrow U$, where S donates seen categories data, U donates unseen categories data and A is the set of attributes of them.

To overcome the difficulty of attribute annotation, we utilize textual descriptions in encyclopedias to extract implicit attributes and use them to displace manually annotated attributes. For each category of both seen and unseen categories, we automatically obtain the textual descriptions by our crawler tool from Wikipedia articles. Then we can define a function to generate a weight vector w_c for category c by:

$$w_c = f_w(t_c) \tag{1}$$

where $f_w(t_c) : R^{d_c} \rightarrow R^d$ transforms textual descriptions of R^{d_c} space to a space R^d. t_c is textual descriptions and can be regarded as a attribute set for category c, which can build the knowledge transfer for seen categories and unseen categories. Specifically, 450-dimensional BOW features are extracted from these textual descriptions and taken as input in the category weight prediction part with two fully-connected layers as shown in Fig. 2(a). Once there is a new description for category c', we can get a w_c' for the new category.

3.3 Image Representation Learning

We aim to generate appropriate features for image representation in this part, we define $g_i(x) : R^{d_i} \rightarrow R^d$ to transform image x in dimensional space R^{d_i} to image feature in space R^d. Recently Convolutional Neural Network (CNN) has made great progress in image classification, object detection and other computer visual tasks. CNN models can be pre-trained on large scale datasets with large number of categories, such as ImageNet [21]. These models have shown good effect for various visual recognition tasks on other image datasets, which are usually used to directly extract CNN visual features of images. Due to the data diversity information included in CNN pre-trained models, we can utilize them to improve prediction for unseen categories data. So we propose to use the pre-trained CNN model that has a similar network structure of AlexNet [22], which contains five convolutional layers and three fully-connected layers. The CNN model is pre-trained by 1.2 million images of 1,000 categories from ImageNet. We extract the output of FC7 layer of pre-trained model after the ReLU, and fine-tune the FC8 layer with 4096-dimensional output as shown in Fig. 2(b).

3.4 Text Representation Learning

In this part we aim to generate appropriate features for text representation, and define $g_t(y) : R^{d_t} \rightarrow R^d$ to transform text y in dimensional space R^{d_t} to text feature in space R^d. We first extract BOW features similar as the textual descriptions in Sect. 3.2. Then we directly build a network with two fully-connected layers to map text features from the original BOW feature space to the output 4096-dimensional space. Similar with the fully-connected layers in CNN, we utilize ReLU as the nonlinear activation function for each fully-connected layer as shown in Fig. 2(c).

3.5   Knowledge Transfer Learning

In this part, our aim is to predict scores using category weight vectors, and a predicted score can be calculated by:

$$\hat{y}_c = w_c^T z \tag{2}$$

where w_c is the weight vector for a particular category c and z is feature vector of a media data. Specifically, for image x or text y, we can get the predicted score of category c by:

$$\hat{y}_{ci} = f_w(t_c) \cdot g_i(x)$$
$$\hat{y}_{ct} = f_w(t_c) \cdot g_t(y) \tag{3}$$

where $g_i(x) : R^{d_i} \rightarrow R^d$ is the output of image representation learning, $g_t(y) : R^{d_t} \rightarrow R^d$ is the output of text representation learning and $f_w(t_c) : R^{d_c} \rightarrow R^d$ is the weight vector for category c. The output of dot product between f and g finally gets through a n_c dimension softmax to produce a probability distribution over n_c categories in a common semantic space, and n_c is the number of categories in category weight vector prediction part. The loss is defined as:

$$Loss = -\frac{1}{m} \sum_{i=1}^{m} y^{(i)} log(h_\theta(x^{(i)})) + (1 - y^{(i)}) log(1 - h_\theta(x^{(i)})) \tag{4}$$

where $h_\theta(x^{(i)})$ is the probability distribution output of the i-th instance $x^{(i)}$, $y^{(i)}$ is the category label of $x^{(i)}$, m is the total category number of the training data, and θ is the parameter of the network.

4   Experiments

This section presents the experiments for verifying the effectiveness of our proposed approach. We adopt 2 widely-used cross-media retrieval datasets and 5 compared methods in the experiments.

4.1   Dataset Introduction

This section introduces the 2 datasets adopted for the experiments, namely Wikipedia dataset and Pascal Sentence dataset.

Wikipedia dataset [2] is widely used for cross-media retrieval evaluation [7,14]. It is based on "featured articles" in Wikipedia, which contains 2,866 image/text pairs with 10 high-level semantic categories. In each pair, the text describes the image with several paragraphs, so they have compact correlation. The dataset is randomly split into two parts: 2,173 pairs are selected as training set and 693 pairs are selected as testing set. We randomly select 3 categories as unseen categories and the other 7 categories as seen categories. We shuffle the categories randomly and use 3 folds to define 3 of those splits. The performance is averaged over the folds.

Pascal Sentence dataset [23] is selected from 2008 PASCAL development kit, which contains 1,000 image/text pairs organized into 20 categories. And each image instance has 5 sentences as description. There are 800 texts selected as training set, 200 texts for testing set. We randomly split unseen and seen categories as the portion of 1:3, so 5 categories are randomly selected as unseen categories and the other 15 are categories as seen categories. We also take average of three times of random selections similar as Wikipedia dataset.

4.2 Details of the Deep Architecture

In the implementation, we adopt TensorFlow[1] to develop our model. We use a base learning rate 0.01, whose decay-step is 200, decay-rate is 0.96, weight-decay is $5e-4$, and batch size is set to be 100. We also apply dropout with probability 0.9 on fully-connected layers to prevent over fitting. For image representation learning, the five convolutional layers along with FC6 and FC7 of AlexNet are pre-trained on ImageNet and FC8 is fine-tuned with the images in each dataset. For text representation learning, two fully-connected layers are adopted with 4096 hidden layer nodes. Category weight vector is generated through two fully-connected layers with 4096 hidden layer nodes of category weight vector prediction. In part of knowledge transfer learning, the output is generated by dot product with category weight vector and image/text feature, and finally gets through a softmax to produce a probability distribution into common semantic representation.

4.3 Compared Methods and Input Settings

5 state-of-the-art methods are compared in the experiments: CCA [24], CFA [4], KCCA [25], JRL [14] and Deep-SM [6]. Among these, CCA, CFA, KCCA and JRL are traditional methods, while Deep-SM is DNN-based method. The 5 compared methods are briefly introduced as follows:

- **CCA** learns a common space for different media types, which is able to maximize the correlation of them.
- **CFA** learns linear projection functions to project the cross-media data to one common space, which minimizes the Frobenius norm between the pairwise cross-media data.

---

[1] https://www.tensorflow.org.

- **KCCA** holds the idea of first projecting the data into a higher-dimensional feature space and then performing CCA. In our experiments, the kernel functions used are radial basis function (RBF).
- **JRL** simultaneously learns linear projections for different media types with semantic information, semi-supervised regularization and sparse regularization.
- **Deep-SM** uses CNN model pre-trained on ImageNet as the feature extractor for images, learns common representation based on DNN framework.

For image, the processing is end-to-end in our approach, and it directly takes the original image as input. Deep-SM also takes original images as input. However, all the other methods including CCA, CFA, KCCA, JRL can only take feature vector as input. For them we take the same pre-trained AlexNet adopted by our approach as feature extractor. Then we extract the output of the FC7 layer as the feature vector. For text, our approach and all the compared methods use the same BOW features. For Wikipedia dataset, the BOW features are of 3,000-dimension, and the 1,000-dimensional BOW features are used for Pascal Sentence dataset. The feature of textual descriptions of each category is a 450-dimensional BOW feature.

4.4 Evaluation Metrics

For two retrieval tasks: Image→Text and Text→Image, we first use all compared methods and our approach to obtain the output features for all testing images and texts. Then taking Image→Text task as example, we take each image as query, and measure the cosine distance between the output feature of the query image and all texts. Finally, we get a ranking list according to the distances and then compute the mean average precision (MAP) to evaluate the retrieval results.

The MAP scores are computed as all queries' mean of average precision (AP), and AP is computed as:

$$AP = \frac{1}{R} \sum_{k=1}^{n} \frac{R_k}{k} \times rel_k \tag{5}$$

where R denotes relevant item number in testing set (according to the label in our experiments), R_k denotes the relevant item number in top k results, n denotes the testing set size, and $rel_k = 1$ means the k-th result is relevant, and 0 otherwise.

4.5 Experimental Results

Table 1 shows the MAP scores in our experiments on the 2 datasets. On Wikipedia dataset, our approach achieves the highest MAP score of 0.225. Comparing with the best compared method Deep-SM, our approach obtains an inspiring improvement of 0.055. Similar trends can be seen on Pascal Sentence dataset, where our approach remains the highest MAP score of 0.227. This is because these compared methods only learn information from seen categories data and

Table 1. MAP scores of our approach and compared methods.

Dataset	Method	Task		
		Image→Text	Text→Image	Average
Wikipedia dataset	**Ours**	**0.277**	**0.174**	**0.225**
	CCA	0.141	0.152	0.146
	CFA	0.169	0.159	0.164
	KCCA	0.157	0.168	0.162
	JRL	0.160	0.166	0.163
	Deep-SM	0.184	0.156	0.170
Pascal Sentences dataset	**Ours**	**0.256**	**0.198**	**0.227**
	CCA	0.097	0.096	0.096
	CFA	0.169	0.193	0.181
	KCCA	0.182	0.211	0.197
	JRL	0.150	0.154	0.152
	Deep-SM	0.189	0.183	0.186

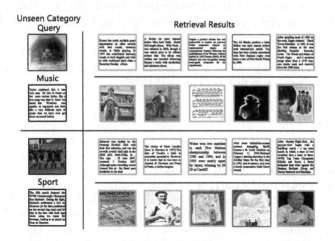

Fig. 3. Some zero-shot cross-media retrieval results of our approach on Wikipedia dataset. There are four examples of unseen category queries on left row. Top five retrieval results are shown on the right. The correct results are of green boxes and wrong results of red boxes. (Color figure online)

give no considerations to unseen categories. So the performances of them are not effective with unseen categories data retrieval. Our approach can make use of external knowledge from encyclopedias and automatically obtain attribute information of both seen and unseen categories. Besides, both multimedia and external knowledge information is considered in a neural network to map cross-media data to a common semantic representation. Some result examples of our approach on Wikipedia dataset are shown in Fig. 3.

5 Conclusion

This paper has proposed the new approach on zero-shot cross-media retrieval, which is designed to utilize the external knowledge transfer for unseen categories data and generate common semantic representation for cross-media data. Our approach first obtains textual descriptions from online encyclopedias, and then learns category weight vectors for both seen and unseen categories, which contain rich implicit external knowledge. Then we model the multimedia and external knowledge information to generate output features into common semantic representation, by joint optimization of category weight vectors and media features in a deep neural network. The proposed approach can explore semantic correlation of different media types and utilize the external knowledge transfer at the same time for zero-shot cross-media retrieval, and get better results on zero-shot cross-media retrieval. Experimental results on 2 widely-used datasets compared with state-of-the-art methods verify the effectiveness of our proposed approach.

The future work lies in two aspects: First, the utilization of external knowledge is only from textual descriptions and not involved with other types such as images and videos in online encyclopedias. So we intend to incorporate external knowledge of various types into our framework. Second, for text data processing, we will apply more effective model such as RNN or LSTM to make better use of textual information.

Acknowledgments. This work was supported by National Natural Science Foundation of China under Grants 61371128 and 61532005.

References

1. Lew, M.S., Sebe, N., Djeraba, C., Jain, R.: Content-based multimedia information retrieval: state of the art and challenges. ACM Trans. Multimed. Comput. Commun. Appl. (TOMM) **2**(1), 1–9 (2006)
2. Rasiwasia, N., Costa Pereira, J., Coviello, E., Doyle, G., Lanckriet, G.R., Levy, R., Vasconcelos, N.: A new approach to cross-modal multimedia retrieval. In: ACM International Conference on Multimedia (ACM MM), pp. 251–260 (2010)
3. Ranjan, V., Rasiwasia, N., Jawahar, C.: Multi-label cross-modal retrieval. In: IEEE Conference on Computer Vision and Pattern Recognition (CVPR), pp. 4094–4102 (2015)
4. Li, D., Dimitrova, N., Li, M., Sethi, I.K.: Multimedia content processing through cross-modal association. In: ACM International Conference on Multimedia (ACM MM), pp. 604–611 (2003)
5. Peng, Y., Huang, X., Qi, J.: Cross-media shared representation by hierarchical learning with multiple deep networks. In: International Joint Conference on Artificial Intelligence (IJCAI), pp. 3846–3853 (2016)
6. Wei, Y., Zhao, Y., Lu, C., Wei, S., Liu, L., Zhu, Z., Yan, S.: Cross-modal retrieval with CNN visual features: a new baseline. IEEE Trans. Cybern. (TCYB) **47**(2), 449–460 (2017)
7. Feng, F., Wang, X., Li, R.: Cross-modal retrieval with correspondence autoencoder. In: ACM International Conference on Multimedia (ACM MM), pp. 7–16 (2014)

8. Palatucci, M., Pomerleau, D., Hinton, G.E., Mitchell, T.M.: Zero-shot learning with semantic output codes. In: Annual Conference on Neural Information Processing Systems (NIPS), pp. 1410–1418 (2009)
9. Larochelle, H., Erhan, D., Bengio, Y.: Zero-data learning of new tasks. In: AAAI Conference on Artificial Intelligence (AAAI), pp. 646–651 (2008)
10. Lampert, C.H., Nickisch, H., Harmeling, S.: Attribute-based classification for zero-shot visual object categorization. IEEE Trans. Pattern Anal. Mach. Intell. (TPAMI) **36**(3), 453–465 (2014)
11. Akata, Z., Perronnin, F., Harchaoui, Z., Schmid, C.: Label-embedding for attribute-based classification. In: IEEE Conference on Computer Vision and Pattern Recognition (CVPR), pp. 819–826 (2013)
12. Elhoseiny, M., Saleh, B., Elgammal, A.: Write a classifier: zero-shot learning using purely textual descriptions. In: IEEE International Conference on Computer Vision (ICCV), pp. 2584–2591 (2014)
13. Ba, J.L., Swersky, K., Fidler, S., Salakhutdinov, R.: Predicting deep zero-shot convolutional neural networks using textual descriptions. In: IEEE International Conference on Computer Vision (ICCV), pp. 4247–4255 (2016)
14. Zhai, X., Peng, Y., Xiao, J.: Learning cross-media joint representation with sparse and semisupervised regularization. IEEE Trans. Circuits Syst. Video Technol. (TCSVT) **24**(6), 965–978 (2014)
15. Ngiam, J., Khosla, A., Kim, M., Nam, J., Lee, H., Ng, A.Y.: Multimodal deep learning. In: International Conference on Machine Learning (ICML), pp. 689–696 (2011)
16. He, Y., Xiang, S., Kang, C., Wang, J., Pan, C.: Cross-modal retrieval via deep and bidirectional representation learning. IEEE Trans. Multimed. (TMM) **18**(7), 1363–1377 (2016)
17. Kankuekul, P., Kawewong, A., Tangruamsub, S., Hasegawa, O.: Online incremental attribute-based zero-shot learning. In: IEEE Conference on Computer Vision and Pattern Recognition (CVPR), pp. 3657–3664 (2012)
18. Wu, S., Bondugula, S., Luisier, F., Zhuang, X., Natarajan, P.: Zero-shot event detection using multi-modal fusion of weakly supervised concepts. In: IEEE Conference on Computer Vision and Pattern Recognition (CVPR), pp. 2665–2672 (2014)
19. Farhadi, A., Endres, I., Hoiem, D., Forsyth, D.: Describing objects by their attributes. In: IEEE Conference on Computer Vision and Pattern Recognition (CVPR), pp. 1778–1785 (2009)
20. Parikh, D., Grauman, K.: Relative attributes. In: IEEE International Conference on Computer Vision (ICCV), pp. 503–510 (2011)
21. Deng, J., Dong, W., Socher, R., Li, L.J., Li, K., Fei-Fei, L.: ImageNet: a large-scale hierarchical image database. In: IEEE Conference on Computer Vision and Pattern Recognition (CVPR), pp. 248–255 (2009)
22. Krizhevsky, A., Sutskever, I., Hinton, G.E.: ImageNet classification with deep convolutional neural networks. In: Annual Conference on Neural Information Processing Systems (NIPS), pp. 1097–1105 (2012)
23. Farhadi, A., Hejrati, M., Sadeghi, M.A., Young, P., Rashtchian, C., Hockenmaier, J., Forsyth, D.: Every picture tells a story: generating sentences from images. In: Daniilidis, K., Maragos, P., Paragios, N. (eds.) ECCV 2010. LNCS, vol. 6314, pp. 15–29. Springer, Heidelberg (2010). https://doi.org/10.1007/978-3-642-15561-1_2
24. Hotelling, H.: Relations between two sets of variates. Biometrika **28**(3/4), 321–377 (1936)
25. Hardoon, D.R., Szedmák, S.R., Shawe-Taylor, J.R.: Canonical correlation analysis: an overview with application to learning methods. Neural Comput. **16**(12), 2639–2664 (2004)

Regular Poster Papers

A Novel Computer-Aided Diagnosis Method of Nasopharyngeal Carcinoma Based on Magnetic Resonance Images

Xiang Tian[1], Yan Zhang[1], Qingbin Wu[2(✉)], Changzheng Shi[3], Xiaoping Li[3], Chunmei Qing[1], and Lin Shu[1]

[1] School of Electronic and Information Engineering,
South China University of Technology, Guangzhou, Guangdong, China
xtian@scut.edu.cn
[2] Information Department, The First Affiliated Hospital of Jinan University,
Guangzhou, Guangdong, China
spgoal@163.com
[3] Medical Imaging Center, The First Affiliated Hospital of Jinan University,
Guangzhou, Guangdong, China

Abstract. A novel computer-aided method based on magnetic resonance images (MRI) was proposed for the early detection and diagnosis of nasopharyngeal carcinoma (NPC). A local Chan-Vese level-set model, which integrated the maximum interclass-variance method with the Chan-Vese model, was built to detect foci with unobvious boundaries. For each of the suspected foci, 26 features, including suspected focus texture, shape, and grayscale characteristics, were extracted, and then classified with a support-vector-machine (SVM) classifier. The method was tested with 289 brain images of 48 patients with nasopharyngeal carcinoma and 33 healthy adults, which obtained an average successful-diagnosis rate of 90.74%.

1 Introduction

The incidence of nasopharyngeal carcinoma is the highest among the malignant tumors in head and neck cancer. Nasopharyngeal cancer can be successfully cured in 90% of cases when early detected [1]. Magnetic resonance imaging has a high resolution for soft tissue, and it is far less harmful compared with X-ray, CT, etc. Therefore, magnetic resonance imaging is commonly used and plays an important role in computer-aided diagnosis of nasopharyngeal carcinoma [2].

The study of computer-aided diagnosis based on medical images has been mainly focused on the diagnosis of breast cancer, lung cancer, colon cancer and other diseases [3], but relatively few attentions have been paid to nasopharyngeal carcinoma. And those about nasopharyngeal carcinoma have been focused on the segmentation of suspected foci rather than diagnosis. Chanapai et al. [4] proposed an automatic segmentation method of nasopharyngeal neoplasms based on CT images, in which, according to the location of nasopharyngeal carcinoma, three

© Springer Nature Singapore Pte Ltd. 2018
B. Huet et al. (Eds.): ICIMCS 2017, CCIS 819, pp. 215–225, 2018.
https://doi.org/10.1007/978-981-10-8530-7_21

probability functions were established, and then points with the highest probabilities were chosen as seed points for the region growth. Ritthipravat et al. [5] proposed an improved method of regional growth to realize segmentation of nasal mucosa region in CT enhanced images. However, this method required an iterative operation for each CT fault, which was time consuming. Fitton et al. [6] realized segmentation of nasopharyngeal carcinoma foci for weighted CT-MRI images, in which, a rough outline of the tumor was sketched, and then the Snake method was used to accurately segment foci from a CT-MRI registration image. The method was a semi-automatic method that required manual intervention. Han et al. [7] used a modified Markov random field model to realize semi-automatic segmentation of head and neck tumors in PET-CT images.

The eventual aim of image processing herein is not segmentation itself but diagnosis, therefore, in this paper, we establish a computer-aided diagnostic method for nasopharyngeal carcinoma based on magnetic resonance images.

Since foci can usually be found in the nasal-mucosa regions for a nasopharyngeal carcinoma patient, we propose a method to segment suspected foci from nasal-mucosa regions in brain MRI images, so as to improve the accuracy of diagnosis of nasopharyngeal carcinoma. The boundaries of nasopharyngeal carcinoma foci are unobvious, which makes it rather difficult to segment them from magnetic resonance images. We tackle this problem by improving the Chan-Vese model: Firstly, the Ostu threshold segmentation method is used, and the local image containing the nasal mucosa regions is constructed according to the symmetry of the brain. Then the Chan-Vese model is used to segment the nasal mucosa regions in the local image. By using principal component analysis, we extract features of the nasal mucosa regions from the aspects of texture, shape, and gray scale. Finally, using the support vector machine as a classifier to aid diagnosis.

The rest of the paper is organized as follows: Sect. 2 introduces the workflow of the proposed method in this paper. In Sect. 3, we briefly review the Chan-Vese model and describe our local Chan-Vese model, the proposed model is validated by some experiments on real magnetic resonance images. In Sect. 4, the method for feature extraction and classification are presented. Finally, some conclusive remarks are included in Sect. 5.

2   Framework of the Method

As shown in Fig. 1, the computer-aided diagnosis of nasopharyngeal carcinoma based on magnetic resonance images is implemented in the following four steps: (1) Magnetic resonance image pre-processing, (2) segmentation of the region of interest: in this paper, the region of interest refers to the nasopharyngeal mucosa region in the brain MRI, (3) feature extraction and selection, (4) classification and identification: by using the support vector machine as a classifier.

A surgeon usually makes diagnosis of nasopharyngeal carcinoma by considering the image features at the cross-sectional areas of brain MRI. And nasopharyngeal carcinoma foci exhibit medium and even high signal intensity in T2 sequence, which makes it easy to segment the areas of interest [8]. Therefore, the method proposed herein is carried out on the T2-weighted sequence of the cross-sectional areas of brain MRI. In line with the imaging principle of MRI, artifacts and noises may form due to the non-uniformity of the magnetic field, the movement of the patient during imaging process, etc., and the images usually require appropriate pre-processing to reduce or eliminate the noise [9]. The experimental data of this paper are provided by the First Affiliated Hospital of Jinan University. In this paper, median filter is used to smooth the images. Meanwhile, the boundaries of nasopharyngeal carcinoma foci are unobvious, therefore, the histogram transformation is used to adjust the contrast, and enhance the denoised MR images.

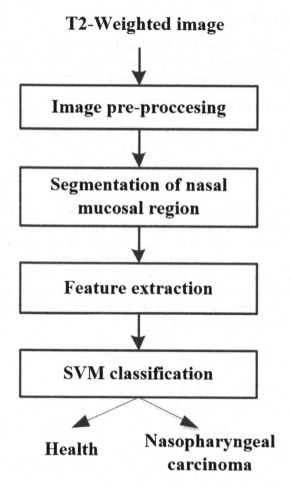

Fig. 1. Automatic diagnosis workflow

3   Segmentation

Foci can usually be found in the nasal-mucosa regions for a nasopharyngeal carcinoma patient, so we mainly consider the segmentation of nasal mucosa in brain MRI images. Due to the low contrast ratio of Brain MR images, the complexity and diversity of the tissues and organs of a brain, the diversity among individuals, the ambiguity of the boundary between the nasal mucosa and the adjacent soft tissues, etc., the segmentation of nasal mucosal regions is the core and most difficult problem of computer aided diagnosis of nasopharyngeal carcinoma. To tackle it, we propose a local Chan-Vese level set model for nasal-mucosal region segmentation.

3.1   Chan-Vese Model

The Chan-Vese model proposed by Chan and Vese in 2001 is the most popular model based on the boundary level set method [10]. It searches for the real image boundary by minimizing the energy function defined in (1) [10].

$$
\begin{aligned}
E(c_1, c_2, \Gamma) &= \mu length(\Gamma) \\
&+ \lambda_1 \int \int_{inside(\Gamma)} |u(x, y) - c_1|^2 dxdy \\
&+ \lambda_2 \int \int_{outside(\Gamma)} |u(x, y) - c_2|^2 dxdy
\end{aligned} \tag{1}
$$

Where $u(x, y)$ is a given image, represents a closed curve that divides an image into a target and a background, μ, λ_1 and λ_2 are positive constants, c_1 and c_2 are the intensity averages of $u(x, y)$ inside Γ and outside Γ, respectively.

To solve this minimization problem, the level set method [11] is used which replaces the unknown curve Γ by the level-set function $\phi(x, y)$, in which $\phi(x, y) > 0$ if the point (x, y) is inside Γ, $\phi(x, y) < 0$ if (x, y) is outside Γ, and $\phi(x, y) = 0$ if (x, y) is on Γ. Thus, the energy function defined in (1) is reformulated in terms of the level set function ϕ as shown in (2).

$$
\begin{aligned}
E(\phi, c_1, c_2) &= \mu \int \int_{\Omega} \delta_\varepsilon(\phi) |\nabla \phi| dxdy \\
&+ \nu \int \int_{\Omega} H_\varepsilon(-\phi) |\nabla \phi| dxdy \\
&+ \lambda_1 \int \int_{\Omega} |u(x, y) - c_1|^2 H_\varepsilon(\phi) dxdy \\
&+ \lambda_2 \int \int_{\Omega} |u(x, y) - c_2|^2 (1 - H_\varepsilon(\phi)) dxdy
\end{aligned} \tag{2}
$$

Where the regularized approximation of Heaviside function $H_\varepsilon(\phi)$, denoted as $H(\phi)$, and the regularized approximation of Dirac delta function $\delta_\varepsilon(\phi)$, denoted as $\delta(\phi)$, are defined in (3) and (4), respectively.

$$H(z) = \begin{cases} 1, & if z >= 0 \\ 0, & if z < 0 \end{cases} \tag{3}$$

$$\delta(z) = \frac{d}{dz}H(z) \tag{4}$$

Turning the minimization problem into an Euler-Lagrange equation, and then updating the level set function ϕ by means of the gradient descent method, we have (5).

$$\frac{\partial \phi}{\partial t} = \delta_\varepsilon(\phi)[\mu \cdot \kappa - \nu - \lambda_1(\mu - c_1)^2 + \lambda(\mu - c_2)^2] \tag{5}$$

Where $\kappa = \nabla(\nabla\phi/|\nabla\phi|)$ stands for the average curvature of the closed curve Γ, and the points on the boundary curve Γ at moment t satisfy $\phi_t = 0$.

Let ϕ be equal, and minimize $E(\phi, c_1, c_2)$, thus we can update c_1 and c_2, respectively, at each iteration following (6) and (7), respectively.

$$c_1(\phi) = \frac{\int \int_\Omega u(x,y)H_\varepsilon(\phi)dxdy}{\int \int_\Omega H_\varepsilon(\phi)dxdy} \tag{6}$$

$$c_2(\phi) = \frac{\int \int_\Omega u(x,y)(1 - H_\varepsilon(\phi))dxdy}{\int \int_\Omega (1 - H_\varepsilon(\phi))dxdy} \tag{7}$$

When one segments the target region with the Chan-Vese model, the evolution velocity and direction of the contour curve are independent of the gradient information of the target boundary. Therefore, satisfactory segmentation effect can be achieved even when the boundary of the target region is blur. However, the energy function of the Chan-Vese model assumes that there are only two homogeneous regions of the target and the background. When there are more homogeneous regions in the image, the model can not convergence to right target edge [12].

Local Chan-Vese Model. To overcome the shortcoming of the Chan-Vese model on multi-target image segmentation, this paper proposes a local Chan-Vese level set model for the segmentation of nasal mucosal regions. Firstly, the entire brain image is segmented using the maximum interclass variance method (Ostu method), and local images including the nasal mucosa region are constructed according to the symmetry of the brain. Then the initial contours are defined in the local images, and the nasal mucosa region is precisely segmented using the Chan-Vese model. Since the gray scales of different organizations in brain MR images are uneven, there are holes and noise in the brain region of the binary image segmented by the Ostu method. Then the binary image is processed by mathematical morphology to obtain the complete brain region, and the position of the vertical symmetry axis of the brain is estimated. Considering the facts that the nasal mucosa is symmetrical about the vertical symmetry axis of the brain, and the nasal mucosa region locate substantially in the upper part of the brain region, four control points are chosen according to the brain region and vertical symmetry axis position to form a rectangular region which includes the nasal mucosa region. The size of the fixed rectangle is 150×150. The rectangular area obtained is the local image of the entire nasal mucosa region. Then define an initial contour in the local image, and solve the numerical approximation of Eq. (7), as shown in (8), by means of discrete network and the finite difference method. The initial contours defined in this paper are rectangular contours whose sizes are smaller than the local image sizes.

$$
\begin{aligned}
\frac{\phi_{i,j}^{n+1} - \phi_{i,j}^{n}}{\Delta t} &= \delta_{\varepsilon}(\phi_{i,j}^{n})[\frac{\mu}{h^2}\Delta^x - \left(\frac{\Delta_+^x \phi_{i,j}^{n+1}}{\Delta_+^x \phi_{i,j}^{n}/h^2 + (\phi_{i,j+1}^{n} - \phi_{i,j-1}^{n})^2/h^2}\right) \\
&+ \frac{\nu}{h^2}\Delta^y - \left(\frac{\Delta_+^y \phi_{i,j}^{n+1}}{\Delta_+^y \phi_{i,j}^{n}/h^2 + (\phi_{i,j+1}^{n} - \phi_{i,j-1}^{n})^2/h^2}\right) \\
&- \lambda_1(u(i,j) - c_1(\phi^n))^2 + \lambda_2(u(i,j) - c_2(\phi^n))^2]
\end{aligned}
\tag{8}
$$

Algorithm 1 below describes the main steps of the proposed local Chan-Vese level set model.

Algorithm 1. Local Chan-Vese level set model

Input: the magnetic resonance image after pre-processing;
  1: Segmentation of the entire brain region using the Ostu method;
  2: Construct the local image containing the nasal mucosa region using the symmetry of the brain;
  3: Define the initial contour in the local image;
  4: **for** $n = 1, 2, \cdots, N$ **do**
  5:     Determine the value of the current level set function ϕ^n, then figure out $c_1(\phi^n)$, $c_2(\phi^n)$, and the curvature $\kappa(\phi_n)$ of current contour;
  6:     Figure out the value of the level set function at the next moment, and update the contour curve;
  7:     **if** the current contour curve converges to the boundary of the nasal mucosal region **then**
  8:         Stop iteration, and output the final contour curve;
  9:     **else**
 10:         Repeat step 5, continue iterations;
 11:     **end if**
 12: **end for**
Output: the nasal mucosa region

3.2   Segmentation Experiments

The experimental data, which contains 48 cases of brain MR images of nasopharyngeal carcinoma patients, and 33 cases of brain MR images of healthy adults, are provided by the First Affiliated Hospital of Jinan University. For each nasopharyngeal carcinoma patient or healthy adult, we select from the cross-section T2 weighted sequence 3 to 5 frames of images which contain the nasopharynx. Totally 120 frames of images are selected from the brain MR images of the 33 healthy adults, and 169 frames of images are selected from those of the 48 nasopharyngeal carcinoma patients. Several magnetic resonance images of patients with nasopharyngeal carcinoma are shown in Fig. 2. The initial rectangle contour is defined in local image containing the nasopharynx, and the number of iterations is 200. The traditional Chan-Vese model is used to segment the nasal mucosa region, the experimental results are shown in Fig. 3. The proposed local Chan-Vese model is also used to segment the nasal mucosa region, and the experimental results are shown in Fig. 4.

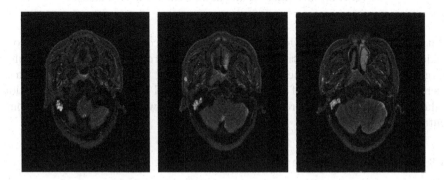

Fig. 2. Initial magnetic resonance images

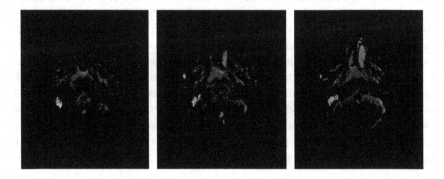

Fig. 3. Segmentation results using Chan-Vese model

According to the experimental results, the local Chan-Vese level set method proposed in this paper has the following advantages compared with the traditional Chan-Vese model: Firstly, the Otsu method is used to obtain the brain region, and local images containing the nasal mucosa region are constructed according to the symmetry of the brain, which can reduce manual intervention.

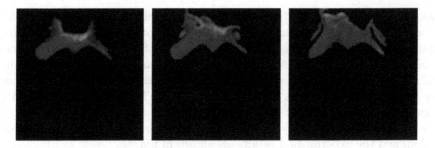

Fig. 4. Segmentation results using local Chan-Vese model

Rather than the whole image, only the local image containing the nasal mucosa region is used for segmentation, so as to avoid the problem of segmenting multi-target region. Moreover, the local image containing the nasal mucosa region is merely a very small part of the original image, and only the level-set function value in the local image is required to be updated, which greatly reduced computation cost.

3.3   Error Performance

The programming language is MATLAB. The experimental platform is Intel Pentium P6100 with speed 2.00 GHz, and memory 2 GBs. The size of each of the original magnetic resonance images is 512×512. The proposed segmentation algorithm is further evaluated with three commonly used measures: reliability, accuracy, and segmentation efficiency [2]. And the results are: The reliability of the segmentation algorithm is between 78.4% and 90.27%, with an average of 84.06%. The accuracy is between 78.39% and 91.92%, with an average of 85.82%. It costs the traditional Chan-Vese model about 35 s to segment a magnetic resonance image, and the segmentation results are shown in Fig. 3. As shown in Fig. 3, the obtained images contain some noise. It costs the method proposed in this paper about 20 s to segment a magnetic resonance image, and the segmentation results are shown in Fig. 4. As shown in Fig. 4, the proposed method could effectively segment the nasal mucosa area. The experimental results show that the segmentation algorithm proposed in this paper could effectively improve the speed and precision of segmentation.

4   Feature Extraction and Classification

According to the characteristics of the medical images of nasopharyngeal carcinoma patients and healthy adults, shape, size, and grayscale information of nasopharyngeal mucosal are usually considered in the subjective diagnosis of nasopharyngeal carcinoma. Therefore, during the implementation of classification, features are extracted from these three aspects of the nasal mucosa region.

In this paper, the gray-level co-occurrence matrix method [14] is used to describe the texture features of the nasal mucosa region. For each nasal mucosa region, the gray-level co-occurrence matrix in four directions, $0°$, $45°$, $90°$, $145°$, are determined, and the energy, contrast, correlation and entropy are figured out for each direction of the co-occurrence matrix, then the mean and standard deviation of the four features in all directions are also figured out. Thus, the final extracted texture feature is an 8-dimensional eigenvector.

The shape features of the nasal mucosa region are described by the geometrical features and the Hu seventh order invariant moments. As a highly generalized image feature, Hu seventh order invariant moment possesses invariance under translation, rotation, scale, and other distortion. Furthermore, five geometric shapes features, including area, circumference, elongation, rectangle, and circularity, are also extracted. The final extracted shape feature is a 12-dimensional eigenvector.

The gray features extracted are statistical features based on histogram, including gray mean, variance, inclination, peak state, energy, and entropy, which forms a 6-dimensional eigenvector.

Thus, the features extracted for the nasal mucosa region form a 26-dimensional vector. Principal components are then chosen from these 26 features to reduce redundancy. Apply the principal component analysis to the data, and the results show that, the first eight principal components contribute more than 95% of the characteristic information. Therefore, the original 26-dimensional eigenvector is compressed into an 8-dimensional eigenvector.

Then, we use support vector machine (SVM) as classifier [16]. The feature set contains 289 samples, 60% of which are randomly selected as training samples, and the remaining 40% ones are as test samples. The kernel function used in the SVM classifier is the Gaussian radial basis function. The classification results are shown in Table 1.

Table 1. SVM classification results

	Accuracy of training	Accuracy of test
NPC	95.45%	88.14%
Health	92.11%	86.36%
Overall	94.09%	87.38%

As shown in Table 1, the correctness rate of the training is 94.09%, and that of the classification is 87.38%. The average correct rate of the support vector machine is 90.74%.

We further compare the performance of the support vector machine with that of random forest (RF) and neural network (NN), with the results shown in Table 2.

Table 2. Comparison of different classification methods

	SVM	RF	NN
Accuracy of train	94.09%	100%	100%
Accuracy of test	87.38%	84.46%	82.52%

As shown in Table 2, the support vector machine (SVM) is not as good as random forest and neural network in training, but the accuracy of the test is higher; the random forest and the neural network method are obviously over-fitted; In general, the support vector machine exhibits better generalization ability.

5   Conclusions

A computer-aided diagnosis method of nasopharyngeal carcinoma based on brain MR images was proposed. In the method, a local Chan-Vese model was introduced to segment the nasal mucosa region; 26 features were extracted from the nasal mucosa region, and then compressed into 8 principal components; finally, classification and diagnosis were implemented with a support vector machine. The experiment results demonstrated a satisfactory performance of the classifier.

However, the diagnosis of nasopharyngeal cancer is rather complex and difficult. There are still lots to be done, e.g., optimization of model parameters, improvement of the segmentation algorithm, extraction of better features, etc., in our future study.

Acknowledgments. This work is supported in part by the Guangzhou Key Lab of Body Data Science (201605030011) and the Diabetes Intelligent Wear Monitoring Equipment and Complications Prevention and Control Cloud Platform (2016B010108008) and the Research and Application of Mobile Medical Technology (2015B010106008).

References

1. Prasad, U., Pathmanathan, R., Sam, C.K., Rampal, L., Singh, J.: Early diagnosis of nasopharyngeal carcinoma: a multi-pronged approach. In: Ablashi, D.V., Faggioni, A., Krueger, G.R.F., Pagano, J.S., Pearson, G.R. (eds.) Epstein-Barr Virus and Human Disease Experimental Biology and Medicine. EBAM, vol. 20. Humana Press, New York (1989). https://doi.org/10.1007/978-1-4612-4508-7_58
2. Liu, D.J., Yuan, L.I., Wei-Min, A.N., et al.: Study on liver cancer computer-aided diagnosis based on medical imaging. Chin. Med. Equip. (2015)
3. Wang, X.F., Nie, S.D., Wang, Y.J.: Progress in computer-aided detection for brain tumor using MRI. Chin. J. Med. Phys. **1**, 11 (2014)
4. Chanapai, W., Bhongmakapat, T., Tuntiyatorn, L., et al.: Nasopharyngeal carcinoma segmentation using a region growing technique. Int. J. Comput. Assist. Radiol. Surg. **7**, 413–422 (2012)

5. Ritthipravat, P., Tatanun, C., Bhongmakapat, T., et al.: Automatic segmentation of nasopharyngeal carcinoma from CT images. In: International Conference on BioMedical Engineering and Informatics, vol. 2, pp. 18–22 (2008)
6. Fitton, I., Cornelissen, S.A.P., Duppen, J.C., et al.: Semi-automatic delineation using weighted CT-MRI registered images for radiotherapy of nasopharyngeal cancer. Med. Phys. **38**, 4662–4666 (2011)
7. Han, D., Bayouth, J., Song, Q., Taurani, A., Sonka, M., Buatti, J., Wu, X.: Globally optimal tumor segmentation in PET-CT images: a graph-based co-segmentation method. In: Székely, G., Hahn, H.K. (eds.) IPMI 2011. LNCS, vol. 6801, pp. 245–256. Springer, Heidelberg (2011). https://doi.org/10.1007/978-3-642-22092-0_21
8. Dvořák, P., Kropatsch, W.G., Bartušek, K.: Automatic brain tumor detection in T2-weighted magnetic resonance images. Meas. Sci. Rev. **13**(5), 223–230 (2013)
9. Ghanavati, S., Li, J., Liu, T., et al.: Automatic brain tumor detection in magnetic resonance images. In: 2012 9th IEEE International Symposium on Biomedical Imaging (ISBI), pp. 574–577 (2012)
10. Chan, T.F., Vese, L.A.: Active contours without edges. IEEE Trans. Image Process. **10**(2), 266–277 (2001)
11. Osher, S., Sethian, J.A.: Fronts propagating with curvature-dependent speed: algorithms based on Hamilton-Jacobi formulations. J. Comput. Phys. **79**(1), 12–49 (1988)
12. Wang, X.F., Huang, D.S., Xu, H.: An efficient local Chan-Vese model for image segmentation. Pattern Recogn. **43**(3), 603–618 (2010)
13. Otsu, N.: A threshold selection method from gray-level histograms. IEEE Trans. Syst. Man Cybern. **9**(1), 62–66 (1979)
14. Zacharaki, E.I., Wang, S., Chawla, S., et al.: Classification of brain tumor type and grade using MRI texture and shape in a machine learning scheme. Magn. Reson. Med. **62**(6), 1609–1618 (2009)
15. Saha, M., Mukherjee, R., Chakraborty, C.: Computer-aided diagnosis of breast cancer using cytological images: a systematic review. Tissue Cell **48**(5), 461–474 (2016)
16. Jayachandran, A., Dhanasekaran, R.: Brain tumor detection and classification of MR images using texture features and fuzzy SVM classifier. Res. J. Appl. Sci. Eng. Technol. **6**(12), 2264–2269 (2013)

A Real-Time Distributed Index Based on Topic for Microblogging System

Zhikun Chen[1(✉)], Lu Wang[1,2], and Shuqiang Yang[2]

[1] Naval Academy of Armament (NAA), Beijing, China
zkchen@nudt.edu.cn
[2] Computer Department, National University of Defense Technology,
Changsha, Hunan, China

Abstract. With the development of internet technology and widely used in mobile devices, the microblogging systems such as Twitter and Sina Weibo in China have become the most important platform for people to retrieve information and communicate with each other. The real-time search became a big challenge for microblogging systems because of the volume of data and users. Existing approaches build all microblogs in an index which will increase the cost of index update and query. The search results could not satisfy users' timely and high quality requirements. In this paper, we propose a new real-time distributed index based on topic (RDIBT), which can build index for each topic. Those topical indices will be distributed to many sites, so it can improve the concurrently of queries. Extensive experiments demonstrate the effectiveness and efficiency of RDIBT on the real dataset.

Keywords: Social network · Real-time search · Topic model
Microblog · Index

1 Introduction

The Information Retrieval technology is a mature technology in traditional web context. The traditional web search engines such as Google, Yahoo!, or Bing which can get relative pages from several billion pages in milliseconds. The key technologies of web search engine, include Web crawling [9, 18], indexing [1], and rank algorithms [4, 5, 8, 10, 14, 15], etc. Recently years, microblogging system has become the most popular manner to gain information with the development of Internet technology and mobile device. Most of people select microblogging system to gain the real-time social events or break news instead of web search engines [19]. That is because the social events can be real-time propagated in the microblogging system. So the research of microblog's real-time search is necessary.

In microblogging system, users can post short, 140-character messages, called\ microblog", to their "follower" (other users who following this user). Conversely, users can receive microblogs from people who they following via a number of mechanisms, including web clients, mobile clients, and SMS. In additional, users can repost or reply microblogs which are posted by their following users by their interest. So the information of microblogging system is large, and the propagative speed is very fast.

One salient aspect of microblogging systems is that users demand to know what's happening right now, especially in response to breaking news. So the two major requirements of microblog real-time search, include processing large number of searching requirements quickly and making the new microblogs can be searchable in few seconds after creations. The traditional Web search engines do not have the ability to deliver microblogs to users in a timely fashion.

Recently, several real-time indexing technologies have been developed by many researchers. And those technologies were all been used in some applications. Such as literature [20] proposed the Log-Structured Inverted Indices (LSII). It can solve the problem of inaccuracy results by the index technologies of literatures [6, 7]. Literature [12] proposed real-time indexing for personalized search. With a same search, the system returns different searching results for different users according to users' personalization. But all microblogs' index will be created in a same index file by those indexing technologies. The system not only cannot search the index in parallel for a search, but also have to scan most content of index. So, we can know that those indices are not only have high update cost, but also have high searching cost.

The contributions of this paper are as follows:

(1) We design and implement a real-time distributed index based on topic for microblogging system.
(2) We use the Twitter-LDA [21] to infer the topic of microblogs.
(3) We evaluate the effectiveness and performance of our solution with a real microblog dataset.

The remainder of this paper is organized as follows. Section 2 reviews the topic model of Twitter-LDA model. Section 3 states the framework of our solution. The implementation of indexing module and search are introduced in Sects. 4 and 5, respectively. In Sect. 6 states the experiments study in the real dataset. Section 7 concludes this paper.

2 Twitter-LDA Model

The topic model is a type of statistical model for discovering the abstract "topics" that occur in a collection of documents in machine learning and natural language processing. The traditional topic model such as Latent Dirichlet Allocation (LDA) [3, 13, 17] has been used for topic mining in a lot of applications, but it does not work well in the microblogging system. The major reasons are the short length (the maximum length of a microblog is 140-character and noisy words of microblog (literature [16] has described that the LDA does not work well in the short documents). This paper will use the Twitter-LDA model to infer the topic of microblog. That is because the twitter-LDA has the following characteristics: (1) In this model, it models one microblog as a single topic; (2) In this model, the noisy word will be labeled as background word. The Twitter-LDA had been used in Twitter. The remainder of this section will introduce the philosophy of Twitter-LDA.

So $\theta^u \sim Dir(\alpha)$ is a parameter of Dirichlet distribution, whose probability density function takes Eq. (1), where α is a T dimensions vector.

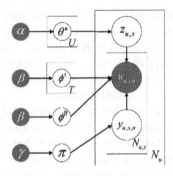

Fig. 1. The graphical model of Twitter-LDA

$$p(\theta|\alpha) = \frac{\Gamma(\sum_{i=1}^{T} \alpha_i)}{\prod_{i=1}^{T} \Gamma(\alpha_i)} \prod_{i=1}^{T} \theta_i^{\alpha_i - 1} \tag{1}$$

In Eq. (1), $\Gamma(x) = \int_0^\infty t^{x-1} e^{-t} dt$ is a Gamma function, and the T dimensions vector has to satisfy Eq. (2):

$$\sum_{i=1}^{T} \theta_i = 1, \theta_i > 0 \tag{2}$$

The graphical presentation of Twitter-LDA is shown in Fig. 1. The detail of generative process of it is shown in Fig. 2. The parameters which will be used in this model are listed in Table 1.

---

1)   Sample $\phi^B \sim Dir(\beta)$ and $\pi \sim Dir(\gamma)$

2)   **for** every topic $t = 1, 2, \cdots, T$

3)   Sample $\phi^t \sim Dir(\beta)$

4)   **for** each user $u = 1, 2, \cdots, U$

5)   Sample $\theta^u \sim Dir(\alpha)$

6)   **for** each microblog from user u, $s = 1, 2, \cdots, N_u$

7)   Sample $z_{u,s} \sim Multi(\pi)$

8)   **if** $y_{u,s,n} = 0$

9)   Sample $w_{u,s,n} \sim Multi(\phi^B)$

10)   **if** $y_{u,s,n} = 1$

11)   Sample $w_{u,s,n} \sim Multi(\phi^{z_{u,s}})$

Fig. 2. Twitter-LDA: the generative process of microblog

Table 1. Parameters in Twitter-LDA model

Symbol	Description
T	The number of topics in the system
U	The number of users in the training data set
α, β, γ	The hyper-parameters
π	The Bernoulli distribution that governs the choice between background words and topic words
θ^u	The topic vector of user u
ϕ^t	The topic word vector
ϕ^B	The background word vector
N_u	The number of microblogs of user u
N_u^i	The number of microblogs of ith topic for user u
$t_{u,s}$	The sth microblog of user u
$W_{u,s}$	The word set of $t_{u,s}$
$N_{u,s}$	The number of words in $t_{u,s}$
$z_{u,s}$	The topic label of $t_{u,s}$
$w_{u,s,n}$	The nth word of $t_{u,s}$
$y_{u,s,n}$	The label of $w_{u,s,n}$

3   The Architecture of Our Solution

This section will introduce the architecture of our solution. It contains four modules, namely data pre-processing, indexing, search, and ranking algorithm, as shown in Fig. 3.

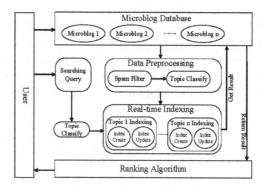

Fig. 3. The architecture of our solution

3.1   Data Preprocessing

The goal of data pre-processing is to reduce the amount of spam microblogs and infer the topic of the incoming microblog, the detail of data pre-processing is shown in Fig. 4.

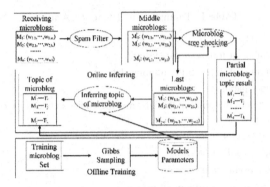

Fig. 4. The process of pre-processing

The data pre-processing contains two components, namely filtering spam microblog and inferring topic of microblog. This paper uses a simple manner to filter spam microblog (reducing the cost of pre-processing)-the spam user's microblog is spam microblog. The users who following the spam users will be confirmed as spam users.

Inferring the topic of microblog is the main work of data pre-processing module. This component contains two parts—inferring the topic according to the characteristics of microblog, and the other according to the content of the microblog. The microblogging system contains the relation of repost and reply. So if a microblog reposts or replies other microblog, then they belong to the same topic. We use a tree model to represent the relation of microblogs, which is shown in Fig. 5. Microblogs in this microblog tree all belong to the same topic which is decided by the root microblog—microblog A. There are some microblogs also do not been inferred after the microblog tree checking, such as the primitive microblog or those microblogs which do not sign any symbol. This paper uses the Twitter-LDA to infer the topic of those microblogs. The topic model based on Twitter-LDA contains offline training and online inferring. We use Gibbs Sampling [13] model to gain some global statistic parameters in the offline training, such as word-topic matrix $\{\phi^t\}_{t=1}^T$, the topic vector of background word ϕ^B, and the Bernoulli distribution that governs the choice between background words and topic words π. We use parameters which are gained from the offline training step to infer the topic of the new incoming microblogs in the online inferring step.

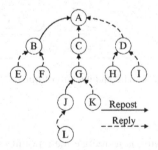

Fig. 5. The tree structure of microblogs

3.2   Indexing

The indexing module maintains the index structure when the new microblog is incoming, which should guarantee the new microblogs are searchable in few seconds after creation. Every topic creates an index, and those topics' indices will be distributed to many nodes. Every topic index has the same index structure which refers to the ETIS structure of literature [11]. The index structure contains three components, includes index creation, index updater, and index replication, the detail of them will be stated in Sect. 4.

(1) Creation: creating a new index block when some layer's index is larger than the threshold.
(2) Update: updating some layer's index block when new index inserts to this layer.
(3) Replication: replicating some layer's index to the next layer when this layer's index is larger than the threshold.

3.3   Search

The goal of search module responses the search requirement of user. This module will infer topics of the keywords which are given by users, and distribute the search requirement to corresponding topic indices. After that, it will merge the results which are produced by the topic index, and return the merged results to user. The detail of search processing will be stated in Sect. 5.

3.4   Rank Algorithm

The rank algorithm of our solution refers to literature [7], it not only considers the time of microblog and user's authority, but also considers the popular of the topic, the expression of this rank algorithm is shown in Eq. (3). This paper does not focuses on the rank algorithm, so we do not state the detail of it, and the implementation detail of rank algorithm can gain from literature [7].

$$Rank(d,q) = \omega_1 \cdot sig(d.user) + \omega_2 \cdot sim(d,q) + \omega_3 \cdot fresh(ts_d, ts_q) \tag{3}$$

Such that:

(1) $\omega_1 + \omega_2 + \omega_3 = 1$, and $\omega_1, \omega_2, \omega_3 > 0$,
(2) $sig(d.user)$ represents the user's authority of this microblog d,
(3) $sim(d,q)$ quantifies the similarity of microblog d with query q,
(4) $fresh(ts_d, ts_q)$ measures the freshness of microblog d with query q based on the timestamps of d and q.

4   The Implementation of Indexing

The index is the key module for search engine. The index of this paper is a distributed inverted index based on content, where each index is created by Lucene [2] which is an open-source text search engine library.

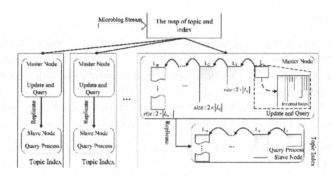

Fig. 6. The architecture of RDIBT

The velocity of new incoming microblogs is rapidly, so how to efficient maintain the index is a large challenge for search engine. RDIBT will create index according to the topic, every topic has a single index structure. So the system always maintains a map relation of topic with index structure, and the map relation is stored in the memory. The architecture of RDIBT is shown in Fig. 6.

The topic index is named Multiple Capacity Index Set (MCIS), the structure is composed by a series of inverted index $L_0, L_1, \cdots, L_m$. The capacity of every layer cannot larger than a threshold, we assume as $\tau_i (0 \leq i \leq m)$. And the threshold of ith layer is multiple of $(i-1)^{th}$ layer, we assume as 2 times in the description of our solution, so $\tau_i = 2 \times \tau_{i-1}$.

Maintaining MCIS structure contains two parts—index creation and index merger. The index creation is invoked when a new topic index needs to be created or a new layer's index needs to be created in the MCIS structure. The index merger is invoked when the capacity of a layer's index is larger than threshold, and there are new indices inserted. So we should merge the lower layer's index into the higher layer. This process may cause cascaded merger operation. We assume a topic's index is composed by L layers, and the lowest layer's (the 0 layer) capacity threshold is m. So the ith layer's capacity threshold of this topic index is $2^i m$. The index of L_0 is created based on new incoming microblogs, while the remainder indices $(l \geq 1)$ are built by merging the index at lower layer $(l-1$ layer). The new incoming microblogs' index of every topic will be created in L_0. So it can update the new incoming microblogs' index with a lower update cost, which can make the new incoming microblogs searchable immediately.

Algorithm 1—Maintain(MC,m,t) is used to maintain the MCIS index structure, where MC is the index of a specially topic, m is the capacity threshold of the 0th layer, t is the multiple of capacity threshold of a layer with its next layer, $\tau_i = t\tau_{i-1} = t^i m$, we assume $t = 2$ in the description of RDIBT. A new index will be created in L_0 when the new incoming microblog is the first microblog of this topic (at lines 3–5). If the total capacity of L_0 and new microblog is larger than the capacity threshold of 0th layer, then a new index I_{new} will be created in the 0th layer. The new incoming microblog's index will be inserted to I_{new}. After that, a new thread will be invoked to merge the indices of

L_0 layer and L_1 layer. Finally the I_{new} will be the L_0 (at lines 6–12). The detail of Merger operation is shown in algorithm 2.

Algorithm 1 Maintain(M C,m ,t)

Input:

 The index for a special topic, M C;

 The capacity threshold of the 0th layer, m;

 The multiple of capacity threshold of a layer with its next layer, t;

1: **while** True **do**

2: **if** a new incoming microblog which belongs to this topic arrives

3:   **if** M C == null **then**

4:    Create the 0-layer's index of M C,L $_0$;

5:   **end if**

6:   if|L$_0$j + l _size(M icb) > m

7:    Create a new index I$_{new}$ for M C;

8:    M C Ã M C[fI$_{new}$g

9:    Add this microblog into I$_{new}$;

10:    Invoke Merge(M C, L $_0$) algorithm in a new thread to merger indices;

11:    Remove the old index of L $_0$;

12:    $L_0 \leftarrow I_{new}$;

13:   **else**

14:    Add this microblog into the L_0 layer index of MC;

15:   **end if**

16: **end if**

17: **end while**

Algorithm 2 Merge(MC, L_i)

Input:

 The index for a special topic, MC;

 The layer of index which need to be merged, L_i;

1: **if** $|L_i| + |L_{i+1}| > \tau_{i+1}$ **then**

2: Create new index file in $i + 1$ layer of MC, I_{new};

3: $I_{new} \leftarrow L_i$;

4: Merge(MC, L_i);

5: $L_{i+1} \leftarrow I_{new}$;

6: **else**

7: Batch merging the indices of L_i into L_{i+1};

8: **end if**

9: Remove the old index of L_i;

10: Replicate(SN, L_{i+1});

The merger operation will be invoked if one layer's capacity is larger than the capacity threshold. If the total capacity of L_i and L_{i+1} is larger than capacity threshold of L_{i+1}, then we should merge L_{i+1} to L_{i+2} first before merging L_i into L_{i+1}, so it is an iterative process (at lines 1–5). If merging L_i into L_{i+1} does not cause merger operation of L_{i+1}, then we will batch merging the indices of L_i into L_{i+1} (at line 7). After that, we should remove the old index of L_i (at line 9). Finally, we replicate the higher layer's indices which have been changed to the slave node, which can guarantee the consistent of the master node with slave node (at line 10). The detail of replication is shown in algorithm 3, we do not state the detail in this paper.

The MCIS has the following properties from the structure of MCIS.

Property 1: The higher layer's index is older than the lower layer. Assume $0 \leq L_i < L_j \leq L$ (L is the height of this index), the index of L_j is older than L_i.

Property 2: The new incoming microblogs are only processed at 0th layer. And L_0 is stored in the memory, so it can be processed quickly.

Property 3: The index structure of Slave node is consistent with Master node, but Slave node does not have the 0-layer index.

So we can know that the MCIS can index new incoming microblogs quickly, and it also can response user's search requirement quickly.

Algorithm 3 Replicate(SN, L_i)

Input:
    The index of Slave Node, SN;
    The index of layer need to be replicated in the master node, L_i;
1:    Create a new index in the ith layer of SN, I_{new};
2:    Replicate i^{th} layer's index of Master Node to the I_{new} of Slave Node, $I_{new} \leftarrow L_i$;
3:    Remove the old i^{th} layer's index of Slave Node;
4:    $SN(L_i) \leftarrow I_{new}$;

5　Search

This section will state the searching process by our index. In our solution, index is built by topic. So we can filter the topic of the keywords to reduce the amount of index which we need to scan. Second, the index is distributed, so the search can be executed in parallel. The process of search is shown in Fig. 7. We can know that the process is composed by four steps, namely topic inferring, dispatch search, search index, and merged results.

5.1　Topic Inferring

The RDIBT is organized by topics, every topic will create an index. At first, we have to infer the topics of the keywords in the process of search. So we can reduce the amount of indices which need to be scanned.

The keywords which are proposed by users are very short, so it is hard to infer them to a special topic. We will use LDA to infer the topic distribution of keywords in this step. LDA model can return a topic distribution vector, assume as $\theta = (\theta^1, \theta^2, \cdots \theta^k)^T$, where θ^i is the probability of the keywords in topic i,k is the amount of topic. So we can know topics which are referred by keywords, and we do not need to scan the topic indices which are not referred by keywords.

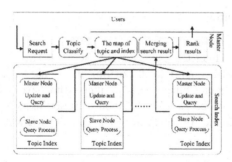

Fig. 7. The process of search

5.2 Search Distribution

We should dispatch the search requirement after inferring the topics of keywords. The process of dispatching search is finished in master node. It will dispatch the search requirement to nodes which store the topic indices that are referred by keywords. The location of topic index can be found by the map of topic with topic index, which is stored in the memory all the time.

5.3 Searching Index

The search requirement is dispatched to many nodes. Every topic index will finish its search individually. The search in a topic index contains the search of master node and slave node. The search of L_0 is finished by master node, other layers' searches are finished by slave node, which can reduce the load of master node. So the master mode can pay more attention to maintain the index, which can guarantee the efficiency of index update. Slave node will search other layers' indices. The search results of master node and slave node have to be merged and sorted according the rank principle. And the finally results of this topic index will be sent to system's master node.

5.4 Merging Results

Every topic index's search result has to return results to system's master node. The master node will merge and sort the results according to the rank algorithm. Every topic indices' results are ordinal, so it can sort all results very quickly. In additional, the results which belong to a microblog tree will be organized as a hierarchical structure. The rank of this hierarchical structure is the maximum rank of this structure's microblogs. The root of the hierarchical structure is the root of this microblog tree. So it can more clearly represent the evolution or development of some important or beak events.

6 Experiments and Results Analyze

In this section, we evaluate the efficiency of indexing and search, and scalability of the system upon real Twitter data set.

6.1   Experiment Setting

All experiments executed in a HBase Cluster which is composed by 11 nodes (every node with a dual-core Intel CPU at 2.8 GHZ, 8G of RAM, 1 TB disks and gigabit Ethernet, run at Ubunt10 system). In all experiments, we use a real Twitter dataset. The set of Twitter data about Chinese-based twitters who have published at least one Chinese tweet was prepared as follows. About 260 000 users and 2.7 million tweets were collected through the API of Twitter. The default parameter settings are listed in Table 2.

Table 2. Default parameter setting

Parameter	Default	Description
Microblogs	1000	# incoming microblogs per second
t	2	The multiple of higher layer
m	64	The capacity threshold of the 0th layer
Searchcount	10000	# search per second

The performance of the index is measured by the following factors: (i) Average Cost Time, the average time consumption on indexing per microblog. (ii) Average Operation Time, the elapsed time to response a search. (iii) Rat, the completeness of the search result, which is represented by Eq. (4), where *Numi* is the amount of microblogs which is returned by RDIBT, *Rnum* is the actual amount of microblogs which are related to the search. And we also evaluate the scalability of RDIBT according to the average Cost Time and Average Operation Time when adding processing node to the RDIBT.

$$Rat = \frac{Numi}{Rnum} \tag{4}$$

6.2   Efficiency of Indexing

We use average cost time per microblog to evaluate the efficiency of the index by varying the amount of incoming microblogs per second. Figure 8 illustrate the average cost time to maintain the RDIBT, where Fig. 8(a) and (b) is in different t and m, respectively. When the amount of incoming microblogs per second is increasing, the average cost time of each microblog increases. The reasons are as following. First, the more incoming microblogs will increase system's load, and the indexing will use more resources. Second, the more incoming microblogs will cause more merger and replication operations, and the cost of those operations also in the cost of indexing.

Figure 8(a) illustrates the average cost time in different t. The larger t will increase the capacity threshold of higher layer (> 0). $t = 3$ has the higher cost than $t = 2$ when the amount of incoming microblogs is lower (in our experiments is less than 6000) because the cost of merger and replication operation of $t = 3$ is larger than $t = 2$. But

$t = 3$ has lower indexing cost than $t = 2$ when the amount of incoming microblogs is high because the frequency of merger and replication operations in $t = 3$ is lower than $t = 2$, then the cost in merger and replication operations is lower.

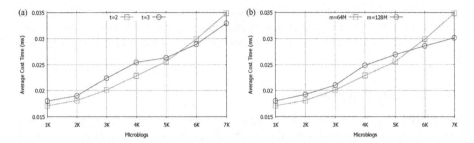

Fig. 8. The efficiency of indexing with t and m

Figure 8(b) illustrates the average cost time in different m. The m also changes the capacity thresholds of index layers. So it has the similar trend with t. And reasons are all similar. So we do not state it again.

6.3   Efficiency of Search

We illustrate the average operation time and the complete rat by varying the amount of incoming microblogs and search to verify the efficiency of search. We will compare the performance of RDIBT with LSII. In the experiments, we implement a simply version of LSII according to the philosophy of LSII, and we also deploy it in the same environment of RDIBT. We select the LSII is because the structure of LSII is also hierarchical. And the parameters environment of LSII are the same with RDIBT.

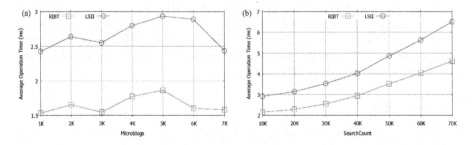

Fig. 9. The efficiency of search with microblogs and searchcount

Figure 9 compares the average operation time of LSII and RDIBT by varying the amount of incoming microblogs and search. In Fig. 9(a), the average operation time consumptions of RDIBT and LSII have no clear tendency when the amount of incoming microblogs increase, which demonstrates that RDIBT and LSII both strike a well balance between search and update costs. The new incoming microblogs will not affect the performance of search. But the average operation time of RDIBT is less than LSII because it can reduce the amount of indices that need to be scanned. And it also can execute the search in parallel. In Fig. 9(b), the average operation time consumptions of RDIBT and LSII both increase when the amount of searches increases. The reason is that the more amount of searches will add system's load, and the process nodes need to use more resources to execute searches, which will increase the search's time. And the RDIBT also has higher performance than LSII, which is the same with Fig. 9(a).

6.4   Complete Rate of Results

The RDIBT is an index schema based on topic, so the search also needs to scan relative indices to get the result. And does the search can scan the complete indices is important for the search result. This subsection will verify the complete rat of search result in RDIBT.

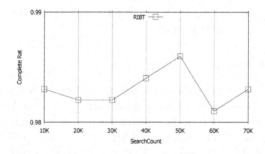

Fig. 10. The complete rate of result

Figure 10 illustrates the complete rate of search result by varying the quantity of searches. The quantity of searches will not affect the complete rate of the search result. We also can know that the complete rate of search result in RDIBT is very high which approximates to 99%. And the most important microblogs are all returned. So we can conclude that the result of RDIBT is complete.

6.5   Scalability

The RDIBT is a distributed schema, so the scalability is an important factor to evaluate the performance of index. In the experiments, we will start with 10 process nodes, and add more processing nodes to cluster one by one until 20 process nodes. We record both the average cost time and average operation time for varying the number of processing node, and the results are shown in Fig. 11.

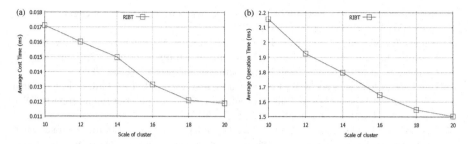

Fig. 11. The scalability of RDIBT in index cost time and operation time

Figure 11(a) illustrates the average cost time by varying the number of processing node. The more processing nodes will decrease the average cost time of microblog because the new node can apportion other nodes' work. So some new incoming microblogs can be indexed in the new node. RDIBT is an index schema based on topic, so the index work in which node is based on the topics of new incoming microblogs. So the speed up rat is not linear, but it approximates to linear. Figure 11(b) illustrates the average operation time by varying the number of processing node. The result is similar with Fig. 11(b), and they have the same reasons. So we can conclude that the RDIBT has high scalability.

7   Conclusion

Real-time indexing of microblogs recently has become a hot research field because the traditional indexing and search methods cannot satisfy requirements of microblog real-time search. The large volume of fast arriving microblog data, along with the large number of concurrent queries, poses significant technical challenges. We have proposed RDIBT, a real-time distributed index based on topic. It can execute the real-time indexing in distributed to improve the performance of real-time indexing and the search. The experiments on a real Twitter dataset demonstrate the effectiveness of the index schema, the performance of search in RDIBT index schema, and the scalability . of RDIBT.

Acknowledgment. Thanks to the anonymous reviewers for their insightful comments.

References

1. Abiteboul, S., Vianu, V.: Queries and computation on the Web. In: Afrati, F., Kolaitis, P. (eds.) ICDT 1997. LNCS, vol. 1186, pp. 262–275. Springer, Heidelberg (1997). https://doi.org/10.1007/3-540-62222-5_50. Author, F.: Article title. Journal **2**(5), 99–110 (2016)
2. Apache. Apache lucene (2012). http://lucene.apache.org/core/
3. Blei, D.M., Ng, A.Y., Jordan, M.I.: Latent dirichlet allocation. J. Mach. Learn. Res. **3**, 993–1022 (2003)

4. Brin, S., Page, L.: The anatomy of a large-scale hypertextual web search engine. Comput. Netw. ISDN Syst. **30**(1), 107–117 (1998)
5. Burges, C., Shaked, T., Renshaw, E., Lazier, A., Deeds, M., Hamilton, N., Hullender, G.: Learning to rank using gradient descent. In: Proceedings of the 22nd International Conference on Machine Learning, Bonn, Germany, pp. 89–96. ACM (2005)
6. Busch, M., Gade, K., Larson, B., Lok, P., Luckenbill, S., Lin, J.: Earlybird: real-time search at Twitter. In: Proceedings of 28th International Conference on Data Engineering (ICDE), Washington, DC, USA, pp. 1360–1369. IEEE (2012)
7. Chen, C., Li, F., Ooi, B.C., Wu, S.: TI: an efficient indexing mechanism for real-time search on tweets. In: Proceedings of the 30th International Conference on Management of Data, Athens, Greece, pp. 649–660. ACM (2011)
8. Chu, W., Keerthi, S.S.: Support vector ordinal regression. Neural Comput. **19**(3), 792–815 (2007)
9. Diligenti, M., Coetzee, F., Lawrence, S., Giles, C.L., Gori, M., et al.: Focused crawling using context graphs. In: Proceedings of 26th International Conference on Very Large Data Bases, Cairo, Egypt, pp. 527–534. ACM (2000)
10. Freund, Y., Iyer, R., Schapire, R.E., Singer, Y.: An efficient boosting algorithm for combining preferences. J. Mach. Learn. Res. **4**, 933–969 (2003)
11. Gao, M., Jin, C., Qian, W., Gong, X.: Real-time search over a microblogging system. In: Proceedings of the 2nd International Conference on Cloud and Green Computing, Xiangtan, Hunan, China, pp. 352–359. IEEE (2012)
12. Gao, M., Jin, C., Qian, W., Gong, X.: Real-time and personalized search over a microblogging system. Comput. J. **57**(9), 1281–1295 (2013)
13. Griffiths, T.L., Steyvers, M.: Finding scientific topics. Proc. Nat. Acad. Sci. U.S. Am. **101** (Suppl 1), 5228–5235 (2004)
14. Herbrich, R., Graepel, T., Obermayer, K.: Support vector learning for ordinal regression. In: Proceedings of 9th International Conference on Artificial Neural Networks, Edinburgh, Scotland, pp. 97–102. IEEE (1999)
15. Kleinberg, J., Tomkins, A.: Applications of linear algebra in information retrieval and hypertext analysis. In: Proceedings of the 18th SIGMOD-SIGACT-SIGART Symposium on Principles of Database Systems, Philadelphia, Pennsylvania, pp. 185–193. ACM (1999)
16. Lu, Y., Zhai, C.: Opinion integration through semi-supervised topic modeling. In: Proceedings of the 17th International Conference on World Wide Web, Beijing, China, pp. 121–130. ACM (2008)
17. Minka, T., Lafferty, J.: Expectation-propagation for the generative aspect model. In: Proceedings of the 18th Conference on Uncertainty in Artificial Intelligence, Edmonton, Alberta, Canada, pp. 352–359. Morgan Kaufmann Publishers Inc. (2002)
18. Pant, G., Srinivasan, P., Menczer, F.: Crawling the web. In: Pant, G., Srinivasan, P., Menczer, F. (eds.) Web Dynamics, pp. 153–177. Springer, Heidelberg (2004). https://doi.org/10.1007/978-3-662-10874-1_7
19. Teevan, J., Ramage, D., Morris, M.R.: Twittersearch: a comparison of microblog search and web search. In: Proceedings of the 4th International Conference on Web Search and Data Mining, HongKong, China, pp. 35–44. ACM (2011)
20. Wu, L., Lin, W., Xiao, X., Xu, Y.: LSII: an indexing structure for exact real-time search on microblogs. In: Proceedings of the 29th International Conference on Data Engineering, Brisbane, Australia, pp. 482–493. IEEE (2013)
21. Zhao, W.X., Jiang, J., Weng, J., He, J., Lim, E.-P., Yan, H., Li, X.: Comparing Twitter and traditional media using topic models. In: Clough, P., Foley, C., Gurrin, C., Jones, G.J.F., Kraaij, W., Lee, H., Mudoch, V. (eds.) ECIR 2011. LNCS, vol. 6611, pp. 338–349. Springer, Heidelberg (2011). https://doi.org/10.1007/978-3-642-20161-5_34

Auto-Segmentation of Pathological Lung Parenchyma Based on Region Growing Method

Jiyang Dong[1(✉)], Ke Lu[1], Shuangfeng Dai[2], Jian Xue[1], and Rui Zhai[2]

[1] University of Chinese Academy of Science, Beijing, China
dongjiyang12@mails.ucas.ac.cn, {luk,xuejian}@ucas.ac.cn
[2] Institute of Remote Sensing and Digital Earth, Chinese Academy of Sciences,
Beijing, China
daisf@radi.ac.cn, zhairui11b@mails.ucas.ac.cn

Abstract. Lung parenchyma extraction is a precursor to the diagnosis and analysis of lung diseases. In this study, we propose a fully automated lung segmentation method that is able to extract lung parenchyma from both normal and pathological lung. First, we adapt the threshold algorithm to perform image binary, and then utilize the connected domain labeling method to select seed for region growing segmentation method which will be performed next. Then region growing image segmentation method is adopted and a rudimentary lung volume is established. A further refinement is performed to include the areas that might have been missed during the segmentation by an improved convex hull algorithm. We evaluated the accuracy and efficiency of the proposed method on 10 3D-CT scan sets. The results show that the improved convex hull algorithm can repair the concavities of lung contour effectively and the proposed segmentation method can extract the lung parenchyma precisely.

Keywords: Automated segmentation · Pathological lung
Automatic seed selection · Region growing

1 Introduction

Pulmonary diseases are one of the major causes of deaths around the world [11]. The segmentation of lung parenchyma is the current standard in the routine computer-aided diagnosis and analysis, and its accuracy and degree of automation affect the tasks of clinicians and radiologists directly.

Although current state-of-the-art lung segmentation algorithms work well for certain situations, they usually need manual participation which aggravate the tasks of clinicians and radiologists. Besides, current algorithms are not generic enough due to the diversity and irregularity of lung diseases.

Threshold segmentation methods [2,8] are used frequently because of their efficiency. However, such methods have limited effects because they simply take

© Springer Nature Singapore Pte Ltd. 2018
B. Huet et al. (Eds.): ICIMCS 2017, CCIS 819, pp. 241–251, 2018.
https://doi.org/10.1007/978-981-10-8530-7_23

intensity of each pixel into consideration. Therefore threshold-based methods are usually utilized with other segmentation algorithms instead of being used alone.

Region-based segmentation methods have been used widely in CT image segmentation. Region growing method [4,5,16] is found useful in segmenting small structures. It is able to segment the lung area quickly and maintain the contour correctly. However, the method requires manual seed selection and the growing criterion is sensitive to parameters. Graph-based methods [3,12,13] introduced the graph theory into image segmentation. By minimizing energy function with max-flow/min-cut method, region of interest (ROI) can be extracted from images. The methods have already shown their potential in medical image segmentation. However, most of graph-based methods are interactive when they are used. Besides, the computational cost of this type of methods are relatively high.

For more advanced methods, the utility of prior models have been proved beneficial for medical cases [6,7]. These methods align a statistical shape model of an anatomical structure to ROI in the image using an optimization procedure. They have a good constraint on local shapes and a strong robustness to noise and pseudo boundaries. However, as commonly known, the primary drawbacks of the methods using prior model are the requirement of modeling large amount of training data with high variations and accurate anatomical correspondences among the shape instances [10].

Deep learning approaches have gained growing attention in medical image segmentation due to their strong abilities and robustness. These methods [9,14] can learn and extract features automatically, which is different from traditional feature selection (points, lines and shapes). However, the most challenging step of learning-based methods is how to obtain a labeled data set with significant amount for training, which is still a heavy task for now.

As discussed above, the segmentation of lung parenchyma is a pivotal procedure for helping clinicians to conduct clinical diagnosis and guided surgery, and the research of it has attracted a lot of attention persistently. Finding out a segmentation method with high efficiency, full automation and precise results is the primary aim of current research. In this paper, we proposed a novel approach that is able to extract 3D lung parenchyma for CT image sets. We implement the method based on 3D region growing which has a good balance between accuracy and efficiency. Aiming at eliminating the interaction during segmentation, we design a novel procedure that can select the seed for region growing automatically. The results after segmentation are commonly incomplete due to the existence of abnormal areas such as nodules and cavities. We then utilize connecting domain labeling method and convex hull algorithm for post-processing the segmentation results. Our automated 3D lung segmentation method was tested on the chest CT images provided by the General Hospital of Ningxia Medical University, China and the public image sets provided by LIDC-IDRI [1].

The rest of manuscript gives more details of our method and its performance. In Sect. 2 we describe the problem and introduce the proposed method. Section 3 presents the experimental results and some discussion, followed by the conclusion and plan about future work in Sect. 4.

2 Theory and Methodology

In the proposed approach, there are four main stages: (1) the automated selection of seed for region growing, (2) region growing segmentation method with improved growing strategy, (3) the elimination of cavities and tracheas, (4) the refinement of segmentation.

2.1 Automated Seed Selection

Each pixel in a CT image is denoted by a CT value which represents the density of human body tissue where this pixel belongs to. The higher the density is, the larger the CT value shows. The CT value distribution of human body tissues is shown in Fig. 1.

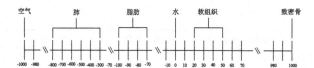

Fig. 1. CT value distribution of human body tissues

It is obvious that the air (background), the lung parenchyma, the muscles and the bones, which are the main components of human chest, have totally different values in a CT image, and the parenchyma that we are interesting in has relatively lower values. So if we employ a binarization of the initial image with a threshold method, it is reasonable to believe that the main lung parenchyma areas with some straightforward analysis, such as connecting domain labeling method. The seed for region growing can be extracted randomly from the approximate lung parenchyma areas. In this work, we adopt Otsu's method [15] for binarization and select the centroid of the extracted lung parenchyma areas for the seed.

Assume the gray values of pixels in a image vary in the range $[0, L-1]$, and make n_i represents the number of pixels that have gray value i. The total number of pixels is $N = sum_{i=0}^{L-1} n_i$ and the probability of gray value i is $p_i = \frac{n_i}{N}$. Otsu assumed k is the threshold that divides all the pixels of the image into two parts (class C_0 and class C_1) and defined two measures which represents the between-class variance and the within-class variance respectively as below:

$$\sigma_B^2 = \omega_0(\mu_0 - \mu_G)^2 + \omega_1(\mu_1 - \mu_G)^2 \tag{1}$$

$$\sigma_W^2 = \sigma_G^2 - \sigma_B^2 \tag{2}$$

where

$$\omega_0 = Pr(C_0) = \sum_{i=0}^{k} p_i \tag{3}$$

$$\omega_1 = Pr(C_1) = 1 - \omega_0 \tag{4}$$

$$\mu_0 = \sum_{i=0}^{k} ip_i \tag{5}$$

$$\mu_1 = \sum_{i=k+1}^{L-1} ip_i \tag{6}$$

$$\mu_G = \sum_{i=0}^{L-1} ip_i \tag{7}$$

The best threshold is the value k that makes $\frac{\sigma_B^2}{\sigma_W^2}$ max.

The more details about the automated seed selection is described in Algorithm 1.

Algorithm 1. Automated selection of seed for region growing

Input: I ← input image
Output: s_1 ← seed for left lung and **s_2** ← seed for right lung
   $m \times n$ ← sizes of the image
   Obtain the best threshold T by adopting Otsu method
   Employ binarization for the image according to T
   I_t ← the binary image
   I_t ← $1 - $**$I_t$**
   Divide the image **I_t** into two parts, **I_1** ← left part and **I_2** ← right part
   for $i = 1$ to 2 **do**
      Adopt connecting domain labeling method to **I_i**
      LN ← number of connecting domain
      $j \leftarrow 1$
      $flag \leftarrow 0$
      while $flag = 0$ **and** $j \leq LN$ **do**
         if There are pixels with label j on more than 2 boundaries of **I_i** **then**
            $j = j + 1$
         else
            $flag = 1$
         end if
      end while
      s_i ← the centroid of pixels with label j
   end for

2.2   Region Growing Method

The main work of region growing method is putting the pixels with similar properties together to form a region. The seed merges those similar pixels and becomes a new seed region. Repeat the step until all the pixels in the image have been searched. As for 3D CT image sets, we start with a seed in a 2D slice. Then we take a traversal of its 4-neighborhood and let the centroid of the seed and the pixels similar with it denotes the new seed for the slices next to the current slice. We adopt a loop to ensure the whole 3D lung is extracted.

Another pivotal aspect of region growing is growing strategy. We let u_0, u_i and u_x denote the intensity value of seed, an extracted pixel during the i-th growing and a pixel in the 4-neighborhood of it, respectively. There are two thresholds to judge whether a pixel belongs to foreground area. The formula is shown below:

$$\begin{cases} |u_x - u_1| \leq T_1 \\ |u_x - u_0| \leq T_2 \end{cases} \tag{8}$$

In the formula, T_1 controls the local intensity value variety, and T_2 controls the global intensity value variety correspondingly. If the pixel with u_x intensity value meets the conditions, we categorize it as foreground area and define ti as a pixel during the $(i + 1)$-th growing.

2.3   Automatic Trachea Extraction

The lung parenchyma and bronchial tree always have similar intensity value, which is obvious in Fig. 1. So the bronchial tree is often extracted along with lung parenchyma. However, trachea and airways are typically evaluated separately from the lung parenchyma in clinical practice. Hence, remove of trachea is needed at this situation. We adopt a method based on connecting domain analysis to eliminate bronchial tree in this work. We first perform the connecting domain analysis on the image after region growing segmentation. All the foreground areas have been labeled after this step. Then we calculate the area size of each connecting area. In view of the fact that the trachea areas are far smaller than lung parenchyma area, we set a threshold to classify the connecting areas. Those with area size smaller than the threshold are judged to be bronchial tree and will be set as foreground.

2.4   Refinement of Segmentation

Due to the existence of nodules in lung, the mask of parenchyma obtained by segmentation usually has cavities and concavities. Hence, a refinement work is needed in the next step. It is obvious that the area per slice of a normal lung has a smooth transition along the Z-axis. But the 2-D areas change abruptly if there are abnormalities in scans due to the fact that abnormal imaging areas may be not captured by segmentation.

We perform a refinement method for lung parenchyma segmentation based on convex hull algorithm. We first obtain the boundary point set from the segmentation result. Then we adopt the Graham scanning method to extract all the convex points on the boundary, which is followed by checking each two adjacent convex points. If the distance between two adjacent convex points is small, we believe that there is a depression that needs to be repaired between them. On the other hand, when the distance is big, we believe the two points locate at the inside edge near heart. In this situation, we can not simply replace the boundary between the two points with a line segment. So we perform a second convex hull method to refine the boundary between the two points. By this means, the proposed method has a good performance when there are nodules near the pleura or mediastinum. The details about the refinement is described in Algorithms 2 and 3.

Algorithm 2. Refinement of segmentation result

Input: $\mathbf{I}_b \leftarrow$ image before refinement
    $T_D \leftarrow$ threshold for two convex points' distance
Output: $\mathbf{I}_{out} \leftarrow$ final segmentation result
  Extract the boundary point sets $\mathbf{P}$ from $\mathbf{I}_b$
  $N_p \leftarrow$ number of points in $\mathbf{P}$
  $\mathbf{Q} = \text{GRAHAM}(\mathbf{P})$
  $N_Q \leftarrow$ number of points in $\mathbf{Q}$
  for $i = 1$ to $N_Q - 1$ **do**
    if $\text{DIST}(\mathbf{Q}_i, \mathbf{Q}_{i+1}) < T_D$ **then**
      Remove the points between $\mathbf{Q}_i$ and $\mathbf{Q}_{i+1}$ in $\mathbf{P}$
    else
      $\mathbf{P}_t \leftarrow$ the points between $\mathbf{Q}_i$ and $\mathbf{Q}_{i+1}$ in $\mathbf{P}$
      $\mathbf{Q}_t = \text{GRAHAM}(\mathbf{P}_t)$
      Replace $\mathbf{P}_t$ with $\mathbf{Q}_t$
    end if
  end for
  return the area in boundary $\mathbf{P}$

  function $\text{DIST}(\mathbf{p}, \mathbf{q})$
    return $\sqrt{(p_x - q_x)^2 + (p_y - q_y)^2}$
  end function

---

3   Results and Discussion

We utilize 10 CT data sets of chest for evaluating the performance of the proposed algorithm. Among them, one is a scanning set from healthy lungs, and the others are lungs with diversity of nodules. Part of the data sets were provided by the General Hospital of Ningxia Medical University, China, and the other sets

---

Algorithm 3. Graham scanning method

---

function GRAHAM(**P**)

$N_P \leftarrow$ number of points in **P**

$pos \leftarrow 1$

for $i = 1$ to N_P **do**

    if $pos < 4$ **then**

        $\mathbf{Q}_{pos} \leftarrow \mathbf{P}_i$

        $pos = pos + 1$

    else

        if $(\mathbf{P}_i - \mathbf{Q}_{pos-2}) \times (\mathbf{Q}_{pos-1} - \mathbf{Q}_{pos-2}) < 0$ **then**

            $\mathbf{Q}_{pos} \leftarrow \mathbf{P}_i$

            $pos = pos + 1$

        else

            $pos = pos - 1$

        end if

    end if

end for

return Q

end function

---

were downloaded from LIDC-IDRI (Lung Image Database Consortium–Image Database Resource Initiative). The format of the image sets are DICOM.

The whole process of our method in segmenting lung parenchyma is shown in Fig. 2.

It is obvious that the proposed algorithm has significant performance in extracting the lung parenchyma, especially when there exist pathologies. To quantify the accuracy of segmentation results, we take the overlap area of the segmentation results obtained by segmentation methods and those obtained by manual extraction as the measurement, which is shown below.

$$Correct rate = \frac{Area_{overlap}}{Area_{total}} \tag{9}$$

We calculate the correct rate of every slice, and take the average of it as an assessment of the 3D CT data set. The details of experiment results is shown in Table 1.

On the 10 3D CT data sets, the average correct rate of our method is 94.89%, while that of region growing method is 90.58% (Fig. 3).

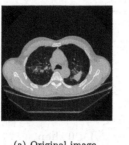
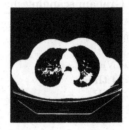

(a) Original image

(b) Image after threshold segmentation and binary

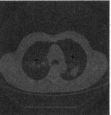

(c) Seed by automated selection

(d) Segmentation result after region growing

(e) Segmentation result after eliminating trachea

(f) Boundary obtained by our method

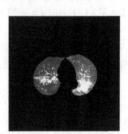

(g) Mask of lung parenchyma

(h) Final segmentation result

Fig. 2. The whole process of the proposed method

 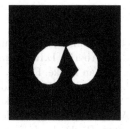

(a) Boundary obtained by original (b) Segmentation result by original
convex hull   convex hull

Fig. 3. Results of original convex hull

Table 1. Average correct rate

Cases	Average correct rate		Number of slices
	Region growing	Ours	
1	91.11	95.21	62
2	92.41	96.96	70
3	92.02	98.55	69
4	86.96	90.52	66
5	92.08	95.33	71
6	90.31	94.14	85
7	90.60	98.49	80
8	91.13	93.34	84
9	88.59	91.01	85
10	90.82	95.88	80

4 Conclusions

The precise and efficient segmentation of lung parenchyma is very important to
lung diseases' diagnosis and treatment. In this work, an automated segmentation
algorithm for pathological lung parenchyma is proposed. The method is based
on 3D region growing, and take a refinement step with an improved convex hull
method. The proposed method is able to extract the lung parenchyma at both
the normal and pathological situations. Besides, the automation property makes
it superior.

Acknowledgments. Thanks are due to the NSFC (Grant No. U1301251, 61671426,
61471150), and Beijing National Science Foundation (No. 4141003) for funding.

References

1. Armato, S.G., McLennan, G., Bidaut, L., McNitt-Gray, M.F., Meyer, C.R., Reeves, A.P., Zhao, B., Aberle, D.R., Henschke, C.I., Hoffman, E.A., Kazerooni, E.A., MacMahon, H., Van Beeke, E.J.R., Yankelevitz, D., Biancardi, A.M., Bland, P.H., Brown, M.S., Engelmann, R.M., Laderach, G.E., Max, D., Pais, R.C., Qing, D.P.Y., Roberts, R.Y., Smith, A.R., Starkey, A., Batrah, P., Caligiuri, P., Farooqi, A., Gladish, G.W., Jude, C.M., Munden, R.F., Petkovska, I., Quint, L.E., Schwartz, L.H., Sundaram, B., Dodd, L.E., Fenimore, C., Gur, D., Petrick, N., Freymann, J., Kirby, J., Hughes, B., Casteele, A.V., Gupte, S., Sallamm, M., Heath, M.D., Kuhn, M.H., Dharaiya, E., Burns, R., Fryd, D.S., Salganicoff, M., Anand, V., Shreter, U., Vastagh, S., Croft, B.Y.: The lung image database consortium (LIDC) and image database resource initiative (IDRI): a completed reference database of lung nodules on CT scans. Med. Phys. **38**(2), 915–931 (2011). https://doi.org/10.1118/1.3528204
2. Brown, M.S., McNitt-Gray, M.F., Mankovich, N.J., Goldin, J.G., Hiller, J., Wilson, L.S., Aberie, D.R.: Method for segmenting chest CT image data using an anatomical model: preliminary results. IEEE Trans. Med. Imaging **16**(6), 828–839 (1997). https://doi.org/10.1109/42.650879
3. Dai, S., Lu, K., Dong, J., Zhang, Y., Chen, Y.: A novel approach of lung segmentation on chest CT images using graph cuts. Neurocomputing **168**, 799–807 (2015). https://doi.org/10.1016/j.neucom.2015.05.044
4. De Nunzio, G., Tommasi, E., Agrusti, A., Cataldo, R., De Mitri, I., Favetta, M., Maglio, S., Massafra, A., Quarta, M., Torsello, M., Zecca, I., Bellotti, R., Tangaro, S., Calvini, P., Camarlinghi, N., Falaschi, F., Cerello, P., Oliva, P.: Automatic lung segmentation in CT images with accurate handling of the hilar region. J. Digit. Imaging **24**(1), 11–27 (2011). https://doi.org/10.1007/s10278-009-9229-1
5. Gill, G., Beichel, R.R.: An approach for reducing the error rate in automated lung segmentation. Comput. Biol. Med. **76**, 143–153 (2016). https://doi.org/10.1016/j.compbiomed.2016.06.022
6. Hong, R., Hu, Z., Wang, R., Wang, M., Tao, D.: Multi-view object retrieval via multi-scale topic models. IEEE Trans. Image Process. **25**(12), 5814–5827 (2016). https://doi.org/10.1109/TIP.2016.2614132
7. Hong, R., Zhang, L., Zhang, C., Zimmermann, R.: Flickr circles: aesthetic tendency discovery by multi-view regularized topic modeling. IEEE Trans. Multimed. **18**(8), 1555–1567 (2016). https://doi.org/10.1109/TMM.2016.2567071
8. Kemerink, G.J., Lamers, R.J.S., Pellis, B.J., Kruize, H.H., van Engelshoven, J.M.A.: On segmentation of lung parenchyma in quantitative computed tomography of the lung. Med. Phys. **25**(12), 2432–2439 (1998). https://doi.org/10.1118/1.598454
9. Lee, W.-L., Chang, K., Hsieh, K.-S.: Unsupervised segmentation of lung fields in chest radiographs using multiresolution fractal feature vector and deformable models. Med. Biol. Eng. Comput. **54**(9), 1409–1422 (2016). https://doi.org/10.1007/s11517-015-1412-6
10. Mansoor, A., Bagci, U., Xu, Z., Foster, B., Olivier, K.N., Elinoff, J.M., Suffredini, A.F., Udupa, J.K., Mollura, D.J.: A generic approach to pathological lung segmentation. IEEE Trans. Med. Imaging **33**(12), 2293–2310 (2014). https://doi.org/10.1109/TMI.2014.2337057

11. McGuire, S.: World Cancer Report 2014. Geneva, Switzerland: World Health Organization, International Agency for Research on Cancer, WHO Press, 2015. Adv. Nutr. (Bethesda, Md.) **7**(2), 418–419 (2016). https://doi.org/10.3945/an.116. 012211

12. Ming, J.T.C., Noor, N.M., Rijal, O.M., Kassim, R.M., Yunus, A.: Enhanced automatic lung segmentation using graph cut for Interstitial Lung Disease. In: 2014 IEEE Conference on Biomedical Engineering and Sciences (IECBES), pp. 17–21. https://doi.org/10.1109/IECBES.2014.7047479

13. Nakagomi, K., Shimizu, A., Kobatake, H., Yakami, M., Fujimoto, K., Togashi, K.: Multi-shape graph cuts with neighbor prior constraints and its application to lung segmentation from a chest CT volume. Med. Image Anal. **17**(1), 62–77 (2013). https://doi.org/10.1016/j.media.2012.08.002

14. Ngo, T.A., Carneiro, G.: Lung segmentation in chest radiographs using distance regularized level set and deep-structured learning and inference. In: 2015 IEEE International Conference on Image Processing (ICIP), pp. 2140–2143. https://doi.org/10.1109/ICIP.2015.7351179

15. Otsu, N.: A threshold selection method from gray-level histograms. IEEE Trans. Syst. Man Cybern. **9**(1), 62–66 (1979). https://doi.org/10.1109/TSMC.1979.4310076

16. Zhou, H., Goldgof, D.B., Hawkins, S., Wei, L., Liu, Y., Creighton, D., Gillies, R.J., Hall, L.O., Nahavandi, S.: A robust approach for automated lung segmentation in thoracic CT. In: 2015 IEEE International Conference on Systems, Man, and Cybernetics, pp. 2267–2272. https://doi.org/10.1109/SMC.2015.396

Classification of Heart Sounds Based on Convolutional Neural Network

Tianya Li, Chunmei Qing[✉], and Xiang Tian

School of Electronic and Information Engineering,
South China University of Technology, Guangzhou, China
1343202195@qq.com, {qchm,xtian}@scut.edu.cn

Abstract. In this paper, we present a new method to categorize the heart sound signals into Normal, Murmur, Extra Heart Sound and Artifact with Convolutional Neural Network (CNN) model. The experimental dataset are from the PASCAL heart sound classification workshop, 2011. Our method mainly contains three steps as follows. Firstly, we propose cross- cutting and framing to enlarge the data. The data used for training and test is three times than before. Secondly, we manage the heart sound signals via Butterworth filter and Fast Fourier Transform simply. Finally the captured frequency features are input into the CNN model for classification. Compared with the traditional heart sounds classification approaches-selecting features and designing classifier, our method overcomes the uncertain in selecting features and improves the self-learning ability. The experimental results show that deep learning network model have higher classification effectiveness for the data with much noise. The global identification rate reaches 98%, more effective than previous related studies.

Keywords: Heart sounds · Cross-framing
Fast Fourier Transform (FFT) · Convolutional Neural Network (CNN)

1 Introduction

Heart sound signal is the concentrated expression of heart and vessels movements. Heart sound auscultation has been a critical part of the clinical examination of cardiovascular diseases, and the clinic doctor make decisions by distinguishing the murmur and distortion of heart sound. Nowadays, electrocardiogram (ECG), echocardiogram, carotic pulse graph, Apex cardiogram and phonocardiogram (PCG) all have provided direct and accurate evidences of cardiovascular diseases. PCG and heart sound auscultation have more advantages because of lower cost, simple operation, and portability. Cardiovascular diseases have been the leading causes of deaths worldwide recently. With the sick crowed and hospital reception enlarging rapidly, the doctors have challenge in less misdiagnosis rate and rich clinical knowledge. Intelligent diagnostic system of cardiovascular diseases becomes necessary in reducing cost effective and improving accuracy.

© Springer Nature Singapore Pte Ltd. 2018
B. Huet et al. (Eds.): ICIMCS 2017, CCIS 819, pp. 252–259, 2018.
https://doi.org/10.1007/978-981-10-8530-7_24

Traditionally, the major approach of classifying heart sound contains four steps: The Prepossessing Procedure, The Segmentation of heart sound, Extracting features, Designing Classifier. In the prepossessing procedure, discrete wavelet transforms (decomposition and reconstruction with selected coefficients) and band-pass filter have been used for removing the murmur components. In segmentation procedure, the soft-threshold (based on Shannon energy and modified by peak conditioning process) method is used to detect the corresponded S1 peaks and S2 peaks [5]. The periodic signal is segmented into systole, S1, diastole and S2. In the feature extraction process, many researchers have a try from different domains. The correlation dimension based on empirical mode decomposition (EMD) [1], Lyapunov exponent [5], the statistical measures of four segmentation components (Mean, Standard Deviation of S1 and S2 peak values) [3], the autocorrelation function coefficients of average Shannon energy envelop [4], Fractal and Mel Frequency Cepstrum Coefficients (MFCC) [6] all have been used as features to classify the heart sound by researchers. Partial least squares regression method was used to reduce the dimension of extracting feature vectors [7].

Support Vector Machine (SVM), Artificial Neural Network (ANN) and Gaussian Mixture Model (GMM) are the common classifiers in traditional methods. A weighted fuzzy C-means algorithm was proposed to modify the GMM model [2]. A Random Forest is used as classifier [3], which consists of 70 tree-structured classifiers. The results show it works well in over-fitting on a big database. A non-learning static rule-based classification tree [5] is proposed for classification. The developed model is tested on twenty-two datasets of normal and murmur heart sounds with accuracy of 95.5%.

In the approaches of classifying heart sounds mentioned above, researchers are aimed to make improvements in selecting features and designing classifier. However, it is flexible and skillful for choosing features. Furthermore, it has already been ripe in study of selecting features. Avoiding the challenge of selecting features, our study propose a method of designing intelligent diagnosis system which has more effective classification but use simple and common features. Deep learning network has been widely used in speech analysis and image recognition, which captures the essential feature representation of data with the multiple-hidden-layer artificial neural networks. Besides, it reduces the training complexity with initialization of weights layer by layer. Compared with the feature constructing artificially, the self-learning feature can describe the data much more intrinsically. In this paper, we will build a convolutional neural network as classifier without segmentation of the heart sounds. The approach will be tested on a publicly available heart sound classification dataset [9]. The CNN model learns the heart sound structure information successfully and improves the classification effectiveness obviously.

2   Methods

2.1   CNN Introduction

Convolutional neural network [10] has already been the research focus in speech analysis and image recognition. The local receptive field and weight sharing are two distinct characteristics in CNN. They reduce the complexity and number of weights in the training processing. CNN is a Multilayer non-linear perception identifying 2-D shape, which has high invariance in translation, zoom and rotation. Besides, it can extract more adequate feature maps by multiple convolution kernels. As for the extracted feature maps, an aggregate statistical operation named pooling reduces the dimension and improves effectiveness. Multilayer convolution can extract more comprehensive features. In CNN, dropout is a simple and effective technique of preventing networks from over-fitting. The term 'dropout' refers to dropping out units (hidden and visible) in a neural network randomly and temporarily [8]. Each unit is retained with a fixed probability p independent of other units, where p can be chosen using a validation set or can simply be set at 0.5. Figure 1 shows a simple framework of CNN. The input produces six feature maps in C1 with six convolution kernels. After pooling, dropout, the feature maps are activated by a sigmoid function in S2. In C3 and S4 the operation are the same as C1 and S2 with more convolution layers. Finally, the rasterization data from S4 are input into a neural network.

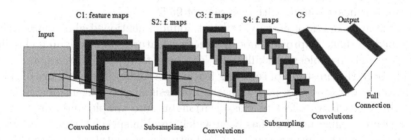

Fig. 1. Concept demonstration of CNN model

2.2   The Prepossessing Procedure

The experimental data from set-A are gathered via the iStethoscope Pro iPhone app at home, which has big noise because of the friction between stethoscope and clothes, skin. The heart sound mainly consists of the first heart sounds and the second heart sounds, which are all in approximate frequency bands. The background noise has much more detail frequency bands. Considering that the input of CNN model must have same size, we cut heart sound signals into 5 s cross-over. The time-frequency graphs of four heart sounds are shown in Fig. 2.

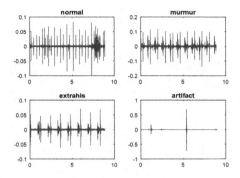

Fig. 2. time-frequency graph of original heart sound signal

Sub Sampling, Butterworth Filter and Normalization. The original experimental heart sound signal $X(i)$ gathered in 44100 Hz and the natural frequency of heart sound is less than 1000 Hz. We down sample the experimental heart sound signal into 2205 Hz to simplification based on sampling theorem. Then the signal is filtered with a band-pass, zero-phase, Butterworth filter order 6 (25–900 Hz) to eliminate out of the band noise. Next, the processed signal $\hat{X}(i)$ is normalized as follows:

$$\bar{X}(i) = \frac{\hat{X}(i)}{\max\limits_{i}\left(\left|\hat{X}(i)\right|\right)}$$

Framing and Fast Fourier Transform. We select 0.1 s as frame duration, and 0.05 s as frame step. The signal lasted for 5 s is divided into 24 sub-frames, whose frame length is 882. Considering the periodicity, a heart sound signal record with size 24 × 882 was reshaped into 3 × 84 × 84. After cross-framing, the data is enlarged three times than before.

Then we get the frequency information as extracted features by using Fast Fourier Transform. Finally a matrix with size 84 × 84 is input into the model we construct below, which is selected as feature vector of experimental signal.

CNN Model of Heart Sounds Classification. In this paper, we build a CNN model with two hidden layers considering the not too big data, exploring whether a deep learning network with fewer layers could be more effective than traditional classifiers (SVM, ANN etc.). Each convolution layer has 64 convolution kernels. Figure 3 shows the framework and parameters setting of CNN in our experiment. We take learning rate as 0.01 and probability of dropout as 0.5 in the training procedure.

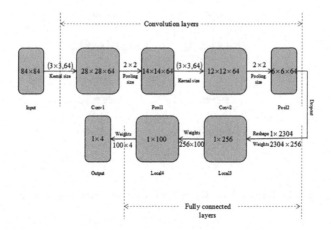

Fig. 3. Framework of CNN

3   Results and Classification

3.1   Datasets

The heart sound data used in experiment was obtained from the 2011 PASCAL Classifying Heart Sounds Challenge [9]. The data are grouped into two sets A and B which are gathered from the flowing sources accordingly: (a) general public via the iStethoscope Pro iPhone app, and (b) clinic trial in hospitals using the digital stethoscope DigiScope. Dataset A is divided into four categories: Normal (31 samples), Murmur (34), Extra Heart Sound (19) and Artifact (40); Dataset B has three categories: Normal (319), Murmur (95), Extrasystole (46). All the data vary in length and last about 8 s.

A heart sound cycle last from 1 to 2 s. The input into the CNN model must have same size. We cut every heart sound data provided from Classifying Heart Sounds Workshop into 5 s by using cool edit 2.0. Cutting the data cross-over, the experimental data was enlarged three times. Eventually, with discarding the data less than 5 s, we have 327 heart sounds from Dataset A used for experiment, which have the same size, 5 s. 70% of them are used for training the module and 30% are used for testing the effectiveness of classification, e.t Normal (84), Murmur (95), Extra Heart Sound (43), Artifact (105).

3.2   Classification Results

Using the measurements proposed in the 2011 PASCAL Classifying Heart Sounds Challenge Workshop [9], we evaluate the classification performance compared with the award papers in the competition, which using UCI [11], J48 [12] and MLP [12] as classifier respectively. Besides, the proposed method is also compared with the two papers [3,4], which using the same experimental sets. In paper [3], traditional methods of selecting features after segmentation and random forests classifier are proposed. In paper [4], without the segmentation, the autocorrelation feature and diffusion maps are proposed. The precision (PPV), sensitivity (Se) and specificity (Sp) are defined as follows:

$$PPV = \frac{TP}{TP + FP}$$

$$Se = \frac{TP}{TP + FN}$$

$$Se = \frac{TP}{TP + FN}$$

Here the true precision is shorted for TP. The false positive is shorted for FP. The true negative is shorted for TN. The false negative is shorted for FN. The several papers' results are summarized in Table 1.

Table 1. Classification results for Dataset-A

Measures	UCI [11]	J48 [12]	MLP [12]	DWT-RF [3]	DM-SVM [4]	Ours
Precision of normal	0.45	0.25	0.35	0.48	0.62	0.96
Precision of murmur	0.31	0.47	0.67	0.62	0.91	1.00
Precision of extrasystole	0.11	0.27	0.18	1.00	1.00	0.98
Precision of artifact	0.58	0.71	0.92	0.82	0.64	1.00
Artifact sensitivity	0.43	0.63	0.69	0.88	1.00	1.00
Artifact specificity	0.44	0.39	0.44	0.53	0.58	1.00
Total precision	0.36	0.43	0.53	0.73	0.79	0.98

Paper [3,4] have the highest precision on Extra Heart Sound dataset. With the CNN model, the classification performance improves highly for the noisy dataset, and the highest precision reaches on normal, murmur and artifact heart sounds dataset for the six classification methods. It reaches 100% in classifying the artifact heart sound. The total precision on all test data is 98%, which is 19% higher than the best of remain five previous related studies.

The CNN model above has two convolution layers with sixty four convolution kernels. To explore the number of layers' influence on classification effectiveness, the classification results with different number of convolution layers are summarized in Table 2. In the training process, we have 690 training samples. The batch size is 30, and we set the epoch as 1000 times to optimize network weights.

The CNN model with one convolution layer and two convolution layers all have better classification effectiveness. Their convolution kernel size is 3 × 3. In the four experiments, the model with four convolution layers has the longest time for training, which is almost four times than others. However, the test accuracy are less than the CNN model with two convolution layers. Besides, in the first 300 epochs training process, its accuracy is only 0.32. The first two experiments' training accuracy reaches 0.9 in 200 epochs. The results show that the CNN model has better classification effectiveness on the not too large heart sound

Table 2. Comparison results with different convolution layer

Number of convolution layers	1	2	3	4
Precision of normal	0.95	0.96	0.77	0.89
Precision of murmur	0.99	1.00	0.97	1.00
Precision of extrasystole	0.97	0.98	0.98	0.98
Precision of artifact	1.00	1.00	1.00	1.00
Total precision	0.97	0.98	0.93	0.97

dataset, and it doesn't need too deep network. The training accuracy from 0.3 in the previous hundreds epochs can reach 0.99 in the end. The CNN model has strong self-learning ability.

4   Conclusion

The heart sound signal contains important information for the cardiovascular diseases diagnosis. In classification of heart sound, traditional methods have challenges in segmentation and selecting features. The papers using UCI, J48 and MLP classifier have lower precision because of failing to accurately segment the heart sound and estimate the cardiac period. Our proposed method avoids the two difficulties in classifying heart sounds. Without segmentation, the frequency features acquired from FFT simply are input into the CNN model, and the classification result reveals that the model could learn the heart sound signal's structure successfully. Compared with the paper [4] which used SVM as classifier without segmentation, the CNN model learns the inner features more deeply and modifies the classification efficiency evidently. Our methods try to build a deep learning network to classify the heart sound and the precision increases by 19% than the best one in the same experimental datasets. The heart sound signal has obviously periodic structure. It has great invariance in time axis. Hence the CNN model with fewer convolution layers has better classification effectiveness than some traditional methods. In the future, the more specific classification of abnormal heart sound has practical significance for clinic diagnosis, and it also is our striving direction.

Acknowledgments. This work is supported in part by the National Natural Science Founding of China (61171142, 61401163, U1636218), Science and Technology Planning Project of Guangdong Province of China (2014B010111003, 2014B010111006), the Fundamental Research Funds for the Central Universities (2017MS045), the Diabetes Intelligent Wear Monitoring Equipment and Complications Prevention and Control Cloud Platform (2016B010108008), and Guangzhou Key Lab of Body Data Science (201605030011).

References

1. Guo, X., Yuan, Z., Zhang, W.: Heart sound recognition based on EMD correlation dimension and multi-fractals spectrum. Chin. J. Sci. Instrum. **35**(4), 827–833 (2014)
2. Zhang, W., Guo, X., Weng, J.: Application of improved GMM in classification and recognition of heart sound. Vibr. Shock **33**(6), 29–34 (2014)
3. Balili, C.C., Sobrepena, M.C.C., Naval, P.C.: Classification of heart sounds using discrete and continuous wavelet transform and random forests. In: IAPR Asian Conference on Pattern Recognition, pp. 655–659 (2015)
4. Deng, S.W., Han, J.Q.: Towards heart sound classification without segmentation via autocorrelation feature and diffusion maps. Future Gener. Comput. Syst. **60**, 13–21 (2016). Elsevier Science Publishers B. V.
5. Karar, M.E., Elkhafif, S.H., Elbrawany, M.A.: Automated diagnosis of heart sounds using rule-based classification tree. J. Med. Syst. **41**(4), 60 (2017)
6. Hamidi, M., Ghassemian, H., Imani, M.: Heart sound classification using fractal and MFCC (Printed in Persian). In: International Conference on Signal Processing and Intelligent Systems (2016)
7. Zhang, W., Han, J., Deng, S.: Heart sound classification based on scaled spectrogram and partial least squares regression. Biomed. Sig. Process. Control **32**, 20–28 (2017)
8. Srivastava, N., Hinton, G., Krizhevsky, A., et al.: Dropout: a simple way to prevent neural networks from overfitting. Mach. Learn. Res. **15**, 1929–1958 (2014)
9. Bentley, P., Nordehn, G., Coimbra, M., Mannor, S.: The PASCAL classifying heart sounds challenge 2011 (CHSC 2011) results. http://www.peterjbentley.com/heartchallenge/index.html
10. Zouxy: Deep learning series of summarized notes (seven). http://blog.csdn.net/zouxy09/article/details/8781543
11. Deng, Y., Bentley, P.: A robust heart sound segmentation and classification algorithm using wavelet decomposition and spectrogram. http://www.peterjbentley.com/heartwokshop/challengepaper3.pdf
12. Gomes, E., Pereira, G.: Classifying heart sounds using peak location for segmentation and feature construction. http://www.peterjbentley.com/heartworkshaop/challengepaper1.pdf

Content-Based Similar Document Image Retrieval Using Fusion of CNN Features

Mao Tan$^{(\boxtimes)}$ ⓘ, Siping Yuan ⓘ, and Yongxin Su ⓘ

The College of Information Engineering, Xiangtan University,
Xiangtan 411105, China
mr.tanmao@gmail.com

Abstract. Rapid increase of digitized document images give birth to high demand of document image retrieval. While conventional document image retrieval approaches depend on complex OCR-based text recognition and text similarity detection, this paper proposes a new content-based approach, in which more attention is paid to feature extraction and feature fusion methods. In the proposed approach, multiple features of document images are extracted by different CNN models. After that, the extracted CNN features are reduced and fused into weighted average feature. Finally, the document images are ranked based on the feature similarity to query image. Experimental procedure is performed on a group of document images that transformed from academic papers, which contain both English and Chinese document, the results show that the proposed approach has good ability to retrieve document images with similar text content, and the fusion of CNN features can improve the retrieval accuracy.

Keywords: Text retrieval · Document image retrieval
Convolutional neural networks · Feature fusion · Multi models fusion

1 Introduction

Due to development of digital media technology, the scale of multimedia resources including the document images is getting bigger and bigger. Document image retrieval, the task of which is to find useful information or similar document images from a large dataset for a given user query, has become an important research domain in natural language processing. Many approaches based on Optical Character Recognition (OCR) have been proposed, which recognize text content from images and then use text similarity detection to implement document image retrieval system.

Conventional document image retrieval depends on complex model of the OCR-based approach, has some weaknesses such as high computational cost, language dependency, and it is sensitive to image resolution. Direct recommendation and retrieval on the basis of arbitrary multi-character text in unconstrained image require a recognition-free retrieval approach to learn and recognize deep visual features in images. The new document image recognition-free retrieval approach will be conducive to detect the re-contributed and re-published text content on the database of academic journals theses, or query the relevant literature in massive resources.

© Springer Nature Singapore Pte Ltd. 2018
B. Huet et al. (Eds.): ICIMCS 2017, CCIS 819, pp. 260–270, 2018.
https://doi.org/10.1007/978-981-10-8530-7_25

Pre-processing is the first step of document image retrieval, document images may be noisy, distorted, and skewed, digitized text need to treated using different pre-processing methods. According to the type of document image dataset, various pre-processing methods are applied to the document images. In some cases, converting colorful images to grayscale images, adjustment of images' sizes, border removal [1] and normalization of the text line width [2] in the initial steps can enhance document images.

In early studies on text recognition and retrieval, the extraction of features requires layout analysis, line segmentation, word segmentation, word recognition, etc. But over the last decade, deep learning based features extraction has become an key research direction. Among various deep learning models, the Convolutional Neural Networks (CNNs) are the most powerful networks in image processing tasks. When CNNs are trained in images database, a deep representation of the image is constructed to make object information increasingly explicit along the processing hierarchy [3]. During the CNN feature training phase, Redmon et al. [4] proposed an improved model that inspired by the GoogLeNet model [5] for image classification. They pre-trained the model's convolutional layers on ImageNet dataset for approximately a week, and used the initial convolutional layers of the network to extract features from the image while the fully connected layers to predict the result. Gatys et al. [6] obtained a style representation of an input image and generated results on the basis of the VGGNet, which is a CNN that rivals human performance on a common visual object recognition benchmark task [7]. As for learning visual features of multi-character text, Goodfellow et al. [8] proposed a unified approach that integrates the localization, segmentation, and recognition steps via the use of a deep convolutional neural network that operates directly on the image pixels.

However, compared with other similar methods, the parameter space of CNN network is too large to train a CNN model in a short time. Fortunately, there are some open pre-trained models that we can easily use, such as MatConvNet [9]. Besides that, training the CNN features on a large dataset and fine-tuning by target dataset can significantly improve the performance [10]. Furthermore, we can use the PCA method to reduce the dimension of the CNN features according to the investigation in reference [11], which is mainly to evaluate the performance of compressed neural codes, and it declared that plain PCA or a combination of PCA with discriminative dimensionality reduction can result in very short codes and good (state-of-the-art) performance.

To the best of our knowledge, model fusion is a very powerful technique to increase accuracy on a variety of machine learning tasks. The most basic and convenient way to fusion is to ensemble the features or predictions from multiple different models on the test set, which is a quick way to ensemble already existing model when teaming up. When averaging the outputs from multiple different models, not all predictors are perfectly calibrated or the predictions clutter around a certain range. Fusion methods is key to the solutions, better results can be obtained, if it is given by a linear combination of the ensemble the features or predictions. In this case, the combination coefficients have to be determined by some optimization procedure [12]. A ranking average is proposed in [13] that first turn the predictions into ranks, and then averaging these ranks, which do well on improving the exact same fusion used an average. Moreira et al. [14] specifically tested two un-supervised rank aggregation approaches well known in the information retrieval literature, namely CombSUM and CombMNZ.

These algorithms are used to aggregate the information gathered from different outputs or features in order to achieve more accurate ranking results than using individual scores.

Similarity measurement is another key technique to determine the effectiveness of the retrieval system. There are many ways to measure the similarity of image content. An efficient and widespread method is computing pair-wise image cosine similarity based on visual features of all images, and then used this parameter value to retrieve the high similarity images [15].

In this paper, we try to establish a content-based approach to document image retrieval with the purpose of finding out the similar document through a query document image. We choose a document image similarity retrieval method with CNN feature extraction and cosine similarity matching as a basic framework. At the same time, a multiple models fusion method is proposed, which using Rank_avg of each CNN network to obtain the weighted average fusion feature, and then integrate these methods in the framework in order to improve the accuracy of retrieval system. In the experimental procedure, we slice a batch of English and Chinese academic papers into document images as the image dataset, a group of document images with changed text content is used as the query image, several case studies are provided to evaluate the adaptability and accuracy of the proposed method in different conditions.

2 Methodology

In this section, we mainly discuss several key steps of the document image similarity retrieval based on the multiple CNN models fusion features of images. Firstly, we fine-tune the pre-trained CNN models using MatConvNet, and set repeatedly the crop size of experimental document image. After that, we use multiple different fine-tuned CNN models to extract diverse CNN features from experimental document image dataset, which can convert the visual content into a deep representation. As the CNN feature matrix trained by the CNN model are high-dimensional, we further perform the PCA method to reduce the dimensions and make the each CNN feature matrix has identical dimension in order to subsequent model fusion. Then ensemble the multiple CNN feature matrix by corresponding combination coefficients that calculated from the Rank_avg of its CNN network, obtain a weighted average fusion feature. After that, we compute and rank the cosine similarity of document images to the query images based on the weighted average fusion feature, output the final retrieval result. In the following section, we elaborate on each of steps in detail, the entire processes are shown in Fig. 1.

As shown in Fig. 1, firstly, we convert original images to processed images by using some mature pre-processing methods. We extract the CNN feature to obtain the deep visual representations by fine-tune the multiple pre-trained CNN network model on the target document image dataset. After obtaining the CNN feature matrix, we reduce the dimension of the matrix and improve the efficiency of the algorithm by PCA. Then, we ensemble the various features from multiple network models based on *Rank_avg* value. We measure the cosine similarity between the query document image and each image in the training dataset based on multiple model fusion features, and show the most similar images.

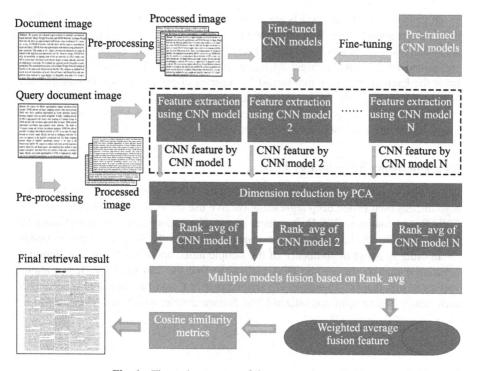

Fig. 1. The entire process of the proposed approach.

2.1 CNN Feature Extraction

It is necessary to extract the primitive features of document image as the constructive parameter of the training model. The quality of the feature extraction directly determines the retrieval effect. Recently, CNNs have achieved impressive results in some areas such as image recognition and object detection. It can input image into the network directly, avoiding the complex feature extraction and data reconstruction process in traditional recognition algorithm. As described above, we choose some state-of-the-art CNN models that submitted for the ImageNet challenge over the last 5 years as the training network. Among them, AlexNet, the first entry that use a deep neural network in 2012 ImageNet competition, has strong generalization ability in computer vision tasks. VGGNet is a preferred multi-layer neural network model for extracting the CNN features of image. The VGGNet use small-size convolution filters and deep network layers, which also has strong generalization ability in many computer vision applications and other image recognition datasets. GoogLeNet can improve utilization of the computing resources inside the network by a carefully crafted design, which allows for increasing the depth and width of the network while keeping the computational budget constant, has good prediction performance in image classification. In addition, ResNet uses a residual learning framework to ease the training of deeper networks but still owes low complexity of the network, and it outperforms the human level accuracy in the 2015 ImageNet competition.

In general, most CNN models are trained by composing simple linear or non-linear filtering operations, while their implementation need to be trained on large dataset and learned from vast amounts of data. Therefore, we fine-tune the above mentioned pre-trained models on the target document image dataset. At the training phase, we input the fixed-size images that turned by a series of pre-processing to multiple networks and removes the mean. After that, we retain the CNN feature matrix of the penultimate layer of this deep CNN representation, which can be used as a powerful image descriptor applicable to many types of datasets.

2.2 Dimension Reduction by PCA

After CNN feature extraction with various CNN model, we obtain some high-dimensional image deep representation. We use the PCA method to compress the CNN feature matrix to 256-D. It reduces some information redundancy, and make the CNN feature matrix has identical dimension to facilitate the subsequent model fusion.

In order to avoid the influence of the sample units, and simplify the calculation of covariance matrix, we use the PCA method to find the 256 largest variation feature vectors in this matrix. Therefore, covariance matrix C can be calculated according to each feature vector x_i in normalized CNN feature matrix, which can be expressed as

$$C = \frac{1}{n} \sum_{i=1}^{n} x_i x_i^T,$$ (1)

where C represents the covariance matrix of the feature matrix, and n represents the number of feature vectors.

After that, the eigenvalue equation based on C can be expressed as

$$\lambda_i \mu_i = C \mu_i,$$ (2)

where λ_i is the eigenvalue of the covariance matrix, and μ_i is the corresponding eigenvector of the covariance matrix.

Then, we use the resulting 256 normalized feature vectors to constitute the main feature matrix to form a 256-D space. Based on that, we project the high-dimensional CNN feature matrix onto the 256-D dimensional space. Finally, the CNN feature projection matrix is indexed to improve the retrieval efficiency.

2.3 Fusion of CNN Features

Through the above method, we obtain various fine-turned CNN models to extract image features. It has been confirmed that creating ensembles from multiple individual files can reduces the generalization error. Therefore, we fuse the features from multiple different existing models respectively, propose the multiple models fusion method based on *Rank_avg*.

The features trained by different CNN models might represent different characteristics of document image, and utilizing different features effectively through multiple models fusion method will have positive effect on document image similarity retrieval.

We improve the model fusion method that based on ranking average in [13], ensemble the features from multiple model by corresponding combination coefficients that calculated from the *Rank_avg* of its model network.

A small scale document image dataset is created in advance to calculate the *Rank_avg* of each model, which include 422 pair similar document images and the index of each pair of images. Then, the *Rank_avg* of each model can be calculated according to the retrieval results that learned by corresponding model on this dataset, which is more adaptable to ensemble different models that have significant difference. The *Rank_avg* can be calculated as

$$Rank\_avg = \sum_{i=1}^{n} \frac{score}{rank_i}, \tag{3}$$

where $n = 422$, *score* is the mean accuracy in the top-5 similar images to the each query when using certain model, $rank_i$ is the ranking of the i-th image's similar image in its retrieval result.

After that, normalizing the *Rank_avg* between 0 and 1 can get the corresponding combination coefficient ε. Finally, we ensemble the three CNN feature matrix M_{VD}, M_{VE} and M_G trained by VGGNet-D, VGGNet-E and GoogLeNet respectively according to corresponding ε and obtain the weighted average fusion feature that can be expressed as

$$M = \varepsilon_{VD} * M_{VD} + \varepsilon_{VE} * M_{VE} + \varepsilon_G * M_G, \tag{4}$$

where ε_{VD}, ε_{VE} and ε_G are the corresponding coefficients for the feature matrix to ensemble, and $\varepsilon_{VD} + \varepsilon_{VE} + \varepsilon_G = 1$.

2.4 Similarity Metric

Cosine similarity has been proved to be an effective metric system because of its accuracy. The 256-D weighted average fusion feature matrix $[z_1, z_2, \ldots, z_n]^T$ could describe the main CNN features of the document images in the dataset, where n is the number of document images in the datasets. The cosine similarity calculated from CNN feature vector can approximately measure the similarity between document images.

For each pair of feature vector (Z_u, Z_v) where $u \neq v$, the pair-wise image cosine similarity T_s can be expressed as

$$T_s(Z_u, Z_v) = \frac{\sum_{i=1}^{k} F(Z_u, u_i) * F(Z_v, v_i)}{\sqrt{\sum_{i=1}^{k} F(Z_u, u_i)^2} * \sqrt{\sum_{i=1}^{k} F(Z_v, v_i)^2}}, \tag{5}$$

where $K = 256$, and $F(Z_u, u_i)$ is the value of the i-th column element of the 256-D dimensional feature vector corresponding to the document image Z_u. $T_s(Z_u, Z_v)$ is the pair-wise document image cosine similarity. Through Eq. (5), we can retrieve out some high similarity document images to query image.

3 Experiments

3.1 Data Collection and Evaluation Metric

In this work, to evaluate the proposed method, we collect a group of English and Chinese academic papers as the text database, and cut them into many small pieces of heterogeneous document image to construct a training dataset, which contains 2017 images totally. Then, we select some text paragraphs from the original article and edit them by various ways. After that, we store the edited text paragraphs as images to construct an query image dataset including 422 images totally, which is used to evaluate the accuracy of the proposed approach in various situations. In addition, we select the 422 query images and their original images to construct a small scale document image dataset, and create a **<query image name, original image name>** index to calculate the *Rank_avg* of each CNN network in advance.

We performed different experiments with different CNN model. 422 query document images is selected to retrieve out the similar document images in image dataset. The proposed method is evaluated using the accuracy value measured based on the results ranked among the Top-1, Top-3, Top-5 and Top-10 similar images to a query document image.

3.2 Experimental Results and Analyses

The training and query dataset includes English and Chinese document images, and there are 10 types edited images in query dataset, including retranslating by Google, changing the font color, adding another statement in the content, omitting lots of content, adjusting the line spacing of the text and reversing the word order, and so on. Therefore, we retrieve separately different images each time to see the retrieval effect of different text language and content, or local deformation of layout. At first, we choose an English document image as query image, which is converted from the abstract of the an English article, The query document image is shown as Fig. 2(a). After that, we calculate the query document image's similarity to each document image in training dataset by using MMF (VGGNet-D + VGGNet-E + GoogLeNet), the original document image that is shown in Fig. 2(b) can be retrieved out in first.

Another case study is provided to evaluate the retrieval effect when querying through Chinese document image, which is re-translated by Google and modified in its original text content. The Top-1 retrieval result image is shown in Fig. 3, and in these result we can see that similar text content with some different characters and visual presentations can be recognized by the proposed approach.

Then we consider the Top-1, Top3, Top5 and Top-10 accuracy in ranked result using various individual CNN model, and compare them with the accuracy that obtained by multiple models using weighted average fusion feature. The condition that fuse the features of AlexNet and VGGNet-E is named MMF-1, the fusion of AlexNet, VGGNet-D and VGGNet-E is named MMF-2, the fusion of AlexNet and GoogLeNet is named MMF-3, and MMF-4 represents fusion of AlexNet and ResNet-152. According to experimental performance, for GoogLeNet and ResNet, the crop size of

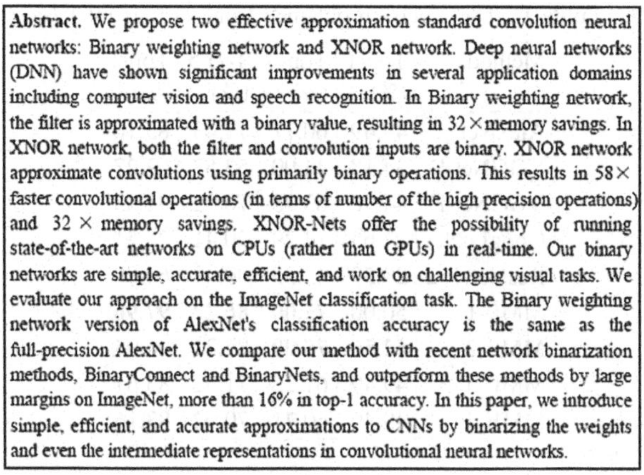

Abstract. We propose two effective approximation standard convolution neural networks: Binary weighting network and XNOR network. Deep neural networks (DNN) have shown significant improvements in several application domains including computer vision and speech recognition. In Binary weighting network, the filter is approximated with a binary value, resulting in 32 ×memory savings. In XNOR network, both the filter and convolution inputs are binary. XNOR network approximate convolutions using primarily binary operations. This results in 58× faster convolutional operations (in terms of number of the high precision operations) and 32 × memory savings. XNOR-Nets offer the possibility of running state-of-the-art networks on CPUs (rather than GPUs) in real-time. Our binary networks are simple, accurate, efficient, and work on challenging visual tasks. We evaluate our approach on the ImageNet classification task. The Binary weighting network version of AlexNet's classification accuracy is the same as the full-precision AlexNet. We compare our method with recent network binarization methods, BinaryConnect and BinaryNets, and outperform these methods by large margins on ImageNet, more than 16% in top-1 accuracy. In this paper, we introduce simple, efficient, and accurate approximations to CNNs by binarizing the weights and even the intermediate representations in convolutional neural networks.

(a)

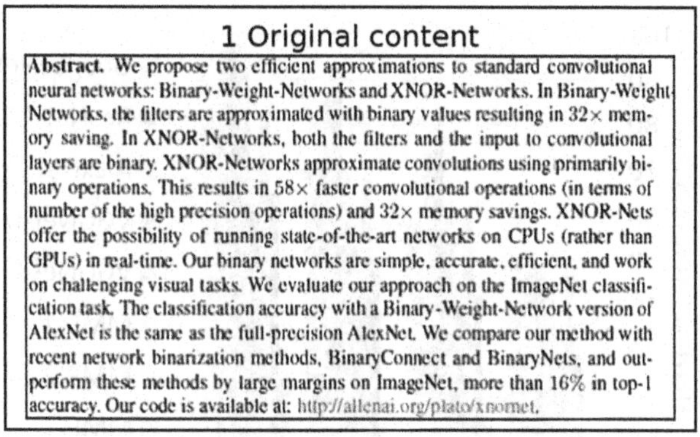

1 Original content

Abstract. We propose two efficient approximations to standard convolutional neural networks: Binary-Weight-Networks and XNOR-Networks. In Binary-Weight-Networks, the filters are approximated with binary values resulting in 32× memory saving. In XNOR-Networks, both the filters and the input to convolutional layers are binary. XNOR-Networks approximate convolutions using primarily binary operations. This results in 58× faster convolutional operations (in terms of number of the high precision operations) and 32× memory savings. XNOR-Nets offer the possibility of running state-of-the-art networks on CPUs (rather than GPUs) in real-time. Our binary networks are simple, accurate, efficient, and work on challenging visual tasks. We evaluate our approach on the ImageNet classification task. The classification accuracy with a Binary-Weight-Network version of AlexNet is the same as the full-precision AlexNet. We compare our method with recent network binarization methods, BinaryConnect and BinaryNets, and outperform these methods by large margins on ImageNet, more than 16% in top-1 accuracy. Our code is available at: http://allenai.org/plato/xnornet.

(b)

Fig. 2. The Top-1 similarity retrieval of English document image. (a) Query image. (b) Result image.

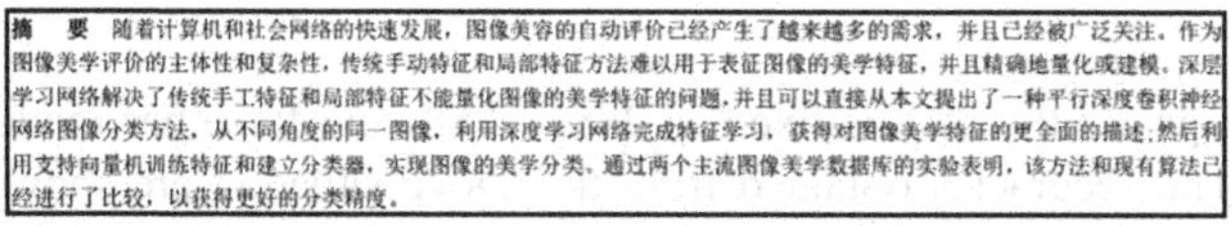

摘 要 随着计算机和社会网络的快速发展，图像美容的自动评价已经产生了越来越多的需求，并且已经被广泛关注，作为图像美学评价的主体性和复杂性，传统手动特征和局部特征方法难以用于表征图像的美学特征，并且精确地量化或建模，深层学习网络分类图像的问题，从不同角度的同一图像，利用深度学习网络完成特征学习，获得对图像美学特征的更全面的描述；然后利用支持向量机训练特征和建立分类器，实现图像的美学分类，通过两个主流图像美学数据库的实验表明，该方法与现有算法已经进行了比较，以获得更好的分类精度。

(a)

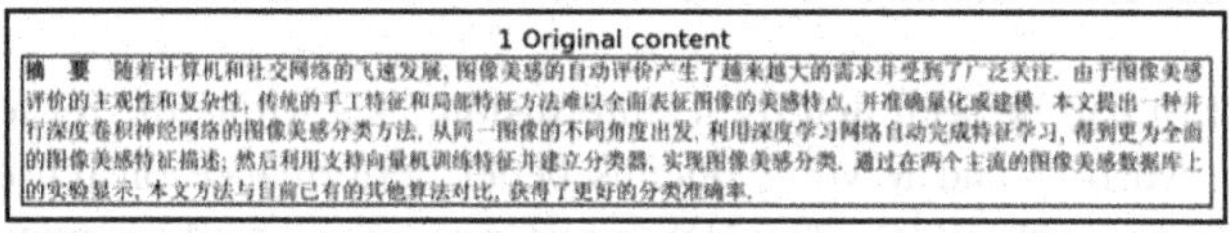

1 Original content

摘 要 随着计算机和社交网络的飞速发展，图像美感的自动评价产生了越来越大的需求并受到了广泛关注。由于图像美感评价的主观性和复杂性，传统的手工特征和局部特征方法难以全面表征图像的美感特点，并准确量化或建模。本文提出一种并行深度卷积神经网络的图像美感分类方法，从同一图像的不同角度出发，利用深度学习网络自动完成特征学习，得到更为全面的图像美感特征描述；然后利用支持向量机训练特征并建立分类器，实现图像美感分类。通过在两个主流的图像美感数据库上的实验显示，本文方法与目前已有的其他算法对比，获得了更好的分类准确率。

(b)

Fig. 3. The Top-1 similarity retrieval of Chinese document image. (a) Query image. (b) Result image.

Table 1. The precision obtained from various models.

Methods	Top-1 (%)	Top-3 (%)	Top-5 (%)	Top-10 (%)
AlexNet	49.49	60.71	71.43	83.16
VGGNet-D	34.18	44.90	53.57	63.27
VGGNet-E	44.90	63.78	70.92	91.33
GoogLeNet	7.65	14.29	20.41	25.51
ResNet-152	29.59	42.35	49.49	64.80
MMF-1	50.00	**75.00**	**86.22**	**97.96**
MMF-2	**52.55**	**75.00**	85.71	96.94
MMF-3	49.49	61.22	71.92	83.67
MMF-4	49.49	60.71	70.92	83.16

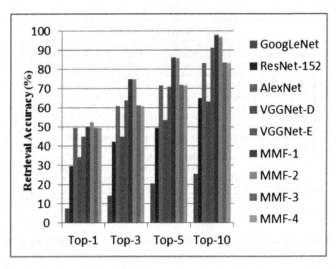

Fig. 4. The retrieval accuracy obtained from the proposed fusion method and some single model.

document images in the case is fixed as 288 × 288, and for other models it is set to 256 × 256. The accuracies obtained from the above situation are shown in Table 1. During the model fusion, we got the Rank_avg and ε of each CNN network in advance, which is obtained by training each network with the small scale document image dataset.

In Table 1, it can be seen that by feature fusion, as a whole the retrieval precision are improved, MMF-1 and MMF-2 obtains better performance on retrieval accuracy than the best individual models AlexNet in our case, which result is mainly caused by good individual models. At the same time, it should be noted that the accuracy improvement fluctuate slightly if GoogLeNet or ResNet-152 is adopted in features fusion. We can see that minor performance improvement in MMF-3 but slight accuracy decreases of MMF-4 in TOP-5 retrieval, which should be caused by the low accuracy of individual model in the two fusion models. The above results show us that the chosen of individual CNN model with good performance is important for the proposed fusion approach. Further in more, Fig. 4 illustrates intuitively that the similarity retrieval results through various individual models and the proposed fusion method.

4   Conclusions

In this paper, a new content-based approach to document image retrieval is proposed. All of the experimental results indicate that the proposed approach is effective to realize document image recognition-free retrieval for different language characters without using OCR. By using Rank_avg to fuse the features obtained from several classical CNN model, the retrieval accuracy can be significantly improved in most of conditions with different transformations of text content or layout. In our next works, for obtaining higher retrieval accuracy, more methods will be chosen and tested to fuse multiple CNN models. When this approach is further improved to adapt more complex transformations, it is expected to be applied in paper plagiarism identification or literature recommendation.

Acknowledgments. This work was partially supported by the National Research Foundation of China (61402391).

References

1. Gatos, B., Pratikakis, I.: Segmentation-free word spotting in historical printed documents. In: 10th International Conference on Document Analysis and Recognition, pp. 271–275. IEEE, Barcelona, Spain (2010)
2. Frinken, V., Fischer, A., Manmatha, R., et al.: A novel word spotting method based on recurrent neural networks. IEEE Trans. Pattern Anal. Mach. Intell. **34**(2), 211–224 (2012)
3. Gatys, L.A., Ecker, A.S., Bethge, M.: Texture synthesis and the controlled generation of natural stimuli using convolutional neural networks. arXiv:1505.07376 (2015)
4. Redmon, J., Divvala, S., Girshick, R., et al.: You only look once: unified, real-time object detection. In: IEEE Conference on Computer Vision and Pattern Recognition, pp. 779–788. IEEE, Las Vegas, NV (2016)
5. Szegedy, C., Liu, W., Jia, Y., et al.: Going deeper with convolutions. In: Proceedings of the IEEE Conference on Computer Vision and Pattern Recognition, pp. 1–9. IEEE, San Francisco (2015)
6. Gatys, L.A., Ecker, A.S., Bethge, M.: A neural algorithm of artistic style. Computer Science (2015)
7. Simonyan, K., Zisserman, A.: Very deep convolutional networks for large-scale image recognition. arXiv:1409.1556 (2014)
8. Goodfellow, I.J., Bulatov, Y., Ibarz, J., et al.: Multi-digit number recognition from street view imagery using deep convolutional neural networks. Computer Science (2013)
9. Vedaldi, A., Lenc, K.: MatConvNet: Convolutional neural networks for MATLAB. In: Proceedings of the 23rd ACM International Conference on Multimedia, pp. 689–692. ACM, Brisbane, Australia (2014)

10. Chatfield, K., Simonyan, K., Vedaldi, A., et al.: Return of the devil in the details: delving deep into convolutional nets. Computer Science (2014)
11. Babenko, A., Slesarev, A., Chigorin, A., Lempitsky, V.: Neural codes for image retrieval. In: Fleet, D., Pajdla, T., Schiele, B., Tuytelaars, T. (eds.) ECCV 2014. LNCS, vol. 8689, pp. 584–599. Springer, Cham (2014). https://doi.org/10.1007/978-3-319-10590-1_38
12. Jahrer, M., Töscher, A., Legenstein, R.: Combining predictions for accurate recommender systems. In: Proceedings of the 16th ACM SIGKDD International Conference on Knowledge Discovery and Data Mining, pp. 693–702. ACM, Washington (2010)
13. Kaggle Ensembling Guide. https://mlwave.com/kaggle-ensembling-guide/. Accessed 11 June 2015
14. Moreira, C., Martins, B., Calado, P.: Using rank aggregation for expert search in academic digital libraries. arXiv:1501.05140 (2015)
15. Sejal, D., Rashmi, V., Venugopal, K.R.: Image recommendation based on keyword relevance using absorbing Markov chain and image features. Int. J. Multimedia Inf. Retrieval 5(3), 1–15 (2016)

Continuous Dropout Strategy for Deep Learning Network

Jianchao Fei[1], Ting Rui[1(⊠)], Xiaona Song[1], You Zhou[2], and Sai Zhang[1]

[1] College of Filed Engineering, PLA University Science and Technology, Nanjing 210007, China
rtinguu@sohu.com
[2] Jiangsu Institute of Commerce, Nanjing 210007, China

Abstract. Recent years, more and more attractive results are achieved by deep learning. However, large numbers of parameters generally cause overfitting in the training stage. Hinton [17] proposed dropout to address this problem in 2012. During our research, we find that there is a balance between generalization and accuracy. Dropout can increase generalization, decrease overfitting and thus increase accuracy by using appropriate dropout rate. However, too high generalization may lead to relatively low accuracy. So, we propose a continuous dropout rate strategy that we gradually decrease the dropout rate during training instead of a constant one. In this way, we can obtain high generalization in the beginning and high accuracy in the end. Experiment results show that our proposed strategy can achieve higher accuracy compared to the traditional dropout.

Keywords: Deep learning · Generalization · Overfitting · Dropout

1 Introduction

Deep learning has been demonstrated to be an successful way in various areas such as classification [1, 2], detection [3–5] and segmentation [6–8]. Compared to traditional neural network, convolutional neural network (CNN), as one of the most famous deep learning algorithms, benefits from its special structure design: local receptive field, shared weights, and pooling operation. CNN contains multiple nonlinear hidden layers which make it powerful in presenting complicated relationships between inputs and outputs. To some extent, deeper CNN structure performs higher ability of nonlinear representation with more parameters, and thus achieves higher accuracy. Recent years, researchers add more and more layers to CNN, obtaining supervising results on many famous benchmark datasets. Zisserman and Simonyan increase the VGG net depth to 16 (or 19) which decreases the ImageNet top-5 error to 7.3%, 55% improvement compared with AlexNet [9, 10]. In ILSVRC 2015, ResNet achieves an amazing result (4.3%, top-5) by 152 layers [11].

Generally, we cannot stack layers to CNN directly. As more and more layers added, we may face overfitting problem [14]. When CNN becomes complex, it has large numbers of parameters with limited training data. As a result, the CNN model may overreact to minor fluctuations in the training data and describe random error or noise

B. Huet et al. (Eds.): ICIMCS 2017, CCIS 819, pp. 271–279, 2018.
https://doi.org/10.1007/978-981-10-8530-7_26

instead of the underlying relationship. Many methods have been developed for reducing this problem. Among them, dropout [17] is now most widely used in many deep learning models addressing overfitting problem which has been demonstrated to be very successful.

According to [20], dropout can be applied to CNN, NN, and DBN, showing significant improvements on various datasets such as Mnist, Cifar-10 and ImageNet. It can been seen as an way to combine many different neural network architectures efficiently. With deep study on dropout, we find that dropout rate is constant during training and it varies from different models and datasets. Constant dropout rate yields relatively constant generalization ability. In the start stage of training, we prefer to obtain high generation ability, however, in the ending stage we pay more attention to the accuracy. Obviously, constant dropout rate cannot meet this request. In this paper, we propose a continuous dropout rate strategy instead of the traditional (constant) one.

2   Related Work

Overfitting must be taken account into when we train deep learning network. Decreasing overfitting, i.e. increasing generalization can help improve network performance. So many researchers devote to finding a way to address this problem. The existing methods include early stopping [15], weight decay [16] and dropout [17].

Early stopping is realized by adding validation datasets. We automatically stop the training process as soon as performance on a validation dataset starts to get worse. This method can prevent the model from continuing to overfit. In another word, it just stop the model from getting worse when overfitting happens but cannot eliminate or decrease overfitting. The weight decay parameter governs the regularization term which is added to the network's loss to compute the backprop gradient. It encourages weights close to zero based on the idea that a zero weight cost little bits to be specified, thus being simple which can often improve generalization obviously [18]. Dropout is a technique dropping out units (hidden or visible) in a model. Standard backpropagation learning generally yields brittle co-adaptations which works for training data but do not generalize to test data. Dropout can break up these co-adaptions by randomly making any particular hidden units unreliable and thus improve the generalization.

Methods discussed above mainly focus on decreasing overfitting, but pay little attention to the accuracy although accuracy may increase as overfitting decrease to some extent. However, we find that there is a balance between overfitting (i.e. generalization) and accuracy. Too high or too low generalization both cannot obtain higher accuracy. So we proposed a continuous dropout rate strategy instead of a constant one. To our best knowledge, there is no previous work that adopts this strategy. The details will be shown in the next paragraph.

3   Methods

3.1   Model Design

The main goal we try to demonstrate is the effectiveness and superiority of our method rather than getting state-of-the-art results. Followed by this basic principle, a simple default CNN structure in LightNet [19] is adopted in our main experiments instead of a sophistical one which is specially designed for achieving higher accuracy or beating the state-of-the-art. The overall CNN architecture is depicted in Fig. 1. The size of data we use is (or resized to) 32 × 32, so we simply use the same hyperparameters on all datasets.

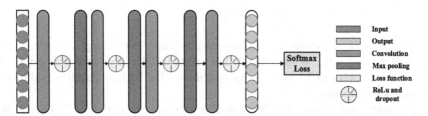

Fig. 1. An illustration of the architecture of our model. This model contains five layers with weights: the first four are convolution layers and the last one is the output. The kernel size of first three convolution layers is 5 × 5 with pad of 2, the fourth is 4 × 4 with pad of 0 and the last one is 1 × 1 with pad of 0. Relu activation function is deployed on the output of every convolution layer acting as the non-linear feature mapping. The max pooling operation is adopted with size of 3 and stride of 2. The number of feature maps in this model is given by 32-32-64-64-n (n is the number of class).

3.2   Formula Design

s Let z^l denote the vector of input into layer l, y^l denote the vector of outputs from layer l, and b^l denote the bias of layer l. The feedforward operation of a standard neural network can be describe as

$$z^l = w^{l+1}y^l + b^{l+1},$$
$$y^{l+1} = f(z^{l+1}), \tag{1}$$

where f is a activation function.

Dropout is technique to drop out units randomly. That is to say, each unit is retained with a fix probability independent of other units. So, the feedforward operation changes to

$$r^l \sim Bernoulli(p),$$
$$\widetilde{y}^l = r^l * y^l,$$
$$z^{l+1} = w^{l+1}\widetilde{y}^l + b^{l+1}, \tag{2}$$
$$y^{l+1} = f(z^{l+1}).$$

The main idea of our method is to change the dropout rate during training instead of a fixed one. Let *epoch* denote the number of training time, n denote a scalar that controls the decreasing speed of dropout rate, m denote the start dropout rate. Then the formulas turn into

$$
\begin{aligned}
r^l &= epoch * n + m, \\
\widetilde{y}^l &= r^l * y^l, \\
z^{l+1} &= w^{l+1}\widetilde{y}^l + b^{l+1}, \\
y^{l+1} &= f(z^{l+1}).
\end{aligned}
\tag{3}
$$

$epoch$ and n determine the ending dropout rate. For example, $epoch = 100$, $n = -0.001$, $m = 0.5$, dropout rate will decrease 0.001 every epoch during training, and change from 0.5 to 0.1 after the whole training. The back propagation is similar to the traditional dropout.

The traditional dropout can be treated as training a collection of 2^n thinned networks (if the neural network has n units) according to [20]. In another word, the traditional dropout increases the feature space to a larger fixed size which significantly reduces overfitting and improves generalization ability. In this way, accuracy can be increased due to lower overfitting and larger generalization ability. However, as the training continues, this fixed size feature space may be redundant. Moreover, generalization ability is not always proportional to accuracy. Too large generalization ability may decrease accuracy. We hope that the network can have larger generalization ability to reduce overfitting in the start training stage and relatively lower generalization ability to obtain higher accuracy in the ending training stage.

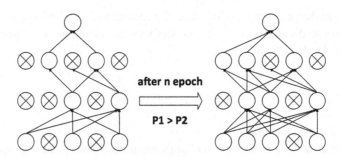

Fig. 2. The left figure note the network which is trained in the beginning, and the right one note the network which is trained after n epoch. $P1$ represents the dropout rate when the network is trained in the beginning, $P2$ is dropout rate after n epoch. According to our strategy, dropout rate is decreasing by epoch, so $P1 > P2$.

Our continuous dropout rate strategy can meet these requirements:

(1) Continuous dropout can gradually simplify the feature space as the dropout rate decrease. Figure 2 shows the difference.
(2) We believe that there is a balance between generalization and accuracy. From Fig. 5 we can see that during the network training with our continuous strategy, higher accuracy is obtained in the later stage with lower dropout rate.

4 Methods

4.1 Datasets

We select three datasets to validate our strategy: Mnist, Cifar-10, SVHN and self-make dataset.

Mnist. It is a digit handwritten dataset of 0–9 with 60000 training images and 10000 test images. All the images are in gray mode. The task is to classify the images into 10 classes. Although the best classification accuracy of MNIST is very high (over 99%), it still can be seen as a standard dataset to validate models. We resize the images to 32 × 32 in order to use the same model with other datasets.

Cifar-10. It was collected by Krizhevsky, Nair, and Hinton which consists of 60000 32 × 32 color images in 10 classes, with 6000 images per class. There are 50000 training images and 10000 test images. It is an common computer-vision dataset used for object recognition.

SVHN. The Street View House Number (SVHN) dataset is a real-world image dataset for developing machine learning and object recognition. It consists of house numbers collected by Google Street View.

Self-make dataset. Our self-make dataset consists of 30000 training images and 8000 test images collected from bridges. These images contain cracks on the bridge surface. The goal is to estimate if there is a crack in one image. All the images are 32 × 32 in gray mode.

4.2 Test on Datasets

All the images in these three datasets are (or resized to) 32 × 32. So we apply the same model (shown in Sect. 3.1) to them (except the input layer and output layer as the channels and classes are different). We set $epoch = 100$, $n = -0.004$, $m = 0.5$. So the continuous dropout rate function becomes

$$r = -epoch * 0.004 + 0.5 \tag{4}$$

During our experiments, we consider another case: change Eq. 4 to a step function, which is named as the step dropout. The step function is

$$r = \begin{cases} 0.5, & epoch < 20 \\ 0.3, & 20 \leq epoch \leq 40 \\ 0.1, & 40 < epoch \leq 100 \end{cases} \tag{5}$$

Step dropout can also meet the requirements mentioned in Sect. 3.2. In the first stage, dropout rate is 0.5 (named starting dropout rate). The main goal is to obtain high generation and reduce overfitting. In the last stage, dropout decrease to 0.1 (named ending dropout rate). And thus the main goal becomes to increase the accuracy.

In order to show the superiority of continuous dropout rate, we conduct four tests on every dataset: model with dropout, model with step dropout and model with continuous dropout. Figure 3 shows the results.

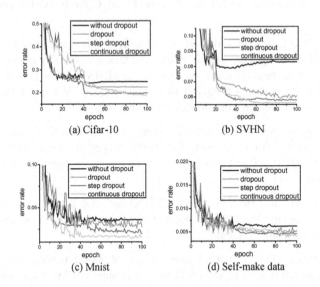

(a) Cifar-10   (b) SVHN

(c) Mnist   (d) Self-make data

Fig. 3. Tests on four datasets

From Fig. 3, we can see that dropout indeed increases the accuracy compared with the model without dropout. Obviously, step dropout and continuous dropout obtain higher accuracy while continuous dropout is slightly better. In fact, we conduct many tests on step dropout through changing different conditional breakpoints such as 0.5–0.3–0.05, however, continuous dropout is still the best. Perhaps continuous dropout has more feature space to select as the dropout rate is changing every epoch.

Next we mainly focus on explaining the reason why continuous dropout is better than traditional dropout.

Firstly, we visualize the weights of first layer of dropout model and continuous model in Fig. 1. As is shown in Fig. 4, more distinct and detailed information is displayed in the continuous dropout model. That is to say, continuous dropout model extracts better features for classification than traditional dropout model.

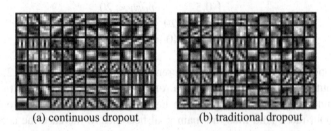

(a) continuous dropout   (b) traditional dropout

Fig. 4. Weights visualization

Then we compare the loss and training error of the two models during training. We find that continuous dropout model has lower loss and the loss decrease by epoch while dropout obtain higher loss and the loss has the trend to become horizon in the last training stage. At the same time, training error of continuous dropout model is lower than traditional dropout model's which indicates that continuous dropout model do better in the balance between generalization and accuracy. As we know, a lower loss and training error indicates a better convergence. This can be another convincing evidence to explain why continuous dropout performs better than traditional dropout model.

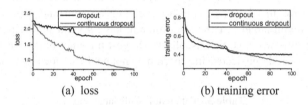

(a) loss   (b) training error

Fig. 5. Loss and training error during training

4.3 Test on Datasets

In order to further study continuous dropout, several tests are done aimed to show the effects of different parameters in Eq. 4.

(1) set the same ending dropout rate $r = 0.1$, and test on different n. In this case, the training epoch will vary with n. Different n deicide the decreasing speed of dropout rate. From Table 1, we can see that $n = 0.2$ yields best performance. Lower n with more training epoch and higher n with less training epoch both cannot obtain highest accuracy. A proper decreasing speed leads to better performance.

Table 1. Different n with same ending dropout rate

n	0.001	0.003	0.005	0.007	0.009
Test error	0.187	0.189	0.193	0.219	0.24

(2) set the same $n = 0.001$ with different ending dropout rate. The training epoch also varies as different ending dropout rate. Different ending dropout rates indicate network will converge in different feature space according to our analysis in Sect. 3. Obviously, large ending dropout rate has relatively bad performance. However, different small ending dropout rates almost yield the same good performance. There is a reasonable explanation that the front stage of training has large effect on the network as the network may escape from poor local optimum to a better optimum in this stage. While in the last stage of training, accuracy will not

be improved significantly even when the network converge in a more simplified feature space with lower ending dropout rate due to the local optimum obtained in front stage (Table 2).

Table 2. Different ending dropout rate with same n

Ending dropout rate	0	0.1	0.2	0.3	0.4
Test error		0.188	0.185	0.192	0.211	0.225

(3) set the same $epoch = 100$ with different n, and thus different ending dropout rate. Results show that lower n with larger ending dropout rate gets lower accuracy compared with larger n. However, different large n yield similar performance. At the same time, we note that usually the largest n cannot obtain best performance because severe large decreasing speed may not get better local optimum (Table 3).

Table 3. Different n with same epoch

n	0.001	0.002	0.003	0.004	0.005
Test error	0.225	0.206	0.201	0.189	0.191

Through these tests on different parameters, we find that parameters have large effects on the eventual results. Proper n and ending dropout rate, not larger n or lower ending dropout, obtain better performance.

5   Conclusions

In this paper, we propose continuous dropout to replace the traditional one. Models with continuous dropout can converge in a more simplified feature space and balance the generalization and accuracy. Extensive experiments are conducted on different datasets to validate our strategy. Results shows that continuous dropout outperforms traditional one. Moreover, we discuss the effects of parameters and give reasonable explanations.

Acknowledgment. This work was supported in part by National Natural Science Foundation of China (Grant No. 61473444). This foundation is mainly focus on multimedia and machine learning.

References

1. Al Rahhal, M.M., Bazi, Y., AlHichri, H., et al.: Deep learning approach for active classification of electrocardiogram signals. Inf. Sci. **345**, 340–354 (2016)
2. Zeiler, M.D., Fergus, R.: Visualizing and understanding convolutional networks. In: Fleet, D., Pajdla, T., Schiele, B., Tuytelaars, T. (eds.) ECCV 2014. LNCS, vol. 8689, pp. 818–833. Springer, Cham (2014). https://doi.org/10.1007/978-3-319-10590-1_53. Author, F., Author, S., Author, T.: Book title, 2nd edn. Publisher, Location (1999)

3. Girshick, R., Donahue, J., Darrell, T., Malik, J.: Rich feature hierarchies for accurate object detection and semantic segmentation. In: Proceedings of the IEEE Conference on Computer Vision and Pattern Recognition, pp. 580–587 (2014)
4. Shin, H.C., Roth, H.R., Gao, M., et al.: Deep convolutional neural networks for computer-aided detection: CNN architectures, dataset characteristics and transfer learning. IEEE Trans. Med. Imaging **35**(5), 1285–1298 (2016)
5. Hong, R., Hu, Z., Wang, R., Wang, M., Tao, D.: Multi-view object retrieval via multi-scale topic models. IEEE Trans. Image Process. **25**(12), 5814–5827 (2016)
6. Farabet, C., Couprie, C., Najman, L., LeCun, Y.: Learning hierarchical features for scene labeling. IEEE Trans. Pattern Anal. Mach. Intell. **35**(8), 1915–1929 (2013)
7. Chen, L.C., Papandreou, G., Kokkinos, I., et al.: Deeplab: semantic image segmentation with deep convolutional nets, atrous convolution, and fully connected CRFs. arXiv preprint arXiv:1606.00915 (2016)
8. Hong, R., Yang, Y., Wang, M., Hua, X.-S.: Learning visual semantic relationships for efficient visual retrieval. IEEE Trans. Big Data **1**(4), 152–161 (2015)
9. Simonyan, K., Zisserman, A.: Very deep convolutional networks for large-scale image recognition. arXiv preprint arXiv:1409.1556 (2014)
10. Krizhevsky, A., Sutskever, I., Hinton, G.E.: Imagenet classification with deep convolutional neural networks. In: Advances in Neural Information Processing Systems, pp. 1097–1105 (2012)
11. He, K., Zhang, X., Ren, S., et al.: Deep residual learning for image recognition. arXiv preprint arXiv:1512.03385 (2015)
12. Hochreiter, S., Bengio, Y., Frasconi, P., Schmidhuber, J.: Gradient flow in recurrent nets: the difficulty of learning long-term dependencies. In: Kremer, S.C., Kolen, J.F. (eds.) A Field Guide to Dynamical Recurrent Neural Networks. IEEE Press (2001)
13. Nair, V., Hinton, G.E.: Rectified linear units improve restricted Boltzmann machines. In: Proceedings of the 27th International Conference on Machine Learning (ICML-2010), pp. 807–814 (2010)
14. Hawkins, D.M.: The problem of overfitting. J. Chem. Inf. Comput. Sci. **44**(1), 1–12 (2004)
15. Caruana, R., Lawrence, S., Giles, C.L.: Overfitting in neural nets: backpropagation, conjugate gradient, and early stopping. In: Advances in Neural Information Processing Systems, pp. 402–408 (2001)
16. Krogh, A., Hertz, J.A.: A simple weight decay can improve generalization. In: Advances in Neural Information Processing Systems, pp. 950–957 (1992)
17. Hinton, G.E., Srivastava, N., Krizhevsky, A., et al.: Improving neural networks by preventing co-adaptation of feature detectors. arXiv preprint arXiv:1207.0580 (2012)
18. Hinton, G.E., Van Camp, D.: Keeping the neural networks simple by minimizing the description length of the weights. In: Proceedings of the Sixth Annual Conference on Computational Learning Theory, pp. 5–13. ACM (1993)
19. Ye, C., Zhao, C., Yang, Y., et al.: LightNet: a versatile, standalone Matlab-based environment for deep learning. arXiv preprint arXiv:1605.02766 (2016)
20. Srivastava, N., Hinton, G., Krizhevsky, A., et al.: Dropout: a simple way to prevent neural networks from overfitting. J. Mach. Learn. Res. **15**(1), 1929–1958 (2014)

Cross-Media Semantic Matching
via Sparse Neural Network Pre-trained
by Deep Restricted Boltzmann Machines

Bin Zhang, Huaxiang Zhang(✉) ⓘ, Jiande Sun, Zhenhua Wang, Hongchen Wu,
and Xiao Dong

Department of Computer Science, Shandong Normal University, Jinan 250300, China
huaxzhang@163.com

Abstract. Cross-media retrieval arouses considerable attentions and becomes a more and more worthwhile research direction in the domain of information retrieval. Different from many related works which perform retrieval by mapping heterogeneous data into a common representation subspace using a couple of projection matrices, we input multi-modal media data into a model of neural network which utilize a deep sparse neural network pre-trained by restricted Boltzmann machines and output their semantic understanding for semantic matching (RSNN-SM). Consequently, the heterogeneous modality data are represented by their top-level semantic outputs, and cross-media retrieval is performed by measuring their semantic similarities. Experimental results on several real-world datasets show that, RSNN-SM obtains the best performance and outperforms the state-of-the-art approaches.

Keywords: Cross-media retrieval · Semantic matching
Sparse coding · Neural network · Deep restricted Boltzmann machines

1 Introduction

Traditional single-media retrieval is text-based or content-based [1–3]. However, in such an era of big data, multimodal data increase rapidly. Cross-media retrieval arouses considerable attentions and becomes a more and more worthwhile research direction in the domain of information retrieval, and a significant number of works named subspace learning focus on mapping the low-level features of multi-modal media data into an isomorphic subspace using a couple of projection matrices, so that it can learn common representations of multi-modal data and perform similarity comparison.

However, the methods mentioned above have a few drawbacks. On the one hand, the projection matrices used by the methods is just a single-layer projection. As we all know, fully-connected neural network could be seen as a multi-layer projection, and it has a better performance. On the other hand, we apply the sparsity regularization to fully-connected neural networks which can reduce

© Springer Nature Singapore Pte Ltd. 2018
B. Huet et al. (Eds.): ICIMCS 2017, CCIS 819, pp. 280–289, 2018.
https://doi.org/10.1007/978-981-10-8530-7_27

noise in data and enforce models to learn useful information. Lastly, the first step of the methods is using random or all-zero data to initialize a couple of projection matrices. Differently, we employ restricted Boltzmann machines (RBM) to initialize the weights of the fully-connected network to regularize the model. What's more, the semantic information is high-level abstraction which come form human understanding and doesn't need clear interpretation of features, e.g. line, edge or word, sentence, and it's very useful for retrieval approaches to learn discriminative information. Consequently, we attempt to use absolutely semantic information for cross-media in this paper. Our method is simple but effective.

In this paper, we mainly focus on cross-media retrieval between texts and images and use three models of neural networks to map them into a semantic subspace. We input images and texts into three models of neural networks (i.e. fully-connected neural network named NN [4,5], sparse neural network named SNN [6], and sparse neural network pre-trained by deep restricted Boltzmann machines named RSNN [7,8]) and output their semantic understanding. So all heterogeneous samples are represented by the top-level semantic outputs of neural networks.

2   Related Work

A classical method named Canonical Correlation Analysis (CCA) learns a pair of projection matrices to project the low-level features of multi-modal media data into a common subspace by maximizing the correlations among them [9]. Its unsupervised, others like BLM [10] and PLS [11]. Then, some methods of cross-media retrieval are successfully proposed based on CCA. CCA-3V introduces a third view (i.e. semantic view) to the isomorphic subspace of CCA [12]. And GMA is proposed to extract feature of multi-modal data [13]. Whats more, MFA and LDA are introduced to cross-media retrieval, and GMMFA (GMA + MFA) and GMLDA (GMA + LDA) are performed well in cross-media retrieval [13].

3   Cross-Media Retrieval Based on Semantic Matching

The process of cross-media retrieval is shown as follows: the first step is extracting features of input data; then, based on the low-level feature representations of texts and images, we use three models of neural networks to map texts and images into a semantic subspace, and perform retrieval based on their semantic similarities; and lastly, based on the ranking of the retrieved results, the model returns similarly matching images responding to a text query or similarly matching texts responding to an image query.

3.1   Semantic Matching

We use three models of neural networks to map texts and images into a semantic subspace, and in our models, inputs of the neural network are the low-level features of texts and images, and the top-level outputs are considered as their semantic space. In the semantic space, there is a semantic vocabulary $L = (l_1, \ldots, l_k)$ of class collection, e.g. "Building" or "animal". We use T to represent texts and I for images, and their low-level features are represented as $V_T^{q \times n}$ and $V_I^{p \times n}$ respectively, where q and p are the dimensions of textual features and visual features respectively, and n is number of samples (Texts and images are pairwise). Semantic matching maps texts and images into a common semantic space:

$$M_T : V_T^{q \times n} \to S^{k \times n} \tag{1}$$

$$M_I : V_I^{p \times n} \to S^{k \times n} \tag{2}$$

where k is the number of categories.

We use the model to map texts and images into a semantic subspace S^k since they share a common vocabulary L. We use the labeled samples as training data, and the unlabeled ones as testing data. After the neural network for texts and images has been trained respectively, the corresponding top-level outputs of the testing samples can be obtained by the neural networks. And cross-media retrieval is performed as follows: given a query text T, we obtain its representative $\pi_T^k \in S^k$, and find the most closely matching image $\pi_I^k \in S^k$ by minimizing the distance between them:

$$D(T, I) = distance\left(\pi_T^k, \pi_I^k\right) \tag{3}$$

So does using an image to retrieve texts.

The algorithm of semantic matching based on neural networks is shown as follows:

Algorithm 1. Semantic matching based on neural networks

Input: Low-level features of texts or images and their labels.
Output: The retrieval results.
1: Construct the neural networks N_1 for texts and N_2 for images respectively.
2: Train N_1 and N_2 by labeled texts and images respectively.
3: Obtain the semantic representatives of the testing texts and images using N_1 and N_2 respectively.
4: Given a query text or image, find the most closely matching images or texts by minimizing the distance $D(T, I)$ between their representatives.

3.2 The Models of Neural Networks

We use three models of neural networks for semantic matching: fully-connected neural network; sparse neural network; sparse neural network pre-trained by deep restricted Boltzmann machines.

3.2.1   Fully-Connected Neural Network

Fully-connected neural network is a basic and classic model of neural networks, it uses Back Propagation (BP) algorithm to adjust the weights of neural network, even as for deep learning. In this paper, we use traditional fully-connected neural networks for semantic matching and name it Neural Network-Semantic Matching (NN-SM). The networks adjust the weights iteratively by minimizing the deviation between actual outputs and target outputs [4,5]:

$$E_d\left(w\right) = \frac{1}{2}\sum_j \left(t_j - o_j\right)^2 \tag{4}$$

where t_j and o_j are target output and actual output of unit j.

3.2.2   Sparse Neural Network

Researchers find that visual cortex of human exists sparse coding, that is to say, rare neurons in human brain are activated when he or she see a text or an image. Since the ideas of sparse coding and neural network are both motivated by visual cortical mechanism of human, we apply sparsity regularization to fully-connected neural networks and apply the novel model to semantic matching, named Sparse Neural Network-Semantic Matching (SNN-SM). The sparse restriction can reduce noise in data and enforce models to learn useful information, so it could improves the recognition performance [6].

Similar to human's brain neurons, we think the output units of network are active if the values of them are close to 1, or inactive if they are close to 0, and we want to enforce the neural network to be sparse by making the activation value of the units to be near zero. Consequently, we apply a penalty term named KL (Kullback-Leibler) divergence to the objective function of neural network, so that it can enforce the activation value of units to be near zero.

Now, we apply the penalty term to the objective function of fully-connected neural network, Eq. (4), and rewrite it as:

$$E_d\left(w\right) = \frac{1}{2}\sum_j \left(t_j - o_j\right)^2 + \beta\sum_j KL\left(p\|\hat{p}_j\right) \tag{5}$$

where β is a small parameter that controls the penalty term, p is a small value near zero, and $\hat{p}_j$ represents the average activation value of unit j.

To compute the gradient descent of the loss function $E_d\left(w\right)$ with the KL divergence penalty term, there is a trick which just needs a small change. For each hidden unit, we just need to change its error term as follows:

$$\delta_j = o_j(1 - o_j)\left(\sum_{k \in outputs} \delta_k w_{kj} + \beta\left(-\frac{p}{\hat{p}_j} + \frac{1-p}{1-\hat{p}_j}\right)\right) \tag{6}$$

We describe the algorithm of sparse neural network in Algorithm 2:

Algorithm 2. Sparse Neural Network

Input: Training samples, number of hidden units m, learning rate ε, number of iterations r, sparse target p and its control parameter β.

Output: Top-level outputs of neural networks.

1: Initialize the weight matrix w randomly.
2: **for** 1 to r **do**
3:     //Feed forward propagation:
4:     **for all** hidden unit h, compute its outputs o_h and average activation value $\hat{p}_h$, **do**
5:         $o_h = \sigma(\sum_i w_{hi} x_{hi})$
6:         $\hat{p}_h = \frac{1}{m} \sum_{i=1}^{m} o_h(x_i)$
7:     **end for**
8:     **for all** output unit k, compute its outputs o_k, **do**
9:         $o_k = \sigma(\sum_h w_{kh} o_{kh})$
10:    **end for**
11:    //Back propagation:
12:    **for all** output unit k, compute its error term δ_k, **do**
13:        $\delta_k \leftarrow o_k(1 - o_k)(t_k - o_k)$
14:    **end for**
15:    **for all** hidden unit j, compute its error term δ_j, **do**
16:        $\delta_h \leftarrow o_h(1 - o_h)\left(\sum_{k \in outputs} w_{kh}\delta_k + \beta\left(-\frac{p}{\hat{p}_h} + \frac{1-p}{1-\hat{p}_h}\right)\right)$
17:    **end for**
18:    Update every weight w_{ji}:
19:    $w_{ji} \leftarrow w_{ji} + \Delta w_{ji}$ where $\Delta w_{ji} = \varepsilon \delta_j x_{ji}$ (j represents h or k)
20: **end for**

3.2.3   Sparse Neural Network Pre-trained by Deep Restricted Boltzmann Machines

Since the weights of fully-connected neural network are randomly initialized, we employ restricted Boltzmann machines (RBM) [7,8] to initialize the weights of the fully-connected network. Now the weights are learned form input data and could be initialized to some sensible values, and this pretraining can regularize the model of the network, so it could approach global optimum and get a better performance. We use this model for semantic matching and name it sparse neural network pre-trained by deep restricted Boltzmann machines-semantic matching (RSNN-SM).

RBM is a model of stochastic neural network which can also be seen as an undirected graph. Where v and h are states of visible layer and hidden layer, and w is weights between the two layers.

We use v_i to represent the state of visible unit i, and h_j for hidden unit j. So given a state (v, h), the energy function of RBM model is defined as follows [7,8]:

$$E\left(v, h | \theta\right) = -\sum_{i=1}^{n} a_i v_i - \sum_{j=1}^{m} b_j h_j - \sum_{i=1}^{n} \sum_{j=1}^{m} v_i w_{ji} h_j \qquad (7)$$

where n and m are numbers of visible units and hidden units, w_{ji} is the weight between visible unit i and hidden unit j, a_i and b_j are the biases of unit i and unit j, and $\theta = \{w_{ji}, a_i, b_j\}$ is the real parameters of RBM. Based on the energy function, we can get joint probability distribution of (v, h):

$$P(v, h | \theta) = \frac{e^{-E(v,h|\theta)}}{Z(\theta)}, \quad Z\left(\theta\right) = \sum_{v,h} e^{-E(v,h|\theta)} \qquad (8)$$

where $Z(\theta)$ is normalization factor.

Then, RBM is trained using Contrastive Divergence (CD) algorithm [7,8] which constructs the network one layer at a time and then uses the output layer of the obtained RBM as the input layer of another RBM. All RBMs are stacked as a multi-layer RBM which is named deep RBM. We learn the weights of deep RBM using the training data, and transfer the weights of deep RBM to sparse neural network.

4   Experiments

In this section, we do experiments on three real-world datasets, i.e. Wiki dataset, NUS-WIDE dataset and Wiki dataset with CNN features based on NN-SM, SNN-SM and RSNN-SM. The experimental results show that, among the three models, RSNN-SM obtains the best performance and outperforms the state-of-the-art approaches.

4.1   Evaluation: Mean Average Precision (MAP) and Precision-Recall (PR)

We mainly focus on cross-media retrieval between texts and images, and employ the widely used mean average precision (MAP) and precision-recall (PR) to evaluate the performance of retrieval algorithms [9,14,15].

In order to evaluate which distance metric is suitable for the proposed algorithms to measure the correlations of texts and images, we use five distance functions [9] for RSNN-SM on Wiki dataset: centered correlation (CC), normalized correlation (NC), Kullback-Leibler divergence (KL), L1 distance and L2 distance. The results shown in Table 1 demonstrate that CC obtains the best MAP scores, so we use CC as distance function for our retrieval methods in all experiments.

4.2   Experimental Results

We compare our methods with some other cross-media retrieval methods on NUS-WIDE dataset, Wiki dataset and Wiki dataset with CNN features, which

Table 1. MAP scores using different distance metric based on RSNN-SM on Wiki dataset

Methods	Distance function	Image query	Text query	Average
RSNN-SM	L1	0.2328	0.2301	0.2315
	L2	0.2177	0.2340	0.2259
	KL	0.2397	0.2324	0.2361
	NC	0.3027	0.2401	0.2714
	CC	**0.3374**	**0.2409**	**0.2892**

contain BLM, PLS, JFSSL, LCFS, SliM2, CDFE, GMLDA, GMMFA, CCA-3V, LSCMR, Bi-LSCMR, M3R, etc. [14]. The MAP scores shown in Table 2 demonstrate that, RSNN-SM obtains the best results and improves the retrieval performance significantly on both Wiki dataset and NUS-WIDE dataset, especially on NUS-WIDE dataset.

Table 2. MAP scores on Wiki dataset and NUS-WIDE dataset

Methods	Wiki dataset			NUS-WIDE dataset		
	I2T	T2I	Avg	I2T	T2I	Avg
PLS	0.2375	0.1723	0.2049	0.2752	0.2661	0.2706
BLM	0.2562	0.2023	0.2293	0.2976	0.2809	0.2892
CCA	0.2405	0.1835	0.2120	0.2872	0.2840	0.2856
LSCMR	0.2021	0.2229	0.2125	0.1424	0.2491	0.1958
Bi-LSCMR	0.2123	0.2528	0.2326	0.1453	0.2380	0.1917
CDFE	0.2655	0.2059	0.2357	0.2595	0.2869	0.2732
GMMFA	0.2750	0.2139	0.2445	0.2983	0.2939	0.2961
GMLDA	0.2751	0.2098	0.2425	0.3243	0.3076	0.3159
CCA-3V	0.2752	0.2242	0.2497	0.3513	0.3260	0.3386
SliM2	0.2548	0.2021	0.2285	0.3154	0.2924	0.3039
M3R	0.2298	**0.2677**	0.2488	0.2445	0.3044	0.2742
LCFS	0.2798	0.2141	0.2470	0.3830	0.3460	0.3645
JFSSL	0.3036	0.2275	0.2669	0.4035	0.3747	0.3891
NN-SM	0.2934	0.2224	0.2579	0.3907	0.3695	0.3801
SNN-SM	0.3198	0.2310	0.2754	0.4235	0.3884	0.4060
RSNN-SM	**0.3374**	0.2409	**0.2892**	**0.4529**	**0.4079**	**0.4304**

We select CCA, JFSSL and compare them with the proposed algorithms, and then show the results in Fig. 1. The results in Fig. 1a include the MAP scores per class for text query, image query and average performance respectively obtained by RSNN-SM, SNN-SM, NN-SM, JFSSL and CCA on Wiki dataset, and the results in Fig. 1b include the PR curves for text query and image query obtained by our methods, JFSSL and CCA on Wiki dataset. The results demonstrate that our methods obtain better performance than others for most categories and most levels of recall. What's more, RSNN-SM obtains the best results.

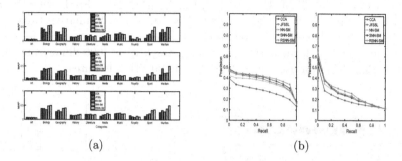

(a)   (b)

Fig. 1. (a) MAP scores for image query (top), text query (middle) and average performance (bottom); (b) precision-recall curves for image query (left), text query (right)

Wiki dataset is designed for cross-media retrieval and suitable for evaluating its performance, however, its number of samples is small. To the best of our knowledge, neural network is suitable for large data processing. Because large number of samples can accelerate the convergence of a neural network and improve its performance. For this reason, we also evaluate the performance of our methods on NUS-WIDE dataset, which is much larger than Wiki dataset. Furthermore, similar to the experiments on Wiki dataset, Fig. 2a and b also show that our methods obtain better performance than others for most categories and most levels of recall. What's more, RSNN-SM obtains the best results and improves the performance significantly.

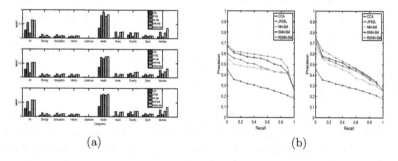

(a)   (b)

Fig. 2. (a) MAP scores for image query (top), text query (middle) and average performance (bottom); (b) precision-recall curves for image query (left), text query (right)

Recently, deep learning is becoming more and more popular since its good performance. And it is worth mentioning that CNN visual features perform better than others since it extract features from images automatically and without any human experience. So based on CNN visual features, some cross-media retrieval approaches obtain a better performance than some other features [15]. Consequently, we also compare some methods of cross-media retrieval which include CCA, PLS, BLM, CCA-3V, GMLDA, GMMFA, JFSSL with the proposed algorithms on Wiki dataset with CNN features. Similarly, Table 3 and Fig. 3 also show that our methods obtain better performance. And as we can see, all methods perform better on Wiki dataset with 4096-dimensional CNN features than Wiki dataset with 128-dimensional SIFT features.

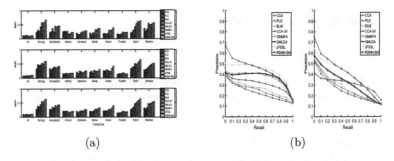

(a)   (b)

Fig. 3. (a) MAP scores for image query (top), text query (middle) and average performance (bottom); (b) precision-recall curves for image query (left), text query (right)

Table 3. MAP scores on Wiki dataset with CNN features. From method 1 to method 8 are CCA, PLS, BLM, CCA-3V, GMLDA, GMMFA, JFSSL and RSNN-SM respectively.

Methods	CCA	PLS	BLM	CCA-3V	GMLDA	GMMFA	JFSSL	RSNN-SM
I2T	0.226	0.250	0.263	0.310	0.372	0.371	0.402	**0.422**
T2I	0.246	0.252	0.266	0.316	0.322	0.322	0.375	**0.386**
Avg	0.236	0.251	0.265	0.313	0.347	0.346	0.389	**0.404**

5   Conclusion

In this paper, we use three models of neural networks in which input is multimodal media data and output is their semantic understanding, and map heterogeneous data into a high-level semantic subspace. Since sparse restrictions can reduce data noise and enforce the model to learn useful information, we apply the idea of sparse coding to traditional fully-connected neural network, and propose a method named SNN-SM. Then, we utilize deep RBM to initialize the weights of the SNN as pre-training, since the weights are initialized to some sensible values, they may come closer to global optimum, and this pretraining can regularize the model of the network. Consequently, the algorithm could get a better performance. Experimental results demonstrate the effectiveness of the proposed approach.

References

1. Zhao, M., Zhang, H., Meng, L.: An angle structure descriptor for image retrieval. China Commun. **13**(8), 222–230 (2016)
2. Zhao, M., Zhang, H., Sun, J.: A novel image retrieval method based on multi-trend structure descriptor. J. Vis. Commun. Image Represent. **38**(c), 73–81 (2016)
3. Hong, R., Wang, M., Li, G., Nie, L., Zha, Z.J., Chua, T.S.: Multimedia question answering. IEEE Multimed. **19**(4), 72–78 (2012)
4. Mitchell, T.M., Carbonell, J.G., Michalski, R.S.: Machine Learning. China Machine Press, Beijing (2003)
5. Zhang, H., Ji, H., Wang, X.: Transfer learning from unlabeled data via neural networks, pp. 173–187 (2012)
6. Lee, H., Ekanadham, C., Ng, A.Y.: Sparse deep belief net model for visual area V2. In: International Conference on Neural Information Processing Systems, pp. 873–880 (2007)
7. Hinton, G.E., Osindero, S., Teh, Y.W.: A fast learning algorithm for deep belief nets. Neural Comput. **18**(7), 1527–1554 (2014)
8. Sun, J., Liu, X., Wan, W., Li, J., Zhao, D., Zhang, H.: Video hashing based on appearance and attention features fusion via DBN. Neurocomputing **213**, 84–94 (2016)
9. Rasiwasia, N., Pereira, J.C., Coviello, E., Doyle, G., Lanckriet, G.R.G., Levy, R., Vasconcelos, N.: A new approach to cross-modal multimedia retrieval. In: International Conference on Multimedia, pp. 251–260 (2010)
10. Tenenbaum, J.B., Freeman, W.T.: Separating style and content with bilinear models. Neural Comput. **12**(6), 1247–1283 (2014)
11. Rosipal, R., Krämer, N.: Overview and recent advances in partial least squares. In: Saunders, C., Grobelnik, M., Gunn, S., Shawe-Taylor, J. (eds.) SLSFS 2005. LNCS, vol. 3940, pp. 34–51. Springer, Heidelberg (2006). https://doi.org/10.1007/11752790_2
12. Gong, Y., Ke, Q., Isard, M., Lazebnik, S.: A multi-view embedding space for modeling internet images, tags, and their semantics. Int. J. Comput. Vis. **106**(2), 210–233 (2014)
13. Sharma, A., Kumar, A., Daume, H., Jacobs, D.W.: Generalized multiview analysis: a discriminative latent space. In: Computer Vision and Pattern Recognition, pp. 2160–2167 (2012)
14. Wang, K., Yin, Q., Wang, W., Wu, S., Wang, L.: A comprehensive survey on cross-modal retrieval (2016)
15. Wei, Y., Zhao, Y., Zhu, Z., Wei, S., Xiao, Y., Feng, J., Yan, S.: Modality-dependent cross-media retrieval. ACM Trans. Intell. Syst. Technol. **7**(4), 57 (2016)

Deep Auto-Encoder Based on Supervised Learning for Damaged Face Reconstruction

Ting Rui[1,2], Sai Zhang[1(✉)], Junhua Zou[1], You Zhou[3], and Jian Tang[1]

[1] College of Filed Engineering, PLA Army Engineering University,
Nanjing, China
466908114@qq.com
[2] State Key Laboratory for Novel Software Technology, Nanjing University,
Nanjing, China
[3] Jiangsu Institute of Commerce, Nanjing, China

Abstract. Based on the reconstruction idea of auto-encoder (AE) and image reconstruction, we present a new idea that the classical auto-encoder can be polished up by supervised learning. We also present a novel supervised deep learning framework for damaged face reconstruction after analyzing the deep model structure. The proposed model is unlike the classical auto-encoder which is unsupervised learning. In this paper, the deep supervised auto-encoder model is illustrated, which has a set of "progressive" and "interrelated" learning strategies by multiple groups of supervised single-layer AE. In this structure, we define a Deep Supervised Network with the supervised auto-encoder which is trained to extract characteristic features from damaged images and reconstruct the corresponding similar facial images, and it improves the ability to express the feature code. Extensive experiment on AR database demonstrates that the proposed method can significantly improve the smoothness of the damaged face reconstruction under enormous illumination, expression change. Experiments show that the proposed method has good contribution and adaptability to the damaged face reconstruction.

Keywords: Auto-encoder · Supervised learning · Deep structure
Image reconstruction

1 Introduction

The damaged data (one, two or more dimensions) are also affected in the retrieval [1]. Many damaged photos (two dimensions) are available online, and current photo restoration solutions either provide unsatisfactory results, or require an advanced understanding of image editing software. We narrowed our scope to what we consider the most interesting subproblem of photo restoration: facial image completion. The image completion problem we attempted to solve was as follows, given an image of a face with some rectangular sections of the image set to be white, fill in the missing pixels. Nowadays, deep learning [2] has been a hot spot and an effective way in image processing [3–5]. Deng [6, 7] presented methods both leverage a large image database to find similar faces to use to complete the missing patch, but results are only shown for

© Springer Nature Singapore Pte Ltd. 2018
B. Huet et al. (Eds.): ICIMCS 2017, CCIS 819, pp. 290–299, 2018.
https://doi.org/10.1007/978-981-10-8530-7_28

low resolution grey scale images. Pathak et al. [8–10] restored images by image semantic information. Yang [11] inferred missing information by content and texture information based on convolutional neural networks. Huanga [12] built a depth framework based on a special Denoising Auto-Encoder (DAE) for face recognition. Yeh [13–15] proposed a novel method for image inpainting based on a Deep Convolutional Generative Adversarial Network (DCGAN).

Auto-encoder is one of the classical models in deep learning, and it completes the training through unsupervised learning (maybe self-supervise learning is more accurate). Auto-encoder not only can finish structure extraction and expression of low dimensional data, but also can reconstruct data information through concise expression in deep network. However, the expression of the data is only limited to compression of the inherent information. If the training data is damaged, it can lead to the feature extraction incomplete, and produce inevitable impact on the follow-up reconstruction.

In summary, we propose a new deep supervised auto-encoder model which is based on the classical unsupervised auto-encoder. Applying the supervised learning strategy, we use the priori information efficiently to get more abundant feature representation from the damaged images and more abstract features from the deep structure simultaneously. Our experiment indicates that the proposed method has an extraordinary performance when used to reconstruct the damaged facial image.

2 Supervised Auto-Encoder

2.1 Unsupervised Auto-Encoder

Auto-encoder (AE) is one of the classical models in deep learning. In 1986, Rumelhart [16] proposed the concept of auto-encoder and applied it to high-dimensional and complex data processing. AE is a deep network that can be stacked over multiple single-layers AE, and the goal of the single-layer AE is to minimize the average reconstruction error between the input data X and the reconstructed data Z, the cost function is:

$$J(W, b) = \frac{1}{m} \sum_{i=1}^{m} (\frac{1}{2} \|Z_i - X_i\|^2) \tag{1}$$

Where m is the number of training samples, Z_i represents the i_{th} reconstruction sample, X_i represents the i_{th} input sample.

It uses back propagation algorithm to train the shallow network, learn an approximate identity function, and use the forward propagating to turn the original input X into low dimensional expression X_e of the hidden layer by encoding which makes the low dimensional data encoding can approximately reconstruct the original form of input data.

The output goal of AE is to train the data self-recovery by setting the output target as the input. It can learn the representative feature from labeled data, approximate the original input data.

2.2 Supervised Single-Layer Auto-Encoder

AE is closely related to the form of training samples and the feature representation. If the training sample of unsupervised AE is damaged, the feature representation must be incomplete.

In order to make up for the limitation on feature representation and take full advantage of supervised learning, we propose a new supervised learning method for the classical unsupervised AE. The new model transforms the objective function of the classical unsupervised AE into the minimum mean reconstruction error between the supervised label X_{label} and the reconstructed sample Z. The cost function becomes:

$$J(W,b) = \frac{1}{m}\sum_{i=1}^{m}(\frac{1}{2}\|Z^i - X^i_{label}\|^2) \tag{2}$$

where m is the number of training samples, X^i_{label} represents the i_{th} supervised sample (X^i_{label} is not equivalent to the input sample X_i. X^i_{label} is lossless sample, but X_i is damaged sample). The model structure is shown in Fig. 1.

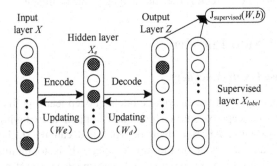

Fig. 1. Framework of supervised single-layer AE.

For the learning of feature representation, we start reversing to calculate the residuals of each node from the output layer by back propagation algorithm, and then calculate the weight of the update. Finally, we use the gradient descending method to update the feature weights under the framework of the supervised learning, calculated as follows:

$$W = W - \alpha * \nabla_{W(l)} J_{supervised}(W,b) \tag{3}$$

Feature representation of unsupervised AE is limited, and the feature extracted by training is only the inherent characteristic of input samples. In this paper, the classical AE model is supervised, which improves the uniqueness and limitation of the characteristic expression ability of the classical AE model.

This new method allows the unsupervised AE model trained by the new idea to be able to learn more diverse features than its inherent characteristics. This method makes up for the lack of feature representation in the classical AE model, making the feature more robust.

3 Supervised Deep Auto-Encoder Designing and Training

In this paper, the proposed model and the classical deep AE are significant differences in the model structure and training methods. The deep structure of the classical AE is achieved through an unsupervised greedy algorithm, which is implemented in a stacked form. Each layer of the training process will produce a feature representation, the deeper the number of layers stacked, the more abstract features obtained. For the supervised deep AE model, multi-layer stacking is also to obtain more abstract, more diversified feature representation (the weight W). Since the supervised label which is used to supervise each layer of the deep AE model is not the input of this layer, the classical AE stacking method and the training strategy cannot be used. In this paper, we propose a new deep network structure and training method.

In this paper, the training of the new model is divided into three groups, as shown in Fig. 2. Each group of training is based on a supervised learning single-layer AE model, and each training model is independent, but the entire training process is interrelated. The first group of training is the training of the input layer (the training of the first layer) in the new model, as shown in Fig. 2(a). In the training process, we describe the result of the hidden layer as the feature code, and the connection weight (W_e) from the input layer to the hidden layer is called the encoded feature representation. The connection weight from the hidden layer to the output layer (W_d) is called the decoded feature representation; The second group of training is called the training of the output layer (the training of the third layer). Firstly, the first group of reconstructed data is extracted as the input of the second model, and the supervised learning is carried out again with the lossless samples. In this paper, the learning process which is from the training of the first group to the second group is called "progressive learning". The purpose of learning is in order to further reduce the errors between the reconstructed data and lossless data. At the same time, we can obtain the decoded feature representation in the output layer on the basis of the first group of reconstructed data, as shown in Fig. 2(b); The training of the last group is called the training of the middle layer in the new model (the training of the second layer), as shown in Fig. 2(c). By extracting the feature codes of the first group as input, the feature code of the second group is extracted as a supervisor. The purpose of this part is to establish the relevance between the encoded feature representation in the input layer and the decoded feature representation in the output layer through the learning of the layer. The learning process of this part is called "correlation coding". The supervised learning of the two groups of the feature code further improves the ability of deep feature representation and the coding of the features. In the training of each group of supervised single-layer AE models, the sigmoid function $f(\cdot)$ is used as an activation function to map the feature representation, and the learning process is as follows:

$$f_e^i(x) = f(W_e^i * x + b_e^i)$$
$$f_d^i(f_e^i) = f(W_d^i * f_e^i + b_d^i)$$

(4)

where f_e^i is the coding result of the i_{th} supervised AE model, and f_d^i is the decoding result of the i_{th} supervised AE model;

This paper completes the training of the new model through "progressive learning" and "relevance coding". The new model can achieve the abstract characteristic code from the deep structure, and overcomes the limitation of the classical AE about the learning of the feature representation.

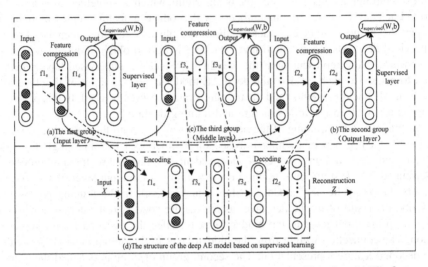

Fig. 2. Training framework of deep AE model based on supervised learning. (a) The first group of supervised training processes; (b) the second group of progressive learning; (c) the third group of relevance codes; (d) the structure of the deep AE model based on supervised learning.

4   Image Reconstruction with Deep Supervised Auto-Encoder Model

The training of the model is completed by the training method of the model in Sect. 3. The feature representation in the model is extracted according to the method in Sect. 3, the characteristic weight W. According to the pre-coded and re-decoded network structure, a stacking AE model is constructed with two layers coding and two layers decoding. The network structure is shown in Fig. 2(d). Firstly, the deep feature is extracted and encoded from the damaged sample, and then the decoded feature representation is used to reconstruct sample from damaged sample to the near-destructive sample by the feature code. For the trained model, the damaged sample reconstruction is done in a feedforward manner. The preprocessing process is as follows:

$$\begin{aligned}
f_e^1(x) &= f(W_e^1 * x + b_e^1) \\
f_e^3(f_e^1) &= f(W_e^3 * f_e^1 + b_e^3) \\
f_d^3(f_e^3) &= f(W_d^3 * f_e^3 + b_d^3) \\
f_d^2(f_d^3) &= f(W_d^2 * f_d^3 + b_d^2)
\end{aligned} \tag{5}$$

5 Experiment and Analysis

5.1 Experimental Dataset Description

The AR database contains over 4000 face images from 126 people (56 women and 70 men). These images contain frontal faces with different facial expression, illuminations, and occlusions (sun glasses and scarf). Some face images from AR are illustrated in Fig. 3. According to the experimental requirements, we extracted 100 validators from this database (50 males and 50 females) to complete the validation of the proposed method in this article, for each person corresponding to 26 faces, with a total of 2600 faces. The experiment took these samples from the AR database into four parts. In first part including 40 men and 40 women, for each person corresponding to 14 faces, we choose the facial images with neutral expression, frontal pose and different illumination as a lossless training set, with a total of 1120 faces, as shown in Fig. 3(a); The second part is to create a corresponding loss set for the lossless training set by manually corrupt the area of each lossless face to simulate the damaged face samples. The same is a total of 1120 faces, as shown in Fig. 3(b); The third is the test set that is made up of another 20 people who are different from the training set, including 10 males and 10 females, for each person corresponding to 14 damaged faces, as shown in Fig. 3(c); The fourth part is labels that test set corresponding to the lossless samples, as shown in Fig. 3(d).

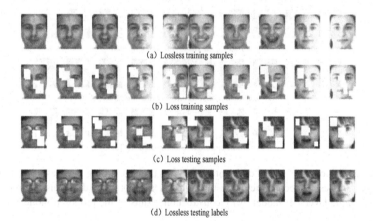

(a) Lossless training samples

(b) Loss training samples

(c) Loss testing samples

(d) Lossless testing labels

Fig. 3. Training set and test set. (a) Lossless training samples; (b) corresponding damaged training samples; (c) damaged testing samples; (d) test the label faces of the samples.

5.2 Experimental Framework and Results Analysis

In this experiment, the reconstructed face samples were used to quantitatively describe the effect of different reconstruction methods by using Pearson correlation [17] and equivalent numbers of looks (ENL). The experimental framework is shown in Fig. 4. Using the above models, the reconstructed results of the damaged faces are shown in Fig. 5.

It can be seen that the reconstructed face of the supervised AE model is superior to that of the unsupervised AE model, as shown in Fig. 5(c) and (d). As shown in Fig. 5(e),

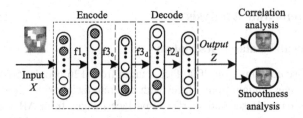

Fig. 4. The experimental framework of the proposed model.

the results show that the deep AE model which is based on supervised learning is still superior to the supervised AE model. From the subjective vision, the face reconstruction through the deep network has the best reconstruction effect on the local detail and the smoothness.

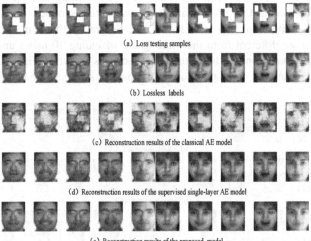

(a) Loss testing samples

(b) Lossless labels

(c) Reconstruction results of the classical AE model

(d) Reconstruction results of the supervised single-layer AE model

(e) Reconstruction results of the proposed model

Fig. 5. Reconstruction results of different models. (a) Damage testing samples; (b) test the label faces of the samples; (c) reconstruction results of classical AE model; (d) reconstruction results of supervised single-layer AE model; (e) reconstruction results of the proposed model.

In order to quantitatively describe the difference of the reconstructed performance of the above model, we use Pearson correlation to analyze the reconstruction results of different models. The Pearson correlation coefficient and is defined as follows:

$$r = \frac{\sum\limits_{i=1}^{n}(X_{label} - \overline{Z})(X_{label}^2 - \overline{Z^2})}{\sqrt{\sum\limits_{i=1}^{n}(X_{label} - \overline{Z})^2}\sqrt{\sum\limits_{i=1}^{n}(X_{label}^2 - \overline{Z^2})^2}} \tag{6}$$

Where n represents the number of samples, X_{label} represents the label face, and Z represents the reconstructed face.

The experimental analysis results shown in Table 1, and the result is the average of 14 test faces for each tester.

Table 1. The results of the correlation analysis.

Model	Unsupervised AE model	Supervised AE model	Supervised deep AE model
1	0.6599	0.9161	0.9173
2	0.7238	0.9523	0.9405
3	0.5876	0.9074	0.9095
......	......	......	......
18	0.7081	0.9455	0.9489
19	0.6740	0.9428	0.9457
20	0.7536	0.9614	0.9635
Average	0.71	0.93	0.93

As shown in Table 1, the supervised single-layer AE model is superior to the classical AE model for the damaged face reconstruction, and the correlation of single sample increased by 0.2 to 0.4. The average correlation of all test samples is improved 0.22. The change of the classical unsupervised AE model to the supervised AE model proved to be effective. Based on the supervised deep AE model, the reconstruction results of damaged images are similar to those of the supervised single-layer AE models in correlation. But from the subjective point of view, the reconstruction effect of the supervised deep AE model is better than the supervised single-layer AE model.

We objectively evaluate the reconstructed image based on the smoothness analysis. ENL is an indicator of the relative intensity of speckle noise in an image. When the ENL value is bigger, it indicates the image is smoothed well. The smoothness is defined as follows:

$$ENL = \frac{\mu^2}{\sigma^2} \tag{7}$$

where μ represents the average of the regions of interest in the reconstructed image, and σ represents the variance of the region of interest in the reconstructed image.

The analysis results shown in Table 2, and the result is the average of 14 test faces for each tester. Figure 6. shows the statistical results of part of the testers, including men and women.

The experiments show that the reconstruction of the supervised learning AE model is smoother than the classical AE model, the smoothness of single sample increased by 0.4 to 1. The average smoothness of all test samples is improved 0.38. For the supervised deep AE model, the smooth effect is further improved on the basis of supervised single-layer AE model, which is improved by 0.43. The experiments show that the proposed model is effective.

Through the above two objective evaluation criteria, the validity of the proposed model is proved in the evaluation of correlation and smoothness analysis.

Table 2. The results of smoothness analysis.

Model	Unsupervised AE model	Supervised AE model	Deep supervised AE model
1	3.7483	4.7312	5.0157
2	6.5009	6.9301	7.4391
3	6.7242	7.5998	7.8264
......	......	......	......
18	3.8266	4.2054	4.6285
19	5.3089	6.2248	6.683
20	6.5796	6.8913	7.1612
Average	8.73	9.21	9.64

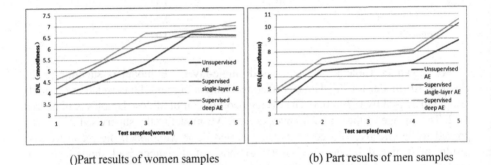

()Part results of women samples   (b) Part results of men samples

Fig. 6. A statistical chart of the average smoothness.

6   Conclusions

In summary, we have performed both an experimental and theoretical study of the classical unsupervised learning auto-encoder and the supervised learning auto-encoder. In view of the above study, we propose a new method of the damaged face reconstruction by using the deep auto-encoder model which is based on supervised learning, and it is unlike the classical auto-encoder or the deep auto-encoder based image reconstruction method, our method considers the priori information from training samples in the deep learning procedure and can make up for the missing feature representation in the damaged image. Specifically, a deep network structure which is based on the supervised learning is presented, which is trained to extract characteristic features from corrupted facial images and reconstruct the corresponding similar facial images. The reconstruction is realized by a deep neural network that learns to feature face images into a low-dimensional vector and to reconstruct the respective corresponding face images from the feature vectors.

Having trained the deep auto-encoder which is based on supervised learning, a new face image can be reconstructed by comparing its reconstruction image with individual lossless image during training. The proposed method has shown its contribution by the experiments.

References

1. Hong, R., Hu, Z., Wang, R., et al.: Multi-view object retrieval via multi-scale topic models. IEEE Trans. Image Process. **25**(12), 5814–5827 (2016)
2. Hinton, G.E., Osindero, S., Teh, Y.W.: A fast learning algorithm for deep belief nets. Neural Comput. **18**(7), 1527 (2006)
3. Bengio, Y.: Learning deep architectures for AI. Found. Trends Mach. Learn. **2**(1), 1–81 (2009). S1935-8237
4. Zhang, C., Zhang, Z.: Improving multiview face detection with multi-task deep convolutional neural networks. In: Applications of Computer Vision, pp. 1036–1041. IEEE (2014)
5. Längkvist, M., Karlsson, L., Loutfi, A.: A review of unsupervised feature learning and deep learning for time-series modeling. Pattern Recogn. Lett. **42**(1), 11–24 (2014)
6. Deng, Y., Li, D., et al.: Partially occluded face completion and recognition. IEEE International Conference on Image Processing, pp. 4145–4148. IEEE (2010)
7. Deng, Y., Dai, Q., et al.: Graph Laplace for occluded face completion and recognition. IEEE Trans. Image Process. **20**(8), 2329–2338 (2011). A Publication of the IEEE Signal Processing Society
8. Pathak, D., Krahenbuhl, P., et al.: Context encoders: feature learning by inpainting. In: IEEE Conference on Computer Vision and Pattern Recognition, pp. 2536–2544. IEEE Computer Society (2016)
9. Hong, R., Zhang, L., Zhang, C., et al.: Flickr circles: aesthetic tendency discovery by multi-view regularized topic modeling. IEEE Trans. Multimed. **18**(8), 1555–1567 (2016)
10. Hong, R., Yang, Y., Wang, M., et al.: Learning visual semantic relationships for efficient visual retrieval. IEEE Trans. Big Data **1**(4), 152–161 (2017)
11. Yang, C., et al.: High-Resolution Image Inpainting Using Multi-scale Neural Patch Synthesis (2016)
12. Huanga, R., Chang, L., et al.: Adaptive deep supervised autoencoder based image reconstruction for face recognition. Math. Probl. Eng. (2016)
13. Yeh, R., Chen, C., Lim, T.Y., et al.: Semantic image inpainting with perceptual and contextual losses (2016)
14. Denton, E., Chintala, S., Szlam, A., et al.: Deep generative image models using a Laplacian pyramid of adversarial networks **2015**, 1486–1494 (2015)
15. Radford, A., Metz, L., Chintala, S.: Unsupervised representation learning with deep convolutional generative adversarial networks. Comput. Sci. (2015)
16. Rumelhart, D.E., Hinton, G.E., Williams, R.J.: Learning representations by back-propagating errors. Nature **323**, 533–536 (1986)
17. Pearson, K.: Mathematical contributions to the theory of evolution (III): regression, heredity, and panmixia. Philos. Trans. R. Soc. London. Ser. A Contain. Pap. Math. Phys. Character **187**, 253–318 (1895)

Design and Implementation of Secure Multimedia Storage System

Guang-yu Gu[1], Qing Yi[2], Hao Zheng[3], Shu-juan Zhang[1],
and Bo-wu Sun[4,5(✉)]

[1] State Grid Anhui Electric Power Research Institute, Hefei, China
[2] Anhui Electrical Engineering Professional Technique College, Hefei, China
[3] State Grid Anhui Electric Power Company, Hefei, China
[4] State Key Laboratory of Information Security,
Institute of Information Engineering, CAS, Beijing, China
sunbowu@iie.ac.cn
[5] School of Cyber Security, The University of Chinese Academy of Sciences,
Beijing, China

Abstract. To keep the users' multimedia data secure and private in the cloud, this paper designs and implements a secure multimedia storage system based on HDFS platform. The system provides different client software for windows and android to encrypt users' data before outsourcing to the cloud. And only the data user owns the encryption key so that it will prevent sensitive information leakage from the cloud server or malicious attackers. This paper designs an experiment to show the validity and effectiveness of the system.

Keywords: Multimedia security · Cloud computing · Transparent encryption

1 Introduction

With the increasing demand for information sharing and multi terminal (e.g. cellphones and computers) access, the cloud storage service has been developing rapidly in recent years. Users usually outsource their multimedia data including videos, photos, and files to the cloud for convenient access. However, most of the multimedia data are sensitive. These data leakage incident would cause personal privacy violation problems or economy loss [1, 2], such as the incident of iCloud photos in 2014. Recently the hackers are blackmailing the Disney Company due to the unreleased movie leakage. Multimedia storage security [3–5] has gradually become the focus of enterprises and individual users.

Cloud computing integrate massive computing and storage capabilities into a unified resource pool using virtualization technology and provide public service. Generally, in order to make the most of limited resources, cloud storage service providers may store data in plain text and lack of isolation between different user data. Once the cloud service providers are under attack, vulnerable protection mechanism would lead to a large number of user data leakage. Meanwhile in the cloud mode, data ownership and management authority are separated. Users lose the ability to manage their data, and then the cloud service providers can completely control these

© Springer Nature Singapore Pte Ltd. 2018
B. Huet et al. (Eds.): ICIMCS 2017, CCIS 819, pp. 300–309, 2018.
https://doi.org/10.1007/978-981-10-8530-7_29

sensitive data. It is a severe challenge to prevent cloud service providers from unauthorized access of users' private data.

This paper presents a method to realize the encrypted multimedia storage system based on transparent encryption and decryption technology, and developed a Hadoop based distributed file system (HDFS) server, Windows platform client and Android platform client. In this system, the user data is managed in the client software, both the transmission process and the cloud storage are encrypted. The user has the authority to manage the data by controlling the key, which would effectively prevent the cloud service provider or attackers from unauthorized access. Even if the terminal (e.g. cellphone or computer) is lost or service provider stops operating, encrypted multimedia data stored in the cloud and terminals will not disclose the privacy information. In addition, the application of transparent encryption and decryption technology ensures that the user does not have to change the original file operating habits, which brings great convenience.

2 Background and Related Work

At present, many enterprises provide cloud storage services include Amazon S3 (Amazon Simple Storage Service), Alibaba cloud and so on. Cloud storage client tools obtain the cloud file meta information and users can directly access their multimedia data through the client. But in the above services, the data are plain text form in the local or in the cloud, there are security risks of multimedia data leakage.

To protect the security and privacy of users' multimedia data, one solution is to encrypt data locally, and then upload the encrypted data to the cloud [6], such as Securedropbox [7] and a domestic file encryption tool named Cryptsync. These two schemes are based on the local encryption and decryption tools. The data in the local will be encrypted to the corresponding cipher text folder, users need to manually upload encrypted data to the cloud. The combination of these tools and cloud storage system can effectively solve the problem of cloud data storage in plain text form and semi-trusted service providers, but due to cloud storage stage and synchronization stage need user interaction, it will change the users' habits.

Part of the cloud storage service providers also make an effort to protect user data security, for example, Apple Corp's iCloud uses cloud data encryption storage mode, this scheme can effectively prevent malicious attackers to steal data in the cloud, but because the encryption key is not mastered in the hands of users, this scheme does not solve the problem that service provider abuses their authority.

3 Transparent Encryption and Decryption Technology

Transparent encryption and decryption technology means that it will not change the user's habit of accessing the data. The client's encryption and decryption function is running automatically in the background. Thus the user can not feel the existence of encryption and decryption process. But once out of the environment, the data is unreadable because it is not correctly decrypted, which could ensure the data security.

Transparent encryption technology mainly includes tree methods: encrypting file system (EFS), filter driver layer transparent encryption and API hook transparent encryption.

EFS is a hybrid encryption mechanism provided by Windows based on asymmetric public key encryption algorithm RSA and symmetric encryption algorithm DES. Firstly, the operating system generates a public key pair based on the user's security identifier. When encrypting files, the system generates a pseudo-random number as the file encryption key (FEK). DES algorithm is used to encrypt the file and FEK is encrypted by the public key. When decrypting files, the system uses the current user's private key to decrypt the FEK, and then use FEK to decrypt cipher text.

Transparent encryption and decryption of filter driver layer works in the kernel layer. The filter driver is a special drive of the kernel, which depends on the host drive, and the filter driver intercepts and modifies the host drive request. The scheme adds a filter driver layer between the file system driver layer and the I/O manager. Filter driver layer intercepts input and output request packet before transmitting message (i/o request package, IRP) and analyzes the properties of the IRP package.

API hook transparent encryption and decryption method works in the application layer. Applications in the Windows platform or Android platform are generally in the user state. Programs working at this level cannot manipulate the address space arbitrarily. Programs must call the system API if they want to perform file operations. The hook method is realized by modifying the API function entry address. The process is as follows: (1) inject the hook procedure to the target process; (2) modify the file read and write function of the entrance address to the encryption and decryption function; (3) use the original function to complete the read and write operation.

In the above three methods, EFS is convenient to develop but it has strict requirements on the operating system version and the file system format, which limits its applicability. As to the transparent encryption in filter driver layer, it is based on dynamic encryption and has high efficiency. But implementing this method needs more efforts due to driving layer development. And adding the filter driver layer may be conflict with other driving, which will lead to compatibility problems. The third API hook method works in the application layer, which has the advantages of good compatibility, stability and low cost of development and maintenance. But this method is based on static encryption, the operating efficiency of large files is relatively low. Considering the security, system compatibility, stability and development difficulties, the system uses API hook transparent encryption and decryption method.

4   System Design and Implementation

4.1   Design Goals and System Architecture

The design goal of the secure multimedia storage system is to provide users with cloud storage services while protecting their data security. The core idea is to store and transmit data in cipher text form, and the user masters the key to control the data management authority. The operating environment of the system applies the following assumptions: (1) cloud storage platform is semi-trusted. That is, cloud storage platform will faithfully execute data access function, but it will be curious about the content of users' multimedia data. (2) The terminal device for the user to access to the cloud storage is heterogeneous and is easy to lose, but the client is credible after the authentication. The specific goals of the system include:

(1) Confidentiality of data. Transparent encryption and decryption technology protects the users' data in the terminal. The transmission process and the storage are encrypted, which provides confidentiality protection for users.
(2) Data availability. Using data synchronization based on the cloud platform, users can access the data stored in the cloud at any time through the internet.
(3) Support heterogeneous terminal. Terminal includes at least Windows system and Android system. Different terminals provide uniform data view on traditional PC and mobile phones.
(4) Support cloud platform expansion. The system can connect to the third-party cloud platform.

Figure 1 is the cloud storage system architecture diagram, the system includes three parts: client, server and data storage platform. The client provides the interactive interface to the user, and carries out the data encryption and data synchronization. The server performs the user management, key management and data synchronization. The data storage platform provides the storage service, including HDFS distributed storage platform and third party cloud platform such as Amazon S3, Tencent cloud and Alibaba cloud.

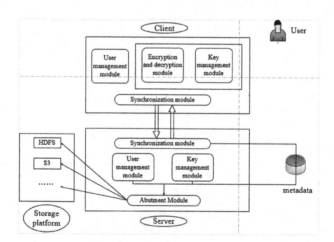

Fig. 1. System architecture of ciphertext cloud storage system.

4.2 Windows Client Transparent Encryption and Decryption

Windows client includes user management module, encryption and decryption module, key management module and synchronization module. Encryption and decryption module and key management module are the core module of the system. They achieve data transparent encryption and decryption.

Encryption and decryption module. API Hook method is used in the encryption and decryption module, which could modify the entrance of the API function. But the Windows system processes are independent of each other. In other words, in a process, we cannot directly modify the function entrance address of another process. However, the Windows system provides a message handling mechanism called hook, which allows an application to install subroutines in other programs and monitor the specified type of messages in the target program. Before the message reaches the target window, the hook program captures the message and get control, then the hook program can modify the message to continue to pass, and it also could directly terminate the message delivery.

Figure 2 shows the basic principles of API Hook transparent encryption and decryption in Windows system. The steps of the implementation are as follows.

Step 1: open the target process and acquire the LoadLibrary function address.

Step 2: apply for memory in the target process and write the Dll path, then, start remote thread which entrance address is LoadLibrary function's address and inject the Dll path into the parameter. The injected Dll code will run during loaded, then find the function library and export table of read and write function.

Step 3: modify the export table, change the entrance address of the system read and write function into encryption and decryption function's entrance address.

Step 4: call the original read and write functions in the encryption and decryption function.

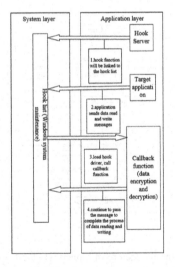

Fig. 2. Windows system API hook transparent encryption and decryption.

Key management module. This module implements the management of the master key and the encryption key, including functions of key generation, authentication, update, backup, reset and etc. The system uses the symmetric encryption algorithm, which is fast and efficient. However, because the algorithm is open, its security level only depends on the encryption key. To ensure the security of the key, the system uses a two-level key scheme. Level one is the master key and level two is the encryption key. The master key is set by the user and is used to encrypt the encryption key. In addition, the encryption key is generated by the system for data encryption and decryption. The two-level key management mechanism effectively guarantees security of the key. Both the privileged user and the malicious attacker cannot obtain the master key in the system.

4.3   Android Client Transparent Encryption and Decryption

Android client encryption and decryption module is also based on API Hook imple-mentation, but the specific implementation is different from Windows.

Android system according to the programming language, can be divided into Java layer, NativeC layer and Linux Kernel layer. In the NativeC layer, the functions pro-vided by Linux can be directly used by Java Native Interface (JNI). So the transparent encryption and decryption module that is based on API Hook can be achieved in the NativeC layer. In Android system, opening and closing operations of files use JNI to achieve the open function and close function, which is corresponding to the dynamic library named "libnativehelper.so". The core of transparent encryption and decryption module is to hook the dynamic library, so that the reading and writing operations of files perform newly opening and closing functions that are injected with the encryption and decryption module. The programs of NativeC layer are in the Linux user state and each process has a separate process space. We must enter its process space to modify codes in the memory in order to make its hook. Moreover, the process "ptrace" of tracking function that Linux provide can achieve this function. The function can bind a target process, query and modify memory space and registers of the process.

In the specific implementations, the structure of target process will be very difficult to achieve if we inject all codes into the target process. Therefore, we put the open and close function which are include the encryption and decryption into a dynamic-link library named mylib.so. Thus we place mylib.so and target process in the same process space and the target process can load and call that functions. Figure 3 shows the specific procedure.

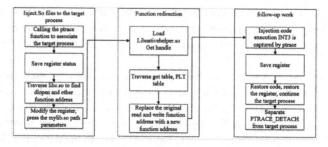

Fig. 3. Android system API hook transparent encryption and decryption.

4.4   Server

The server includes a user management module, a key management module, a synchronization module and a docking module, and each module maintains a data table in a database to storage user's information, key information, file meta information and cloud platform mount information respectively.

User management module. In this module, it will achieve user registration, account activation, user login, password reset and other basic functions. The password in this module is only used for user authentication and independent of the key in the key management module.

Key management module. Key management is mainly implemented in the client, and the server only achieve the key backup and key recovery. When a user first sets the key or performs a key reset, the client sends a request to the server to back up the key. If the user does not log in for the first time but none key information is existed on the client, the client would request to recover the key from the server.

Synchronous module. It uses a centralized synchronization mechanism that is based on WebDAV protocol for data synchronization. Taking file uploads as an example, the file uploads includes file content uploads and writing file meta information to database. When the server receives the client request, firstly it will initialize and start the WebDAV Server, and check WebDAV methods and paths from WebDAV. Then use the PUT method to upload files and return operation results to the client.

Docking module. It mounts the data storage platform and have a unified file management interface to access the data in the storage platform. This module is divided into two parts: the mount sub-module and the general operation sub-module. The latter provides a unified abstract data access interface, and implements the interface function for different cloud platforms.

4.5   Data Storage Platform

The system uses HDFS as the default storage platform. It also could adopt the third-party cloud platform such as Amazon S3 to expand the underlying storage resources.

Hadoop is an open source distributed computing platform. HDFS is the primary distributed storage used by Hadoop applications. A HDFS cluster primarily consists of a NameNode that manages the file system metadata and DataNodes that store the actual data.

The Amazon S3 is Amazon's public network storage services, users pay their costs according to the actual use of storage space and data traffic. It is based on bucket to storage data files, a user can create multiple buckets, and each Bucket's name is globally unique. The Amazon S3 does not have user interface, but it provides a programmable function interface for the developers to perform the data file upload, delete, rename and other basic operations.

5   System Test

5.1   Operating Results

The system designed in this paper provides users with free trial, which can be downloaded from the link http://159.226.94.60/Pcloud/.

The system development environment and operating environment are as follows.

Server: CentOS release 6.4, PHP 5.3.3 + Apache 2.2.15 + MySQL 5.1.73 + JDK 1.7.0_40.

Windows client: development tools QT, development language C++, operating environment Win7/Win8.

Android client: development tools Eclipse, development language Java, operating environment Android2.2 and above.

Using the current common PC system Win7 and Android4.0 version of the phone to run the system to show the effect. The users first log in and complete the master key authentication of the system. Then the users can view their multimedia files in the main interface, different terminals provide a unified view of the data, as is shown in Fig. 4.

Fig. 4. System user interface (windows client and android client).

In this system, the user data in the terminal, the transmission process and the cloud are in the form of ciphertext. When the user is opening the file, the system background transparently decrypts the file and then presents the user with the plain text. Take the windows client as an example, when the user opens the file in the windows client and could edit and modify the file normally; if the user directly opens the local file, the file is not correctly decrypted and would appear garbled.

5.2   Performance Test

The experiment is designed to verify the effect of encryption time on file transfer. The test environment is 100 Mbps Ethernet, the client is Intel (R) Core (TM) i7-2600 CPU @ 3.40 GHz, 4G memory, 900G hard disk and the server is the Intel (R) Core (TM) i7-2600 CPU @ 3.40 GHz, 16G memory, 1T hard drive. The dataset is a set of audio files of different sizes. The experiment records the file encryption time and the total time including the file encryption and transferring. The results are shown in Fig. 5. Experimental results show that the proportion of the encryption time to the total time is small, which basically maintained at 4% to 5%. Thus due to the introduction of the file encryption, the performance loss is acceptable.

Fig. 5. The impact of encryption time on file uploads.

6   Conclusion

In this paper, a ciphertext cloud storage system based on transparent encryption and decryption technology is designed and implemented. The system can protect the users' multimedia data in the computers and mobile phones. The data storage in the cloud are encrypted in order to prevent the users' privacy disclosure. The system has good scalability in encryption and decryption algorithms and cloud storage providers. By default, HDFS-based private cloud storage is used to achieve high reliability and high performance data storage. At the same time, the system could apply to common third-party cloud platforms including Amazon S3, Tencent cloud and Alibaba Cloud to further expand storage capacity. The system has been successfully used in the broadcasting industry to ensure the security of audio files.

References

1. Yu, S., Wang, C., Ren, K., Lou, W.: Achieving secure, scalable, and fine-grained data access control in cloud computing. In: Proceedings of the 29th Conference on Information Communications (INFOCOM 2010). IEEE Press, Piscataway, pp. 534–542 (2010). https://doi.org/10.1109/infcom.2010.5462174
2. Shaikh, F.B., Haider, S.: Security threats in cloud computing. In: Proceedings of 2011 International Conference for Internet Technology and Secured Transactions (ICITST 2011). IEEE Press, Piscataway, pp. 214–219 (2011). https://doi.org/10.1109/ccaa.2015.7148450
3. Huang, C.T., Qin, Z., Kuo, C.C.J.: Multimedia storage security in cloud computing: an overview. In: Proceedings of 2011 IEEE 13th International Workshop on Multimedia Signal Processing (MMSP 2011). IEEE Press, Piscataway, pp. 1–6 (2011). https://doi.org/10.1109/mmsp.2011.6093775

4. Villn, R., Voloshynovskiy, S., Koval, O., Pun, T.: Multilevel 2-D bar codes: toward high-capacity storage modules for multimedia security and management. IEEE Trans. Inf. Forensics Secur. 1(4), 405–420 (2006). https://doi.org/10.1109/TIFS.2006.885022

5. Yang, J., Wang, H., Lv, Z., Wei, W., Song, H., Erol-Kantarci, M., Kantarci, B., He, S.: Multimedia recommendation and transmission system based on cloud platform. Future Gener. Comput. Syst. 70, 94–103 (2017)

6. Huang, K.Y., Luo, G.H., Yuan, S.M.: SSTreasury+: a secure and elastic cloud data encryption system. In: Proceedings of Sixth International Conference on Genetic and Evolutionary Computing (ICGEC 2012). IEEE Press, Piscataway, pp. 518–521 (2012). https://doi.org/10.1109/icgec.2012.132

7. Chen, M.-Y., Liu, C.-W., Hwang, M.-S.: SecureDropbox: a file encryption system suitable for cloud storage services. In: Proceedings of the 2013 ACM Cloud and Autonomic Computing Conference (CAC 2013). ACM, New York (2013). Article 21, 2 p. http://dx.doi.org/10.1145/2494621.2494642

Emotion Recognition from EEG Using RASM and LSTM

Zhenqi Li[1], Xiang Tian[1], Lin Shu[1(✉)], Xiangmin Xu[1], and Bin Hu[2]

[1] School of Electronic and Information Engineering,
South China University of Technology, Guangzhou, Guangdong Province, China
shul@scut.edu.cn
[2] School of Information Science and Engineering,
Lanzhou University, Lanzhou, Gansu Province, China

Abstract. In the field of human-computer interaction, automatic emotion recognition is an important and challenging task. As a physiological signal that directly reflects the brain activity, EEG has advantages in emotion recognition. However, previous studies seldom consider together the temporal, spatial, and frequency characteristics of EEG signals, and the reported emotion recognition accuracy is not adequate for applications. To address this issue, this study proposes a new approach which extracts RASM as the feature to describe the frequency-space domain characteristics of EEG signals and constructs a LSTM network as the classifier to explore the temporal correlations of EEG signals. It is implemented on the DEAP dataset for a trial-level emotion recognition task. In a comparison with a number of relevant studies on DEAP, its mean accuracy of 76.67% ranks the first, which approves the effectiveness of this new approach.

Keywords: EEG · LSTM · Emotion recognition
Human-computer interaction

1 Introduction

Emotions play an important role in communication, as it contains a wealth of information, such as personality, hobbies and interests. Therefore, emotion recognition has been adopted in human-computer interaction (HCI) for the improvement of the interactive experience. With the rapid development of HCI, automatic emotion recognition is becoming more and more important and has attracts more attentions.

Emotion recognition from EEG (electroencephalogram) has been viewed as a promising way as EEG is the general response of the electrophysiological activity of brain nerve cells, and is associated with human psychological and physiological activities. It has a high temporal resolution and is relatively easy to be collected.

© Springer Nature Singapore Pte Ltd. 2018
B. Huet et al. (Eds.): ICIMCS 2017, CCIS 819, pp. 310–318, 2018.
https://doi.org/10.1007/978-981-10-8530-7_30

From a biological point of view, the active regions of the brain are not the same under different emotions [7]. So many of the studies have focused on the features regarding the frequency domain and the space domain, such as the frequency energy, entropy, spectral density and their differences between two symmetric electrodes. Kollia extracted the power spectral density (PSD) of EEG for each frequency band and classified emotions using random forest (RF), based on which an adequate accuracy of $88.4 \pm 3.55\%$ of personalized models experiment was achieved, while the mean accuracy of both valence and arousal was 65% in subject-independent experiment [4]. Zheng investigated stable patterns of EEG over time for emotion recognition, such as power spectral density (PSD), differential entropy (DE), differential asymmetry (DASM), rational asymmetry (RASM), asymmetry (ASM) and differential caudality (DCAU) [10].

Emotions are often described in a two-dimensional continuous space [5,9], therefore we assume that the change of emotional state refers to a continuous process. The current emotional state is affected by the past emotional state, and this effect is reflected in the temporal correlations of EEG signals. In the field of machine learning, Long-short-term-memory recurrent neural networks (LSTM-RNN) is usually used to explore the correlations of the time series. Soleymani compared the recognition performance of four classifiers, LSTM-RNN, continuous conditional random fields (CCRF), support vector regression (SVR) and multi-linear regression (MLR) [8], among which LSTM-RNN was reported as the model with a best performance. Li [6] designed a hybrid deep learning model that combined the Convolutional Neural Network (CNN) and LSTM-RNN, and the performance of their method was close to that of Chen's method [2].

This study presents a method that considers both the frequency and spatial domain features of EEG signals, as well as the temporal correlations. In the second sector, a new method using RASM and LSTM is presented, where the RASM features that reflect frequency and spatial characteristics of EEG signals are extracted. In order to explore the temporal correlation of EEG signals, an LSTM classifier is constructed. In the third sector, the accuracy of the new method is evaluated via experiments using the DEAP dataset, and is validated by a comparison with traditional methods. Finally, a conclusion is made and the limitations and future work are discussed.

2   Method

A new method using RASM and LSTM is proposed in this sector, which represents the frequency and spatial characteristics and explores temporal correlations of EEG signals. It utilizes the comprehensive characteristics of EEG signals in temporal, frequency and spatial domains to achieve automatic emotion recognition with a high accuracy. The whole diagram of this new method is shown in Fig. 1.

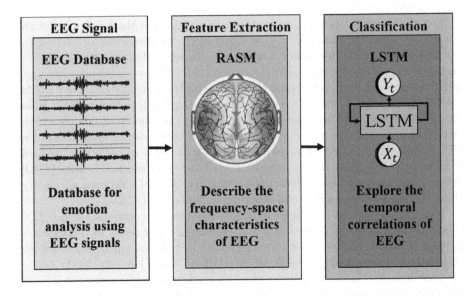

Fig. 1. Diagram of the new method.

2.1 Feature Extraction

The changes in emotion state can cause changes in brain activity. So the RASM (rational asymmetry) features are utilized in the study, which reflects the changes in spectral power in bilateral brain regions.

As seen in Fig. 2, a short-time Fourier transform (STFT) with a half-overlapped 1-s Hanning window was applied to each of the 32 channels of the EEG signals to compute the spectral time series, which were divided into four frequency bands of theta (θ: 4–7 Hz), alpha (α: 8–13 Hz), beta (β: 14–30 Hz) and gamma (γ: 31–50 Hz) band. Next, we adopted the hemispheric asymmetry

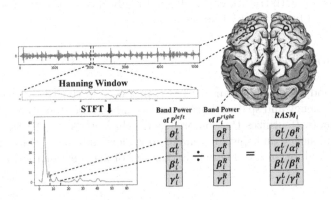

Fig. 2. Diagram of the feature extraction.

index of the spectral power [7]. According to the international 10–20 system, 14 asymmetry indexes can be derived from 14 symmetric electrode pairs, namely Fp1-Fp2, AF3-AF4, F3-F4, F7-F8, FC5-FC6, FC1-FC2, C3-C4, T7-T8, CP5-CP6, CP1-CP2, P3-P4, P7-P8, PO3-PO4, and O1-O2. The asymmetry indexes were then calculated by power division and called rational asymmetry of 14 electrode pairs (RASM14). The brief process of our feature extration is illustrated in Fig. 2, where $i \in [1, 14]$, P_i^{left} and P_i^{right} denote the ith left and right electrode of the ith symmetric electrode pair respectively, $RASM_i$ is the RASM feature of the ith symmetric electrode pair; θ_i^L, α_i^L, β_i^L, γ_i^L are the theta, alpha, beta and gamma band power of P_i^{left}, respectively.

2.2   Classification

In our assumption, emotions change continuously, and this continuity is reflected in the temporal correlations of EEG signals. To explore the correlations, the classification method of Long Short-Term Memory networks (LSTM) is adopted.

LSTM is a special kind of Recurrent Neural Networks (RNN). RNN is the networks with loops in it and the information is passed from the current loop to the next loop. This chain-like nature reveals that RNN is the natural architecture of neural network to use for sequences and lists, for example, the time series. However, standard RNN has the problem of long-term dependencies [1]. It means that RNN may lose the ability to connect information when the gap between loops grows. While LSTM is capable of learning long-term dependencies due to the explicitly design of its repeating module. The structure of a standard RNN and LSTM that have been used in this study is shown in Fig. 3. As LSTM has the advantage in learning long-term dependencies of time series, it is used in the study to explore the temporal correlations of EEG signals.

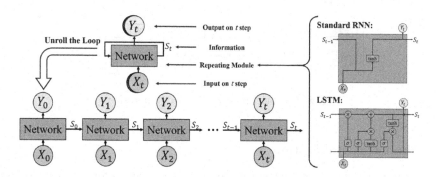

Fig. 3. The structure of standard RNN and LSTM.

3   Experiment and Result

The effectiveness of the new method using RASM and LSTM is evaluated on EDAP and is compared with conventional methods for emotion recognition.

3.1   Experimental Dataset

The dataset used to validate the new method is DEAP [3], a database of various physiological signals for emotion analysis. It includes 32-channel EEG signals and 8-channel peripheral physiological signals collected from 32 subjects. Each subject watched 40 one-minute-long excerpts of music videos and the signals were recorded during those trials. After each trial, subjects rated each video in terms of valence, arousal, dominance, familiarity and like/dislike. The ratings were continuously distributed from 1 to 9 in each dimension. We divided the trials into two classes based on the value of valence and labeled the divisions positive if its valence was higher than 6, and negative if the valence value was lower than 4. 895 trials in total were obtained, with 63-s data for each. And 125 segments for each trial were obtained using a half-overlapped 1-s Hanning window. 28 channels of EEG signals were selected out of 32 channels in the DEAP database to calculate RASM14. Figure 4 shows the whole feature of a trial, which includes 125 RASM14 vectors, where each vector is 56-byte length and consists of 4 frequency band power of total 14 pairs. Finally, we got 895 features as our experimental dataset. The brief process of data preparation is illustrated in Fig. 4, where X_1–X_{125} represent the features of 125 segments; θ_i, α_i, β_i and γ_i represent the RASM of the ith symmetric electrode pair in four frequency bands, respectively.

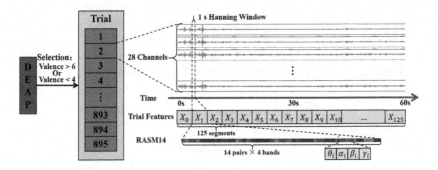

Fig. 4. The brief process of data preparation.

3.2   Experimental Setting

The structure and the detailed settings of hyper parameters for the new method is illustrated in Fig. 5, where the inputs are the trial features that have been extracted, reflecting the EEG characteristics of frequency-space domain. The first layer of our model is a LSTM layer, which is used to find the temporal correlations of EEG signals. The second layer is the full-connect layer, which is used as the classifier. To prevent overfitting, 'dropout' is adopted in the LSTM layer and the full-connect layer.

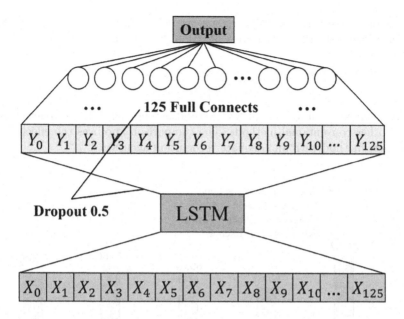

Fig. 5. The structure and settings of LSTM in emotion recognition.

The 10-folds cross validation methods are used to evaluate the performance of our approach. The accuracies of the 10-folds validation processes are averaged so that it can give a relatively impartial evaluation of the proposed new method, and a mean accuracy of 76.67% were achieved. For a comparison, a method of the Support Vector Machine (SVM) classifier with RASM features was evaluated using the same data and the validation approach. Since we focus on the trial-oriented recognition rather than some segment-oriented recognition or subject-oriented recognition tasks, we only select those relevant studies out for a comparison. The brief information for these methods is shown in Table 1.

Table 1. Information of the methods in the comparison

Algorithm	Database	Features	Classifier
Our approach	DEAP	RASM	LSTM
Baseline approach	DEAP	RASM	SVM
Zhang [10]	DEAP	DE	GELM
Chen [2]	DEAP	Fusion feature	HMM
Li [6]	DEAP	Wavelet energy	CRNN

The average recognition accuracy was calculated by the following formula, where Acc represents the average recognition accuracy, N_{test} represents the number of the testing samples, $N^k_{correct}$ is the number of samples that have been classified correctly in the kth validation, k $\in$ [1, 10].

$$Acc = \frac{1}{10} \sum_{k=1}^{10} \frac{N^k_{correct}}{N_{test}} \qquad (1)$$

The average accuracy of our new method is reported in Fig. 6 together with that of other conventional methods. The comparison approves the effectiveness of our new method with an adequate recognition accuracy.

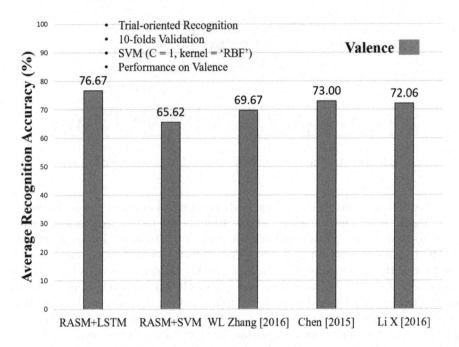

Fig. 6. Performance comparison among relevant methods.

4   Discussion

Compared with other conventional methods, the new approach of RASM+LSTM we proposed achieves better performance in the emotional recognition task. The reason might be as follows. The SVM classifier did not have the ability to calculate the temporal correlations of EEG signals. The method by Zhang [10] using the GELM classifier also exhibited the same problem. The performance on Valence dimension in the work of Chen [2] was good, as the HMM was used to establish the relationship between the current state and the previous state. However, performance of the HMM would decline when the input sequence was quite long and had variable lengths, as each step's output of the HMM was only related to a few previous states. The CRNN framework for emotion recognition proposed in [6] using CNN to extract EEG features required a huge set of training data which was extremely difficult to achieve. In this case, the CRNN's performance was weaker than our approach.

To sum up, for EEG-based emotion recognition, RASM is a considerable feature and LSTM is a suitable classifier. As the new approach focuses on the trial-oriented recognition, which is limited with a minute-level time resolution. It might not perform well in short time recognition. We then tested our approach in segment-oriented emotion recognition, where the data had the second-level time resolution, and the trial labels were used as the segment labels. Then we got a mean accuracy of 71.96%, which was lower than the trial-oriented recognition, as the emotion labels in the database were set for the trials instead of the segments.

Although the accuracy of our experiment is more than 75%, it is not good enough for applications. The task of the future work is to improve the recognition accuracy. More features will be tried especially those reflect the characteristics of EEG signals in frequency-space domain. On the other hand, we will try to modify the proposed classifier for enabling its ability in learning more comprehensive contextual information from EEG signals.

5   Conclusion

In this paper, we proposed a new method using RASM and LSTM for emotion recognition from EEG, which took advantages of the frequency-space features and temporal correlations of EEG signals. The comparison experiment results show the effectiveness of our approach as the emotion recognition accuracy of our approach is better than the compared methods.

Acknowledgment. This work was supported by National Natural Science Founding of China (U1636218), the Guangzhou Key Lab of Body Data Science (201605030011) and the Science and Technology Program of Guangzhou of China (201704020043) and the Fundamental Research Funds for the Central Universities (2017MS041).

References

1. Bengio, Y., Simard, P., Frasconi, P.: Learning long-term dependencies with gradient descent is difficult. IEEE Trans. Neural Netw. **5**(2), 157–166 (2002)
2. Chen, J., Hu, B., Xu, L., Moore, P., Su, Y.: Feature-level fusion of multimodal physiological signals for emotion recognition. In: IEEE International Conference on Bioinformatics and Biomedicine, pp. 395–399 (2015)
3. Koelstra, S., Muhl, C., Soleymani, M., Lee, J.S., Yazdani, A., Ebrahimi, T., Pun, T., Nijholt, A., Patras, I.: Deap: a database for emotion analysis; using physiological signals. IEEE Trans. Affect. Comput. **3**(1), 18–31 (2012)
4. Kollia, V.: Personalization effect on emotion recognition from physiological data: an investigation of performance on different setups and classifiers (2016)
5. Lang, P.J.: The emotion probe. Studies of motivation and attention. Am. Psychol. **50**(5), 372 (1995)

6. Li, X., Song, D., Zhang, P., Yu, G., Hou, Y., Hu, B.: Emotion recognition from multi-channel EEG data through convolutional recurrent neural network. In: IEEE International Conference on Bioinformatics and Biomedicine, pp. 352–359 (2017)
7. Lin, Y.P., Wang, C.H., Jung, T.P., Wu, T.L., Jeng, S.K., Duann, J.R., Chen, J.H.: EEG-based emotion recognition in music listening. IEEE Trans. Biomed. Eng. **57**(7), 1798–1806 (2010)
8. Soleymani, M., Asghari-Esfeden, S., Fu, Y., Pantic, M.: Analysis of EEG signals and facial expressions for continuous emotion detection. IEEE Trans. Affect. Comput. **7**(1), 17–28 (2016)
9. Verma, G.K., Tiwary, U.S.: Affect representation and recognition in 3D continuous valence-arousal-dominance space. Multimedia Tools Appl. 1–25 (2016)
10. Zheng, W.L., Zhu, J.Y., Lu, B.L.: Identifying stable patterns over time for emotion recognition from EEG (2016)

Exemplar-Based Photo Color Correction by Exploring Visual Aesthetics

Zhenkun Zhou$^{(\boxtimes)}$, Shijie Hao, and Mingyu Liu

Hefei University of Technology, Hefei, China
zhouzhenkun.arsenal@gmail.com

Abstract. With the prevalence of mobile imaging devices, large amount of photos are produced in each day. Automatic image enhancing models, such as exemplar-based color correction model, are highly needed. Based on feature correspondence between the exemplars and the target photo, the model optimizes the correction parameters by solving a matrix factorization problem. However, current models do not consider how to obtain reliable exemplars. In this paper, a simple but effective idea is employed to address this issue. We introduce an aesthetics evaluation stage, which measures the quality of the exemplars, to only select aesthetically good exemplars into the color correction model. This pre-selection strategy makes the exemplars more reliable in the correction model, and thus improves the visual quality of the results. Visual and quantitative experiments validate our improved model.

Keywords: Image enhancement · Color correction · Image aesthetics

1 Introduction

As digital imaging devices, especially mobile phones, are entering everyone's daily life, tremendous amount of photos have been produced [1]. However, the quality of these photos is usually not high due to the following reasons. On one hand, most amateur users are less known about photographing skills, e.g. the rule of thirds and the rule of balance. On the other hand, the photo quality is usually vulnerable to various external factors, such as low light, overcast sky and foggy weather.

In this context, it is highly desirable to develop image enhancement techniques that are able to adjust the photo appearance and improve its quality. Adobe Photoshop is an acceptable choice. However, it usually requires many kinds of human interactions and sufficient manual editing skills. Therefore, various automatic enhancement methods have been developed, such as illumination enhancement [2], detail enhancement [3]. However, many enhancing models [2, 3] only process the target image individually, while they do not consider the guidance from exemplars, i.e. visually similar images. Recently, novel color enhancing models that utilize the correspondence between the target images and its exemplars have been proposed [4–6]. Their key idea is that several exemplar images jointly guide the color correction process of the target image. Different from the traditional methods that rely on pre-determined assumption, exemplar-based methods learn an appropriate correction model configuration directly from exemplar images. Of note, the exemplar images are assumed to be of good

© Springer Nature Singapore Pte Ltd. 2018
B. Huet et al. (Eds.): ICIMCS 2017, CCIS 819, pp. 319–326, 2018.
https://doi.org/10.1007/978-981-10-8530-7_31

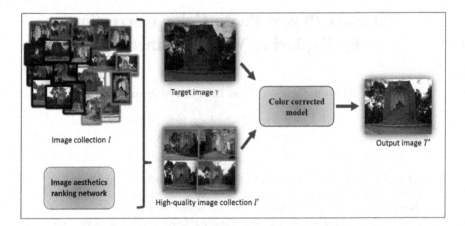

Fig. 1. The schematic illustration of the proposed framework

quality, e.g. clear edge, vivid color, proper composition, etc. We note that, however, these exemplars are not always straightforward to collect in real-world applications. For example, image search engines can help a tourist to obtain sufficient similar images as candidate exemplars. Although these candidate images are semantically similar to the target, their image quality is not guaranteed. In this situation, the effectiveness of color correction can be weakened when low-quality images are included in the exemplar set. Existed methods [5, 6] do not consider this issue, and assume good exemplar collection is always at hand (Fig. 1).

To address this issue, we propose an improved gamma enhancement model by exploring visual aesthetics of the candidate exemplars. The basic roadmap of our method is to actively select aesthetically appealing candidate images, and use them as the exemplars to jointly determine the correction parameters of the target photo. To fulfill our goal, we quantitatively assess the visual aesthetics of the candidate images, which is used as the exemplar selection criterion. Of note, different from the traditional image quality evaluation lays more emphasis on the noise level, the aesthetic evaluation considers more imaging factors, and is more suitable for selecting visually appealing candidates in our research. The contribution of our method is that we extend the exemplar based color correction model by making itself aware of selecting reliable exemplars. Both qualitative and quantitative experiments show the effectiveness of our method.

2   Related Work

Since our work is closely related to color correction and aesthetics evaluation, we briefly review the methods of these two topics in this section.

Traditional methods for color correction often rely on human interactions [7] or natural image statistics [8, 9]. When facing large number of photos for processing, these methods tend to be less efficient as huge human efforts or computational sources are needed. HaCohen et al. [5] propose to propagate color information from exemplar images to the target. However, dense correspondence between images is a prerequisite, which introduces heavy computational load for real-world applications. Recently, Park et al. [6] propose a novel method called Efficient and Robust Color Correction (ERCC), which estimates optimal correction parameters through a matrix factorization model. They achieve the state-of-the-art correction result. However, their exemplars are all assumed to be of good aesthetics, and they do not consider the situation when less aesthetic images are included.

Recently, image aesthetics assessment has attracted much attention from related research communities. Beyond traditional image quality, aesthetics assessment focuses on if an image provides mental satisfaction to users according to its visual appearance [10, 11]. Traditional methods evaluate image aesthetics by combining multiple image features, including global and local ones, and building regression or classification models for quantitative description. Due to the well-known semantic gap [12–15], these models are less effective to keep up with human evaluation. In recent years, more advanced features have been extracted from CNN models [16], which are more semantically aware than the handcrafted features. Several CNN-based models have been proposed for the aesthetics evaluation task [17, 18]. Xin et al. formulate the aesthetics evaluation task as a binary classification problem [17]. Differently, Kong et al. formulate a regression model and obtain more precise aesthetics description at a finer scale, which is suitable for selecting good candidate images as exemplars.

3   Proposed Model

3.1   Color Correction Model

Suppose the target image T is less visually appealing. We aim at enhancing the aesthetic quality of the target image by the groupwise ERCC model [6]. A collection of semantically similar images $T = \{I\_1, I\_2, ..., I\_n\}$ are pre-assumed to be collected. In general, the applied color correction method globally transfers the color information from T to T. The general color correction model is represented as:

$$I = (cI')^{\gamma} \tag{1}$$

where I is an image for correction, and I' is the desired image, c is a parameter controlling the white balance, and γ is the non-linear gamma mapping. This model could be viewed as the combination of the white balance model and the gamma correction model. Since T and $\mathfrak{T}$ generally have the same scene, the group-wise correspondence across T and $\mathfrak{T}$ can be built by extracting their SIFT features and matching them based on the nearest neighbor rule. We denote all images for processing as $I_i \in \{I_1, I_2, ..., I_u\}$ $(u = n + 1)$, and denote all v 3D matched positions as $\{p_j\}_{j=1}^{v}$. The 2D image projection of the matching points p_j on images I_i is denoted as x_{ij}. According to Eq. (1), we further have point-wise correction model:

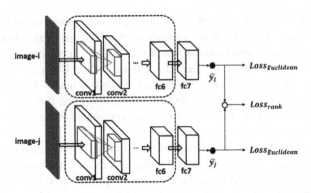

Fig. 2. The network structure for scoring image aesthetics

$$I_i(x_{ij}) = (c_i a_j e_{ij})^{\gamma_i} \tag{2}$$

where $I_i(x_{ij})$ is the intensity of x_{ij} in image I_i, a_j is the intensity of p_j, c_i and γ_i are unknown global parameters of image I_i. Of note, we add a per-pixel error e_{ij} that represents unstable factors, such as the light change. Taking logarithms of Eq. (2), we can obtain:

$$\log(I_i(x_{ij})) = \gamma_i \log(c_i) + \gamma_i \log(a_j) + \gamma_i \log(e_{ij}) \tag{3}$$

With v points for all u images, we can further rewrite Eq. (3) in the matrix form:

$$P = C + A + E \tag{4}$$

where $P \in \mathbb{R}^{u \times v}$. We apply a matrix factorization-based formulation is to solve Eq. (4), and obtain the value of each c_i and γ_i for image I_i. (The details can be found in [6].) Therefore, from the solved results, we naturally obtain the corresponding c and γ for our target image T, where the basic correction model in Eq. 1 is applied.

$$T = (cT')^{\gamma} \tag{5}$$

3.2   Exemplar Selection with a CNN-Based Aesthetics Evaluation Model

The above model described in Sect. 3.1 assumes all collected candidates in T have good visual aesthetics, which is usually not the case in real-world applications. In contrary, the aesthetic quality of images across T can be inconsistent, where poor-quality images can be included. The matched pixels from these images would have a negative influence on color correction, which thus lower the performance of the color correction. To address this issue, we equip the color correction method with a CNN based image aesthetic assessment, which is able to select high quality images from T as exemplars.

Fig. 3. The 10 target images for experimental validation

Fig. 4. Visual comparison of the results produced by [6] and our method (four exemplars are used). The upper row shows the original target images and several zoomed-in patches. The middle row is the results of our method. The bottom row is the results of [6], of which the exemplars are randomly selected

We choose the AlexNet as the basic structure and fine-tune the network, in which we replace the softmax loss with a Euclidean loss to predict aesthetic scores (Fig. 2). In order to enhance the model reliability, image pairs are sent to the Siamese network structure. These image pairs are sigh as image-i and image-j. y_i and y_j are the ground-truth ratings for image-i and image-j. $\hat{y}_i$ and $\hat{y}_j$ are the estimated scores produced by the CNN model. Then a pairwise ranking loss of relative rankings of image pairs is introduced:

$$Loss_{rank} = \frac{1}{2N} \sum_{i,j}^{N} max\left(0, \alpha - \delta\left(y_i \geq y_j\right)\left(\hat{y}_i - \hat{y}_j\right)\right) \qquad (6)$$

where the function δ is expressed as:

$$\delta\left(y_i \geq y_j\right) = \begin{cases} 1, & \textbf{if } y_i \geq y_j \\ -1, & \textbf{if } y_i < y_j \end{cases}$$

and α is a specified margin parameter. Combining the Euclidean loss and the ranking loss together, we formulate a unified optimization:

$$Loss_{rank+Euclidean} = Loss_{Euclidean} + w_r Loss_{rank} \qquad (7)$$

where w_r is weight parameter for ranking loss and empirically set as 1 in our experiments. This model is able to provide scores more consistent with human raters. As for the aesthetic scoring dataset used for training the network, the AADB dataset published in [18] is used.

For images in the collection $\mathfrak{T}$, we sent them to the trained network above and obtain their aesthetic scores $S = (s_1, s_2, \ldots, s_n)$. By sorting them and selecting the first m exemplars $\mathfrak{T}' = \{I'_1, I'_2, \ldots, I'_m\} \subseteq \mathfrak{T}$, we can conduct the color correction based on the refined exemplars. The overall framework of our gamma enhancement is to (1). select the exemplar set $\mathfrak{T}'$ at first, and then (2). apply the correction model described in Sect. 3.1, where $\mathfrak{T}$ is replaced with the refined set $\mathfrak{T}'$.

4   Experiments

We choose 10 images as experimental target images which depict different scenes from the Internet (Fig. 3). For each image, we collect 50 images as a candidate set T. Each share of 50 images represents a scene that is consistent with their target image, but they vary in different aesthetic qualities. In order to select the high aesthetic images from the candidate set. We sorted these images respectively in a descending order. For example, in Fig. 5, we sort the pictures of the Hall of Supreme Harmony and show several high (the first row) and low-score (second row) candidates. It is obvious that the images in the first row are more visually appealing than the ones in the second row in terms of their color and light conditions. The aesthetic partition is consistent with the human preference.

Fig. 5. An example of sorted candidates based on the aesthetics evaluation model

We first demonstrate the effectiveness of our correction method by means of aesthetic scores. In our experiments, we select top 4 exemplar images from the 50 candidates for correcting each target image ($m = 4$). As for measuring quantitative aesthetics of result images, we also use the network based regressive model in [18]. We compare the scores before and after the color correction process in Table 1. We can observe that most processed images (9 out of 10) achieve better aesthetic scores. In average, our method achieves 10.3% improvement (0.4481 vs. 0.4050).

Table 1. Aesthetic scores before and after the proposed color correction model.

T	Img1	Img2	Img3	Img4	Img5	Img6	Img7	Img8	Img9	Img10
[6]	0.3853	0.4739	0.5650	0.2918	0.4120	**0.3199**	0.3215	0.3496	0.6071	0.3241
Ours	**0.4372**	**0.6229**	**0.5687**	**0.3091**	**0.4920**	0.2682	**0.3427**	**0.4443**	**0.6501**	**0.3457**

Table 2. Increments of ratings of our method than randomly select reference images.

Δ_s m	Img1	Imag2	Imag3	Img4	Img5	Img6	Img7	Img8	Img9	Img10
1	-0.0045	0.0418	0.0327	0.1087	0.0141	0.0708	0.1278	0.0519	0.0208	0.0489
4	0.0124	0.1141	-0.0072	0.0381	0.0036	-0.0104	0.0164	0.0817	0.0440	0.0047
9	0.0045	0.0551	0.0372	0.0200	0.0072	0.0065	0.0057	0.0781	0.0181	0.0300
14	0.0093	0.0669	0.0482	0.0077	0.0089	0.0671	0.0149	0.1094	0.0216	0.0466
19	0.0012	0.0792	0.0345	-0.0004	0.0040	0.0369	0.0035	0.0312	0.0219	0.0367

We also conduct quantitative comparison with the original model in [6]. For fair comparison, we chose the same number of exemplars (m = 1, 4, 9, 14, 19) for both methods throughout the experiments. The only difference is that our method selects m exemplars based on aesthetics scores while are its counterpart [6] select them randomly. We denote the difference between the result scores of our method and the method in [6] as Δ_s. From Table 2, we can see that our method generally obtains better scores (positive Δ_s) than its counterpart. This empirically validates the usefulness of only selecting aesthetically appealing image as exemplars. The visual comparison between the original ERCC and our method is shown in Fig. 4. We can see that our results generate better color contrast, and also preserve the color naturalness in general. From the zoomed-in patches, we can see that more texture details can be clearly exhibited based on our method. Since the exemplars are selected by the aesthetic evaluation network, they have high aesthetic quality in terms of good light conditions, vivid colors, and clear textures. In this context, proper correction parameters can be jointly estimated by the group wise correction model in Eq. 4.

5 Conclusions

In this paper, we present an improved color correction method. Unlike the traditional model, we adopt image aesthetic evaluation to select reliable exemplar photo for the correction model. In the experiments, the qualitative and quantitative results demonstrate the effectiveness of our method. Of note, we only use the general aesthetic scores of the candidate images. We plan to conduct the future research in the following aspects. First, we can apply other novel models [19] to solve the optimal correction parameter. Second, we plan to explore the fine grained aesthetic attributes of images and embed this information [20] into our color correction model.

References

1. Zhu, W., Cui, P., Wang, Z., Hua, G.: Multimedia big data computing. IEEE Multimed. **22**(3), 96–100 (2015)
2. Xiaojie, G., Li, Y., Ling, H.: LIME: low-light image enhancement via illumination map estimation. IEEE Trans. Image Process. **26**(2), 982–993 (2016)
3. Hao, S., Guo, Y., Hong, R., Wang, M.: Scale-aware spatially guided mapping by combining multiple level-of-details. IEEE Multimed. **23**(3), 34–42 (2016)
4. Hong, R., Zhang, L., Tao, D.: Unified photo enhancement by discovering aesthetic communities from Flickr. IEEE Trans. Image Process. **25**(3), 1124–1135 (2016)
5. HaCohen, Y., Shechtman, E., Goldman, D., Lischinski, D.: Optimizing color consistency in photo collections. ACM Trans. Graph. (TOG) **32**(4), 38 (2013)
6. Park, J., Tai, Y., Sinha, S., So Kweon, I.: Efficient and robust color consistency for community photo collections. In: Proceedings of CVPR (2016)
7. Lischinski, D., Farbman, Z., Uyttendaele, M., Szeliski, R.: Interactive local adjustment of tonal values. ACM Trans. Graph. (TOG) **25**(3), 646–653 (2006)
8. Hong, R., Zhang, L., Zhang, C., Zimmermann, R.: Flickr circles: aesthetic tendency discovery by multi-view regularized topic modeling. IEEE Trans. Multimed. **18**(8), 1555–1567 (2016)
9. Gijsenij, A., Gevers, T.: Color constancy using natural image statistics and scene semantics. IEEE Trans. Pattern Anal. Mach. Intell. **33**(4), 687–698 (2011)
10. Zhang, H., Shang, X., Luan, H., Wang, M., Chua, T.-S.: Learning from collective intelligence: feature learning using social images and tags. ACM Trans. Multimed. Comput. Commun. Appl. **13**(1), 1–23 (2016). article 1
11. Joshi, D., Datta, R., Luong, Q.-T., Fedorovskaya, E., Wang, J.Z., Li, J., Luo, J.: Aesthetics and emotions in images: a computational perspective. IEEE Sig. Process. Mag. **28**(5), 94–115 (2011)
12. Zhang, H., Zha, Z.-J., Yang, Y., Yan, S., Gao, Y., Chua, T.-S.: Attribute-augmented semantic hierarchy: towards bridging semantic gap and intention gap in image retrieval. In: Proceedings of ACM Multimedia (2013)
13. Datta, R., Joshi, D., Li, J., Wang, J.Z.: Studying aesthetics in photographic images using a computational approach. In: Leonardis, A., Bischof, H., Pinz, A. (eds.) ECCV 2006. LNCS, vol. 3953, pp. 288–301. Springer, Heidelberg (2006). https://doi.org/10.1007/11744078_23
14. Hong, R., Yang, Y., Wang, M., Hua, X.-S.: Learning visual semantic relationships for efficient visual retrieval. IEEE Trans. Big Data **1**(4), 152–161 (2015)
15. Liu, X., Wang, M., Yin, B.-C., Huet, B., Li, X.: Event-based media enrichment using an adaptive probabilistic hypergraph model. IEEE Trans. Cybern. **45**(11), 2461–2471 (2015)
16. Zhang, H., Kyaw, Z., Chang, S.-F., Chua, T.-S.: Visual translation embedding network for visual relation detection. In: Proceedings of CVPR (2017)
17. Xin, L., Lin, Z., Jin, H., Yang, J., Wang, J.: Rating image aesthetics using deep learning. IEEE Trans. Multimed. **17**(11), 2021–2034 (2015)
18. Kong, S., Shen, X., Lin, Z., Mech, R., Fowlkes, C.: Photo aesthetics ranking network with attributes and content adaptation. In: Leibe, B., Matas, J., Sebe, N., Welling, M. (eds.) ECCV 2016. LNCS, vol. 9905, pp. 662–679. Springer, Cham (2016). https://doi.org/10.1007/978-3-319-46448-0_40
19. Zhang, H., Shen, F., Liu, W., He, X., Luan, H., Chua, T.-S.: Discrete collaborative filtering. In: Proceeding of SIGIR (2016)
20. Zhang, H., Zha, Z.-J., Yang, Y., Yan, S., Chua, T.-S.: Robust (semi) nonnegative graph embedding. IEEE Trans. Image Process. **23**(7), 2996–3012 (2014)

Fast Nearest Neighbor Search Based on Approximate k-NN Graph

Jie Yang[1], Wan-Lei Zhao[1(✉)] ⓘ, Cheng-Hao Deng[1], Hanzi Wang[1] ⓘ, and Sangwhan Moon[2]

[1] Fujian Key Laboratory of Sensing and Computing for Smart City, Xiamen University, Fujian, China
{jyang,chenghaodeng}@stu.xmu.edu.cn, {wlzhao,hanzi.wang}@xmu.edu.cn
[2] Odd Concepts Inc., Seoul, Korea
sangwhan@oddconcepts.kr

Abstract. Nearest neighbor search is known as a challenging issue that has been studied for several decades. Recently, this issue becomes more and more imminent in viewing that the big data problem arises from various fields. According to recent study, graph-based methods are effective to address this issue. However, the k-nearest neighbor graph construction of the existing solutions is computationally inefficient, which becomes the processing bottleneck. To address this issue, a novel k-nearest neighbor graph construction method is proposed. As indicated by extensive experiments, satisfactory performance is achieved on different datasets while the graph construction cost has been reduced to low level. In addition, a comparative study on various approximate nearest neighbor search methods, such as the space partitioning, compressional, hash and the graph-based is presented. As indicated in the experiment, our method makes the best trade-off between search quality and computational cost.

Keywords: Nearest neighbor search · k-NN Graph · Two means tree

1 Introduction

Nearest neighbor search (NNS) generally arises from a wide range of subjects, such as database, machine learning, computer vision, and information retrieval. Due to the fundamental role it plays, it has been studied in many computer fields for several decades. The nearest neighbor search problem can be simply defined as follows. Given a query vector ($q \in R^d$), and n candidates that are under the same dimensionality. It is required to return sample(s) for the query that are closest to it according to certain metric.[1]

Traditionally, this issue has been addressed by various space partitioning strategies [3,11]. However, these methods are hardly scalable to high dimensional

---

[1] In our study, the discussion of nearest neighbor search issue is restricted to l_2-distance.

© Springer Nature Singapore Pte Ltd. 2018
B. Huet et al. (Eds.): ICIMCS 2017, CCIS 819, pp. 327–338, 2018.
https://doi.org/10.1007/978-981-10-8530-7_32

(e.g., $d > 20$), large-scale and dense vector space. Most of the traditional methods such as K-D tree [3], R-tree [11] and locality sensitive hashing (LSH) [7] are unable to return decent results.

Recently, there are two major trends in the literature. In one direction, the nearest neighbor search is conducted based on k-nearest neighbor graph (k-NN Graph) [9,12,21,24], in which the k-NN Graph is constructed offline. Alternatively, NNS is addressed based on vector quantization [2,13,23]. The primary goal of this way is to compress the reference set by vector quantization. Such that it is possible to load the whole reference set (after compression) into the memory in the case that the reference set is extremely large.

In k-NN Graph based methods, the primary issue is about the efficient construction of the k-NN Graph, given the original problem is at the complexity of $O(d \cdot n^2)$. This issue has been addressed by the scheme "divide-and-conquer" [4,22] and nearest neighbor descent [8]. The combination of these two schemes is also seen from recent work [9]. With the support of k-NN Graph, nearest neighbor search is conducted by traversing the k-NN Graph with hill-climbing strategy [8,12]. As shown in different contexts, graph based methods show promising performance. However, the memory cost during the k-NN Graph construction or online search are still relatively high, which could be several times over the size of reference dataset.

Considering the heavy memory consumption of the traditional methods, the issue of NNS is addressed based on vector quantization. The representative methods are product quantizer (PQ) [13], additive quantizer (AQ) [2], composite quantizer (CQ) [23] and stacked quantizer (SQ) [17]. In all these methods, vectors in the reference set are compressed via vector quantization. On one hand, the candidate vectors have been compressed (typically the memory consumption is one order of magnitude lower than the size of reference set), which makes it possible to scale-up the nearest neighbor search to very large range. On the other hand, the distance computation between query and all the candidates becomes very efficient when it is approximated by the distance between query and vocabulary words. However, due to the approximation in both vector representation and distance calculation, high recall is undesirable with the compressional methods.

In this paper, a light-weight k-NN Graph construction method is presented. The nearest neighbor search is therefore conducted by hill-climbing strategy with the support of constructed k-NN Graph. The effectiveness of the proposed method is studied in comparison to recent graph based methods. In addition, a comparative study is made for all four categories of NNS methods in the state-of-the-art. By this way, on one hand, we show the proposed method achieves the best trade-off between search quality and computational cost. On the other hand, a clear picture about the progress on NNS in the literature is presented.

The remaining of this paper is organized as follows. In Sect. 2, a brief review about the literature of NNS is presented. Section 3 shows an efficient k-NN Graph construction method based on two means tree. Experimental results and analysis are presented in Sect. 4. Section 5 concludes the paper.

2   Related Work

In this section, four categories of nearest neighbor search methods are reviewed. Namely, they are space partitioning methods, compressional methods, hash methods and k-NN Graph based methods. For each category, the general idea as well as its advantages and pitfalls are discussed.

2.1   Space Partitioning Methods

The basic idea of these methods is to partition the space into embedded hierarchical sub-spaces. The NNS is performed by traversing over one or several branches to probe the nearest neighbor. The space partitioning aims to restrict the search taking place within minimum number of sub-spaces. However, the partition scheme does not excludes the possibility that nearest neighbor resides outside of these candidate sub-spaces. Therefore, extensive probing over the large number of branches in K-D tree becomes inevitable. For this reason, NNS with K-D tree could be very slow. In the worst case, K-D tree performs as slow as the linear scan. Similar comments apply to R-tree [11] and its variants despite that a more sophisticated design on the partition strategy is proposed in these tree structures. In recent released nearest neighbor search package FLANN [18], two space partitioning methods, namely K-D tree and hierarchical k-means are integrated. It turns out to be quite efficient for the applications that does not require high search quality.

2.2   Locality Sensitive Hashing

In general, methods based on locality sensitive hashing (LSH) [7] convert a vector into a series of hash keys via a collection of locality sensitive hash functions. In the search stage, two steps are involved. Namely, step *1.* collects the candidates that share the same or similar hash keys as the query; step *2.* performs exhaustive comparison between the query and all these selected candidates to find out the nearest neighbor. Similar as FLANN, LSH is good for the application that only requires approximate nearest neighbor. Moreover, in order to support the fast comparison in step *2*, the number of hash tables should be large enough which causes a lot of memory consumption.

2.3   Compressional Methods

For all the compressional methods, they share two things in common. Firstly, the candidate vectors are all compressed via vector quantization. This makes it easier than previous methods to hold the whole dataset in the memory. Secondly, NNS is conducted between the query and the compressed candidate vectors. The distance between query and candidates is approximated by the distance between query and vocabulary words that are used for quantization. These quantization based methods can be generally grouped into two categories, namely, divisive methods [10,13,19] and compositional methods [5,23]. Comparing with other types of methods, compressional methods holds a unique advantage. It is no need to load the original reference set into the memory. For this reason, it becomes very scalable to large-scale search task in terms of its memory complexity. However, due to the approximation in distance calculation, good search quality is hardly achievable.

2.4 k-NN Graph Based Methods

Two major steps are involved in k-NN Graph based methods. Namely, they are the offline k-NN Graph construction and online nearest neighbor search. At the offline stage, an approximate k-NN Graph is constructed which retains the first k nearest neighbors for each individual data point. Since the complexity of building an exact k-NN Graph is $O(d \cdot n^2)$, recent works [8,9,15,16] only intend to search for approximate solution. As the k-NN Graph plays a key role for online search, in the following, representative k-NN Graph construction methods, notably from [8,9,15,16], are reviewed.

k-nearest neighbor Graph (KGraph). The idea of KGraph [8] is inspired by the observation that "a neighbor of a neighbor is also likely to be a neighbor". The construction of nearest neighbor list of each data point starts from random set of neighbors. The nearest neighbor list is refined iteratively by exploring its neighbors' neighborhoods. Although efficient, the memory cost is still relatively high. In addition, according to our observation, the quality of k-NN Graph drops dramatically as the scale of data increases to very large.

Diversified proximity graph (DPG). DPG [15] is proposed as an improvement over k-NN Graph constructed by KGraph [8]. Namely, two post-processing operations are applied on k-NN Graph from [8]. Firstly, neighbors of one sample, which are closer to others than they are to the sample, are removed from the k-NN list of the sample. In addition, the reverse nearest neighbors (points which view one sample as their neighbor) in the diversified k-NN Graph are appended to k-NN list of one sample. As indicated in [15], these two post-processing schemes lead to considerable performance boost. For this reason, in our k-NN Graph construction method, these two post-processing operations are also adopted.

Hierarchical navigable small world (HNSW). [16] Different from other graph based methods, HNSW builds graphs of several layers. The graphs in the upper layer only keep a portion of the samples. Specifically, the samples of upper layer are a subset of samples from the lower layer. As a result, it forms a coarse-to-fine indexing for the reference set. The graph of each layer is built by incrementally inserting points into the graph. Superior performance is achieved based on hierarchical navigable small world graph. Unfortunately, it takes a lot of memory in both construction and online search. In addition, the graph construction could be very slow for large-scale dataset.

Once the k-NN Graph is built, it is used to support the online search, which generally follows a hill-climbing scheme. The search starts from a group of randomly selected seeds. Seeds are compared to the query. A priority queue is maintained to keep the closest k candidates for the query. The search is expanded to more candidates by considering the data samples from the k-NN list of unexpanded candidate in the queue. The priority queue is updated with closer candidates in each round. This greedy search continues until there is no new candidate in the priority queue to be expanded.

3 k-NN Graph Based Nearest Neighbor Search

In viewing the high computational cost of k-NN Graph construction of existing methods, an efficient and light-weight k-NN Graph construction method is presented. Basically, we follow the strategy of divide-and-conquer [4,9,22]. While different from [4,9,22], the division over the vector space is undertaken by two means clustering [20].

3.1 k-NN Graph Construction

The motivation behind this algorithm is based on the observation that samples in one cluster are most likely neighbors. The general procedure that constructs the k-NN Graph is divided into two steps. Firstly, the input dataset is partitioned into small clusters, where the size of each cluster is no bigger than a threshold. This could be efficiently fulfilled by bisecting the dataset repeatedly with two means clustering [20]. In the second step, an exhaustive distance comparison is conducted within each cluster. The k-NN list for each cluster member is therefore built or updated. This general procedure could be repeated for several times to refine the k-NN list of each sample.

Algorithm 1. *k-NN Graph construction*

```
 1: Input: X_{n×d}: reference set, k: scale of k-NN Graph
 2: Output: k-NN Graph G
 3: Initialize G_{n×k}; t ← 0;
 4: for t < I_0 do
 5:     Apply two means clustering on X_{n×d}
 6:     Collect clusters set S
 7:     for each S_m ∈ S do
 8:         for each < i, j >_{(i<j)} ∈ S_m × S_m do
 9:             if < i, j > is NOT visited then
10:                 Update G[i] and G[j] with d(x_i, x_j);
11:             end if
12:         end for
13:     end for
14:     t ← t + 1
```

15: **end for**
16: Apply diversification on G
17: **for** each $G[i]$ **do**
18:     Collect reverse nearest neighbors for i
19:     Join reverse nearest neighbors of i into $G[i]$
20: **end for**

end

As shown in Algorithm 1, the k-NN Graph construction mainly relies on two means clustering, which forms a partition on the input reference set in each round. Comparing with K-D tree that is adopted in [9], two means produces ball shape clusters instead of cubic shape partition, which fits well to the l_2-space. With the clustering result of each round, the brute-force comparison is conducted within each cluster. Due to the small scale of each cluster, this process could be very efficient. The k-NN Graph G is refined as new and closer neighbors join in. Similar as [15], each k-NN list in the graph is diversified and the reverse nearest neighbors are appended. Due to these two operations, the length of k-NN list of one data sample could be different from another.

In Algorithm 1, the major cost is spent on partitioning the dataset into small subsets, which is carried out by two means tree. According to [20], its complexity is $n \cdot log(n) \cdot d$. As a result, the overall complexity of the k-NN Graph construction is $O(I_0 \cdot n \cdot log(n) \cdot d)$, where I_0 is a constant. According to our observation, it is sufficient to set I_0 to 16 for million level dataset. Once the k-NN Graph is ready, the same hill-climbing procedure as [9,15] is adopted for nearest neighbor search.

Besides the speed efficiency, very few amount of extra memory are required in Algorithm 1. The extra memory are allocated to maintain the k-NN Graph. As revealed in the experiment, compared with recent k-NN Graph construction methods [8,9,16], it is efficient and light-weight.

4   Experiments

In this section, the comparative study is made between the proposed method and other graph based methods, i.e. DPG [15], EFANNA [9] and HNSW [16]. In addition, the comparisons are extended to four categories of NNS methods, such as space partitioning, compressional and hash based methods. The performance of representative methods from each category is presented. Namely, the performance from FLANN [18], E2LSH [1,7], product quantizer [13] is presented. The effectiveness of all the methods are evaluated in terms of online search efficiency, quality (in terms of *recall@1*), time cost of offline indexing and memory consumption. Codes of all the methods are compiled with GCC 5.4. All the experiments are conducted with single thread on a PC with 3.6 GHz CPU and 96 GB memory setup.

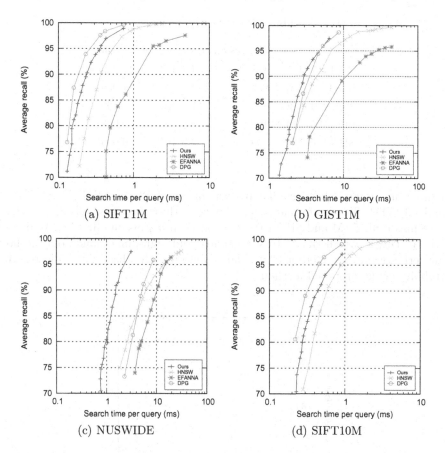

Fig. 1. NNS recall against search time for graph-based methods tested on four datasets.

4.1 Datasets

Four datasets are adopted in the evaluation, which are SIFT1M, GIST1M, NUSWIDE and SIFT1B. Due to the memory constraint, only two subsets of SIFT1B are used. The first *10* million and *100* million vectors are extracted as SIFT10M and SIFT100M respectively. The general information of these datasets are summarized in Table 1.

4.2 Comparison to Graph-Based Methods

In this section, the performance of proposed method is presented in comparison to three graph-based methods including EFANNA [9], HNSW [16] and DPG [15], which are all recently proposed.

Online Search Performance. The curves of average recall against search time are presented in Fig. 1 for all the methods on four datasets. As shown in the

Table 1. Overview of datasets

	Dimension	Dataset size	# Query
SIFT1M [13]	128	1×10^6	10,000
GIST1M [13]	960	1×10^6	1,000
NUSWIDE [6]	500	2.7×10^5	1,000
SIFT10M [14]	128	1×10^7	10,000
SIFT100M [14]	128	1×10^8	10,000

figure, our method shows similar performance as DPG on SIFT1M, SIFT10M and GIST1M. The performance gap between these two methods is less than *0.08* ms on SIFT1M and SIFT10M and less than *0.4* ms on GIST1M. While on NUSWIDE, in which the vectors are sparse and high-dimensional, our method outperforms all the methods by a large margin. This basically indicates the stability of the proposed method.

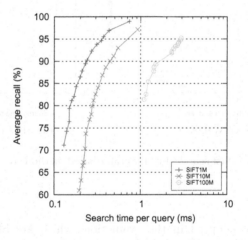

Fig. 2. Search efficiency of our method in SIFT1M, SIFT10M and SIFT100M.

In addition, the scalability test is conducted for the proposed method by varying the dataset size from *1*M to *100*M of SIFT vectors. Due to the heavy memory cost at the offline stage, it is infeasible to pull out the similar test for DPG, HNSW and EFANNA on SIFT100M. For this reason, only the performance of our method is presented. As shown in Fig. 2, our method only takes *0.24* ms, *0.44* ms and *1.51* ms on SIFT1M, SIFT10M and SIFT100M respectively, to reach to *0.9* recall for a query. The search time increases only less than *7* times as the size of reference set increases *100* times. The complexity of our method is therefore sublinear to the size of reference set, which demonstrates a good scalability on such high dimensional data.

Offline Construction Cost. In this section, the offline construction time cost and memory consumption for graph based methods are reported. The memory cost is measured by the ratio between the real memory consumption (including the reference set) and the reference set size. The time cost is reported in Fig. 3(a). While the memory cost spent on offline k-NN Graph construction of all the methods are reported in Fig. 3(b).

As shown from Fig. 3(a) and (b), our method takes minimum time for k-NN Graph construction among all graph based methods. Even for dataset as big as SIFT100M, it takes only *37.58* h to produce the k-NN Graph by a single thread. While for the same task, it would take several days for HNSW and DPG. In addition, our method also shows lowest memory consumption among all graph based methods.

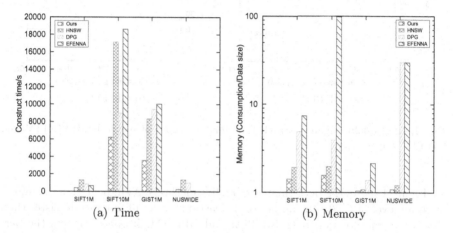

(a) Time   (b) Memory

Fig. 3. Index construction time cost and memory cost of graph-based methods in four datasets respectively.

4.3   Comparison to State-of-the-Art Methods

In this section, the comparative study of our method are conducted against methods of four categories. Representative methods from these categories are considered. Namely, they are FLANN (space partitioning method), E2LSH (hash method), PQ (compressional method). The performance from EFANNA are presented again as the representative of graph-based methods. The comparative study is made on SIFT1M and GIST1M.

Online Search Performance. In the first part, we study the efficiency of different types of methods. Below are the default settings of the key parameters of the algorithms.

– FLANN. The parameter *precision* in FLANN is varied from *0.6* to *1* to produce the time-recall curve.

- E2LSH. The parameter *search radius* in E2LSH is varied from *0.45* to *0.68* to produce the time-recall curve.
- PQ. Coarse word number is fixed to *8192*; segmentation number is fixed to *8* and the word number in each subcodebook is fixed to *256*.

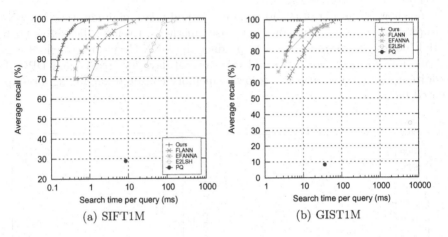

Fig. 4. NNS quality against search time for four types of methods for SIFT1M and GIST1M respectively.

Figure 4 shows the performance of all five methods. As indicated in the figure, at recall level of *0.90*, our method is at least one order of magnitude faster than the rest of methods on both SIFT1M and GIST1M. If one compares the performance reported in Fig. 4 to the performance reported in Fig. 1, it is clear to see that graph based methods achieve superior performance. While compressional method (IVFPQ) and hash based method demonstrate poor performance in most of the cases.

Offline Construction Cost. In this section, the performance of five NNS methods are studied in terms of their offline construction/indexing cost. The indexing time cost and relative memory consumption are presented in Fig. 5(a) and (b) respectively.

As shown in Fig. 5, our method still shows the best trade-off between construction memory and construction time among all the methods considered in this study. In contrast, another graph based method, namely EFANNA shows highest memory consumption due to the use of K-D trees for indexing. Although PQ only requires minimum memory for indexing, its online performance turns out to be very poor. While E2LSH is computationally expensive in terms of both memory and time consumptions.

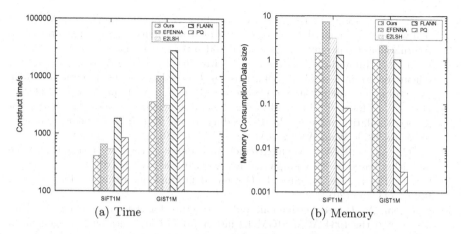

Fig. 5. Index construction time cost and memory cost of four types of methods when *recall*@1 equals to *0.9* in SIFT1M and GIST1M respectively.

5 Conclusions

We have presented an efficient and light-weight *k*-NN Graph construction method, based on which satisfactory performance is achieved for nearest neighbor search across several large-scale and high dimensional datasets. It shows the best trade-off between offline computational cost and online search effectiveness. With the proposed method, it is possible to achieve real time image search on billion level dataset with single thread given sufficient memory are available. In addition, a comparative study over four categories of NNS methods is presented. It is clear to see graph based methods demonstrate superior performance on large-scale search tasks over methods of other categories.

Acknowledgments. This work is supported by National Natural Science Foundation of China under grants 61572408. The authors would like to express their sincere thanks to ODD Concepts Inc. from Seoul, South Korea for their financial support.

References

1. Andoni, A.: E2LSH Searching Toolkit. http://www.mit.edu/~andoni/LSH/
2. Babenko, A., Lempitsky, V.: Additive quantization for extreme vector compression. In: CVPR, pp. 931–938 (2014)
3. Bentley, J.L.: Multidimensional binary search trees used for associative searching. Commun. ACM **18**(9), 509–517 (1975)
4. Bentley, J.L.: Multidimensional divide-and-conquer. Commun. ACM **23**(4), 214–229 (1980)
5. Chen, Y., Guan, T., Wang, C.: Approximate nearest neighbor search by residual vector quantization. Sensors **10**, 11259–11273 (2010)

6. Chua, T.-S., Tang, J., Hong, R., Li, H., Luo, Z., Zheng, Y.-T.: NUS-WIDE: a real-world web image database from national university of Singapore. In: ACM International Conference on Image and Video Retrieval (2009)

7. Datar, M., Immorlica, N., Indyk, P., Mirrokni, V.S.: Locality-sensitive hashing scheme based on p-stable distributions. In: Proceedings of the Twentieth Annual Symposium on Computational Geometry. ACM, New York, pp. 253–262 (2004)

8. Dong, W., Moses, C., Li, K.: Efficient k-nearest neighbor graph construction for generic similarity measures. In: Proceedings of the 20th International Conference on World Wide Web, WWW 2011, pp. 577–586 (2011). ACM, New York

9. Fu, C., Cai, D.: EFANNA: an extremely fast approximate nearest neighbor search algorithm based on kNN graph. arXiv.org (2016). arXiv:1609.07228

10. Ge, T., He, K., Ke, Q., Sun, J.: Optimized product quantization. Trans. PAMI **36**(4), 744–755 (2014)

11. Guttman, A.: R-trees: a dynamic index structure for spatial searching. In: Proceedings of the 1984 ACM SIGMOD international conference on Management of data, vol. 14, pp. 47–57. ACM, New York, June 1984

12. Hajebi, K., Abbasi-Yadkor, Y., Shahbazi, H., Zhang, H.: Fast approximate nearest-neighbor search with k-nearest neighbor graph. In: International Joint Conference on Artificial Intelligence, pp. 1312–1317 (2011)

13. Jégou, H., Douze, M., Schmid, C.: Product quantization for nearest neighbor search. Trans. PAMI **33**(1), 117–128 (2011)

14. Jegou, H., Tavenard, R., Douze, M., Amsaleg, L.: Searching in one billion vectors: re-rank with source coding. In: ICASSP (2011)

15. Li, W., Zhang, Y., Sun, Y., Wang, W., Zhang, W., Lin, X.: Approximate nearest neighbor search on high dimensional data–experiments, analysis and improvement. Arxiv.org (2016). https://arxiv.org/abs/1610.02455

16. Malkov, Y.A., Yashunin, D.A.: Efficient and robust approximate nearest neighbor search using hierarchical navigable small world graphs. Arxiv.org (2016). https://arxiv.org/abs/1411.2173

17. Martinez, J., Hoos, H.H., Little, J.J.: Stacked quantizers for compositional vector compression. Arxiv.org (2014). https://arxiv.org/abs/1411.2173

18. Muja, M., Lowe, D.G.: Scalable nearest neighbor algorithms for high dimensional data. Trans. PAMI **36**, 2227–2240 (2014)

19. Norouzi, M., Fleet, D.J.: Cartesian k-means. In: CVPR, pp. 3017–3024 (2013)

20. Verma, N., Kpotufe, S., Dasgupta, S.: Which spatial partition trees are adaptive to intrinsic dimension? In: Proceedings of the Twenty-Fifth Conference on Uncertainty in Artificial Intelligence, pp. 565–574 (2009)

21. Wang, J., Li, S.: Query-driven iterated neighborhood graph search for large scale indexing. In: Proceedings of the 20th ACM International Conference on Multimedia, pp. 179–188. ACM, New York (2012)

22. Wang, J., Wang, J., Zeng, G., Tu, Z., Gan, R., Li, S.: Scalable k-NN graph construction for visual descriptors. In: CVPR, pp. 1106–1113 (2012)

23. Zhang, T., Du, C., Wang, J.: Composite quantization for approximate nearest neighbor search. In: ICML, pp. 838–846 (2014)

24. Zhou, W., Yuan, C., Gu, R., Huang, Y.: Large scale nearest neighbors search based on neighborhood graph. In: International Conference on Advanced Cloud and Big Data (2013)

Image Recommendation
on Content-Based Bipartite Graph

Lifang Wu, Lei Zhang, Meng Jian$^{(\boxtimes)}$, Dai Zhang, and Haiying Liu

Faculty of Information Technology, Beijing University of Technology,
Beijing 100124, China
lfwu@bjut.edu.cn, zhangleiaurora@163.com, jianmeng648@163.com,
davidzhangdai@aliyun.com, liuhaiying@emails.bjut.edu.cn

Abstract. Recently, online social curation networks attract lots of users due to its convenience to retrieve, collect, sort and share multimedia content with each other. And high quality recommendation on social curation networks becomes urgent in current complex information environment. In this paper, we proposed a content-based bipartite graph algorithm for social curation network recommendation. Bipartite graph employs relationships between users and items to infer user-item association for recommendation. Beyond the traditional bipartite graph, we introduce the content of items into bipartite graph to extend the recommendation scope and improve its recommendation diversity simultaneously. Furthermore, content similarity is employed for recommendation reranking to improve visual quality of recommended images. Experimental results demonstrate that the proposed method enhance the recommendation ability of bipartite graph effectively in diversity and visual quality.

Keywords: Bipartite graph · Online social networking sites
Content-based

1 Introduction

In recent years, online social networking websites, such as Facebook, Twitter, Weibo, Pinterest and Flickr, are emerging to change the way people communicate and successfully make conversations more convenient with various kinds of contents. Some investigation reports illustrate that users are more likely to know strangers by his own friends and family [1]. It shows the role of social network. In 2009, a content curation social networks (CCSNs) Pinterest [2,3], was published and became the fourth largest social network websites in America. In China, several similar social network sites such as Huaban, Meilishuo and so

M. Jian—This work was supported in part by the Beijing Municipal Education Commission Science and Technology Innovation Project (KZ201610005012) and in part by the China Postdoctoral Science Foundation funded project (2017M610026 & 2017M610027).

© Springer Nature Singapore Pte Ltd. 2018
B. Huet et al. (Eds.): ICIMCS 2017, CCIS 819, pp. 339–348, 2018.
https://doi.org/10.1007/978-981-10-8530-7_33

on have been published. With the rapid development of CCSNs, there appears many related research topics remaining on such networks. For example, Cinar et al. [4] use text and images to infer users' interests on social media, user profiling by social curation [5], boards recommendation in pinterest [6].

The graph model [7,8] is capable to represent social relations with its intrinsic property revealing affinities between samples. Therefore a lot of graph based models are elaborately constructed for social recommendation. As a generalized graph model, bipartite graph is constructed to reveal relations between two aspects of samples and intuitively employed for recommendation with collaborative filtering. It is one of collaboration filtering recommendation algorithms. The typical bipartite graph assume that there are a few of user-item links. And it is effective in word alignment, male-female contact networks [9], human romance or partnership networks [10] and so on. Besides, some works focused on analyzing bipartite graph [11,12]. Zhang et al. [13] proposed a bipartite graph recommendation based on heat conduction process. And Sheng and Zhang [14] proposed a diffusion based recommendation scheme, which used the user, item and tags for recommendation and used the frequency of tags as the edge weight to improve the accuracy. Zhou et al. [15] proposed Network Inference algorithm (Network-Based Inference, NBI) which adopts the resource-allocation process of bipartite networks to improve the performance of the CF algorithm in recommendation.

We figure out a phenomenon that contents are dominant on CCSNs. Could we introduce the item relations into bipartite recommendation algorithms? Although there exists no explicit item relations, we could investigate such relations using the content similarity. We proposed an improved content-based bipartite graph (CBG) recommendation algorithm. As shown in Fig. 1, first, we compute the similarity between items by measure image similarity in the deep learning space. And then, we combine the similarity of items with the bipartite graph to improve the bipartite graph recommendation scheme. Finally, the recommendation results are reranked over the similarity of pins. The contribution of the proposed method for image recommendation are summarized as follows.

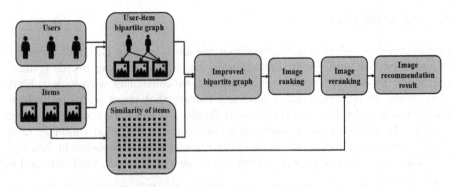

Fig. 1. The framework of the proposed CBG algorithm for image recommendation.

- We employ *AlexNet* for feature extraction and content similarity measurement for image recommendation.
- CBG involves the content similarity of items in the bipartite graph based image recommendation to extend the recommendation scope and improve recommendation ability in diversity.
- CBG leverages content similarity to rerank the recommendation results which improves the visual quality of recommended items.

Experimental results demonstrate the proposed CBG method has a good ability of recommending broader images compared to traditional bipartite graph based method.

The remaining parts of this paper are arranged as follows: in Sect. 2, the proposed algorithm is described in details. The experiments and the corresponding analysis are provided in Sect. 3. Finally, the work is concluded in Sect. 4.

2 The Proposed Algorithm

2.1 Bipartite Graph Based Recommendation

For the general bipartite graph $G(x, y, z)$, where $X = [x_1, x_2, x_3, \ldots x_n]$ and $Y = [y_1, y_2, y_3, \ldots y_m]$ denote item set and user set respectively, and E is the set of edges. In the traditional bipartite graph method, each item corresponds a resource. We use resource-allocation to construct the w_{ij} which represents resource assigned from item x_j to item x_i over bipartite graph. Therefore the resource w_{ij} assigned from item x_j to item x_i can be calculated by

$$w_{ij} = \frac{1}{k(x_j)} \sum_{l=1}^{m} \frac{a_{il} a_{jl}}{k(y_l)} \tag{1}$$

where $i, j \in (1, 2, 3, \ldots, n)$, $k(x_j)$ is the degree of x_j, which is the number of links connected to x_j, $k(y_l)$ is the degree of y_l and a_{il} is an $n \times m$ adjacency matrix.

$$a_{il} = \begin{cases} 0 & x_i y_l \notin E \\ 1 & else \end{cases} \tag{2}$$

Finally, image recommendation can be performed with probability of item x_i to user y_l as

$$f_l(x_i) = \sum_{j=1}^{n} w_{ij} a_{jl} \tag{3}$$

By ranking $f_l(x_i)$, the item x_i of $top - N$ are recommended to user y_l.

In traditional bipartite graphs, $f_l(x_i)$ will be zero when there exist no common items between the user y_l and the one which belongs to. As shown in Fig. 2, $user_l$ owns $item_l$–$item_3$, $user_2$ owns $item_3$–$item_5$ and $user_3$ owns $item_5$–$item_6$. The probability of $item_1$ to $user_3$ calculated by bipartite graph algorithm mentioned above is:

$$f_3(x_1) = w_{11} a_{13} + w_{12} a_{23} + w_{13} a_{33}$$
$$+ w_{14} a_{43} + w_{15} a_{53} + w_{16} a_{63}$$

Thus the $item_1$ would not be recommended to $user_3$. However, as illustrated in Fig. 2, it is reasonable to recommend $item_1$ to $user_3$ in case that $item_1$ and $item_6$ are similar to each other. Therefore, in this work we employ item similarity in bipartite graph and propose content-based bipartite graph (CBG) for image recommendation.

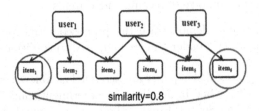

Fig. 2. An example of bipartite graph between users and items, and that of similarity between items.

2.2   Framework of CBG for Recommendation

In this work, we propose content-based bipartite graph (CBG) for image recommendation, which further involves content similarity between items over bipartite relations. Figure 1 provides the framework of the proposed CBG algorithm for recommendation. First, given user-item relations are utilized to construct a user-item bipartite graph. Moreover, we compute the item similarity by measuring image content similarity with deep learning feature extraction. Then to consider intrinsic relationship between items in recommendation, the user-item bipartite graph is improved by combining with the similarity of items. Finally, the ranking results of the improved bipartite graph are further reranked by using the similarity of items for recommendation.

2.3   Content Similarity

As mentioned in Fig. 1, the proposed CBG algorithm employs similarity of items in bipartite graph based image recommendation. The content similarity of items is measured over deep learning based feature extraction by *AlexNet*. *AlexNet* [16] is a deep learning model which is trained from *ImageNet* for image classification. Because the *ImageNet* include about Millions of images in training set, the features space in *AlexNet* is thought effective for image representation. And the finetuned *AlexNet* is usually utilized in image analysis related applications [17,18]. In this work, we also fine-tune the *AlexNet* model to extract image features and evaluate cosine similarity sim_{ij} between items in the feature space. We use 13158 images in the training set and 3291 images in the verification set for fine-tuning and use 30 categories on CCSNs as tags.

Algorithm 1. Recommendation results reranking

Input: U – Set of users;

U_O_{TOP100} – Recommendation top 100;

$Feature_{item}$ – List of the feature of items.

Output: $U\_O_{NEW,TOP20}$ – Top 20 recommendation items.

Step 1. For $i = 1$ to $-U-$;

Step 2.   Select the set of top 100 recommendation items of each

u_i as $U\_O_{TOP100,i}$;

Step 3.   For $j = 1$ to $U\_O_{TOP100,i}$;

Step 4.   Select set of items linked with each user u_l as

O_l;

Step 5.   Calculate the list of similarity between O_i and

$U\_O_{TOP100,ij}$;

Step 6.   Reranking the list;

Step 7.   Get the top 20 of this list.

2.4 Improved Bipartite Graph

Depending on the traditional bipartite graph, w_{ij} Eq. (1) be considered as the relation between item x_i and item x_j. As illustrated in Fig. 1, the proposed CBG employs content similarity in bipartite graph to improve w_{ij} as follows.

$$W_{NEW,ij} = \beta w_{ij} + (1 - \beta)\, sim_{ij}$$

$$= \beta \left(\frac{1}{k(x_j)} \sum_{l=1}^{m} \frac{a_{il} a_{jl}}{k(y_l)} \right) + (1 - \beta)\, sim_{ij} \tag{4}$$

Then, the image recommendation could be implemented by ranking the probability $f_l(x_i)$ of item x_i to user y_l in Eq. (3). Thanks to the similarity of items sim_{ij}, the ranking results could be used to recommend items to the user who shares no common items with the users which the items belong to. The proposed CBG image recommendation method is capable to recommend more high quality items compared to traditional bipartite graph methods. This implies the improved bipartite graph helps extend the recommendation scope and improve recommendation ability in diversity.

2.5 Recommendation Results Reranking

We observe a phenomenon that among the items with similarity inference probabilities of bipartite graph, the user prefers the items with similar visual appearance to the given items of him. Therefore we consider to adopt visual similarity to further rerank the recommendation results of bipartite graph. First, we achieve the top 100 recommendation items to each user by the improved bipartite graph based method in Sect. 2.4. To rerank the 100 items, we measure the similarity between the top 100 items and the items linked with users. And then rerank the items by their content similarity. Finally, The detailed reranking algorithm is described in Algorithm 1.

3   Experiments

To verify the effectiveness of the proposed CBG for image recommendation, we conduct a series of experiments. First, we conduct experiments on the influence of in improved bipartite graph construction of CBG. Second, we provide analysis of the proposed CBG method on the diversity of recommendation results. Finally, we compare the recommendation performance of CBG with some other recommendation methods. Users and images used in experiments are crawled from Huaban.com which is a CCSNs like Pinterest. Bipartite graph in CBG is constructed on both users and images, and content similarity in improving the bipartite graph is calculated by measuring similarity of images. Huaban.com includes 34 categories such as *"funny"*, *"web_app_icon"*, *"desire"* et al. The composition of Huaban.com is given in Fig. 3. The top of the picture is the logo of Huaban.com. Under the logo is the data structure of Huaban.com. Each user is allowed to collect lots of pins, i.e., pictures, and each pin corresponds a board which consists of pictures from a certain category. In this work, 4737 users, 33926 pins and 100873 relation between them are crawled from Huaban.com. In this work, we use a NVIDIA Tesla K40C GPU to fine-tune the *AlexNet* model for feature extraction and content similarity measurement.

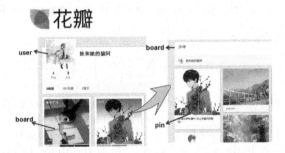

Fig. 3. The data composition of Huaban.com.

3.1   Influence of β in CBG

In Sect. 2.4, to consider intrinsic relationship between items in recommendation we combine the user-item bipartite graph with the similarity of items. β plays a trade-off between resource relation w_{ij} and content similarity sim_{ij} in Eq. (4). In this experiment, we perform image recommendation with varying β from 0.1 to 0.9 with step size of 0.1 and analyze the influence of β in CBG based recommendation performance. With each β, we obtain the top 5 recommended items to each user. We calculate the maximum similarity between the recommended

5 items and the items belonging to the corresponding users. And the average similarity of the recommended 5 items and the mean average of all the users is used to evaluate the performance. Figure 4 provide the mean average similarity between given items of all the users and the recommended 5 items with varying β in CBG, where the horizontal axis is the value of varying β and the vertical axis is the mean average similarity between recommended items and the items belonging to the users. Figure 4 shows that with $\beta = 0.2$ the proposed CBG achieves the best performance of 0.486. It indicates that with $\beta = 0.2$ the improved bipartite graph consists of 20% original bipartite graph and 80% content similarity. It means in image recommendation systems, the content similarity are more important than associate relations in bipartite graph.

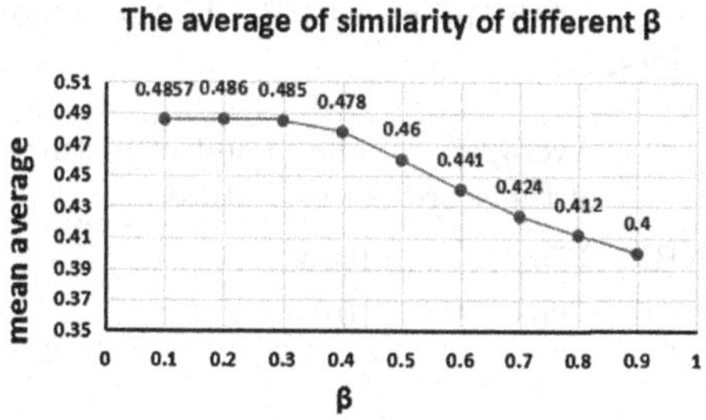

The average of similarity of different β

Fig. 4. The mean average similarity between given items of all the users and recommended items with varying β in CBG.

3.2   Diversity Analysis on Recommendation Results of CBG

With the help of content similarity, the improved bipartite graph extend the image recommendation scope. In order to reveal the effectiveness of content similarity in improving recommendation ability of bipartite graph, Fig. 5 provides the recommendation results with $w_{ij} = 0$ as Eq. (1). As shown in Fig. 5, there are four group pictures which is the example recommendation results by CBG with $w_{ij} = 0$. In each group, the first three are the items belonging to the corresponding user with black boundary, and the last one is the recommended item by CBG with red boundary. We can see that the proposed CBG recommend various images like expression images, scenery images, aesthetic images, anime et al. It means that the proposed CBG improve w_{ij} in case of zero resulting in a probability $f_l(x_i)$ for every item x_i to user y_l as Eq. (3). Therefore, it can recommend diverse items than the traditional bipartite graph method. The statistical results show that almost 18% of the recommendation results have $w_{ij} = 0$ in CBG. In other words, the proposed CBG method is capable to recommend items 18% more than traditional bipartite graph method.

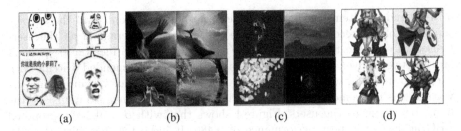

(a)   (b)   (c)   (d)

Fig. 5. Examples of recommendation results by CBG which are not recommended by traditional bipartite graph based method. In each group, the first three images with black boundary are items from a user and the last one with red boundary is the recommended image by CBG. (Color figure online)

Table 1. The average score of the proposed CBG by user study compared with NBI on recommendation results.

	Average of the score	The mount of pictures in user study
NBI	3.75	1016
CBG	3.86	1019

3.3 Experimental Comparison

We further compare the proposed CBG with the traditional bipartite graph method NBI [15] for image recommendation. Average score, which is the similarity between the recommended items and the items belonging to the user by user study, is employed to quantitatively evaluate the performance. User study make volunteers give a score for the recommended items. For the 4737 users, we recommended 5 pins to each user. There are total 23685 recommended pins. We have total 10 volunteers for user study. For each volunteer, 100 recommended images are randomly selected and for each recommended image top three most similar images are provided as reference of users' preference. Figure 6 provides examples of recommendation results by CBG compared with NBI. In each group of Fig. 6, the first 3 images given from the user and the last one is the recommended image. It can be observed that the recommended results by CBG take more visual similarity to the users' items than those by NBI. If the recommended image looks similar to anyone of the 3 images of the user, it is considered as *"perfectmatch"* and scored as 5. If it is almost similar to anyone of the 3, it is considered as *"goodmatch"* and scored as 4. And so on, the score is given from 5 to 1. The average score for the recommendation results are provided in Table 1. We can see from Table 1 that the proposed CBG obtains the better average score than NBI on the recommended results. It intuitively illustrates that in image recommendation systems, users tend to prefer the items with visual similarity to their own items. It can be concluded that the proposed CBG is capable to recommend diverse items to users due to the improved bipartite graph with content similarity and provide high quality recommendation in visual with the help of content similarity.

(a)   (b)   (c)   (d)

Fig. 6. Examples of recommendation results by CBG compared with NBI. (a) and (b) are results of CBG. (c) and (d) are the results of NBI. In each group, the first three images with black boundary are items from a user and the last one with red boundary is the recommended image by CBG. (Color figure online)

4   Conclusions

In this paper, we proposed content based bipartite graph (CBG) to recommend items for users on content curation social networks. The proposed CBG combine the similarity of items with bipartite graph to improve diversity in recommendation. We further employ content similarity to rerank the recommendation results of improved bipartite graph and enhance the visual quality of recommendation. Experimental results and corresponding analysis demonstrate the proposed CBG method has a good ability of recommending broader images compared to traditional bipartite graph based method. And the proposed CBG method is able to result in varies recommendation results.

CCSNs provides valuable category information. In our future work, we would consider to leverage board category information in recommendation systems to improve its performance.

References

1. Liben-Nowell, D., Novak, J., Kumar, R., et al.: Geographic routing in social networks. Proc. Nat. Acad. Sci. **102**(33), 11623–11628 (2005)
2. Zarro, M., Hall, C.: Pinterest: social collecting for linking using sharing. In: Proceedings of the National Academy of Science ACM, pp. 417–418 (2012)
3. Catherine, H., Michael, Z.: Social curation on the website Pinterest.com. Proc. Am. Soc. Inf. Sci. Technol. **49**(1), 1–9 (2012)
4. Cinar, Y.G., Zoghbi, S., Marie-Francine, M.: Inferring user interests on social media from text and images. In: Proceedings of the IEEE International Conference on Data Mining Workshop, pp. 1342–1347 (2015)
5. Geng, X., Zhang, H., Song, Z., et al.: One of a kind: user profiling by social curation. In: Proceedings of the ACM, pp. 567–576 (2014)

6. Yang, X., Li, Y., Luo, J.: Pinterest board recommendation for twitter users. In: Proceedings of the ACM, pp. 963–966 (2015)
7. Pham, T., Li, X., Cong, G., et al.: A general graph-based model for recommendation in event-based social networks. In: Proceedings of the IEEE International Conference on Data Engineering, pp. 567–578 (2015)
8. Li, J., Ma, S., Hong, S.: Recommendation on social network based on graph model. In: Proceedings of the Control Conference, pp. 7548–7551. IEEE (2012)
9. Ergn, G.: Human sexual contact network as a bipartite graph. Proc. Phys. A Stat. Mech. Appl. **308**(1), 483–488 (2001)
10. Bearman, P.S., Moody, J., Stovel, K.: Chains of affection: the structure of adolescent romantic and sexual networks. Proc. Am. J. Sociol, **110**(1), 44–91 (2004)
11. Holme, P., Liljeros, F., Edling, C., et al.: Network bipartivity. Proc. Phys. Rev. E Stat. Nonlinear Soft Matter Phys. **68**(5 Pt 2), 056107 (2003)
12. Lambiotte, R., Ausloos, M.: N-body decomposition of bipartite author networks. Proc. Phys. Rev. E Stat. Nonlinear Soft Matter Phys. **72**(2), 066117 (2005)
13. Zhang, Y.C., Blattner, M., Yu, Y.K.: Heat conduction process on community networks as a recommendation model. Proc. Phys. Rev. Lett. **99**(15), 12505–12508 (2008)
14. Sheng, M.S., Zhang, Z.K.: Diffusion-based recommendation in collaborative tagging systems. Proc. Chin. Phys. Lett. **26**(11), 250–253 (2009)
15. Zhou, T., Ren, J., Medo, M., et al.: Bipartite network projection and personal recommendation. Proc. Phys. Rev. E Stat. Nonlinear Soft Matter Phys. **76**(2), 70–80 (2007)
16. Krizhevsky, A., Sutskever, I., Hinton, G.E.: ImageNet classification with deep convolutional neural networks. In: Proceedings of the International Conference on Neural Information, pp. 1097–1105 (2012)
17. Lecun, Y., Bengio, Y., Hinton, G.: Deep learning. Proc. Nature **521**(7553), 436–444 (2015)
18. Schmidhuber, J.: Deep learning in neural networks: an overview. Proc. Neural Netw. Off. J. Int. Neural Netw. Soc. **61**, 85–117 (2014)

Initialized Frame Attention Networks for Video Question Answering

Kun Gao[1(✉)], Xianglei Zhu[2], and Yahong Han[1]

[1] School of Computer Science and Technology, Tianjin University, Tianjin, China
{gaokun,yahong}@tju.edu.cn
[2] China Automotive Technology and Research Center, Tianjin, China
zhuxianglei@catarc.ac.cn

Abstract. Video Question Answering (Video QA) is one of the important and challenging problems in multimedia and computer vision research. In this paper, we propose a novel framework, called initialized frame attention networks (IFAN). This framework uses long short term memory (LSTM) networks to encode visual information of videos, then initializes the language model by the encoded features. Based on the visual and semantic features, we can get an appropriate answer. In particular, in this IFAN framework, we effectively integrate temporal attention mechanism to focus on the salient frames of videos, which are associated to the questions. In order to verify the effectiveness of the proposed framework, we conduct experiments on TACoS dataset. It achieves good performances on both hard level and easy level of TACoS dataset.

Keywords: Visual information · Initialize · Attention mechanism

1 Introduction

The recent development of deep learning technologies has achieved successes in many visual and natural language processing (NLP) tasks. Deep convolutional neural networks (CNNs) have promoted the development of many visual tasks, such as action recognition [14], image classification [13], and object retrieval [18–20]. In addition, recurrent neural networks (RNNs), particularly LSTM [1], play an important role in the NLP field. Recently, there has been attracted great interest in many integration tasks, which bridge the visual and the semantic information, and these tasks aim at deeply understanding the visual contents. A great way of showing one's comprehension about videos is to be able to answer questions about them. Thus, this paper proposes the IFAN framework for the Video QA task.

Research on Video QA is mostly driven by video captioning [21,22] and image question answering (Image QA) tasks. In contrast to Image QA, Video QA confronts many challenges, such as background noises, motion speed, view point changes and so on. In particular, the temporal information among consecutive video frames aggravates the difficulty of Video QA. On the other hand, many

© Springer Nature Singapore Pte Ltd. 2018
B. Huet et al. (Eds.): ICIMCS 2017, CCIS 819, pp. 349–359, 2018.
https://doi.org/10.1007/978-981-10-8530-7_34

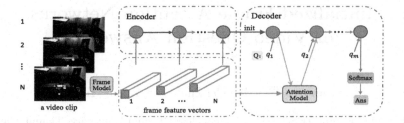

Fig. 1. The proposed initialized frame attention networks framework for Video QA.

creative ideas of video captioning can be transferred to Video QA task. For video captioning, Venugopalan et al. [3] proposed an encoder-decoder framework to generate the video descriptions. In the encoder part, it aggregates deep frame features to the video representation by average pooling. However, this aggregated mode might ignore the difference of frames and does not highlight the important frames. So Yao et al. [4] integrated the attention mechanism to increase the attention weights of semantically associated video frames, which are vital for generating descriptions.

Based on the above discussions, we can analyse two key points to solve the Video QA task. Firstly, how to utilize the temporal information to deeply understand visual contents of videos. Secondly, how to benefit from the idea of attention mechanism which is successfully applied in other visual tasks, and consequently build a close link between textual questions and video frames. Many related work also focuses on these aspects. The first work on video-based question answering was proposed by Tu et al. [9], which builds a question answering system based on a joint parse graph from videos and texts. Then Zhu et al. [10] presented an encoder-decoder approach to learn temporal structures of videos and answer multiple-choice questions by a ranking loss. This work focuses on the temporal domain and intends to train the encoder part in an unsupervised method with large number of video data. However, this temporal model and question pair model are trained in separated way which weakens the relation between the video contents and the texts. Based on the current research work, there are some problems which need to be addressed on Video QA task.

Motivated by the above discussions, we present a novel framework named IFAN for Video QA, as illustrated in Fig. 1. Our proposed framework is composed of two components: encoder part and decoder part. At first, we generate the frame feature vectors by our designed frame model. Then in the encoder part, we use LSTM model to encode these frame features to generate the overall visual representation, and utilize this representation to initialize the language model of decoder part. Meanwhile, for decoder part, we integrate the frame attention mechanism to decode visual information of question-related frames. Finally, we use softmax classifier to choose the best answer. We conduct experiments on the public dataset: TACoS dataset.

This paper mainly makes three-fold contributions for the Video QA. We summarize the contributions as follows: (1) We utilize the visual information and design an integral framework which can be learned by end to end fashion. The network can effectively bridge visual and semantic features. (2) We integrate the frame attention to the language LSTM. Thus, this model combines questions and video frames effectively and has the ability to focus on question-related frames. (3) We conduct extensive experiments on TACoS dataset, and the results demonstrate that the proposed IFAN is effective.

2   The Proposed Method

In this section, we describe our proposed IFAN framework in detail. First, we introduce the process of generating frame feature vectors by using frame model. Then in the encoder part, we use LSTM model to generate the overall visual representation, and utilize it to initialize the language model of decoder part. We also integrate the frame attention mechanism to attend to the question-related video frames. Finally, we detailed discuss how to choose the best answer.

2.1   Generating the Frame Feature Vectors Using Frame Model

In this subsection, we describe the process of generating video representation. Besides, we obtain the video representation by analysing consecutive video frames.

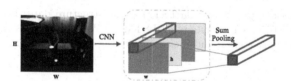

Fig. 2. Frame model based on CNN.

Given a video clip V, we sample N frames and extract the convolutional feature of each frame by using designed frame model, as shown in Fig. 2. For each frame f_k we extract the convolutional feature maps F_k with VGGNet [11], then we generate the frame feature vector v_k by sum pooling strategy.

$$F_k = CNN_{vgg}(f_k), \tag{1}$$

$$v_k = SumPooling(F_k). \tag{2}$$

Unlike previous studies which use features from the last fully connected layer, we get the feature maps F_k from the last convolutional layer, which retain the spatial structure information of the original frame. In order to explain the process of generating the frame feature vector clearly, we make the following definition: the input frame size is $H \times W$, and the dimension of the extracted feature maps F_k is $c \times h \times w$, where $h \times w$ is the spatial scale of each channel on F_k, and c

is the number of channels. In addition, we aggregate the extracted feature maps by sum pooling to get the frame feature vector with dimension of c. Thus, for each frame f_k, we generate the vector v_k with the dimension of c. Finally, for the given video clip V, we obtain the frame feature vectors $\{v_1, v_2, \ldots, v_N\}$, and regard them to represent the given video clip.

2.2   The Encoder Part

The visual information in videos is essential for Video QA task. It provides a holistic understanding of video contents. From the perspective of overall information, we have a good comprehension of characters, environment and so on. In this encoder part, we utilize the LSTM model to generate deep visual representation.

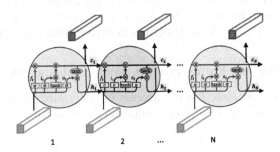

Fig. 3. The encoder part based on LSTM (This structure dates from http://colah. github.io/posts/2015-08-Understanding-LSTMs/). We input the frame feature vectors to LSTM model in sequence, and then generate the deep visual representation.

After obtaining frame feature vectors $\{v_1, v_2, \ldots, v_N\}$, we put them into the nodes of LSTM model in sequence, as described in Fig. 3. For each frame feature vector, we use a basic LSTM unit to encode the visual information. In the following part, we first describe the structure of the basic LSTM unit, then we describe the process of generating deep visual representation.

LSTM is wildly applied to process sequence problems [12]. In the basic LSTM unit structure, there is a unit called the memory cell. It records the state variation from the current moment to the next step, and it is regulated by three gates: input gate, forget gate, and output gate. All these gates determine whether the information could be passed from them. Specifically, for the frame feature vector $v_k (k = 1, 2, \ldots, N)$, the input gate i encodes the input v_k and the former hidden state h_{k-1}, then decide how much information alters the memory cell state. Besides, the forget gate f controls whether to forget the former memory state c_{k-1} or not. In addition, the output gate o modulates what percentage of memory cell information could be transformed to the current hidden unit h_k. Thus, for the frame feature vector v_N, we get the last hidden state h_N and the last memory cell state c_N, and regard the concatenate vector of $\{h_N, c_N\}$ as the ultimate visual representation of whole video clip.

2.3 The Decoder Part

After getting the visual representation $\{h_N, c_N\}$, we utilize it to initialize the language model of decoder part. As described in Subsect. 2.2, we initialize the language model with the deep visual representation. By initializing, the language model has an advanced perception of visual information. In this subsection, we depict how to utilize the language model to decode visual information, and establish a close relationship between vision and questions.

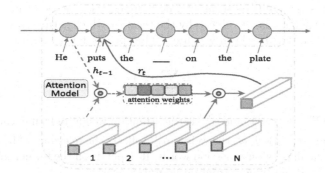

Fig. 4. The decoder part. We utilize the encoded feature to initialize the language model and integrate frame attention to focus on question-related frames.

Note that, modeling questions is vital for Video QA task. The commonly employed strategy is to use CNNs [5] or RNNs [16] to extract semantic vectors. This general method gives rise to the resulting question representations lack visual information from the videos, which is essential for understanding the video contents. Thus, we integrate the attention mechanism to the language model to selectively focus on the question-related frames. As shown in Fig. 4, the unit of language model we proposed is an extension of the basic LSTM unit structure, for the reason that other than the current sequence input, there is another input to each LSTM node, which is introduced by attention mechanism term.

Given a question $Q = \{q_1, q_2, \ldots, q_m\}$, we learn the word tokens as follows:

$$p_i = OH(q_i), \tag{3}$$

$$x_i = W_e p_i. \tag{4}$$

Where $OH(\cdot)$ transforms a word q_i to its one hot representation p_i, a vector that there is only one nonzero value in the position i corresponding to the word vocabulary. The matrix W_e transforms the one hot vector p_i into the d_e dimensional embedding space x_i. These embedding vectors $\{x_1, x_2, \ldots, x_m\}$ are fed into the language LSTM model in sequence. The update rules can be defined as follows:

$$i_t = \sigma(W_{xi}x_t + W_{hi}h_{t-1} + W_{ri}r_t + b_i), \tag{5}$$

$$f_t = \sigma(W_{xf}x_t + W_{hf}h_{t-1} + W_{rf}r_t + b_f), \tag{6}$$

$$o_t = \sigma(W_{xo}x_t + W_{ho}h_{t-1} + W_{ro}r_t + b_o), \tag{7}$$

$$g_t = \emptyset(W_{xg}x_t + W_{hg}h_{t-1} + W_{rg}r_t + b_g), \tag{8}$$

$$c_t = f_t \odot c_{t-1} + i_t \odot g_t, \tag{9}$$

$$h_t = o_t \odot \emptyset(c_t). \tag{10}$$

Where $\sigma(\cdot)$ is the sigmoid activation function, $\emptyset(\cdot)$ is the tanh activation function, and $\odot$ is the multiplication operator among relevant elements. The frame attention mechanism is introduced by the term r_t, which is the representation of the video frame that has been weighted. The specific formulation is as follows:

$$r_t = \sum_{k=1}^{N} \alpha_k^{(t)} v_k \tag{11}$$

Where $\sum_{k=1}^{N} \alpha_k^{(t)} = 1$, and $\alpha_k^{(t)}$ is the attention weight of frame feature vector v_k at t-th time step. Besides, the weight $\alpha_k^{(t)}$ reflects the relevance of frame feature vector v_k with all previous question words. It depends on the former hidden state h_{t-1} and is modeled by an attention neural network.

$$e_k^{(t)} = w^T tanh(W_{he}h_{t-1} + 2DTempConv(F)) \tag{12}$$

In this formulation, F denotes the whole frame feature vectors, which are obtained in Subsect. 2.1, with the dimension of $Num \times Dim$, where Num denotes the number of video frames, and Dim denotes the dimension of each frame feature vector. We conduct 2D convolution on F. Next, we get the unnormalized relevance score $e_k^{(t)}$. Then we normalize it to get the frame attention weight $\alpha_k^{(t)}$.

$$\alpha_k^{(t)} = exp\{e_k^{(t)}\}/\sum_{k=1}^{N} exp\{e_k^{(t)}\} \tag{13}$$

Consequently, under the effect of language LSTM structure with M nodes, we get the last hidden state h_M and memory cell state c_M from the last language LSTM node. Contrast to the conventional approach [5,10] which makes the last hidden state h_M to be the final representation, we regard the concatenate vector of h_M and c_M as the ultimate representation of the whole question Q.

2.4   Learning and Inference

After getting the ultimate question representation, we vectorize the representation to be a hidden vector, then execute ReLU and dropout on it. Afterwards, we vectorize it to the length as same as the number of candidate vocabulary. We train the network with RMSProp update rule, mini-batch size of 100, and a global learning rate of 3×10^{-4}. Besides, we apply the standard accuracy metric to evaluate the performance.

3   Experiments

In this section, we first introduce the TACoS dataset, which is used for evaluating the performance. Then we introduce the experimental setup. In the following part, we evaluate our proposed IFAN framework from three aspects: the function of initialization of decoder part, the advantage of frame attention mechanism, and the approach of feature concatenation. At last, comparison with the previous methods which are conducted on TACoS dataset and discussions are presented.

3.1   Dataset

We use the TACoS dataset [10] for Video QA task, which generates question answering pairs in the cooking scenario. It includes 127 long videos with total 18227 video clips. This dataset generates two difficult levels: hard level and easy level. And they are divided into three splits, separately. For each split, it includes three parts: past part, present part, and future part. In our work, we use the present part to evaluate our proposed IFAN. In this dataset, the present part is divided into training, validation, and testing sets.

3.2   Experimental Setup

In this subsection, we introduce the experimental setup, and choose the hyper-parameters via the validation set. For each video clip, we sample 26 frames, and resize these frames to 240×320. Correspondingly, in the encoder part, the nodes of LSTM model are set to 26. For the decoder part, we set the number of language LSTM nodes to the same number. The dimensions of these two LSTM hidden units are all set to 256, and the embedding size is set to 512. After filtering out the lower frequency words, we set 650 as the number of answer vocabulary for easy level, and set 2000 for hard level.

3.3   Evaluation of Initialization of Decoder Part

In order to evaluate the performance of the initialization, we remove the encoder part and build the compared framework, named frame attention networks (FAN). In this FAN framework, the initialization states of the hidden units in the language model are set to zero. In this subsection, we compare and analyze the frameworks of IFAN and FAN with the same parameters.

From Table 1, we can see that the performance of the proposed IFAN has 0.61% and 0.22% improvements than FAN framework on hard level and easy level of TACoS. According to the results, we know that the encoder-decoder structure is more efficient. Through initialization of encoded features, the language LSTM has a clear command of the visual information, which is benefit for the language model to generate the appropriate answer.

Table 1. Comparison of IFAN and FAN on TACoS hard level and easy level.

Method	Hard				Easy			
	$split_1$	$split_2$	$split_3$	Mean	$split_1$	$split_2$	$split_3$	Mean
IFAN	85.57%	85.74%	84.32%	85.21%	92.60%	92.96%	91.16%	92.24%
FAN	85.09%	85.41%	83.28%	84.60%	92.30%	92.74%	91.03%	92.02%

3.4   Evaluation of the Attention Mechanism

In the IFAN framework, we integrate the attention mechanism to the language LSTM. By this strategy, this framework generates the attention distribution over the video frames, and establishes a close contact between the semantic and the visual information. In this subsection, we evaluate the effectiveness of this attention strategy. In order to verify conveniently, we remove the attention mechanism in the decoder part, and in the language model, we only input the question tokens in sequence, named initialized language LSTM networks (ILLN). The compared results of IFAN and ILLN frameworks are shown in Table 2.

Table 2. Comparison of IFAN and ILLN on TACoS hard level and easy level.

Method	Hard				Easy			
	$split_1$	$split_2$	$split_3$	Mean	$split_1$	$split_2$	$split_3$	Mean
IFAN	85.57%	85.74%	84.32%	85.21%	92.60%	92.96%	91.16%	92.24%
ILLN	85.37%	85.63%	83.77%	84.92%	92.22%	92.52%	91.02%	91.92%

From Table 2, we can see the accuracy of IFAN is higher than ILLN on both hard and easy levels. The results demonstrate that the attention strategy is applicable to bridge the vision and language to tackle the problem of video-based question answering.

3.5   Evaluation of the Feature Concatenation

In the language model of IFAN framework, different with the commonly method [10] which only regards the last hidden state to be the ultimate representation, we also utilize the memory cell state to strengthen the semantic information. To evaluate the effectiveness of this proposal, we design the IFAN_h framework which only regards the hidden state to be the final feature. The results conducted on hard and easy levels are shown in Table 3.

In Table 3, we can see that the performance of IFAN is better than IFAN_h on two difficult levels of TACoS dataset. By comparing and analyzing, we conclude that the memory cell state can enhance the semantic information effectively.

Table 3. Comparison of IFAN and IFAN_h on hard level and easy level.

Method	Hard				Easy			
	$split_1$	$split_2$	$split_3$	Mean	$split_1$	$split_2$	$split_3$	Mean
IFAN	85.57%	85.74%	84.32%	85.21%	92.60%	92.96%	91.16%	92.24%
IFAN_h	84.49%	84.98%	83.12%	84.20%	91.90%	92.08%	90.50%	91.49%

3.6 Comparison with Previous Methods

In this subsection, we compare our results with several methods conducted on TACoS dataset for Video QA task. They are GRUmodel method [10], ConvNets method [10], and the CCA method [10].

Table 4. Comparison with previous methods on hard level and easy level.

Method	Hard				Easy			
	$split_1$	$split_2$	$split_3$	Mean	$split_1$	$split_2$	$split_3$	Mean
IFAN	85.57%	85.74%	84.32%	85.21%	92.60%	92.96%	91.16%	92.24%
GRUmodel [10]	66.90%	66.20%	68.20%	67.10%	79.10%	81.90%	78.10%	79.70%
ConvNets [10]	–	–	–	65.50%	–	–	–	76.30%
CCA [10]	–	–	–	–	67.10%	64.90%	63.20%	65.10%

As shown in Table 4, compared with GRUmodel method, our IFAN has a 18.11% advantage on hard level and 12.54% on easy level. Besides, it outperforms the ConvNets method 19.71% on hard level and 15.94% on easy level. It also boosts the performance of CCA by 27.14% on easy level of TACoS dataset.

4 Conclusion

In this paper, we propose a novel IFAN framework for Video QA task. This framework is designed based on the encoder-decoder architecture, which learn visual and semantic information by end-to-end fashion. The encoder part encodes the viusal information, which is benefit for language model to decode semantic information. Besides, the strategy of frame attention mechanism automatically assists the language model to fix its attention on the salient frames which are associated to questions. Besides, the memory cell state in the language model effectively strengths the semantic information. Thus, our proposed IFAN achieves good performances on both hard and easy levels on TACoS dataset.

Acknowledgment. This work was supported by the NSFC (under Grant U1509206, 61472276).

References

1. Hochreiter, S., Schmidhuber, J.: Long short-term memory. Neural Comput. **9**(8), 1735–1780 (1997)
2. Zhu, Y., Groth, O., Bernstein, M., Fei-Fei, L.: Visual7W: grounded question answering in images. In: Proceedings of the IEEE Conference on Computer Vision and Pattern Recognition, pp. 4995–5004 (2016)
3. Venugopalan, S., Xu, H., Donahue, J., Rohrbach, M., Mooney, R., Saenko, K.: Translating videos to natural language using deep recurrent neural networks. arXiv preprint arXiv:1412.4729 (2014)
4. Yao, L., Torabi, A., Cho, K., Ballas, N., Pal, C., Larochelle, H., Courville, A.: Describing videos by exploiting temporal structure. In: Proceedings of the IEEE International Conference on Computer Vision, pp. 4507–4515 (2015)
5. Yang, Z., He, X., Gao, J., Deng, L., Smola, A.: Stacked attention networks for image question answering. In: Proceedings of the IEEE Conference on Computer Vision and Pattern Recognition, pp. 21–29 (2016)
6. Xu, H., Saenko, K.: Ask, attend and answer: exploring question-guided spatial attention for visual question answering. In: Leibe, B., Matas, J., Sebe, N., Welling, M. (eds.) ECCV 2016. LNCS, vol. 9911, pp. 451–466. Springer, Cham (2016). https://doi.org/10.1007/978-3-319-46478-7_28
7. Shih, K.J., Singh, S., Hoiem, D.: Where to look: focus regions for visual question answering. In: Proceedings of the IEEE Conference on Computer Vision and Pattern Recognition, pp. 4613–4621 (2016)
8. Chen, K., Wang, J., Chen, L.C., Gao, H., Xu, W., Nevatia, R.: ABC-CNN: an attention based convolutional neural network for visual question answering. arXiv preprint arXiv:1511.05960 (2015)
9. Tu, K., Meng, M., Lee, M.W., Choe, T.E., Zhu, S.C.: Joint video and text parsing for understanding events and answering queries. IEEE MultiMed. **21**(2), 42–70 (2014)
10. Zhu, L., Xu, Z., Yang, Y., Hauptmann, A.G.: Uncovering temporal context for video question and answering. arXiv preprint arXiv:1511.04670 (2015)
11. Simonyan, K., Zisserman, A.: Very deep convolutional networks for large-scale image recognition. arXiv preprint arXiv:1409.1556 (2014)
12. Karpathy, A., Fei-Fei, L.: Deep visual-semantic alignments for generating image descriptions. In: Proceedings of the IEEE Conference on Computer Vision and Pattern Recognition, pp. 3128–3137 (2015)
13. Krizhevsky, A., Sutskever, I., Hinton, G.E.: Imagenet classification with deep convolutional neural networks. In: Advances in Neural Information Processing Systems, pp. 1097–1105 (2012)
14. Simonyan, K., Zisserman, A.: Two-stream convolutional networks for action recognition in videos. In: Advances in Neural Information Processing Systems, pp. 568–576 (2014)
15. Ma, L., Lu, Z., Li, H.: Learning to answer questions from image using convolutional neural network. In: AAAI, p. 16 (2016)
16. Zeng, K.H., Chen, T.H., Chuang, C.Y., Liao, Y.H., Niebles, J.C., Sun, M.: Leveraging video descriptions to learn video question answering. In: AAAI, pp. 4334–4340 (2017)
17. Vilariño, D.L., Brea, V.M., Cabello, D., Pardo, J.M.: Discrete-time CNN for image segmentation by active contours. Pattern Recogn. Lett. **19**, 721–734 (1998)

18. Hong, R., Zhang, L., Zhang, C., Zimmermann, R.: Flickr circles: aesthetic tendency discovery by multi-view regularized topic modeling. IEEE Trans. Multimed. **18**, 1555–1567 (2016)
19. Hong, R., Hu, Z., Wang, R., Wang, M., Tao, D.: Multi-view object retrieval via multi-scale topic models. IEEE Trans. Image Process. **25**, 5814–5827 (2016)
20. Hong, R., Yang, Y., Wang, M., Hua, X.S.: Learning visual semantic relationships for efficient visual retrieval. IEEE Trans. Big Data **1**, 152–161 (2015)
21. Yang, Z., Han, Y., Wang Z.: Catching the temporal regions-of-interest for video captioning. In: Proceedings of the ACM International Conference on Multimedia, MM 2017. ACM (2017)
22. Li, G., Ma, S., Han, Y.: Summarization-based video caption via deep neural networks. In: Proceedings of the 23rd ACM International Conference on Multimedia, pp. 1191–1194 (2015)

MFCC: An Efficient and Effective Matrix Factorization Model Based on Co-clustering

Wenjuan Yang$^{(\boxtimes)}$, Le Wu, Xueliang Liu, and Chunxiao Fan

Hefei University of Technology, Hefei, China
xiaobie.hfut@gmail.com

Abstract. Collaborative Filtering (CF) is a popular way to build recommender systems and has been widely deployed by many e-commerce websites. Generally, there are two parallel research directions on CF, one is to improve the prediction accuracy ~ (i.e., effectiveness) of CF algorithms and others focus on reducing time cost of CF algorithms ~ (i.e., efficiency). Nevertheless, the problem of how to combine the complementary advantages of these two directions, and design a CF algorithm that is both effective and efficient remains pretty much open. To this end, in this paper, we provide a Matrix Factorization based on Co-Clustering (MFCC) algorithm to address the problem. Specifically, we first adopt a co-clustering algorithm to cluster the user-item rating matrix into several separate sub rating matrices. After that, we provide an efficient matrix factorization algorithm by utilizing the strong connections of users and items in each cluster. In the meantime, this process is also efficient as we can simultaneously compute the matrix factorization for each cluster as there exists little interactions among different clusters. Finally, the experimental results show both the effectiveness and efficiency of our proposed model.

Keywords: Co-clustering · Matrix factorization · Collaborative filtering

1 Introduction

The rapid development of Internet has brought massive information to users for their different types of demand in the information age [7, 10, 13, 25, 26]. However, it brings a new issue called the problem of information overload, which causes difficulties for users to choose their individual information and correspondingly reduces the utilization rate. To solve the problem, the recommender system begins to emerge [1, 2].

Collaborative filtering (CF) is one of the most widely used algorithms for many e-commerce sites in recommender systems [1–3] until now. It identifies users whose tastes are similar to those of the active users. Then it recommends items that those users have liked. And many online companies such as Yahoo and Amazon apply CF to provide recommendations to their customers [2]. In particular, CF mainly includes two types of algorithms: the neighbor-based CF [3] and model-based CF [4]. The neighbor-based CF algorithm is simple and easy to interpret. Nevertheless, these neighbor-based CF suffers from high time complexity and relatively low accuracy as it is hard for them to find reliable neighbors when the user-item rating matrix is sparse. On the contrary, the latent based models show good accuracies from both research and industry area.

© Springer Nature Singapore Pte Ltd. 2018
B. Huet et al. (Eds.): ICIMCS 2017, CCIS 819, pp. 360–370, 2018.
https://doi.org/10.1007/978-981-10-8530-7_35

The core idea of these latent factor models is to project both users and items in the low latent space, then the predicted rating can be computed in this latent space [4, 9]. Despite the success of these latent based models, in the real world, since there are millions of users and items in the recommender systems, the time efficiency of these CF algorithms needs to be further improved. Hence, how to improve these CF algorithms' efficiency turns to another research problem.

In fact, in order to solve the above problem, many researchers have integrated clustering methods into recommender systems [6, 8]. As a result, these algorithms can cluster the original user-item rating matrix into several sub small matrices, then the traditional CF algorithms can be applied in these small matrices. However, as reported by the current research results, the clustering stage can reduce the effectiveness to some degree.

In this paper, we study the problem of how to improve both efficiency and effectiveness of the CF algorithms, and propose a novel Matrix Factorization based on Co-Clustering (MFCC) algorithm to solve this problem. The core idea of this method is that it utilizes the properties of the clustering algorithm into the CF algorithm. Specifically, we first group the original user-item rating matrix into multiple small sub rating matrices by a co-clustering algorithm. Due to the properties of each sub matrix, the users and items in this matrix are strongly connected. We push these strong connections in each sub matrix into the latent models, and ensure the factorization of each user and item in each cluster are similar. As a result, the time complexity of the training phase is significantly reduced, and the effectiveness of the final prediction is guaranteed. Experiments on a publicly available dataset have demonstrated both the efficiency and effectiveness of the proposed MFCC.

The remainder of this paper is constructed as follows: we first introduce the related works on recommender systems, description of problem definitions and related knowledge in second part. In Sect. 3, we introduce the framework of this paper and the related description. Our experiments and conclusion are illustrated in the Sects. 4 and 5 separately.

2　Related Work

As the most popular technique in recommender systems, collaborative filtering (CF) has received a great success in various applications [2, 23, 24]. Specifically, CF mainly includes the neighbor-based CF and the model-based CF algorithm, moreover, the model-based CF has a better performance. Probabilistic Matrix Factorization (PMF) [9] is a classical model-based CF, which can not only handle large-scale datasets quickly, but also obtain a reasonable accuracy. So many algorithms are developed to further improve its effectiveness. For example, the NHPMF [5] algorithm significantly enhanced the accuracy than PMF.

Although the model-based CF has been widely studied, with the rapid increase of data size, the algorithm tends to be inefficient to meet the requirement of real-world applications. Applying clustering to CF [6, 19] is mainly due to the following reasons. Firstly, the sizes of generated classes by clustering are reduced. Secondly, the clustering can also reduce the scarcity of ratings. At first, many scholars only considered the application of clustering to items [6, 11] or users [12] to improve the efficiency.

However, these methods only consider one dimension of the matrix information and lost the other one. To address this issue, the co-clustering based on CF approaches are proposed [8]. Compared with the classical clustering methods, the co-clustering can effectively find the hidden clustering structure of the user-item rating matrix and cluster the above two dimensions at the same time.

Earlier, a co-clustering algorithm for information theory [14] was proposed. Later, Agarwal [15] developed a method by utilizing a generalized linear model to smooth the error function. Subsequently, several researchers suggested how to set the reference standard of the number of cluster categories [16]. But all these methods are hard clustering [17], namely, each user, item and rating only belongs to a single cluster. Therefore, some scholars proposed to employ the fuzzy clustering [18, 20, 21] to relax the restrictions on the attribution of categories.

As we can see, although model-based algorithms can obtain high accuracies, they are insufficiently efficient. And co-clustering algorithms can accelerate the process of handling large-scale datasets. However, they will sacrifice the accuracy. In this paper, we propose to combine the matrix factorization and co-clustering and present a method called MFCC, where the efficiency of the algorithm is improved and a reasonable accuracy is insured.

3   Description of the Recommendation Algorithm

As shown in Fig. 1, the overall flow chart of MFCC includes two main steps: co-clustering and rating training. The first step is to divide the user-item rating matrix into several small ones. The second step is used to predict the unknown ratings of these small matrices with matrix factorization in parallel. Based on the above strategy, we can recommend items based on the obtained ratings.

3.1   The Proposed Algorithm

The mathematical notations used in co-clustering are shown in Table 1. As mentioned above, the co-clustering algorithm groups the original matrix into several small clusters, and each small cluster is closely related. According to the close relations, we can obtain less computation and higher accuracy in the second step.

Suppose we want to divide the user-item rating matrix into small ones. Different from classical clustering approaches, in each iteration, co-clustering will first cluster all the users, items, and ratings respectively and assign them probabilities, namely, one for each cluster. Then the co-clustering integrates these obtained soft assignments to improve the next round of clustering. The above process will repeat until it is converged.

In particular, suppose is the probability that the user, item and rating will be assigned to the cluster. According to the co-clustering, we can formulate it as

$$p(k|u, v, r) = \frac{[p(k|u) + a] \times [p(k|v) + b] \times [p(r|k) + c]}{\sum_{k' \in K} [p(k'|u) + a] \times [p(k'|v) + b] \times [p(r|k') + c]} \tag{1}$$

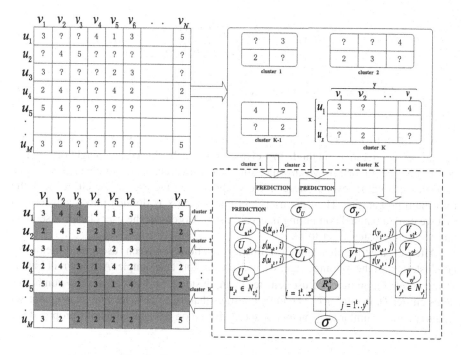

Fig. 1. Framework of MFCC recommendation

Table 1. Notations used in co-clustering.

Notations	Description
U, u	User sets, the current user
V, v	Item sets, the current item
K, k	Cluster sets, the current cluster
R, r	Rating matrix, the current rating
$p(k\|u)$	Probability of cluster given user
$p(k\|v)$	Probability of cluster given item
$p(k\|u, v, r)$	Probability of given user, item and rating

where $p(k|u)$, $p(k|v)$ and $p(r|k)$ denotes the probability that each element will be assigned to the cluster k. In practice, we set a, b, c to 0.00000001 to avoid the denominator from being zero. Meanwhile, the above mentioned probabilities can be estimated as:

$$p(k|u) = \frac{\sum_{v \in V(u)} p(k|u, v, r)}{\sum_{k' \in K} \sum_{v \in V(u)} p(k'|u, v, r)} \tag{2}$$

$$p(k|v) = \frac{\sum_{u \in U(v)} p(k|u, v, r)}{\sum_{k' \in K} \sum_{u \in U(v)} p(k'|u, v, r)} \qquad (3)$$

$$p(r|k) = \frac{\sum p(k|u, v, r)}{\sum_r \sum p(k|u, v, r')} \qquad (4)$$

According to Eqs. (2), (3) and (4), when the above co-clustering process is converged by an iterative method, the elements in each cluster are neighbors, which constitute a neighbor set. Meanwhile, since the above cluster assignment is soft, one user may belong to several clusters. We simply assign the user to the cluster with the maximum probability. Then the user-item rating matrix is divided into K clusters, so that we can do parallel computing in each cluster. Moreover, the user cluster is set to C and the item cluster is set to D.

After excavating the mutual influence relations between users and items by co-clustering, in the training stage, we take cluster k as an example. As shown in Fig. 1, x^k represents the number of user cluster C_i in cluster k, and y^k denotes the number of items cluster D_j in cluster k. The model ensures that user i behaves like its neighbor set C_i and item j is similar to its neighbor set D_j. Based on this, the equations proposed are as follows:

$$U_i^k = \sum_{a \in C_i} s(i, a) * U_i^k + \phi_{U^k}, \quad \phi_{U^k} \sim N(0, \sigma_U^2 \omega) \qquad (5)$$

$$V_j^k = \sum_{a \in D_j} t(j, a) * V_j^k + \phi_{V^k}, \quad \phi_{V^k} \sim N(0, \sigma_V^2 \omega) \qquad (6)$$

From the above two formulas, we can see that the latent feature vectors of each user (item) consist of two terms. The first term is the weighted average of the user's (item's) neighbors, where s represents the similarity between user i and user a, and t represents the similarity between item j and item a. The second term is the divergence between each user and item parameterized by the variance σ_U^2 and σ_V^2. It is clear that Eqs. (5) and (6) can be transformed into the following formulas when the variance is zero:

$$p(U^k|S, \sigma_U^2) = \prod_{i=1^k}^{x^k} N(\sum_{a \in C_i} s(i, a) * U_a^k, \sigma_U^2 \omega) \qquad (7)$$

$$p(V^k|T, \sigma_V^2) = \prod_{j=1^k}^{y^k} N(\sum_{a \in D_j} t(j, a) * V_a^k, \sigma_V^2 \omega) \qquad (8)$$

Through the above two equations and the observed rating data, we define the following expression:

$$p(R^k|U^k, V^k, \sigma^2) = \prod_{i=1^k}^{x^k} \prod_{j=1^k}^{y^k} [N(R_{ij}^k|U_i^{kT} V_j^k, \sigma^2)]^{\omega_{ij}} \qquad (9)$$

where ω_{ij} is an indicator function that is equal to 1 if user i rated item j and equal to 0 otherwise. According to Eqs. (7), (8) and (9), the following equation can be obtained from the Bayesian inference:

$$p(U^k, V^k | R^k, \sigma^2, \sigma_U^2, \sigma_V^2) \propto p(U^k | S, \sigma_U^2) * p(V^k | T, \sigma_V^2) * p(R^k | U^k, V^k, \sigma^2) \quad (10)$$

Fixing the hyperparameters $(\sigma^2, \sigma_U^2, \sigma_V^2)$, the maximization of Eq. (10) is equivalent to minimizing the following cost function:

$$
\begin{aligned}
E^k = \; & \frac{1}{2} \sum_{i=1^k}^{x^k} \sum_{j=1^k}^{y^k} \omega_{ij} (R_{ij}^k - U_i^{kT} V_j^k)^2 \\
& + \frac{1}{2} \lambda_U \sum_{i=1^k}^{x^k} \left\| U_i^k - \sum_{a \in C_i} s(i,a) * U_a^k \right\|_F^2 \\
& + \frac{1}{2} \lambda_V \sum_{j=1^k}^{y^k} \left\| V_j^k - \sum_{a \in D_j} t(j,a) * V_a^k \right\|_F^2
\end{aligned}
\quad (11)
$$

In the above equation, $\lambda_U = \sigma^2 / \sigma_U^2$, $\lambda_V = \sigma^2 / \sigma_V^2$. Obviously, it consists of three parts. The first is the relations between the actual ratings and the predicted ratings. The following two terms are the neighbors information and they are smoothed by the parameter λ_U and λ_V. What's more, the parameter λ_U controls how much the user neighbor influences while λ_V controls how much the item neighbor influences on the cost function. In order to reach the minimum value of Eq. (11), we use the random gradient descent method on U_i^k and V_j^k for each user and item. So we give the functions as follows:

$$
\begin{aligned}
\frac{\partial E^k}{\partial U_i^k} = \; & \sum_{j=1^k}^{y^k} \left(R_{ij}^k - U_i^{kT} V_j^k \right) \left(-V_j^k \right) + \lambda_U \left(U_i^k - \sum_{a \in C_i} s(i,a) * U_a^k \right) \\
& - \lambda_U \sum_{i \in C_a} s(a,i) \left(U_a^k - \sum_{j \in C_a} s(j,a) * U_j^k \right)
\end{aligned}
\quad (12)
$$

$$
\begin{aligned}
\frac{\partial E^k}{\partial V_j^k} = \; & \sum_{i=1^k}^{x^k} \left(R_{ij}^k - U_i^{kT} V_j^k \right) \left(-U_i^k \right) + \lambda_V \left(V_j^k - \sum_{a \in D_j} t(j,a) * V_a^k \right) \\
& - \lambda_V \sum_{j \in D_a} t(a,j) \left(V_a^k - \sum_{i \in D_a} t(i,a) * V_i^k \right)
\end{aligned}
\quad (13)
$$

3.2 Time Complexity Analysis

In this paper, the calculation process mainly includes three parts. For the first part of co-clustering, the time complexity is $O(iter1 \times L \times K)$, where $iter1$ is the number of iterations, generally within 20, L denotes non-zero values of rating matrix, and K means the number of clusters. The time complexity of computing users' and items' similarity is $O(M^2 + N^2)$. The third part is the time complexity of training. Since we first do co-clustering, we can perform the parallel computation of each cluster in the training stage. Then the time complexity of the partial derivative of the user is

$O(iter2 \times (L \times D + xMD)/K)$, and according to Eq. (13), the time complexity of the item cluster can be computed as $O(iter2 \times (L \times D + yND)/K)$. Thus in total, the time complexity is $O(iter2 \times (L \times D + xMD + yND)/K)$, where $iter2$ denotes the number of iterations on the training stage, D denotes the dimension, x denotes the number of each user cluster, and y denotes the number of each item cluster.

3.3   Discussion on MFCC

The MFCC algorithm incorporates the co-clustering into matrix factorization for recommendation. Theoretically, the model unifies advantages of the two algorithms. So we analyze the model from two aspects, efficiency and effectiveness. On one hand, the algorithm first splits the user-item rating matrix into K small clusters, and then each cluster of users (items) is equivalent to a neighbor set. When we do parallel computing on each cluster, the time complexity is reduced to $1/K$ of the training stage without co-clustering. On the other hand, MFCC can preserve a comparable accuracy even though it deals with large-scale datasets. It is significant in real-world applications.

4   Experiments

4.1   Dataset

We choose the considerably classical MovieLens 10M dataset (http://www.movielens. org) frequently used in recommender systems for evaluation. The dataset selected in this paper contains 71567 users of 10000054 rating records (0.5 to 5) for 10,681 movies, including 95580 tags.

4.2   Evaluation

In this paper, root mean square error (RMSE) is used to measure the performance of rating prediction [22]. Specifically, with smaller RMSE, the prediction accuracy is higher. Assuming that the rating vector of N movies is expressed as $\{p_1, \ldots, p_N\}$ and the corresponding actual rating vector is $\{r_1, \ldots, r_N\}$, then the RMSE of the algorithm is:

$$RMSE = \sqrt{\frac{\sum_{i=1}^{N} (p_i - r_i)^2}{N}} \qquad (14)$$

4.3   Comparative Methods

In this paper, we compare our proposed method with the following four baselines:

(1) PMF: It is a classical matrix factorization algorithm for recommendation [9]. Specifically, this algorithm models the rating matrix as a product of two lower-rank user and movie matrices. Then it recommends movies by the two matrices. Although the algorithm obtains a favorable efficiency, its effectiveness has room for improvement.

(2) Co-Clustering: This algorithm [19] splits the user-item rating matrix into several small matrices, and in each cluster, the elements are similar. Then the scholars utilize WNMF (weighted non-negative matrix factorization) to predict the unknown ratings. The method has some advantages for dealing with large-scale datasets, but its effectiveness is relatively poor.

(3) Co-Clustering + PMF (CCPMF): The method mainly includes two stages. The first stage is to cluster the user-item rating matrix to several sub rating matrices. In the second stage, we use PMF to get user and item matrices in each cluster, then we can know the missing values by the two matrices. As CCPMF is the combination of Co-Clustering and PMF, it can improve effectiveness less.

(4) NHPMF: To improve the accuracy of recommendations, NHPMF [5] uses extra information to select neighbors of each user and each item, then it does matrix factorization on each user's and item's latent feature vector. The proposed method has good performance on effectiveness, but the time cost can be much less.

As we can see from the above four baselines, NHPMF uses external information to improve accuracy. To be fair, similar as the experimental setup in NHPMF [5], we explore the external data source such as tag information in our experiments. Hence, we remove the tags with less than five different users and movies. For each user and movie, less than five different tags are also deleted. Finally, the dataset contains 447 users and 2335 items with 148183 ratings and 1389 tags.

4.4 Experimental Results and Analysis

4.4.1 The Effect of Parameter λ on the Algorithm

The experiments first observe the effect of parameter λ on MFCC's accuracy. The dimension D is set to be 10 and 25, $\lambda_U = \lambda_V = \lambda$, where λ indicates the degree that the user (item) is affected by its neighbors. Figure 2 shows that λ has a great impact on RMSE. As λ increases, the algorithm's accuracy is improved. But when λ surpasses 15, the algorithm's accuracy decreases. This indicates that λ is too large to lead to overfitting, thus we set $\lambda = 10$ in subsequent experiments. In the course of the experiment, as λ increases, the number of iterations increases when RMSE reaches the minimum. In other words, its increase slows down the convergence of RMSE to the minimum. The experimental results are shown in Fig. 3.

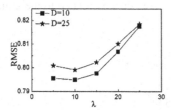

Fig. 2. λ on the impact of RMSE

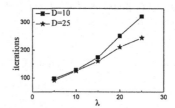

Fig. 3. λ on the impact of iterations

4.4.2   Comparative Evaluation of Different Methods

In Table 2, we compare MFCC with other CF algorithms by setting the feature vectors' dimension D to 5, 10, 15, 20, and 25 respectively.

The above experimental results demonstrate that MFCC outperforms PMF and Co-Clustering in terms of RMSE. This is mainly because the relations modeled by PMF and Co-Clustering are simpler. Moreover, MFCC uses the validity of the information such as tag information and neighbor relations to improve the accuracy. Owing to the similar reasons, the accuracy of CCPMF is much lower than MFCC's. In addition, MFCC achieves very close performance compared with NHPMF. Since the error of MFCC in the co-clustering stage leads to the improvement of the unreliability of neighbor sets, which affects the accuracy of training stage. However, as shown in Table 4, MFCC is more effective than NHPMF. Considering the big data, it can be applied in a wide range of fields and be more feasible in the practical application.

Table 2. RMSE comparisons for different latent feature dimension D

Models	D				
	5	0	15	20	25
PMF	0.8027	0.8538	0.8863	0.9021	0.9540
NHPMF	0.7878	0.7771	0.7747	0.7722	0.7705
Co-clustering	1.0901	1.0440	1.0258	1.0102	1.0095
CCPMF	1.0126	1.0117	1.0134	1.0032	1.0043
MFCC	0.7996	0.7991	0.7975	0.7965	0.7949

4.4.3   Algorithms' Run Time Comparison

In this section, we experimentally compare the time it takes to update the algorithm at each iteration. The experimental environment for the operation is Intel Core i5 CPU, 3.00 GHZ frequency, Windows10 system, 12 GB memory.

(1) We calculate the correlation between the number of clusters and the training time. The results are shown in Table 3.

As can be seen from Table 3, the time shows a rapid growth trend with the increasing number of clusters. This is mainly because the time complexity of the co-clustering phase is $O(iter1 \times L \times K)$, and the time is linearly related to the number of clusters K.

Table 3. Time on the impact of K

Number of clusters	Time(s)
K = 1	5.81
K = 5	8.38
K = 10	11.34
K = 20	17.11
K = 50	33.21

Table 4. Time on the impact of models

Models	Time(s)
PMF	0.14
NHPMF	5.61
Co-clustering	2.10
CCPMF	0.29
MFCC	0.13

(2) We set $\lambda_U = \lambda_V = \lambda$, and when D is 10, the run time comparison results of each algorithm are as follows:

From the experimental results, we can see that PMF and MFCC are more efficient, because PMF doesn't take into account neighbor relations, and the time complexity of PMF is only relevant to the amount of non-zero rating entries. NHPMF not only considers the relations between neighbors, but also joins the tag information, which results in a surprising time complexity. MFCC is theoretically the fusion of two algorithms, so the time complexity will be higher. But because of the parallel computing, it runs at a speed of more than 40 times than NHPMF algorithm with a comparable accuracy at the same time. Obviously, this effect is considerable.

5 Conclusions

In this paper, we propose the MFCC model to improve the time efficiency based on maintaining a comparable accuracy. In the proposed method, we utilize co-clustering into matrix factorization, and the method combines advantages of the two algorithms. Moreover, the experimental results on the MovieLens dataset show our method outperforms many typical recommendation algorithms.

Acknowledgements. This work was supported in part by the National Natural Science Foundation of China (NSFC) under grants 61472116 and 61502139, Natural Science Foundation of Anhui Province under grant 1608085MF128 and 1708085QF155, and the Open Projects Program of National Laboratory of Pattern Recognition under grant 201600006 and 201700017.

References

1. Adomavicius, G., Tuzhilin, A.: Toward the next generation of recommender systems: a survey of the state-of-the-art and possible extensions. IEEE TKDE **17**, 734–749 (2005)
2. Linden, G., Smith, B., York, J.: Amazon.com recommendations: item-to-item collaborative filtering. IEEE Internet Comput. **7**, 76–80 (2003)
3. Sarwar, B., Karypis, G., Konstan, J., et al.: Item-based collaborative filtering recommendation algorithms. In: WWW, pp. 285–295 (2001)
4. Koren, Y., Bell, R., Volinsky, C.: Matrix factorization techniques for recommender systems. Computer **42**, 30–37 (2009)

5. Wu, L., Chen, E., Liu, Q., et al.: Leveraging tagging for neighborhood-aware probabilistic matrix factorization. In: CIKM, pp. 1854–1858 (2012)
6. Najafabadi, M.K., Mahrin, M.N., Chuprat, S., et al.: Improving the accuracy of collaborative filtering recommendations using clustering and association rules mining on implicit data. Comput. Hum. Behav. **67**, 113–128 (2017)
7. Hong, R., Hu, Z., Wang, R., Wang, M., Tao, D.: Multi-view object retrieval via multi-scale topic models. IEEE Trans. Image Process. **25**, 5814–5827 (2016)
8. Wu, Y., Liu, X., Xie, M., et al.: Improving collaborative filtering via scalable user-item co-clustering. In: WSDM, pp. 73–82 (2016)
9. Mnih, A., Salakhutdinov, R.R.: Probabilistic matrix factorization. In: NIPS, pp. 1257–1264 (2007)
10. Zhang, H., Shen, F., Liu, W., He, X., Luan, H., Chua, T.-S.: Discrete collaborative filtering. In: SIGIR, pp. 325–334 (2016)
11. Wang, Z., Wang, X., Qian, H.: Item type based collaborative algorithm. In: CSO, pp. 387–390 (2010)
12. Shi, X.Y., Ye, H.W., Gong, S.J.: A personalized recommender integrating item-based and user-based collaborative filtering. In: ISBIM, pp. 264–267 (2008)
13. Zhang, H., Zha, Z.-J., Yang, Y., Yan, S., Chua, T.-S.: Robust semi nonnegative graph embedding. IEEE Trans. Image Process. **23**, 2996–3012 (2014)
14. Dhillon, I.S., Mallela, S., Modha, D.S.: Information-theoretic co-clustering. In: KDD, pp. 89–98 (2003)
15. Agarwal, D., Merugu, S.: Predictive discrete latent factor models for large scale dyadic data. In: SIGKDD, pp. 26–35 (2007)
16. Xiao-Guang, L., Ge, Y., Da-Ling, W., et al.: Latent concept extraction and text clustering based on information theory. JSW, 2276–2284 (2008)
17. Geiger, B.C., Amjad, R.A.: Hard Clusters Maximize Mutual Information (2016)
18. Hu, L., Chan, K.C.C.: Fuzzy clustering in a complex network based on content relevance and link structures. TFS **24**, 456–470 (2016)
19. Hu, W.U., Wang, Y.J., Wang, Z., et al.: Two-phase collaborative filtering algorithm based on co-clustering. JSW **21**, 1042–1054 (2010)
20. Mei, J.P., Wang, Y., Chen, L., et al.: Large scale document categorization with fuzzy clustering. TFS **25**, 1239–1251 (2016)
21. Bu, J., Shen, X., Xu, B., et al.: Improving collaborative recommendation via user-item subgroups. TKDE **28**, 2363–2375 (2016)
22. Chai, T., Draxler, R.R.: Root mean square error (RMSE) or mean absolute error (MAE)? - Arguments against avoiding RMSE in the literature. GMD **7**, 1525–1534 (2014)
23. Liu, Q., Ge, Y., Li, Z., et al.: Personalized travel package recommendation. In: IEEE ICDM, pp. 407–416 (2011)
24. Wu, L., Ge, Y., Liu, Q., et al.: Modeling the evolution of users' preferences and social links in social networking services. IEEE TKDE **29**, 1240–1253 (2017)
25. Hong, R., Zhang, L., Zhang, C., Zimmermann, R.: Flickr circles: aesthetic tendency discovery by multi-view regularized topic modeling. IEEE Trans. Multimed. **18**, 1555–1567 (2016)
26. Wu, L., Liu, Q., Chen, E., Yuan, N.J., Guo, G., Xie, X.: Relevance meets coverage: a unified framework to generate diversified recommendations. ACM TIST **7**, 39 (2016)

Multi-layers CNNs for 3D Model Retrieval

Anan Liu, Shu Xiang, Weizhi Nie[(✉)], and Yuting Su

School of Electrical and Information Engineering, Tianjin University, Tianjin, China
weizhinie@tju.edu.cn

Abstract. Due to the rapid development of 3D capturing scanners and better visual process techniques, there is a huge increase of 3D models being uploaded and captured by users. 3D model retrieval has become a hot topic in computer vision. State-of-the-art methods leverage CNNs to solve this problem. But existing CNN architectures and approaches are unable to fully exploit the information of 3D representations. In order to improve the performance of 3D object retrieval algorithms, we proposed a multi-layers CNNs (MLCNN) structure for 3D model representation. First, we combine the 12 rendered views of a 3D object into one representative view, which becomes the actual input. Second, in order to save the global and local information for each 3D model, we aggregate every convolutional layer's feature into a multi-layers descriptor after a simple PCA compression. Finally, the Euclidean metric is leveraged to compute the similarity between two different 3D models to complete the retrieval problem. The final comparing experiments and corresponding experimental results demonstrate the superiority of our approach.

Keywords: 3D model retrieval · CNN multi-view · PCA

1 Introduction

Recently, the rapid development of computer graphics hardware and 3D technologies for modeling, reconstruction, printing and so on have produced increasing number of 3D models. Thus, 3D model retrieval is becoming mandatory in diverse domains [14], such as computer-aided design, digital entertainment, medical diagnosis, e-business, and location-based mobile applications. Many methods were proposed to handle this problem. However, it is still quite challenging due to the variation of viewpoints, illuminations, model sizes, model styles, etc.

Deep learning provides an effective tool for feature learning. 3D feature extraction algorithms have gradually shifted from hand-designed features to deep learning features. The hand-designed features are usually obtained by extracting the geometry distribution or histogram statistics, such as Heat Kernel Signature, Spin Image, FPFH [11], etc. But when it comes to a particular task, this method gets hard to obtain optimal 3D shape feature representations. Recently, the deep learning model has begun to be applied to the 3D shape feature representation, making significant achievements [37].

© Springer Nature Singapore Pte Ltd. 2018
B. Huet et al. (Eds.): ICIMCS 2017, CCIS 819, pp. 371–383, 2018.
https://doi.org/10.1007/978-981-10-8530-7_36

There are two main types of processing 3D data on CNNs:

- CNNs based upon volumetric representations:
  The key of the volumetric CNNs methods is turning a geometric 3D shape into probability distribution of binary variables on a 3D voxel grid. Each 3D mesh is represented as a binary tensor: 1 indicates the voxel is inside the mesh surface, and 0 indicates the voxel is outside the mesh [34]. These data will be trained on CNNs. For example, Li et al. [34] represent a 3D shape by volumetric fields, which overcome the sparse problems of the 3D voxels;
- CNNs based upon multi-view:
  Experiments demonstrate that training a CNN on multiple 2D views achieves a significantly higher performance. In [32], MVCNN requires picturing from different viewpoints to obtain images of different angles of the object. It generates a single and compact descriptor through view-pooling layer. MVCNN's performance is far higher than that of state-of-the-art 3D shape descriptors.

Though MVCNN presents state-of-the-art results on 3D object classification and 3D object retrieval using sketches, there is still huge space for improvement. Firstly, taking 12 rendered views as inputs, MVCNN requires 12 times training on the network [32] to learn the single detector for a 3D object, which results in huge time cost. In addition, MVCNN divides the Convnet [19] into two parts, view-pooling layer aggregates features of 12 rendered views directly, ignoring the difference between views. Lastly, whether the view-pooling layer is the best way to combine features should be discussed.

Therefore, in this paper, we proposed the multi-layers CNNs (MLCNN) for 3D model representation (Fig. 1). First, we aggregate 12 views of a 3D object directly into a representative view, which is the actual input of our network. Compared with MVCNN, this design puts the view-pooling operation in the visual layer and makes the 12 times training in the network into one time. Second, in order to save the global and local information of 3D model, we extract every convolutional layer's feature during the feed-forward process. These features are then projected to an appropriate dimension space by PCA. After concatenate operation, we obtain the final multi-layers feature. At last, the Euclidean metric is utilized to compute the similarity between two different 3D models to handle retrieval problems.

The main contributions of this paper are summarized as follows:

- We proposed a new architecture to solve 3D shape representation problems based on CNNs. The network costs less time for training and guarantees the performance for classification and retrieval tasks;
- We employed multi-layers descriptor for 3D shape retrieval, which has more comprehensive information. PCA was used to compress the dimension of multi-layers feature to an optimal size, which can effectively improve the performance of our model;
- Our method achieves a classification accuracy of 91.0% and Mean Average Precision 81.5% outperforming the state-of-the-art 3D descriptors.

The rest of the paper is structured as follows: in Sect. 2, we do a survey of the related work. Then we introduce the detail of our methods in Sect. 3, experimental settings and results are introduced in Sect. 4, Sect. 5 will draw conclusions of the paper.

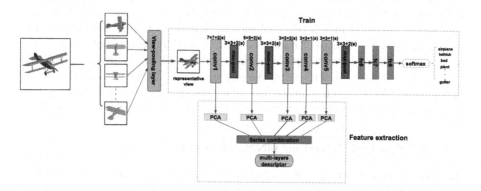

Fig. 1. The framework of MLCNN.

2   Related Work

Our work aims to propose a 3D shape retrieval method based on multi-view CNNs. In this section, we briefly review the representative work in the fields of 3D model retrieval and deep learning architecture.

2.1   3D Object Retrieval Algorithms

With the advent of advanced 3D modeling tools and 3D capturing devices, numerous shape descriptors have been developed. They can be classified into two broad categories [8,13]: view-based descriptors that represent 3D object by multiple views, and descriptors based on 3D models; respectively, model-based algorithms [22,27,28,30] and view-based algorithms [7,9,15,23,29].

Model-based algorithms: Prior approaches largely belong to model-based algorithms, such as the spherical harmonics and moments [25], volumetric descriptor [24], polygon meshes like triangle areas [33] and the surface similarity [4]. The core of this kind of algorithms is extracting hand-designed features from 3D models. For example, Bu et al. [36] represent a geometric 3D shape as a probability distribution of binary variables on a 3D voxel grid. Xie et al. [3] extract the multi-scale histogram of the 3D shape's Heat Kernel Signature as an input to the self-encoding machine. Instead, researchers start to work on the voxel-based representations of 3D objects. Xu et al. [16] extract and combine each layer of the 3D voxels into a binary image. Wu et al. [34] learn shape descriptors from the voxel-based representation of an object through 3D convolutional nets. In [2], Hypergraph Analysis can explore higher order relationship among objects without using the distance between objects.

View-based algorithms: Though shape-based features enable significant performance over a variety of tasks, they require 3D models to be explicit enough, which limits the efficiency of practical applications. Instead, view-based techniques have attracted more and more attention in recent years. Liu et al. [1] propose an original multi-modal clique graph (MCG) to represent an individual 3D model with multi-view and multi-modal information. Wang et al. [5] present an images-based 3D model retrieval method where each model is described by six 2D images. Six images of each model are naturally divided into three pairs, and the similarity between two models is calculated by summing up the distances of all corresponding pairs. Ansary et al. [35] propose Adapting Views Clustering (AVC), which is utilized to select an optimal number of views, then uses probabilistic Bayesian method for 3D-model retrieval from these views.

2.2   3D Research Based on CNNs Networks

The convolutional network (ConvNet) architecture is a kind of artificial neural network, which has become a hotspot in the field of speech analysis and image recognition. Pioneered by Lecun and collaborators [20], CNNs now produce state-of-the-art performances on many visual recognition tasks. There have been numbers of works on recognizing 3D objects with CNNs. Maturana et al. proposed VoxNet [26], an architecture to tackle 3D recognition problem by integrating a volumetric Occupancy Grid representation with a supervised 3D Convolutional Neural Network (3D CNN). VoxNet achieves accuracy beyond the state-of-the-art while labeling hundreds of instances per second.

In [31], Deep Pano's method directly learns from the panoramic views of 3D models. The panoramic view is a cylinder projection of a 3D model around its principle axis. To make the learned deep features invariant to the rotation around the principle axis, a special layer named Row-Wise Max-Pooling (RWMP) layer is presented and inserted between the convolutional layers and the fully-connected layers. Proposed by Kalogerakis and collaborators [17], a series of shadows and depth maps of 3D shapes are obtained at different viewpoints and scales. FCN network is employed to obtain shape descriptors. Another image-based method [21] utilizes two concatenated views (binocular images) as input, outputs a single compact descriptor through CNNs. In experiments based on projected images, researchers have plenty of methods. Su et al. (MVCNN) [32] represent a 3D object by views generated from the projection at 12 different viewpoints, and then use VGG-M convolution neural network to learn the features of each view, finally, the features of the multi-view are pooled and sent to the next CNN network to get the final shape descriptors. MVCNN dramatically outperform any previously published results.

3   Our Approach

Based on the conclusions above, this paper will introduce the following 3 steps to solve 3D object retrieval problems. First, network training, the view-pooling layer is employed to generate a representative view. Our network, which has been pretrained on ImageNet1k then trained on the representative views. Second, in order to reduce the errors caused by redundant information, we extract features from every convolutional layer with PCA compression to project convolutional features into lower dimension. Then we connect them to a compact multi-layers descriptor. Finally, Euclidean distance is utilized to compute the similarity between different 3D objects. The detail will be shown in the next subsections.

3.1 Network Training

By adopting MVCNN, we create 12 rendered views by placing 12 virtual cameras around the mesh every 30° (see Fig. 1). In this step, we pay close attention to network training. We designed our network based on image-based CNNs. In our network, 12 rendered images in a 3D shape are initially passed through view-pooling layer, which is an element-wise maximum operation across the views [32]. As a result, our trainable network has only one input actually, which greatly reduce the training time without performance decline. View-pooling layer is closely related to max-pooling layers and max-out layers [12], in the 12 rendered images, taking the max operation in the same place. Besides, our CNNs network consists of mainly five convolutional layers with Relu and max-pool layer, followed by three fully connected layers and a softmax classification layer. The network is pre-trained on ImageNet images from 1k categories and then fine-tuned on all 2D views of the 3D shapes in training set.

3.2 Multi-layers Feature Extraction and Optimization

In order to obtain complete information from a 3D object, we desire to capture a multi-layers descriptor for 3D shapes. Here, we noticed that every convolutional layer consists of different level features [39, 40], once we combine them by a specified method, the final descriptor will own both local and global information. In regard to per convolutional layer, we extract their feature separately, whose dimension depends on their filter size. After that, we obtained five convolutional features for one 3D object. In many algorithms, the compressed dimension algorithm becomes part of the data preprocessing [38, 42]. Usually, the original high-dimensional space contains redundant information and noise information, resulting in errors and lower accuracy. Thus, we project these convolutional features into PCA space separately to obtain the most appropriate dimension. Then we concatenate these compressed features into a multi-layers descriptor, which is utilized to represent 3D shapes.

3.3 Similarity Measurement

Retrieval tasks require a similarity or distance measurement. We use Euclidean distance to compute the distance between different 3D objects. The reason we choose ℓ_2 distance is that our purpose is demonstrating a multi-layers descriptor. Euclidean distance is help to highlight the role of features.

$$S_1(x_i, y_j) = \frac{1}{\sqrt{(f(x_i) - f(y_j))^2}} \tag{1}$$

where, x_i and y_i represent different 3D models respectively. $f(.)$ represents the feature mapping function, which is used to extract feature for each 3D model.

$$S_2(Q, M) = \arg \min_{i,j}^{n,m} S_1(x_i, y_j) \tag{2}$$

Given a query 3D model, all the distances between the query 3D model and other 3D models in the dataset can be calculated. $\tilde{M}$ represents the candidate model set, M_i is the candidate model, Q is the query model. The retrieved model with the highest similarity score can be achieved as follows:

$$M^* = argmax_{M_i \in \tilde{M}} S_2(Q, M_i) \tag{3}$$

4 Experiments

4.1 Dataset

We utilize ModelNet dataset for our training and testing. ModelNet contains 127,915 3D CAD models from 662 categories. ModelNet includes a subset, ModelNet40, a 40-class well annotated subset containing 12,311 shapes from 40 common categories, which can be downloaded from ModelNet website[1].

4.2 Evaluation Criteria

The following criteria are employed as the evaluation measures of the retrieval performance:

- Nearest Neighbor (NN): The percentage of the closest match models belongs to the query category.
- First Tier (FT): The recall for the first K relevant match samples, where K is the cardinality of the query category.
- Second Tier (ST): The recall for the first 2K relevant match samples, where K is the cardinality of the query category.
- F-measure: Asynthetical measurement of precision and recall for a fixed number of retrieved results.
- Discounted Cumulative Gain (DCG): A statistical measure that assigns higher weights to relevant results occupying the top-ranking positions.
- Average Normalized Modified Retrieval Rank (ANMRR): It measures the rank performance by a ranking list, which considers the ranking information of relevant objects among the top retrieved objects.
- PrecisionCRecall curve (PR): A crucial indicator that shows the relationship between the precision and the recall. The mean Average Precision (mAP) of PR-Curve can be calculated for quantitative evaluation.

---

[1] http://modelnet.cs.princeton.edu/.

4.3 The Optimal Parameters

In the step of feature extraction, in order to save local and global information of 3D models, we extract information from each convolutional layer. However, different convolutional layer has different dimension feature vector. The simple fusion will make these features have different weights and obviously influence the final performance [41]. In order to handle this problem, PCA is utilized to make these features into one same dimension for more robust feature fusion. Thus, the compression rates of PCA is a key parameter in this method. The corresponding experiment is shown in Fig. 2. Here, different compression rates were completed and the final performance of mAP is utilized to find the be compression rate.

From the final experimental results, we can find that the best retrieval result appears when the compression rate is 512. Meanwhile, we also compared the retrieval performance on different criteria. The 512 dimensions also achieved the best performance. Thus, it was chosen for further comparison with existing 3D shape descriptors.

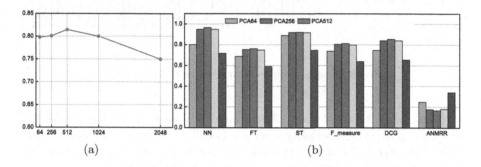

Fig. 2. Results of dimensionality reduction by PCA

4.4 Comparison with Different Number Views

In this paper, the biggest difference is the location of view-pooling operation. This decision effectively reduces the time cost of training and the complexity of the network. In order to demonstrate the performance of our approach, we compared with MVCNN using different number of views in classification and retrieval. Here, we randomly choose 5 views and 10 views to represent each 3D model. The experimental results are shown in Table 1. From this table, we can find that more views can lead higher accuracy and mAP. The reason is that more views can represent more visual information or structure information, guaranteeing the robust of the final visual feature. Meanwhile, we also find that MLCNN outperforms MVCNN on this experiment, which means MLCNN can provide more robust feature than MVCNN.

We also make the comparison experiment on retrieval problems. The experimental results are shown in Fig. 3. Here, Fig. 3(a) shows the Precision-Recall Curve on different number views and Fig. 3(b) shows the related evaluating results.

Table 1. Performance of different number views on classification

Method	Accuracy (%)	mAP (%)
MVCNN-5	76.67	69.1
MLCNN-5	81.67	70.4
MVCNN-10	85.11	72.5
MLCNN-10	86.67	78.7
MVCNN-12	89.9	79.9
MLCNN-12	**91.0**	**81.5**

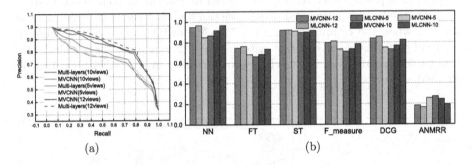

(a)   (b)

Fig. 3. Results of different number views on retrieval

Remarkably, MLCNN with different number of views outperforms MVCNN, which also proves the superiority of our method. The experiment not only demonstrates the superiority of our approach but also demonstrates that view-pooling operation designed in first layer can save main visual information.

4.5 Comparison to State-of-the-Art on Retrieval

In order to evaluate the performance of our method, we choose some state-of-the-art methods as comparison methods on retrieval tasks. These methods are followed as:

- Nearest Neighbor (NN): It is the percentage of queries which is the closest match belongs to the query's category.
- Adaptive views clustering (AVC) [2]: The adaptive views clustering method provides an optimal selection of 2D views from a 3D model and a probabilistic Bayesian method for 3D model retrieval from these views. The characteristic views selection algorithm is based on an adaptive clustering algorithm and uses statistical model distribution scores to select the optimal number of views.
- Camera constraint-free view-based (CCFV) [10]: For each query object, all query views are clustered to generate the view cluster, which is then used to build the query models. The CCFV model is generated on the basis of the

query Gaussian models by combining the positive matching model and the negative matching model.

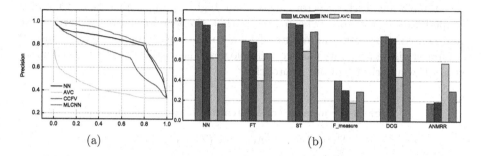

Fig. 4. Results of different retrieval methods

The experimental resutls are shown in the Fig. 4. Figure 4(a) shows the precision-recall curves on ModelNet40, Fig. 4(b) presents the performance by different evaluation criteria. From these experimental results, we have the following observations.

- CCFV and AVC can be seen as a statistical model. CCFV utilized the Gaussian model to describe the feature distribution. AVC utilized the Bayesian model to describe each 3D model. However, AVC considers each view as an independent individual. CCFV utilizes the Gaussian model, which considers the changes of views in feature space. The final experimental results also demonstrate that CCFV outperforms AVC;
- NN is simple but it outperforms CCFV and AVC. The reason is that NN applied the CNN feature. CCFV and AVC applied the Zernike moments as the feature of each view. Thus, the superiority of CNNs leads that NN has a better retrieval result than CCFV and AVC.
- Our approach has the best results. The reason is that we proposed a robust feature extraction methods, which can effectively save local and global information for each 3D model. Meanwhile, the network of CNN can learn better statistical information than CCFV and AVC. Thus, MLCNN has the best retrieval results.

4.6 Comparison with State-of-the-Art Methods on Classification

In this paper, MLCNN can be seen as modified MVCNN. In order to demonstrate that our approach can provide better feature description than MVCNN, classification experiment is also made on the related dataset. Here, our MLCNN are compared against the 3D ShapeNets by Wu et al. [34], Spherical Harmonics descriptor (SPH) by Kazhdan et al. [18], the LightField descriptor (LFD) by Chen et al. [6], and Fisher vectors extracted on the same rendered views.

Experimental results are summarized in Table 2. The CNN baseline, MVCNN, and our method are all pre-trained on ImageNet1K, fine-tuned on ModelNet40 dataset. In Table 2, the top 3 are results using state-of-the-art volumetric-based descriptors. Remarkably the view-based methods in our experiment including Fisher vector, achieve far higher performance than that of 3 shape-based descriptors. The reason is that shape information is hard to be represented. However, the feature of view can be easily represented because of computer vision has more mature technologies. The final experiment also demonstrate the superiority of our approach.

Table 2. Performance of different methods on classification

Method	Acurracy (%)	mAP (%)
SPH	68.2	33.3
LFD	75.5	40.9
3D ShapeNets	77.3	49.2
Fisher vector	84.8	43.9
CNN	88.6	62.8
MVCNN	89.9	79.9
MLCNN	**91.0**	**81.5**

5   Conclusion

In this paper, we proposed a novel CNN architecture MLCNN for 3D model representation. The pooling operation of the visual layer can effectively reduce the time cost of training. The multiple layers feature extraction can effectively save local and global information for each 3D model. We compared some state-of-the-art methods on classification and retrieval problem. The final experimental results also demonstrate the performance of our approach and prove the effectiveness of our design. In the future, We will continue to figure out how much views are informative, try different combinations of images, present other feature extraction method, and explore better method on Volumetric CNNs.

References

1. Akgül, C.B., Sankur, B., Yemez, Y., Schmitt, F.J.M.: 3D model retrieval using probability density-based shape descriptors. IEEE Trans. Pattern Anal. Mach. Intell. **31**(6), 1117–1133 (2009)
2. Ansary, T.F., Daoudi, M., Vandeborre, J.: A Bayesian 3-D search engine using adaptive views clustering. IEEE Trans. Multimedia **9**(1), 78–88 (2007)
3. Bu, S., Liu, Z., Han, J., Wu, J., Ji, R.: Learning high-level feature by deep belief networks for 3-D model retrieval and recognition. IEEE Trans. Multimedia **16**(8), 2154–2167 (2014)

4. Bustos, B., Keim, D.A., Saupe, D., Schreck, T., Vranic, D.V.: Feature-based similarity search in 3D object databases. ACM Comput. Surv. **37**(4), 345–387 (2005)
5. Cao, B., Kang, Y., Lin, S., Luo, X., Xu, S., Lv, Z.: Style-sensitive 3D model retrieval through sketch-based queries. J. Intell. Fuzzy Syst. **31**(5), 2637–2644 (2016)
6. Chen, D., Tian, X., Shen, Y., Ouhyoung, M.: On visual similarity based 3D model retrieval. Comput. Graph. Forum **22**(3), 223–232 (2003)
7. Cheng, Z., Shen, J.: On very large scale test collection for landmark image search benchmarking. Sig. Process. **124**, 13–26 (2016)
8. Deng, J., Dong, W., Socher, R., Li, L., Li, K., Li, F.: Imagenet: a large-scale hierarchical image database. In: 2009 IEEE Computer Society Conference on Computer Vision and Pattern Recognition (CVPR 2009), 20–25 June 2009, Miami, Florida, USA, pp. 248–255 (2009)
9. Gao, Y., Dai, Q.: View-based 3D object retrieval: challenges and approaches. IEEE MultiMedia **21**(3), 52–57 (2014)
10. Gao, Y., Tang, J., Hong, R., Yan, S., Dai, Q., Zhang, N., Chua, T.: Camera constraint-free view-based 3-D object retrieval. IEEE Trans. Image Process. **21**(4), 2269–2281 (2012)
11. Gao, Y., Wang, M., Tao, D., Ji, R., Dai, Q.: 3-D object retrieval and recognition with hypergraph analysis. IEEE Trans. Image Process. **21**(9), 4290–4303 (2012)
12. Goodfellow, I.J., Warde-Farley, D., Mirza, M., Courville, A.C., Bengio, Y.: Maxout networks. In: Proceedings of the 30th International Conference on Machine Learning, ICML 2013, Atlanta, GA, USA, 16–21 June 2013, pp. 1319–1327 (2013)
13. Hong, R., Hu, Z., Wang, R., Wang, M., Tao, D.: Multi-view object retrieval via multi-scale topic models. IEEE Trans. Image Process. **25**(12), 5814–5827 (2016)
14. Hong, R., Yang, Y., Wang, M., Hua, X.: Learning visual semantic relationships for efficient visual retrieval. IEEE Trans. Big Data **1**(4), 152–161 (2015)
15. Hu, F., Xia, G., Hu, J., Zhang, L.: Transferring deep convolutional neural networks for the scene classification of high-resolution remote sensing imagery. Remote Sens. **7**(11), 14680–14707 (2015)
16. Irfanoglu, M.O., Gökberk, B., Akarun, L.: 3D shape-based face recognition using automatically registered facial surfaces. In: 17th International Conference on Pattern Recognition, ICPR 2004, Cambridge, UK, 23–26 August 2004, pp. 183–186 (2004)
17. Kalogerakis, E., Averkiou, M., Maji, S., Chaudhuri, S.: 3D shape segmentation with projective convolutional networks. CoRR abs/1612.02808 (2016)
18. Kazhdan, M.M., Funkhouser, T.A., Rusinkiewicz, S.: Rotation invariant spherical harmonic representation of 3D shape descriptors. In: First Eurographics Symposium on Geometry Processing, Aachen, Germany, 23–25 June 2003, pp. 156–164 (2003)
19. Krizhevsky, A., Sutskever, I., Hinton, G.E.: Imagenet classification with deep convolutional neural networks. In: Advances in Neural Information Processing Systems 25: 26th Annual Conference on Neural Information Processing Systems 2012, Proceedings of a Meeting Held 3–6 December 2012, Lake Tahoe, Nevada, USA, pp. 1106–1114 (2012)
20. LeCun, Y., Haffner, P., Bottou, L., Bengio, Y.: Object recognition with gradient-based learning. In: Forsyth, D.A., Mundy, J.L., di Gesú, V., Cipolla, R. (eds.) Shape, Contour and Grouping in Computer Vision. LNCS, vol. 1681, pp. 319–345. Springer, Heidelberg (1999). https://doi.org/10.1007/3-540-46805-6_19
21. LeCun, Y., Huang, F.J., Bottou, L.: Learning methods for generic object recognition with invariance to pose and lighting. In: 2004 IEEE Computer Society Conference on Computer Vision and Pattern Recognition (CVPR 2004), with CD-ROM, 27 June–2 July 2004, Washington, DC, USA, pp. 97–104 (2004)

22. Liu, A.A., Nie, W.Z., Gao, Y., Su, Y.T.: View-based 3-D model retrieval: a bench-mark. IEEE Trans. Cybern. **48**(3), 916–928 (2017)
23. Liu, A., Nie, W., Gao, Y., Su, Y.: Multi-modal clique-graph matching for view-based 3D model retrieval. IEEE Trans. Image Process. **25**(5), 2103–2116 (2016)
24. Liu, A., Wang, Z., Nie, W., Su, Y.: Graph-based characteristic view set extraction and matching for 3D model retrieval. Inf. Sci. **320**, 429–442 (2015)
25. Liu, Q.: A survey of recent view-based 3D model retrieval methods. CoRR abs/1208.3670 (2012)
26. Maturana, D., Scherer, S.: VoxNet: a 3D convolutional neural network for real-time object recognition. In: 2015 IEEE/RSJ International Conference on Intelligent Robots and Systems, IROS 2015, Hamburg, Germany, 28 September–2 October 2015, pp. 922–928 (2015)
27. Nie, L., Wang, M., Zha, Z.J., Chua, T.S.: Oracle in image search: a content-based approach to performance prediction. ACM Trans. Inf. Syst. **30**(2), 13:1–13:23 (2012)
28. Nie, L., Wang, M., Zha, Z., Li, G., Chua, T.S.: Multimedia answering: enriching text QA with media information. In: Proceedings of the 34th International ACM SIGIR Conference on Research and Development in Information Retrieval, SIGIR 2011, pp. 695–704. ACM (2011)
29. Nie, L., Yan, S., Wang, M., Hong, R., Chua, T.S.: Harvesting visual concepts for image search with complex queries. In: Proceedings of the 20th ACM International Conference on Multimedia, MM 2012, pp. 59–68. ACM (2012)
30. Saupe, D., Vranic, D.V.: 3D model retrieval with spherical harmonics and moments. In: Proceedings of the 23rd DAGM-Symposium Pattern Recognition, Munich, Germany, 12–14 September 2001, pp. 392–397 (2001)
31. Shi, B., Bai, S., Zhou, Z., Bai, X.: DeepPano: deep panoramic representation for 3-D shape recognition. IEEE Signal Process. Lett. **22**(12), 2339–2343 (2015)
32. Su, H., Maji, S., Kalogerakis, E., Learned-Miller, E.G.: Multi-view convolutional neural networks for 3D shape recognition. In: 2015 IEEE International Conference on Computer Vision, ICCV 2015, Santiago, Chile, 7–13 December 2015, pp. 945–953 (2015)
33. Tangelder, J.W.H., Veltkamp, R.C.: Polyhedral model retrieval using weighted point sets. Int. J. Image Graph. **3**(1), 209 (2003)
34. Wu, Z., Song, S., Khosla, A., Yu, F., Zhang, L., Tang, X., Xiao, J.: 3D shapenets: a deep representation for volumetric shapes. In: IEEE Conference on Computer Vision and Pattern Recognition, CVPR 2015, Boston, MA, USA, 7–12 June 2015, pp. 1912–1920 (2015)
35. Xie, J., Dai, G., Zhu, F., Wong, E.K., Fang, Y.: Deepshape: deep-learned shape descriptor for 3D shape retrieval. IEEE Trans. Pattern Anal. Mach. Intell. **39**(7), 1335–1345 (2017)
36. Xu, X., Corrigan, D., Dehghani, A., Caulfield, S., Moloney, D.: 3D object recognition based on volumetric representation using convolutional neural networks. In: Perales, F.J.J., Kittler, J. (eds.) AMDO 2016. LNCS, vol. 9756, pp. 147–156. Springer, Cham (2016). https://doi.org/10.1007/978-3-319-41778-3_15
37. Yang, S., Ramanan, D.: Multi-scale recognition with DAG-CNNs. In: 2015 IEEE International Conference on Computer Vision, ICCV 2015, Santiago, Chile, 7–13 December 2015, pp. 1215–1223 (2015)
38. Zhang, H., Shang, X., Luan, H., Wang, M., Chua, T.: Learning from collective intelligence: feature learning using social images and tags. TOMCCAP **13**(1), 1:1–1:23 (2016)

39. Zhang, H., Shang, X., Yang, W., Xu, H., Luan, H., Chua, T.: Online collaborative learning for open-vocabulary visual classifiers. In: 2016 IEEE Conference on Computer Vision and Pattern Recognition, CVPR 2016, Las Vegas, NV, USA, 27–30 June 2016, pp. 2809–2817 (2016)
40. Zhang, H., Shen, F., Liu, W., He, X., Luan, H., Chua, T.: Discrete collaborative filtering. In: Proceedings of the 39th International ACM SIGIR conference on Research and Development in Information Retrieval, SIGIR 2016, Pisa, Italy, 17–21 July 2016, pp. 325–334 (2016)
41. Zhang, H., Zha, Z., Yang, Y., Yan, S., Chua, T.: Robust (semi) nonnegative graph embedding. IEEE Trans. Image Process. **23**(7), 2996–3012 (2014)
42. Zhang, H., Zha, Z., Yang, Y., Yan, S., Gao, Y., Chua, T.: Attribute-augmented semantic hierarchy: towards bridging semantic gap and intention gap in image retrieval. In: ACM Multimedia Conference, MM 2013, Barcelona, Spain, 21–25 October 2013, pp. 33–42 (2013)

Multispectral Image Denoising Based on Non-local Means and Bilateral Filtering

Xueyan Zhen[1], Ning He[2($\boxtimes$)], Xin Sun[2], and Yuqing Zhang[1]

[1] Beijing Key Laboratory of Information Services Engineering,
Beijing Union University, Beijing 100101, China
zhen15811114253@163.com, zyuqing1104@163.com
[2] College of Intellectualized City, Beijing Union University,
Beijing 100101, China
xxthening@buu.edu.cn, Sunx5232@163.com

Abstract. Multispectral images are obtained by taking multiple images of the different wave bands of the same target, which provides a more comprehensive and clearer description of the scene. However, in practice, multispectral images are always degraded by various types of noise. In this paper, an image denoising method based on non-local means and bilateral filtering is proposed. The method uses the non-local means algorithm to denoise the image, and then uses the bilateral filter to enhance it. The proposed method is compared with the BM3D denoising algorithm, non-local means algorithm and bilateral filtering. The experimental results show that the proposed method not only improves the visual effect but also the value of structural similarity and feature similarity.

Keywords: Multispectral images · Non-local means · Bilateral filtering
BM3D

1 Introduction

The Multispectral images can provide more information about real scenes. However, in reality, multispectral images usually contain some degree of noise because of the external conditions, which can adversely affect the subsequent processing.

Xie et al. proposed a new denoising method based on tensors that considers the two intrinsic properties of multispectral images, namely, spectral global correlation and spatial non-local self-similarity [1]. This method is superior to other algorithms that only consider an intrinsic characteristic. Peng et al. proposed a method for multispectral image denoising using an optimized vector bilateral filter. The parameter optimization program is based on Stein's unbiased estimation [2], and the optimized vector bilateral filter provides improved denoising performance on multispectral images. Scheunders proposed a multispectral image denoising technique using inter-band correlation [3] in which redundant wavelet transform is applied and denoising is applied by thresholding wavelet coefficients. The technique was shown to outperform single band wavelet thresholding on multispectral images. Dabov et al. [4] proposed the 3D block matching (BM3D) algorithm, which is an algorithm with good denoising performance. However, when BM3D is used to denoise multispectral images, the image distortion is serious,

© Springer Nature Singapore Pte Ltd. 2018
B. Huet et al. (Eds.): ICIMCS 2017, CCIS 819, pp. 384–391, 2018.
https://doi.org/10.1007/978-981-10-8530-7_37

and the original structure of the image cannot be well maintained. Buades et al. [5] proposed the non-local means (NL-means) algorithm using the idea of neighborhood average denoising, and the restored pixel is the weighted average of all pixels in the image. When the NL-means algorithm is used to denoise the multispectral images, the image can keep its original structure better, but the residual noise is increased.

Hence, to reduce the residual noise of the images and maintain image edges, this paper presents an image denoising method based on both NL-means and bilateral filtering. The method uses the NL-means algorithm to denoise the image and then uses bilateral filtering to filter it. The experimental results show that the visual effects and image quality are improved.

2 Image Denoising Based on NL-Means and Bilateral Filtering

The BM3D algorithm is currently one of the best image denoising algorithms available. However, when BM3D is used to denoise a multispectral image, the result contains a noticeable fuzzy region. The disadvantage of the NL-means algorithm is that a high level of residual noise will remain in the image after denoising, especially in the edges of the image. To further improve the image quality, this paper presents a denoising method based on NL-means and bilateral filtering. First, the image is denoised by NL-means, and the initial denoised image is obtained. Then, the image is further denoised by bilateral filtering.

2.1 Obtaining the Initial Denoising Image Using NL-Means

Although the non-local algorithm uses neighborhood average denoising theory, its neighborhood range is non-local, that is, not limited to the target pixel as the center of the neighborhood, and image blocks are used to compare the similarity of the target pixel.

The NL-means algorithm [6] is as follows: if the noise image is $v = \{v(i)|i \in I\}$ and the image after denoising is $NL[v]$, then the gray value for pixel i can be calculated as follows:

$$NL[v](i) = \sum_{j \in I} w(i,j)v(j) \tag{1}$$

where $w(i,j)$ represents the degree of similarity between two image blocks centered on pixel i and j, calculated using:

$$w(i,j) = \frac{1}{Z(i)} \exp(-\frac{||v(N_i) - v(N_j)||_2^2}{h^2}) \tag{2}$$

$$Z(i) = \sum_j \exp(-\frac{||v(N_i) - v(N_j)||_2^2}{h^2}) \tag{3}$$

where, $Z(i)$ is the normalization factor, $v(N_i)$ is the gray scale vector of the corresponding window centered on pixel i, h is the filter smoothness parameter, and the value of $w(i,j)$ is between 0 and 1.

2.2 Further Denoising Using Bilateral Filtering

The bilateral filter is a non-linear filter designed based on the analysis of Overton et al. and classical Gaussian filtering algorithm [7]. It has non-iterative, local, and simple features.

Bilateral filtering not only considers the proximity of space, but also the similarity of gray scale relations. Using a non-linear combination of the two, the bilateral filter obtains a smooth image [8]. The formula is as follows:

$$\hat{I}(x,y) = \frac{\sum\limits_{(i,j)\in M_{x,y}} \omega_s(i,j)\omega_r(i,j)I(i,j)}{\sum\limits_{(i,j)\in M_{x,y}} \omega_s(i,j)\omega_r(i,j)} \tag{4}$$

$$\omega_s(i,j) = \exp(-\frac{|i-x|^2 + |i-y|^2}{2\sigma_s^2}) \tag{5}$$

$$\omega_r(i,j) = \exp(-\frac{|I(i,j) - I(x,y)|^2}{2\sigma_r^2}) \tag{6}$$

where $\hat{I}$ is the filtered image, $M_{x,y}$ denotes the $(2N+1) \times (2N+1)$ spatial neighborhood pixel set centered on (x,y), $I(x,y)$ denotes the center point pixel value of $M(x,y)$, $I(i,j)$ denotes the pixel value at (i,j) in $M_{x,y}$, $\omega_s(i,j)$ is the spatial proximity factor, $\omega_r(i,j)$ is the gray level similarity factor, and σ_s σ_r are filtering parameters. If we assume that $\omega(i,j)$ is the weight coefficient, then $\omega(i,j) = \frac{\omega_s(i,j)\omega_r(i,j)}{c}$, where c is a constant.

A high level of noise remains in the image when NL-means denoising is used, and bilateral filtering can effectively reduce the image noise and while maintaining the image edges. Combining the two methods for image denoising can achieve a good denoising effect.

SSIM is a reference image quality evaluation index that measures the brightness, contrast, and structure [9]. FSIM is an image quality evaluation algorithm based on the underlying features [10]. The performance of the algorithm is evaluated using SSIM and FSIM values.

3   Experimental Results and Analysis

All experiments in this paper were simulated by adding Gaussian white noise with standard deviations of $\sigma = 10$ and 20 to real images. The performance of the algorithm is evaluated using subjective evaluation and objective SSIM and FSIM values. In this

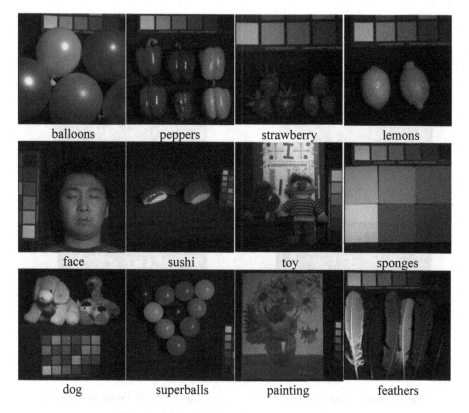

Fig. 1. Original images used in the experiment.

paper, we compare the proposed method with the BM3D algorithm, NL-means algorithm, and bilateral filtering. Their parameters are set as follows. The BM3D algorithm uses an 8×8 fixed size image block. The NL-means algorithm search window radius is set to 5, its similarity window radius is set to 2, and its smoothing parameter is set to 10. The bilateral filtering template radius is set to 8. These parameters are the optimal values obtained after a large number of experiments. For this study, we use multiple images for testing. Figure 1[1] shows the original images used in the experiment. Tables 1 and 2, respectively, show the performance evaluation results for noise levels of $\sigma = 10$ and $\sigma = 20$ for each of the four methods.

We choose two images, "balloons" and "peppers," to discuss in detail. Figure 2 shows a balloon noisy image where $\sigma = 10$, and Fig. 3 shows the image after denoising using the proposed method. For further comparison, peppers images corrupted by noise are processed using the BM3D algorithm, NL-means algorithm, bilateral filtering, and the proposed method. Figure 4 shows the noisy image with $\sigma = 10$, and Fig. 6, shows the results after all methods have been applied. Table 1 shows the resulting values of the

---

[1] http://www1.cs.columbia.edu/CAVE/databases/multispectral.

Fig. 2. Noisy image

Fig. 3. Image after denoising

Fig. 4. Noisy image ($\sigma = 10$)

Fig. 5. Noisy image ($\sigma = 20$)

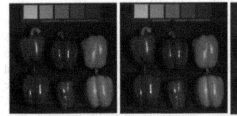

Fig. 6. Images after denoising using (left to right) BM3D, NL-means, bilateral filtering, and the proposed method ($\sigma = 10$).

performance evaluation metrics for the four methods for all images. Figure 5 shows the noisy image at $\sigma = 20$, and Fig. 7 shows the results after all methods have been applied.

Moreover, Table 2 shows the resulting values of the performance evaluation metrics for all four methods. Subjectively, the proposed method obtains a clearer image

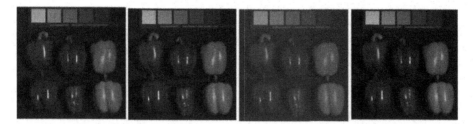

Fig. 7. Images after denoising using (left to right) BM3D, NL-means, bilateral filtering, and the proposed method ($\sigma = 20$).

Table 1. Performance evaluation of the four methods for $\sigma = 10$.

	SSIM	FSIM	SSIM	FSIM	SSIM	FSIM
	Balloons		*Peppers*		*Strawberry*	
BM3D	0.998618	0.989710	0.996654	0.986546	0.994613	0.991211
Bilateral filtering	0.999682	0.990189	0.999027	0.986816	0.999245	0.995256
NL-means	0.756735	0.948691	0.763018	0.967027	0.761760	0.968309
Proposed method	**0.999949**	**0.993487**	**0.999966**	**0.967027**	**0.999590**	**0.993403**
	Lemons		*Face*		*Sushi*	
BM3D	0.999209	0.988221	0.997708	0.994010	0.999146	0.947712
Bilateral filtering	0.998936	0.995785	0.998935	0.996355	0.999002	0.985050
NL-means	0.755789	0.966747	0.758137	0.964739	0.737577	0.960536
Proposed method	**0.999948**	**0.994115**	**0.999928**	**0.995318**	**0.999970**	**0.975081**
	Toy		*Sponges*		*Dog*	
BM3D	0.998605	0.997111	0.999455	0.989820	0.999445	0.997021
Bilateral filtering	0.999359	0.996933	0.999561	0.991859	0.998737	0.997889
NL-means	0.793203	0.973994	0.759860	0.973994	0.778577	0.972676
Proposed method	**0.999962**	**0.996706**	**0.999966**	**0.994348**	**0.999982**	**0.997550**
	Superballs		*Painting*		*Feathers*	
BM3D	0.999133	0.980010	0.999667	0.993603	0.999112	0.994401
Bilateral filtering	0.998808	0.993517	0.999286	0.994794	0.999234	0.996049
NL-means	0.741390	0.966301	0.785226	0.969749	0.783850	0.973148
Proposed method	**0.999970**	**0.989861**	**0.999826**	**0.992659**	**0.999932**	**0.995031**

with less noise. Moreover, the values of the objective evaluation metrics are also higher. Therefore, this method is superior to the other three at removing noise and preserving edges. The results of the two experiments show that when σ is small, the effect of this method is better. When σ is large, the denoising and edge-preserving performance decrease, but are still better than those of the other three methods.

Table 2. Performance evaluation of the four methods for $\sigma = 20$.

	SSIM	FSIM	SSIM	FSIM	SSIM	FSIM
	Balloons		*Peppers*		*Strawberry*	
BM3D	0.998542	0.978311	0.996566	0.981545	0.997571	0.984121
Bilateral filtering	0.998941	0.966502	0.997325	0.991137	0.996282	0.991402
NL-means	0.473582	0.869075	0.494226	0.827927	0.494187	0.905239
Proposed method	**0.999942**	**0.981393**	**0.999955**	**0.953449**	**0.999837**	**0.991367**
	Lemons		*Face*		*Sushi*	
BM3D	0.996783	0.983312	0.996453	0.986901	0.997765	0.939502
Bilateral filtering	0.996973	0.988743	0.995684	0.987443	0.996914	0.980245
NL-means	0.475592	0.902011	0.482508	0.901384	0.453553	0.894366
Proposed method	**0.999954**	**0.991497**	**0.999947**	**0.992567**	**0.999964**	**0.97443**
	Toy		*Sponges*		*Dog*	
BM3D	0.997715	0.992900	0.996911	0.987811	0.995634	0.992422
Bilateral filtering	0.997787	0.995375	0.998587	0.978701	0.996533	0.994977
NL-means	0.545068	0.921793	0.475206	0.875805	0.513566	0.916205
Proposed method	**0.999950**	**0.995378**	**0.999931**	**0.986685**	**0.999967**	**0.995793**
	Superballs		*Painting*		*Feathers*	
BM3D	0.996944	0.971212	0.996442	0.983921	0.998841	0.988602
Bilateral filtering	0.996863	0.990906	0.997580	0.995128	0.998463	0.994548
NL-means	0.480543	0.909665	0.545358	0.927185	0.526506	0.923356
Proposed method	**0.999971**	**0.988392**	**0.999890**	**0.991642**	**0.999940**	**0.993679**

4   Conclusions

In this paper, the NL-means and bilateral filtering methods were combined for image denoising. Compared with the BM3D algorithm and bilateral filtering, the details are more prominent, the picture is clearer, and there is less noise remaining when this method is used. Compared with the results of the NL-means algorithm, the algorithm proposed in this paper has noticeably better results and better denoising performance with respect to subjective visual effect, SSIM, and FSIM.

Acknowledgments. This work was supported by the National Natural Science Foundation of China (Grant Nos. 61370138, 61572077, 61271435, and U1301251) and Beijing Municipal Natural Science Foundation (Grant Nos. 4152017 and 4162027).

References

1. Xie, Q., Zhao, Q., Meng, D., et al.: Multispectral images denoising by intrinsic tensor sparsity regularization. In: IEEE Conference on Computer Vision and Pattern Recognition, pp. 1692–1700 (2016)
2. Peng, H., Rao, R., Dianat, S.A.: Multispectral image denoising with optimized vector bilateral filter. IEEE Trans. Image Process. **23**(1), 264–273 (2014)

3. Scheunders, P.: Denoising of multispectral images using wavelet thresholding, vol. 5238 (2003)
4. Dabov, K., Foi, A., Katkovnik, V., et al.: Image denoising by sparse 3-D transform-domain collaborative filtering. IEEE Trans. Image Process. **16**(8), 2080–2095 (2007)
5. Buades, A., Coll, B., Morel, J.M.: A non-local algorithm for image denoising. In: 2005 IEEE Computer Society Conference on Computer Vision and Pattern Recognition, vol. 2, pp. 60–65 (2005)
6. Xizheng, C.: Image denoising algorithm based on edge preservation. Xidian University (2014)
7. Zhang, Z., Wang, W.: An improved bilateral filtering algorithm. J. Image Graph. **14**(3), 443–447 (2009)
8. Zhang, H., Tan, J.: Improved bilateral filtering algorithm. J. Hefei Univ. Technol. (Nat. Sci.) (9), 1059–1062 (2014)
9. He, J., Li, Y.: An image quality evaluation based on structural similarity. J. Changchun Univ. Sci. Technol. (Nat. Sci. Ed.) (3), 105–108 (2014)
10. Miao, Y., Yi, S., He, J., et al.: Feature similarity image quality evaluation based on gradient information. J. Image Graph. **20**(6), 749–755 (2015)

Probabilistic Collaborative Representation with Kernels for Visual Classification

Jie Meng$^{(\boxtimes)}$, Yanjiang Wang, and Bao-Di Liu

College of Information and Control Engineering,
China University of Petroleum (East China), Qingdao, Shandong, China
1556485553@163.com, yjwang@upc.edu.cn, thu.liubaodi@gmail.com

Abstract. Non-parametric subspace classifier, such as collaborative representation based classification, sparse representation based classification obtains superior performance to conventional parametric model method, such as support vector machine and softmax regression, for visual classification. Recently, a probabilistic collaborative representation based classifier, which utilizes a hybrid representation (shared representation and class specific representation) to a test sample, leading to state-of-the-art classification performance. However, the probabilistic collaborative representation based classification does not consider the nonlinear characteristics hidden in visual features. In the paper, we propose to utilize kernel technique to extend the probabilistic collaborative presentation based classification method. Experimental results on several benchmark datasets demonstrate that our propose method obtains favourable classification performance.

Keywords: Probabilistic collaborative representation
Kernel method · Visual recognition

1 Introduction

Visual recognition [1,2] is one of the fundamental issue in computer vision areas. In the past decades, a sea of visual recognition methods emerged [3–6]. Generally speaking, the conventional visual recognition methods can be categorized into two types. One is parametric methods and the other is non-parametric methods. For the former methods, they focus on learning the parameters of the visual recognition models from the training data, e.g., support vector machine method [7]. For the latter, they directly utilize the training samples to predict the labels of the test samples, e.g., nearest neighbor method.

Non-parametric methods attract thousands of scholars and researchers due that it is easy to implement, avoid over-fitting, and superior performance. The nearest subspace methods are classical non-parametric classifiers. The principle of such classifier is to assign a test sample to the class which has the shortest distance to it. Wei *et al.* [8] proposed to classify images through comparing the reconstruction error of each category. Wright *et al.* [9] described a sparse

© Springer Nature Singapore Pte Ltd. 2018
B. Huet et al. (Eds.): ICIMCS 2017, CCIS 819, pp. 392–402, 2018.
https://doi.org/10.1007/978-981-10-8530-7_38

representation based classification (SRC) system and achieved impressive performance for face recognition. Given a test sample, the sparse representation technique [10] represents it as a sparse linear combination of the train samples. The predicted label is determined by the residual error from each class. Zhang *et al.* [11] illustrated a collaborative representation based classification (CRC) system. Similar to SRC, CRC represents a test sample as the linear combination of almost all the training samples. Moreover, they demonstrated that it was the collaborative representation rather than the sparse representation that makes the nearest subspace method powerful for classification. Under the framework of SRC and CRC, a variety of nearest subspace method [12] was proposed to enhance the visual recognition performance. Yang *et al.*[13] learned a dictionary for each class with sparse coefficients and applied it for face recognition. Wang *et al.* [14] introduced a modified sparse model and a supervised class-specific representation method for classification. Liu *et al.* [15–17] proposed a class specific representation algorithm which can find the intrinsic relationship between the base vectors and the original image features. Wang *et al.*[18] proposed a label constrained specific representation approach to preserve the structural information in the feature space. Recently, Cai *et al.* [19] proposed a probabilistic collaborative representation based classification method. The probabilistic collaborative representation based classification method employed a probabilistic collaborative representation framework to jointly maximize the probability that a test sample belongs to each class. In fact, the probabilistic collaborative representation based classficiation method utilized the shared collaborative representation and class specific collaborative representation to obtain a more robust and stable solution. The probabilistic collaborative representation based classification leads to state-of-the-art classification results.

In this section, motivated by the superior performance on visual recognition achieved by the probabilistic collaborative representation based classification (ProCRC), we propose to extend the ProCRC to arbitrary kernel space. The structural of our proposed probabilistic collaborative representation based classification with kernels is shown in Fig. 1. Our work focuses on twofold.

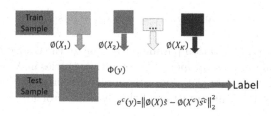

Fig. 1. Structural of the probabilistic collaborative representation with kernels.

1. We propose method to extend the probabilistic collaborative representation based classification method to arbitrary kernel space to find the nonlinear structures hidden in the data samples.

2. The proposed probabilistic collaborative representation based classification method is evaluated on six benchmark visual recognition datasets and achieve superior performance to the conventional methods, such as CRC and ProCRC.

The rest of the paper are organized as follows. Section 2 overviews the two classical visual recognition algorithms. Section 3 proposes our hybrid collaborative representation based classification with kernels. Then, experimental results and analysis are shown in Sect. 4. Finally, discussions and conclusions are drawn in Sect. 5.

2   Related Work

In this section, we will review some related work about collaborative representation based classification (CRC) and probabilistic collaborative representation based classification (ProCRC).

2.1   Overview of CRC

Zhang *et al.* [11] proposed the collaborative representation based classification (CRC). The proposed CRC achieved superior performance compared with conventional methods, such as support vector machine (SVM) and Nearest Neiborhood (NN). Here, collaborative representation can be considered as methods of rearranging the structure of the original data with a linear combination of bases vectors. Specifically, given the training samples $X = [X^1, X^2, \cdots, X^C] \in \mathbb{R}^{D \times N}$, $X^c \in \mathbb{R}^{D \times N_c}$ represents the training samples from the c_{th} class, C represents the number of classes, N_c represents the number of training samples in the c_{th} class $(N = \sum_{c=1}^{C} N_c)$, and D represents the dimensions of the samples. Supposing that $y \in \mathbb{R}^{D \times 1}$ is a test sample, the collaborative representation algorithm aims to solve the following objective function,

$$\hat{s} = \arg \min_s \left\{ \|y - Xs\|_2^2 + \beta \|s\|_2^2 \right\}. \tag{1}$$

Here, β is the regularization parameter to control the tradeoff between fitting goodness and collaborative property (i.e., multiple entries in X participating into representing the test samples). The collaborative representation based classification is to find the minimum value of the residual error for each class,

$$id(y) = \arg \min_c \|y - X^c \hat{s}^c\|_2^2. \tag{2}$$

The procedure of CRC is shown in Algorithm 1. Collaborative representation based classification effectively utilize all training samples for face recognition and the objective function of CRC has analytic solutions.

Algorithm 1. Algorithm for CRC

Require: Training samples $X \in \mathbb{R}^{D \times N}$, β, and test sample y
1: Code y with the dictionary X via collaborative representation (Eq. (1)).
2: **for** $c = 1; c \leq C; c{+}{+}$ **do**
3:    Compute the residuals $e^c(y) = \|y - X^c \hat{s}^c\|_2^2$
4: **end for**
5: $id(y) = \arg min_c \{e^c\}$
6: **return** $id(y)$

2.2 Overview of ProCRC

Cai *et al.* [19] proposed the probabilistic collaborative representation based classification (ProCRC) method. The proposed ProCRC maximizes the possibility that the test sample belongs to each of multiple classes. The objective function can be written as follows,

$$\hat{s} = \arg \min_{s} \left\{ \|y - Xs\|_2^2 + \beta \|s\|_2^2 + \frac{\tau}{C} \sum_{c=1}^{C} \|Xs - X_c s_c\|_2^2 \right\} \qquad (3)$$

In Eq. (3), the first two terms, which find the optimal collaborative representation for the test sample y, form the conventional collaborative representation. The third term is to further represent the test sample y with the class specific description (Here, $y \approx Xs$). The parameter β and τ balance the role of the three terms. When the parameter $\tau = 0$, Eq. (3) will degenerate to conventional CRC. The ProCRC is to find the minimum value of the residual error for each class, as follows,

$$id(y) = \arg min_c \|Xs - X^c \hat{s}^c\|_2^2. \qquad (4)$$

3 Probabilistic Collaborative Representation Based Classification in Reproducing Kernel Hilbert Space

The ProCRC method achieves state-of-the-art performance on a variety of challenging visual datasets. However, it does not consider the nonlinear characteristics hidden in image features. As a matter of fact, many real word images require complex nonlinearity in visual classification tasks due to their distribution. In this section, we propose method to extend the probabilistic collaborative representation based classification to arbitrary kernel space.

3.1 Extend the ProCRC to Arbitrary Kernel Space

Suppose there exists a kernel function $\phi : R^D \rightarrow R^K (D < K)$, function ϕ map the image features to the high dimensional feature space. The training samples $\phi(X) = [\phi(X^1), \phi(X^2), \cdots, \phi(X^C)] \in R^{K \times N}$. The testing sample $\phi(y) = \in R^{K \times 1}$.

The objective function of probabilistic collaborative representation based classification with kernels (ProKCRC) is as follows,

$$\hat{s} = \arg\min_{s} \left\{ \|\phi(y) - \phi(X)s\|_2^2 + \beta\|s\|_2^2 + \frac{\tau}{C}\sum_{c=1}^{C}\|\phi(X)s - \phi(X_c)s_c\|_2^2 \right\} \quad (5)$$

3.2 Optimization the Objective of ProKCRC

In Eq. (5), the map ϕ is unknown. However, the ϕ in the objective function (Eq. (5)) can be replace with the kernel function $\kappa(x, y) = \phi(x)^T \phi(y)$. Using the "kernel trick", we obtain Eq. (6) for probabilistic collaborative representation as follows,

$$
\begin{aligned}
f(s) &= \|\phi(y) - \phi(X)s\|_2^2 + \beta\|s\|_2^2 + \frac{\tau}{C}\sum_{c=1}^{C}\|\phi(X)s - \phi(X_c)s_c\|_2^2 \\
&= \|\phi(y) - \phi(X)s\|_2^2 + \beta\|s\|_2^2 \\
&\quad + \frac{\tau}{C}\sum_{c=1}^{C}\|\phi(X)s - [0,\cdots,\phi(X_c),\cdots,0]s\|_2^2 \\
&= trace\left\{\kappa(y,y) - 2\kappa(y,X)s + s^T\kappa(X,X)s\right\} + \beta trace\left\{s^T s\right\} \\
&\quad + \tau trace\left\{s^T\kappa(X,X)s\right\} - 2\frac{\tau}{C}trace\left\{s^T\kappa(X,X)s\right\} \\
&\quad + \frac{\tau}{C}trace\left\{s^T\begin{bmatrix}\kappa(X_1,X_1) & 0 & 0 \\ 0 & \cdots & 0 \\ 0 & 0 & \kappa(X_C,X_C)\end{bmatrix}s\right\}
\end{aligned}
\quad (6)
$$

Here, $trace\{A\}$ represents the trace of matrix A.

Remove the irrelvant term $trace\{\kappa(y,y)\}$, Eq. (6) can be simplified as follows,

$$
\begin{aligned}
f(s) &= trace\left\{s^T\left\{\left(1+\tau-\frac{2\tau}{C}\right)\kappa(X,X) + \beta I\right\}s\right\} \\
&\quad + \frac{\tau}{C}trace\left\{s^T\begin{bmatrix}\kappa(X_1,X_1) & 0 & 0 \\ 0 & \cdots & 0 \\ 0 & 0 & \kappa(X_C,X_C)\end{bmatrix}s\right\} \\
&\quad - 2trace\left\{\kappa(y,X)s\right\}
\end{aligned}
\quad (7)
$$

Here, I represent the identity matrix.

Let $P = \begin{bmatrix}\kappa(X_1,X_1) & 0 & 0 \\ 0 & \cdots & 0 \\ 0 & 0 & \kappa(X_C,X_C)\end{bmatrix}$. The solution to s can be obtained efficiently, as follows,

$$\hat{s} = \left\{\left(1+\tau\frac{C-2}{C}\right)\kappa(X,X) + \beta I + P\right\}^{-1}\kappa(X,y) \quad (8)$$

Algorithm 2. Algorithm for ProKCRC

Require: Training samples $X \in \mathbb{R}^{D \times N}$, β, and test sample y
1: Code y with the dictionary X via ProKCRC (Eq. (8)).
2: **for** $c = 1$; $c \leq C$; $c{+}{+}$ **do**
3:    Compute the residuals $e^c(y) = \|\phi(X)\hat{s} - \phi(X^c)\hat{s}^c\|_2^2$
4: **end for**
5: $id(y) = \arg \min_c \{e^c\}$
6: **return** $id(y)$

After obtain the code $\hat{s}$, The ProKCRC is to find the minimum value of the residual error for each class, as follows,

$$id(y) = \arg \min_c \|\phi(X)\hat{s} - \phi(X^c)\hat{s}^c\|_2^2. \tag{9}$$

The procedure of ProKCRC is shown in Algorithm 2.

4 Experimental Results

In this section, we compare our proposed ProKCRC algorithm with CRC algorithm on six datasets, including two handwritten recognition datasets, such as MNIST [20] dataset and USPS [20] dataset; three face recognition datasets, such as the AR [21] dataset, Extended YaleB [22] and CMU PIE dataset [23]; and one image classification dataset, Caltech-101 [24] dataset. In the following subsections, first, we list the parameter settings for all the experiments. Second, we present the experimental results on these six datasets to show the performance of our proposed algorithm. Third, we further analyze the experimental results.

4.1 Experimental Settings

For all datasets, to eliminate the randomness of the experiment, the data are randomly split into the training set and the testing set 10 times, respectively. The mean of the face recognition rate are reported.

We use four different kernels: the linear kernel ($\kappa(x,y) = x^T y$), the Hellinger kernel ($\kappa(x,y) = \sum_{d=1}^{D} \sqrt{x_d y_d}$), the polynomial kernel (POLY, $\kappa(x,y) = (p + x^T y)^q$), and the radial basis function kernel (RBF, $\kappa(x,y) = \exp(-\gamma \|x - y\|_2^2)$). Here, we set $p = 4$, $q = 2$ and $\gamma = 0.3$.

For face recognition datasets, 5 and 10 samples per class are used for training and testing, respectively. Each face image is cropped to 32×32. Then, all images are pulled into column vector, and ℓ_2 normalized to form the raw ℓ_2 normalized feature. For handwritten recognition datasets, 10 and 10 samples per class are used for training and testing, respectively. The size of each image is 28×28 and 16×16 for MNIST dataset and USPS dataset, respectively. All images are pulled into column vector, and ℓ_2 normalized to form the raw ℓ_2 normalized feature. For image classification dataset, 5 and 10 samples per class are used for training and testing, respectively. For image features, we use VGG-verydeep-19 [25] to extract CNN features. We use the activations of the last fourth layers as a local feature. The final feature of each image is ℓ_2 normalized with 4,096 demensions.

4.2 Experiment on Handwritten Recognition Datasets

For MNIST dataset, it consists of 70,000 images that belongs to 10 classes and the dimensionality of each image is 784. In Fig. 2, we list some samples belonging to this dataset. The parameter β is ranged from 2^{-5} to 2^5. The parameter τ is ranged from 2^{-5} to 2^8. The optimal parameter β and τ are $(2^{-1}, 2^{-2})$, $(2^3, 2^2)$, $(2^{-4}, 2^7)$, $(2^1, 2^{-4})$ for linear kernel, Hellinger kernel, RBF kernel, and POLY kernel, respectively. Table 1 shows the recognition rate of CRC and ProKCRC. From Table 1, we can see that the optimal kernel function is Hellinger and the classification rate with Hellinger kernel is 1.6% higher than the classification rate with linear kernel (i.e. the conventional ProCRC method).

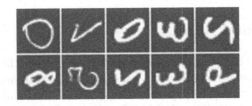

Fig. 2. Samples in MINIST dataset.

For USPS dataset, it consists of 11,000 images that belongs to 10 classes and the dimensionality of each image is 256. The parameter β is ranged from 2^{-4} to 2^6. The parameter τ is ranged from 2^{-5} to 2^5. The optimal parameter β and τ are $(2^{-1}, 2^{-1})$, $(2^5, 2^2)$, $(2^0, 2^3)$, $(2^1, 2^{-4})$ for linear kernel, Hellinger kernel, RBF kernel, and POLY kernel, respectively. Table 1 shows the recognition rate of CRC and ProKCRC. From Table 1, we can see that the optimal kernel function

Table 1. The comparison of classification rate between CRC And ProKCRC in six datasets (%)

Methods\Datasets	MNIST	USPS	Caltech-101	AR	Extended Yale B	CMU PIE
CRC (linear)	76.9	75.1	87.70583	91.68	79.07896	73.2353
CRC (Hellinger)	78.5	77.5	87.98039	92.09	89.44738	75.23528
CRC (rbf)	74.2	74.9	88.39217	92.2	77.26316	73.51471
CRC (poly)	75.5	75.9	88.14704	92	77.71054	76.63159
ProKCRC (linear)	77.2	78.1	87.72549	93.48	81.3158	77.97057
ProKCRC (Hellinger)	**78.8**	**79.4**	87.99019	93.77	**91.28947**	**79.38236**
ProKCRC (rbf)	75.3	78.1	**88.40196**	**94.03**	80.9999	77.95589
ProKCRC (poly)	76.3	76.3	88.38235	93.73	80.86341	78.17648

is Hellinger and the classification rate with Hellinger kernel is 1.3% higher than the classification rate with linear kernel (i.e. the conventional ProCRC method).

Experiment on Image Classification Datasets. For Caltech-101 dataset, it consists of $9,144$ images that belongs to 102 classes, one of which is the background. The parameter β is ranged from 2^{-6} to 2^2. The parameter τ is ranged from 2^{-12} to 2^{-5}. The optimal parameter β and τ are $(2^{-2}, 2^{-9})$, $(2^2, 2^{-7})$, $(2^{-5}, 2^{-10})$, $(2^0, 2^{-7})$ for linear kernel, Hellinger kernel, RBF kernel, and POLY kernel, respectively. Table 1 shows the recognition rate of CRC and ProKCRC. From Table 1, we can see that the optimal kernel function is RBF and the classification rate with RBF kernel is 0.67% higher than the classification rate with linear kernel (i.e. the conventional ProCRC method).

Experiment on Face Recognition Datasets. For the AR dataset, there are over 4,000 frontal faces for 126 individuals. A subset consisting of 50 male and 50 female categories is used here. There are 26 face images for each class. The AR dataset contains many facial variations, such as illumination change, various expressions, and facial disguises. Figure 3 shows some samples face images from the dataset. The parameter β is ranged from 2^{-13} to 2^{-5}. The parameter τ is ranged from $\{2^{-12}\}$ to $\{2^{-5}\}$. The optimal parameter β and τ are $(2^{-9}, 2^{-8})$, $(2^{-6}, 2^{-9})$, $(2^{-12}, 2^{-11})$, $(2^{-6}, 2^{-9})$ for linear kernel, Hellinger kernel, RBF kernel, and POLY kernel, respectively. Table 1 shows the recognition rate of CRC and ProKCRC. From Table 1, we can see that the optimal kernel function is RBF and the classification rate with RBF kernel is 0.55% higher than the classification rate with linear kernel (i.e. the conventional ProCRC method).

Fig. 3. Samples in AR dataset.

For the Extended YaleB dataset, there are 2,414 frontal face images and 38 individuals in total. All the images are captured under varying illumination conditions. The parameter β is ranged from 2^{-15} to 2^{-5}. The parameter τ is ranged from 2^{-8} to 2^0. The optimal parameter β and τ are $(2^{-14}, 2^{-1})$, $(2^{-6}, 2^{-7})$, $(2^{-13}, 2^{-5})$, $(2^{-8}, 2^{-1})$ for linear kernel, Hellinger kernel, RBF kernel, and POLY kernel, respectively. Table 1 shows the recognition rate of CRC and ProKCRC. From Table 1, we can see that the optimal kernel function is Hellinger and the classification rate with Hellinger kernel is 9.97% higher than the classification rate with linear kernel (i.e. the conventional ProCRC method).

The CMU PIE dataset contains 41,368 images of 68 individuals in total. Each individual is under 13 different poses, 43 different illumination conditions, and with 4 different expressions. Each individual thus may lie on multiple manifolds. Five near frontal poses (C05, C07, C09, C27, C29) and all different illuminations and expressions are used in our experiment. There are about 170 images for each individual and 11,554 images in total. The parameter β is ranged from 2^{-13} to 2^{-4}. The parameter τ is ranged from 2^{-10} to 2^{-1}. The optimal parameter β and τ are $(2^{-7}, 2^{-3})$, $(2^{-5}, 2^{-7})$, $(2^{-12}, 2^{-9})$, $(2^{-9}, 2^{-2})$ for linear kernel, Hellinger kernel, RBF kernel, and POLY kernel, respectively. Table 1 shows the recognition rate of CRC and ProKCRC. From Table 1, we can see that the optimal kernel function is Hellinger and the classification rate with Hellinger kernel is 1.41% higher than the classification rate with linear kernel (i.e. the conventional ProCRC method).

Analysis of the Experimental Results. From the experimental results, we have the following conclusions.

1. The classification rate on these six datasets with the ProKCRC method is higher than that with CRC method in each kernel space. That is to say, the ProKCRC method achieves superior performance to the CRC method.
2. For handwritten recognition datasets, the ProKCRC method in Hellinger kernel space achieves the optimal classification rate. For image classification dataset, the ProKCRC method in RBF kernel space obtains the highest classification rate among the ProKCRC method in these kernel spaces. For face recognition datasets, the ProKCRC method in Hellinger kernel space obtains better classification rate than the ProKCRC method in other kernel spaces. Notability, the classification rate is increased by 9.97% with ProKCRC method from linear kernel to Hellinger kernel for Extended YaleB dataset.
3. Our proposed ProKCRC method is capable of efficiently promoting the performance of visual classification.

In addition, the comparison of running time between CRC and ProKCRC on Extended YaleB dataset is shown in Table 2.

Table 2. The comparison of running time (s) between CRC and ProKCRC on Extended YaleB dataset

Methods	linear	Hellinger	rbf	poly
CRC	1.055	1.194	1.769	1.078
ProKCRC	6.830	7.083	7.530	6.976

5   Conclusions

In this paper, we propose to extend the probabilistic collaborative representation based classification method to arbitrary kernel space. The proposed probabilistic collaborative representation based classification method is capable of finding nonlinear structures hidden in the image features. The ProKCRC method has the close form solution and is easy to implement. Our experiments on handwritten recognition, image classification and face recognition tasks validated its superiority to CRC and ProKCRC in the linear kernel space.

Acknowledgment. This paper is supported partly by the National Natural Science Foundation of China (Grant No. 61402535, No. 61271407), the Natural Science Foundation for Youths of Shandong Province, China (Grant No. ZR2014FQ001), the Natural Science Foundation of Shandong Province (Grant No. ZR2017MF069), Qingdao Science and Technology Project (No. 17-1-1-8-jch), and the Fundamental Research Funds for the Central Universities, China University of Petroleum (East China) (Grant No. 16CX02060A), International S And T Cooperation Program of China (Grant No. 2015DFG12050).

References

1. Liu, W., Tao, D., Cheng, J., Tang, Y.: Multiview Hessian discriminative sparse coding for image annotation. Comput. Vis. Image Underst. **118**(1), 50–60 (2013)
2. Tao, D., Li, X., Wu, X., Maybank, S.J.: General tensor discriminant analysis and gabor features for gait recognition. IEEE Trans. Pattern Anal. Mach. Intell. **29**(10) (2007)
3. Liu, T., Tao, D.: On the performance of Manhattan nonnegative matrix factorization. IEEE Trans. Neural Netw. Learn. Syst. **27**(9), 1851–1863 (2016)
4. Liu, T., Gong, M., Tao, D.: Large-cone nonnegative matrix factorization. IEEE Trans. Neural Netw. Learn. Syst. **28**(9), 2129–2142 (2017)
5. Yu, J., Rui, Y., Tao, D.: Click prediction for web image reranking using multimodal sparse coding. IEEE Trans. Image Process. **23**(5), 2019 (2014)
6. Yu, J., Tao, D., Wang, M., Rui, Y.: Learning to rank using user clicks and visual features for image retrieval. IEEE Trans. Cybern. **45**(4), 767–779 (2015)
7. Tao, D., Tang, X., Li, X., Xindong, W.: Asymmetric bagging and random subspace for support vector machines-based relevance feedback in image retrieval. IEEE Trans. Pattern Anal. Mach. Intell. **28**(7), 1088–1099 (2006)
8. Wei, C.-P., Chao, Y.-W., Yeh, Y.-R., Wang, Y.-C.F.: Locality-sensitive dictionary learning for sparse representation based classification. Pattern Recogn. **46**(5), 1277–1287 (2013)
9. Wright, J., Yang, A.Y., Ganesh, A., Sastry, S.S., Ma, Y.: Robust face recognition via sparse representation. IEEE Trans. Pattern Anal. Mach. Intell. **31**(2), 210–227 (2009)
10. Liu, B.-D., Wang, Y.-X., Shen, B., Zhang, Y.-J., Hebert, M.: Self-explanatory sparse representation for image classification. In: Fleet, D., Pajdla, T., Schiele, B., Tuytelaars, T. (eds.) ECCV 2014. LNCS, vol. 8690, pp. 600–616. Springer, Cham (2014). https://doi.org/10.1007/978-3-319-10605-2_39
11. Zhang, L., Yang, M., Feng, X.: Sparse representation or collaborative representation: which helps face recognition? In: Proceedings of the 13th ICCV, pp. 471–478. IEEE (2011)
12. Tao, D., Li, X., Wu, X., Maybank, S.J.: Geometric mean for subspace selection. IEEE Trans. Pattern Anal. Mach. Intell. **31**(2), 260–274 (2009)
13. Yang, M., Zhang, L., Yang, J., Zhang, D.: Metaface learning for sparse representation based face recognition. In: Proceedings of the 17th ICIP, pp. 1601–1604. IEEE (2010)

14. Wang, H., Yuan, C., Weiming, H., Sun, C.: Supervised class-specific dictionary learning for sparse modeling in action recognition. Pattern Recogn. **45**(11), 3902–3911 (2012)
15. Liu, B.D., Shen, B., Wang, Y.X.: Class specific dictionary learning for face recognition. In: International Conference on Security, Pattern Analysis, and Cybernetics, pp. 229–234 (2014)
16. Liu, B.D., Shen, B., Gui, L., Wang, Y.X., Li, X., Yan, F., Wang, Y.J.: Face recognition using class specific dictionary learning for sparse representation and collaborative representation. Neurocomputing **204**, 198–210 (2016)
17. Liu, B.D., Gui, L., Wang, Y., Wang, Y.X., Shen, B., Li, X., Wang, Y.J.: Class specific centralized dictionary learning for face recognition. Multimedia Tools Appl. **76**(3), 1–19 (2017)
18. Wang, W., Yan, Y., Winkler, S., Sebe, N.: Category specific dictionary learning for attribute specific feature selection. IEEE Trans. Image Process. **25**(3), 1465–1478 (2016)
19. Cai, S., Zhang, L., Zuo, W., Feng, X.: A probabilistic collaborative representation based approach for pattern classification. In: Computer Vision and Pattern Recognition (2016)
20. Lecun, Y., Cortes, C.: The MNIST database of handwritten digits (2010)
21. Martinez, A.M.: The AR face database. CVC Technical report, 24 (1998)
22. Georghiades, A.S., Belhumeur, P.N., Kriegman, D.J.: From few to many: illumination cone models for face recognition under variable lighting and pose. IEEE Trans. Pattern Anal. Mach. Intell. **23**(6), 643–660 (2001)
23. Sim, T., Baker, S., Bsat, M.: The CMU pose, illumination, and expression (PIE) database. In: IEEE International Conference on Automatic Face and Gesture Recognition, Proceedings, pp. 46–51 (2002)
24. Fei-Fei, L., Fergus, R., Perona, P.: Learning generative visual models from few training examples: an incremental Bayesian approach tested on 101 object categories. Comput. Vis. Image Underst. **106**(1), 59–70 (2007)
25. Simonyan, K., Zisserman, A.: Very deep convolutional networks for large-scale image recognition. arXiv preprint arXiv:1409.1556 (2014)

Probability Matrix SVM+ Learning for Complex Action Recognition

Fang Liu, Xiangmin Xu$^{(\boxtimes)}$, Chunmei Qing, and Jianxiu Jin

South China University of Technology, Guangzhou, China
xmxu@scut.edu.cn

Abstract. Complex action recognition is a hot topic in computer vision. When training a robust model, a large amount of labeled data is required. However, labeling complex actions is often time-consuming and expensive. Considering that each complex action is composed of a sequence of simple actions, we propose a new perspective to provide more information during training in order to solve the problem of insufficient labeled data. The probability matrix is then designed by manual annotation, which encodes a probability distribution of simple actions in complex actions. So the probability matrix is only available during training but unavailable during testing. Finally, a probability matrix is regared as privileged information in a SVM+ framework, and we regard this setting as probability matrix SVM+(pmSVM+). To validate the proposed model, extensive experiments are carried out on complex action datasets. Experiment results show the effectiveness of pmSVM+ for complex action recognition.

Keywords: Privileged information · Relative probability matrix
Simple action · Complex action recognition

1 Introduction

Complex action recognition has attracted considerable attention because of its many applications, such as intelligent video surveillance, content-based video search and retrieval, and human-computer interactions. Complex action recognition has the great challenge due to the following reasons. Firstly, complex action videos contain cluttered backgrounds, view point changes, motion speed variations, and large intra-class variations within the same category of actions. Secondly, each complex action has a longer temporal structure. To address the above problems, recognizing complex action requires a large amount of labeled training data.

A large number of approaches have been proposed for recognizing complex actions. However, these methods can achieve promising performance depends on the size of labeled training samples. But Manual labeling complex action videos is often expensive and time-consuming. Considering that each complex action is composed of a sequence of simple actions, which can be easily acquired

© Springer Nature Singapore Pte Ltd. 2018
B. Huet et al. (Eds.): ICIMCS 2017, CCIS 819, pp. 403–410, 2018.
https://doi.org/10.1007/978-981-10-8530-7_39

from existing simple action datasets. We expect to recognize complex action recognition from a new perspective.

While privileged information has shown promising performance in image classification and action recognition [4,14,15,19]. Privileged information can provide more information at the training stage, it can effectively solve the problem of insufficient labeled training data. Therefore a critical aspect is finding beneficial information as privileged information to help machine learning. According to [14], there are different types of privileged information, such as textual descriptions, attributes and so on. These privileged information can boost the performance of machine learning by offering more information related to target images or videos during training.

Different from these privileged information learning approaches, we design privileged information from a sequence of simple actions. As different complex actions can be composed of different simple actions, but all complex actions share these simple actions, so complex action can be considered as a probability distribution of simple actions. Then the probability matrix is designed by manual annotation. In this situation, the probability matrix can not be obtained in the test videos, we treat it as privileged information for complex action recognition. In addition, we observe that the probability matrix contains more information than the complex action data alone to learn a robust model. Therefore, the probability matrix can provide helpful information for recognizing complex actions.

To this end, we design privileged information from a sequence of simple actions. Then a probability matrix is developed as the privileged information and put it into a SVM+ framework for video-based human action recognition.

The remainder of this paper is organized as follows. Section 2 presents a brief review of related works. In Sect. 3, we introduce the proposed model for complex action recognition in more detail. Extensive experimental results are described in Sect. 4. Finally, we conclude the paper in Sect. 5.

2   Related Work

This section describes related work on complex action recognition and privileged information.

Complex action recognition: A considerable amount of approaches have been proposed for recognizing complex actions. These methods exploit temporal structure, attribute, parts and other methods to recognize complex actions. In the aspect of temporal structure [9], Niebles et al. [9] proposed modeling the temporal decomposition of human complex actions. In the aspect of the attribute [5,20], Zhang et al. [20] used the attributes for complex action recognition. In the aspect of part [3,18], Wang et al. [18] proposed using a set of spatiotemporal parts called motionlet for complex action recognition.

Privileged information: In 2009, Vapnik and Vashist [15] firstly proposed the concept of privileged information, which was only available at the training stage, but not available for testing. The ideal was implemented based on SVM method, called SVM+, which was effective solved in [10]. A variety of approaches [15,19] have been proposed for task classification by using privileged information. Types of privileged information were explored in [14], such as attributes, bounding box, textual description and so on. For example, Wang et al. [19] proposed using relative attributes as privileged information to improve the performance of age estimation.

3   Proposed Method

The probability matrix is designed for the training samples, and our goal is to utilize the designed probability matrix to improve the performance of complex action recognition. Details of the designed probability matrix are described as follows.

3.1   Probability Matrix as Privileged Information

As in [7], each complex action is composed of a sequence of simple actions. Different complex actions can be composed of different simple actions, e.g., the javelin throw action is composed of running and boxing and the bowling action is composed of bending, boxing and walking, as shown in Fig. 1.

While all complex actions share these simple actions. Traditional approaches only use these complex actions as training data to recognize complex actions, which require a large number of training samples in order to learn robust model. However, labeled complex actions is difficult to obtain. Fortunately, these simple actions is easily obtained from existing simple action datasets.

We utilize these simple actions to facilitate complex action recognition. Therefore, the probability matrix by manual annotation is designed to capture the each simple action probability in the complex action videos. When performing complex action recognition, knowing the each simple action probability in the training data is regarded as privileged information, and the probability matrix contains a large amount of information about complex actions to facilitate their learning.

We use a sequence of simple actions for which the probability matrix annotation is available, which encodes the each simple action probability in complex actions. For all complex actions, we can obtain the probability matrix $P \in R^{nS \times T}$. Finally, we consider it as privileged data X^* for complex action recognition.

The main task of this section is to design a probability matrix for building the privileged information of training data. Different from the aforementioned privileged information, the privileged information used in our model is learned from simple actions, and it conveys more information to facilitate recognizing complex actions.

Subsequently, an effective method will be proposed to use the above privileged data. In the following section, we describe the proposed pmSVM+ in more detail.

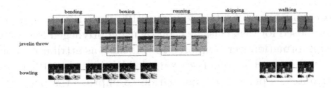

Fig. 1. Example of complex actions described by a sequence of simple actions.

3.2 Probability Matrix SVM+(pmSVM+)

In the following part, we will introduce the designed probability matrix as the privileged information to recognize complex human actions.

Vapnik and Vashist [15] introduced a new learning paradigm called Learning Using Privileged Information (LUPI). The privileged information is available for training samples, but is not available for testing samples.

LUPI exploits the privileged information X^* to help train a robust model. The LUPI paradigm can be implemented in a SVM algorithm, called SVM+ [15], $\varphi(x) = sign(wx + b)$ is a decision function and $\phi(x_i^*) = sign(wx_i^* + b)$ is a correcting function. Then the corresponding optimization problem of SVM+ is formulated as follows:

$$\min_{w,b,w^*,d} \frac{1}{2}\|w\|_2^2 + \frac{\gamma}{2}\|w^*\|_2^2 + C\sum_{i=1}^n (w^* \cdot x_i^* + d),$$
$$s.t. \forall 1 \leq i \leq n, y_i(w \cdot z_i + b) \geq 1 - (w^* \cdot x_i^* + d),$$
$$\forall 1 \leq i \leq n, w^* \cdot x_i^* + d \geq 0,$$

the triplets (x_i, x_i^*, y_i) are given data, where $x_i \in X$, $x_i^* \in X^*$, $y_i \in \{-1, 1\}$. $C > 0$ and $\gamma > 0$ are hyperparameters, and z_i^* is a feature map of x_i^*. The term $\frac{\gamma}{2}\|w^*\|_2^2$ constraints the capacity of the correcting space.

For complex action recognition, in the above equation, X are the feature vectors of the complex action videos and X^* are the probability of complex actions. In our work, we used the X^* to estimate the value of slacks with Eq. (1).

As suggested in [10], we use the alternating SMO to solve the SVM+ and the parameters are set as suggested by [11]. In SVM+, we consider the designed probability matrix as the privileged information and have $(T(T+1))/2$ decision functions, where T is the number of complex action classes. We expect that the designed probability matrix as the privileged information can improve the performance of complex action recognition. More details about the experiments are discussed in the next section.

4   Experiments

4.1   Datasets

The simple action dataset consists of 26 action categories, 21 action categories are chosen from the KTH dataset [13], Weizmann dataset [2], HMDB51 dataset

Fig. 2. Sample frames from simple action dataset, Olympic Sports dataset and YouTube Action dataset.

[6], and 5 action categories are captured action videos by our lab. It contains bending, boxing, clapping, catching, circling, climb, diving, falling, fencing, high throwing, low throw, normal throw, kick ball, waving, jacking, jogging, jumping, pjumping, running, ride horse, ride bike, swing baseball, sword, skipping, stand, waiting and walking. Some video frames are shown in the first row of Fig. 2. We employ all the samples from the Weizmann dataset [2], 30 samples from the KTH dataset [13], HMDB51 dataset [6] and captured action videos for each class respectively.

The Olympic Sport dataset [9] consists of 16 action classes from You Tube videos: bowling, basketball layup, clean and jerk, discus throw, high jump, hammer throw, platform, springboard, javelin throw, pole vault, long jump, snatch, shot put, triple-jump, tennis-serve and vault, some video frames are shown in the second row of Fig. 2. The experiment setting is suggested by [3], we use 649 video clips for training and 134 for testing, and we report the average accuracy for the proposed approach.

The YouTube Action dataset [8] have 11 action categories and 1168 videos. Some video frames are shown in the third row of Fig. 2. We follow the experiment setting in [8] and use Leave-One-Out Cross-Validation for the given 25 groups. We also report the average accuracy for the proposed methods.

The UCF50 dataset [12] contains 50 action classes and 6618 realistic videos taken from You Tube, some video frames are shown in the fourth row of Fig. 2. Following the experiment setup described in [1], we use 5%, 10%, 20% of the training samples to implement our experiment and report the average accuracy for the proposed method.

4.2 Experimental Results

In this subsection, we will report the results on the complex action datasets. As we know, DT features [16] and IDT features [17] have promising performance for action recognition, thus we compare our proposed method with two baselines: DT features [16] and IDT features [17]. Details of comparison results are described as follows.

Table 1. Recognition results for the Olympic Sports dataset with different percentages of training samples.

Percentage	10%	20%	30%
Dense trajectory	44.5%	52.7%	57.2%
pmSVM+	50.7%	62.9%	65.1%

Table 2. Recognition results for the YouTube Action dataset with different percentages of training samples.

Percentage	10%	20%	30%
Dense trajectory	53.9%	65.9%	72.7%
pmSVM+	55.6%	67.8%	74.3%

Using DT features

– Olympic Sports: The SVM+ algorithm can be solved according to [10] with the parameters set based on [11]. We randomly choose 10%, 20%, 30% of the training samples for each class. The results of the experiments with dense trajectory and with our method are shown in Table 1. The proposed method remarkably outperforms the dense trajectory method. The results show that the probability matrix as privileged information can improve the performance of complex action recognition.
– YouTube Action: We also randomly choose 10%, 20%, 30% of the training samples to conduct the experiments. The results of experiments with dense trajectory and with the proposed method are shown in Table 2. In our experiments, our proposed method performs well compared to the dense trajectory method. Thus, the probability matrix as privileged information can help complex action learning and demonstrates that simple actions facilitate complex action learning.

Using IDT features

– Olympic Sports: We randomly choose 5%, 10%, 20% of the training samples for each class. The results of the experiments with improved dense trajectory and with our method are shown in Table 3. The proposed method remarkably outperforms the improved dense trajectory method. This also demonstrates that the probability matrix from simple actions can offer more information, and boost the performance of complex action recognition.
– UCF50: We also randomly choose 5%, 10%, 20% of the training samples to conduct the experiments. The results of experiments with improved dense trajectory and with the proposed method are shown in Table 4. In our experiments, our proposed method performs well compared to the improved dense trajectory method. Thus, the experiment results show that pmSVM+ is a promising method to improve the performance of complex action recognition by using the probability matrix from a sequence of simple actins.

Table 3. Recognition results for the Olympic Sports dataset with different percentages of training samples.

Percentage	5%	10%	20%
Improved dense trajectory	38.5%	49.8%	62.4%
pmSVM+	44.4%	51.4%	66.3%

Table 4. Recognition results for the UCF50 dataset with different percentages of training samples.

Percentage	5%	10%	20%
Improved dense trajectory	56.5%	68.4%	76.6%
pmSVM+	57.7%	70.2%	77.2%

5   Conclusions

In order to recognize few labeled complex actions, privileged information is applied in our model. In this model, we employ a probability matrix as the privileged information learned from simple actions to recognize complex actions. A probability matrix is then regared as privileged information in a SVM+ framework, which can deal with the situation of insufficient training samples.

Extensive experiments on published complex action datasets show that the proposed approach achieves significantly improvement compared to existing approaches. Our future work mainly concentrates on to explore more beneficial information from simple actions to help complex action learning.

Acknowledgment. This work is supported in part by the National Natural Science Founding of China (61171142, 61401163, U1636218), Science and Technology Planning Project of Guangdong Province of China (2014B010111003, 2014B010111006), the Fundamental Research Funds for the Central Universities (2017MS045), and Guangzhou Key Lab of Body Data Science (201605030011).

References

1. Corso, J.J., Sadanand, S.: Action bank: a high-level representation of activity in video. In: IEEE Conference on Computer Vision and Pattern Recognition, pp. 1234–1241 (2012)
2. Gorelick, L., Blank, M., Shechtman, E., Irani, M., Basri, R.: Actions as space-time shapes. IEEE Trans. Pattern Anal. Mach. Intell. **29**(12), 2247–2253 (2007)
3. Hong, R., Hu, Z., Wang, R., Wang, M., Tao, D.: Multi-view object retrieval via multi-scale topic models. IEEE Trans. Image Process. **25**(12), 5814–5827 (2016)
4. Hong, R., Yang, Y., Wang, M., Hua, X.S.: Learning visual semantic relationships for efficient visual retrieval. IEEE Trans. Big Data **1**(4), 152–161 (2017)

5. Hong, R., Zhang, L., Zhang, C., Zimmermann, R.: Flickr circles: aesthetic tendency discovery by multi-view regularized topic modeling. IEEE Trans. Multimedia **18**(8), 1555–1567 (2016)
6. Kuehne, H., Jhuang, H., Garrote, E., Poggio, T., Serre, T.: HMDB: a large video database for human motion recognition. In: International Conference on Computer Vision, pp. 2556–2563 (2015)
7. Liu, F., Xu, X., Qiu, S., Qing, C.: Simple to complex transfer learning for action recognition. IEEE Trans. Image Process. Publ. IEEE Sig. Process. Soc. **25**(2), 949–960 (2015)
8. Liu, J., Luo, J., Shah, M.: Recognizing realistic actions from videos in the wild. In: IEEE Conference on Computer Vision and Pattern Recognition, CVPR 2009, pp. 1996–2003. IEEE (2009)
9. Niebles, J.C., Chen, C.-W., Fei-Fei, L.: Modeling temporal structure of decomposable motion segments for activity classification. In: Daniilidis, K., Maragos, P., Paragios, N. (eds.) ECCV 2010. LNCS, vol. 6312, pp. 392–405. Springer, Heidelberg (2010). https://doi.org/10.1007/978-3-642-15552-9_29
10. Pechyony, D., Izmailov, R., Vashist, A., Vapnik, V.: SMO-style algorithms for learning using privileged information. In: International Conference on Data Mining, Dmin 2010, 12–15 July 2010, Las Vegas, Nevada, USA, pp. 235–241 (2010)
11. Pechyony, D., Vapnik, V.: Fast optimization algorithms for solving SVM+. Stat. Learn. Data Sci. (2011)
12. Reddy, K.K., Shah, M.: Recognizing 50 human action categories of web videos. Mach. Vis. Appl. **24**(5), 971–981 (2013)
13. Schüldt, C., Laptev, I., Caputo, B.: Recognizing human actions: a local SVM approach. In: Proceedings of the 17th International Conference on Pattern Recognition, ICPR 2004, vol. 3, pp. 32–36. IEEE (2004)
14. Sharmanska, V., Quadrianto, N., Lampert, C.H.: Learning to rank using privileged information. In: IEEE International Conference on Computer Vision, pp. 825–832 (2013)
15. Vapnik, V., Vashist, A.: A new learning paradigm: learning using privileged information. Neural Netw. **22**(5), 544–557 (2009)
16. Wang, H., Kläser, A., Schmid, C., Liu, C.L.: Action recognition by dense trajectories. In: 2011 IEEE Conference on Computer Vision and Pattern Recognition (CVPR), pp. 3169–3176. IEEE (2011)
17. Wang, H., Schmid, C.: Action recognition with improved trajectories. In: IEEE International Conference on Computer Vision, pp. 3551–3558 (2013)
18. Wang, L., Qiao, Y., Tang, X.: Motionlets: mid-level 3D parts for human motion recognition. In: Proceedings of the IEEE Conference on Computer Vision and Pattern Recognition, pp. 2674–2681 (2013)
19. Wang, S., Tao, D., Yang, J.: Relative attribute SVM+ learning for age estimation. IEEE Trans. Cybern. **46**(3), 827–839 (2016)
20. Zhang, Z., Wang, C., Xiao, B., Zhou, W., Liu, S.: Attribute regularization based human action recognition. IEEE Trans. Inf. Forensics Secur. **8**(10), 1600–1609 (2013)

Progressive Lifelong Learning by Sharing Representations for Few Labeled Data

Guoxi Su$^{(\boxtimes)}$, Xiangmin Xu, Chaowen Chen, Bolun Cai, and Chunmei Qing

South China University of Techonology,
381 Wushan Road, Guangzhou 510640, China
su.guoxi@mail.scut.edu.cn, {xmxu,qchm}@scut.edu.cn,
czwmtnh@gmail.com, caibolun@gmail.com

Abstract. Lifelong Machine Learning (LML) has been receiving more and more attention in the past few years. It produces systems that are able to learn knowledge from consecutive tasks and refine the learned knowledge for a life time. In the optimization process of classical full-supervised LML systems, sufficient labeled data are required for extracting inter-task relationships before transferring. In order to leverage abundant unlabeled data and reduce the expenditure of labeling data, an progressive lifelong learning algorithm (PLLA) is proposed in this paper with unsupervised pre-training to learn shared representations that are more suitable as input to LML systems than the raw input data. Experiments show that the proposed PLLA is much more effective than many other LML methods when few labeled data is available.

Keywords: Lifelong machine learning · Representation learning
Few labeled data

1 Introduction

Over the last few decades there have been critical progresses in machine learning theory and algorithms which aims to enable machines to learn intelligently like human. However, the capacity of machines for persistent learning has a large gap from that of human. And it is now appropriate to more seriously consider the nature of systems that are capable of learning, retaining and using knowledge over a life time [1]. It has a variety of related applications such as robotic controlling [2], online image retrieval [3,4] and topic modelling [5–7].

Among all the LML algorithms, ELLA (Efficient Lifelong Learning Algorithm) [8] is a representative and effective algorithm which achieves nearly identical performance to batch Multi-task Learning (MTL) [9] with three orders of magnitude speedup in learning time. ELLA develops an efficient procedure of updating shared knowledge between each learned task and improved performance of learned task through reverse transfer. However, ELLA is a supervised learning algorithm so that its training procedure needs plenty of labeled data while labeling data needs the expenditure of much time and work especially

© Springer Nature Singapore Pte Ltd. 2018
B. Huet et al. (Eds.): ICIMCS 2017, CCIS 819, pp. 411–418, 2018.
https://doi.org/10.1007/978-981-10-8530-7_40

under the current big data environment. The lack of labeled training data may also restrict the model of ELLA to scale up. On the other hand, future machine learning algorithms tend to learn without supervision.

In order to effectively exploit unlabeled data, this paper proposed an progressive lifelong learning algorithm (PLLA) based on ELLA and Deep Belief Network (DBN) [10,11]. This is based on the fact that unsupervised deep learning methods can capture underlying regularities in the data and project all the raw input data to a shared feature representation. When used to learn multifarious and consecutive tasks, experiments show that hierarchically learned features help to capture commonalities between tasks and gets much better performance than ELLA and other LML methods when using less training labeled data.

2 Related Work

In this section, we introduce some LML and online multi-task learning (OMTL) frameworks which is related to our work in sharing representations or integrating hypothesis. Differences between PLLA and other methods are also illustrated.

Inspired by the short-term and long-term learning in psychology, Silver proposed an algorithm of LML based on multi-task learning (MTL) neural network [12]. In this framework, the input layer and hidden layer are shared among tasks to transfer knowledge and the output nodes are task specific. Recently, Lifelong Learning of Discriminative Representations (LLDR) [13,14] extended the MTL neural networks in order to deal with high dimensional problems and large amount of tasks in actual lifelong learning. This framework is similar to our work with shared hierarchical representations and task specific hypothesis. But we have further considerations on the transferring of the hypothesis functions and updating the representations with inherited gradients.

Compared to the above OMTL and LML paradigms where all tasks are in a single group [15–17], learning task grouping may be a better way to transfer knowledge between tasks in LML.

Disjoint grouping MTL (DG-MTL) [9] presented a model that can share representations among tasks in the same group while learning the disjoint grouping simultaneously. More recently, Mishra extended DG-MTL to fit in lifelong learning setting [18] which learned both partition functions and parameters online. These algorithms have different assumptions on task grouping from ours where tasks in different groups are totally untransferable.

Against the disjoint grouping models, the Grouping and Overlapping MTL (GO-MTL) algorithm [19] is a rich model of underlying task structure exploiting a sparsely shared basis. It automatically learns overlapping groups of tasks that allowing two tasks from different groups to share knowledge by one or more basis in common. Efficient Lifelong learning Algorithm (ELLA) [8] is developed employing GO-MTL as its starting point, greatly reducing its running time while retaining nearly identically performance. This work has been extended by the authors in multiple ways as in [2,20]. This efficient LML framework of integrating hypothesis is a fundamental part of our work. We adapt it for shared representations and introduce a new online updating strategy to ensure efficiency.

3   Progressive Lifelong Learning with Shared Representations

Lifelong Machine Learning considers systems that can learn many tasks from one or more domains over its lifetime [1]. We employ a lifelong learning framework in which the agent faces a series of supervised learning tasks $\mathcal{Z}^{(1)}$, $\mathcal{Z}^{(2)}$,...,$\mathcal{Z}^{(T_{max})}$. Each learning task $\mathcal{Z}^{(t)} = (\hat{f}^{(t)}, \mathbf{X}^{(t)}, \mathbf{y}^{(t)})$ is defined by a hidden function $\hat{f}^{(t)}:\mathcal{X}^{(t)} \to \mathcal{Y}^{(t)}$ from an instance space $\mathcal{X}^{(t)} \subseteq \mathbb{R}^d$ to a set of labels $\mathcal{Y}^{(t)}$ where $t = 1, 2, ..., T_{max}$. To learn $\hat{f}^{(t)}$, the agent is given n_t training instances $\mathbf{X}^{(t)} \in \mathbb{R}^{d \times n_t}$ with corresponding labels $\mathbf{y}^{(t)} \in \mathcal{Y}^{(t)^{n_t}}$ given by $\hat{f}^{(t)}$. Its goal is to construct task-specific hypothesis function $f^{(t)}$ for each task t to ensure the accuracy of labeling new data.

To model the relationships between tasks, it is assumed that the parameter vectors $\boldsymbol{\theta}^{(t)}$ can be represented using a linear combination of k shared latent model components from $\mathbf{L} \in \mathbb{R}^{d \times k}$ by computing $\boldsymbol{\theta}^{(t)} = \mathbf{L}\mathbf{s}^{(t)}$ where the weight vector $\mathbf{s}^{(t)} \in \mathbb{R}^k$ is encouraged to be sparse.

PLLA is formed by two layers. The upper layer is the inferring layer based on features extracted from the lower one. The lower layer is the shared hierarchical feature model initialized by unsupervised pre-training. The structure of PLLA is illustrated in Fig. 1.

Since we have integrated the shared feature representations and the potential knowledge basis into a new model, the objective function is changed from that of ELLA: (assume that the representations have only one layer of hidden units for brevity)

$$e_T(\mathbf{L}, \mathbf{W}) = \frac{1}{T} \sum_{t=1}^{T} \min_{\mathbf{s}^{(t)}} \left\{ \frac{1}{n_t} \sum_{i=1}^{n_t} \mathcal{L}(f(sigmoid(\mathbf{W}^{\top}\mathbf{x}_i^{(t)}); \right.$$

$$\left. \mathbf{L}\mathbf{s}^{(t)}), y_i^{(t)}) + \mu\|\mathbf{s}^{(t)}\|_1 \right\} + \lambda\|\mathbf{L}\|_2^F. \tag{1}$$

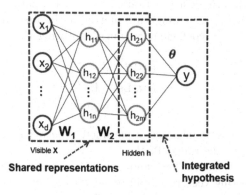

Fig. 1. The framework of PLLA with DBN representations and integrated hypothesis.

Algorithm 1. PLLA

Require: labeled data set $(\mathbf{X}_l^{(t)}, \mathbf{y}^{(t)})$ of current task t
Ensure: the library of learned knowledge $\mathbf{L}$
    and the hypothesis function $f^{(t)}$ with its parameters $\theta^{(t)}$
1: initialize $\mathbf{W}_l$ of each layer l with $\bigcup_{t=1}^{T_c} \mathbf{X}^{(t)}$ by CD-k algorithm, (T_c is the number
    of candidate tasks)
2: **while** isMoreTaskToLearn() **do**
3:    $(\mathbf{X}_l^{(t)}, \mathbf{y}^{(t)}, t) \leftarrow$ getTrainningDataSet()
4:    apply visible to hidden algorithms to get $\mathbf{H}^t$
5:    $\theta^{(t)} = argmin_\theta \frac{1}{n_t} \sum_{i=1}^{n_t} \mathcal{L}(f(\mathbf{h}_i^{(t)}; \theta^{(t)}), y_i^{(t)})$
6:    $\mathbf{s}^{(t)} = argmin_{\mathbf{s}^{(t)}} f_l(\mathbf{L}, \mathbf{s}^{(t)}, \theta^{(t)}, \mathbf{D}^{(t)})$, where $\mathbf{D}^{(t)}$ is the Hessian matrix of the
    loss function on task t
7:    compute $\gamma_t = (cos < \mathbf{s}^{(t)}, \mathbf{s}^{(t-1)} > +1)/2$
8:    **for** $i = 1$ to maxepoch **do**
9:        apply visible to hidden algorithms to get $\mathbf{H}^t$
10:      $\theta^{(t)} = argmin_\theta \frac{1}{n_t} \sum_{i=1}^{n_t} \mathcal{L}(f(\mathbf{h}_i^{(t)}; \theta^{(t)}), y_i^{(t)})$
11:      **for** $l = n_l - 1$ downto 0 **do**
12:        if $(i == 1) and (t \geq 1)$
13:        $g\mathbf{W}_l^t = \gamma_t g\mathbf{W}_l^{t-1} + \nabla_{\mathbf{w}_l} \mathcal{L}(f(\mathbf{H}^t; \theta^{(t)}), y_i^{(t)})$
14:        else
15:        $g\mathbf{W}_l^t = \gamma_c g\mathbf{W}_l^t + \nabla_{\mathbf{w}_l} \mathcal{L}(f(\mathbf{H}^t; \theta^{(t)}), y_i^{(t)})$
16:        end if
17:        $\mathbf{W}_l = \mathbf{W}_l - \alpha g\mathbf{W}_l^t$
18:      **end for**
19:    **end for**
20:    get the new $\theta^{(t)}$ by single task learners from $(\mathbf{H}^t, \mathbf{y}^t)$
21:    $\mathbf{L} \leftarrow argmin_{\mathbf{L}}(\lambda \|\mathbf{L}\|_2^F + \frac{1}{T} \sum_{t=1}^{T} f_l(\mathbf{L}, \mathbf{s}^{(t)}, \theta^{(t)}, \mathbf{D}^{(t)}))$
22: **end while**

However, Eq. 1 is not jointly convex in $\mathbf{L}$ and $\mathbf{W}$, it is difficult and inefficient to optimize them simultaneously. As described in the block of Algorithm 1, we make an online strategy that optimizing the feature representation matric $\mathbf{W}$ firstly by minimizing the lost function on the labeled data of current task. The gradients for updating each weighting matric at the first iteration is inherited from the last one by a coefficient γ which capturing the relatedness between tasks:

$$\begin{aligned} \gamma_t &= dist(\theta^{(t)}, \theta^{(t-1)}) \\ &= dist(\mathbf{Ls}^{(t)}, \mathbf{Ls}^{(t-1)})) \\ &= cos < \mathbf{s}^{(t)}, \mathbf{s}^{(t-1)} >, \end{aligned} \qquad (2)$$

where $dist()$ is the cosine distance of parameters between task t and task $t - 1$. We also rescale γ_t to the range $[0, 1]$.

The intuition is if current task and learned task are closely related, the angle between their selecting vectors should be nearly the same. During the following iterations, gradients are maintained with a hyper parameter γ_c.

4   Experiments

In this section, we evaluate our proposed PLLA model against five baselines: Single task learning (STL), Disjoint grouping MTL (DG-MTL)[9], LLDR [13], ELLA [21] and Online multi-task boosting (OMB)[22]. In experiments, we reduced the amount of labeled data of each task to [10%, 20%, ..., 100%]. We ensure that all models exploit the same amount labeled data in the experiments. We evaluate the performance on prediction over two databases: the Land Mine Data set and the London School Data set.

4.1   Parameter Settings

All the comparing models have some hyper-parameters need to be confirmed by the user. We also use gridsearch procedure if the algorithm has multiple hyper-parameters which need to be selected.

In the STL mehtod, the regularization coefficient of regression is picked in $\{exp(-5), exp(-4), ..., exp(5)\}$.

In DG-MTL, the number of groups are chosen from a pool of $\{2, 3, 4, 5\}$ and the values of regularization parameters are picked from $\{0.001, 0.01, 0.1, 1, 10, 100\}$.

In ELLA, The parameter values of k and λ are selected independently for each algorithm and data set using a gridsearch over values of k (the number of hidden basis) from 2 to 10 and values of the ridge term for single task learner, λ_1 from the set $\{exp(-5), exp(-4), ..., exp(5)\}$. We also pick the regularization parameters for the basis and the sparsity constraint from $\{exp(-10), exp(-5), exp(-2), exp(1), exp(4)\}$. Other parameter settings follow the default settings in the code that provided by the authors.

In PLLA and LLDR, the number of hidden layers n_l is chosen over values $n_l \in \{1, 2\}$. Since the size of the database is not huge, it is unnecessary to build deeper architectures. Hyper parameter γ_c in PLLA is picked in $\{0.1, 0.2, ..., 0.9\}$ by grid-search and the learning rate α is chosen in $\{0.01, 0.02, 0.05, 0.1, 0.2, 0.5, 1, 2, 5\}$. The regularization coefficient for single task learning was selected in $\{exp(-5), exp(-4), ..., exp(5)\}$.

In OMB, the number of base learners is chosen from 5 to 20 and we exploit Naive Bayesian classfiers as the base learners.

4.2   Land Mine Detection

In the Land Mine data set [23], the goal is to detect whether or not a land mine is present in an area based on RADAR images. The 10 input features (plus a bias term) are extracted from radar data. The data set consists of 14,820 instances in total, divided into 29 different geographical regions. We treat each region as a different task.

In this database, one hidden layer is formed in PLLA $n_l = 1$ and the number of hidden variables m is 10. In this database, the number of total labeled data for each task varies from 449 to 690.

Since the land mine data is real-valued, we use Gaussian-Binary DBN in our model instead of binary DBN.

4.3   London School Data

The London School data set consists of examination scores from 15,362 students in 139 schools from the Inner London Education Authority. We treat the data from each school as a separate task. The goal is to predict the examination score of each student with 27 different features.

In this database, one hidden layer is formed in PLLA $n_l = 1$ and the number of hidden variables m is 30. We also set a decreasing learning rate since this dataset has much more tasks than others.

4.4   Results

Figure 2 left shows the results of the performance on prediction (AUC) with few labeled data over the Land Mine Data set. The given average and the standard deviation results are computed over running 100 times. It can be observed that our proposed PLLA gets about 8% improvement than ELLA when only 10% labeled data is leveraged.

Figure 2 right depicts the similar regularity on the London School Data set. PLLA is always more efficient than ELLA when few labeled data are exploited. On the other hand, the result with only 30% of labeled data in PLLA is nearly identical to the result of ELLA with 100% labeled data. DG-MTL does not fit for this situation again with so many tasks to be learned. Its efficiency and performance are both the worst.

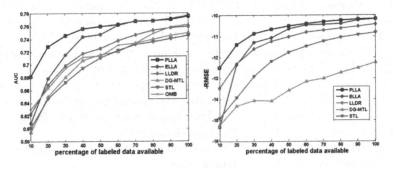

Fig. 2. The results of training with different amount of labeled data on left: land mind detection; right: London school

5   Conclusion

In order to reduce human effort in labeling data for supervised lifelong machine learning, it is motivated to consider how to improve the performance on prediction when few labeled data is available. In this paper, we proposed an effective algorithm called PLLA. It can discover and leverage the hidden structures in the unlabeled data to enhance the performance on prediction of supervised learning especially when few label data is available.

Acknowledgements. This work is supported in part by the National Natural Science Founding of China (61171142, 61401163, U1636218), Science and Technology Planning Project of Guangdong Province of China (2014B010111003, 2014B010111006), the Fundamental Research Funds for the Central Universities (2017MS045), and Guangzhou Key Lab of Body Data Science (201605030011).

References

1. Silver, D.L., Yang, Q., Li, L.: Lifelong machine learning systems: beyond learning algorithms. In: AAAI Spring Symposium: Lifelong Machine Learning (2013)
2. Ammar, H.B., Eaton, E., Ruvolo, P., Taylor, M.: Online multi-task learning for policy gradient methods. In: Proceedings of the 31st International Conference on Machine Learning (ICML-14), pp. 1206–1214 (2014)
3. Banko, M., Etzioni, O.: Strategies for lifelong knowledge extraction from the web. In: Proceedings of the 4th International Conference on Knowledge Capture, pp. 95–102 (2007)
4. Hong, R., Yang, Y., Wang, M., Hua, X.S.: Learning visual semantic relationships for efficient visual retrieval. IEEE Trans. Big Data **1**, 152–161 (2017)
5. Chen, Z., Liu, B.: Topic modeling using topics from many domains, lifelong learning and big data. In: International Conference on International Conference on Machine Learning, pp. 703–711 (2014)
6. Hong, R., Hu, Z., Wang, R., Wang, M., Tao, D.: Multi-view object retrieval via multi-scale topic models. IEEE Trans. Image Process. **25**, 5814–5827 (2016)
7. Hong, R., Zhang, L., Zhang, C., Zimmermann, R.: Flickr circles: aesthetic tendency discovery by multi-view regularized topic modeling. IEEE Trans. Multimedia **18**, 1555–1567 (2016)
8. Ruvolo, P., Eaton, E.: Ella: an efficient lifelong learning algorithm. In: Proceedings of the 30th International Conference on Machine Learning (ICML-13), June 2013
9. Kang, Z., Grauman, K., Sha, F.: Learning with whom to share in multi-task feature learning. In: Proceedings of the 28th International Conference on Machine Learning (ICML-11), pp. 521–528 (2011)
10. Hinton, G.E., Osindero, S., Teh, Y.W.: A fast learning algorithm for deep belief nets. Neural Comput. **18**, 1527–1554 (2006)
11. Hinton, G.E., Salakhutdinov, R.R.: Reducing the dimensionality of data with neural networks. Science **313**, 504–507 (2006)
12. Silver, D.L., Mercer, R.E.: The task rehearsal method of life-long learning: overcoming impoverished data. In: Cohen, R., Spencer, B. (eds.) AI 2002. LNCS (LNAI), vol. 2338, pp. 90–101. Springer, Heidelberg (2002). https://doi.org/10.1007/3-540-47922-8_8
13. Alsharif, O., Bachman, P., Pineau, J.: Lifelong learning of discriminative representations. CoRR (2014)
14. Alsharif, O., Bachman, P., Pineau, J.: Representation as a service. arXiv preprint arXiv:1404.4108 (2014)
15. Archambeau, C., Guo, S., Zoeter, O.: Sparse bayesian multi-task learning. In: Advances in Neural Information Processing Systems, pp. 1755–1763 (2011)
16. Evgeniou, A., Pontil, M.: Multi-task feature learning. Adv. Neural Inf. Process. Syst. **19**, 41 (2007)
17. Bakker, B., Heskes, T.: Task clustering and gating for bayesian multitask learning. J. Mach. Learn. Res. **4**, 83–99 (2003)

18. Mishra, M., Huan, J.: Learning task grouping using supervised task space partitioning in lifelong multitask learning. In: Proceedings of the 24th ACM International on Conference on Information and Knowledge Management, pp. 1091–1100. ACM (2015)
19. Kumar, A., Daume III, H.: Learning task grouping and overlap in multi-task learning. ArXiv e-prints (2012)
20. Ruvolo, P., Eaton, E.: Online multi-task learning via sparse dictionary optimization. In: Twenty-Eighth AAAI Conference on Artificial Intelligence (AAAI-14) (2014)
21. Ruvolo, P., Eaton, E.: Active task selection for lifelong machine learning. In: Proceedings of the 27th AAAI Conference on Artificial Intelligence (AAAI-13) (2013)
22. Wang, B., Pineau, J.: Online boosting algorithms for anytime transfer and multi-task learning. In: Twenty-Ninth AAAI Conference on Artificial Intelligence (2015)
23. Xue, Y., Liao, X., Carin, L., Krishnapuram, B.: Multi-task learning for classification with dirichlet process priors. J. Mach. Learn. Res. 8, 35–63 (2007)

Refining Eye Synthetic Images via Coarse-to-Fine Adversarial Networks for Appearance-Based Gaze Estimation

Tongtong Zhao[1], Yafei Wang[1,2], and Xianping Fu[1(✉)]

[1] Information Science and Technology College, Dalian Maritime University,
Dalian 116026, China
{zhaotongtong,wangyafei,fxp}@dlmu.edu.cn
[2] School of Physics and Optoelectronic Engineering, Dalian University of Technology,
Dalian 116024, China

Abstract. Recently, several models have achieved great success in terms of reducing the gap between synthetic and real image distributions with large unlabeled real data. However, collecting such large amounts of real data costs a lot of labouring and training them requires high memory. To reduce the gap with less real data, we propose a coarse-to-fine refine eye image method combining coarse model net and fine model net through adversarial training. Coarse model net is a feed-forward convolutional neural network aiming to transform synthetic eye images into coarse images. Fine model net is a modified Generative Adversarial Networks (GANs) which add realism to coarse images using unlabeled real data. Experimental results show that the proposed method achieves similar distributions as recent work but decreasing real data at least one order of magnitude. In addition, a significant accuracy improvement for gaze estimation with refined synthetic eye images is observed.

Keywords: Feed-forward convolutional neural network
Image synthesis · Generative Adversarial Networks

1 Introduction

Learning high-level feature representations to improve the realism of synthetic images from large amount of unlabeled real datasets is becoming increasingly tractable with recent progress in graphics. However, collecting such large amounts of training data costs a lot of labouring and training them requires high memory. Furthermore, feature representations between synthetic images and real images are always hard to generalize. Thus the idea of good intermediate representations with reducing the quantity of real data has become appealing.

X. Fu—This work was supported in part by the National Natural Science Foundation of China Grant 61370142 and Grant 61272368, by the Fundamental Research Funds for the Central Universities Grant 3132016352, by the Fundamental Research of Ministry of Transport of P. R. China Grant 2015329225300.

© Springer Nature Singapore Pte Ltd. 2018
B. Huet et al. (Eds.): ICIMCS 2017, CCIS 819, pp. 419–428, 2018.
https://doi.org/10.1007/978-981-10-8530-7_41

Train feed-forward convolutional neural network is one approach for solving image transformation tasks, the tasks can be explained as a system that receives input image and transforms it into an output image. Feed-forward convolutional neural network is widely used. For instance, in the area of super-resolution [2], colorization [3], segmentation [4], and style transformation [2]. Recent work has shown that high-quality images can be generated using perceptual loss functions with high-level image feature representations which extracted from pre-trained convolutional neural networks. In parallel, Generative Adversarial Networks (GANs) can be trained with missing data and can provide predictions on inputs that are missing data, this characteristic also can be used as refine images [5].

Previous work usually directly generate synthetic images using the model that learning from real images [1,5,7]. In this paper, we combine the benefits of feed-forward convolutional neural network and GANs, and propose a coarse-to-fine eye synthesis method through adversarial training, where the goal is to learn intermediate representations. Figure 1 gives an overview of our method, our method mainly involves two net: coarse model net and refine model net, few real images are chose to train the coarse model as target, and the rest of the real images are used to add realism to synthetic images. Coarse model net consists of two components: train net and the loss net. We train the train net using a fully convolutional neural network rather than a fully connected encoder network. Moreover, similar to [2], we train the loss net using feed-forward convolutional neural network, but rather than using per-pixel loss functions depending only on low-level pixel information, we train our networks using perceptual loss functions that depend on high-level features from a pretrained loss network. The refine model net is a modified GANs, but with coarse generate images as inputs instead of random vectors and change the loss function according to [7] for avoiding the problem of mode collapse. In this paper, we make the following contributions:

1. We propose a coarse-to-fine eye synthesis method through adversarial training to speed up reducing the gap between synthetic and real image distributions.
2. We train a coarse model net to transform synthetic images into coarse images using high-level features from a pretrained network. By training this net, synthetic images can learn distributions from target images.
3. We make several key modifications to the GANs [1] to make the net become an efficient refine model net. And refine model net can speed up learning distributions and adding realism to synthetic images with coarse generate images from coarse model net.
4. Compared to the recent method based on Generative Adversarial Networks, our networks give similar qualitative results but reduce the quantity of real data by more than one order of magnitude. In addition, we qualitatively evaluate the generated images by training models for gaze estimation and experiment shows a significant improvement over using refined synthetic eye images with the baseline methods.

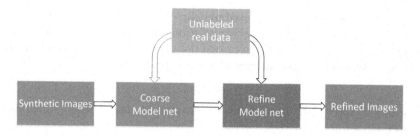

Fig. 1. An overview of our method. As figure shows that unlabeled real data is divided into two parts, few of real data serve to train coarse net for generating coarse images that have similar distributions with these real data. And the rest of real data are used for training the fine net which is a modified GANs.

2   The Proposed Approach

The goal of coarse-to-fine eye synthesis is to refine synthetic images $\tilde{\alpha}$ with a coarse-to-fine net $N(\alpha)$ using a set of unlabeled real eye images β. The proceeding can be shown as:

$$\tilde{\alpha} \longleftarrow N(\alpha). \tag{1}$$

We divided the coarse-to-fine net $N(\alpha)$ into two parts: coarse model net $C(\alpha)$ and refine model net $F(\hat{\alpha})$, where $\hat{\alpha}$ represents the coarse images generated by $C(\alpha)$ as output. Coarse model net transforms the synthetic images into visually realistic images with similar distributions as target images. Target images are real eye images. With the distributions, the output images can be refine with less unlabeled real data and achieve similar or better effect on gaze estimation.

2.1   Coarse Model Net

To speed up bridging the gap between synthetic and real image distributions and reduce the quantity of real data, we need to learn intermediate features about the image content and overall spatial structure. To this end, we train a feed-forward network $C(\alpha)$ to generate coarse images with intermediate features. As shown in Fig. 2, our coarse model net consists of two components: train net $T_\omega(\alpha)$ and loss

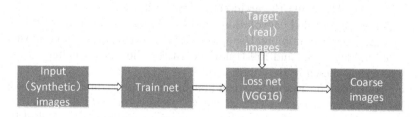

Fig. 2. Our coarse model net consists of two components: train net $T_{\omega_i}(\alpha)$ and loss net $L(\alpha', \beta_i)$

net $L(\alpha', \beta)$. Loss net $L(\alpha', \beta)$ is used to define several loss functions $l_1, l_2, \ldots, l_j$. Train net $T_{\omega_i}(\alpha)$ is a deep residual convolutional neural network with parameter weights ω_i, we choose i images from real data and set one weight per β_i. Train net $T_\omega(\alpha)$ generates output images α' via mapping

$$\alpha' = T_\omega(\alpha). \tag{2}$$

According to the weight ω_i of β_i, we set distribution target as α'' which can be represented as:

$$\alpha'' = \sum_{i=1} \omega_i \beta_i. \tag{3}$$

Each loss function calculates a scalar value $l_i(\alpha', \beta_i)$ measuring the difference between the output images α' and target images α''. Each convolution we set an equal weight W. Furthermore, train net is trained using Adaptive Moment Estimation (Adam) to minimize a weighted combination of loss functions because of the characteristic of low space, which can be represent as:

$$W^* = \arg \min_W E_{\alpha, \{\alpha''\}} [\Sigma_{i=1} \lambda_i l_i (T_\omega(\alpha), \alpha'')]. \tag{4}$$

To make sure the coarse images learning the intermediate features that closely resemble the real images' distributions, we draw inspiration from recent works that generate images via optimization [1,2,8]. In these methods, pretrained convolutional neural networks have the ability of perceptual information. Thus, a perceptual loss function is defined to measure high-level perceptual information. And we also use a pretrained network $L(\alpha', \beta)$ and remain fixed during the training process in order to define our loss functions. Similar to [2], loss net $L(\alpha', \beta)$ is trained by deep convolutional networks as well.

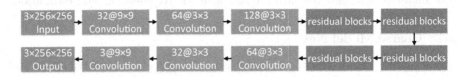

Fig. 3. Network architecture of train net.

Train net. Train net is trained by COCO dataset [6] because the dataset is rich in content. Following the architectural guidelines of DCGANs [9] and sim-GANs [5], we use strided convolutions and fractionally strided convolutions for downsampling and upsampling. Use spatial batch normalization and remove fully connected hidden layers and ReLU nonlinearities. The exact architectures of all our networks is shown in the Fig. 3.

Our train net consists of four residual blocks. All residual blocks use 3×3 kernels. As shown in Fig. 4, residual blocks' architecture add dropout to basic residual blocks [10]. Furthermore, spatial batch normalization and ReLU follow all non-residual convolutional layers except for the output which uses tanh instead.

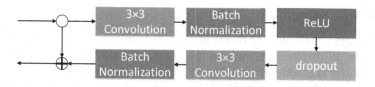

Fig. 4. Structure of residual blocks.

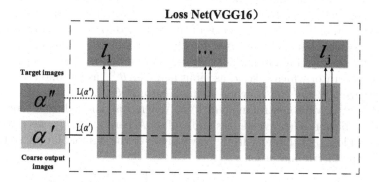

Fig. 5. Network architecture of loss net.

Loss net. We wish to preserve some detailed messages such as colors, common patterns, etc. To achieve this, loss net is designed. To make use of loss net $L(\alpha', \beta)$ which is a pretrained network, we define a perceptual loss function to measure high-level perceptual information. ImageNet dataset is used to train this loss net. As Fig. 5 shows, we use the 16-layer VGG network and minimize loss for several layers. β_i is chose as the template to generate images which from the real unlabeled datasets.

Similar to [8], rather than encouraging exactly match the output image α' with target images α'', which is equal to $\sum_{i=1} \omega_i \beta_i$, we represent the loss as:

$$l_j(\alpha', \alpha'') = \frac{1}{C_j H_j W_j} \|L_j(\alpha') - L_j(\alpha'')\|_2^2. \tag{5}$$

which $C_j \times H_j \times W_j$ is the shape of feature map and j is the jth layer of the loss net. We try to find an image α' for a number of layers j which minimizes the loss $l_j(\alpha', \alpha'')$ by optimization. Thus, the output images $\hat{\alpha}$ which we called coarse images can be represent as:

$$\hat{\alpha} = \arg\min_{\alpha'} \lambda_l l_j(\alpha', \alpha'') + \lambda_{TV} l_{TV}(\alpha') \tag{6}$$

$l_{TV}(\alpha')$ is total variation regularizer for spatial smoothness in the output image $\hat{\alpha}$. λ_l and λ_{TV} are scalars.

2.2   Refine Model Net

When we get coarse images $\hat{\alpha}$, we get the distributions of the template at the same time. With the distributions, we try to generate details to improve the realism of the synthetic images using unlabeled real data. As Fig. 6 shows that our refine model net can be divided into two networks: Generate Network G and Discriminator Network D. G represents the generate network which creates images that are intended to come from the same distribution as the unlabeled real data. D represents an adversarial discriminator network that is trained to classify images as real or generated. In terms of the cost used for the discriminator, $J^{(D)}$ seldom changed but the cost used for the generator $J^{(G)}$ different from each other. D is the discriminator which takes x as input and uses $\theta^{(D)}$ as parameters. G is the generator which takes $\hat{\alpha}$ as input and uses $\theta^{(G)}$ as parameters. D wishes to minimize $J^{(G)}(\theta^{(D)}\theta^{(G)})$ while controlling only $\theta^{(D)}$. G wishes to minimize $J^{(G)}(\theta^{(D)}\theta^{(G)})$ while controlling only $\theta^{(G)}$. When $\hat{\alpha}$ is sampled from some simple prior distribution, $G(\hat{\alpha})$ yields a sample of x. According to [7], we rewrite the function of loss, but different from [7], we preserve the sigmoid layers, so the cost used for the discriminator is:

$$J^{(G)}(\theta^{(D)}\theta^{(G)}) = -\frac{1}{2}E[D(x)] - \frac{1}{2}E[(1 - D(G(\hat{\alpha})))] \qquad (7)$$

This is equivalent to minimize standard cross-entropy cost when training a standard binary classifier with a sigmoid output. The only difference is that the classifier training on two mini-batches of data, one coming from the dataset where the label is 1 for all examples, and one coming from the generator, where the label is 0 for all examples. For training this network, each min-batch randomly involved real images which are x in the equation. $D(x)$ is the probability of the input being a coarse image, and $1 - D(G(\hat{\alpha}))$ that of a real one. We update the parameters by taking a stochastic gradient descent (SGD) step for mini-batch on the mini-batch loss.

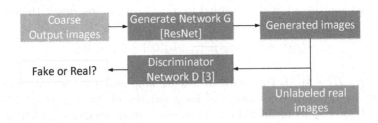

Fig. 6. Architecture of refine model net.

3   Results and Discussion

To verify the effectiveness of the proposed method, we perform experiments to assess both the quality of our refined images and their suitability for appearance-based gaze estimation. We use COCO dataset to train the train net of coarse model net. And few of images from MPIIGaze dataset are chosen as target images. The gaze estimation dataset consists of 28,332 synthetic images from eye gaze synthesizer UnityEyes-fine dataset, six subjects of UTview datset and 350,428 real images from the MPIIGaze dataset. For UTview [16], the data of subjects S0, S2, S3, S4, S6 and S8 in UTView are used as subject 1–6 in our dataset. In total, there are 144 (head pose) × 160 (gaze directions) × 6 (subjects) = 138,240 training samples and 8 (head pose) × 160 (gaze directions) × 6 (subjects) = 7680 testing samples.

3.1 Appearance Based Gaze Estimation

Figure 7 shows a large improvement from training on more training data. As our approach achieves comparable performance to state-of-the-art deep learning based methods which is simGANs [5]. We compare our method with vary training dataset, %t refers to the percentage of the training dataset. As Fig. 8 shows that our network achieves similar distribution but the quantity of real data is decreased with at least one order of magnitude of training data. Importantly, our coarse-to-fine network does not require labeling the real images as well.

We evaluate the ability of our method for appearance-based gaze estimation from real dataset and synthetic image dataset. ALR [11], SVR [12], RF [13], convolution neural network [15] and KNN [15] are compared with our method as

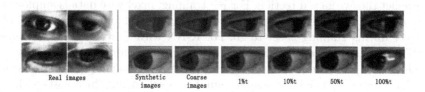

Fig. 7. Example output of our method for the UnityEyes dataset [15]. As images show that vary numbers of training real images can generate different result -here %t refers to the percentage of the training dataset. We observe a large improvement from training on more training data.

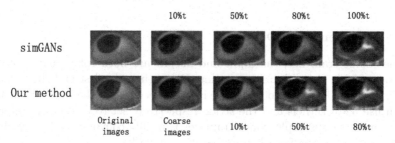

Fig. 8. Comparison of our method to simGANs [5]. As figure shows, our network achieves similar distribution with less training data -here %t refers to the percentage of the training dataset.

Table 1. Comparison of our method to the state-of-the-art on the part of MPIIGaze dataset of real eyes which contains 350,428 images and UnityEyes dataset of synthetic images which contains 28,332 images of UnityEyes-fine dataset. The third column indicates whether the methods are trained on Real/Synthetic data. The error means eye gaze estimation error in degrees.

Method	Error	R/S
ALR [11]	16.7	R
SVR [12]	16.6	R
RF [13]	15.4	R
CNN with UT [16]	13.2	R
K-NN with UT (ours)	8.9	R
CNN with UT (ours)	10.2	R
K-NN with refined UnityEyes [15]	10.2	S
CNN with refined UnityEyes [15]	11.5	S
CNN with refined UnityEyes (SimGANs [5])	8.0	S
K-NN with refined UnityEyes (ours)	8.3	S
CNN with Refined UnityEyes (ours)	7.7	S

baseline methods. Similar to [14], we train a convolution neural network (CNN) to predict the eye gaze direction. For RF training, pixel-wise data is employed to represent the original eye image by converting it to column vector, the number of trees during training is set to 20. For K-NN with UnityEyes refined images or UTview real images, considering that the computation cost increases with neighbor samples number, it can be found that a high-quality gaze estimator is obtained when the neighbor samples number is set to 50, which costs a shorter operating time. A comparison to the state-of-the-art can be shown in Table 1. Training the CNN on the refined images outperforms the state-of-the-art on the part of MPIIGaze dataset. We observe a large improvement in performance from training on the refined images and an significant improvement compared to the state-of-the-art.

3.2 Implementation Details

In the coarse train net, the input and output are both color images of shape $3 \times 256 \times 256$ in the training processing. Other than the first and the last layers which use 9×9 kernels and the stride is 1, the second and the last but one layers which use 3×3 kernels and the stride respectively set to 2 to downsample the input and $\frac{1}{2}$ to upsample. Since train net is a fully-convolutional network, any resolution can be applied when we test the network.

In the refine generate network G, images from coarse net are passed through eight 3×3 convolutional layers containing 64 feature maps. Then the output is passed through a 1×1 convolutional layer to produce 1 feature map.

In the refine discriminator network D, similar to [5], the network consists of five convolution layers and two max-pooling layers. First convolutional layer uses 3×3 kernels, stride set to 2, feature maps are 96. Second convolutional layer uses 3×3 kernels as well, stride set to 2, feature maps are 64. Max-pooling layer uses 3×3 kernels and stride set to 1. Third convolutional layer uses 3×3 kernels, stride set to 1, feature maps are 32. The last two convolutional layers use 1×1 kernels, stride set to 1, and feature maps are 32 and 2 respectively.

We train generate network G for 500 steps, and discriminator network D for 100 steps. Then we update generate network G twice while updating discriminator network D once.

References

1. Gatys, L.A., Ecker, A.S., Bethge, M.: A neural algorithm of artistic style. arXiv preprint arXiv:1508.06576 (2015)
2. Johnson, J., Alahi, A., Fei-Fei, L.: Perceptual losses for real-time style transfer and super-resolution. In: Leibe, B., Matas, J., Sebe, N., Welling, M. (eds.) ECCV 2016. LNCS, vol. 9906, pp. 694–711. Springer, Cham (2016). https://doi.org/10. 1007/978-3-319-46475-6_43
3. Cheng, Z., Yang, Q., Sheng, B.: Deep colorization. In: IEEE International Conference on Computer Vision, pp. 415–423 (2015)
4. Long, J., Shelhamer, E., Darrell, T.: Fully convolutional networks for semantic segmentation. In: IEEE Conference on Computer Vision and Pattern Recognition, pp. 3431–3440 (2015)
5. Shrivastava, A., Pfister, T., Tuzel, O., et al.: Learning from simulated and unsupervised images through adversarial training (2016)
6. Lin, T.-Y., Maire, M., Belongie, S., Hays, J., Perona, P., Ramanan, D., Dollár, P., Zitnick, C.L.: Microsoft COCO: common objects in context. In: Fleet, D., Pajdla, T., Schiele, B., Tuytelaars, T. (eds.) ECCV 2014. LNCS, vol. 8693, pp. 740–755. Springer, Cham (2014). https://doi.org/10.1007/978-3-319-10602-1_48
7. Arjovsky, M., Chintala, S., Bottou, L.: Wasserstein gan. arXiv preprint arXiv:1701.07875 (2017)
8. Mahendran, A., Vedaldi, A.: Understanding deep image representations by inverting them. In: IEEE Conference on Computer Vision and Pattern Recognition(CVPR), pp. 5188–5196 (2015)
9. Radford, A., Metz, L., Chintala, S.: Unsupervised representation learning with deep convolutional generative adversarial networks. arXiv preprint arXiv:1511.06434 (2015)
10. Zagoruyko, S., Komodakis, N.: Wide residual networks. arXiv preprint arXiv:1605.07146 (2016)
11. Lu, F., Sugano, Y., Okabe, T., et al.: Adaptive linear regression for appearance-based gaze estimation. IEEE Trans. Pattern Anal. Mach. Intell. **36**(10), 2033–2046 (2014)
12. Schneider, T., Schauerte, B., Stiefelhagen, R.: Manifold alignment for person independent appearance-based gaze estimation. In: 2014 22nd International Conference on Pattern Recognition (ICPR), pp. 1167–1172. IEEE (2014)
13. Sugano, Y., Matsushita, Y., Sato, Y.: Learning-by-synthesis for appearance-based 3D gaze estimation. In: IEEE Conference on Computer Vision and Pattern Recognition (CVPR), pp. 1821–1828 (2014)

14. Wood, E., Baltrušaitis, T., Morency, L.P., Robinson, P., Bulling, A.: Learning an appearance-based gaze estimator from one million synthesised images. In: Biennial ACM Symposium on Eye Tracking Research & Applications, pp. 131–138 (2016)
15. Wood, E., Baltrušaitis, T., Zhang, X., Sugano, Y., Robinson, P., Bulling, A.: Rendering of eyes for eye-shape registration and gaze estimation. In: IEEE International Conference on Computer Vision (ICCV), pp. 3756–3764 (2015)
16. Zhang, X., Sugano, Y., Fritz, M., Bulling, A.: Appearance-based gaze estimation in the wild. In: IEEE Conference on Computer Vision and Pattern Recognition (CVPR), pp. 4511–4520 (2015)

Robust Steganography via Patch-Based Texture Synthesis

Zhengcai Qin[1,2,3], Meng Li[1,2,3], and Bin Wu[1,2,3]($\boxtimes$)

[1] State Key Laboratory of Information Security,
Institute of Information Engineering, Chinese Academy of Sciences,
Beijing 100093, China
wubin@iie.ac.cn
[2] Shenzhen Key Laboratory of Media Security, Shenzhen University,
Shenzhen 518060, China
[3] School of Cyber Security, University of Chinese Academy of Sciences,
Beijing 100049, China

Abstract. We propose a novel patch-based texture synthesis approach for steganography, which has the characteristics of high quality, high embedding capacity and even can be applied to the pictures with lossy compression. Our scheme is to embed the information in the process of generating the texture image, and ensure the high similarity between the synthetic texture and the source texture. Our approach has the following advantages. First, our method can offer different embedding capacity which depends on the size of the synthetic image. Second, our method not only can be well used in the images with lossless compression, but also can be applied to the images with lossy compression and has an extremely low bit error rate. Experimental results have verified that our method achieves state-of-the-art results on steganography with lossy compression.

Keywords: Steganography · Texture synthesis · Lossy compression
Noise attack · Hash

1 Introduction

In the last decade, the digital media research has made a lot of progress and breakthroughs, and also attracted the attention from the field of digital steganography. Steganography [1] is a convert communication technology that will hide information in multimedia carrier and avoid eavesdroppers' suspicion. In general, the host medium used in the steganographic includes digital image, text,

B. Wu—This work was supported by the Joint Funds of the National Natural Science Foundation of China (Grant No. U1536202), Fundamental theory and cutting edge technology Research Program of Institute of Information Engineering, CAS (Grant No. Y7Z0391102), SKLOIS Key Deployment Project (Grant No. Y7D0061102) and CAS Key Technology Talent Program.

© Springer Nature Singapore Pte Ltd. 2018
B. Huet et al. (Eds.): ICIMCS 2017, CCIS 819, pp. 429–439, 2018.
https://doi.org/10.1007/978-981-10-8530-7_42

audio, video, 3D model [2], but most of the steganographic methods [3–6] are for digital images. Many image steganography algorithms [7] use existing images as the communication carrier, and the cost of embedding information in the picture is the distortion encountered in the stego image. However, this leads to two problems, first of all, when the image is selected, the size of the image is determined. The greater the amount of embedding information, the greater the distortion, which results in poor image quality. The second problem is that the transmission is not lossless, for example, when we upload pictures to social networks, the service provider will always compress the pictures, which will lead to a lot of steganographic methods that do not consider the robustness fail, and the receiver can not correctly extract information.

In this paper, we propose a patch-based texture synthesis steganography algorithm. Different from the method of information embedding by modifying the carrier, our method embeds the information in the process of texture image generation. We can generate the texture image with different sizes which depend on the length of information to embed without decreasing the quality of the image. Our method not only can be well used to hide the information in the lossless picture, but also achieves state-of-the-art results in JPEG image with lossy compression after some slight modification of the procedure.

2   Related Works

The study of steganography based on texture synthesis [8,9] has attracted a great deal of attention. Now the main work of texture synthesis is divided into two directions, one is pixel-based texture synthesis, the other one is patch-based texture synthesis.

The pixel-based texture synthesis methods use spatial neighborhood comparisons to choose the most similar pixel in a sample texture. Since each output pixels is determined by the already synthesized pixels, any wrongly synthesized pixels during the process influence the rest of the result causing propagation of errors. Otori and Kuriyama [10] pioneered the work of pixel-based texture synthesis. They use the feature vector LBP as a unit to embed information, and synthesize a texture image that contains secret message. Later, Otori and Kuriyama [11] proposes to fill the blank pixels in the order of the Hibert curve, that will synthesize the texture picture with higher quality, and does not arouse any suspicion. But stego images that are sythesized by [10,11] can't deal with the lossy compression, the receiver can not extract message successfully when stego images are compressed lossily.

Patch-based texture synthesis method [12] pastes the patches which has small error of overlapped region with the synthesized texture. Because the size of a patch block is much larger than a pixel, it retains the features of the original texture image, and it is easy to find the seam line that does not make people suspect in the overlap between patch boundary and generated content. Wu and Wang [4] proposed to select candidate patches whose MSEO rank value equals to information value and use image quilting [13] to synthesize texture picture. The method has the characteristics of large embedding capacity and high quality, but only for lossless pictures. Qian [5] has proposed a steganography approach by using texture synthesis based on patches, that provides a capability of countering JPEG compression. But the error rate is not low enough.

Inspired by the works in [4,5,14], we proposed a patch-based texture synthesis steganography method that not only can be well used to hide the information in the lossless picture, but also achieves excellent results in JPEG image with lossy compression. We will describe our approach in the next section.

3   Proposed Method

In this section we will clarify our approach in detail as shown in Fig. 1. First of all, we will introduce some basic definitions. The basic unit that we use in steganography is called a patch. Figure 2(a) is a patch. The patch has a kernel block with size of $K_w * K_h$, surrounded by a boundary area with a depth of P_d. K_w, K_h, P_d are variable, specified by the user. Given a source texture with size of $S_w * S_h$, we can generate many candidate patches. The concept of candidate patches is simple: we use a window $P_w * P_h$ and then travel the source texture by shifting a pixel each time in the order of the scan-line, as shown in Fig. 2(b). Let $CP = \{cp_i | i = 0, 1, \ldots, CP_n - 1\}$ represents a candidate patch set, where $CP_n = \|CP\|$ represents the number of elements in the CP. We can use (1) to derive CP_n.

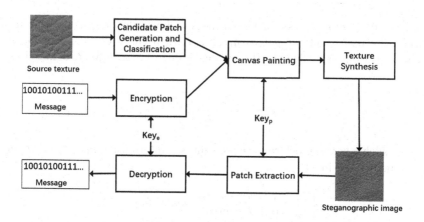

Fig. 1. The flow chart of the proposed steganography

$$CP_n = \|CP\| = (S_w - P_w + 1) \times (S_h - P_h + 1) \tag{1}$$

Each patch has a kernel block. Thus, we can get $KB_n(KB_n = CP_n)$ core blocks. KB represents the set of all generated core blocks, and $\|KB\|$ represents the number of all the elements in the set. We can employ the indexing for each kernel block kb_i, i.e., $KB = \{kb_i | i = 0, \ldots, \|KB\| - 1\}$.

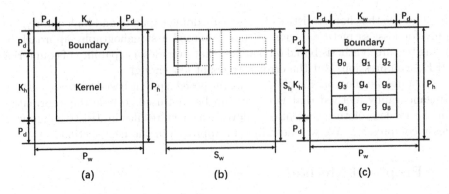

Fig. 2. Patch, candidate patch generation process, the division of kernel blocks. (a) The diagram of a patch. The interior is the core area, surrounded by the boundary area. (b) The illustration of candidate patch generation process. (c) An illustration of the division of kernel block, the kernel block is divided into $N = G_r * G_c$ grids, $G_r = G_c = 3$ by default.

Next, we divide the kernel block of each patch. We need to divide the kernel block into N grids($N = G_r * G_c$), as shown in Fig. 2(c), we can derive the size of each grid $G_w * G_h$ using (2).

$$G_w = \frac{K_w}{G_r}, G_h = \frac{K_h}{G_c} \tag{2}$$

Then we number for each small grid in the scan-line order (Zigzag or other means can also be used), and we get $g_0, g_1, \ldots, g_8$ when $G_r = G_c = 3$. For $G_w * G_h$ pixels in grid g_k, we calculate the average value of attribute R, denoted as I_k. We can derive I_k using (3).

$$I_k = \frac{\sum_{i=1}^{G_w} \sum_{j=1}^{G_h} R(i,j)}{G_w G_h} \tag{3}$$

And such a kernel block represents eight bits information $h_0 h_1 h_2 h_3 h_4 h_5 h_6 h_7$, h_i can be derived in (4).

$$\begin{cases} h_i = 1 \ if \ I_{i+1} \geq I_i \\ h_i = 0 \ otherwise \end{cases}, where \ 0 \leq i \leq 7 \tag{4}$$

Thus, each candidate patch represents a specific hash message.

3.1 Information Embedding Process

The generation of candidate patches. The first step in the message embedding process is to generate a candidate patch set. The candidate patch is generated by sampling the source texture, and it is used as the basic unit for the generation of the new texture image. Assuming the size of the given source texture is $S_w * S_h$, and the size of candidate patch block is $P_w * P_h$, we will generate candidate patches by following scan-line order and shifting a pixel each time. The set CP contains all candidate patches that are generated directly from the source texture image. We set $K_w = K_h$ and $G_c = G_r$ by default.

Candidate patch classification. According to the internal kernel block of the patch, you can extract the specific hash message represented by the patch. In the case of $G_c = G_r = 3$, we divide the kernel region of each patch into nine lattices with the size of $G_w * G_h$, and a kernel block can be hash for the 8 bites message, then we create a index table which has 256 rows, each row represents a category $\prod_i$, where $i = 0, 1, 2, \ldots, 255$. We add the candidate patch which has the decimal value v of the eight bits hash message $h_0 h_1 h_2 h_3 h_4 h_5 h_6 h_7$ to the category $\prod_v$. When all the candidate patches are added to the corresponding category, the index table is obtained. We can use the index table to find the candidate patch whose hash message is equal to the value that needs to be embedded.

Message encryption and segmentation. The sender and the receiver share a pair of keys K_e. The sender encrypts the information with the key K_e and converts the ciphertext into a binary bit string M. Next, M is segmented by the length of the hash message, and then we get segments $m_1, m_2, \ldots, m_n$, where n is the total number of segments.

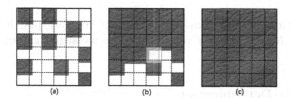

Fig. 3. Texture synthesis process. (a) Paint message patches, (b) Paint blank districts, (c) Synthesized steganographic image

Texture synthesis process. The texture synthesis process is shown in Fig. 3. The sender and the receiver also share a pair of keys K_p for selecting the positions to paint patches to hide secret message. A blank canvas of size $[(K_w + P_d) * W_r] * [(K_h + P_d) * W_c]$ is constructed, where W_r, W_c are integers and satisfies (5).

$$W_r \times W_c \geq 4n \tag{5}$$

In order to guarantee the quality of the generated picture, the sender selects a part of location in the blank canvas to hide secret message, and the other blank blocks are painted by choosing the optimal candidate patch. The sender and the receiver share the location key. The number of positions n is selected with the key k_p, all these positions must are not directly adjacent to the others and do not exist overlapped area. Select the segment m_i from $m_1, m_2, \ldots, m_n$ in order, and randomly choose an candidate patch in the corresponding category to paint the selected blank position.

$$MSEO = \frac{1}{P_w \times P_h} \sum_{i \in OL} (p_i^c - p_i^s)^2 \tag{6}$$

And we choose the patch which has the minimal MSEO (mean square error of the overlapped area) value in all candidate patches to paint blank portion in scan-line order, and use the image quilting method [13] to quilt the overlapped area. After painted all blank districts, a texture image with hidden message is synthesized. The equation of MSEO is shown in (6), where OL stands for the overlapped area of the working location, p_i^c stands for the pixel i of the candidate patch in the OL, p_i^s stands for the pixel i of the synthesized area in OL.

3.2   Message Extraction

Message segments extraction. After receiving the texture picture, the receiver uses the key K_p to determine the locations of the patches which represent the secret message first. Then receiver divides the kernel area into grids according to the same method as sender, and extracts bit message by comparing the average value of all pixels in grid in agreed order. In this way, we can extract all the secret message segments hidden in the steganographic synthetic texture, and combine them into the secret bit string M.

The decryption of the message. The receiver decrypts the bit string M using the key K_e. So the receiver will get the message that sender hid in the texture picture.

3.3   Capacity Determination

The embedding capacity of the proposed method is mainly related to the size of the synthetic texture image. The size of the synthetic texture image is $T_w * T_h$, the kernel block size is $K_w * K_h$, the width of the boundary area around the kernel block is P_d, and the number of lattices in each kernel block is N, the maximum total capacity (TC) our algorithm can offer is shown in (7).

$$TC = \left\lfloor \frac{\left\lfloor \frac{T_w}{K_w + P_d} \right\rfloor \times \left\lfloor \frac{T_h}{K_h + P_d} \right\rfloor}{4} \right\rfloor \times (N - 1) \tag{7}$$

Supposed that we intend to generate a synthetic texture $T_w * T_h = 1024 * 1024$, and the kernel block size $K_w * K_h = 24 * 24$, the boundary depth $P_d = 8$ pixels, the number of grids in each kernel blocks $N = 9$, then the maximum total embedding capacity is $TC = 2048$ bits. Compared to most image steganography methods [14], this is already a very large embedding capacity.

4 Application in JPEG Compression

Now most of picture-based steganography methods are unable to effectively deal with JPEG compression. And we propose the method that can against JPEG compression after a slight modification. Even being compressed, it can extract message normally, the bit error rate is much lower than other methods. In order to apply our proposed method to JPEG compression, we make the following modifications:

1. The size of the grid in the kernel block and the width of the boundary around the kernel block are multiple of 8. Because the basic unit of the DCT transform is a block of $8*8$ pixels. In order to ensure the local feature of each grid, we expect that each grid contains the complete unit of the DCT transform.
2. The attribute value R takes the upper left corner of the DCT coefficient matrix. Because the non-zero coefficients of each $8*8$ pixel DCT coefficient matrix are mainly concentrated in the upper left corner. Thus, $I_k = DCT\_Array[0][0]$, where DCT_Array is the DCT coefficient matrix.
3. Filter the candidate patches. For every candidate patches in each category, we calculate the minimum absolute value δ of the differences between the adjacent grids, and we sort these candidate patches according to the value of δ in descending order. We selected the first N_p patches as the last candidate patch set for that category. The smaller the number N_p of patches to be selected, the better the anti-compression performs.

4.1 Message Embedding Process

The generation of candidate patches. Assuming the size of the source texture is $S_w * S_h$, candidate patch block with the size of $P_w * P_h$, we employ a window and travel the source texture by shifting a pixel each time following the scan-line order to generate candidate patches. The size of the grid in the kernel block and the width of the boundary around the kernel block are multiple of 8. After traversing the source textures, all candidate patches make up the candidate patch set. If $K_w = K_h$, $G_w = G_h$, we can rotate or flip candidate patches, so that the number of candidate patches expanded to 8 times than the previous.

Patch classification and filtration. Because of the internal division of the patch, different patches can represent different information. According to the hash message the patch represents, patches will be classified into the corresponding category. We use the following rules to filter patches and remain the patches which meet the conditions. For every candidate patch in each category, we calculate the minimum absolute value δ of the differences between the adjacent grids, and we sort these candidate patches by the value of δ in descending order. We selected the first N_p patches as the last candidate patch set for that category.

$$\delta = \min(\{|I_{i+1} - I_i| | i = 0, 1, \ldots, N - 2\}) \tag{8}$$

Message encryption and segmentation. The sender and the receiver share a pair of keys K_e for encryption and decryption. The sender encrypts the information with the key and converts the ciphertext into the information bit string M. Next, M is segmented by the length of the hash message, and we get segments $m_1, m_2, \ldots, m_n$, where n is the total number of segments.

Texture synthesis process. The sender and the receiver also share a pair of keys K_p for selecting the positions to paint patches to hide secret message. A blank canvas of size $[(K_w + P_d) * W_r] * [(K_h + P_d) * W_c]$ is constructed, where W_r, W_c are integers and satisfies (5).

The number of positions n is selected with the key k_p, all these positions must are not directly adjacent to the others and do not exist overlapped area. Select the segment m_i from $m_1, m_2, \ldots, m_n$, and randomly choose the candidate patch in the corresponding category to paint the selected patch position. And we choose the patch which has the minimal MSEO value in all candidate patches to paint blank portion in scan-line order. And finally, a texture image with hidden message is synthesized.

4.2 Message Extraction

The receiver uses the key K_p to determine the locations of the patches which represent the secret message, and then obtain the message segments according to the internal division. Combine the message segments according their order and get the message string M. Finally, the receiver decrypts the string with the key K_e, and obtains the secret information sent by the sender.

5 Experimental Results and Analysis

5.1 Synthesized Texture Quality

Figure 4 is part of our experimental results. In order to verify that the texture picture we generated is very similar to the source texture image. We use the PPMC [15] scheme to measure the similarity of the synthesized texture image with the source texture image. PPMC (Pearson Product Moment Correlation) is

Table 1. Comparison of pearson correlation coefficients

	Case-A	Case-B
	(a)vs.(b)	(a)vs.(c)
Fabric	0.9990	0.9986
Rope net	0.9984	0.9980
Marble	0.9991	0.9989
Leather	0.9993	0.9990

Fig. 4. Results for the synthetic textures with lossless compression and the synthetic textures with lossy compression. (a) Source texture. (b) The texture generated by the method described in Sect. 3. (c) The texture generated by the modified method described in Sect. 4.

a measure of the correlation of two variables. The scheme produces a correlation coefficient range of 1 to −1. The result 1 means that the two variables are absolutely positive correlation, and the result is 0.5 to 1.0 for a high degree of correlation.

Table 1 shows the PPMC for the 3-channel RGB of the experimental picture. In Case-A, we show the correlation coefficients between the source texture and the steganographic synthetic texture with lossless compression. In Case-B, the correlation coefficients of source texture and steganographic synthetic texture with JPEG compression are recorded. The correlation coefficient shown in Case-A is very close to 1.0. This shows that the steganographic synthetic texture with lossless compression is highly similar with the source texture. In Case-B, the correlation coefficients between source texture and JPEG-compressed texture are also very closed to 1. It indicates that the texture image our steganographic algorithm synthesized has a strong similarity with the source texture image.

5.2   JPEG Compression

On the fight against JPEG compression, we carried out a lot of experiments. As shown in Fig. 5, we carried out three groups of experiments with N_p values of 10, 50, 100, and in each experiment, JPEG compression quality factor were taken 90, 70, 50, 30, 10. From Fig. 5, we can find that with the decrease of QF, the bit error rate presents a gradual upward trend, but the bit error rate is always less than 19%, in good cases it less than 0.5%, such as $N_p = 10$, $QF = 50$. Thus, we can conclude that our method, even in the presence of JPEG compression, still has a very high transmission accuracy.

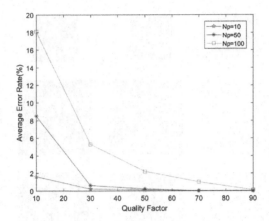

Fig. 5. Error rate of data extraction corresponding to quality factors of JPEG compression

Table 2. Average error rate of data extraction after compressing the stego images

Quality factor	90	70	50
[4]	14.5%	24.0%	26.3%
[5]	0	5.6%	7.7%
Proposed	0	1.0%	2.2%

We also chose 80 source pictures from the database "Brodatz Textures" [16] to carry on experiment. The source texture are rescaled to the size of 128 * 128. The embedding rate 0.5 bits per patch are selected to generate stego images for the proposed method and the methods in [4,5]. And the quality factors are used from 50 to 90. We extracted hidden data and calculated the average error rates. The results are shown in Table 2. These results indicate that we proposed steganography method has better capability of countering JPEG compression than methods in [4,5].

6   Conclusion and Future Work

This paper proposes a steganographic algorithm for synthesizing texture images by selecting patch with specific hash information. For a given texture image, we can produce steganographic texture image of any size. And the approach can not only be used in lossless image, it can also be used in lossy JPEG compression pictures with the state-of-the-art performance. We believe that our proposed method extends the usage scenarios of images in steganography.

One of our future works is to propose a steganographic method that can recover the hidden information correctly under the malicious tailoring attack, and improve the anti-attack capability of stego texture images.

References

1. Johnson, N.F., Jajodia, S.: Exploring steganography: seeing the unseen. Computer **31**(2), 26–34 (1998)
2. Cheng, Y.M., Wang, C.M.: A high-capacity steganographic approach for 3D polygonal meshes. Vis. Comput. **22**(9), 845–855 (2006)
3. Petrowski, K., Kharrazi, M., Sencar, H.T., Memon, N.: PSTEG: steganographic embedding through patching [image steganography]. In: IEEE International Conference on Acoustics, Speech, and Signal Processing, Proceedings, vol. 2, pp. 537–540. IEEE Xplore (2005)
4. Wu, K.C., Wang, C.M.: Steganography using reversible texture synthesis. IEEE Trans. Image Process. **24**(1), 130–139 (2014)
5. Qian, Z., Zhou, H., Zhang, W., Zhang, X.: Robust steganography using texture synthesis. Advances in Intelligent Information Hiding and Multimedia Signal Processing. SIST, vol. 63, pp. 25–33. Springer, Cham (2017). https://doi.org/10.1007/978-3-319-50209-0_4
6. Xu, J., Mao, X., Jin, X., Jaffer, A., Lu, S., Li, L., et al.: Hidden message in a deformation-based texture. Vis. Comput. **31**(12), 1653–1669 (2015)
7. Fridrich, J.: Steganography in Digital Media: Principles, Algorithms, and Applications. Cambridge University Press, Cambridge (2009)
8. Efros, A.A., Leung, T.K.: Texture syntesis by non-parametric sampling. In: The Proceedings of the Seventh IEEE International Conference on Computer Vision. IEEE, vol. 2, p. 1033 (1999)
9. Han, C., Risser, E., Ramamoorthi, R., Grinspun, E.: Multiscale texture synthesis. ACM Trans. Graph. **27**(3), 1–8 (2008)
10. Otori, H., Kuriyama, S.: Data-embeddable texture synthesis. In: Butz, A., Fisher, B., Krüger, A., Olivier, P., Owada, S. (eds.) SG 2007. LNCS, vol. 4569, pp. 146–157. Springer, Heidelberg (2007). https://doi.org/10.1007/978-3-540-73214-3_13
11. Otori, H., Kuriyama, S.: Texture synthesis for mobile data communications. Comput. Graph. Appl. IEEE **29**(6), 74–81 (2009)
12. Liang, L.: Real-time texture synthesis by patch-based sampling. ACM Trans. Graph. **20**(3), 127–150 (2001)
13. Efros, A.A., Freeman, W.T.: Image quilting for texture synthesis and transfer. In: Conference on Computer Graphics and Interactive Techniques, pp. 341–346. ACM (2001)
14. Zhou, Z., Sun, H., Harit, R., Chen, X., Sun, X.: Coverless image steganography without embedding. In: Huang, Z., Sun, X., Luo, J., Wang, J. (eds.) ICCCS 2015. LNCS, vol. 9483, pp. 123–132. Springer, Cham (2015). https://doi.org/10.1007/978-3-319-27051-7_11
15. Rodgers, J.L., Nicewander, W.A.: Thirteen ways to look at the correlation coefficient. Am. Stat. **42**(1), 59–66 (1988)
16. Brodatz Texture, Texture Image Database. http://multibandtexture.recherche.usherbrooke.ca/original_brodatz.html

Saliency Cuts on RGB-D Images

Yuantian Wang, Lei Huang$^{(\boxtimes)}$, Tongwei Ren, and Yunfei Zhang

State Key Laboratory for Novel Software Technology,
Nanjing University, Nanjing, China
{wangyt,141250197}@smail.nju.edu.cn,
{leihuang,rentw}@nju.edu.cn

Abstract. Saliency cuts aims to segment salient objects from a given
saliency map. The existing saliency cuts methods focus on dealing with
RGB images and videos, but ignore the exploration of depth cue, which
limit their performance on RGB-D images. In this paper, we propose a
novel saliency cuts method on RGB-D images, which utilizes both color
and depth cues to segment salient objects. Given a saliency map, we first
generate segmentation seeds with adaptive triple thresholding. Next, we
extend GrabCut by combining depth cue, and use it to generate a roughly
labeled map. Finally, we refine the boundary of the salient object adaptively, and produce an accurate binary mask. To the best of our knowledge, this method is the first specific saliency cuts method for RGB-D
images. We validated the proposed method on the largest RGB-D image
dataset for salient object detection, named NJU2000. The experimental
results demonstrate that our method outperforms the state-of-the-art
methods.

Keywords: Saliency cuts · RGB-D image · Depth-aware GrabCut
Adaptive boundary refinement

1 Introduction

As a special task in object segmentation, saliency cuts aims to automatically
segment salient objects from a given saliency map [1]. It can be used in numerous applications, such as object classification [2,3], retrieval [4–6], social media
analysis [7–9], and image annotation [10,11]. Different to traditional object segmentation methods [12–15], saliency map generated by saliency detection algorithm [16,17] is the main input of saliency cuts. In contrast, original images or
videos are ignored [18,19] or used to improve refinement [20,21].

The existing saliency cuts methods are proposed to deal with RGB images
and videos. For example, Otsu *et al.* produced segmentation results using thresholds from gray-Level histograms of saliency maps [18]. Achanta *et al.* segmented
from the saliency value and luminance of saliency map [19]. Fu *et al.* generated
saliency cuts results via professional labels [1]. Cheng *et al.* used a fixed threshold to binarize the saliency maps and produced results from iterative GrabCut
calculation [21]. Li *et al.* fed segmentation seeds generated with adaptive triple

© Springer Nature Singapore Pte Ltd. 2018
B. Huet et al. (Eds.): ICIMCS 2017, CCIS 819, pp. 440–448, 2018.
https://doi.org/10.1007/978-981-10-8530-7_43

thresholding method to GrabCut algorithm to produce segmentation results [20]. Banica *et al.* segmented video object via salient segment chain composition [22].

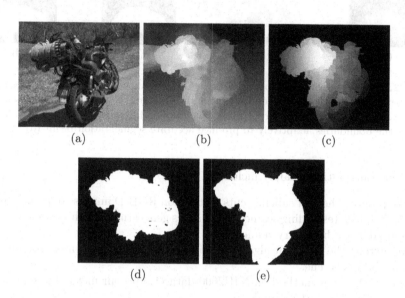

(a)   (b)   (c)

(d)   (e)

Fig. 1. An example of the effect of depth cue in saliency cuts. The saliency cuts result (e) using color cue (a), depth cue (b) and saliency map (c) is better than the one (d) only using color cue and saliency map.

However, these methods ignore the exploration of depth cue, which prevent them to produce better performance on RGB-D images than on RGB images. Figure 1 shows an example of the effect of depth cue in saliency cuts. The saliency cuts result of motorcycle (Fig. 1(d)) is incomplete using only color cue (Fig. 1(a)) and saliency map (Fig. 1(c)), because of the complexity and diversity of motorcycle's appearance in color cue. However, the motorcycle's appearance in depth cue (Fig. 1(b)) is relatively simpler, which can help segmenting the motorcycle from the background. Hence, a possible improvement of saliency cuts is to combine color cue with depth cue to produce a better saliency cuts result (Fig. 1(e)).

Based on the above observation, we propose a novel saliency cuts method on RGB-D images. Figure 2 shows an overview of the proposed method. We first use adaptive triple thresholding algorithm [20] to generate segmentation seeds from a given saliency map. Then, we feed the segmentation seeds to depth-aware GrabCut algorithm to generate roughly labeled map. Finally, we produce an accurate binary mask via adaptive boundary refinement. As far as we know, it is the first specific saliency cuts method on RGB-D images. We validated our method on the largest RGB-D image dataset for salient object detection, named NJU2000 [23]. The experimental results show that our method outperforms the state-of-the-art saliency cuts methods on RGB-D images.

Seeds generation via   Depth aware   Adaptive
adaptive triple thresholding   GrabCut extension   boundary refinement

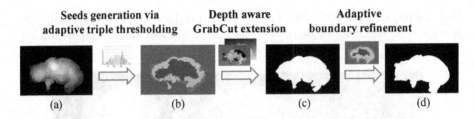

(a)   (b)   (c)   (d)

Fig. 2. An overview of our proposed method. Given a saliency map (a), we first generate segmentation seeds (b) using adaptive triple thresholding. Next, we feed these segmentation seeds to depth-aware GrabCut to generate roughly labeled map (c). Finally, we refine the boundaries adaptively to produce accurate segmentation result (d).

Our contributions mainly include:

- We propose the first saliency cuts method on RGB-D images combining adaptive triple thresholding segmentation seeds generation, depth-aware GrabCut, and adaptive boundary refinement.
- We extend the GrabCut algorithm on RGB-D images via combining the color cue and depth cue.
- We validate our method on NJU2000 dataset, and our method is superior to the state-of-the-art methods.

2   Our Method

2.1   Segmentation Seeds Generation via Adaptive Triple Thresholding

We generate segmentation seeds from saliency map using adaptive triple thresholding [20]. Assume the value range of saliency map is $[0, H]$, where H equals 255 in our experiments. t_l, t_m and t_h are the three thresholds used to divide saliency map M^s into four parts: $M^s = \Omega^s_{cb} \cup \Omega^s_{pb} \cup \Omega^s_{pf} \cup \Omega^s_{cf}$. Here, Ω^s_{cb}, Ω^s_{pb}, Ω^s_{pf} and Ω^s_{cf} denote certain background, probable background, probable foreground and certain foreground, which contain the pixels whose saliency values are in the value range of $[1, t_l]$, $[t_l + 1, t_m]$, $[t_m + 1, t_h]$ and $[t_h + 1, H]$, respectively. Obviously, the intersection of each two in Ω^s_{cb}, Ω^s_{pb}, Ω^s_{pf} and Ω^s_{cf} is $\emptyset$. Assume n is the number of pixels on M^s, and n_{cb}, n_{pb}, n_{pf} and n_{cf} are the numbers of pixels on Ω^s_{cb}, Ω^s_{pb}, Ω^s_{pf} and Ω^s_{cf}, respectively. t_l, t_m, t_h are calculated as follows:

$$\{t_l, t_m, t_h\} = \arg\max\{\omega_{cb}\omega_{pb}(\mu_{cb} - \mu_{pb})^2 + \omega_{cf}\omega_{pf}(\mu_{cf} - \mu_{pf})^2\}, \quad (1)$$

where ω_{cb}, ω_{pb}, ω_{pf} and ω_{cf} are the weights of Ω^s_{cb}, Ω^s_{pb}, Ω^s_{pf} and Ω^s_{cf}, which equal $\frac{n_{cb}}{n}$, $\frac{n_{pb}}{n}$, $\frac{n_{pf}}{n}$ and $\frac{n_{cf}}{n}$, respectively; μ_{cb}, μ_{pb}, μ_{pf} and μ_{cf} are the average saliency value of Ω^s_{cb}, Ω^s_{pb}, Ω^s_{pf} and Ω^s_{cf}, respectively.

2.2   Depth-Aware GrabCut

The segmentation procedure in GrabCut algorithm can be considered as a mini-cut problem [24]. We extend the energy function E of GrabCut by combining depth cue:

$$E = \alpha E'(L, K^c, \theta^c, Z^c) + (1 - \alpha)E'(L, K^d, \theta^d, Z^d), \qquad (2)$$

where L is the label set; K^c and K^d are the parameter sets of GMM model on color cue and depth cue; θ^c and θ^d are gray histogram of foreground or background on color cue and depth cue; Z^c and Z^d are the gray value sets of color cue and depth value set of depth cue; α is a parameter for combination, which equals 0.5 in our experiments; $E'(L, K, \theta, Z)$ is the energy function of color cue and depth cue, which is defined as follows:

$$E'(L, K, \theta, Z) = U(l_i, k_i, \theta, z_i) + V(L, Z), \qquad (3)$$

where $U(l_i, k_i, \theta, z_i)$ is the data term; $V(L, Z)$ is the smooth term, which is calculated as follows:

$$V(L, Z) = \gamma \sum_{(m,n) \in C} [l_n \neq l_m] \exp -\beta Dis(z_m, z_n)^2, \qquad (4)$$

where constant γ equals 50 [25]; C is the set of pairs of neighboring pixels; $\beta = (2\langle (z_m - z_n)^2 \rangle)^{-1}$ and $\langle \cdot \rangle$ in β denotes expectation over an colorful image; $Dis(z_m, z_n)$ denotes the distance between pixels m and n.

Referring to [26], we use Euclidean distance $Dis^c(z_m, z_n)$ on color cue and geodesic distance $Dis^d(z_m^d, z_n^d)$ on depth cue, respectively, because geodesic distance can better extract the spatial property of depth cue. We define $Dis^c(z_m, z_n)$ as follows:

$$Dis^c(z_m^c, z_n^c) = ||z_m^c - z_n^c||, \qquad (5)$$

where z_m^c and z_n^c are the gray value of pixel m and n on color cue, respectively, and define $Dis^d(z_m^d, z_n^d)$ as follows:

$$Dis^d(z_m^d, z_n^d) = \min\{\varphi_{m,n}\}, \qquad (6)$$

where $\varphi_{m,n}$ denotes the distance of a path between pixel m and n, which is calculated as follows:

$$\varphi_{m,n} = \max_{i,j \in P_{m,n}} \{||z_i^d - z_j^d||\}, \qquad (7)$$

where i and j are two neighbor pixels on path $P_{m,n}$; z_i^d and z_j^d are the depth value of i and j on depth cue.

Based on the above depth-aware GrabCut algorithm, we generate a roughly labeled map M^{rl}, which contains Ω_{cb}^{rl}, Ω_{pb}^{rl}, Ω_{pf}^{rl} and Ω_{cf}^{rl} with the similar definition to Ω_{cb}^s, Ω_{pb}^s, Ω_{pf}^s and Ω_{cf}^s, after we feed the segmentation seeds M^s.

2.3   Adaptive Boundary Refinement

To obtain more accurate salient objects, we adaptively refine the object boundaries generated by M^{rl} [27].

In order to avoid containing background in the segmented salient objects, we
erode Ω_{cf}^{rl} as follows:

$$\Omega_{cf}^{rl'} = f_e(\Omega_{cf}^{rl}, \lambda_1 R(\Omega_{cf}^{rl})), \tag{8}$$

where $R(\Omega_{cf}^{rl})$ is the radius of circumcircle of Ω_{cf}^{rl}; λ_1 is a parameter, which
equals 0.1; $f_e(\Omega, R)$ is a function to erode Ω with a radius R.
Ω_{pf}^{cl} is also updated as follows:

$$\Omega_{pf}^{cl'} = (\Omega_{cf}^{rl} \backslash \Omega_{cf}^{cl'}) \cup \Omega_{pf}^{rl}. \tag{9}$$

Meanwhile, to improve the completeness of the segmented salient objects, we
dilate the foreground region, $i.e.$, the union of Ω_{cf}^{rl} and Ω_{pf}^{rl}, and refine probable
background as the union of Ω_{pb}^{rl} and the newly covered region in dilation, which
is defined as follows:

$$\Omega_{pb}^{cl'} = (f_d((\Omega_{cf}^{rl} \cup \Omega_{pf}^{rl}), \lambda_2 R(\Omega_{cf}^{rl} \cup \Omega_{pf}^{rl})) \backslash (\Omega_{cf}^{rl} \cup \Omega_{pf}^{rl})) \cup \Omega_{pb}^{rl}, \tag{10}$$

where $R(\Omega_{cf}^{rl} \cup \Omega_{pf}^{rl})$ is the radius of circumcircle of $\Omega_{cf}^{rl} \cup \Omega_{pf}^{rl}$, λ_2 is a parameter,
which equals 0.1; $f_d(\Omega, R)$ is a function to dilate Ω with a radius R.
$\Omega_{cb}^{cl'}$ is also updated as follows:

$$\Omega_{cb}^{cl'} = \Omega_{cf}^{rl} \backslash \Omega_{pb}^{cl'}. \tag{11}$$

We re-feed the segmentation seeds $M^{cl'}$ to depth-aware GrabCut to generate
the accurately labeled map M^{dl}, which contains Ω_{cb}^{dl}, Ω_{pb}^{dl}, Ω_{pf}^{dl} and Ω_{cf}^{dl}, and
produce the accurate binary mask by defining the binary value of pixels in Ω_{cf}^{dl}
and Ω_{pf}^{dl} as 1, denoting object, and defining the binary value of pixels in Ω_{cb}^{dl} and
Ω_{pb}^{dl} as 0, denoting background, respectively.

3   Experiments

3.1   Dataset and Experiment Settings

We validated our method on the largest RGB-D image dataset for salient object
detection, named NJU2000, which contains 2, 000 RGB-D images with manually
segmented salient object in ground truth [23]. Saliency maps are generated using
Feng's method [28], because it is a state-of-the-art saliency detection method on
RGB-D images.

All the experiments were conducted on a computer with 2.9 GHz Intel Core
i5 CPU and 8 GB memory. The average processing time per image of our method
is 2.12 s. We apply the default settings of author suggestions for all the saliency
cuts methods we used in our experiments.

3.2   Component Analysis

We first validate the effectiveness of three components in our method, namely adaptive triple thresholding segmentation seeds generation, depth-aware Grab-Cut, and adaptive boundary refinement.

We compare our method with three baselines. *Fixed* denotes the method with segmentation seeds generation using fixed thresholds which uniformly divide saliency value range (*i.e.*, (t_l, t_m, t_h) equals $(64, 128, 192)$), original GrabCut and no boundary refinement, and add three components of our method in sequence to generate the comparison methods. *Ours-A* denotes the method with adaptive triple thresholding segmentation seeds generation, original GrabCut and no boundary refinement. *Ours-AD* denotes the method with adaptive triple thresholding segmentation seeds generation, depth-aware GrabCut and no boundary refinement. *Ours* denotes our proposed method, which uses adaptive triple thresholding segmentation seeds generation, depth-aware GrabCut and adaptive boundary refinement.

Figure 3 shows the precision, recall and F_β values of method Fixed, Ours-A, Ours-AD and Ours, here $\beta^2 = 0.3$ [29]. We can see that the recall and F_β value grow from method Fixed to Ours while precision value keeps relatively consistent. It indicates that each component in our method can help generating better saliency cuts results via improving the completeness of salient object segmentation.

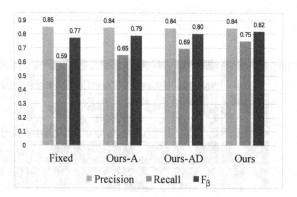

Fig. 3. Effectiveness validation of different components in our method. Fixed, Ours-A, Ours-AD, and Ours are shown in Sect. 3.2.

3.3   Comparison with State-of-the-Arts

We also compare our method with four state-of-the-art saliency cuts methods, namely Otsu [18], FT [19], AL [1], and ASRE [21]. Here, Otsu and FT use only saliency maps as input; AL and ASRE generate segmentation seeds from saliency maps, and feed segmentation seeds and RGB images to GrabCut algorithm. To make fair comparison, we extend AL and ASRE to AL* and ASRE* by

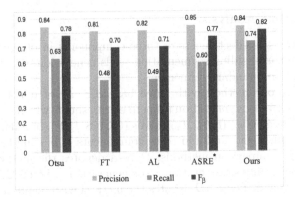

Fig. 4. Effectiveness comparison of our method and four state-of-the-art saliency cuts methods, namely Otsu [18], FT [19], AL* [1], and ASRE* [21].

replacing GrabCut with depth-aware GrabCut, because the later obtains better segmentation performance on RGB-D images.

Figure 4 shows the comparison results of five methods. We can see that our method outperforms other methods on F_β value, because it achieves the best balance between precision and recall. It indicates that our method segments the most complete and accurate salient objects in all five methods. Figure 5 shows some segmentation results generated by five saliency cuts methods on RGB-D images. It shows that our method produces the best segmentation results on various salient objects, such as car, animal, and person.

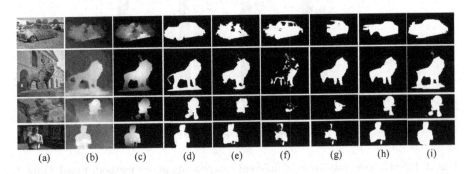

Fig. 5. Examples of saliency cuts results of different methods. (a) Color cue. (b) Depth cue. (c) Saliency map. (d) Ground truth. (e) Otsu. (f) FT. (g) AL*. (h) ASRE*. (i) Ours.

4   Conclusion

In this paper, we proposed the first saliency cuts method on RGB-D images, which utilizes segmentation seeds generation using adaptive triple thresholding, depth-aware GrabCut and adaptive boundary refinement. The proposed method was validated on NJU2000 dataset. The experimental results show that our method is superior to the state-of-the-art saliency cuts methods on RGB-D images.

Acknowledgments. This work is supported by National Science Foundation of China (61321491, 61202320), National Undergraduate Innovation Project (G201610284069), and Collaborative Innovation Center of Novel Software Technology and Industrialization.

References

1. Fu, Y., Cheng, J., Li, Z., Lu, H.: Saliency cuts: an automatic approach to object segmentation. In: CVPR, pp. 1–4 (2012)
2. Athanasiadis, T., et al.: Integrating image segmentation and classification for fuzzy knowledge-based multimedia indexing. In: Huet, B., Smeaton, A., Mayer-Patel, K., Avrithis, Y. (eds.) MMM 2009. LNCS, vol. 5371, pp. 263–274. Springer, Heidelberg (2009). https://doi.org/10.1007/978-3-540-92892-8_29
3. Hong, R., Zhang, L., Zhang, C., Zimmermann, R.: Flickr circles: aesthetic tendency discovery by multi-view regularized topic modeling. TMM **18**, 1555–1567 (2016)
4. Nie, L., Yan, S., Wang, M., Hong, R., Chua, T.S.: Harvesting visual concepts for image search with complex queries. In: MM, pp. 59–68. ACM (2012)
5. Hong, R., Hu, Z., Wang, R., Wang, M., Tao, D.: Multi-view object retrieval via multi-scale topic models. TIP **25**, 5814–5827 (2016)
6. Hong, R., Yang, Y., Wang, M., Hua, X.S.: Learning visual semantic relationships for efficient visual retrieval. TBD **1**, 152–161 (2017)
7. Li, Z., Tang, J.: Weakly supervised deep matrix factorization for social image understanding. TIP **26**, 276–288 (2016)
8. Sang, J., Xu, C., Liu, J.: User-aware image tag refinement via ternary semantic analysis. TMM **14**, 883–895 (2012)
9. Nie, L., Wang, M., Zha, Z., Chua, T.S.: Oracle in image search: a content-based approach to performance prediction. TOIS **30**, 13:1–13:23 (2012)
10. Tang, J., Hong, R., Yan, S., Chua, T.S., Qi, G.J., Jain, R.: Image annotation by kNN-sparse graph-based label propagation over noisily tagged web images. TIST **2**, 14 (2011)
11. Nie, L., Wang, M., Zha, Z., Li, G., Chua, T.S.: Multimedia answering: enriching text QA with media information. In: SIGIR, pp. 695–704. ACM (2011)
12. Xu, N., Bansal, R., Ahuja, N.: Object segmentation using graph cuts based active contours. In: CVPR, vol. 2, pp. II-46–53 (2007)
13. Shi, J., Malik, J.: Normalized cuts and image segmentation. TPAMI **22**, 888–905 (2000)
14. Song, H., Liu, Z., Du, H., Sun, G., Le, M.O., Ren, T.: Depth-aware salient object detection and segmentation via multiscale discriminative saliency fusion and bootstrap learning. TIP **PP**, 1 (2017)
15. Ye, L., Liu, Z., Li, L., Shen, L., Bai, C., Wang, Y.: Salient object segmentation via effective integration of saliency and objectness. TMM **PP**, 1 (2017)
16. Hou, X., Zhang, L.: Saliency detection: a spectral residual approach. In: CVPR, pp. 1–8 (2007)
17. Guo, J., Ren, T., Huang, L., Bei, J.: Saliency detection on sampled images for tag ranking. Multimed. Syst. 1–13 (2017)

18. Otsu, N.: A threshold selection method from gray-level histograms. SMC **9**, 62–66 (2007)

19. Achanta, R., Hemami, S., Estrada, F., Susstrunk, S.: Frequency-tuned salient region detection. In: CVPR, pp. 1597–1604 (2009)

20. Li, S., Ju, R., Ren, T., Wu, G.: Saliency cuts based on adaptive triple thresholding. In: ICIP, pp. 4609–4613 (2015)

21. Cheng, M.M., Zhang, G.X., Mitra, N.J., Huang, X., Hu, S.M.: Global contrast based salient region detection. In: CVPR, pp. 409–416 (2011)

22. Banica, D., Agape, A., Ion, A., Sminchisescu, C.: Video object segmentation by salient segment chain composition. In: ICCV Workshops, pp. 283–290 (2013)

23. Ju, R., Liu, Y., Ren, T., Ge, L., Wu, G.: Depth-aware salient object detection using anisotropic center-surround difference. SPIC **38**, 115–126 (2015)

24. Rother, C., Kolmogorov, V., Blake, A.: "GrabCut": interactive foreground extraction using iterated graph cuts. TOG **23**, 309–314 (2004)

25. Blake, A., Rother, C., Brown, M., Perez, P., Torr, P.: Interactive image segmentation using an adaptive GMMRF model. In: Pajdla, T., Matas, J. (eds.) ECCV 2004. LNCS, vol. 3021, pp. 428–441. Springer, Heidelberg (2004). https://doi.org/10.1007/978-3-540-24670-1_33

26. Ge, L., Ju, R., Ren, T., Wu, G.: Interactive RGB-D image segmentation using hierarchical graph cut and geodesic distance. In: Ho, Y.-S., Sang, J., Ro, Y.M., Kim, J., Wu, F. (eds.) PCM 2015. LNCS, vol. 9314, pp. 114–124. Springer, Cham (2015). https://doi.org/10.1007/978-3-319-24075-6_12

27. Liu, J., Ren, T., Wang, Y., Zhong, S.H., Bei, J., Chen, S.: Object proposal on RGB-D images via elastic edge boxes. NEUCOM **236**, 134–146 (2017)

28. Feng, D., Barnes, N., You, S., Mccarthy, C.: Local background enclosure for RGB-D salient object detection. In: CVPR, pp. 2343–2350 (2016)

29. Borji, A., Cheng, M.M., Jiang, H., Li, J.: Salient object detection: a benchmark. TIP **24**, 5706–5722 (2015)

Same-Style Products Mining for Clothes Retrieval

Zhenwei Shen[1]([✉]) [iD], Zhiwei Fang[2,3] [iD], and Jing Liu[2] [iD]

[1] Shandong University of Science and Technology, Qingdao, China
shenzhenwei@outlook.com
[2] National Lab of Pattern Recognition, Institute of Automation,
Chinese Academy of Sciences, Beijing, China
{zhiwei.fang,jliu}@nlpr.ia.ac.cn
[3] University of Chinese Academy of Sciences, Beijing, China

Abstract. Same-style clothes retrieval is a task to search images which contain exactly the same designing style clothes. For such a task, too limited training data makes the problem of how to gain suitable same-style feature representations challenging but significant. In this paper, we adopt a memory-augmented deep neural network, also called as a few-shot learning model, to collect possibly same-style images. Besides, we present an object-aware clothes retrieval framework to further enhance the same-style feature representations, in which object focusing regions through object detection are first obtained, and a multi-task Siamese network is designed for ranking feature learning provided with some same-style or non-same-style image pairs. Experiments results show that our proposed solution is effective to discover more same-style images precisely, and further achieve the satisfied performance on same-style clothes retrieval.

Keywords: Clothes retrieval · Same-style products mining
Few-shot learning

1 Introduction

With the advances of mobile smart devices and e-commerce, online clothing shopping by taking photos as queries is becoming an increasingly popular manner. How to search the same-style clothes with queries, i.e., same-style clothes retrieval (SSCR), is a necessary and challenging research problem. Different from traditional clothing retrieval [1–3], SSCR focuses on images with same texture, fabric and same design style, as illustrated in Fig. 1. The main difficulties in SSCR are the high variations in clothing pose and the uncontrolled conditions where images are taken. It is essential to use large training dataset to learn a strong feature representation to cover the complex conditions of clothing images. Although existing datasets are annotated with massive attributes or clothing masks [4–6], they cannot solve those problems confronted by SSCR.

© Springer Nature Singapore Pte Ltd. 2018
B. Huet et al. (Eds.): ICIMCS 2017, CCIS 819, pp. 449–458, 2018.
https://doi.org/10.1007/978-981-10-8530-7_44

Fig. 1. Same-style clothes are those with same texture, fabric and same design style. The top row shows the same-style examples, the middle and bottom rows show the non-same-style examples. The top row images also indicate that they don't need to be the exactly same one

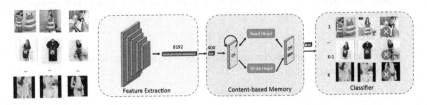

Fig. 2. Pipeline of same-style products mining. At the first stage, features are extracted from a Convolutional Neural Network model, then some clusters of images are selected, At the second stage, we use a few-shot learning model to filter false images in those clusters.

Therefore lack of training data is one of the fundamental problems that need to be addressed.

Directly annotating same-style clothes in large scale image dataset is time-consuming and costly. A more practical method is to mine images from existing huge image databases. But neither traditional methods nor Feedforward Deep Convolutional Neural Network (FDCNN) could deal with this problem: traditional methods (e.g. clustering) are not strong enough to pick right images from false, and without large datasets traditional FDCNN models couldn't generalize to explore never-before-seen data.

In this paper, we propose a few-shot-learning based method to conduct same-style clothes mining. It is a kind of memory-augmented deep neural network (MANN). With the recent development, MANN has gained the ability to rapidly assimilate new data, and leverage new data to make accurate recognition after only one-shot or few-shot learning [7–10]. Our model mainly consists of five components: a controller, read and write heads, an content-based memory and a classifier. The controller can slowly learn an abstract method for obtaining useful representations of raw data via gradient descent. Meanwhile, the memory and other rest parts make it also have the ability to bind new information after a few presentation. These great strengths have open the way to dig out new pictures from the existing datasets with only a few training data. However, its drawback is that it can not process many categories of objects concurrently, that means it cannot be applied directly to the SSCR task, which should generalize to a myriad of clothing styles theoretically. To overcome this shortcoming, we simplify the SSCR problem as a task to identify clothing style question which only need to recognize one or several clothing styles when mining the training data. In order to achieve this, traditional or other weak retrieval methods and the few-shot learning technique are combined. Specifically, a unsupervised clustering method is first adopt to dig out coarse same-style clothing clusters, then a few-shot learning model is trained to conduct more fine-grained recognition between true same-style clothes and false ones. New training and test strategy has been adopted for our few-shot learning model. With this scheme, we propose a novel pipeline, as shown in Fig. 2, to excavate the same-style clothing photos for a certain seed image using few-shot learning model. First, we obtain k clusters of images each of which composed of several same-style clothing images and several noise images according to CNNs features. Second, a few-shot learning model is used to denoise non-same-style images.

We exploit image retrieval framework in [11], additional training data we obtained with the above mining approach are used and experimental results show that this new framework leads to improved performance.

2   Approach

In this section, we first introduce our proposed "same-style products mining pipeline" in detail. Then the specific implementation process of our modified object-aware clothing image retrieval framework is described (Fig. 3).

2.1   Same-Style Products Mining Pipeline

As shown in Fig. 2, the workflow consists of two phases: (1) obtaining k coarse clusters for k seed images; (2) removing false same-style images from those clusters.

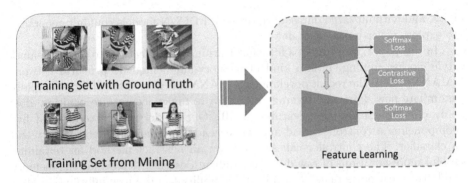

Fig. 3. Illustration of the proposed framework for SSCR. Product mining part is loaded onto framework in [11] and the original softmax losses are modified to be better suited to SSCR task.

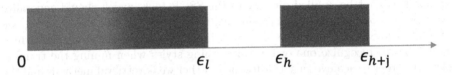

Fig. 4. The composing of one group images for testing. The proportion of same-style images in blue block is higher than in red blocks. (Color figure online)

Fig. 5. Examples of same-style products mining results.

In the first stage, we adopt $\epsilon - NN$ method with random seeds to dig out k coarse same-style clusters. For a random seed, we choose a lower ϵ_l and a higher ϵ_h based on statistical methods. Images whose distance to corresponding seed image falls into $[0, \epsilon_l]$ are the candidate same-style samples. The top q images which are more likely to be the same-style images are used as positive samples during testing stage. The same-style probability threshold of top q images is 0.8 in this paper. The images which fall into the range $[\epsilon_h, \epsilon_{h+j}]$ will be treat as the negative samples. ϵ_{h+j} denotes there are j images within the range $[\epsilon_h, \epsilon_{h+j}]$. The components of one group images are illustrated in Fig. 4. The clustering method is based on cosine distance. Inspired by [11], we choose VGG-CNN-S [12] which is pre-trained on ImageNet [13] as feature extractor and add an max-pooling layer pool6 (kernel size $= 3 \times 3$ and stride $= 1$)to the output of pool5. In addition, dimension reduction algorithm is applied to the output of "pool6", 8196-D features are compressed to 400-D. In this paper, we simply use principal component analysis algorithm (PCA).

In the second stage, the few-shot learning model plays a critical role to identify image's clothing style. Our five-part model mainly consists of a controller, read heads, write heads, a content-based memory and a classifier. The controller in our experiments are Long Short-Term Memories (LSTMs). It receives some concatenated input (x_t, y_{t-1}), y_{t-1} is the class label for image feature x_{t-1}. The content-based memory is for restoring knowledge with two operations: reading and writing. For an input x_t, the controller learns a key, k_t, which is then either stored in a row of memory matrix M_t, or used to read information from M_t. When to read the encoded information in memory, we obtain the read weight vector w_t^r using the cosine measure according to a softmax. The cosine distance is calculated between the query key and each individual row in memory, i.e., $M_t(i)$:

$$K(k_t, M_t(i)) = \frac{k_t \cdot M_t(i)}{\|k_t\| \|M_t(i)\|}$$

$$w_r^t(i) \leftarrow \frac{exp(K(k_t, M_t(i)))}{\sum_j exp(K(k_t, M_t(j)))}$$

The information we read from memory r_t is then retrieved using w_t^r:

$$r_t \leftarrow \sum_i w_t^r(i) M_t(i)$$

Then r_t is concatenated with the LSTMs controller hidden state h_t. (r_t, h_t) will be the input of final classifier. For more details, we recommend [8].

The most important improvements for the few-shot learning model we have made are the new training and test strategies. We use $C + N$ classes samples every episode in training and testing. When training the model we choose C random clothing styles with s images in every class and N non-same-style classes with s images, $N \leq s$. We set $C = 1$, $s = 10$ in this paper. More concretely, to obtain training set, we choose s images in one ground truth group as class 0 samples. For the non-same-style samples (class 1), we first pick an image from class 0 randomly, then take it as the query image. We retrieve its nearest neighbors pictures from retrieval set, and s images in the retrieval result but not in the ground truth will be chosen as class 1 samples. In test phase, for a random clothing style, we choose top s images most similar to the seed image and bind label "0", and another s images whose cosine distances are more than ϵ_h as non-same-style class images, as indicated in Fig. 4. The number of images in range $[0, \epsilon_l]$ should be larger than s. The few-shot learning model works as a rapidly learned binary classifier.

2.2   Object-Aware Clothes Retrieval Framework

We adopt a object-aware clothes retrieval framework which is akin to the one in [11]. It includes two modules: object detection and feature extraction.

Object detection module is an essential part of the framework. The same as [11], the object model is based on AlexNet [14] with typical Faster R-CNN [15] framework. All the images before loaded into a feature extractor are cropped by the object detection boxes.

The Multi-task Siamese Network (MSN) is based on Siamese Network [16], and include three loss functions: two softmax loss and a contrastive loss. Two CNN branches share weights and also based on VGG-CNN-S [12]. The original softmax loss in [11] is defined on "sub-categories", e.g. plaid shirt,hoodie. Sub-category attribute features will be learned by this definition, but it will also narrow the gap among different clothing styles from the same sub-category. Experimental results show this adjustment is beneficial for the SSCR task. The contrastive loss is defined as [11].

For comparison, we use VGG-CNN-S [12] or AlexNet [14] as base model in this paper. More powerful network structure or more accurate detector, e.g. VGG16 [17], ResNet [18], FPN [19], Deformable Faster R-CNN [20], may continue improve our performance. It will be the future work.

3   Experiments

3.1   Dataset

In this paper we use a subset of the dataset from Alibaba Large-scale Image Search Challenge 2015 (ALISC2015). All images in ALISC2015 are divided into 10 categorise. In this paper, we use three of them, i.e., coat, skirt, pants. The subset is composed of two parts: retrieval set (1433007 images) and validation set (649 query images and their ground truth images). Its test set is not released, follow [21], we divide the validation set into val1 and val2 two parts. Images in val2 are composed of one-third (218/649) of all validation set which are used as test set. Data used to train object detector are provided by [11].

3.2   Implementation Details

Few-shot learning model. Our few-shot learning model uses one-hot vectors to represent class label, i.e., [1, 0] and [0, 1]. We define [0, 1] as non-same-style images. We train the model with val1 and test it on val2, In every episode, we

Fig. 6. Retrieval results and the benefit with more training data. The pictures in leftmost column are query images, others are the answers.

randomly choose one class clothing style as class 0. And we assign the first two images to class 0. Before training the few-shot binary classifier, we first pre-train the few-shot learning model in accordance with the instructions in [8] with data val1, and training occurs for 2 million episodes. $5 \times 10 \times batchsize$ images are used in every episode The final model was trained 100 000 episodes after that using training strategy in Sect. 2.1. During the training process, the parameters are shown as follow: learning rate (1e−4), batchsize (16), memory slots (128), memory size (40), LSTM hidden units (200), weight decay (0.99), number of reads from memory (4). **MSN.** We set initial learning rate as 1e−4, and adopt a lower one according to the performance on val2.

3.3   Results

Same-style products mining. We evaluate our same-style products mining result on val2. Same-style products mining task should focuses on the precision of mining result. We use N false samples precision (NFSP) to denote the precision of same-style image after N non-same-style images have been presented before test. Note that when N non-same-style images have been fed to model, the number of occurrences of samples from class 0 is $2 + n_r$, n_r is a random integer number within $[0, 8]$. In theory, given a larger n, we tend to obtain a larger n_r. Thus, the model will grasp more same-style and non-same-style characteristics when n is larger.

We test our performance on val2, results are shown in Table 1. The pipeline exhibits high classification accuracy on the second presentation of a sample from non-same-style clothes within an episode (81.97%), which manifests the powerful capability to extract features for a given clothing style. The precision reaches up 93.48% after the tenth. We also present some mining results in Fig. 5. The variation among a group of images illustrates that our proposed same-style products mining pipeline can learn the essential characteristics in one clothing style. It can weaken the effects of context, posture, light and colour.

Table 1. Same-style products mining results on val2. NFSP (N false samples precision) denotes the precision of same-style image after N false same-style images have been presented before test.

N	1	5	10
NFSP	81.97%	86.10%	93.48%

Same-style clothes retrieval. Table 2 shows the results on three methods, "MSN*" stands for the method according to [11], "Ours" referes to the approach we proposed in this paper, "Ours+" means our approach trained with additional 145 groups images (1/3 of the original data). All methods are tested on the val2 set. Comparing with the top two rows in Table 2, it can be see that softmax losses with defined on same clothing styles played a significant role, result are promoted 2.73% in MAP@20. MAP@20 is calculated according to ALISC2015 official evaluation metrics. To explore role of the new sample, we contrast the two results with and without our mined data. It has be promoted to 38.49% with extra 2.01% gain since our mined data were used.

To intuitively represent the benefit of more training data, we show some retrieval results in Fig. 6. The first column images are query seeds, right four columns are retrieval results with our retrieval framework, pictures with "Ours+" ticks are the new ones appear in "Ours+" approach results. Those pictures are taken under different scenarios (indoor or outdoor) and clothes exhibit variations. The result shows that our method has the ability of retrieval cross-scenario. We achieve a satisfied performance even those photographs are in multiscale (third row), taken from different angles (first row) or in different positions (second and second row). Figure 6 also demonstrates that more data lead to better expression ability.

Table 2. Result on the ALISC-clothes dataset. "SC" or "SCS" refers to softmax losses defined on sub-categories or same clothing styles, "SSPM" means same-style products mining.

Methods	Softmax loss	SSPM	MAP@20
MSN* [11]	SC	w/o	33.96%
Ours	SCS	w/o	36.48%
Ours+	SCS	w	38.49%

4   Conclusions

This work proposes a novel same-style products mining pipeline. It contains two stages: weak mining and denoising. We adopt a few-shot learning model in the second stage. It rapidly learns same-style clothing representation in a few-shot. The new image groups excavated by our method can achieve 93.48% precision in val2. Our work alleviate the problem of lacking of training samples. With our proposed same-style clothes retrieval framework, we achieve 4.53% improvement.

Acknowledgments. This work was supported by National Natural Science Foundation of China (61332016 and 61472422).

References

1. Liang, X., Lin, L., Yang, W., Luo, P.: Clothes co-parsing via joint image segmentation and labeling with application to clothing retrieval. IEEE Trans. Multimedia **18**(6), 1 (2016)
2. Liu, S., Song, Z., Wang, M., Xu, C., Lu, H., Yan, S.: Street-to-shop: cross-scenario clothing retrieval via parts alignment and auxiliary set. In: IEEE Conference on Computer Vision and Pattern Recognition, pp. 3330–3337 (2012)
3. Veit, A., Kovacs, B., Bell, S., Mcauley, J., Bala, K., Belongie, S.: Learning visual clothing style with heterogeneous dyadic co-occurrences. In: IEEE International Conference on Computer Vision, pp. 4642–4650 (2015)
4. Luo, P., Wang, X., Tang, X.: Pedestrian parsing via deep decompositional network. In: IEEE International Conference on Computer Vision, pp. 2648–2655 (2013)
5. Yamaguchi, K., Kiapour, M.H., Berg, T.L.: Paper doll parsing: retrieving similar styles to parse clothing items. In: IEEE International Conference on Computer Vision, pp. 3519–3526 (2014)
6. Kiapour, M.H., Han, X., Lazebnik, S., Berg, A.C., Berg, T.L.: Where to buy it: matching street clothing photos in online shops. In: IEEE International Conference on Computer Vision, pp. 3343–3351 (2015)
7. Kaiser, L., Nachum, O., Roy, A., Bengio, S.: Learning to remember rare events. arXiv preprint arXiv:1703.03129 (2017)
8. Santoro, A., Bartunov, S., Botvinick, M., Wierstra, D., Lillicrap, T.: One-shot learning with memory-augmented neural networks. arXiv preprint arXiv:1605.06065 (2016)
9. Vinyals, O., Blundell, C., Lillicrap, T., Wierstra, D., et al.: Matching networks for one shot learning. In: Advances in Neural Information Processing Systems, pp. 3630–3638 (2016)
10. Ravi, S., Larochelle, H.: Optimization as a model for few-shot learning. In: International Conference on Learning Representations, vol. 1, p. 6 (2017)
11. Fang, Z., Liu, J., Wang, Y., Li, Y., Hang, S., Tang, J., Lu, H.: Object-aware deep network for commodity image retrieval. In: Proceedings of the 2016 ACM on International Conference on Multimedia Retrieval, pp. 405–408. ACM (2016)
12. Chatfield, K., Simonyan, K., Vedaldi, A., Zisserman, A.: Return of the devil in the details: delving deep into convolutional nets. arXiv preprint arXiv:1405.3531 (2014)

13. Deng, J., Dong, W., Socher, R., Li, L.J., Li, K., Fei-Fei, L.: Imagenet: a large-scale hierarchical image database. In: IEEE Conference on Computer Vision and Pattern Recognition, CVPR 2009, pp. 248–255. IEEE (2009)

14. Krizhevsky, A., Sutskever, I., Hinton, G.E.: Imagenet classification with deep convolutional neural networks. In: Advances in Neural Information Processing Systems, pp. 1097–1105 (2012)

15. Ren, S., He, K., Girshick, R., Sun, J.: Faster R-CNN: towards real-time object detection with region proposal networks. In: Advances in Neural Information Processing Systems, pp. 91–99 (2015)

16. Chopra, S., Hadsell, R., LeCun, Y.: Learning a similarity metric discriminatively, with application to face verification. In: IEEE Computer Society Conference on Computer Vision and Pattern Recognition, CVPR 2005, pp. 539–546 (2005)

17. Simonyan, K., Zisserman, A.: Very deep convolutional networks for large-scale image recognition. arXiv preprint arXiv:1409.1556 (2014)

18. He, K., Zhang, X., Ren, S., Sun, J.: Deep residual learning for image recognition. In: Proceedings of the IEEE Conference on Computer Vision and Pattern Recognition, pp. 770–778 (2016)

19. Lin, T.Y., Dollár, P., Girshick, R., He, K., Hariharan, B., Belongie, S.: Feature pyramid networks for object detection. arXiv preprint arXiv:1612.03144 (2016)

20. Dai, J., Qi, H., Xiong, Y., Li, Y., Zhang, G., Hu, H., Wei, Y.: Deformable convolutional networks. arXiv preprint arXiv:1703.06211 (2017)

21. Wang, X., Sun, Z., Zhang, W., Zhou, Y., Jiang, Y.G.: Matching user photos to online products with robust deep features. In: ACM on International Conference on Multimedia Retrieval, pp. 7–14 (2016)

Scattering Wavelet Based Deep Network for Image Classification

Wenyou Huang[1,2]($\boxtimes$), Xiaoyi Zou[2], and Rui Qiao[2]

[1] China Nuclear Power Technology Research Institute, Shenzhen, Guangdong, China
huangwenyou@cgnpc.com.cn
[2] School of Electronic and Information Engineering,
South China University of Technology, Guangzhou, Guangdong, China
zouxy09@foxmail.com, eeruiq@mail.scut.edu.cn

Abstract. Scattering representation which is invariant to translation, rotation, scale and linear transformation of image, has good power to describe signal classes with a deformable structure. However, natural images contain general object classes with far more complex sources of variability, including occlusions, clutter or complex changes of shape and/or texture. The variability of physical transformations such as translation or rotation is universal and does not need to be learnt, but for complex data, learning becomes important in order to address more complex sources of variability. This paper proposes a novel framework by combining scattering transform and deep learning architecture to address the limitations of ScatNet. Wavelet scattering networks may provide the first two layers of general deep architectures to avoid the learning of large number of low-level filters for deep network. The proposed method is proved experimentally efficient.

Keywords: Scatering transform · Deep learning
Wavelet scatering network

1 Introduction

Image classification is a very challenging task, many hand-crafted low-level features are proposed to counter this problem, and have achieved excellent results for some specific data and tasks. Such as, Haar-like [1], LBP [2], HOG [3] and SIFT [4] etc. However, designing outstanding features for new conditions manually usually needs knowledge from new domain and cannot be simply adapted to new conditions because of the lack of adaptability [18–20].

In recent years, deep learning is gaining more and more attention due to its excellent ability for extracting the abstract features to represent data. A large number of deep learning based methods have achieved great success in various fields [5,17]. The common deep learning frameworks learn a series of filters mapping the raw pixels of data to the output directly. As we all know, the dimensionality of image is always huge. Because of the 'curse of dimensionality' [6], more hidden layers or hidden units are needed to learn the complex filters.

© Springer Nature Singapore Pte Ltd. 2018
B. Huet et al. (Eds.): ICIMCS 2017, CCIS 819, pp. 459–469, 2018.
https://doi.org/10.1007/978-981-10-8530-7_45

In addition, with the size of the image becoming larger, more training data are needed to prevent overfitting, e.g., in [7], Le et al. The model they proposed takes three days for training on a cluster with 1,000 machines by using parallelism technique on a dataset which has 10 million samples. They speculate that it is the lack of high-level features that lead to such a long training time. And in [8], a big neural network, is trained on two GTX 580 3GB GPUs with 1.2 million training images for six days. However, these resources are not available for general users, which make the large scale deep learning algorithms nontrivial. Besides, learning a network which is useful for accurate classification depends on expertise of parameter tuning and some ad hoc tricks.

For the traditional deep convolution networks, their excellent results are usually based on experience, but wavelet scattering networks (ScatNet) [9,10] is an exception, which has clear mathematical derivation. The convolutional filters in ScatNet are prefixed, hence no learning process is needed at all. It is unexpected that for the ScatNet which has a similar multistage architecture of deep convolution networks, has outstanding performance in several challenging vision tasks [9,10] than deep convolution networks or DNNs.

However, such a prefixed architecture does not generalize so well to natural images which contain general object classes with far more complex sources of variability, including occlusions, clutter or complex changes of shape and/or texture. The variability of physical transformations such as translation or rotation is universal and does not need to be learnt, but for complex data, learning becomes important in order to address more complex sources of variability.

In this study, we present a novel framework by combining scattering transform and deep learning architecture to address the limitations of ScatNet. On one hand, wavelet scattering networks may provide the first two layers of general deep architectures to avoid the learning of large number of low-level filters for deep network. The invariance and stability properties of scattering operators have the capacity to eliminates translation or rotation variability of input and simplify the learning task of subsequent layers, since they map image patches into a regular manifold thanks to their Lipschitz continuity properties. On the other hand, construct a deep network above these scattering coefficients can learn unknown far more complex sources of variability which the scattering transform cannot describe.

2   Methodology Overview

2.1   Datasets

In order to demonstrate the effectiveness of the proposed approaches, our experiments are performed on standard MNIST digit dataset [12], MNIST variation dataset [13] and cifar-10 dataset [14].

2.2   Description of the Proposed Approach

This paper proposes a novel framework by combining scattering transform and deep learning architecture to address the limitations of ScatNet, whose filters are

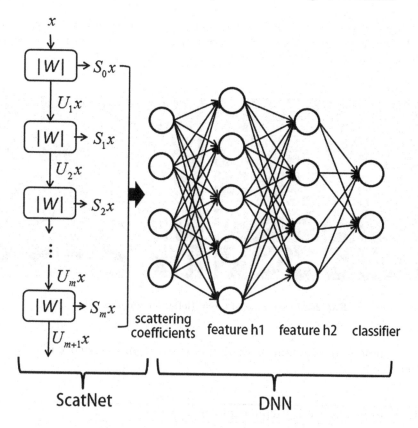

Fig. 1. Scattering transform based deep learning

prefixed and does not generalize so well to natural images which contain general object classes with far more complex sources of variability that the scattering transform cannot describe. The framework is shown in Fig. 1. Firstly, an image x is feed into a Scatnet and outputs multiple layers of scattering invariant coefficients. A locally translation invariant scattering representation is obtained by concatenating the scattering coefficients as a vector, orderly

$$Sx = \{S_m x\}_{0 \leq m \leq M}. \tag{1}$$

Secondly, this scattering representation is used as the input of deep network, and the successive layers are trained by unsupervised and supervised manner. This framework can be extended to other deep learning architectures because of the excellent generality of scattering representation.

We use Morlet wavelet to form the filter bank. The Morlet wavelet Ψ is shown in Eq. 2:

$$\Psi(u) = \alpha(e^{iu\xi} - \beta)e^{-|u|^2/(2\sigma^2)}, \tag{2}$$

The Morlet wavelet with $\sigma = 0.85$ and $\xi = 3\pi/4$ is shown in Fig. 2, used in all classification experiments in this paper. Besides, the low-pass filter is defined by $\varphi(u) = (1/(2\pi\sigma^2))e^{-|u|^2/(2\sigma^2)}$.

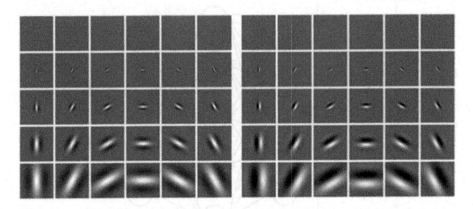

Fig. 2. Morlet wavelets, real (left), imaginary (right)

The procedure to obtain scattering representation of image x is showen in Algorithm 1.

Algorithm 1. Scattering representation of image x

Input: image x
1: Initialize: $U_0x = x, j_0 = 0$
2: **for** $\forall m < M$ **do**
3:     **for** $\forall p$ in $|p| = m$ **do**
4:         **for** $\forall j > j_{|p|}$ and $r \in G$ **do**
5:             $S_m[p + (j, r)]x = U_m[p]x * \varphi_J$
6:             $U_{m+1}[p + (j, r)]x = |U_m[p]x * \Psi_{\lambda_{m+1}}|$
7:         **end for**
8:     **end for**
9: **end for**
Output: $Sx = \{S_mx\}_{0 \leq m \leq M}$

Here m is the length of the iterative path p, that is, the number of layers of the network ($0 \leq m \leq M$), j is the scale parameter and J is the max scale selected by user, r is the rotation parameter, S_mx is the invariant scattering coefficient, $U_{m+1}x$ is the covariant wavelet modulus coefficient, $\Psi_\lambda(u) = 2^{2j}\Phi(2^j r^{-1}u)$ is the two-dimensional multi-resolution direction wavelet function, $\varphi_J(u) = 2^{-2J}\varphi(2^{-J}u)$.

Two typical types of deep learning models are trained above the scattering representation of image x. The discriminative model: Sparse Auto-encoders and the generative model: Deep Belief Nets. The training algorithm of SAE and DBN can be unified to a same framework namely layer-wise greedy learning algorithm which is showed in Algorithm 2.

Algorithm 2. Layer-wise greedy learning algorithm

Input: training set $\{x_{scat}^{(i)}y^{(i)}\}, x_{scat}^{(i)} = Sx^{(i)}$
  1: Initialize: Initialize the model parameter θ randomly
  2: Step 1: Use $x_{scat}^{(i)}$ as the input of first layer, train the parameters θ in unsupervised learning manner
  3: Step 2: Fix the parameters of pre-layers, use the output of pre-layers to feed the current layer and train the parameters of current layer
  4: Step 3: Repeat step 1 and step 2 until the desired number of layers are obtained
  5: Step 4: Stack all pre-trained layers, and add a classification layer on the top of them. Then fine-tune all parameters of entire network in supervised manner
Output: the optimal model parameter θ

---

3   Experimental Results and Discussion

3.1   Experiments for WST Based SDAE

We experiment with different setting of scattering wavelet and different architectures to evaluate the recognition performance on testing dataset. Especially, for all experiments, we adopt two-hidden layer sparse autoencoders, and empirically fix parameter $\lambda = 0.2$ and $\beta = 1.0$. The probability p used in Dropout is set to 0.2. Classification is based on 10 classes softmax classifier. In the training process, the training set is divided into a series of mini-batches which has 100 samples, and for all training stages, the value of training epoch is the same. The framework is entirely implemented on a PC with 128GB RAW and Intel Xeon E5-2640 2.0 GHz CPU in Matlab.

Evaluations on Different Setting of WST. In the experiments, we train sparse autoencoders with varying settings of wavelet scattering transform for MNIST-rot dataset. We test three parameters for wavelet scattering transform, include max scale J, max order M and number of orientation L. We adopt two-hidden layer sparse autoencoders and its number of hidden units is fixed to 500×500 during these experiments. And the results are shown in Tables 1, 2, and 3. The best accuracy is in bold.

As showed in Table 1, we fix $L = 8$, $M = 2$, and test four settings for J. We can observe that when J increases, there is a slight fluctuation in recognition accuracy, and reduced number of scattering wavelet coefficients resulted in reduced training time.

Table 1. Performance under different J

(L = 8, M = 2)	J = 3	J = 4	J = 5	J = 6
Accuracy	**95.18%**	94.49%	94.60%	94.90%
#coefficients	3472	1668	1223	1009
Training time/min	183.97	102.17	95.26	80.26

Table 2. Performance under different M

(J = 3, L = 4)	M = 0	M = 1	M = 2	M = 3
Accuracy	34.17%	94.15%	**95.20%**	94.80%
#coefficients	16	208	976	2000
Training time/min	25.23	54.73	71.90	132.89

As showed in Table 2, we fix $L = 4$, $J = 3$, and test four settings for M. We can observe that when $M = 0$, only low-pass filter and subsample are applied to raw images, which lead to the much loss of high frequency information. In this case, the discrimination between images becomes weak which makes accuracy lower. The energy of images will concentrate on lower levels, so $M = 1$ can bring good accuracy, and $M = 2$ will be better because it can bring more discrimination thanks to the second order information. However, the third-order parameter only contains insignificant energy and the impact of classification accuracy is trifling, but will bring a sharp increase in the computational costs. Besides, with the increase of M, the training time will increase because of the increase of scattering wavelet coefficients.

Table 3. Performance under different L

(J = 3, M = 1)	L = 2	L = 4	L = 6	L = 8	L = 10
Accuracy	90.14%	94.15%	**94.61%**	94.60%	94.56%
#coefficients	112	208	304	400	496
Training time/min	47.20	54.73	57.14	49.92	65.87

As showed in Table 3, we fix $J = 3$, $M = 1$, and test five settings for L. Overall, we can obtain more directions of image information when wavelet filter types increase with L increases. It means that, scattering descriptors can distinguish more types of image edge, which will usually improve the classification performance. However, it may have some difference between different properties of specific dataset for different classification tasks, as showed in Table 3 from $L = 6$ to $L = 10$. Besides, when L increases, the training time will increase because of the increase of scattering wavelet coefficients. We get less training time in $L = 8$, this may be associated with the scheduling of CPU.

Evaluations on Different Setting of SDAE. In these experiments, we train different settings of sparse autoencoders while fix $J = 3$, $M = 2$, and $L = 8$. We test different architectures (the number of hidden units in each hidden layer is different) and parameters, and choose different training epochs. We train a multi- classification linear Support Vector Machine directly on the coefficients of scattering wavelet as the baseline for experiments. The optimal hyper-parameters in linear SVM is obtained by cross verification. The results are shown in Table 4. The best accuracy is marked in bold.

Table 4. Performance of SDAE in six dataset

Dataset	Accuracy	Accuracy	Accuracy	Accuracy
(Learning rate, sparsity) (Architectures, epochs)	(1, 0.05) (500 × 500, 200)	(1, 0.05) (1000 × 1000, 500)	(0.2, 0.2) (1000 × 1000, 1000)	Linear SVM
mnist	99.33%	99.29%	**99.49%**	99.43%
mnist-rot	92.46%	92.85%	**95.29%**	91.84%
mnist-bg-rand	88.21%	88.21%	**88.36%**	83.21%
mnist-bg-img	82.86%	82.88%	**84.69%**	81.78%
mnist-bg-img-rot	49.38%	50.16%	**57.28%**	48.33%
cifar-10	65.21%	65.80%	**71.96%**	65.59%

As showed in Table 4, the best accuracy is obtained when the network architecture is 1000×1000, epochs is 1000 and the values of sparsity parameter and learning rate are both 0.2. The proposed model obtains average 4% promotion in six datasets when compare to linear SVM. We can conclude that constructing a deep network above these scattering coefficients will improve the accuracy in some extent. However, as shown in Table 4, the performance of all the methods is all very well and the gap is very small. This is because the amount of samples in the MNIST dataset is more, so the difference between performance is not so statistically meaningful.

3.2   Experiments for WST Based DBN

We experiment with different setting of scattering wavelet and different architectures of DBN to evaluate the recognition performance on testing dataset. Especially, for all experiment, we adopt DBN with two RBMs, and use cross entropy as our object function. Because the scattering descriptor is real-values, the GBRB [11] is adopted as the bottom layer of DBN, and the top one use BBRBM [15]. In the experiment, we initialize w_{ij} randomly between $\pm 1/(D+F)$. Both bias b_i and a_i are initialized to 0. The variance σ_i is initialized to 1. We add momentum to the gradient update terms to speed the convergence rate and set it to 0.9. Learning rate is fixed to 0.1. Besides, the learning rate of GBRBM is set to a more small value 0.003 due to its unstable properties. In the training process, the training set is divided into a series of mini-batches which has 100 samples, and for all training stages, the value of training epoch is the same. The framework is entirely implemented on a PC with 128GB RAW and Intel Xeon E5-2640 2.0 GHz CPU in Matlab.

Evaluations on Different Setting of WST. In the experiments, we train DBN with varying settings of wavelet scattering transform for MNIST-rot dataset. We adopt two-layer DBN and its number of hidden units is fixed to 200×200 and fix epochs to 500 during these experiments. And the results are shown in Tables 5, 6, and 7. The best accuracy is in bold.

Table 5. Performance under different J

$(L = 8, M = 2)$	$J = 3$	$J = 4$	$J = 5$	$J = 6$
Accuracy	91.34%	91.07%	92.03%	**92.15%**
#coefficients	3472	1668	1223	1009
Training time/min	48.20	30.38	27.84	22.84

As showed in Table 5, we fix $L = 8$, $M = 2$, and test four settings for J. Consistent with the previously described, when J increases, there is a trifling fluctuation in recognition accuracy, and the training time decreases.

Table 6. Performance under different M

$(J = 3, L = 4)$	$M = 0$	$M = 1$	$M = 2$	$M = 3$
Accuracy	70.66%	93.54%	**93.58%**	91.72%
#coefficients	16	208	976	2000
Training time/min	65.59	70.53	69.20	76.83

As showed in Table 6, we fix $L = 8$, $J = 4$, and test four settings for M. When $M = 0$, we can only obtain a very low accuracy because of the much loss of high frequency information. The energy of images will concentrate on lower levels, so $M = 1$ and $M = 2$ can bring good accuracy, and $M = 2$ will be better because it can bring more discrimination thanks to the second order information. However, the higher level will contain much less energy, so it is useless to increase the order to higher. This can be shown for $M = 3$. Besides, when M increases, the training time will increase because of the increase of scattering wavelet coefficients.

Table 7. Performance under different L

$(J = 3, M = 1)$	$L = 2$	$L = 4$	$L = 6$	$L = 8$	$L = 10$
Accuracy	89.86%	93.54%	**93.71%**	93.56%	93.23%
#coefficients	112	208	304	400	496
Training time/min	101.32	105.93	108.14	121.58	123.33

As showed in Table 7, we fix $J = 3$, $M = 1$, and test five settings for L. Overall, we can obtain more directions of image information when wavelet filter types increase with L increases. It means that, scattering descriptors can distinguish more types of image edge, which will usually improve the classification performance. Besides, when L increases, the training time will increase because of the increase of scattering wavelet coefficients.

Evaluations on Different Setting of DBN. In these experiments, we train different settings of DBN while fix $J = 3$, $M = 2$, and $L = 8$. We test different architectures (the number of hidden units in each hidden layer is different) and different training epochs. We train a multi-classification linear Support Vector Machine directly on the coefficients of scattering wavelet as the baseline for experiments. The optimal hyper-parameters in linear SVM is obtained by cross verification. The results are shown in Table 8. The best accuracy is marked in bold. Linear SVM is better in dataset MNIST and MNIST-bg-img. However, DBN is better in the other four datasets.

Table 8. Performance of DBN in six dataset

Dataset	Accuracy	Accuracy	Accuracy	Accuracy
(Architectures, epochs)	$(500 \times 500, 500)$	$(100 \times 100, 1000)$	$(1000 \times 1000, 200)$	Linear SVM
mnist	99.03%	98.94%	99.07%	**99.43%**
mnist-rot	91.64%	91.64%	**91.96%**	91.84%
mnist-bg-rand	85.63%	84.14%	**87.85%**	83.21%
mnist-bg-img	79.57%	78.94%	78.61%	**81.78%**
mnist-bg-img-rot	**51.20%**	48.56%	48.95%	48.33%
cifar-10	65.60%	**66.09%**	62.79%	65.59%

3.3 The Comparison Between Proposed Models and Others

We also compare to other methods. The result is shown in Table 9. Some results are directly from [16].

The comparisons with support vector machine and other different deep learning methods are shown in Table 9. The results of our approach reported in Table 9 are picked up from the best accuracy in Tables 4 and 8 when using WST. For easy comparison, the table directly takes the performance reported in [16] for a Support Vector Machine with RBF kernels (SVMrbf), two DBN which have 1 and 3 hidden layers, named DBN1 and DBN3 respectively, a 3 hidden layer stacking autoencoders (SAE-3) and stacking denoising autoencoders (SDAE-3). PCANet-2 is from [16]. The proposed method achieved excellent recognition accuracy even without a hyper-parameter search procedure using validation set. Furthermore, the proposed model is flexibility for choosing the dimension of input for deep networks, and it can achieve excellent performance with much lower computational costs. It is worth to know that the proposed model have obtained the best performance on the MNIST-rot dataset.

Table 9. Performance between different models

Model	MNIST	rot	bg-rand	bg-img	bg-img-rot
SVM(rbf)	98.60%	88.89%	85.42%	77.39%	44.82%
DBN-1	98.79%	85.31%	90.20%	83.85%	47.79%
SAE-3	98.60%	89.70%	88.72%	77.00%	48.07%
DBN-3	98.76%	89.70%	93.27%	83.69%	52.61%
SDAE-3(v)	98.72%	90.47%	89.70%	83.32%	56.24%
ssPGRM	-	-	88.02%	79.68%	40.81%
RBM	-	-	82.57%	76.29%	36.06%
PCANet-2	**99.34%**	92.63%	**93.81%**	**89.05%**	**64.52%**
DCT+SDAE	98.39%	83.27%	88.54%	75.64%	41.56%
DCT+DBN	98.43%	86.53%	89.02%	76.67%	45.07%
Scat+SDAE	99.33%	**95.29%**	88.36%	84.69%	57.28%
Scat+DBN	99.07%	91.96%	87.85%	79.57%	51.20%

4 Conclusion

A novel framework by combining scattering transform and deep learning architecture to address the limitations of ScatNet is proposed in this study. On one hand, wavelet scattering networks may provide the first two layers of general deep architectures to avoid the learning of large number of low-level filters for deep network. The invariance and stability properties of scattering operators have the capacity to eliminate translation or rotation variability of input and simplify the learning task of subsequent layers, since they map image patches into a regular manifold thanks to the Lipschitz continuity properties. On the other hand, constructing a deep network above these scattering coefficients can learn unknown far more complex sources of variability which the scattering transform cannot describe.

Acknowledgments. This work is supported by the Science and Technology Planning Project of Guangdong Province of China (No. 2014B010111003, 2014B010111006, 2016B010108008), Guangzhou Key Lab of Body Data Science under Grant 201605030011 and National Natural Science Founding of China under Grant 61401163.

References

1. Viola, P., Jones, M.J.: Robust real-time face detection. Int. J. Comput. Vis. **57**, 137–154 (2004)
2. Ojala, T., Pietikainen, M., Maenpaa, T.: Multiresolution gray-scale and rotation invariant texture classification with local binary patterns. IEEE Trans. Pattern Anal. Mach. Intell. **24**, 971–987 (2002)

3. Dalal, N., Triggs, B.: Histograms of oriented gradients for human detection. In: IEEE Computer Society Conference on Computer Vision and Pattern Recognition (CVPR), pp. 886–893 (2005)
4. Lowe, D.G.: Object recognition from local scale-invariant features. In: The Proceedings of the Seventh IEEE International Conference on Computer Vision, pp. 1150–1157 (1999)
5. Bengio, Y., Courville, A., Vincent, P.: Representation learning: a review and new perspectives. IEEE Trans. Softw. Eng. **35**, 1798–1828 (2014)
6. Bellman, R.: Dynamic programming and lagrange multipliers. In: Proceedings of the National Academy of Sciences of the United States of America, vol. 42, p. 767 (1956)
7. Le, Q.V.: Building high-level features using large scale unsupervised learning. In: IEEE International Conference on Acoustics, Speech and Signal Processing (ICASSP), pp. 8595–8598 (2013)
8. Krizhevsky, A., Sutskever, I., Hinton, G.E.: Imagenet classification with deep convolutional neural networks. In: Advances in Neural Information Processing Systems, pp. 1097–1105 (2013)
9. Bruna, J., Mallat, S.: Invariant scattering convolution networks. IEEE Trans. Pattern Anal. Mach. Intell. **35**, 1872–1886 (2013)
10. Sifre, L., Mallat, S.: Rotation, scaling and deformation invariant scattering for texture discrimination. In: IEEE Conference on Computer Vision and Pattern Recognition (CVPR), pp. 1233–1240 (2013)
11. Hinton, G.E., Salakhutdinov, R.R.: Reducing the dimensionality of data with neural networks. Science **313**, 504–507 (2006)
12. LeCun, Y.: http://yann.lecun.com/exdb/mnist/
13. Larochelle, H., Erhan, D., Courville, A., Bergstra, J., Bengio, Y.: An empirical evaluation of deep architectures on problems with many factors of variation. In: Proceedings of the 24th International Conference on Machine Learning, pp. 473–480 (2007)
14. Krizhevsky, A., Hinton, G.: Learning multiple layers of features from tiny images. Computer Science Department, University of Toronto. Technical report 1, 7 (2009)
15. Fischer, A., Igel, C.: An Introduction to restricted Boltzmann machines. In: Alvarez, L., Mejail, M., Gomez, L., Jacobo, J. (eds.) CIARP 2012. LNCS, vol. 7441, pp. 14–36. Springer, Heidelberg (2012). https://doi.org/10.1007/978-3-642-33275-3_2
16. Vincent, P., Larochelle, H., Lajoie, I., Bengio, Y., Manzagol, P.A.: Stacked denoising autoencoders: learning useful representations in a deep network with a local denoising criterion. J. Mach. Learn. Res. **11**, 3371–3408 (2010)
17. Zabalza, J., Ren, J., Zheng, J., et al.: Novel segmented stacked autoencoder for effective dimensionality reduction and feature extraction in hyperspectral imaging. Neuro Comput. **185**, 1–10 (2016)
18. Hong, R., Zhang, L., Zhang, C., et al.: Flickr circles: aesthetic tendency discovery by multi-view regularized topic modeling. IEEE Trans. Multimed. **18**, 1555–1567 (2016)
19. Hong, R., Hu, Z., Wang, R., et al.: Multi-view object retrieval via multi-scale topic models. IEEE Trans. Image Process. **25**, 5814–5827 (2016)
20. Hong, R., Yang, Y., Wang, M., et al.: Learning visual semantic relationships for efficient visual retrieval. IEEE Trans. Big Data. **1**, 152–161 (2017)

Scene Text Detection with Cascaded Filtering and Grouping Modules

Lifei Zhang and Xinguang Xiang[✉]

Nanjing University of Science and Technology, Nanjing, China
lfzhang_1030@163.com, xgxiang@njust.edu.cn

Abstract. In this paper, we present a new scene text detection approach with cascaded filtering and grouping modules. Firstly, a coarse-to-fine distance based pair validation scheme is proposed to determine the pairwise relations of character candidates after the extraction and filtering of Extremal Regions. Secondly, an additional module is added to detect text lines with single character or two characters behind the text lines' grouping module. Thirdly, a text-line-level classifier based on the similarity of characters is designed to exclude non-text objects. Experimental results on ICDAR 2011 and ICDAR 2013 robust reading competition datasets demonstrate that our method yields state-of-the-art performance both in recall and precision.

Keywords: Scene text detection · Single or two characters detection
Text line analysis

1 Introduction

Scene text detection plays an important role in many camera-based applications, such as content-based image and video retrieval [1–4], multilingual translation from pictures and OCR in the Wild [5], and automatic driving with traffic markers [6]. It has attracted increasing attention from the computer vision community in recent years, but still remains an open problem due to the wide variety of text appearance and uncontrolled environment [7].

Most of the existing approaches to scene text detection can be roughly classified into three categories: region-based, connected component (CC)-based and hybrid. Region-based approaches [8,9] compute global features from sliding windows on all locations in multiple scales and estimate the likelihood of text with classifiers. These methods are robust to distortions and unconnected characters detection and can achieve high recall rates. The main drawback is the heavy computational cost. The CC-based methods [10–12] first extract character candidates as CCs at pixel-level, then group them into text regions if they have similar geometric and appearance properties, CCs analysis or text-line-level elimination may be added to filter out false positives. Stroke Width Transform (SWT) [10] and Maximally Stable Extremal Regions (MSERs) [13] are widely used to extract CCs, which are efficient and invariant to scale and rotation. The challenge is

© Springer Nature Singapore Pte Ltd. 2018
B. Huet et al. (Eds.): ICIMCS 2017, CCIS 819, pp. 470–478, 2018.
https://doi.org/10.1007/978-981-10-8530-7_46

many non-text candidates are generated. Many non-text components are quite similar to text ones when analysing individually. It is quite difficult to design a fast and also reliable CC analyzer to eliminate false positives without losing the text components. Hybrid approaches [14] combine both of the aforementioned kinds.

Our work is inspired by [12], which is a CC-based method. It uses two stage classifiers to filter the Extremal Regions (ERs) and applies the exhaustive search to group text lines. This method is efficient and robust to blur and low contrast. However, it suffers from the following problems. Firstly, two stage classifiers filter out some true characters, which then result in the missing or incorrect detection of words. Secondly, the grouping stage can only detect text lines longer than three character regions due to the low precision of the detection for character candidates. In reality, single character text lines and text lines with two characters may exist. Thirdly, some text-line outliers are also detected because they are difficult to be filtered out by the character level classifiers.

Our goal is to ease the limitations of these problems. We design a coarse-to-fine scheme to estimate if character candidates are valid pairs. Characters in a word share similar properties, such as spatial location, color, size and stroke width, etc. We enumerate all the character candidates pairs in a channel, the coarse step efficiently filters out invalid pairs with loose constraints. The fine step is based on the distance between them and their appearance similarity which mitigate the distance constraints when they share high appearance similarity. So we can detect text lines with missing characters. We add a single or two characters text lines detection module after character grouping stage. We use multi-channel information to increase the detection accuracy and add this module to the whole pipeline. We also design a new text-line-level classifier based on the similarity and statistical information of the character candidates in a text line to filter out non-text sequences.

The rest of the paper is structured as follows: the proposed method is described in Sect. 2. In Sect. 3, experiments and results are presented. The paper is concluded in Sect. 4.

2   Cascaded Filtering and Grouping Approach

Figure 1 shows the pipeline of our text detection approach. ER selection method in [12] is used to extract character candidates. We design pairwise rules to measure if two ER regions can be valid pair, and then adopt exhaustive search [15] to group text lines. A special module is added to detect text lines with only one character or two characters. We reject non-text sequences with characters' statistic information and their similarity.

ER Extraction. We adopt the ER selection method [12] to extract character candidates. Because it is fast with small computational cost and can detect more than 90% characters with multi-channel combination. What's more, ER features such as bounding box and convex hull ratio are gathered for later processing.

Fig. 1. The pipeline of our approach

We train the character level classifiers with positive character samples from ICDAR 2013 pixel level training dataset [16], negative samples from ICDAR 2013 training dataset and SVT dataset [17].

2.1 Text Line Grouping

We use the exhaustive search [15] to group character candidates into text lines. But different to [15], we use a coarse-to-fine and distance based method to determine the pairwise relations of ERs. We define that two ERs are adjacent when both are text components in the same text line and their interval distance is less than five of their minimum width. The distance contraint decreases the search space as well as connecting more nearby candidate characters in a text line, thus decreasing the influence of missing characters in between.

We get a bounding box of each ER. Given an ER i and denote its width, height, stroke width, as w_i, h_i and s_i respectively. R_i, G_i, B_i, a_i and b_i are the average channel color values of ER i. And the horizontal interval distance and vertical overlap are denoted as d_{ij} and v_{ij} (Fig. 2).

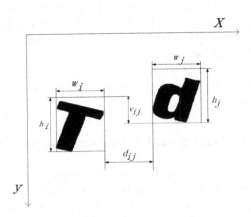

Fig. 2. Two ERs' properties

We use the following features to determine if two characters are adjacent, similar rules have been used in many previous works [11,18,19].

Normalized interval distance: $d_{ij}/min(w_i, w_j)$

Normalized vertical overlap : $v_{ij}/min(h_i, h_j)$

Height ratio: h_i/h_j

Stroke width ratio: s_i/s_j

RGB color difference and Lab color difference:

$abs(R_i - R_j) + abs(G_i - G_j) + abs(B_i - B_j)$

$abs(a_i - a_j) + abs(b_i - b_j)$

We add x-coordinate information to height ratio and stroke width ratio. It's common that the leading capital letter is bigger and taller than the following lower-case letter, and text lines' orientations are often from left to right, which means that if one character is bigger than another, and it lays left of another, they are more likely to be valid pair than bigger one lays right of another. We let 'i' be the left region, 'j' be the right region.

Because of the character filtering in the ER extraction stage, some real characters may be filtered out, the distance between two neighboring characters in a text line may be far. We design a coarse-to-fine and distance based method to determine if two character candidates can be valid pair. Our goal is to connect as much character candidates in a text line as possible and minimize the connection between character and background noise, the algorithm is as shown in the following:

Algorithm 1. Distance based pair validation

Require: a set of ER regions in one channel
Ensure: a set of valid pairs P
 1: filter out pairs when $d_{ij} > 5 \parallel d_{ij} > -0.4 \parallel v_{ij} < 0.5$
 2: use stricter rules on the feature set when $2 < d_{ij} < 5$
 3: use looser rules on the feature set when $-0.4 < d_{ij} < 2$
 4: add valid pairs to set P

In the coarse step, we filter out the impossible pairs according to the normalized distance and vertical overlap, the distance threshold is set intuitively, and the vertical overlap threshold is adapted from [18]. Other rules such as one character don't contain another character; two characters' left coordinate don't overlap [15] are also used. This stage can efficiently reduce the search space yet keep the high recall of pairs for later processing. When the distance is between 2 and 5, which means that two ERs are not so close, we use stricter rules on the feature set, that is their appearance should be more similar. If the distance is between -0.4 and 2, we use looser rules on the feature set. All the parameters are set based on experiments on the training database [16].

The following text line grouping method is based on [15]. First, selecting valid pairs with common regions into triplets, and then selecting triplets with distance and topological constraints into text lines. We detect text lines on multi-channels and multi-scales individually, and then we recover all the scales of text line boxes to the original size. If two text line boxes' overlapping area is over 50% for each text line box, then the union box of the two original boxes is generated. We add the union box into the final result instead of the two original boxes. In our experiment, we use the Y-Cb-Cr and the H(Hue)-S(saturation) color spaces as well as the grad channel and two Gaussian scale space pyramid of the Y channel.

2.2   Text Lines with Single Character or Two Characters Detection

One limitation of the exhaustive search is that only text lines longer than 3 regions [15] can be detected. In reality, text lines shorter than 3 regions are exist. In order to detect these regions, we add single character or two character detection module with high accuracy.

Firstly, we pick out valid pairs which are not included into triplets; we filter these pairs with harsh pair features and character features, and ensure they have no overlap with existing text lines. Rules based on character features require aspect ratio, area ratio and convex hull ratio of each region fall within a given interval obtained in a training stage, which means we should combine the character confidence in text lines with two characters detection stage. Secondly, we pick out character candidates which are not included into pairs; and ensure they have no overlap with existing text lines. We filter these character candidates with additional features like opposite pixel ratio, area ratio, position to enhance the accuracy of character detection.

We also combine multi-channel information into this module, which means a same region on the image should be detected in more than one channel. In our experiment, we keep a pair as valid text line when it appears in more than two channels; keep the single character as valid text line when it appears in more than four channels.

2.3   Non-text Filtering

Some text-like components, such as railings, bricks and some symbols have similar local structures with true text components, such as 'U' and 'l'. Thus they are difficult to be distinguished solely by character-level filtering. In text-line-level, it is very rare that one word contains many repeating characters. Based on these observations, we propose a text-line-level classifier using these properties to filter out non-text lines. Figure 3 shows some examples of non-text objects.

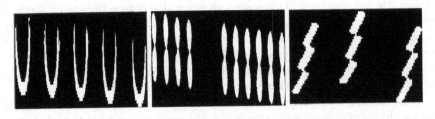

Fig. 3. Non-text objects examples

First, We make the ERs in a text line to be white and the background to be black to get the text line image. Then, We use template match to measure if an ER is similar to all the ERs in the text line image, every ER is measured. We store all the match count in a vector. We define the repeating ratio as Algorithm 2.

Algorithm 2. Get repeating ratio

Require: rectangle contains ER and the text line image.
Ensure: the text line's repeating ratio
 1: For each rectangle containing ER, do template match with the text line image
 2: Summarize the area count with match score > 0.8, store it in a vector
 3: Sort the vector in increasing order
 4: Get the median value $m(v)$ of the vector
 5: if $m(v) > \frac{1}{2}ERNum$, repeating ratio $R_r = 1$
 6: else repeating ratio $R_r = 0$

The meaning behind this is when half of the text line's ERs are repeated, the text line is repeated, $R_r = 1$. We filter out repeating text lines with high accuracy.

3   Experiments

We implemented the proposed method in C++ with OpenCV 3.0 and evaluated its performance on the ICDAR 2011 [20] and ICDAR 2013 [16] Robust Reading competition datasets. Both datasets have been widely used as the standard benchmarks for text detection in natural images, for fair comparison with previous works, we show our results on both datasets. The ICDAR 2011 dataset contains 229 training images and 255 testing ones, and the ICDAR 2013 dataset use the same training set as ICDAR 2011, but with less testing images. Both datasets are evaluated in word level, and the evaluation protocols are all based on [21], but with some small differences as shown on [16]. We show our text detection results on Tables 1 and 2. The method achieves state-of-the-art performance. The coarse-to-fine distance based pairwise rules which connect more character ERs with less background noise can improve the detection recall rate with high accuracy. Our single character or two characters detection module and non-text filtering module also contribute to the final performance. In order to validate the contribution of our modules, we conducted experiments on the ICDAR 2011 dataset without these two modules. The result is shown on Table 3.

Table 1. Text detection results on ICDAR2011 dataset

Method	Recall	Precision	F-measure
Proposed method	0.705	0.803	0.751
Koo et al. [11]	0.686	0.814	0.745
Yin et al. [22]	0.622	0.815	0.705
Neumann et al. [12]	0.647	0.731	0.687
Li et al. [23]	0.680	0.630	0.650

Table 2. Text detection results on ICDAR2013 dataset

Method	Recall	Precision	F-measure
Proposed method	0.72	0.80	0.76
Text spotter [16]	0.65	0.84	0.73
CASIA_NLPR [16]	0.68	0.79	0.73
I2R_NUS [16]	0.66	0.73	0.69

Table 3. Contributions of different modules

Method	Recall	Precision	F-measure
Without single or two	0.696	0.802	0.745
Without non-text filtering	0.705	0.798	0.749
With all modules	0.705	0.803	0.751

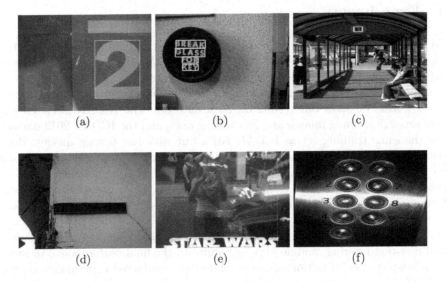

(a)   (b)   (c)

(d)   (e)   (f)

Fig. 4. Samples of positive and negative detection

Our method takes 1.5 s for a 640 ∗ 480 image in average for a standard PC with 2.8 GHz Intel processor. Because the running environments of other works' experiments are different, fair comparisons are hard to make. Figure 4 shows some detection results of our method.

Our method can detect text lines with one or two characters, but there are also some limitations. ER based method can't detect characters whose color is very similar to the background. The character level classifiers filter out multi-character regions due to the lack of training samples. When the text lines' beginning or ending character regions are filtered out, it causes the failure of text detection based on the evaluation scheme [21]. One character or two characters modules can't detect characters appearing in less than four channels or two channels.

4 Conclusions

In this paper, we propose coarse-to-fine distance based valid pair rules to connect more character pairs in a text line with less background noise connection, which can mitigate the character missing caused by the character filtering module. Single or two character detection module is added to detect text lines with a little characters, which is novel and effective. Template match based text line level classification module improves the detection accuracy as well as remaining high recall. Experiments show that our method is valid and useful.

Acknowledgments. This work was supported in part by the Natural Science Foundation of China under Grant 61301106, 61327013 and U1611461.

References

1. Hong, R., Yang, Y., Wang, M., Hua, X.S.: Learning visual semantic relationships for efficient visual retrieval. IEEE Trans. Big Data **1**(4), 152–161 (2015)
2. Hong, R., Zhang, L., Zhang, C., Zimmermann, R.: Flickr circles: aesthetic tendency discovery by multi-view regularized topic modeling. IEEE Trans. Multimedia **18**(8), 1555–1567 (2016)
3. Hong, R., Hu, Z., Wang, R., Wang, M., Tao, D.: Multi-view object retrieval via multi-scale topic models. IEEE Trans. Image Process. **25**(12), 5814–5827 (2016)
4. Li, Z., Tang, J.: Weakly supervised deep metric learning for community-contributed image retrieval. IEEE Trans. Multimedia **17**(11), 1989–1999 (2015)
5. Bissacco, A., Cummins, M., Netzer, Y., Neven, H.: PhotoOCR: reading text in uncontrolled conditions. In: IEEE International Conference on Computer Vision, pp. 785–792 (2014)
6. Zhu, Z., Liang, D., Zhang, S., Huang, X., Li, B., Hu, S.: Traffic-sign detection and classification in the wild. In: Computer Vision and Pattern Recognition, pp. 2110–2118 (2016)
7. Ye, Q., Doermann, D.: Text detection and recognition in imagery: a survey. IEEE Trans. Pattern Anal. Mach. Intell. **37**(7), 1480–1500 (2015)
8. Zhang, Z., Shen, W., Yao, C., Bai, X.: Symmetry-based text line detection in natural scenes. In: Computer Vision and Pattern Recognition, pp. 2558–2567 (2015)
9. Wang, K., Belongie, S.: Word spotting in the wild. In: Daniilidis, K., Maragos, P., Paragios, N. (eds.) ECCV 2010. LNCS, vol. 6311, pp. 591–604. Springer, Heidelberg (2010). https://doi.org/10.1007/978-3-642-15549-9_43
10. Epshtein, B., Ofek, E., Wexler, Y.: Detecting text in natural scenes with stroke width transform. In: Computer Vision and Pattern Recognition, pp. 2963–2970 (2010)
11. Koo, H.I., Kim, D.H.: Scene text detection via connected component clustering and nontext filtering. IEEE Press (2013)
12. Neumann, L., Matas, J.: Real-time scene text localization and recognition. In: IEEE Conference on Computer Vision and Pattern Recognition, pp. 3538–3545 (2012)

13. Matas, J., Chum, O., Urban, M., Pajdla, T.: Robust wide-baseline stereo from maximally stable extremal regions. Image Vis. Comput. **22**(10), 761–767 (2004)
14. Pan, Y.F., Hou, X., Liu, C.L.: A hybrid approach to detect and localize texts in natural scene images. IEEE Trans. Image Process. **20**(3), 800–813 (2011)
15. Neumann, L., Matas, J.: Text localization in real-world images using efficiently pruned exhaustive search. In: 2011 International Conference on Document Analysis and Recognition (ICDAR), pp. 687–691. IEEE (2011)
16. Karatzas, D., Shafait, F., Uchida, S., Iwamura, M., i Bigorda, L.G., Mestre, S.R., Mas, J., Mota, D.F., Almazan, J.A., de las Heras, L.P.: ICDAR 2013 robust reading competition. In: 2013 12th International Conference on Document Analysis and Recognition (ICDAR), pp. 1484–1493. IEEE (2013)
17. Wang, K., Babenko, B., Belongie, S.: End-to-end scene text recognition. In: 2011 IEEE International Conference on Computer Vision (ICCV), pp. 1457–1464. IEEE (2011)
18. Tian, S., Pan, Y., Huang, C., Lu, S., Yu, K., Lim Tan, C.: Text flow: a unified text detection system in natural scene images. In: Proceedings of the IEEE International Conference on Computer Vision, pp. 4651–4659 (2015)
19. Li, Z., Liu, J., Tang, J., Lu, H.: Robust structured subspace learning for data representation. IEEE Trans. Pattern Anal. Mach. Intell. **37**(10), 2085–2098 (2015)
20. Shahab, A., Shafait, F., Dengel, A.: ICDAR 2011 robust reading competition challenge 2: reading text in scene images. In: 2011 International Conference on Document Analysis and Recognition (ICDAR), pp. 1491–1496. IEEE (2011)
21. Wolf, C., Jolion, J.M.: Object count/area graphs for the evaluation of object detection and segmentation algorithms. Int. J. Doc. Anal. Recogn. (IJDAR) **8**(4), 280–296 (2006)
22. Yin, X., Yin, X.C., Hao, H.W., Iqbal, K.: Effective text localization in natural scene images with MSER, geometry-based grouping and AdaBoost. In: 2012 21st International Conference on Pattern Recognition (ICPR), pp. 725–728. IEEE (2012)
23. Li, Y., Shen, C., Jia, W., Hengel, A.V.D.: Leveraging surrounding context for scene text detection. In: IEEE International Conference on Image Processing, pp. 2264–2268 (2013)

Towards Underwater Image Enhancement Using Super-Resolution Convolutional Neural Networks

Xueyan Ding, Yafei Wang, Zheng Liang, Jun Zhang, and Xianping Fu$^{(\boxtimes)}$

Information Science and Technology College,
Dalian Maritime University, Dalian 116026, China
{dingxueyan_meow,wangyafei,zliang,william,fxp}@dlmu.edu.cn

Abstract. Underwater objects detection and recognition is challenging because of the degradation of underwater images, such as color casts, blurring and low contrast. To tackle this problem, a novel underwater image enhancement method is proposed. It consists of two main steps. First, an adaptive color correction algorithm is used to compensate color casts and produce natural color corrected images. Second, a super-resolution convolutional neural network is applied to color corrected images in order to remove blurring. The proposed network learns a relationship which can be employed into image de-blurring from a large amount of blurry images and the corresponding clear images. Based on the relationship, the color corrected image will be de-blurred and sharpened. The experimental results show that the proposed strategy improves the quality of underwater images efficiently and arrives at good results in underwater objects detection and recognition.

Keywords: Underwater image enhancement
Super-resolution convolutional neural networks · Color correction
De-blurring

1 Introduction

Clear and high quality underwater images are necessary for exploring ocean environments and recognizing underwater objects [1,2]. However, capturing clear and high quality underwater images is challenging because of physical particles in underwater environments. Generally, underwater images are degraded by light absorption and scattering. Light absorption reduces energy of light substantially and results in color casts of underwater images. The degree of light absorption depends on different wavelengths of the light. Besides, there are two kinds of scattering: forward scattering and backward scattering. Forward scattering deviates

X. Fu—This work was supported in part by the National Natural Science Foundation of China Grant 61370142 and Grant 61272368, by the Fundamental Research Funds for the Central Universities Grant 3132016352, by the Fundamental Research of Ministry of Transport of P. R. China Grant 2015329225300.

© Springer Nature Singapore Pte Ltd. 2018
B. Huet et al. (Eds.): ICIMCS 2017, CCIS 819, pp. 479–486, 2018.
https://doi.org/10.1007/978-981-10-8530-7_47

light from the object to the camera and leads to a blur scene, and backward scattering reflects light towards the camera before the light reaches the objects and limits the contrast of the images. Affected by these properties of underwater imaging, it is not easy to acquire clear and high quality underwater images. Therefore, an effective underwater image enhancement strategy is desired.

Numerous underwater image enhancement methods have been proposed to improve the quality of underwater images. Traditional image enhancement methods, such as Histogram Equalization (HE) and Contrast Limited Adaptive Histogram Equalization (CLAHE) [3,4], are widely utilized in improving the appearance of degraded underwater images. There was also extensive use of atmospheric scattering model in underwater image enhancement because of the similarity between hazy images and underwater images. As a successful application of atmospheric scattering model, dark channel prior [5,6] is popular in underwater image enhancement. Recently, fusion-based underwater image enhancement methods [7,8] which can achieve better results that traditional single procedures in solving main problems such as noises, low contrast, blurring and color casts. Additionally, learning-based methods are also applied to underwater image enhancement. Farhadifard et al. [9] proposed a learning-based method, which used sparse representation to deblur and adaptive color correction to correct color cast.

Different from traditional underwater image enhancement methods, super-resolution convolutional neural network is introduced into underwater image enhancement in this paper. The proposed underwater image enhancement framework involves two main steps: adaptive color correction and de-blurring with super-resolution convolution networks. First, original degraded underwater image is white balanced by an adaptive color correction algorithm in order to correct color casts. It produces a natural color corrected image. Second, the color corrected image is enhanced by a learning-based de-blurring algorithm with super-resolution convolutional neural networks. For this, the proposed de-blurring network is trained by a large amount of clear images and the corresponding blurry images. Based on the trained network parameters, the blur removed and sharpened image will be obtained.

2   The Proposed Approach

In this section, an efficient underwater image enhancement method which removes color casts and blurring is presented. This method (shown as Fig. 1) involves two main steps: color correction (Sect. 2.1) and de-blurring with super-resolution convolutional neural networks (Sect. 2.2). Color correction algorithm is firstly applied to the original underwater image to remove color casts and obtain natural color corrected image. Then the luminance component (Y) of color corrected image is segmented into patches to feed the proposed de-blurring network to obtain an enhanced luminance component Y^F. Finally, a blur-free and sharpened image can be obtained with the enhanced luminance component Y^F.

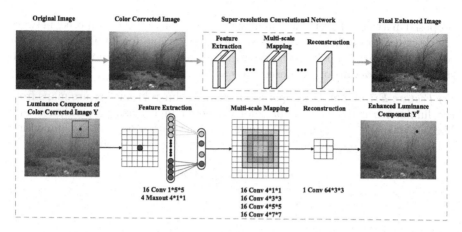

Fig. 1. The overall framework of proposed method. (Color figure online)

2.1 Color Correction

Underwater images are affected by color casts caused by light absorption. In the proposed framework, we firstly employ a white balance method to correct the color of underwater images. More details about the white balance method are available in our previous work [8]. This white balance method removes the color casts efficiently and produce a natural color corrected image. Nevertheless, low contrast and blurring still exist in the color corrected image. To obtain a better enhanced image, de-blurring with super-resolution convolutional network is enforced.

2.2 De-blurring with Super-Resolution Convolutional Network

After color correction, de-blurring with super-resolution convolutional network is carried out. The proposed network directly learns an end-to-end mapping relations between luminance components of blurry images and blur-free images. Figure 1 shows the architecture of the proposed network which involves three parts: feature extraction, multi-scale mapping and reconstruction. The input of the network is luminance component Y of color corrected image in YCbCr color space. The YCbCr image, which contains luminance component Y, blue-difference and red-difference chrominance components (Cb and Cr), represents the equivalent color to the corresponding RGB image. The reason for using YCbCr image instead of RGB image is that we can only consider the luminance and takes no account of chrominance. Layer designs and training process are presented as follows.

Layer Designs

Inspired by super-resolution convolutional network [10], a network which consists of cascaded convolutional layers with nonlinear activation functions employed after some of these layers is proposed. Figure 1 shows the architecture of the proposed network. Layers and nonlinear activations of the proposed network are designed to implement three sequential operations for de-blurring of color corrected images, namely, feature extraction, multi-scale mapping and reconstruction. The details of the designs are as follows.

(1) Feature Extraction: This operation extracts blur-relevant feature maps from the luminance component Y of color corrected image using convolution and Maxout unit [11]. Maxout unit is an unusual activation function for dimension reduction. Based on Maxout unit, the first layer $F_1^i(x)$ is designed as follows:

$$F_1^i(x) = \max_{j \in [1,k]} f_1^{i,j}(x)$$
$$f_1^{i,j}(x) = W_1^{i,j} * Y + B_1^{i,j} \tag{1}$$

where $f_1^{i,j}(x)$ denotes the feature maps obtained by convolutional filters. $\mathcal{W}_1 = \{W_1^{p,q}\}_{(p,q)}^{(n_1,k)}$ and $\mathcal{B}_1 = \{B_1^{p,q}\}_{(p,q)=(1,1)}^{(n_1,k)}$ represent the filters and biases respectively, and $*$ denotes the convolution operation. $\mathcal{W}_1$ applies $k \times n_1$ convolutions on the images, and each convolution has a kernel size 5×5. Maxout unit generates a new feature map by taking a pixel-wise maximization operation over k affine feature maps. Therefore, the layer extracts an n_1-dimensional feature for each patch. Inspired by [12], we set $k \times n_1 = 16$ and $k = 4$.

(2) Multi-scale Mapping: In the second layer, each of these n_1-dimensional vectors is mapped into an n_2-dimensional one using parallel convolutional operations. The size of any convolution filter is among $4 \times 1 \times 1$, $4 \times 3 \times 3$, $4 \times 5 \times 5$ and $4 \times 7 \times 7$, and the number of filters for each scale is set as 16. Therefore, the output of this layer has $n_2 = 64$ dimension. Formally, the output of the second layer F_2^i is written as:

$$F_2^i = W_2^{\lceil i/4 \rceil,(i \backslash 4)} * F_1 + B_2^{\lceil i/4 \rceil,(i \backslash 4)} \tag{2}$$

where $\mathcal{W}_2 = \{W_2^{p,q}\}_{(p,q)=(1,1)}^{(4,n_2/4)}$ and $\mathcal{B}_2 = \{B_2^{p,q}\}_{(p,q)=(1,1)}^{(4,n_2/4)}$ contain n_2 pairs of parameters that is break up into 4 groups. $\lceil \rceil$ takes the integer upwardly and $\backslash$ denotes the remainder operation.

(3) Reconstruction: This operation aggregates the above feature maps to generate the enhanced luminance component of color corrected image.

$$Y^F = \max(0, W_3 * F_2 + B_3) \tag{3}$$

where $\mathcal{W}_3 = \{W_3\}$ corresponds to a filter with size of $64 \times 3 \times 3$ and $\mathcal{B}_3 = \{W_3\}$ contains a bias. Y^F is the enhanced luminance component of color corrected image.

After enhancing luminance component of color corrected image, final blur removed image can be obtained by converting enhanced YCbCr image into RGB image.

Training

(1) Training Data: In this work, we synthesize training pairs of luminance patches from blur-free images and the corresponding luminance patches from blur images. The blur-free images are extracted from Sun Database [13] randomly, and the corresponding blur images are synthesized from these blur-free images by gaussian lowpass filters. The size of training luminance patches is 29×29. The luminance patches from blur images are regarded as training data, and the corresponding luminance patches from blur-free images are regarded as ground truth.

(2) Training Method: In the proposed network, supervised learning requires the mapping relationship F between luminance patches of blur images and blur-free images. Network parameters $\Theta = \{W_1, W_2, W_3, B_1, B_2, B_3\}$ are achieved by minimizing the loss function between the reconstructed luminance Y and the corresponding ground truth Y^F. Given a set of luminance $\{Y_i\}$ of blur images and their corresponding luminance $\{Y_i^F\}$ of blur-free images, we use Mean Squared Error (MSE) as the loss function. $L(\Theta)$ is the loss between Y and Y^F:

$$L(\Theta) = \frac{1}{N} \sum_{i=1}^{N} \|F(Y_i; \Theta) - Y_i^F\|^2 \qquad (4)$$

where N is the number of training samples.

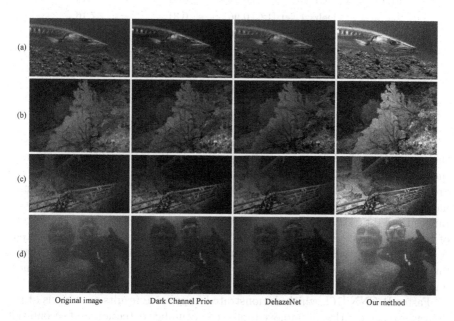

(a)			
(b)			
(c)			
(d)			
Original image	Dark Channel Prior	DehazeNet	Our method

Fig. 2. The experimental results and comparison of underwater image enhancement methods.

3   Results and Discussion

To verify the effectiveness of the proposed method, several experiments involving qualitative comparison, quantitative comparison and application test are conducted. Figure 2 shows the results of the proposed strategy and the comparison with other enhancement methods. In Fig. 2, the first two columns contain original images and our enhanced images. The last two columns show the enhanced images obtained by Dark Channel Prior [5] and DehazeNet [12]. It can be observed that the proposed strategy is able to acquire more pleasing enhanced images with corrected color, enhanced contrast and sharpened details.

Table 1. The PCQI, Blur Metric and entropy values of enhanced images

Image	Method	PCQI [14]	Blur Metric [15]	Entropy
Figure 2(a)	DCP [5]	0.93	0.32	7.50
	DehazeNet [12]	0.96	0.31	7.53
	Our method	**0.98**	**0.25**	**7.67**
Figure 2(b)	DCP [5]	0.96	0.35	7.51
	DehazeNet [12]	0.89	0.35	7.40
	Our method	**1.00**	**0.26**	**7.83**
Figure 2(c)	DCP [5]	0.94	0.31	7.16
	DehazeNet [12]	0.96	0.31	7.16
	Our method	**1.09**	**0.23**	**7.62**
Figure 2(d)	DCP [5]	0.61	0.31	7.17
	DehazeNet [12]	0.58	0.32	6.66
	Our method	**0.62**	**0.24**	**7.62**

Moreover, several evaluation metrics are used to assess the performance of the proposed method. Following other researchers, Patch-based Contrast Quality Index (PCQI) [14], Blur Metric [15] and Entropy are carried out. PCQI was proposed by Wang et al. [14], and the higher PCQI indicates that the image has better contrast. Blur Metric is utilized in assessing blur effect of image. It ranges from 0 to 1 which are respectively the best and the worst quality in term of blur perception. Entropy is used to measure the image information content. A higher entropy value of an image means more information contained in that image. Table 1 shows the PCQI, Blur Metric and Entropy values of enhanced images in Fig. 2.

Faster R-CNN [16], which demonstrated impressive results on various object detection benchmarks, is employed into sea cucumber detection and recognition to evaluate the performance of the proposed method. In our work, Faster R-CNN is applied to original degraded underwater sea cucumber video and as well as the corresponding enhanced video. Table 2 gives the numbers of detection and

Table 2. The detection results of original and enhanced underwater videos.

Data source	Detection	Accurate detection
Original video	30	12
Enhanced video	246	240

accurate detection. It can be observed that the original degraded underwater images show great limitations in underwater objects detection and recognition. By contrast with original underwater images, enhanced images help to reveal more objects. Figure 3 shows four pairs of original degraded images and the corresponding enhanced images extracted from aforementioned two videos. The bounding boxes show the predicted sea cucumber, and the labels represent the probability of prediction. Therefore, the proposed underwater image enhancement method is helpful for underwater objects detection and recognition.

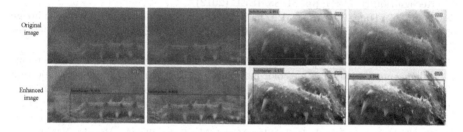

Fig. 3. The detection results of original and enhanced underwater videos.

4   Conclusion

In this paper, an efficient underwater image enhancement strategy combining adaptive color correction and de-blurring with super-resolution convolutional network is presented. The proposed network learns a relationship which can be employed into image de-blurring from a large amount of blurry images and the corresponding clear images. Based on the relationship, the color corrected image will be de-blurred and sharpened. The experimental results show that the proposed method can enhance underwater image effectively and performs well in underwater objects detection and recognition. In future work, we will consider to improve the proposed network to achieve better enhancement, robust adaptation and real-time performance.

References

1. Wang, R., Wang, Y., Zhang, J., Fu, X.: Review on underwater image restoration and enhancement algorithms. In: Proceedings of the 7th International Conference on Internet Multimedia Computing and Service, p. 56. ACM (2015)

2. Schettini, R., Corchs, S.: Underwater image processing: state of the art of restoration and image enhancement methods. EURASIP J. Adv. Signal Process. **2010**(1), 746052 (2010)

3. Hitam, M.S., Awalludin, E.A., Yussof, W.N.J.H.W., Bachok, Z.: Mixture contrast limited adaptive histogram equalization for underwater image enhancement. In: 2013 International Conference on Computer Applications Technology (ICCAT), pp. 1–5. IEEE (2013)

4. Ghani, A.S.A., Isa, N.A.M.: Enhancement of low quality underwater image through integrated global and local contrast correction. Appl. Soft Comput. **37**, 332–344 (2015)

5. He, K., Sun, J., Tang, X.: Single image haze removal using dark channel prior. IEEE Trans. Pattern Anal. Mach. Intell. **33**(12), 2341–2353 (2011)

6. Li, C.-Y., Guo, J.-C., Cong, R.-M., Pang, Y.-W., Wang, B.: Underwater image enhancement by dehazing with minimum information loss and histogram distribution prior. IEEE Trans. Image Process. **25**(12), 5664–5677 (2016)

7. Ancuti, C., Ancuti, C.O., Haber, T., Bekaert, P.: Enhancing underwater images and videos by fusion. In: 2012 IEEE Conference on Computer Vision and Pattern Recognition (CVPR), pp. 81–88. IEEE (2012)

8. Wang, Y., Ding, X., Wang, R., Zhang, J., Fu, X.: Fusion-based underwater image enhancement by wavelet decomposition. In: 2017 IEEE International Conference on Industrial Technology (ICIT), pp. 1013–1018. IEEE (2017)

9. Farhadifard, F., Zhou, Z., von Lukas, U.F.: Learning-based underwater image enhancement with adaptive color mapping. In: 2015 9th International Symposium on Image and Signal Processing and Analysis (ISPA), pp. 48–53. IEEE (2015)

10. Dong, C., Loy, C.C., He, K., Tang, X.: Image super-resolution using deep convolutional networks. IEEE Trans. Pattern Anal. Mach. Intell. **38**(2), 295–307 (2016)

11. Goodfellow, I.J., Warde-Farley, D., Mirza, M., Courville, A., Bengio, Y.: Maxout networks. arXiv preprint arXiv:1302.4389 (2013)

12. Cai, B., Xiangmin, X., Jia, K., Qing, C., Tao, D.: DehazeNet: an end-to-end system for single image haze removal. IEEE Trans. Image Process. **25**(11), 5187–5198 (2016)

13. Xiao, J., Ehinger, K.A., Hays, J., Torralba, A., Oliva, A.: Sun database: exploring a large collection of scene categories. Int. J. Comput. Vis. **119**(1), 3–22 (2016)

14. Wang, S., Ma, K., Yeganeh, H., Wang, Z., Lin, W.: A patch-structure representation method for quality assessment of contrast changed images. IEEE Signal Process. Lett. **22**(12), 2387–2390 (2015)

15. Crete, F., Dolmiere, T., Ladret, P., Nicolas, M.: The blur effect: perception and estimation with a new no-reference perceptual blur metric. In: Human Vision and Electronic Imaging, vol. 12, p. 64920 (2007)

16. Ren, S., He, K., Girshick, R., Sun, J.: Faster R-CNN: towards real-time object detection with region proposal networks. In: Advances in Neural Information Processing Systems, pp. 91–99 (2015)

Traffic Sign Recognition with Inception Convolutional Neural Networks

Jianyun Lu, Yanyun Qu$^{(\boxtimes)}$, and Xiaodong Yang

Computer Science Department, Xiamen University,
Xiamen, People's Republic of China
quyanyun@gmail.com, sikyadjy@gmail.com,
abc8350712@gmail.com

Abstract. Traffic Sign Recognition (TSR) is very important for driverless systems and driver assistance systems. Due to the small size of traffic signs in the wild, the traffic sign becomes very challenging. In this paper, an inception convolutional neural network is designed to solve the traffic sign classification problem. A large receptive field is generated by multiple small filters instead of a single large filter. Moreover, Inspired by Inception V3, inception block is used, which makes the combination of multiple convolution output be optimized. Thus, the coarse cue in the shallow layer and the fine cue in the deeper layer are fused to improve the visual expression capability of the model. The proposed method is evaluated on three famous traffic sign datasets: the German Traffic Sign Recognition Benchmark (GTSRB), the Swedish Traffic Signs Dataset (STSD), and the 2015 Traffic Sign Recognition Competition Dataset. The experimental results demonstrate the effectiveness and robustness of our methods.

Keywords: Traffic sign recognition · Multi feature fusion
Inception convolutional neural networks

1 Introduction

Traffic sign recognition (TSR) is very important to driverless vehicle and driver assistance systems [1]. TSR in the wild is a challenging task, because traffic signs are in the variety of different appearances with the environment changes, such as color fading, illumination, motion-blur, viewpoint variations, occlusions, graffiti, stickers and low resolution. There are many methods to deal with the problem of traffic sign recognition. Some work paid more attentions to the classifiers, and some work paid more attentions to the feature extraction. For the classifiers, many popular machine learning methods are implemented on traffic sign recognition, such as support vector machines (SVM) [3], Bayesian classifiers [4], boosting [5], and random forest classifier [6]. As we know, a multi-class classifier for traffic sign cannot do well without discriminative features. Hand-crafted features such as Scale-Invariant Feature Transform (SIFT) [4, 5] and Histogram of Oriented Gradient (HOG) [7] are usually implemented on traffic sign recognition. In [8], Zaklouta use the tree classifier combining with HOG features. Maldonado [9] designs an end-to-end traffic sign recognition system based on SVMs which included traffic sign detection and recognition and they achieved high

© Springer Nature Singapore Pte Ltd. 2018
B. Huet et al. (Eds.): ICIMCS 2017, CCIS 819, pp. 487–494, 2018.
https://doi.org/10.1007/978-981-10-8530-7_48

recognition accuracy and a very lower detection error rate. Recently, deep learning has greatly succeeded in image classification and speech recognition. Convolutional Neural Networks (CNN) was implemented on large-scale image recognition [10] and achieved the breakthrough performances in ILSVRC2012 [11–13]. Inspired by the success of deep learning on image classification, CNN was used for traffic sign recognition [16–18] in the 2011 International Joint Conference on Neural Networks (IJCNN) competition [14–16]. Sermanet et al. [18] designed a CNNs with multiple scale output in which the last two pooling feature maps are combined in the full connection layer. Their method got better performance because different scales of features are considered and the model was robust to the appearance variation. MCDNN [20] achieved a promising result and win the competition on GTSRB dataset [2].

Since the deep learning methods rise up, the object classification methods are divided into two classes: the traditional methods and the deep learning methods. The disadvantage of the traditional methods for traffic sign recognition is that the feature extraction is separated from the classifier learning, that is, features are hand-crafted and are not related to the classifier. Thus, traffic sign recognition is not optimized in a whole but is only a pipeline system. Deep learning based traffic sign recognition methods can efficiently overcome the disadvantage. However, the current CNNs based traffic sign recognition did not achieve the best performance compared with the traditional methods for traffic sign recognition. We think that bigger convolution kernel used in shallow convolution layers of the current CNN based methods is not suitable for small traffic sign images. In order to solve this problem, we proposed the inception convolutional neural network named Inception-CNN. In our method, small convolution kernels are used in shallow layers instead of bigger convolution kernels, and in inception block two feature maps from different convolutional block are fused to extract the discriminative features.

2 Framework of the Inception CNN

Figure 1 shows the framework of Inception-CNN, which includes nine convolution layers, three maximum pooling layers, and two fully connection layers. Compared with AlexNet, our method uses a small filter kernel in the shallow layers and uses a deeper CNN. Deepening the convolutional layer results in a big receptive field. And the convolutional shortcut makes the features of multi-scales combine in an optimal way. Two adjustments to traditional CNN make the feature more distinctive.

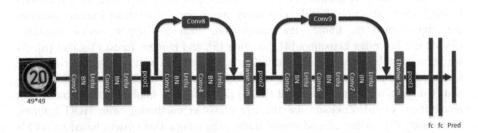

Fig. 1. Inception CNN framework.

In Table 1, we show the whole Architecture, which has 14 layers in total. In Table 1, "mapS" is short for "map size," "chan" for "channel," "kS" for "kernel Size," and "Padding" for "zero padding." Three maximum pooling layers make the features more robust.

Table 1. Architecture of inception CNN

Type	MapS	Chan	kS	Padding
Input	49 × 49	3		
Conv1	49 × 49	60	3 × 3	Yes
Conv2	49 × 49	60	3 × 3	Yes
Pool1	25 × 25	60	2 × 2	
Conv3	25 × 25	120	3 × 3	Yes
Conv4	25 × 25	120	3 × 3	Yes
Conv8	25 × 25	120	1 × 1	
Pool2	13 × 13	120	2 × 2	
Conv5	13 × 13	180	3 × 3	Yes
Conv6	13 × 13	180	3 × 3	Yes
Conv7	13 × 13	180	3 × 3	Yes
Conv9	13 × 13	180	1 × 1	
Pool3	7 × 7	180	2 × 2	
Fc1	1 × 1	200		
Fc2	1 × 1	200		
Soft-max	1 × 1	Class		

3   Implementation Details

In Inception CNN, there are three stages in the inception CNN: the first stage contains conv1, conv2, the second stage contains conv3, conv4, and the third stage contains conv5, conv6, conv7. The convolution kernel size is set to 3*3, followed by Batch normalization and Leaky Relu activation. In [14] and [20], the convolutional kernel size in the first convolution layer is usually 5*5 [14] or 7*7 [20], which got poor performance for small traffic sign recognition. Inspired by VGG [19], we use several small filtering kernels instead of a single large filter kernel. As showed in Fig. 2, a 3*3 region in the first convolutional layer can focus on a pixel of a feature map in its next convolutional layer. More convolutional layers correspond to the larger receptive field.

For the computational complexity, several small convolutional kernels are equal to a larger convolutional kernel with smaller parameters. Intuitively, it is better to choose filters bank with smaller kernel size instead of a large filter. It is because the combination of several small filters can be optimized that the convolution of our method can extract more discriminative features. In the second stage of our method, we fuse the output of the conv8 block and the output of the conv4 block by adding them in an element-wise way. And then we pool the fusion map in Pool2. In the third stage, we fuse the output of the conv9 block and the output of the conv7 block by adding them in an element-wise way. And then we pool the fusion map.

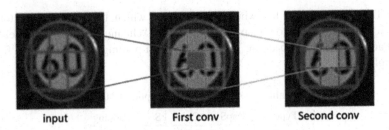

| input | First conv | Second conv |

Fig. 2. The receptive field after two convolutional layers

As showed in Table 1, we get 60 channel feature maps of size 25*25 after the first pooling operation in Pool1. And we get 120 channel feature maps of size 25*25 after conv4 layer. Thus, in the conv8 block which is the shortcut from conv2 to conv4, convolution is implemented on the output of Pool1 with two 1*1 filter kernels. Thus, we get 120 channel feature maps of size 25*25 too. 120 feature maps from conv8 are added with the counterparts from conv4 in an element-wise way.

We use a soft-max function as a classifier which is a multi-class logistic regression function. The soft-max function can compress a real number vector of k dimensions into a probability vector whose elements range from 0 to 1 and the sum of all the elements is 1. The probability of the target class is bigger, and those probability of non-target classes are smaller. We denote X(i) the probability of the ith class and $1\{X(i)\}$ the indicator function. The probability of the jth class is formulated as

$$P(X(j)|X) = \frac{\exp(X(j))}{\sum_{i=1}^{k} \exp(X(i))} \tag{1}$$

The cost function is the likelihood loss function,

$$J = -\sum_{i=1}^{k} 1\{X(i)\} \cdot logP(X(i)|X). \tag{2}$$

When a query image is tested, we use the index of the maximum probability in the probability vector as the target category.

4 Experimental Results

4.1 Datasets

We estimate our method on three traffic sign databases: GTSRB, STSD, and the 2015 Traffic Sign Recognition Competition Dataset (Mutil-72TSD).

GTSRB is famous because it is used in 2011 IJCNN competition of traffic sign recognition [17]. The sizes of traffic sign images vary from 15×15 to 250×250 pixels. It contains 43 classes, there are 39209 training images in the training set and the testing set contains 12630 testing images.

STSD was built in 2011 by the Department of Electronic Engineering in Linkoping University. This dataset is used for traffic sign detection, and we manually crop traffic sign patches from the training images. We build a sub-dataset of STSD named Swedish30 which includes 30 classes with 3129 traffic signs.

Mutil-72TSD is a 72-class traffic sign dataset used in the 2015 China Traffic Sign Detection and Recognition Competition. They are split into 7 main categories: (1) mandatory signs, (2) assist signs, (3) warning signs, (4) road construction safety signs, (5) tourism districts signs, (6) guided signs and (7) prohibitory or restrictive signs. There are great differences in appearance in traffic sign classes, especially in color, shape, scale. We build a dataset that contains 10611 training images and 8520 test images.

To augment the training samples, affine transformations are randomly implemented on the traffic signs with random rotation in the range of $[-10°, 10°]$, and random translation in the range of $[-2, 2]$. Moreover, the brightness is changed randomly, and the gaussian noises are randomly added. Data augmentation can effectively increase the diversity of training samples. We preprocess the data by converting the RGB space into the YUV space, and then only use the Y channel which represents the brightness information. As in [18], it proved that better results are obtained on the Y channel. Some examples of the data augmentation are shown in Fig. 3.

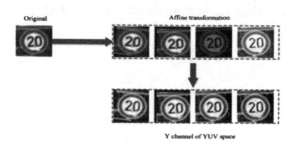

Fig. 3. Augmented samples and data preprocessing

4.2 Results and Analysis

We implement our method in Tensorflow, Pycharm2017 and opencv3.0.0 in ubuntu 16.04 with TitanX, 12 GB memory. We normalized the input image to a certain size of 49*49.

In GTSRB dataset, we train inception CNN with 190000 iterations by using three learning rates: 0.001, 0.0001, 0.00001. We look the whole Inception-CNNs as a neuron of the hidden layer, then constructs 5 Inception-CNNs models for training simultaneously. We add the probability vectors of each network output, and then calculate the maximum probability. The class with the maximum probability will be the prediction class. In this way, the recognition rate of Inception-CNN is 99.303%. We compare our method with six state-of-the-art methods of traffic sign recognition in Table 2. MCDNN [20] and CNN-ELM [21] is superior to our method, but MCDNN trains 25 networks separately for 5 different data preprocessing and CNN-ELM has thousands of neurons in hidden layer, which is time consuming in the training stage. The human performance is at 98.84%, which is below our accuracy. Other methods from the IJCNN 2011 competition such as multi-scale CNNs [18] and random forests on hand-coded histogram of oriented gradient (HOG) feature [8] are inferior to our method.

Table 2. Comparison of Traffic sign recognition methods on GTSRB

Team	Method	Accuracy (%)
IDSIA	MCDNN	99.46
NUDT	CNN-ELM	99.40
Ours	**Inception-CNN**	**99.30**
INI-RTCV	Human performance	98.84
Sermanet	Multi-scale CNNs	98.31
CAOR	Random forests on HOG	96.14
INI-RTCV	LDA on HOG	95.68

We also investigate the effect of conv8 and conv9 in a single neural network model. CNN denotes the traditional CNN without Conv8 and Conv9 layers. We can see from Fig. 4 that CNN learns faster on account of its less number of parameters. Though Inception-CNN converges slower, it can gain higher accuracy and smaller loss which prove that Inception-CNN can improve the classification ability.

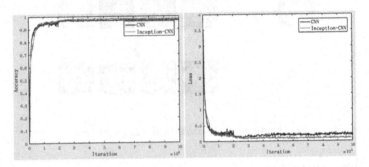

Fig. 4. Curves of recognition rates and loss functions for CNN and inception-CNN

In Table 3, we compare the performance of the two models on three datasets: GTSRB, Swedish30, and Mutil-72TSD. The recognition rates of Inception-CNN on the three datasets are all higher than that of CNN.

Table 3. Comparison of CNN and Inception-CNN

Method	Data		
	GTSRB	Swedish30	Mutil-72TSD
Inception-CNN	98.345%	98.237%	84.683%
CNN	97.838%	97.418%	82.629%

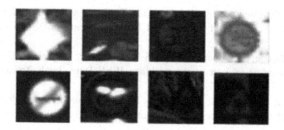

Fig. 5. Error prediction of ours networks

Figure 5 shows some typical samples of recognition failure in GTSRB test sets. It demonstrates that the failure is due to low resolution, strong sunlight, excessive noise, and severe occlusion. Thus, some preprocessing should be implemented on the traffic signs such as super-resolution or denoising before traffic sign recognition.

5   Conclusions

In this paper, we propose Inception-CNN for traffic sign recognition. We use smaller filters in the shallow convolutional layers and use two inception blocks for optimizing the combination of multi-scale feature maps. The proposed method can learn more discriminative features and a better classifier. The proposed method is implemented on the three famous traffic sign recognition datasets: GTSRB, Swedish30, and Mutil-72TSD, and the experimental results demonstrate the effectiveness of our method.

Acknowledgement. This work was supported by the National Natural Science Foundation of China under Grant 61373077.

References

1. Mogelmose, A., Trivedi, M.M., Moeslund, T.B.: Vision-based traffic sign detection and analysis for intelligent driver assistance systems: perspectives and survey. IEEE Trans. Intell. Transp. Syst. **13**(4), 1484–1497 (2012)
2. Stallkamp, J., Schlipsing, M., Salmen, J., Igel, C.: The German traffic sign recognition benchmark: a multi-class classification competition. In: International Joint Conference on Neural Networks (2011)
3. Greenhalgh, J., Mirmehdi, M.: Real-time detection and recognition of road traffic signs. IEEE Trans. Intell. Transp. Syst. **13**(4), 1498–1506 (2012)
4. Meuter, M., Nunn, C., Görmer, S.M., et al.: A decision fusion and reasoning module for a traffic sign recognition system. IEEE Trans. Intell. Transp. Syst. **12**(4), 1126–1134 (2011)
5. Ruta, A., Li, Y., Liu, X.: Robust class similarity measure for traffic sign recognition. IEEE Trans. Intell. Transp. Syst. **11**(4), 846–855 (2010)
6. Zaklouta, F., Stanciulescu, B.: Real-time traffic-sign recognition using tree classifiers. IEEE Trans. Intell. Transp. Syst. **13**(4), 1507–1514 (2012)
7. Dalal, N., Triggs, B.: Histograms of oriented gradients for human detection. In: IEEE Computer Society Conference on Computer Vision and Pattern Recognition, CVPR 2005, vol. 1, pp. 886–893. IEEE (2005)

8. Zaklouta, F., Stanciulescu, B., Hamdoun, O.: Traffic sign classification using kd trees and random forests. In: The 2011 International Joint Conference on Neural Networks (IJCNN), pp. 2151–2155. IEEE (2011)
9. Maldonado-Bascon, S., Lafuente-Arroyo, S., Gil-Jimenez, P., et al.: Road-sign detection and recognition based on support vector machines. IEEE Trans. Intell. Transp. Syst. 8(2), 264–278 (2007)
10. Krizhevsky, A., Sutskever, I., Hinton, G.E.: ImageNet classification with deep convolutional neural networks. In: Advances in Neural Information Processing Systems, pp. 1097–1105 (2012)
11. He, K., Zhang, X., Ren, S., et al.: Deep residual learning for image recognition. arXiv preprint arXiv:1512.03385 (2015)
12. Russakovsky, O., Deng, J., Su, H., et al.: ImageNet large scale visual recognition challenge. Int. J. Comput. Vis. 115(3), 211–252 (2015)
13. Szegedy, C., Vanhoucke, V., Ioffe, S., et al.: Rethinking the inception architecture for computer vision. arXiv preprint arXiv:1512.00567 (2015)
14. Jin, J., Fu, K., Zhang, C.: Traffic sign recognition with hinge loss trained convolutional neural networks. IEEE Trans. Intell. Transp. Syst. 15(5), 1991–2000 (2014)
15. Stallkamp, J., Schlipsing, M., Salmen, J., et al.: The German traffic sign recognition benchmark: a multi-class classification competition. In: The 2011 International Joint Conference on Neural Networks (IJCNN), pp. 1453–1460. IEEE (2011)
16. Cireşan, D., Meier, U., Masci, J., et al.: A committee of neural networks for traffic sign classification. In: The 2011 International Joint Conference on Neural Networks (IJCNN), pp. 1918–1921. IEEE (2011)
17. LeCun, Y., Bottou, L., Bengio, Y., et al.: Gradient-based learning applied to document recognition. Proc. IEEE 86(11), 2278–2324 (1998)
18. Sermanet, P., LeCun, Y.: Traffic sign recognition with multi-scale convolutional networks. In: The 2011 International Joint Conference on Neural Networks (IJCNN), pp. 2809–2813. IEEE (2011)
19. Simonyan, K., Zisserman, A.: Very deep convolutional networks for large-scale image recognition. In ICLR (2015)
20. Ciresan, D., Meier, U., Schmidhuber, J.: Multi-column deep neural networks for image classification. In: Proceedings of IEEE Conference on CVPR, pp. 3642–3649 (2012)
21. Zeng Y., Xu, X., Fang, Y., Zhao, K.: Traffic sign recognition using extreme learning classifier with deep convolutional features. In: The 2015 International Conference on Intelligence Science and Big Data Engineering (IScIDE 2015), Suzhou, China, June 14–16 (2015)

Author Index

Printed in the United States
By Bookmasters